How to Prepare for SAT II:

World History

MARILYNN HITCHENS

and

HEIDI ROUPP

BARRON'S

All inquiries should be addressed to:
Barron's Educational Series, Inc.
250 Wireless Boulevard
Hauppauge, New York 11788

Library of Congress Catalog Card No. 95-46634

International Standard Book No. 0-8120-9294-5

Library of Congress Cataloging-in-Publication Data
Hitchens, Marilynn
     How to prepare for SAT II: World history / by Marilynn Hitchens
and Heidi Roupp
         p.   cm.
     ISBN 0-8120-9294-5
     1. History—Examinations, questions, etc. 2. Scholastic Aptitude
Test—Study guides. 3. College entrance achievement tests—Study
guides. I. Roupp, Heidi II. Title.
D16.3.R68 1996
907.6—dc20   95-46634
                                                    CIP

PRINTED IN THE UNITED STATES OF AMERICA

6789 6500 987654

Contents

UNIT III
SYSTEMS OF SOCIETY AND CULTURE:
THE CLASSICAL AGE
(1000 B.C.E.–500 B.C.E.)

UNIT IV
EXPANDING CLASSICAL SYSTEMS OF SOCIETY AND CULTURE
(100 C.E.–1200 C.E.)

UNIT V
EMERGENCE OF A GLOBAL AGE
(1200 C.E.–1600 C.E.)

UNIT VIII
THE CONTEMPORARY WORLD

MODEL TESTS

Acknowledgments

The authors gratefully acknowledge the following for assistance in providing photos and other visual material:

Page 15: Lascaux Cave Paintings (French Government Tourist Office)

Page 16: Paleolithic and Neolithic Tools (Collection Musée de L'Homme)

Page 18: "Old Times" Cartoon by Roy Katz and Ryan Elston

Page 18: Illustration of Early City by Amber Irene Hasselbring

Page 41: Shiva Nataraja Bronze (photograph © 1995, The Art Institute of Chicago, all rights reserved)

Page 42: Shang Bronze Wine Vessel (photograph © 1995, The Art Institute of Chicago, all rights reserved)

Page 44: Illustration of Ziggurat by Jennifer Hoffman

Page 44: Illustration of Olmec Head by Jennifer Hoffman

Page 44: The Great Wall (China National Tourist Office)

Page 45: Tomb at Luxor (Egyptian Tourist Authority)

Page 45: Pyramids at Giza (David Roupp)

Page 46: Mayan Temple at Chichen (Mexican Government Tourism Office)

Page 46: Mayan Hieroglyphics at Chiapas (Mexican Government Tourism Office)

Page 102: Colosseum (Italian Government Tourist Board)

Page 103: Parthenon (Greek National Tourist Organization)

Page 103: Buddha (photograph © 1995, The Art Institute of Chicago, all rights reserved)

Page 104: Pottery Army (China National Tourist Office)

Page 105: Stupa (David Roupp)

Page 106: Roman Aqueduct (Italian Government Tourist Board)

Page 153: Amed el-Jazzar Mosque (Israel Ministry of Tourism)

Page 153: Gothic Cathedral (French Government Tourist Office)

Page 154: Russian Icon (The Denver Art Museum)

Page 155: Angkor Wat (Marilynn Hitchens)

Page 156: Hokusai *The Tama River in Autumn* (photograph © 1995, The Art Institute of Chicago, all rights reserved)

Page 157: Japanese Rock Garden (David Roupp)

Page 157: Mansa Musa Map (By permission of The British Library)

Page 198: Taj Mahal (India Tourist Agency)

Page 199: Japanese Gunpowder Castle (David Roupp)

Page 200: Dance of Death (Frick Art Reference Library)

Page 201: Benin Bronze Wall Plaque (photograph © 1995, The Art Institute of Chicago, all rights reserved)

Page 202: Machu Picchu (Wright Water Engineers, Inc.)

Page 239: Versailles Palace (French National Tourist Office)

Page 241: Michelangelo *David* (Scala/Art Resource, NY)

Page 241: Slave Ship Lithograph (The Bettmann Archive)

Page 241: Correggio *Virgin and Child with the Young Saint John the Baptist* (photograph © 1995, The Art Institute of Chicago, all rights reserved)

Page 286: Delacroix *The Combat of the Giaour and Hassan* (photograph © 1995, The Art Institute of Chicago, all rights reserved)

Page 286: Monet *The Arrival of the Normandy Train* (photograph © 1995, The Art Institute of Chicago, all rights reserved)

Page 287: Gauguin *Ancestors of Tehamana* (photograph © 1995, The Art Institute of Chicago, all rights reserved)

Page 287: Turkish Mug, Ottoman Empire (photograph © 1995, The Art Institute of Chicago, all rights reserved)

Page 288: Child Labor Engraving (The Bettmann Archive)

Page 345: Shanghai (China National Tourist Office)

Page 345: Picasso *Guernica* (The Bettmann Archive and © 1996 Estate of Pablo Picasso/ARS)

Page 346: Rivera *Zapata* (The Museum of Modern Art, New York)

Page 347: James Irwin on the moon (NASA)

Page 350: Juan Gris *Portrait of Pablo Picasso* (photograph © 1995, The Art Institute of Chicago, all rights reserved)

Page 350: Magritte *Time Transfixed* (photograph © 1995, The Art Institute of Chicago, all rights reserved)

Page 351: Earth seen from the moon (NASA)

Notes to the Student

The SAT II World History test is 60 minutes in length and consists of 95 to 100 multiple-choice questions. According to recent information from the Educational Testing Service, which produces the test, the subject matter is as follows:

Geographical		Chronological	
Europe	50%	Prehistory to 500 CE	10%
Southwest Asia	10%	500–1500 CE	20%
Africa	10%	1500–1900 CE	30%
East Asia	10%	Post–1900 CE	30%
South Asia	5%	Cross-chronological	10%
The Americas			
(excluding the U.S.)	5%		
Cross-regional	10%		

All historical fields are covered—political, intellectual and cultural, social and economic, though, as in most texts, the emphasis is political. Some questions test historical methodology and habits of the mind, for example, concepts essential to historical analysis, such as "change and continuity," the ability to assess quotations from documents, and the capacity to interpret artistic materials. Some questions require understanding of commonly used terms like "civilization," and others test geographical knowledge. It will be helpful to you to obtain the *Official Guide to the SAT II: Subject Tests* prior to taking the test. You can do this by writing to the Educational Testing Service (Princeton, New Jersey 08541) or asking your school counselor.

ABOUT THE BOOK

This book is designed to help you study effectively and to succeed on the SAT II: World History test. The book contents are a synthesis of material presented in commonly used world history textbooks, with attention to test coverage as outlined above, and to world history standards as developed by the National Center for History in the Schools. It also reflects the authors' perceptions of content and understandings that are essential and unique to world history. It anticipates future tests that will continue to move away from Western civilization and an emphasis on the twentieth century, and toward a more chronologically and geographically balanced world history.

The book is divided into eight narrative units. Each unit revolves around a major world history idea that dominates the chronological time period. Facts important to this idea, such as people, places, and terms, are highlighted and defined within the text. They are also listed in the reference index at the back of the book. At the end of each unit is a section called Cross-Regional Developments. This will help you see what is universal about the material and what developments important to human change over time occurred within large areas. There is also a section called Legacies. This will help you remember what the important ideas are in the chapter. Each unit also features visuals, maps, and document excerpts. These will help you prepare for multiple-choice test questions that appear on the exam in picture, map, chart, or quotation form.

Each unit chapter begins with a chronology, key terms, names, and places. A definition or identification of each should be written out or made into flash cards for systematic drill and review. As you progress through the chapters, review the previous lists. While you study the material, locate regions and specific places on a blank world map. A timeline with important events for each era will help you consider how the material from one chapter is related to the next. The units end with a series of recall questions that are designed to test your memory and provide you with practice taking multiple-choice tests. After you have checked your answers, highlight the material that requires further drill.

Document reading requires you to learn to think like an historian. In reading a document, note the time, authorship, place, and historical context of the writing, and then proceed to summarize the main points. Finally, reflect on style, viewpoint, and cardinal characteristics. In tests, you are often asked to identify document excerpts. The documents at the end of each chapter have been chosen to help you with this part of the test. They are of such importance in world history that students who claim world historical literacy should be able to recognize their origins, identify the viewpoint, and discern the legacies of history in them.

The book ends with two sample multiple-choice tests. These questions are designed to replicate the types of questions that might appear on the SAT II test. They are preceded by a number of questions that will give you practice on historical methodology-type questions. Answers to these questions are explained in order to instruct you on the principles of historical research and habits of the mind.

HOW TO PREPARE FOR THE TEST

The best way to prepare for the SAT II: World History test is to use this book as you proceed through your world history course. By presenting the material in a slightly different way from the text you are using, you will be forced to understand, rather than just memorize, world history. This will also help in preparing for the test where questions are phrased differently from the ones in your text. If you do not purchase this book until you have finished your world history course, use it as a short text summary. The most important single technique in studying for the SAT II test is to keep reviewing as you proceed with your course and with the chapters in this book. The book will help you do this because there has been an attempt to refer back to earlier events, but in studying, you should also do the same thing, trying to see relationships and reviewing earlier chapter material along with the chapter under study.

Use the practice tests at the back of the book as diagnostic tests. Allow 55 minutes, complete the test as if you were really taking it, and then analyze your score. If you missed questions pertaining to some particular era or place, review it in this book. Then try the second test example.

HOW TO TAKE THE TEST

Review the essentials of test taking listed below.

1. Get a good night's sleep.
2. Locate your test ticket and review the location of the test. Give yourself adequate time to get there.
3. Bring several sharpened No. 2 pencils.
4. Budget your time. Do not linger over difficult questions. Finish the test and then go back to tackle the difficult questions.
5. Read the entire question. Choose the BEST answer. Words like "always," "never," and "only" are apt to be wrong. Think of chronology. Answers are often wrong because they refer to the wrong chronological era. In questions with EXCEPT or NOT, it sometimes helps to rephrase the question in the positive. Try to find similarities between two or three of the wrong choices in order to eliminate others.
6. Avoid wild guessing. Your score is based on the number right minus one-quarter for every wrong answer.
7. Mark answers clearly and erase thoroughly.
8. If you finish early, review your answers.

Good Luck!

UNIT

I

THE BEGINNINGS OF HUMAN SOCIETY
(4 MILLION B.C.E.–4000 B.C.E.)

CHAPTER 1

The Emergence of Early Human Communities
and the Peopling of the Earth

CHRONOLOGY	Prehistory (3.9 million B.C.E.–4000 B.C.E.)
	Pleistocene (Ice Age) (2 million B.C.E.–11,000 B.C.E.)
	Paleolithic (Old Stone Age) (2 million B.C.E.–10,000 B.C.E.)
	Neolithic (New Stone Age) (8000 B.C.E.–4000 B.C.E.)

TERMS			
	plate tectonics	accelerator mass	bipedal
	prehistory	spectrometry	human language
	fossils	chronology	Multiregional model
	artifacts	hominid	Out of Africa model
	carbon 14 dating	dimorphic	hunter-gatherer
		culture	

PEOPLE			
	paleontologist	Australopithicus afarensis	Homo sapiens
	archaeologist	(Lucy)	(Neanderthal)
	anthropologist	Homo habilis	Homo sapiens sapiens
	Donald Johanson	Homo erectus (Java,	(Cro-Magnon)
	Louis Leakey	Peking man)	
	Mary Leakey		

PLACES			
	Pangaea	Gondwanaland	Olduvai Gorge
	Laurasia	Hadar	

3

The Emergence of Early Human Communities and the Peopling of the Earth

PREHISTORY

The age of the planet Earth is estimated to be between five and six billion years old. Scientists theorize that there was once one supercontinent called **Pangaea**, the center of which is present-day Africa. About 200 million years ago Pangaea broke into two large land masses called **Laurasia**, which formed the northern continents, and **Gondwanaland**, which formed the southern continents. Other pieces split off and began to drift toward their present locations. These splits are explained by theories of **plate tectonics**. According to this theory, rigid plates form the outer layer of the earth's surface, but they float on a soft layer of magma or molten rock near the earth's core. The molten rock pushes continents apart and drifting plates often collide, forming mountains like the Himalayas.

The first inhabitants on earth left no written records. For this reason, this period is called **prehistory**—a time before written history. To understand this period, historians rely on the work of **paleontologists**, scientists who study the **fossils** of plants and animals, **archaeologists**, scientists who study the remains of ancient people (both fossils and **artifacts** or man-made objects), and **anthropologists**, scientists who study physical and cultural characteristics of people. Archaeologists use a method called **carbon 14 dating** to determine the age of various archaeological finds. This process measures the amount of radioactive carbon left in an object. Since all living things absorb radiocarbon from the air and lose it after death at a specific rate over time, the radioactive content can determine just how old a fossil is. The newer **accelerator mass spectrometry** separates smaller fossil samples, just one one-thousandth the size needed for carbon 14 dating, and counts carbon 14 atoms directly. Scientists use genetics to trace the evolutionary patterns of human beings. In this instance, the DNA codes reveal similarities and differences between different **hominid** types.

Since history is the recounting of the human story through time, **chronology** is an important component in the discipline. Time is an artificial creation of the human mind to keep order. Different peoples in different places have told time differently. In the western world, where Christianity predominated, the system of B.C., meaning before the birth of Christ, and A.D., *anno Domini* or the year of the Lord, have predominated. In world history, however, increasingly the system of B.C.E., meaning before the common era, and C.E., meaning common era, are being used to reflect a common universal story. Likewise, from a geographical point of view, world historians prefer to use place names with a world perspective rather than a European one. Thus, the Middle East is referred to in world history as Southwest Asia, the Far East as East Asia, Inner Asia as Central Asia, and India as South Asia.

HOMINID EVOLUTION

The first hominids, or ancestors of present-day humans, have been on earth for about four million years and probably lived in the grasslands of Africa. The oldest known *Australopithecines afarensis* fossils are 3.9 million years old. Archaeologist **Donald Johanson** found the first skeletal remains of *A. afarensis* in 1974.

Discovered in East Africa at a site called **Hadar**, in Ethiopia, Johanson uncovered almost half of the skeletal remains of a female hominid, who lived three million years ago, referred to affectionately now as "Lucy." Subsequent fossil records indicate a **dimorphic** species, a species with two types of individuals. The males were about five feet tall and weighed 110 pounds. Females were about three and one-half to four feet tall and weighed 75 pounds. *A. afarensis* fossil footprints of an adult and child out for a walk 3.5 million years ago in what is now Laetoli, Tanzania, are the first direct evidence for upright walking of human ancestors. Recent research indicates an earlier hominid than *A. afarensis* dating some six million years ago.

In Africa, the **Olduvai Gorge** has become among the most important sites in the world for fossil evidence of human origins. The gorge is a narrow slash cut 300 feet deep by the Olduvai River in Tanzania. The steep, soft sides of the gorge stand almost bare under the African sun, making it easily examined by the human eyes and easily scratched with picks and dug with spades. **Dr. Louis Leakey** and his wife Mary began to examine the gorge in the early 1950s and found a series of tools showing how, with the passage of time, design and workmanship of the chipped stones consistently improved. Then, in 1959 **Mary Leakey** found, at the very lowest level of Olduvai deposits, skull fragments of a human-like creature, *Homo habilis*, "the toolmaker."

Theories of human evolution revolve around the idea that hominids developed unique survival techniques based on **culture** or learned behavior and social organization. In this evolutionary pattern, becoming **bipedal**, or walking upright, was crucial, as two free hands allowed for the development of tools. Tools, in turn, created greater success for hunting and gathering. Most historians today, however, stress social organization and language skills as more important to survival. **Human language** allowed for the development of strategy, group action, and a sense of time and remembered behavior. Mental activity related to increased brain size proved an advantage over physical activity. *A. afarensis* "Lucy" had a brain size of approximately 700 cc, which increased with later hominid types.

Either a drier African climate or increased population drove some primates from the trees to seek hunting grounds on the plains. About two million years ago, *Homo habilis* appeared. He was distinguished by being the first tool maker (as opposed to tool user typical of some other primates) and by having a slightly bigger brain size, about 800 cc. By 1.6 million years ago, *Homo erectus*, also known as the "Java" or "Peking" man, appeared. He had a brain size of 1000 cc, ate a wide range of foods, and used fire and a hand axe. He migrated widely, from East Africa to Europe and East and Southeast Asia.

Between two million and 11,000 years ago, the earth experienced a period that geologists call the **Ice Age**. Four times during the **Pleistocene**, or Ice Age, tremendous sheets of ice advanced southward from the north polar region, covered large portions of the Northern Hemisphere, and then receded. During the middle Pleistocene age, *Homo sapiens*, **Neanderthal**, and other forms of hominids coexisted. With a brain size of modern man, approximately 1500 cc, Neanderthal reacted to and survived the Ice Age by relying on the use of stone tools. However, from 100,000 to 60,000 years ago, *Homo sapiens sapiens,* or **Cro-Magnon**, lived side by side with and then eclipsed Neanderthal. Cro-Magnon was taller and longer limbed and relied more on wits than brawn to survive. Having better clothes and shelter, Cro-Magnon consumed fewer calories to survive, and thus, population increased.

The two competing theories of the origins of modern humans are often called the **Multiregional model** and the **Out of Africa model**. Both agree that human lineage began in Africa about two million years ago with the species *Homo habilis,* which evolved into *Homo erectus* about 1.6 million years ago. The "multiregional" or "candelabra" model says that modern humans evolved simultaneously from *Homo erectus* in many regions of the world, and that interbreeding among these regional populations has caused all modern humans to resemble one another. The "Out of Africa" model argues that modern humans arose as a small population in Africa about 100,000 to 200,000 years ago, then spread throughout the earth, displacing all other descendants of *Homo erectus,* including the

Neanderthal. DNA research has lent credence to the "Out of Africa" model, while the fossil record lends support for the other.

DNA research has also begun to shed light on theories of race. Modern races probably descended from various mixtures of ancestral types. Some black-skinned peoples have been found to share closer DNA characteristics with people outside their race than within it. Skin color seems to have been an adaptation to environment. Dark skins protect humans from tropical ultraviolet rays, while pale skins are an adaptation to the scarcity of sunlight. Thus, different races with black skins live across the equatorial belt in Africa, India, and Australia.

CHAPTER 2

The Development of Agricultural Societies

CHRONOLOGY	Mesolithic (Middle Stone Age) (ca. 10,000 B.C.E.–8000 B.C.E.)		
TERMS	agriculture slash-and-burn girding	root crops river paddy farming	maize pastoralism
PEOPLE	Amurians	Mongoloids	Amerindians
PLACES	Hallan Cemi Jarmo Jericho	Catal Huyuk Banpo	Tehuacan Valley Lascaux

The Development of Agricultural Societies

HUNTER-GATHERER CULTURE

Historians have tended to divide the eras of human development into time periods based on the type of tools that hominids made. Thus, during the **Paleolithic** (*paleo* meaning old, and *lithic* meaning stone) or **Old Stone Age**, which lasted from two million years ago, with the appearance of *Homo habilis,* the tool maker, to 10,000 B.C.E., hominids fashioned tools from stone, wood, and bone by knocking and chipping them from a core. These tools were used for cutting the soft flesh of animals. Carved bone spears, 90,000 years old, with barbed points were found at an ancient fishing site in eastern Zaire. They demonstrate a level of technology not achieved in Europe until 14,000 years ago. Evidence indicates that during the **Neolithic**, or **New Stone Age**, beginning about 8000 B.C.E., stone tools were made by polishing rather than chipping, making them stronger and capable of cutting more deeply. New tools seemed to be a response to the needs of the domestication of plants and animals, which coincided with the New Stone Age. The transitional period from 10,000 B.C.E. to 8000 B.C.E. is known as the **Mesolithic** or **Middle Stone Age**.

During the Paleolithic Era, groups of **hunter-gatherers** migrated from Eurasia into Australia and North and South America to populate all but the most remote parts of the globe. Distances between land masses such as Siberia and Alaska were less during the last Ice Age because ocean levels were lower. This enabled groups of hunter-gatherers to begin crossing from Asia to North America 50,000 and 20,000 years ago. The earliest of these peoples were classified by anthropologists as **Amurians** and the most recent as **Mongoloids**. American Indians, or **Amerindians**, descended from these two

groups. Migrations of peoples continued as a repeating theme throughout human history.

The culture, or behavior patterns, arts, beliefs, and institutions of people like hunter-gatherers, has certain characteristics. Geographically, hunter-gatherers had well-defined territories and settled campsites. They learned to control fire. They knew the habits of animals and relied on plants as an essential part of their diet. They even knew how to plant the seeds of wild plants. Their tools evolved from a stone fist hatchet to harpoons and spears to bows and arrows. They wore sewn clothing. Women's life consisted of searching and gathering foodstuffs, tending campsites, and raising children. Men prepared for and joined in the hunt. Crucial to a successful hunt were communication skills, social and political organization, and actions based on reason not instinct. Beliefs centered around animal spirits and the afterlife. The creation of cave paintings like those at **Lascaux** in France is testament to early man's sense of beauty, time, and spirituality. There, about 15,000 years ago, artists painted amazingly lifelike portraits of the animals they hunted and killed. Located deep within the earth, as much as a half mile from daylight, they were painted either to appease the spirits of animals portrayed, or to persuade the "Earth Mother" to be bountiful.

THE AGRICULTURAL AND PASTORAL REVOLUTIONS

Somewhere in the Mesolithic Era or Middle Stone Age, ca. 10,000 to 8000 B.C.E., hunter-gatherer societies began to cultivate ground and plant crops. This was an activity that had probably been going on for some time, but then was intensified and extended. This was a crucial step in that it liberated humans from bondage to the natural environment. Women probably took the first important steps in this change.

Domestication of Plants

Agriculture, or the breeding, planting, and sowing of foodstuffs, probably originated in Southwest Asian lands or in areas of similar environment. Here, on the western sides of the Zagros Mountains (Iran) and at sites like Jarmo (Iraq), rains supported sustained agriculture. The first successful type of agriculture was **slash-and-burn**, a system that allowed farmers to grow grain in places where it did not grow naturally. **Girding** was a technique to cut the bark around trees, thus killing them, letting in sunlight, and keeping out weeds. After a few years, farmers burned the dead trees so the ashes could improve fertility. Meanwhile, farmers learned how to select strains of seeds that did not fall easily off the stalks, produced abundant harvest, and were resistant to disease and weather. After five or six years, farmers usually had to move on because weeds had overtaken the field or because of exhausted soil. This constant movement helped grain farming to be diffused far and wide. Originating in Southwest Asia about 9000 to 10,000 years ago, it spread to the Nile Valley ca. 5000 B.C.E. Ancestors of the Chinese began farming millet 7000 B.C.E. along the Huang Ho (Yellow River). The first evidence of cultivated maize (corn) was in the Tehuacan Valley of Mexico about 4500 to 4700 years ago.

In other environments the domestication of plants took other forms. In tropical areas of South Asia, root farming began by 5000 B.C.E. Very likely, where "hunter" fishermen frequented suitable harbors, women began to cultivate **root crops** like manioc, taro, cassava, and yams. Unlike grains that were sown and harvested, root farmers planted live shoots from parent plants and waited for the shoots to grow new roots. In cultivated patches, plants at various stages were grown together, indicating that the difference between summer and winter was slight. Another type of farming that had a more dramatic impact on society was rice paddy farming. Developed in the monsoon areas of the world, it very likely developed on the heels of planting methods already known. Rice invaded water soaked fields and soon farmers began planting seedlings into these paddies. Later, methods of regulating water supply to the fields were developed. Historians are divided over the question of whether maize (corn) farming in the Americas developed independently or was carried from Asia. Regardless, its development seems to have followed that of grain farming in which selectively bred seeds are sown and harvested. By about 4000 B.C.E. the domestication of maize took place in central Mexico; by 2000 B.C.E. it was grown in Peru, and by 1000 B.C.E. in the southern United States. While over 100 different crops were domesticated in the Americas, the three main ones were maize, potatoes, and manioc.

Domestication of Animals

Pastoralism, or the domestication of animals, coincided with the development of agriculture. As populations settled down, hunters became pastoralists. This allowed a more reliable source of meat with less energy expended, and it led to the use of animals for carrying and pulling, and to byproduct derivatives like milk and hides. In the plains regions of Asia, Africa, and the Americas, where it was too dry for agriculture, the pastoral cultures took shape. Moving with the flocks and engaging in subsistence agriculture, the nomadic ways of the hunter-gatherers, in part, remained.

The dog was domesticated from the wolf 12,000 years ago. New archaeological discoveries dating back 10,000 years in southeastern Turkey at Hallan Cemi indicate that the pig was the first animal to be domesticated for food. Domestication of animals preceded the transition to agriculture at this site. Taming sheep and cattle in western Asia followed. In the Americas, fewer animals were available to domesticate. Amerindians domesticated dogs, turkeys, and guinea pigs. Early Peruvians tamed llamas and wool-bearing alpacas some 7000 years ago. Water buffalo and chickens originated in southern Asia. Domestication of the rabbit first began in the Roman era on the Iberian Peninsula.

Technology

Technological developments aided the development of agriculture. The soft chipped arrowhead, knives, and spears used for cutting flesh in the Paleolithic period gave way to the polished hard stones of the Mesolithic period. Attached to handles, they could cut down trees in order to clear fields. Soon, animal strength was introduced to pull spades (plows) through the soil, opening up even more land for farming. The wheel was introduced in Egypt and Mesopotamia by 3000 B.C.E. Methods of controlling water supply, grinding grain, and storing it furthered the agricultural process. Boatbuilding and sailing enabled Neolithic peoples to develop long-distance trading networks using nearby rivers for transport.

The results of the agricultural revolution were dramatic. Population increased from two million in Paleolithic times to approximately 60 to 70 million in Neolithic times. While many people remained in Paleolithic or Mesolithic cultures, the agricultural revolution bred two new cultures, agriculturalists and pastoralists, who were often at odds with each other over land. Specialization of the new cultures led to increased trade and its mechanisms like carts and bridles, containers like jars and baskets, and mediums of exchange. It also led to settled communities.

AGRICULTURAL COMMUNITIES

The settled life of the farmer led to a new kind of society. The most visible change was the growth of villages and towns. Sites excavated at **Jarmo** in Iraq, **Jericho** in Jordan, and **Catal Huyuk** in Turkey are dated ca. 7000 B.C.E. Agricultural villages like **Banpo** in China were established along the Yellow River around 5000 to 4000 B.C.E., and settlements existed in the **Tehuacan Valley**, Mexico ca. 4000 B.C.E.

There are architectural similarities among many of these early towns. Their orderly streets reflect planning. They were often built of uniform mud-dried brick. Individual family dwellings were linked. Inhabitants built central squares for trade and ceremony and walls for defense. The society that emerged in these towns reflects growing specialization. Artisans made pottery for cooking vessels or to store grain, wine, and oil. Those skilled in weaving produced baskets or textiles. While some people were artisans, others engaged in trade, or in military, religious, or political endeavors, and still others in farming. New religions based, not on animal beliefs, but on the sun and fertility emerged. Keeping track of cycles and time, and the transmission of such knowledge became important. Growing wealth is reflected in the fine craftsmanship of jewelry, mirrors, and weapons. With these changes, the first civilizations were born.

UNIT REVIEW

Cross-Regional Developments

During the very long period in human history between four million B.C.E. and 8000 B.C.E., human beings developed physically, socially, technologically, and spiritually into a form we are familiar with today. This happened against a backdrop of geologic changes, including four Ice Ages. Physically, hominids became bipedal, increased their brain size, and developed the capability to speak. Socially, hominids began to live in extended groups that worked effectively together to improve hunting and survival possibilities. Technologically, humans fashioned tools to help them in the hunt and to survive the cold weather of the Ice Ages. Spiritually and esthetically, early humans developed a sense of time, learned behavior, ritual religious patterns based on animal spirits, and methods of artistic expression. Throughout this Paleolithic period, change was dominated by the slow process of adaptation to the environment.

During the Neolithic period in the transition from hunting and gathering to agriculture, humans began the process of changing the environment. The domestication of plants and animals revolutionized the lives of *Homo sapiens*. With a surplus of food, populations grew, settled towns were established, specialization of occupations began to appear, new technologies like the wheel, farm implements, irrigation procedures, building, timekeeping, and religions based on fertility were developed. This set the stage for the development of civilization and with it, writing.

Legacies

The human past before the rise of civilizations left many legacies for the modern world. The first global legacy was the peopling of the earth and the astounding story of human adaptation to a variety of contrasting environments in Africa, Eurasia, and the Americas based on a successful hunter-gatherer lifestyle. The second important legacy was the emergence of agrarian societies. Man's successful manipulation of the environment dramatically increased the tempo and nature of change in human history. It set the stage for the rise of civilization.

Documents

WOMEN AND THE AGRICULTURAL REVOLUTION
by Elise Boulding (Reilly)

Successful nomads have a much easier life than do farmers. Among the Kung bushmen today, the men hunt about four days a week and the women only need to work two-and-a-half days at gathering to feed their families. . .

What was it like once bands settled down? This was almost from the first start a woman's world. She would mark out the fields for planting, because she knew where the grain grew best. . . . The agriculture practiced by these first women farmers and their children producing enough food for subsistence only, must be distinguished from the agriculture which developed out of subsistence farming and which produced surpluses and fed nonfarming populations in towns. The first type is commonly called horticulture and is carried out with hand tools only. The second is agriculture proper and involves intensive cultivation with the use of plows and (where necessary) irrigation. . . .

Women also began to spend more time on making tools and containers. No longer needing to hold the family possession down to what they could carry, women could luxuriate in being able to choose larger and heavier grinding stones that crushed grain more efficiently. . . .

The senior women of the family and her daughters and sons formed the property-holding unit of the family.

This document was written by a twentieth-century scholar, Elise Boulding. According to her analysis, women probably played a crucial role in the agricultural revolution; they were the original seed breeders. It also illustrates the changes the agricultural revolution created in society. Division of labor between men and women increased, the place of women became more powerful especially as it became identified with fertility, and leisure time decreased.

MARY LEAKEY FINDS ZINJANTHROPUS (MAIER-ROUPP)

There was indeed plenty of material lying on the eroded surface, some no doubt as a result of the rains earlier that year. But one scrap of bone that caught and held my eye was not lying loose on the surface but projecting from beneath. It seemed to be part of a skull, including a mastoid process (the bony projection below the ear). It had a hominid look, but the bones seemed enormously thick—too thick, surely. I carefully brushed away a little of the deposit, and then I could see parts of two large teeth in place in the upper jaw. They were hominid. It was a hominid skull, apparently *in situ,* and there was a lot of it there. . . .

We devoted the rest of our time at Olduvai in 1959 to extracting it, recovering every fragment we could find by sieving and washing the soil, and to demonstrating that it was indeed in situ on what was clearly part of an extensive living floor with many stone artifacts and animal bones . . . I . . . devoted myself to the task of fitting the fragments of the skull back together.

This document was written by archaeologist Mary Leakey describing the moment she came upon one of the most important fossil finds in world history. It illustrates how important the Olduvai Gorge, Tanzania, has been in the search and discovery for prehistoric remains. The Leakeys called their find Zinjanthropus (from Arabic *Zinj* meaning "East Africa" and Greek *anthropos* meaning "human being"). Today, this fossil species is referred to as *Australopithecus boisei* and is dated at between 1.75 and 1 million years ago. The document also emphasizes the importance of *in situ* ("in its original place") discoveries. When found among tools and remains of animals, archaeologists can not only find remains, but discern how early man lived.

Recall Questions

1. Human racial differences are due to
   (A) descent from different ancestral types.
   (B) differing DNA.
   (C) adaptation to the environment.
   (D) the "Out of Africa" model.
   (E) development of a dimorphic species.

2. The cave paintings at Lascaux illustrate
   (A) how *Homo erectus* lived.
   (B) how early agriculture developed.
   (C) the beliefs of Neolithic man.
   (D) the origins of the pastoral revolution.
   (E) early death rituals of hunters and gatherers.

3. Scientists who study the remains of ancient peoples and their societies are
   (A) anthropologists.
   (B) paleontologists.
   (C) archaeologists.
   (D) historians.
   (E) all of the above.

4. All of the following are considered reasons for the survival of *Homo sapiens* and for successful adaptation to varied or contrasting environments EXCEPT
   (A) social organization.
   (B) language skills.
   (C) physical agility.
   (D) mental acumen.
   (E) learned behavior.

5. Neolithic stone tools can be distinguished from earlier tools because
   (A) they were made of bone, wood, and stone.
   (B) they were shaped principally by chipping or pounding from a core rock.
   (C) they were often spears with barbed points of bone.
   (D) they were shaped by chipping, grinding, and polishing.
   (E) they were often spears with copper or tin points

6. The type of agriculture requiring farmers to move every five to six years in search of new land was
   (A) root farming.
   (B) rice paddy farming.
   (C) maize (corn) agriculture.
   (D) slash-and-burn agriculture.
   (E) irrigated grain farming.

7. The animal domesticated in both Eastern and Western Hemispheres was
   (A) sheep.
   (B) cattle.
   (C) chickens.
   (D) llamas.
   (E) pigs.

8. The difference between agriculture and horticulture is:
   (A) Agriculture involves irrigation and horticulture does not.
   (B) Agriculture is less complex than horticulture.
   (C) Agriculturists use hand tools but do not produce a surplus.
   (D) Agriculture came before horticulture.
   (E) none of the above.

9. Methods used to date prehistoric artifacts and fossils include
    (A) analysis of other artifacts and fossils at the site.
    (B) carbon 14 dating.
    (C) accelerator mass spectrometry.
    (D) analysis of DNA.
    (E) all of the above.

10. Which of the following is arranged in correct chronological order?
    (A) Neolithic, Mesolithic, and Paleolithic
    (B) *Homo habilis, Homo sapiens,* and *Homo erectus.*
    (C) Cro Magnon, Neanderthal, and Java or Peking man
    (D) hunting and gathering, rice paddy farming, and slash-and-burn agriculture
    (E) None of these appear in the correct order.

To check your answers, see page 393.

Lascaux Cave Paintings. *The Lascaux cave paintings give us one of the few views of life in the Paleolithic Age. All Paleolithic people relied primarily on hunting for their survival. These paintings depict the animals normally hunted or those feared. Paleolithic peoples produced the first art. Art bespeaks of one of the most important distinctions between man and animal—the quest for beauty. Beauty goes to the heart of human spirituality and the unseen imagination of the human mind. These paintings reflect the essence rather than the actuality of animals in paleolithic times. They were painted probably as a religious enjoinder for an abundant hunt, as a yearning to control the environment, or to decorate the place used as sanctuaries for ritual initiations and burials.*

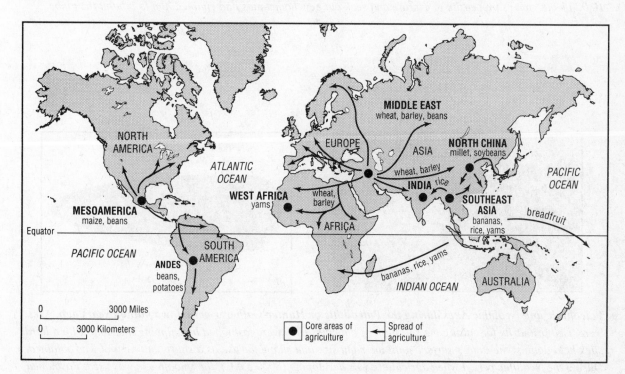

The Spread of Agriculture Beginning About 8000 B.C.E. *The Agricultural Revolution began in Southwest Asia and northern China during the Neolithic period, roughly 8000–5000 B.C.E.*

The Spread of Human Population About 10,000 B.C.E. *Fire to keep warm, tools with which to make clothes and shelters, and the frozen land bridges created by the Ice Ages allowed humans to spread over vast territories. By 10,000 B.C.E., man's propensity to explore and seek out new homelands had enabled him to inhabit the globe.*

Paleolithic and Neolithic Axes during the Paleolithic or Hunter-Gatherer period two million years ago. *Axes were used primarily for cutting the soft flesh of animals. They were fashioned by chipping the stone with a hard stick held against the stone's surface until the right size and shape for use as a sharp cutting tool was obtained. During the Neolithic period when agriculture was developing (8000 B.C.E.), the smooth axe was used. Fashioned by polishing tough-grained stone, it was used to cut down trees in clearing fields. Polishing stone was time-consuming and much more difficult than chipping brittle stones. Farmers often had to work harder than hunters.*

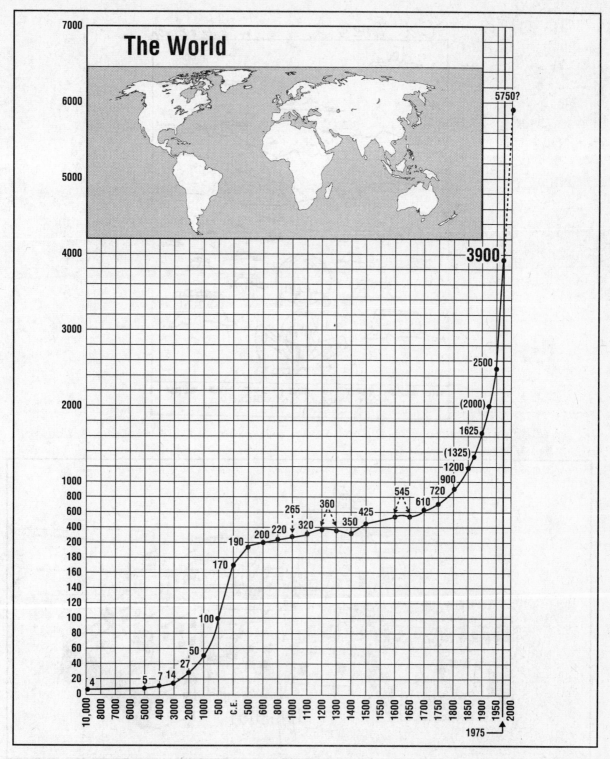

The Rise of World Population 10,000 B.C.E. to Today. *The human species had not only spread across the globe, but increased its numbers dramatically. Major growth in world population had come on the heels of the agricultural and scientific revolutions. Food and medicine were major factors in population explosion.*

Early City. *As a result of the Agricultural Revolution, the early city of Catal Huyuk in the seventh millenium B.C.E. spread over 32 acres and at one time had 6000 inhabitants. The outer houses formed a defense wall of sun-dried mud-brick. Residents climbed a ladder to a hole in the roof to enter their homes. They also used the roof tops to pass from house to house as there were no planned streets, though some random open spaces existed within the settlement. The resemblence to the cliff dwellings of Mesa Verde, a much later agricultural settlement in south-western Colorado, is striking.*

UNIT

II

EARLY CIVILIZATIONS
TO 500 B.C.E.

CHAPTER 3

The Emergence of Civilization
(4000 B.C.E.–1500 B.C.E.)

CHRONOLOGY	Old Kingdom (3100–2200 B.C.E.)
	Middle Kingdom (2100–1700 B.C.E.)
	New Kingdom (1580–1100 B.C.E.)
	Indus River (3000–1750 B.C.E.)
	Archaic (9000–5000 B.C.E.)

TERMS	civilization	calendar	papyrus
	ideograms	polytheism	monotheism
	phonograms	anthopomorphic	Aton
	alluvial	Epic of Gilgamesh	post and lintel
	Fertile Crescent	theocracy	barter
	ziggurat	pyramid	Etesian winds
	Hammurabi's Code	hieroglyphics	matriarchal
	cuneiform	Rosetta Stone	

PEOPLE	Sumerians	Jean Champollion	Howard Carter
	Sargon	King Menes	Ramses II
	Hammurabi	Hyksos	Hatshepsut
	pharaoh	Thutmose III	Olmec
	Cheops	Ikhnaton (Akhenaton)	

PLACES	Mesopotamia	Gizeh	Mohenjo-Daro
	Tigris and Euphrates	Lower Egypt	Mesoamerica
	Rivers	Upper Egypt	San Lorenzo
	Ur	Karnak	La Venta
	Babylonia	Indus River Valley	altiplano
	Nile	Harappa	Chavin de Huantar

The Emergence of Civilization (4000 B.C.E.–1500 B.C.E.)

THE MEANING OF CIVILIZATION

About 4000 B.C.E. village culture gave way to **civilization**. The word civilization can be most closely connected to the word city and involves practices that are connected with city life. Among these practices are:

1. a degree of political order and power;
2. specialization of jobs and class differentiation;
3. city design and building projects that require complex systems of human mobilization and technological skill;
4. establishment of religious centers; and
5. writing systems.

For historians, the notion of civilization has provided a framework for analysis whereby human activity can be broken down into components of political, social, economic, and cultural activities.

The earliest civilizations are closely connected with rivers and successful water system management. They occurred in isolated areas worldwide though their chronological appearance on the Eurasian continent suggests some cultural diffusion in their development. The early civilizations are Mesopotamia—4000 B.C.E., Egypt—4000 B.C.E., Indus Valley—3000 B.C.E., China—2000 B.C.E., Mexican Olmec—1500 B.C.E. and the Chavin culture of Peru—900 B.C.E. All successfully used water to create an agricultural surplus that in turn freed numbers of people to engage in activities other than farming.

Writing

Following the development of speech, the invention of writing during this period was the second great step in communication and marks the boundary between history and prehistory. Writing first began with pictures or pictograms used to convey a message. Certain symbols, known as **ideograms**, were added to represent an abstract idea, such as drawing a heart to stand for the idea of love. Other symbols were developed that represented a particular sound. These symbols, called **phonograms**, could be arranged in various ways to represent the sounds of words. With writing, people were no longer limited by time or distance in their effort to communicate. As more people began to live in complex, urban societies, the need to keep accurate records of tax payments, religious rituals, commerical agreements, and laws created a new class of scribes who often served as an elite corp of record keepers in temples and courts. Writing enabled more people to learn what others knew and led to new discoveries.

COMPARATIVE DEVELOPMENT OF MESOPOTAMIA, EGYPT, INDUS VALLEY, MESOAMERICA, AND PERU

Mesopotamia

In Southwest Asia, stretching in a curve from **Mesopotamia** (the land between the Tigris and Euphrates Rivers) in the east to Palestine in the west, lies an area of rich **alluvial** soil, the product of annual river overflow by the **Tigris and Euphrates Rivers**. By building dams and digging irrigation ditches, people in these valleys were able to grow crops on land that would otherwise have remained part of the desert. From present-day Iraq into Syria, Lebanon, and Israel, this agricultural area has been known in history as the **Fertile Crescent**.

By 4000 B.C.E. the towns in the valley of the Tigris and Euphrates Rivers had grown into full-fledged cities of mudbrick buildings. The city and surrounding territory, or city-state, was governed by a ruler. The city was the residential center for the king, a thriving place of commerce, and a center of worship, as evidenced by the high, terraced pyramid, or **ziggurat**, topped with a temple.

The **Sumerians** in the south laid the foundations for the civilization. Various invaders like the Akkadians came into the valley and adopted Sumerian ways. From time to time, groups of city-states formed alliances, and during the first 1000 years of Mesopotamian history, two empires were formed. About 2400 B.C.E. a great Akkadian warrior, **Sargon**, conquered Mesopotamia and established the first empire. The secret to Sargon's success was a large, standing army that was a mixed blessing. Without a bureaucracy to collect taxes to pay soldiers and resupply the army, he could not sustain them in any one city for very long. He had to plan new military campaigns and was doomed to always be on the move. When Sargon died, his empire fell apart. In the five centuries after the fall of Sargon's empire, the Sumerian city of **Ur** dominated the others. In 1750 B.C.E., the Amorite king of Syria, **Hammurabi**, established a new Mesopotamian empire, **Babylonia**. It fell to the Kassities in 1600 B.C.E.

Politically, the history of Mesopotamia was a stormy one. The region not only suffered internal strife, but was a highway for invasion. It was, perhaps, out of the need for order among various peoples that laws were arranged systematically by topics for easy reference. **Hammurabi's Code** was based on the concept of an eye for an eye and of unequal punishment among classes, the lowest classes receiving harsher punishment than the upper ones. Nevertheless, it provided a notion of justice that was, for the first time, standardized and regularized.

Next to farming, the chief occupation of Mesopotamians was trade. A great part of the trade was carried on or dominated by the priests. Metal ingots were used for currency and the necessity for business records no doubt prompted the invention of a writing system called **cuneiform**. This was based on syllables and words written with a stylus on clay tablets and baked. To aid farmers, a system of time measurement or **calendar** based on lunar patterns was devised. A mathematical system based on scales of twelve was developed. The common problems of farming that ranged from clearing swamp land to creating irrigation systems were aided by development of a political order dominated by chiefs, kings, and priests. The needs of agriculture also produced great technological breakthroughs, among them the plow and use of oxen to pull it, the wheel and cart, and bronze, an alloy of copper and tin, to make sturdier tools.

Classes in Mesopotamia were rigid and fixed by law. They were nobles, freemen, and slaves. Women could hold property and engage in business. Slaves, usually people captured through war or debt, were common. They provided the labor force to build brick temples and other monuments.

The Mesopotamian gods were connected not with animals, as in hunter-gatherer societies, but with the forces of nature. While powerful, immortal, and invisible, the gods of this **polytheistic** religion tended to take on **anthropomorphic** forms, whereby they lived in hierarchies and oversaw human tasks. They were thought to be the architects of natural disasters, and since there were many such disasters, especially those associated with the flooding and rampages of the Tigris and Euphrates, the Mesopotamians tended to look on their gods as wrathful rather than benign. It is in this context that the narration of the Deluge that gave rise to the biblical story of Noah can be understood. In addition to myths, the first great epic poem, the *Epic of Gilgamesh*, was produced. The epic shows the Sumerians wrestling with the enduring questions of life, death, mankind and deity, and immortality.

Egypt

Unlike the Tigris and Euphrates, which are subject to cataracts and torrents of flooding, the **Nile** flooded with annual regularity. With layers of silt to replenish the soil and water to nourish new crops, settled communities along the Nile prospered and united. While Mesopotamia lay open to invasion from all sides, Egypt was protected by the sea, desert, and river cataracts at its borders. Egypt was also nearly self-sufficient with enormous quantities of stone and abundant clay. Copper was obtained from Sinai and timber from Lebanon. Thus, Egyptian civilization emerged confident, tranquil, and insular.

Geographical unity gave rise to political unity under the authority of one king, a **pharaoh**. Pharaohs of the Egyptian **theocracy** were not only absolute rulers and owners of the country, but were also worshipped as gods. The absolute and deific quality of the pharaoh is well demonstrated in the building of the great **pyramids**, which required enormous social organization and architectural skills. The largest was built near Cairo at **Gizeh** by Pharaoh **Cheops** to shelter the body of the pharaoh through death and into the afterlife. The link between politics and religion can also be seen in the development of writing or **hieroglyphics**, priestly writings. Found on tombs and temple walls, hieroglyphics were originally pictograms and later included ideograms and phonograms as well. In 1821 hieroglyphics were decoded by **Jean Champollion**, using the **Rosetta Stone**. The Egyptians also invented a paper-like material called **papyrus**.

The unified political history of Egypt began around 3100 B.C.E., when **King Menes** united **Lower Egypt**, situated in the north on the Nile Delta, with **Upper Egypt**, which extended along the Nile to the First Cataract at Aswan. He established the first of many dynasties, or successions of kings, who ruled Egypt for nearly 3000 years. The first period in Egyptian history is known as the **Old Kingdom**. It lasted until 2200 B.C.E. This was followed by a period of civil wars and unrest until, in 2100 B.C.E. the prince of Thebes made himself ruler and established the **Middle Kingdom**. While the Old Kingdom was noted for its pyramids, the Middle Kingdom was remarkable for literature, art, and ideas. During the period of the Middle Kingdom, the Egyptians reclaimed land in the Nile delta in Lower Egypt through a massive drainage project. Beyond Upper Egypt they occupied Nubia. Trade expanded, linking Mesopotamia, Crete, and the Palestinian coast with Egypt. Like the Old Kingdom, the Middle Kingdom was torn apart by civil war and then by outside invaders, the **Hyksos**, in 1700 B.C.E.

About 1580 B.C.E. the Egyptians rebelled against the Hyksos and established the **New Kingdom**. During the New Kingdom, influences from outside were evident. Egyptians became efficient warriors and during the reign of **Thutmose III**, one of the greatest of the warrior pharaohs, Egypt extended its rule through Syria and Palestine and conquered Nubia to the south. Outside influences were evident under **Ikhnaton** (Akhenaton). The **monotheistic** idea of a single all-powerful god, the sun god **Aton**, permeated the nation's religion. **Howard Carter's** discovery in 1922 of Tutankhamon's tomb provided invaluable artifactual envidence of life during this period. Under **Ramses II**, the last of the great New Kingdom pharaohs, Egypt fought to retain its territory along the shores of the eastern Mediterranean, but by the tenth century B.C.E. Egypt had lost its empire and independence to foreign rule. During the imperial period, temples, rather than pyramids of the Old Kingdom, were the supreme architectural achievement. An outstanding example was at **Karnak**, a huge colonnaded hall built using the **post and lintel** construction, a style later employed by the Greeks.

Numerical System

Egyptian life centered around agriculture. The Egyptians planted, harvested, and ordered their time with a solar calendar of 365 days. Calculating boundaries of fields required a survey that prompted the development of geometry. Government officials collected taxes using a system of numbers and arithmetic based on the decimal. Egyptians, however, did not develop the concept of zero nor did they use money. They traded by **bartering** or swapping one item for another.

Trade moved easily up and down the Nile. The Nile current carried ships downstream in a northerly direction toward the Mediterranean. Seasonal **Etesian winds** worked against the current, propelling ships with sails south or upstream toward Luxor and beyond. Thus, two-way river traffic was accommodated.

Egyptian Society

A stratified society offered individuals some freedom as well as constraints. Even though the majority of Egyptians were servants or laborers, slavery did not become widespread until the New Kingdom and empire. The elite minority served the pharaoh as priests, nobles, and bureaucrats. Upper class women occupied an important place in Egyptian society as dynastic rights were **matriarchal** or traced through the woman's family. **Hatshepsut**, wife and half sister to two successive pharaohs, ruled for 40 years and was the only woman to serve as a pharaoh during this period. Occasionally, humble people, if talented, could rise to the top. Most men and women were probably close to serfs as they could not easily leave their land and were often forced to work as laborers on the pharaoh's projects like the pyramids.

The Indus Valley

About 3000 B.C.E. a third civilization emerged in the **Indus River Valley**. Like the Tigris, Euphrates, and Nile Rivers, the Indus River deposits a rich soil over a vast area, and while not so isolated as the Nile, the Indus Valley is protected. In the north are the towering Himalaya Mountains, in the west, the Hindu Kush Mountains, and to the east, the Great Indian Desert.

In the Indus Valley, two great cities, **Harappa** and **Mohenjo-Daro**, as well as about 70 other ancient towns and villages have been discovered. Far less is known about the Indus Valley than Mesopotamia or Egypt. Still, there is enough archaeological evidence to suggest that the Indus Valley possessed many of the hallmarks of early civilization. Harappa and Mohenjo-Daro were well-planned cities that included a walled central city where the rulers lived and where large granaries stored surplus crops as taxes. The rulers were very likely a strong priestly class. While writing on seals and other artifacts is evident, it has yet to be deciphered. Inhabitants used a standard system of weights and measures. The residents enjoyed piped water, indoor bathrooms, public drainage systems, and ceremonial bathhouses. Upper classes were composed of rulers, priests, and wealthy merchants, while the lower classes lived in smaller dwellings inside and outside the city, primarily as farmers and small artisans.

Like the other civilizations, the Indus Valley was supported by agriculture. But they also traded with Mesopotamia, and they used resources that came from as far away as southern India and Tibet. About 1750 B.C.E. the Indus Valley went through some sort of crisis, either environmental or invasion, and was then abandoned.

Mesoamerica

The process of change from hunter-gatherer society to agricultural is not well-known in **Mesoamerica**. Domestication of plants—beans, peppers, avocados, squash, and maize—probably began with the domestication of maize between 4700 and 4500 years ago. By 2000 B.C.E. villages and pottery of the **Archaic** period are evident. Around 1200 B.C.E. when Tutankhamen ruled in Egypt, the "mother civilization" of Mesoamerica, the **Olmec**, appeared. Major sites are in the wet tropical forests of the gulf coast of eastern Mexico at San Lorenzo (1200–900 B.C.E.) and La Venta (900–500 B.C.E.). Maize cultivation along the rivers provided the basis for a state ruled by a hereditary elite in which ceremonialism of a complex religion dominated much of life.

The Olmec were great carvers in jade and sculpted monumental stone heads with Negroid features and humans with feline attributes. They developed a numerical system based on 20 and a calendar that combined a 365-day year with a 260 ritual cycle. Language and writing systems remain a mystery.

Peru

The geography of South America produced two environments conducive to agriculture. One was the arid coastal valleys of Peru and the other was the highlands or **altiplano** between the two major chains of the Andes. Separation between the two areas and the demands of irrigation created the need for state building projects like large and well-organized irrigation and road and bridge building. Evidence indicates the development of pottery and cotton textiles, domestication of the llama, and construction of large temple platforms and adobe and stone structures between 3000 and 2000 B.C.E. The largest of these ceremonial centers was **Chavin de Huantar** (900–250 B.C.E.).

ACHIEVEMENTS OF EARLY CIVILIZATION

The achievements of early civilization can be enumerated as follows:

1. creation of an agricultural surplus leading to specialization of labor and wealth;
2. creation of systems of irrigation and water control;
3. metallurgy, particularly copper and bronze;
4. cities;
5. governmental systems with legal codes and bureaucracies;
6. writing and math;
7. religious systems closely connected with nature;
8. noteworthy architectural monuments such as temples, ziggurats, and pyramids.

CHAPTER 4

The Age of Metal
(3000 B.C.E.–500 B.C.E.)

CHRONOLOGY	Bronze (4000 B.C.E.)
	Minoan Society
	  (2100–1900 B.C.E.)
	Mycenae (1900 B.C.E.–
	  1100 B.C.E.)
		Shang Dynasty
		  (1500 B.C.E.)
		Non Nok Tha
		  (2500 B.C.E.)
		Dong Son (500 B.C.E.)
			Iron (1200 B.C.E.)
			Assyrian Empire
			  (800–612 B.C.E.)
			Aryan India (1500 B.C.E.)

TERMS	bronze Indo-European The Iliad The Odyssey chariot aristocracy loess bureaucracy nuclear family extended family oracle bones actographic	Pinyin Wade-Giles iron empire cavalry Sanskrit Rig Veda Mahabharata Ramayana monsoon caste transcendental	dharma raj Indra Vedas Shiva Vishnu Brahman asceticism Upanishads reincarnation Hinduism
PEOPLE	Minoans Mycenaeans Homer Heinrich Schliemann Dorians Xia (Hsia) Dynasty Shang Dynasty	Yu vassal patriarch shaman Non Nok Tha Dong Son Thur Dynasty	Hittite Assyrians Persians Aryans Dravidians Brahman
PLACES	Crete Knossos Troy Kazakhstan	Huang Ho (Yellow River) Nineveh steppes Khyber and Bolan Passes	Hindu Kush Ganges River Hindustan

The Age of Metal
(3000 B.C.E.–500 B.C.E.)

BRONZE TECHNOLOGY, NOMADIC INVASIONS, AND THE DEVELOPMENT OF CIVILIZATION IN THE MEDITERRANEAN BASIN, CHINA, AND SOUTHEAST ASIA

Around 4000 B.C.E. copper began to be mixed with tin to make **bronze**. This development occurred around the Black Sea and in Southwest Asia. Use of metal allowed faster manufacture of a greater variety of tools than those of stone or bone. Metal hoes, plows, and other implements proved useful to both agricultural and nomadic societies. This gave rise to a specialized group of artisans and encouraged trade because tin, in particular, was hard to find.

Mediterranean Basin

By 2900–2100 B.C.E. trade had become a motivation for extensive development of sea routes. Minoan society in particular was influenced by this development. The **Minoans** developed a civilized society on the island of **Crete** and traded widely with both Mesopotamia and Egypt. Copying Egyptian art and architectural forms, math, and the alphabet, the Minoans developed important new artistic styles that are reflected in the colossal palace they built at the city of **Knossos**, which was subsequently destroyed by earthquakes and rebuilt. Minoan navies carried their culture to Greece giving rise to a new civilization there called Mycenae.

The **Mycenaeans** were **Indo-European** invaders who spoke a language related to Greek. They entered Greece from the north about 1900 B.C.E and built fortress cities at Sparta, Thebes, Athens, and Tiryns. From these settlements on the mainland, early Greek chieftains advanced throughout the lands around the Aegean Sea. The most famous of these assaults was the siege of the city of **Troy** probably around 1200 B.C.E., described in the great Greek epic poems *The Iliad* and *The Odyssey* by **Homer**. In *The Iliad*, the Mycenaean king Agamemnon kills the Trojan hero Hector, and in *The Odyssey*, Odysseus, a soldier who fought in the Trojan wars, makes an adventurous trip home to Greece. In both stories wisdom is the source of power and victory. In modern times these stories were regarded as myths until **Heinrich Schliemann** excavated ruins at Troy and Mycenae in the late 1800s.

About 1700 B.C.E. the civilized world, extending from the Aegean to the Indus, was overrun by nomadic conquerors. The success of these conquests was closely linked with an important advance in the technique of warfare, the **chariot**. The earliest known chariots, 4000 years old, were found in Central Asian burial mounds in what is now **Kazakhstan**. Mobility, firepower, and armor favored the charioteers. The security of the chariot allowed warriors to launch a barrage of arrows with complete impunity. The weakness of charioteer warfare lay in the expense of the equipment. Bronze weapons and armor, horses, and the skilled leatherwork and carpentry required to construct a serviceable chariot was possible for only a few. The chariot age, therefore, was an age of military **aristocracy**, or rule by an elite upper class.

In Southwest Asia, the significance of chariot warriors was not so great as the civilizations were more firmly rooted and the invaders soon adopted the civilized ways of the places they conquered. For example, from the western end of the Fertile Crescent, the Hyksos invaded Egypt but were driven out by 1570 B.C.E. The Mycenaeans crossed from Central Asia into Greece and were absorbed into the Minoan culture. They, in turn, were overcome in 1200 B.C.E. and 1100 B.C.E. by nomadic peoples from the north, the **Dorians**.

China

Although the **Xia (Hsia) Dynasty**, ca. 2000 to ca. 1600 B.C.E., may have used chariots and bronze, the charioteer invasion of the **Shang Dynasty** left a lasting and indelible record. Like the Tigris and Euphrates, Nile and Indus Rivers, the **Huang Ho** or the **Yellow River** in northern China deposits a rich layer of **loess**, especially at the Ordos bulge, as it flows from its highland source in the Tibetan plateau to the sea. From ancient times, controlling the river by building and maintaining dikes and canals was a major preoccupation of leaders such as the semilegendary founder of China's first kingdom, **Yu** of the Xia (Hsia) Dynasty. By 1500 B.C.E. one of the tribes of the area, the Shang, predominated.

The Shang monarch was seen as the intermediary between the Supreme Being and ordinary mortals. His kingdom was viewed as the center of the world and he directed the affairs of state and bore ritual responsibility for the fertility and well-being of his subjects. While he was served by a sizable regular **bureaucracy** or government officials in the capital city, most of the peasant and artisan population of the kingdom was governed by **vassal** retainers.

In Shang society, peasants worked the land or were servants of aristocratic families. It is likely that slaves were artisans engaged in the manufacture of products that required a high degree of skill, such as weaving silk textiles and casting of bronze, both important inventions of this period. Peasants generally lived in modified **nuclear families** composed of husband, wife, children, and perhaps a grandmother or cousin, while the aristocrats lived in **extended families** consisting of several generations of the family **patriarch**, or the oldest male, who ruled the family.

Shang artistic expression reached its peak in the ornately carved and expertly cast bronze vessels used to make offerings to ensure plentiful harvests. Concern for abundant harvests led the Shang elite to put great stock in the predictions of the **shaman** priests whose prognostications were based on the **oracle bones**, or readings inscribed on bones and shells. Like Egyptian hieroglyphics, Chinese writing was **pictographic**. Over time, the number of characters increased substantially and were the key to Chinese identity and civilization as they united the diverse peoples of the area who spoke an array of languages, but understood the meaning of a symbol within their own language. Just as the symbol 5 refers to the word *cinco* in Spanish and five in English, so do Chinese pictographic symbols refer to words in different languages and dialects that have the same meaning.

The problem of transliterating Chinese characters into English has led to two systems— **Pinyin** and **Wade-Giles**. The newer Pinyin system, which was adopted by the People's Republic of China, is used in periodicals, newspapers, and books about modern China. The older Wade-Giles system, still used in Taiwan and in all English language publications before 1979, appears in this book in parentheses. Chinese words commonly used in English have one spelling.

Southeast Asia

The Bronze Age reached Southeast Asia even before it reached China. By 2500 B.C.E. people in the **Non Nok Tha** culture in ancient Thailand were making bronze tools and implements. Bronze working reached its height around 500 B.C.E. in Vietnam when the **Dong Son** people created huge bronze drums decorated with beautiful designs. The Dong people lived in farming villages but some cities began to appear about 1000 B.C.E. with the rise of the **Thur Dynasty**. This dynasty may have brought Chinese influence into Vietnam, as written references to Vietnam begin with Chinese records of Vietnamese contacts about 200 B.C.E.

IRON TECHNOLOGY AND THE COMPARATIVE DEVELOPMENT OF MILITARY EMPIRES

Iron was probably an accidental by-product of smelting copper or lead in the **Hittite** Empire in present Anatolia (Turkey). Its widespread use began about 1200 B.C.E., following the Hittite decline. The abundance of iron made it cheaper and more accessible, but the necessary technology made it more complex to produce. It had to be heated to higher temperatures and worked rather than poured.

The first major consequence of iron was that it set off another wave of barbarian invasions. The second consequence was economic. Sickle blades, plow shares, and other related agricultural tools were made with iron. This increased the efficiency of agriculture in areas where clayey soils made breaking the earth difficult. The search for new sources of iron ore led to trade and exploration and, thus, spread civilization. It also led to large territorial states called **empires**. The **Assyrian** Empire, the **Persian** Empire and the **Aryan** invasion of India are illustrative of the Iron Age. They built on and spread the legacies of the early civilizations, utilized metallurgy both in the military and civilian sectors, and created large imperial states that set the course of later civilizations in the area.

In Southwest Asia, the Hittites were the first people to work iron and spread the use of iron tools throughout the area. By about 1400 B.C.E. the Hittite kings, after many battles with Babylonians and others, extended their rule over a wide area between the Mediterranean and Black Seas. Yet they were weakened by conflict, and about 1200 B.C.E. were overwhelmed by barbarian invaders. By 800 B.C.E., however, a line of energetic Assyrian kings brought all of Mesopotamia under their rule, creating a vast empire. From their capital at **Nineveh**, they ruled by force, relying on the military and terror to hold it together. In 612 B.C.E., the Assyrians were overthrown, and by 546 B.C.E. the Persians reconquered the area and created a new empire. The successful overthrow of the Assyrians was in part due to the **cavalry** revolution that occurred in the **steppes** (the plains of Eurasia) about this time. By mounting horses, bow in hand, whole tribes of nomads acquired mobility and striking power that hitherto had been reserved only for the aristocratic charioteers. The successful cavalry raids of the Cimmerians and Scythians encouraged revolt by rebellious Babylonians and other dissatisfied subjects for the final overthrow of the Assyrian state.

Aryan Invasion

Metallurgy and nomadic invasions gave definition to Indian society as well. Steppe nomads called Aryans, who spoke an Indo-European language called **Sanskrit**, used the **Khyber** and **Bolan Passes** through the **Hindu Kush** mountain range to invade as early as 1500 B.C.E. The Aryans claimed the land that had been the Indus Valley civilization where they began to settle down and practice agriculture. Some of the native **Dravidians** were conquered; others moved south. Knowledge of this aristocratic charioteer "heroic age" of Indian history can be found in the *Rig Veda*, the oldest religious writings in the world, and the *Mahabharata*, a vast epic poem describing heroic battles between horse-drawn charioteers. The other great epic poem of India was the *Ramayana*, a story of heroic Rama and his wife Sita.

By 900 B.C.E. the use of iron spread to South Asia and, as in Southwest Asia, allowed poor men to protect themselves with armor. It also allowed for the fashioning of new tools that could be used to clear the jungle, especially in the **Ganges River** Valley with its abundant **monsoons** (seasonal winds from the Indian Ocean that bring the summer rains essential to agriculture in South and East Asia). There, rice cultivation, with its higher yields and permanent fields, brought a full-fledged agricultural civilization into being.

Caste

Centralized monarchies supported by courtly centers, high artisan skills, and interregional trade between the Indus and Ganges Valley developed. The unique character of the emergent

Indian civilization centered on the institution of **caste** and the ascetic **transcendental** emphases of Indian religion. The origins of caste are obscure, but historians speculate that it was either a principle upon which the Indus civilization was built, or a way in which Aryan invaders maintained control and separation from those they conquered and ruled. Castes ordered the society into groups and subgroups of families who shared the same occupation inherited the same religious duties or **dharma**, and avoided social contacts with members of other castes. At first, caste practices were not strictly observed. Caste lessened the significance of political and territorial rule and provided a means of bringing new groups into society. New groups became new subcastes. The fragile character of Indian states and the strength of the local princes or **rajes** resulted in large part from caste divisions. This was because the social, economic, and cultural bond of caste was stronger than the political ties of state. Caste also helped maintain priest-led ancient magical rites. Habits of thought related to these ceremonies gave Indian religious tradition a transcendental or metaphysical quality.

Vedas

Surviving records of the Aryans, written in Sanskrit, describe a pantheon of deities, among whom the principal war leader and strongest personality was **Indra**, the destroyer of cities and god of thunder and storm. The similarities between the Indian pantheon of gods and those of Mesopotamians and Greeks suggest a common ancestor in the Indo-European invaders. The priesthood, which developed into the **Brahman** caste, accompanied the invaders to invoke the gods and offer sacrifice. These rituals are found in the *Vedas*, three books of sacred knowledge originally composed and recited orally in Sanskrit. The oldest, the *Rig Veda,* is a collection of hymns to the gods believed to date from 1800 B.C.E. to 1300 B.C.E. By the late Vedic period, the third century B.C.E., the Hindu gods **Shiva** and **Vishnu** prevailed as examples or manfestations of **Brahma**, the universal, eternal force, present in all things. Like fire, Brahma was said to assume many shapes like the god of creation. The many forms or gods believers worshipped were all thought to represent specific aspects of Brahma. Shiva, the god protrayed as a cosmic dancer, was the aspect of Brahma that represented destruction. Another god, Vishnu, was the aspect of Brahma that maintained and preserved what had already been created. Thus, creation, preservation, and destruction, represented by these gods, symbolized the eternal, repeating cyle of life.

Much of Indian society, however, was unwilling to cede authority to the Brahman (Brahmin) caste and so began to develop a rival religious tradition based on **asceticism**. This largely oral tradition recorded in the *Upanishads* conceives of the end of religious life as a quest for release from a cycle of rebirths, or **reincarnations**, by a process of self-annihilation in the All. The truly holy man did not need priests but could find this Truth in self-discipline, meditation, and asceticism. The merger of the Vedic and Upanishadic religious tradition marks the birth of **Hinduism** (a word derived from **Hindustan**, which means riverland).

CHAPTER 5
Regional Interaction
(1000 B.C.E.–600 B.C.E.)

CHRONOLOGY	Kush (1000–672 B.C.E.)	Phoenicia (2000 B.C.E.)	Nok (900–200 B.C.E.)
TERMS	phonograms	Ten Commandments	Messiah
	Dreamtime	covenant	desiccation
	Old Testament	Torah	terra cotta
	Yahweh	ethical monotheism	
	Exodus	corvee labor	
PEOPLE	Phoenicians	Jacob	prophets
	Lydians	Moses	Bantu
	Aborigines	Saul	Nok
	Hebrews	David	
	Abraham	Solomon	
PLACES	Kush	Mount Sinai	Judah
	Meroe	Jerusalem	sahel
	Canaan	Israel	savanna

CHAPTER 5

Regional Interaction (1000 B.C.E.–600 B.C.E.)

COMMERCIAL INTERACTION

Kush

Largely due to expansion efforts of the early civilizations, new civilization centers grew up along the fringes of the early ones. These new civilizations used and improved on the innovations and cultural patterns of the early civilizations and often became conduits of interaction and exchange. To the south of Egypt, the kingdom of **Kush** (present-day Sudan) had become an independent state by 1000 B.C.E. In 715 B.C.E. the Kushites conquered Egypt, but their bronze weapons were no match for the Assyrian iron weapons, so they lost Egypt to the Assyrians in 672 B.C.E. Learning iron technology from the Assyrians, the Kushites established a new capital at **Meroe**, very likely because it was rich in iron deposits. The development of iron agricultural tools and weapons made Kush a powerful economic and military force. The people of Meroe also developed an alphabetic writing and domesticated the elephant. Enterprising traders, the Kushites traded with East Africa, Arabia, and India from ports on the Red Sea.

The Phoenicians

Another group called the **Phoenicians**, located on the eastern Mediterranean coast, or present-day Lebanon, emerged around 2000 B.C.E. They shared this coast with other peoples, including the **Lydians**, who migrated from Greece and are remembered in the West for developing the use of coined money. Tyre, Sideon, Byblos, and Beirut were all ancient Phoenician cities. Phoenicians acquired fame throughout the Mediterranean because of a vivid purple dye they produced from shellfish. The color, used in elegant clothing, came to symbolize royalty in western civilizations. Phoenicians made their living as traders, shipbuilders, sailors, and colonizers. They gradually extended a network of markets across the Mediterranean Basin, along the Atlantic coast as far north as England, and south around the tip of Africa. The Phoenicians borrowed the Babylonian numbering system based on 60, which they, in turn, introduced to others in the course of their trade. Their most famous colony, Carthage, would challenge Rome in the Punic Wars for control of the Mediterranean.

The most significant and lasting contribution of the Phoenicians to world history was their development of a phonetic alphabet. Because of their location, Phoenicians became acquainted with both Egyptian hieroglyphics and Sumerian cuneiform. By 1000 B.C.E. they had developed **phonograms**, a simplified method of writing using 22 consonants that symbolized sounds. Even today, Hebrew and Arabic languages use a writing system without vowels. Unlike the Egyptian system, the Phoenician symbols and the sounds they symbolized were fairly easy to learn and enabled more people to sound out words and understand the message. Thus, reading became less the exclusive activity of a few select scribes. The Greeks later added vowels to the Phoenician consonants that developed into the alphabet for all western European languages.

Southeast Asia

In Southeast Asia a lively seagoing trade developed. Using the monsoon winds and boats with sails, people easily traveled the waters between the subcontinent and the islands of Indonesia. During this period, mariners very likely reached

Australia where they encountered the **Aborigines**, who had probably arrived during the Ice Age when the islands of Indonesia and Australia were connected. There they developed a unique hunter-gatherer culture. Among their beliefs was **Dreamtime** when great ancestors walked the earth. The ancestors' spirit lived in all things and their life force continued to be passed on to new generations.

RELIGIOUS DIASPORA

Besides trade and war, religion became another vehicle of regional interaction. The **Hebrews** trace their origins to a nomadic herder named **Abraham** from the Sumerian city of Ur. According to the **Old Testament**, Abraham left Sumer at the command of his God, **Yahweh** (Jehovah) to found a new nation in **Canaan**, between the Jordan River and the Mediterranean Sea. The tribe of his descendants, led by **Jacob**, migrated to Egypt during a famine, only to be later enslaved by the pharaohs. The book of **Exodus** in the Old Testament describes how **Moses** led the Hebrews out of Egypt about 1240 B.C.E. and traveled to **Mount Sinai** where he received the **Ten Commandments** from God. The Hebrews regarded the Ten Commandments as a **covenant,** or solemn promise, to worship Yahweh and to follow His religious and moral laws as His chosen people. The **Torah**, the first five books of the Old Testament, contains the Law of Moses that requires ethical conduct and belief in one God, **ethical monotheism**. By 1021 B.C.E. a leader named **Saul** united the Hebrew tribes under a single government, Israel, and became the first king. His successor **David** built his capital at **Jerusalem**. David's son, **Solomon**, equipped with chariots, established trade networks, especially with the Phoenicians. Solomon built a huge blast furnace to smelt copper ore from the mines of the nearby Sinai. The copper provided him with a valuable export, but neither it nor the taxes levied on caravans were enough to cover expenses of his building programs, which included the temple in Jerusalem. To make up the difference, taxes and **corvee labor** were imposed. (Corvee labor is a term used in world history to denote labor required of those who could not pay their taxes in money or goods.) When Solomon died, the ten northern tribes revolted and became the kingdom of **Israel**. The two southern tribes united as the kingdom of **Judah**. By the 700s B.C.E., Assyria destroyed the ten tribes of Israel and Judah became a vassal state. When the new Babylonian Empire defeated Assyria, the Hebrews from Judah were led off into captivity. In Babylon, the Hebrew **prophets** reminded the captive people of the word of God and that a savior, or **Messiah**, would come. These religious wanderings illustrate an important aspect of cultural diffusion that took place at this time. The Hebrews absorbed and diffused metal technology and introduced the idea of monotheism far and wide.

ECOLOGY AND MIGRATION

The history of sub-Saharan Africa at this time demonstrates another aspect of regional interaction. Environmental change isolated the area from the crossroads of Southwest Asia and produced a situation in which all the changes of the period from agriculture to metallurgy were diffused into Africa from the outside at a later date. Beginning about 9000 B.C.E., the area of the Sahara Desert began to dry and by 3000 B.C.E. much of the area was desert. This **desiccation** caused populations to move either north toward the Mediterranean or south into the Sudanic region of Africa that is composed of dry **sahel** and grassy **savannas**. The movement south by the **Bantu** is one of the important stories in African history. Over a period of 1000 years, the Bantu expanded over much of the continent, carrying with them agriculture, cattle raising, and iron technology.

Agriculture may have developed independently in Africa, but many scholars believe that the spread of agriculture and iron technology came from centers of civilization in Mesopotamia. The first domesticated crops in Africa were millets and sorghums whose origins are in West Asia. Livestock also came from outside Africa. Horses were apparently introduced by the Hyksos and the camel from the Arabian peninsula, around the first century C.E. Iron technology probably entered either with the Phoenicians, who carried it to Carthage in North Africa and then along the coast or by land across the Sahara into Nigeria, Ghana, and Mali, or by way of Ethiopia where iron objects can be dated to 800 B.C.E. Iron represented power and the blacksmith who made tools and weapons had an important place in society. One of the earliest iron-using cultures of West Africa were the **Nok** people who thrived in the central part of Nigeria between 900 B.C.E. and 200 C.E. Nok artisans produced beautiful **terra cotta** (baked, unglazed pottery) sculptures of human and animal figures. The diffusion of agriculture and iron was accompanied by a great movement of people who may have carried these innovations southward.

UNIT REVIEW

Cross-Regional Developments

Developments that occurred over wide regions of the globe during this period include:

- the development of agricultural surpluses that created complex societies called civilizations;
- the invention of writing systems;
- metallurgy, first copper, then bronze and iron;
- innovations in the military techniques of nomadic people like the chariot and cavalry that allowed them to attack the settled populations with impunity;
- the creation of larger states called empires with their bureaucracies and law codes;
- the diffusion of innovations by means of trade, migration, and invasion;
- the spread of Indo-Europeans across Europe and Asia;
- the origins of the Hindu and Jewish religions.

Legacies

The legacies of this period to world history are numerous:
- improvements in agriculture from irrigation to implements like plows and sickles appeared;
- the development of forms of political systems like kingdoms and empires occurred;
- specialization led to greater artisanry and trade;
- writing systems preserved records and knowledge;
- scientific and mathematical innovations led to great building projects like temples, pyramids, and ziggurats, and walled cities with paved streets and sewers;
- metallurgy progressed from copper to bronze to iron;
- new religious systems were developed that were more human oriented;
- military techniques and weapons were developed that brought the horse, chariot, and broad-based armies to the fore;
- civilization spread.

The basis was set for the classical period.

Documents

HAMMURABI'S CODE

If a man has put out the eye of a free man, they shall put out his eye.

If he breaks the bone of a free man, they shall break his bone.

If he puts out the eye of a villain or breaks the bone of a villain, he shall pay 1 maneh of silver.

If he puts out the eye of a free man's slave or breaks the bone of a free man's slave, he shall pay half his price.

Hammurabi's Code, probably written ca 1760 B.C.E., was the first known attempt in world history to provide a code of law that was applicable to all and that would be the basis of justice. The principles of Hammurabi's Code were an "eye for an eye" and the idea that the higher up the accused was on the social scale, the lesser the punishment.

THE EPIC OF GILGAMESH

The heroes, the wise men, like the new moon, have their waxing and waning. Men will say, "Who has ever ruled with might and with power like Gilgamesh?" As in the dark month, the month of shadows; so without him there is no light. O Gilgamesh, this was the meaning of your dream. You were given the kingship, such was your destiny; everlasting life was not your destiny. . . . Gilgamesh, who do you search? The life you seek you will never find. When the gods created the world, they made death a part of human fate.

About 2000 B.C.E. the Sumerians wrote down the world's oldest story, *The Epic of Gilgamesh*, which went back at least to 6000 B.C.E. in oral form. Gilgamesh was a literary hero based on a real person who had ruled a Sumerian city-state. Gilgamesh does great deeds but is unable to overcome the will of the gods or fate. The poem shows the Sumerians grappling with enduring questions of life and death, mankind and deity. There are many biblical parallels in the poem, including the stories of Adam, the Deluge, Noah's ark, and the trials of Job.

BHAGAVAD GITA (MAHABHARATA)

The spirit that is in all being is immortal in them all: for the death of what cannot die, cease thou to sorrow.

Think thou also of thy duty and do not waver. There is no greater good for a warrior than to fight in righteous war.

There is a war that opens the doors of heaven, Arjuna! Happy the warrior whose fate is to fight such war.

But to forgo this fight for righteousness is to forgo thy duty and honor: is to fall into transgression.

The two greatest epics of Indian literature, the *Mahabharata* and the *Ramayana*, began to take form about 400 to 200 B.C.E. The *Mahabharata* is one of the longest epic poems in world literature. It describes an 18-day struggle between rival families for the throne of a kingdom in northern India. The most famous section is called the *Bhagavad-Gita*. Its message is a religious one—that life is a never-ending journey toward perfection, a perfection that can be attained only by following the codes of conduct of one's caste. In this case, Arjuna is cautioned to fulfill the duties of the warrior caste.

THE TEN COMMANDMENTS

I am the Lord thy God. . . Thou shalt have no other gods before Me. . .

Thou shalt not make unto thee a graven image . . .

Thous shalt not take the name of the Lord thy God in vain. . .

Remember the Sabbath day, to keep it holy . . .

Honor thy father and thy mother . . .

Thou shalt not murder.

Thou shalt not commit adultery.

Thou shalt not steal.

Thou shalt not bear false witness. . .

Thou shalt not covet . . .

The Ten Commandments are important because they provide the ethical basis for both Judaism and Christianity. Their origins appear to be with the fundamental event in Hebrew history—Moses' leadership of the Hebrews from bondage in Egypt ca. thirteenth century B.C.E. The Hebrew god Yahweh ("he causes to be"), or Jehovah, appeared to Moses on Mount Sinai and made a "covenant," or formal contract, with the Hebrews to the effect that if the Hebrews followed the commandments, they would become the "Chosen People" of God. The Ten Commandments are more like Confucian thought than Hindu, Buddhist, and Taoist thought in the sense that the emphasis is on an ordering of human relationships rather than on mysticism, love, and Heaven. The first four commandments deal with the Hebrews' relationship with God, and the last six with their relationships with each other. As a Jew, Jesus embraced the Ten Commandments but added to them the idea of brotherly love, forgiveness, and the promise of a spiritual kingdom "not of this world." The Ten Commandments are contained in the Book of Exodus, one of the Five Books of Moses that make up the Torah.

Recall Questions

1. Aspects of the geography in Shang China that had lasting influence on the people who settled there included
   (A) rich deposits of loess.
   (B) isolation from other civilizations.
   (C) the necessity for irrigation and water control.
   (D) sporadic rainfall.
   (E) all of the above.

2. Which is the greatest epic poem of Sumerian history?
   (A) *Bhagavad Gita*
   (B) *Mahabharata*
   (C) *Gilgamesh*
   (D) *The Iliad*
   (E) *Ramayana*

3. The development and widespread use of iron led to improved agricultural tools and weapons giving a technological advantage to those societies that possessed the metal. The people responsible for the development of iron were
   (A) the Egyptians.
   (B) the Babylonians.
   (C) the Assyrians.
   (D) the Hittites.
   (E) the Phoenicians.

4. The archaeologist who provided evidence to prove that Troy was more than Homer's mythical tale was
   (A) Howard Carter.
   (B) Heinrich Schliemann.
   (C) Richard Leakey.
   (D) Donald Johanson.
   (E) Jean Champollion.

5. Indian religion shaped society through beliefs in the transcendental nature of life with its endless cycle of rebirths or reincarnations. The Hindu god that usually represents destruction is
   (A) Indra.
   (B) Brahman.
   (C) Shiva.
   (D) Vishnu.
   (E) Rama.

6. Which civilization was shaped socially by a belief in castes?
   (A) Minoan
   (B) Egyptian
   (C) Olmec
   (D) Indian
   (E) Chinese

7. Which leader was the first to establish an empire in world history?
   (A) Ramses II
   (B) Hammurabi
   (C) Yu
   (D) Saul
   (E) Sargon

8. Which text is incorrectly linked with the society?
   (A) *Torah*—Hebrew
   (B) *Rig Veda*—Persian
   (C) *Old Testament*—Hebrew
   (D) *Dreamtime*—Aborigines
   (E) *I Ching*—Chinese

9. Which society possessed neither iron nor bronze?
   (A) Nok
   (B) Olmec
   (C) Kush
   (D) Aryan
   (E) Assyrian

10. Based on biblical accounts, which of the following combinations is in the correct chronological order?

  I.   Solomon built the temple

  II.   Abraham left Sumer for Canaan

  III. Jacob migrated to Egypt to avoid famine

  IV. Moses received the Ten Commandments on Mount Sinai

  V.   The Hebrews were enslaved in Babylon where the Prophets reminded them of the promise of a Messiah.

    (A) II. III. IV. I. V.

    (B) II. V. I. III. IV.

    (C) V. II. I. III. IV.

    (D) II. IV. I. III. V.

    (E) III. IV. V. II. I

To check your answers, see page 393.

Mesopotamia 1700–480 B.C.E. Better known as the Fertile Crescent, the area between the Tigris and Euphrates Rivers has often been referred to as the Cradle of Civilization. The geography and climate of this area nourished the development of agriculture. Similar developments occurred along the Nile in Egypt, the Indus River in Pakistan, the Yellow River in China, and the watered plateaus of Mesoamerica.

Shiva. Shiva is one of the Hindu trilogy that includes Vishnu and Brahma. Brahman symbolizes creation, Vishnu the continuance of life, and Shiva destruction. Shiva, who is both male and female, is dancing in a destructive ring of fire. In one hand is a drum symbolizing the sound of creation, and in the other is fire symbolizing destruction. He/she is standing on the dwarf of ignorance. One leg points up toward the heavens and one hand points down toward the earth. Another hand with a flat palm symbolizes peace. The seeming polarity between Heaven and Earth, and creation and destruction, is offset by the ring that unites birth and death into one continuum. This endless cycle is fundamental to the Hindu cosmological and theological world view.

Photograph © 1995, The Art Institute of Chicago,
all rights reserved.

Wine Vessel (Fanglei)-Chinese, Shang Dynasty. These vessels, known as fanglei, were produced for the Shang elite for ritualized ceremonies of ancestor worship and were placed in their tombs when they died. The complex patterns of the outer and inner surface of this jar are designs of many animal forms. The neck of the jar is decorated with birds and dragons; bovine heads form the handles. The abstracted taotie, or horned monster, appears within the triangular design on the side of the vessel. The cicada, a symbol for regeneration also appears in the triangle. The vessel, now a blue-green patina, changed colors as the result of the interaction of bronze and the moist soil in which the vessel had been buried since the twelfth or eleventh century B.C.E.

The Persian Empire 550 B.C.E. Cyrus the Great established one of the world's first empires. To rule such a large area effectively, he built roads, divided the empire into smaller areas called satraps, and pursued a policy of toleration toward differing peoples.

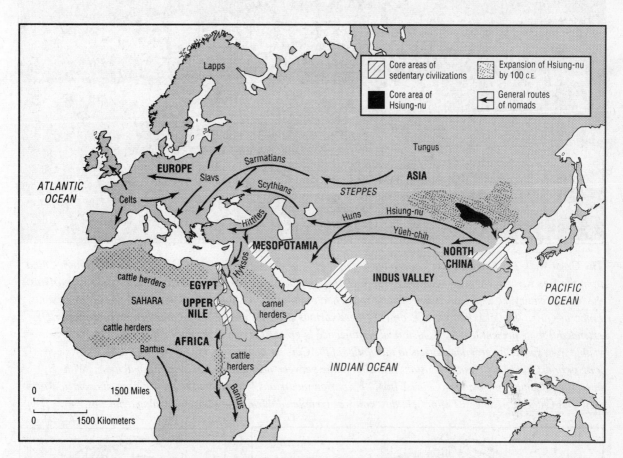

The Earliest Civilizations and the Migrations of Nomadic Peoples Beginning 2000 B.C.E. *All of the earliest civilizations succumbed to the invasion of nomadic people. Nomadic people had the advantage of mobility (the horse) and superior weaponry (bronze and iron technology) on their side. Nomadic people destroyed but they also spread civilization.*

The Great Wall. *The Great Wall of China stretches over hill and through valley across 3000 miles of northern China, from the Yalu River in the east, south of the Gobi Desert, and as far as the Altai Mountains in the west. As early as the fourth century B.C.E., the northern Chinese states had built long walls for protection against the steppe nomads. Emperor Qin in the third century B.C.E. ordered these various stretches of wall linked together. Emperors after Qin extended it to its present length. Its historical significance is great. It is one of the man-made wonders of the world visible from space. Its grandeur attests to the ability of the Chinese civilization to sustain large-scale efforts over long periods. It also reflects the constant Eurasian battle between nomadic and sedentary populations. While it never significantly protected the Chinese from "barbarian incursions," it symbolized the Chinese sinocentric world view and Chinese greatness. The present day wall was completed during the Ming and Ching dynasties.*

Ziggurat. *In southern Mesopotamia, a simple mud-brick temple, located in the center of the city to honor the local god, was periodically rebuilt and enlarged until it became known as a ziggurat or a mountain dedicated to the gods. Ziggurats were terraced, each level slightly smaller and higher than the previous one. The temple at the summit was reached by a triple stairway from the city below. The ziggurat at Ur may have been the model for the Biblical Tower of Babel.*

Olmec. *In the first century C.E. the Olmec civilization of southern Mexico suddenly vanished, leaving behind giant stone heads such as this, which were buried or smashed. The Olmec are noted for several accomplishments that were a legacy to the Mayas. One was a calendar, another, hieroglyphic writing.*

Egyptian Hieroglyphics. *Egyptian hieroglyphics, like this example from Luxor, developed among the Egyptians ca. 3100 B.C.E. from a series of pictures. The pictures were standardized and became the symbol for the object. Soon ideograms of symbols that represented an idea and phonograms or symbols that represented sounds were added to form a complex writing system valuable to priests for recordkeeping and for recording essential information concerning the religion. This system was deciphered in the early 1800s by the Frenchman Jean Champollion.*

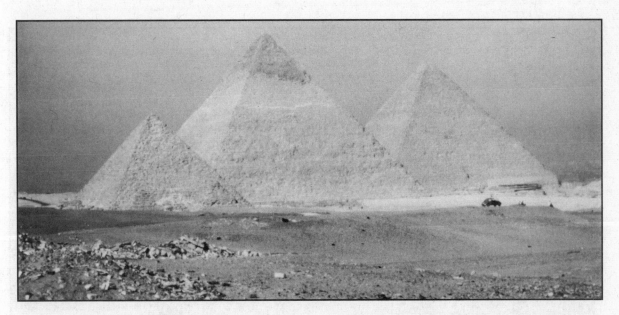

Pyramids at Giza. *The pyramids at Giza were the burial place of the pharaohs of the Old Kingdom and their aristocracy, whose rectangular tombs are visible behind the middle pyramid. The small pyramids at the foot of the foremost pyramid probably belong to the Pharaoh's wives. The pyramid style of architecture can be found in many early civilizations. The ziggurats of the Mesopotamians and the Maya temples are essentially pyramids with flat tops to accommodate religious ceremonies. The first Egyptian pyramid was ordered by pharaoh Zozer who instructed his first minister and brilliant engineer, Imhotep, to design the step pyramid at Sakkara in 1650 B.C.E. This became the model for the pyramids at Giza. The pyramids reflect the pharaoh's ability to command vast resources and labor. The religious significance of the pyramid was its reflection of the pharaoh as god. The pyramid provided the dead king with everything he needed to keep his "ka" or spirit alive. In so doing there was eternal life for all Egyptians. The technology and engineering skills needed to build the tombs furthered the development of mathematics and writing systems, keys to the development of early civilizations.*

Mayan Hieroglyphics at Chiapas. *A mark of all early civilizations was the ability to develop numerical and writing systems. The Mayan number system was based on 20 and depicted by bars and dots. A shell-shaped symbol represented zero. The writing system, like the Egyptian, was based on hieroglyphics or ideograms. The glyphs were carved on slabs of stone called* stelae, *on temples, and on paper from bark or tough maguey cactus fibers. Systems of writing and math allowed the Maya to formulate calendars, make mathematical calculations, and rule large numbers of people through bureaucracies.*

Maya Temple at Chichen Itza. *Chchen Itza "The Well of Itza," is the site of the most extensive and best preserved ruins of Maya civilization. The city, founded about 250 C.E., was a center of religion and government. The well, a round, natural pool, into which priests threw valuable objects as sacrifices to the gods, was a major religious site. The great pyramid, erected about 1100 C.E., was both an imperial tomb and a religious temple. The temple at Chichen Itza resembles a Mesopotamian ziggurat, an Egyptian pyramid, a Hindu temple, and a Buddhist stupa. Why early civilizations all built in similar architectural styles without interaction between them, remains a mystery.*

UNIT
III

SYSTEMS OF SOCIETY AND CULTURE: THE CLASSICAL AGE
(1000 B.C.E.–500 C.E.)

THE MEANING OF CLASSICISM

Between 1000 B.C.E. and 500 C.E., in many parts of the world, civilizations evolved to the point that they began to develop defining political, social, and cultural institutions and characteristics. Thus, for example, China began to develop patterns of thought and culture decidedly different from western Europe or India. In each case, these patterns were highly influenced by religious thought and traditions. Religious or philosophical thought legitimized governments, shaped class structure, and instructed the arts. These patterns became so influential that they impacted other societies and have remained important to this day in understanding cultural differences. The classical period ended between the third and sixth centuries C.E. due to internal decay and a new surge of invasions, but its institutions and ideas endured and have had broad influence over other peoples.

Classicism, therefore, can be understood as defining and long-lasting civilizational patterns shaped by belief systems. Belief systems include both philosophies and religions. Philosophies reach truth by logic while religions seek truth in faith. Philosophies often dwell in secular concerns while religions tend toward concerns of the afterlife and have priests, churches, and rituals. Both search for the meaning of life and are concerned with systems of ethics, that is, right and wrong. In some societies, like China, philosophies overshadowed religions; in others, like India, religions like Buddhism and Hinduism overshadowed philosophy. If there is a connection between the simultaneous rise of classical civilizations and the rise of the world's religions, it can probably be found in the idea that all the great religions of the world deal with patterns of ethics. Ethics tend to order human relationships. Successful ordering led to successful systems of human interaction and successful systems of society. The arts glorified beliefs in these systems. When classical civilizations reach a high point of cultural achievement, it is called a **Golden Age**.

Common to the classical experience were political systems that had institutionalized bureaucracies and armies often tied to religious hierarchies. Political leadership became systematized and legitimized by ideologies of power. Economic systems were expanding and complex, linking agriculture and commerce into large networks tied together by common coinage and rules of exchange. Wealth was created by surplus trade and expansionism. Social classes evolved into hierarchies of power, prestige, and wealth. The institution of slavery took shape. Common also to the classical experience was a tremendous outpouring of art stimulated by increasing wealth, cultural exchange, and cementing of religious tradition. Large urban centers rose as did methods of transportation connecting them. The power and appeal of classical societies caused them to spread, often resulting in large, multinational empires.

CHAPTER 6

Classical Greek Civilization
(600 B.C.E.–200 B.C.E.)

CHRONOLOGY	Hellenic Age (612–339 B.C.E.)
	Golden Age of Greece (Age of Pericles) (457–404 B.C.E.)
	Achaemenid Persia (550–331 B.C.E.)
	Hellenistic Age (323–30 B.C.E.)

TERMS			
	classicism	ephors	Zoroastrianism
	Golden Age	Battle of Marathon	dualism
	Hellenic	Battle of Salamis Bay	Mithra
	polis	Battle of Plataea	Zend Avesta
	civic	Delian League	Hellenism
	acropolis	Peloponnesian Wars	Hellenistic
	oligarchy	humanism	koine
	democracy	rationalism	cosmopolis
	phalanx	anthropomorphic	mystery cults
	archon	materialist	Cynicism
	direct democracy	Golden Mean	Epicureanism
	Assembly	Parthenon	Stoicism
	Council of 500	Doric, Ionian, Corinthian	heliocentric
	ostracism	Royal Road	

PEOPLE			
	Dorians	Sophocles	Cyrus II
	tyrant	Euripides	Darius
	Draco	Aristophanes	satrap
	Solon	Sappho	magi
	Peisastratus	Thales of Miletus	Zoroaster (Zarathustra)
	Cleisthenes	Pythagoras	Alexander the Great
	jury	Hippocrates	Ptolemies
	commander-in-chief	Sophists	Thales
	Pericles	Socrates	Aristarchus
	helots	Plato	Ptolemy
	Miltiades	Aristotle	Nicolaus Copernicus
	Xerxes	Phidias	Euclid
	Philip of Macedon	Herodotus	Archimedes
	Thucydides	Persians	Eratosthenes
	Aeschylus	Medes	

PLACES			
	Mycenae	Peloponnesus	Persepolis
	Ionia	Thermopylae	Macedonia
	Athens	Olympia	Alexandria
	Attica	Delphi	Bactrian Greece
	Sparta	Persia	

Classical Greek Civilization (600 B.C.E.–200 B.C.E.)

THE DEVELOPMENT OF THE GREEK STATE SYSTEM

One of the defining and long-lasting characteristics of Greek, or **Hellenic**, civilization was its political system. Elements of democracy (rule by the majority) reached sophisticated levels of development under the Greeks. This political system was tied to the Greek belief in rationalism. The origins of the Greek political system can be found in its early history.

Mycenae

When the Minoan civilization collapsed about 1400 B.C.E., political and commercial power in the Aegean passed to the mainland Greeks who lived in small city-states grouped under the city of **Mycenae**. Each city-state had a king who was a military general, judge, and priest, but, unlike monarchs in Mesopotamia, his power was not absolute. He was advised by a council composed of heads of important Greek families and he lived a life not dissimilar to other Greeks, plowing his own fields and shearing his sheep.

Dorian Invasion

Shortly after 1200 B.C.E. the **Dorians**, Greek-speaking Indo-Europeans in the north, began moving south, overrunning most of Greece and overthrowing Mycenaean culture. Greece plunged into its Dark Age. The chaos and confusion led to further splintering and an exodus of Greeks to Crete and the Mediterranean coast of Southwest Asia (**Ionia**), where new communities, economically and politically independent of one another, were established.

Polis

Political decentralization, the mountainous Greek landscape, and a historical predisposition toward small states led to the most important political feature of classical Greece, the city-state, or **polis**. Not unlike today's nation-state, the polis was not just a place, but a culture around which a person's meaning and purpose revolved. The word **civic** comes closest to this meaning, that is, it formed the core of an individual's social and political meaning and responsibility. People identified themselves in terms of a community. Loyalty of individuals to their polis and the separation of the polis by geography would later deter Greek attempts to unify the city-states.

The typical city-state (polis) was composed of a city or town and the surrounding countryside of valleys and plains. **Athens**, for instance, included all the towns and villages of the peninsula of **Attica** in eastern Greece, and **Sparta** occupied the valley of a fairly large river. The men who owned the large farms, along with artisans and traders, usually lived in the city that was situated on fortified high ground for protection. Such a hill or citadel was called an **acropolis** or "highest city." The city-state was ruled by a king, and advised by a council of elders. However, between 800 and 600 B.C.E., the kings lost most of their power to the nobility or large landowning aristocrats. Since both officials and the council were elected by a few upper class citizens, this kind of government was called an **oligarchy**, or rule by a few. Sometimes these oligarchs were referred to as **tyrants**, a word that denoted that a leader illegally seized power. Meanwhile, rising population and poor Greek land made Greeks, like the Minoans before them, increasingly turn to trade for a livelihood. The

Greeks exported wine, olive oil, and woolen cloth and imported grain. To increase land and trade, the Greeks began founding new city-states that began to dot the Black Sea area, western Turkey, and southern Italy and France. Soon, the rising wealth of traders and the increasing impoverishment of the farmers and slaves who worked on the lands of the rich, caused Athenian Greeks to challenge the power of the oligarchs. This challenge gave rise to one of the distinctive characteristics of Greek classical culture, **democracy**. In this system, government consisted of officials chosen by vote of the governed and responsible to them.

Origins of Greek Democracy

The reasons for Greek democracy, with its characteristics of equality and freedom of speech, seem to have originated in the economic and military nature of Greek life. In Mesopotamia, warfare was dominated by an aristocracy of horse and chariot, but in Greece, every citizen was also a soldier in the army or a rower in the navy. The army's strength lay in the **phalanx**, or a formation of eight ranks of infantry soldiers, in which all men marched together so closely that their large metal shields overlapped to form a wall. Here, rank and wealth mattered little. It was the free, farm-owning citizen-soldier with enough money to equip himself that provided the basis for Greek city-state security. The economic reason behind Greek democracy was that farmers were simple townspeople who went to their fields each morning and returned in the evening. They were free men, not serfs of great lords. Also, a civilization based on trade must have merchants, manufacturers, and craftsmen. This "middle class" prospered and in their leisure time participated in the affairs of state alongside the aristocracy.

Hellenic Age

The **Hellenic Age** (612–339 B.C.E.) began with the process of democratization in Athens when an aristocrat, **Draco**, codified the laws for the Athenian polis and made them public. This code, though harsh, embodied the idea that the law belonged to all citizens. Then, in 594 B.C.E., the aristocrats elected **Solon** as chief magistrate or **archon**. His reforms included abolition of slavery for debt and limitations on land ownership. This served to empower the commoners who were then given a place in the old aristocratic assembly. In 560 B.C.E. a tyrant named **Peisistratus** supported building programs and arts available to all the commoners, thereby advancing the feeling of equality. Finally, in 508 B.C.E., **Cleisthenes**, a wealthy and prominent aristocrat, institutionalized the Athenian democratic form of government.

Athenian Democracy

Athenian government was a **direct democracy**, meaning that all male citizens over 19 years of age were members of the **Assembly**, which voted on policy and taxes. The **Council of 500**, chosen by lot from the Assembly to serve one year, steered the Assembly. Besides this legislative branch, there was an executive and judicial branch. **Juries** that tried all cases were made up of members of the Assembly chosen by lot. The executive branch was composed of a **commander-in-chief** and nine generals elected annually by the Assembly. Other officials were chosen by lot to serve for one year. By the process of **ostracism**, individuals considered dangerous to the state could be banished by the citizenry. The virtues of the Athenian democratic system were viewed by the Athenian leader **Pericles** in 431 B.C.E., in a funeral speech given in honor of those killed during the war with Sparta. He wrote, "Ours is an unrivaled constitution. So far from owing anything to our neighbors, it sets the standard for them. On account of its popular basis, it has come to be called *Democracy* or *Rule of the Masses*. But, in fact, we enjoy, as between man and man complete equality of legal status. In our public life individual talent is the one thing valued."

Though called a democracy, Athens was not a democracy as envisioned in the contemporary world. Women, slaves, and foreigners could not vote and those groups accounted for over half of the Athenian population. Nor were all Greek city-states democracies. Sparta, for instance, a state settled by Dorians in Laconia, a region of the southern Greek peninsula of **Peloponnesus**, conquered people in the region around their city-state and treated these peoples as slaves, or **helots**. About 25,000 Spartans ruled over 500,000 subjects. The powers of government rested in the hands of five selected officials called **ephors** who were aided by two kings and a council of elders. Rebellions against Spartan masters occurred; therefore, a great deal of Spartan life was directed toward creation of a strong army. When a boy was seven, he was taken away from his family and put in a military school. Spartans did not allow anyone to make a living in any other way but farming. Spartan girls had to undergo physical training to become healthy mothers. Sparta produced no writers or artists. When someone speaks of the "Spartan way of life," they are referring to a simple, vigorous military existence. The differences in values, lifestyles, and political systems between Greek city-states ultimately led to the demise of the Greek classical age.

Persian Wars

The rise of Greece is connected with victory over the Persians. About 500 B.C.E. the Ionian Greek city-states on the eastern shores of the Mediterranean rose in revolt against their Persian master of Southwest Asia. Athens and other Greek city-states came to their defense. In revenge, the Persian king Darius decided to strike at Athens, the richest of the Greek cities, with a powerful fleet. In the **Battle of Marathon** (490 B.C.E.), which followed, the Persians landed an army on the the Plain of Marathon in Greece but were defeated by the Athenians who were led by a brilliant general, **Miltiades**. An Athenian runner ran the 26 miles from the Marathon plain to Athens to convey the good news, giving rise to the "marathon" or 26-mile running race of today. Ten years later the Persian king **Xerxes**, sought revenge. At **Thermopylae**, a narrow mountain pass in Greece, the Persians massacred a Spartan army led by King Leonidas. The Persians then proceeded to conquer northern Greece and burn the city of Athens to the ground. They were finally stopped at the **Battle of Salamis Bay** when the Athenian fleet routed the Persian navy.

Finally, Sparta and Athens teamed up to defeat the Persians at the **Battle of Plataea** in 479 B.C.E. Persian expansion into Europe halted.

Peloponnesian Wars

The battles with Persia confined Greek territory to northern Greece and the Peloponnesus. The Ionic Greek city-states on the eastern coast of the Mediterranean in Southwest Asia were lost. The continuing Persian threat resulted in a naval alliance of Greek city-states eventually dominated by Athens, called the **Delian League** (478 B.C.E.). In this confederation, each member of the League contributed ships, men, and money. Soon, however, Athens began to demand tribute from other members of the league and to use league resources to advance its own trade, building programs, and security. As the leader of the Peloponnesian League, the Spartans became alarmed by the expansion of Athenian interests. This led to the **Peloponnesian Wars** (431–404 B.C.E.). The war pitted Athens and its allies against Sparta and its allies. Ultimately, Sparta triumphed, forcing Athens to become a member of a league of cities headed by Sparta.

Disunity among Greek city-states continued over the next 60 years. This gave **Philip of Macedon** the chance to invade. In 338 B.C.E. he destroyed a joint army of Thebes and Athens and became master of the Greek city-states. As recounted in the history of the Peloponnesian Wars by **Thucydides**, impassioned oratory by **Demosthenes** and **Isocrates** illustrated the inablity of Greeks to unite successfully. Demosthenes pleaded for unity against the Macedonians, but Isocrates argued that outside rule would be preferable to continuing Greek squabbling. Greek rationalism, a hallmark of Greek society, failed to secure Greece's future.

THE CULTURAL ACHIEVEMENTS OF AEGEAN CIVILIZATION

Greek Polytheism

Greek **humanism** is the resounding cultural achievement of the Hellenic way of life. It permeated religion, politics, the arts, and intellectual life of Greece. Humanism refers to a system of thought and action that elevates human beings to the center of existence. Fundamental to this idea was **rationalism**, or the idea that in the mind of man, not the gods, can be conceived order and beauty. The idea of humanism can be traced to Greek religion. The Greek gods were originally connected with nature. Thus, Poseidon was the god of the ocean and Apollo, of the sun. Gradually, they became **anthropomorphic**, that is, they took human form and characteristics. Apollo represented clarity and order, and Athena, wisdom. The many myths that surrounded the gods were stories of human struggles and lessons about life. This Greek religion was both individual and related to the polis. Individuals often went to temples and made sacrifices at altars on matters of personal concern. Gods also formed part of a social and civic life. Each polis tended to favor one deity around which festivals and celebrations revolved. Uniting all Greeks was the pantheon of major gods and the Panhellenic festivals that were held at **Olympia** in honor of Zeus and at **Delphi** in honor of Apollo. The festivities at Olympia included the athletic contests that have inspired the modern Olympic games.

Greek Drama

Greek drama had its origins in religious festivals. The plays were produced in large outdoor theaters and were attended by all people as a method of instruction as well as entertainment. The tragedies were emotionally powerful plays built around the lives of legendary heroes and heroines. **Aeschylus** (524–456 B.C.E., *Orestia* and *Prometheus Bound*), **Sophocles** (496–406 B.C.E., *Oedipus Rex*), and **Euripides** (ca. 480–406 B.C.E., *Trojan Women* and *Medea*), the three greatest Greek writers of tragedy, wrote dramas in which fate, frequently connected with a character flaw, carried the hero from greatness to ruin. Greek comedies dealt in satire and poking fun at political officials and prominent citizens. The most popular writer of comedies was **Aristophanes** (ca. 445–385 B.C.E.). His play *Knights* satirizes corrupt government officials, and *Clouds* ridicules philosophers. One of the greatest poets of the age was **Sappho** (b. ca. 612 B.C.E.). Her poetry, mostly about love, portrayed the complexity of the inner workings of human beings as clearly as Greek sculpture portrayed its outward contours.

Rationalism

The human quality of the popular religion of Greece is connected with the other belief system of the Greeks, especially the Athenians, that of rationalism. Rationalism is the belief that reason or the intellect is the true source of knowledge. Rationalist thought began with Greek observation and speculation about the natural world. The myths and epics of the Mesopotamians and Indians are ample evidence that speculation about the origin of the universe and mankind did not begin with the Greeks. The achievement of the Greeks, however, is that they treated these questions in rational rather than mythological terms. Homer, in *The Iliad*, celebrates this faith in reason by suggesting that the Greek victory over the Trojans was due to superior brains rather than brawn. Early Greek thinkers did not distinguish between philosophy and science as their quest was for an understanding of the universe and an explanation of its principles. Thus, **Thales of Miletus** (ca. 585 B.C.E.), the so-called father of philosophy, described physical reality in terms of earth elements, thereby creating a school of philosophy called **materialist**. **Pythagoras**, a mathematician for whom a geometric theory is named (a theory previously known to the Babylonians), believed that numerical relationships formed the basic principle of the universe, giving rise to the idea of the "harmony of spheres." The distinction between philosophy and science began with **Hippocrates** (ca. 460–377 B.C.E.), the father of medicine. Hippocrates studied the human body and the effect climate and environment have on health. He separated natural science from philosophy, declaring that medicine was a separate craft. This separation was promoted also by the **Sophists**, who agreed that human beings were the proper subject of study. The Sophists traveled the Greek world teaching young men that nothing is absolute, that excellence can be taught, and that by logic and words even the laws of the polis could be put in question.

Philosophers

The most important of the philosopher-scientists were Socrates, Plato, and Aristotle. **Socrates** (ca. 470–300 B.C.E.) studied natural science but then became interested in human behavior and ethics. His fame rested on argument and the challenging of ideas through logically constructed questioning, the so-called "Socratic method." After Athens' defeat in the Peloponnesian Wars, Socrates became a scapegoat for the defeat because he had questioned the common opinions of the city's politicians. He was accused of corrupting the youth of Athens. At his trial, he was condemned to die by an Athenian jury after he refused to admit guilt. Although he could have escaped, he chose to drink the lethal dose of hemlock, arguing that as a citizen he could not defy his polis that had protected and sustained him all of his life. Because Socrates never wrote anything down, we know of his work through his pupil, Plato. **Plato** (427–347 B.C.E.) believed in the primacy of a world of immaterial forms, a philosophy that later provided the intellectual framework for Christian philosophy. In the book *The Republic*, Plato envisioned an ideal state ruled by philosopher-kings who were experts in the theory of forms and persons seasoned by practical experience. **Aristotle** (384–322 B.C.E.), Plato's most distinguished pupil, delved into a wide range of topics. He advocated a life of moderation, or the "**Golden Mean**," to achieve personal happiness. In *Metaphysics*, he argued, contrary to Plato, that all matter was an inseparable unity of form and substance, and he sought to explain the concept of a single God. In *Poetics*, he delineated the nature of poetry, and in *Organon*, he explored two means to acquire knowledge, the deductive and inductive. In *Politics*, he sought not a perfect state as Plato did, but a description of how government worked. He argued that the state should serve all citizens and when it was subjected to special interests, it became perverted. The concerns of philosophy and its methodology, which searched for truth through reason, supported the Greek political system. Citizens were encouraged to participate in the debate using rhetoric and logic, and the educational system supported these abilities. For Greeks, knowledge was virtue.

Arts

Reason and science also supported the Greek achievement in the arts. The concept of beauty involved balance and correct proportion. Architecturally, the Greek concept of beauty found its highest expression in the temples built to the gods. In temple architecture were joined the two belief systems of the Greeks—gods and rationalism. After the Persians destroyed Athens, under the leadership of Pericles, the Athenians crowned the Acropolis with magnificent new temples, the most famous of which was the **Parthenon**. Dedicated to Athena, goddess of Athens and wisdom, the temple is adorned with columns and appears balanced and proportioned from all angles. Columns of the **Doric** (plain), **Ionian** (scroll), and **Corinthian** (acanthus leaves) Greek style still grace buildings all over the western world. In sculpture, humanism is reflected in the realistic and graceful representation of individuals. The greatest of the Greek sculptors, **Phidias**, created the equestrian procession on the Parthenon frieze. Reason also gave birth to the western concept of history. **Herodotus**, the father of history, sought to write history in a new way. Rather than recounting myths, he gathered information for his *History of the Persian Wars*, pointing out to the reader events he could not verify. His successor, Thucydides, took the process a step further by using only facts he could verify and weighing and judging evidence in the *History of the Peloponnesian War*. This tremendous artistic and philosophical output is referred to as the **Golden Age of Greece** (last half of the fifth century B.C.E.) or the **Age of Pericles** (ca. 461–429 B.C.E.) because, during his leadership, Athens became a showplace for Greek achievement.

Greek Society

Alongside the richness of public life, the everyday life of Greeks was simple and stressed moderation. Most Greeks supported themselves by farming and their possessions were few. Slavery was commonplace, most slaves being acquired by war. As in Mesopotamia, slaves received some protection under the law and could buy their freedom. Many served as teachers and household servants, and others worked in mines where treatment and conditions could be cruel. Women led a secluded life and were secondary in a basically patriarchal society. They were protected, however, by a dowry that remained their property throughout married life. Women were often idealized in the nature of Greek goddesses. Courtesans probably lived the freest of all Athenian women. The mistress of Pericles, Aspasia, was noted for her artistic and intellectual abilities as well as her beauty.

Summary

Humanism, in both its rational and religious form, is the hallmark of the Greek classical period. Its emphasis on the human being, on intellect, and on artistic and physical potential for excellence, influenced many other societies and continues to do so to this day. In the Greek ethical system, to know was to be virtuous. The polis, which institutionalized personal political participation, led to the idea of democracy. Philosophy, in its search for truth through logic, led to investigations into human nature and science. In the search for beauty in realism, are architectural and sculptural monuments that are admired to this day. The Greek way of life that stressed excellence, "nothing in excess," and civic participation, remains an ideal.

THE DEVELOPMENT OF CLASSICAL PERSIAN (ACHAEMENID) CIVILIZATION

The **Persians** and **Medes**, the two major groups of Iranian peoples, originated in Central Asia as part of a larger group of peoples known as the Aryans or Indo-Europeans. About 2000 B.C.E. these Iron Age charioteer Iranians moved south into the plateau between the Persian Gulf and the

Caspian Sea. The geographical position of **Persia** (Iran) between India and East Asia to the east and Southwest Asia to the west, has made it an Asian land bridge between cultures. These peoples, like the Hittites, fell under the spell of the more sophisticated cultures of Mesopotamia, but they then went on to create one of the greatest empires of history, encompassing hundreds of peoples and cultures. In the process, they gave definition to their own culture.

In 550 B.C.E. **Cyrus II** (the Great), a Persian warrior, conquered the Medes and created a dynasty, the **Achaemenid**, which lasted until 331 B.C.E. Cyrus the Great organized a powerful army, and in 539 B.C.E. he conquered Mesopotamia, Syria, Palestine, and the Phoenician cities. In 540 B.C.E. he took over the kingdom of Lydia and the Greek city-states of Southwest Asia. Cyrus's son Cambyses conquered Egypt. When **Darius** (521–486 B.C.E.) conquered the Indus Valley ca. 513 B.C.E., the Persians ruled Egypt, all of Southwest Asia, and western India, the largest empire the world had yet known.

In the classical tradition, the Persian empire established by Cyrus the Great created institutions and a culture of long-lasting imprint. In terms of politics, Cyrus gave Persia an identity and an unusual respect for monarchic legitimacy that survived repeated invasions. He also held an enlightened view of empire. Aware that many of the civilizations he conquered were more advanced than his own, he accorded all people respect, toleration, and protection. His subjects retained a large measure of local autonomy. They were free to continue their local customs and practice their religions. He freed the Jews and allowed them to return to Palestine. Furthermore, he broke down barriers between the disparate peoples he conquered, as, for instance, between the insular Egyptians, religiously exclusive Hebrews, and aggressive Hittites. The greatest achievement of the Persians was establishing an effective government for diverse peoples and cultures.

Cyrus's successor, Darius, carried the art of statecraft to an even higher degree. He reorganized the empire into 20 tribute-paying satrapies or provinces. To each he appointed a governor (**satrap**), a military commander, and separate inspectors who reported directly to him. In this way, he was able to keep a close watch on local government. He established a comprehensive code of laws, a stable currency, and an efficient postal system. The Persians did not engage in trade, which they considered a lowly occupation, but they did encourage it and facilitated it by building a network of roads. The most important was the **Royal Road**, which ran from Susa in Persia to Sardis in Anatolia (Turkey), a distance of more than 1500 miles and a journey of seven days. Stations were built every 14 miles to provide travelers with food, water, and horses. Rapid, long-distance communication was a cornerstone of Persian rule.

Zoroastrianism

The culture of Persia was dominated by an essentially ethnic religion, **Zoroastrianism**. Because it sought no converts, there was a policy of tolerance for Judaism, and the Greek, Babylonian, and Egyptian forms of polytheism. Early Iranian religion was polytheistic, though there was a chief god, **Ahuramazda**, the creator and benefactor of all living creatures. **Mithra**, the sun-god, whose cult would later spread through the Roman Empire, saw to justice and redemption. A priestly class, the **Magi**, developed among the Medes to officiate at sacrifices, chant prayers, and tend the sacred flames. Around 600 B.C.E., according to the *Zend Avesta*, a collection of hymns and poems, the prophet **Zoroaster**, or **Zarathustra**, began to preach a new concept of divinity and human life. He taught that life is a constant battleground between two opposing forces, a **dualism** of good as embodied in Ahuramazda and evil as embodied in **Ahriman**. It was the individual's responsibility to choose, and in the end, Ahuramazda, like the Egyptian god Osiris, would judge. The last judgment was linked to the notion of a divine and everlasting kingdom after death. The wicked would be condemned to eternal pain, darkness, and punishment. His ideas converted Darius, the royal family, and many believers throughout the Persian empire. Zorastrianism survived the fall of the Persian Empire at the hands of the Macedonians, and, no doubt influenced religious thought in the age of Jesus and made a vital contribution to Manicheanism, a theology that spread throughout the Byzantine world.

Persian Culture

Persian classicism combined the art of imperial statecraft of the ancient Iranian nomads, Zoroastrianism, and Greek artistic culture. Darius was defeated by the Greeks at the Battle of Marathon and his son Xerxes was similarly defeated, both by sea at Salamis (480 B.C.E.) and at Plataea the following year. But when Darius proceeded to build a capital city, **Persepolis**, to crown his empire, it was to the Ionian Greeks he turned for expertise. Soaring columns and a great ceremonial hall, rivaling the Acropolis, were built to provide a center for the envoys from 23 nations who came bearing gifts each spring. In decorative reliefs and rock sculpture can be seen a blend of Zoroastrianism, the horse, and the balanced role of hierarchy and state executed in Greek humanist style. While Persia was soon to fall to Alexander (the Great) of Macedon, and later to other invaders, the Persian culture and sense of identity established during the classical era remained and reemerged, reaching new heights during the Sassanian Empire and Abassid Caliphate. As a result of the conquests of Alexander, a new synthesis of Greek, Persian, Indian, and Southwest Asian culture emerged.

THE HELLENISTIC SYNTHESIS

When the Greek cities were quarreling among themselves, an able and energetic ruler named Philip became king of **Macedonia** (northern Greece). In 338 B.C.E., he destroyed the joint army of Thebes and Athens and became master of Greece. King Philip was preparing for an invasion of the Persian Empire when he was murdered. His 20-year-old son, known as **Alexander the Great** (336–323 B.C.E.), assumed the throne and began a campaign of conquest. By overthrowing the Persian Empire and by spreading **Hellenism**—Greek culture, thought, and way of life—from Egypt to India, Alexander created a new era of cultural synthesis called **Hellenistic**, an age that lasted from Alexander's death in 323 to 30 B.C.E.

Alexander of Macedonia

Philip had great admiration for Greek culture and had even brought Aristotle to Macedonia to tutor his son Alexander. Emulating the great Greek heroes he had read about, Alexander began a campaign of conquest that over a period of 12 years created the largest empire up to that time, covering about two million square miles. Vowing revenge for the Persian invasion of Greece in 492 and 490 B.C.E., Alexander led an army of Macedonians and Greeks into western Asia where, no doubt, he used the Persian network of roads to his advantage. In 330 B.C.E. he sacked and burned Persepolis. Next, he advanced on Syria, Palestine, and Egypt. At the Nile delta he founded the city of **Alexandria**. Then he pushed east into Afghanistan and Pakistan, crossing the Indus River in 326 B.C.E. and entered India. When his troops refused to go any further, he turned south to the Indian Ocean, and in 323 B.C.E. he died, just before his thirty-third birthday.

Hellenistic Rule

Upon the death of Alexander, his mighty empire broke up between his warring generals. Antigonus became ruler of Macedonia and Greece, Seleucus became ruler of Syria, Palestine, Babylonia, and other Southwest Asian lands, and Ptolemy the first of the Egyptian **Ptolemies**. Over time, smaller independent states emerged like Pergamum and **Bactrian Greece**. The Bactrian Greek kings sent their cavalry probing toward the boundaries of the Chinese empire, and, in the middle of the second century B.C.E. Menander, the philosophic Greek king of the Punjab, fulfilled Alexander's ambition by leading an army of Greeks and Persians down the valley of the Ganges to capture Pataliputra, the capital of Hindustan (India). In rule, these new kings were more eastern than Greek, but Greek culture blanketed the whole area and united it culturally, if not politically.

Hellenistic Trade

The new political developments led to a diffusion of wealth and a great expansion of trade with East Africa, Arabia, India, and Central Asia, with some trade relayed as far east as China. To the west, trade went through the Straits of Gibraltar to Britain and Norway. Silver flowed from Spain, copper from Cyprus, iron from the Black Sea coasts, grains from Egypt, North Africa, and the Crimea, olive oil from Athens, dried fruit from Palestine, woolen goods from Anatolia, timber from Macedonia, marble from Greece, and linen, granite, and papyrus from Egypt. Alexander had found vast sums of gold, silver, and other treasure in Persia. This became the basis for the building programs of the Hellenistic kings. For this, slaves were needed, becoming a common item of trade except in Egypt where they would have competed with free labor. The caravan trade expanded and the Egyptian Ptolemies discovered how to use monsoon winds to establish direct contact with India. A common language emerged called **koine**, a dialect of Greek, which helped to facilitate trade and government.

Diffusion of Greek Culture

Trade transformed the Greek polis into a **cosmopolis** of differing peoples and activities. Cities became economic and cultural centers where people from all over the Mediterranean and Southwest Asia met. While the new kings gave their cities like Antioch, Pergamum, Pella, and, above all, Alexandria all the trappings of the polis like assemblies and councils, they could not afford to give them freedom. In a Hellenistic city, the Greeks represented an elite class of citizens because they were needed to run their kingdoms. This spurred many citizens to assimilate Greek culture in order to rise politically and socially. Opportunities for advancement as well as overpopulation led to an out-migration of Greeks, who then spread all over Southwest Asia. Because the Hellenistic kings could not afford to arm their citizens as in a Greek polis, professional armies emerged, using the Greco-Macedonian style of warfare that proved superior to that of the Southwest Asians. Greeks dominated other professions as well, such as architecture, engineering, and medicine. The Hellenistic idea of kingship that involved royal families, including women, helped elevate the position of women, especially those of the upper class. Thus, Greek culture was diffused but transformed by the eastern traditions of empire and royal statecraft.

Mystery Cults

Since Hellenistic cities lacked the emotional attachment of the polis, people searched for a sense of meaning and belonging in religion. To Hellenistic peoples, Greek cults and polytheistic traditions seemed sterile because of their attachment to ritual, festival, and particular places in the Greek homeland like Olympus. For this reason, eastern religions, especially the **mystery cults** like Serapis and Isis, became popular. Serapis combined elements of the Egyptian god Osiris with aspects of Greek gods. All the mystery religions claimed to save their adherents from fate and promised life for the soul after death.

Hellenistic Philosophy

The cosmopolitan nature of Hellenistic life, its wealth, intermingling of cultural heritages, and its mobility, spawned an explosion in philosophy, science, and medicine. The Library at Alexandria became the repository for all the known knowledge of the ages. Philosophy, in particular, gave people in a changing world a sense of permanence and structure, and the intellectual outlet the polis had once offered. Three philosophies in particular became popular—**Cynicism**, led by Diogenes (ca. 412–323 B.C.E.), **Epicureanism**, advanced by Epicures (340–270 B.C.E.), and **Stoicism**, introduced by Zeno (335–262 B.C.E.). Cynics believed that happiness was possible only by living according to nature and foregoing luxuries. Social conventions contrary to nature were attacked, giving rise to the present meaning of cynicism, a belief that all actions are for selfish motives. This philosophy was particularly appealing to the lower classes who saw its adherents go without warm clothing and sufficient food and housing. Epicureans believed that the principal good of human life was pleasure. It taught followers to ignore politics and issues. Today, an epicurean is one who enjoys food and drink.

Stoics taught that people should participate in politics and world affairs but they ought not to try to change the order of things. Rather, they were to play the role assigned, for the question was not whether they achieved anything, but that they lived virtuous lives. Stoicism today refers to suffering without complaint. The Stoic concept of a universal state government by natural law was one of the great legacies of the Hellenistic world to Rome, as it became a valuable tool for the Romans to rationalize rule of an empire with many different peoples and laws. Duty of individuals to their fellows became a philosophical underpinning for the duties of Roman citizenship.

Hellenistic Science, Math, and Technology

Hellenistic culture's greatest achievement was in science. Mesopotamia, Persia, Egypt, and even India were intermingled with Greek thought. The cosmic observations of the Babylonians provided the raw material for the foundation of astronomy introduced by **Thales**. The most noble Hellenistic astronomer was **Aristarchus** (ca. 310–230 B.C.E.). He argued against Aristotle and **Ptolemy** (an Alexandrian mathematician and astronomer) that the earth was the center of the universe. He propounded, instead, the **heliocentric** theory that the earth and planets move around the sun, a theory that lay dormant until the Polish astronomer, **Nicolaus Copernicus** (1473–1543 C.E.) reinvestigated it. In geometry, Hellenistic thinkers discovered little new but **Euclid** (ca. 300 B.C.E.) completed a valuable textbook of existing knowledge, *The Elements of Geometry*.

The greatest Hellenistic thinker was **Archimedes** (ca. 287–212 B.C.E.), an inventor and mathematician. Among his inventions were the Archimedean screw and the compound pulley. In his book on *Plane Equilibrium*, he dealt for the first time with the principles of mechanics, including the lever. In *On Floating Bodies*, Archimedes founded the science of hydrostatics, advancing the theory that, whenever a solid floats in liquid, the weight of the solid is equal to the volume of liquid displaced. The eclectic geographer, **Eratosthenes** (285–ca. 204 B.C.E.) took doctrines from many schools. Using math, he calculated the circumference of the earth, estimating it almost accurately at 24,675 miles (it is actually 24,860 miles). He declared that a ship could sail from Spain either around Africa to India or directly west to India, a theory not really proven until the voyages of Vasco da Gama (1497–1499 C.E.) and Magellan (1519–1522 C.E.).

In medicine, Herophilus dissected corpses, leading to his conclusion that there were two types of nerves, motor and sensory, and that the brain was the center of intelligence. His dissections led to the invention of new surgical instruments and practices, while Heraclides dedicated himself to observation and the use of medicines. He noted how blood circulated through veins and arteries. One of the mysteries of Hellenistic science is that, although scientists of the period invented such machines as the steam engine, water organ, and air gun, they never used them as labor-saving devices, perhaps because slave labor was so abundant. Inventions were applied to the military, however, in the form of catapults and siege machines, advances that the Romans then used to gain supremacy over the very Hellenistic world that had developed them.

Summary

The Hellenistic Age spread Greek culture and incorporated the ideas and ways of much of Southwest Asia into it. The kingly traditions of the East merged with the Greek polis. Greek humanism and rationalism merged with religious traditions of Egypt and Mesopotamia. Hellenistic commerce flourished under the protection of competitive kingdoms, united by a common Greek language, coinage, and methods of exchange. Wealth brought building, especially of new cities, inventions, and social mobility. The polis became a cosmopolis embracing change and encouraging new ideas. The Hellenistic world later gave the eastern Rome of Constantinople its special forms. To India, Alexander and his successors gave much of its art, especially the techniques of building and carving in stone. Hellenistic art became more realistic, often vividly protraying the lives of ordinary people. Bactrian Greeks developed a syncretic style that mixed the artistic traditions of Greece, India, Persia, and Egypt. Hellenistic rulers continued the concept of a united rule that Chandragupta adopted when he founded the Mauryan empire. When the Arabs finally destroyed the Greek cities of the East, they retained Hellenistic science, math, and medicine. While the kingdoms of the Hellenistic world were busy with their own squabbles, Rome emerged and gradually overtook the Hellenistic world politically. Yet, as has been pointed out by historians, the "Romanization" of the Hellenistic world was slight while the Hellenization of the Latin world was conspicuous.

CHAPTER 7

Classical Roman Civilization

(500 B.C.E.–500 C.E.)

CHRONOLOGY	Roman Republic (509–44 B.C.E.) Punic Wars (264–140 B.C.E.)	Roman Empire (44 B.C.E.–496 C.E.) Age of Augustus (31–27 B.C.E.)	Pax Romana (27–180 C.E.) Sassanian Persian Empire (227–651 C.E.)
TERMS	republic Senate Assembly of Centuries Assembly of Tribes Twelve Tables jus civile jus gentium jus naturale legion Pontifex Maximus Punic Wars Battle of Zama latifundia empiricism First Triumvirate Ides of March	Actium constitutional monarchy Principate princeps civitatis Pax Romana mosaic The Aeneid Latin romance languages barrel and cross vault Pantheon Arch of Constantine collegia Justinian's Code Manicheism Torah	Talmud Diaspora Baptism Eucharist epistles gospels canon law martyrdoms Edict of Milan Cathedral of the Hagia Sophia heresy Nicene Creed Catholic Vulgate edition
PEOPLE	Etruscans patricians plebians consuls tribunes praetors Latins Romulus and Remus Pyrrhus Hannibal Scipio Tiberius and Gaius Gracchus Marius Sulla Spartacus Pompey Julius Caesar	Crassus Brutus Antony and Cleopatra Octavius (Augustus) imperator Caligula Nero Marcus Aurelius Virgil Livy Horace Pliny Plutarch Hadrian Diocletian Sassanids Ardashir Shapur II	Kan Ying Pontius Pilate Zealots rabbis Apocalyptics Gentiles Jesus of Nazareth Paul of Tarsus priests bishops Pope Constantine Aryan Christians Saint Jerome Saint Augustine Huns and Visigoths Alaric Odoacer
PLACES	Tiber River Italy Carthage	Gaul Rubicon River Parthia	Amber Road Silk Road Constantinople

Classical Roman Civilization (500 B.C.E.–500 C.E.)

THE DEVELOPMENT OF ROMAN CIVILIZATION

The Greek humanist tradition and the Roman concept of law and Judeo-Christian ethics are considered the hallmarks of western civilization. From them emerge core values of the western world—individualism, justice, and Christian love. It was in the classical age of Greece and Rome that these concepts emerged. The first of these, humanism, has been investigated in the previous section. The other two emerge during the classical age of Rome. In the first half of Roman history, during the republic, legal traditions developed and evolved to a sophisticated level, and during the second half, the Roman empire, Christianity made its distinctive mark.

Founding of Rome

At about the same time (1000 B.C.E.) the Dorians moved south into Greece and plunged it into a Dark Age, a group of vigorous peoples from Southwest Asia, the **Etruscans**, moved down the Italian peninsula, settling north of the **Tiber River**. Several centuries later, escaping the Doric invasions of Greece, Greek colonists planted new settlements in Sicily and southern Italy. It was the Greeks who gave the name **Italy** to the peninsula. Between the Etruscans in the north and the Greeks in the south, around the Tiber River, lived a group of people called **Latins**. According to ancient Roman tradition, the city of Rome was founded (753 B.C.E.) by two brothers, **Romulus** and **Remus**. Around 700 B.C.E. both Rome and Latium were subjugated by the Etruscans. Like Greece, the city-state of Rome

was ruled by a king (Etruscan), and in 509 B.C.E. large landowners rose in revolt, drove out the Etruscan king, and began to form a new government, a **republic** (power in the hands of the people, not the king). Unlike Greece, the republic was a unified state, instead of a series of independent city-states, able to withstand outside invasion and internal violence.

Roman Republic

The early republican form of government was based on the division of people into two classes—the wealthy landowning class called **patricians**, which made up about 10 percent of the population, and the small farmers, artisans, and shopkeepers called **plebians**. At the head of the republic were two **consuls** who were elected from the patrician class. They commanded the army, presided over religious functions, acted as judges, and could veto one another. In times of emergency, the consuls could turn over their power to a dictator elected for a maximum of six months. The consuls were advised by a 300-member patrician **Senate**, which had been in existence even under the Etruscan king as an advisory body. Senators served for life and provided continuity of policy. The Senate decided questions of peace and war and proposed laws that were voted upon by the **Assembly of Centuries**, a body made up of all male citizens as organized for military purposes in units of 100, called centuries.

As in Greece, this form of government was gradually democratized. In 494 B.C.E., as a result of plebian refusal to serve in the army against one of Rome's neighbors, plebians were given the right to elect their own representatives called **tribunes**. The tribunes were elected by a special assembly of plebeians called the **Assembly of Tribes**. The Assembly of Tribes passed resolutions that tribunes then presented to the Senate for ratification. Gradually, the legal differences between patricians and plebians disappeared altogether. By 376 B.C.E. a plebeian could serve as one of the consuls, and in 287 B.C.E. patricians were admitted to the Assembly of Tribes.

Roman Law

Democratization was also advanced by a law code, the **Twelve Tables** (450 B.C.E.). Soon it became customary for newly elected **praetors** (judges) to announce the laws they intended to enforce and those they considered out of date. In this way, the laws remained responsive to peoples' needs. These statutes, using precedents, customs, and procedures, became the basis of civil law, or *jus civile*. By the third century B.C.E., when trade had become more important, the Romans set up special courts to deal with the problem of differences between foreign and Roman laws. *Jus gentium* was the coalescing of Roman and foreign law. The judge in charge made decisions that seemed fair, thus promoting the idea of justice over the laws of a particular country. This gave rise to the notion of *jus naturale*, or universal law. The sophistication, adaptability, and sturdiness of the Roman legal system, which included (1) a common standard of justice creating a state of laws, not men, (2) judgments based on evidence, (3) an enumeration of rights including those of women, slaves, and property, (4) a reverence for law as reflected in the Roman symbol, the goddess of justice, and (5) the merging of Roman civil law with those of foreigners has endured as an ideal.

Roman Legions

The origins of the Roman system of jurisprudence, republicanism, and democracy can probably be found, as in Greece, in the military and in Roman values. Threatened by the Etruscans, every able-bodied Roman was required to serve in the army. Roman farmers, used to outdoor work, made excellent soldiers. Originally, the Romans used the Greek phalanx system but it gradually gave way to the **legion** system. Legions of from 3000 to 6000 men were made up of companies of about 120 men, loyal to each other and trained to fight, if necessary, by themselves. Equipped with helmets, shields, lances, swords, and later, iron-tipped javelins, they could strike at the enemy from great distances, making them more invincible than the Greek phalanx. Superior arms, discipline, training, and steadfast loyalty soon made the Roman armies masters of the Mediterranean.

Roman Religion

Values and religion also played a role. Early Romans regarded virtue and duty highly. They were careful to show gods the proper respect because they believed whatever happened to them was in the hands of the gods. Romans worshipped many gods, like those that protected home, family, and fields, but there were also, as in Greece, a pantheon of public and semi-anthropomorphic gods common to all Romans. Jupiter, god of the sky, sent rain and inspired magistrates. Mars protected armies. The chief priest, or **Pontifex Maximus**, prescribed prayers and sacrifices in the name of the Roman people. Before these gods, all were equal and all were dutiful.

From Republic to Empire

Conquests and the impact of new values from the Hellenistic world changed Rome and with it, as in Greece, the political system changed. The republic gave way to empire. Rome first conquered the Italian peninsula and then the Mediterranean. In the conquest of Italy, Rome fought numerous wars with its neighbors, but it also used diplomacy and alliances to gain control. Unlike the Greeks, the Romans extended citizenship to many of their allies, thereby spreading the Roman legal system, strengthening the state, and giving it additional wealth and manpower. Between 282 and 272 B.C.E., the Romans engaged in war with the Hellenistic king of Epirus, **Pyrrhus**, who had come across the Adriatic to the aid of Greek cities in southeastern Italy. With his defeat, Rome became master of all Italy.

The most important struggles were the **Punic Wars** (264–146 B.C.E.) which were fought between Rome and Carthage for control of Mediterranean power and wealth. The ancient Phoenician city of **Carthage** was the chief outlet for the lucrative trade of North Africa and the Carthaginian navy controlled the Mediterranean trade lanes of the Hellenistic world. In the First Punic War (264–241 B.C.E.), Rome won control of Sicily. When Rome went on to annex Sardinia and Corsica, Carthage sought revenge. This led to the Second Punic War (218–201 B.C.E.). The leader of the Carthaginian forces, **Hannibal**, daringly led his army, including elephants, through Spain and across the Alps into northern Italy. There he was thoroughly routed by the Romans. Rome then invaded Africa and at the **Battle of Zama** in 202 B.C.E., Hannibal was defeated by the Roman general **Scipio**. The result of the second war was that Carthage was forced to give up Spain. The Third Punic War (149 B.C.E.) led to the complete destruction of the city of Carthage. Because Macedonia had joined Hannibal during the Second Punic War, Rome conquered Macedonia and then Greece (133 B.C.E.) in order to gain control of this politically unstable and fragmented part of the Hellenistic world. By the second century B.C.E., Rome had become master of the whole Mediterranean world.

Consequences of the Punic Wars

The conquests completely changed the economic, social, cultural, and finally, political life of Rome. Economically, Roman soldiers came home to neglected farms that had been bought by wealthy landowners in their absence. These huge estates or **latifundia** were worked by cheap slave labor that had been imported from places of conquest. Without soldiering or farming, these warriors wandered to the cities where they became a class that was dependent on state handouts and entertainment. They fell prey to the politics of their generals who claimed their allegiance above and beyond allegiance to the state. Meanwhile, grain was imported from abroad, from places conquered by the Romans. North Africa, particularly Egypt, became the breadbasket of the Romans. As trade and empire increased, a new class of people arose, composed of merchants and bureaucrats. The wealth of conquest replaced taxation, and booty caused the development of industry to be neglected.

More important, the basic Roman values of simplicity and morality were undermined by the influx of the more urbane and cosmopolitan Hellenistic ideas. Romans fell in love with Hellenistic culture. They were educated by Greek tutors, entertained by Greek plays, intrigued by Greek notions of government and philosophy, delighted by the luxury of the Greek cosmopolis, and tutored by Greeks in the art of moneymaking. Family life, the bulwark of old Rome, weakened. Political corruption became a science, luxury a goal. As the Roman satirical poet Juvenal wrote, "Luxury has fallen upon us—more terrible than the sword. The conquered East has avenged herself by the gift of her vices." Was Rome corrupted? Perhaps the answer can be found in **empiricism** (observations). The Roman state and the empire it ruled lasted for another six centuries. The Golden Age was yet to come. The high tide of prosperity lay in the future. The practical Romans simply took change in stride.

In 44 B.C.E., Rome became an empire despite almost a decade of reformers who attempted to stave off such a turn of events. In 133 B.C.E. **Tiberius Gracchus**, a tribune, attempted to return to the old ways by limiting the amount of land a person could own. In 123 B.C.E. his brother, **Gaius** attempted to get the government to buy grain and sell it to the poor at low prices. Both attempts at economic reform failed due to opposition by wealthy senators. Disorder existed in the provinces as well, giving rise to popular and victorious generals who gained booty that they used to pay off a political following.

The first general to successfully challenge the Senate was **Marius** (ca. 155–86 B.C.E.). He had created a professional army by opening the army to everyone and furnishing recruits with equipment. With a loyal force of soldiers behind him, he was able to override the Senate and have himself reelected consul four times. The Senate then threw its weight behind another general, **Sulla**, who, in 83 B.C.E., took over the government, executed Marius' followers, and restored the Senate to its old position of authority. In reality, he ruled as a dictator until 79 B.C.E., when he retired. Shortly thereafter a massive slave revolt led by the Greek slave **Spartacus** occurred.

Julius Caesar

Rome was plunged into civil war. The major contest that emerged was between **Pompey** (106–48 B.C.E.) and **Julius Caesar** (ca. 102–44 B.C.E.). Pompey had earned his fame by conquests in the East, Julius Caesar by conquest in **Gaul** (France). Pompey was supported by the Senate, Caesar by the people. In 59 B.C.E. Caesar, Pompey, and a wealthy businessman, **Crassus**, agreed to share power and formed the **First Triumvirate**. Caesar left Rome and, while he was away, Crassus died. The Senate and Pompey became increasingly distrustful of the popular Caesar and forbade him to cross the **Rubicon River**, the boundary between Gaul and Rome, with his army. Caesar defied the Senate and, in so doing, brought the republic to an end. Pompey fled to Greece and then Egypt where he was killed. In 46 B.C.E. Caesar was appointed dictator, whereupon he launched a series of reforms including removing citizens from welfare rolls and sending them into the provinces, restoring agricultural self-sufficiency, and reforming provincial administration. However, on March 15, the "**Ides of March**," 44 B.C.E., he was assassinated by a band of senatorial conspirators led by **Brutus**. Rome was once again at war. **Antony** (a former ally of Julius Caesar) and **Cleopatra** (the last of the Ptolemies) were defeated at **Actium**, and in 30 B.C.E. Egypt became part of Rome. The empire was restored to order only in 27 B.C.E., when **Octavius**, a grandnephew of Caesar's, ended almost a century of chaos in which republican institutions had failed to function. He assumed the title of **Augustus**, instituted a **constitutional monarchy**, and inaugurated the empire, a period that lasted 500 years in the West and 1500 in the East.

Augustus Caesar

The age of Augustus is often called the "**Principate**" because Augustus tried to restore the outward framework of republican government like the Senate. In fact, the Senate became only an advisory body, and Augustus was dictator, being, at the same time, chief military general (**imperator**), chief priest (pontifex maximus), and first citizen (**princeps civitatis**). The imperial system had all the strengths and weaknesses of any empire—good emperors who ruled wisely and gave the state a degree of solidarity and order unknown to republican governments, but during the reign of bad emperors, corruption and disorder prevailed. During the reign of Augustus' descendants, the Julio-Claudian Dynasty, for instance, Tiberius and Claudius ruled with steady hands, but **Caligula** (r. 31–41 C.E.) was cruel and incompetent and ultimately was assassinated. His successor, **Nero**, was also excessive and irresponsible. His life ended in suicide.

Pax Romana

In 69 C.E. Vasparian, the first emperor who was not a member of an aristocratic family, assumed power, and in 96 C.E. the Senate elected Nerva to the imperial rule. This illustrated the potential that existed in the Roman system for talented individuals to achieve upward mobility. Nerva's election initiated the rule of the Five Good Emperors—Nerva, Trajan, Hadrian, Pius, and **Marcus Aurelius**. Marcus Aurelius (161–180 C.E.), known as the philosopher-emperor, wrote *Meditations*, a book of spiritual reflections in which he struggled with the paradox that as a man of peace, he spent most of his reign fighting Germans in Britain and on the Parthian (Persian/Iranian) frontier. His writings reflect a Stoic attitude of duty and acceptance. The period from Augustus to Marcus Aurelius (27 B.C.E.–180 C.E.) is often called the **Pax Romana** because it was a time of relative political peace when no major wars threatened the security of the empire. This, in turn, encouraged trade and wealth.

After the death of Marcus Aurelius, a period of disorder ensued in which power passed into the hands of the military and imperial leadership was up for bid.

THE CULTURAL ACHIEVEMENTS OF ROME

The Age of Augustus initiated 400 years of imperial rule that was celebrated both in literature and in stone. Rome was more notable as an imitator than an innovator. As with the rest of the Hellenistic world, Romans became Hellenized, copying Greek culture and then making their own special adaptations. In portraiture, Romans started with the Greek realistic style but by the later imperial period they moved toward idealized representations that were celebratory of Roman victory and achievement. The Romans were innovators, however, in **mosaic** decoration, an art form that reached its zenith in the eastern Roman Empire sometime later.

Roman Literature and Science

The Augustan peace inspired a Roman literary flowering, the "Golden Age" of Latin literature. The tone and ideal of Roman literature, like that of the Greeks, was humanistic and worldly. Though it frequently referred to the gods, it was in human terms. The three titans of the Roman literary world were **Virgil** (70–19 B.C.E.), **Livy** (59 B.C.E.–17 C.E.) and **Horace** (65–8 B.C.E.). Virgil's masterpiece is *The Aeneid*, an epic poem that is the Latin equivalent of *The Iliad* and *The Odyssey*. It recounts the founding of Rome and the exploits of the Roman hero, Aeneas, who escaped to Italy after the fall of Troy. Livy's history of Rome is the prose counterpart of the *The Aeneid*, while Horace is famous for his odes commemorating Augustus's victories. Together, these authors gave the western world not just great literature, but a language, **Latin**, which made a major imprint on the Latin Christian church and on the development of the **romance languages** of Europe—Portuguese, Spanish, French, and Italian. Some important writing was in the field of science, a field in which Romans recapitulated Greek work rather than provide an innovative pure science. **Pliny** produced a multivolume encyclopedia entitled *Natural History*, in which he discussed a range of topics from biology to botany. Claudius Ptolemy produced many works on astronomy and geography. His theory that the earth was the center of the solar system, though wrong, dominated science for 1000 years. **Plutarch** (42–ca. 102 C.E.), whose interest in famous people was in their moral qualities, wrote a collection of biographical sketches of 65 Greek and Romans.

Roman Architecture

Undoubtedly, Rome's principal cultural achievement lay in the field of engineering and building. Central to this building were two innovations—cement and the arch. The Romans learned from the Etruscans how to make rounded arches, but they devised a way to extend the arch into a **barrel vault** and to set two arches at right angles to one another to form a **cross vault**. Thus, the weight of a building was equally distributed and walls no longer needed to be as thick to hold up the roof as in the post and lintel system. The Romans also perfected the dome. Domes, vaults, and arches were used by the Romans to build palaces, theaters, coliseums, public baths, temples, public buildings, and aqueducts. Some of the most beautiful illustrations of Roman architecture are the **Pantheon** and the **Arch of Constantine** because they incorporate the Greek sense of balance and harmony and the Roman genius in building.

Growth of Cities

These building achievements are also notable because they can be found not only in the large urban centers imitative of the Greek cosmopolis, but also in towns. The Roman empire, in contrast to the Hellenistic world, was marked by growth and development of cities besides those of the capitals linked by a system of roads that facilitated trade and communication throughout the empire. There were 160 cities alone that lay beyond the Rhine. Roman cities were self-governing. In the Romanized provinces of the west they had councils like the Senate, assemblies, and magistrates who considered it an honor to serve without pay. Emperors encouraged the growth of cities by passing special decrees. Trajan, for instance, made it possible for municipalities to receive bequests like libraries, temples, aqueducts, and charities. Cities also blossomed due to trade. However, they were vulnerable to outside invasion, plague, and insecure trade routes. In the third and fourth centuries C.E., when they were under attack, people abandoned the cities and fled to the countryside, but the legacy of independent towns was not forgotten.

Roman Society

Even relatively small urban centers were decked out with an impressive array of theaters, triumphal arches, baths, and fountains. Indeed, the provision of reliable drinking water and higher standards of hygiene are one of Rome's contributions to western civilization. The Romans also improved the rural areas by introducing irrigation and drainage systems, as well as better agricultural tools. Tradesmen were organized into guilds (**collegia**) for social and religious purposes rather than for better wages and working conditions. While much has been written about the amusements of Romans, such as gladiator contests, chariot races, and the 159 public holidays that existed under Claudius, ordinary Romans dealt with everyday problems and enjoyed simple pleasures like most people through the ages. Taxes were collected from an imperial population of about 4.5 million, in order to finance public buildings. Taxation for the one million Roman citizens was abolished about 167 B.C.E. In the province of Africa, however, the standard tax for peasant farmers was one-third of their production plus six days' labor service. But they were protected by a powerful corpus of law that gradually offered protection for the poor, and even for slaves against wanton cruelty. Although not fully codified until the sixth century C.E., this body of law, known as **Justinian's Code**, is one of the greatest cultural and political achievements of Rome.

Imperial Law

Law rather than bureaucracies or the military was the Roman apparatus of imperial rule. Generally, the Romans gave a great deal of political autonomy to local governments and maintained small garrisons of soldiers scattered throughout the empire. While local laws continued to apply in many areas, Roman law provided a legal system accessible to citizens at any part of the empire and capable of facilitating commercial exchange. It was implemented by a bureaucracy accountable directly to the emperor. The *jus civile* or civil law, which applied to Romans only and the *jus gentium*, or law of nations, formed the basis of general notions of law, the *jus naturale*. This law focused heavily on private property and family stability, objectivity and fairness, and evolution to meet changing conditions. In this way, law rather than a common social structure, culture, or religion became the glue of the empire.

Summary

Basically, Rome was Hellenistic in culture. It admired and adopted Greek ways and to them it made its own particular contributions. These include law, language, and building. These were diffused far and wide, bringing Roman civilization to northern Europe and the Mediterranean basin. By the first century C.E., a more powerful and distinctive cultural force was added, that of Christianity.

ROMAN DIFFUSION AND CHRISTIANITY

Roman diffusion occurred by conquest and trade. After subduing the Italian peninsula and bringing Carthage to its knees (201 B.C.E.), Rome began an unremitting march to empire. First it turned on those who had helped Hannibal, the Macedonians, and the Celts in northern Italy. Caesar subdued Gaul (France), Augustus settled with **Parthia** (Iran) and then annexed Egypt, Galatia (Turkey), and Judea. Then he advanced over the Alps into the Danube and Rhine areas and conquered Spain. By the time of Hadrian (117–138 C.E.) the empire had reached its farthest extent, including now Britain, Dacia (Romania), Mesopotamia, and Northwest Africa (Morocco). In the east, the ease of conquest can be explained by the fragmentation of the Hellenistic kingdoms. In the west, Romans were striking into new territories in western Europe peopled by various tribes who had moved into the area north of the Alps during the Late Bronze and early Iron Age. This had occurred around 1000 B.C.E., when a group of tribes called the Urnfield culture divided into four main groups— Celts in the west, Slavs in the north, Italic-speaking in the south, and Ilyrians in the southeast. Outside this ring in the north were Germans and Balts. During the first millennium B.C.E., the Celts expanded at the expense of others in northern Europe, but in the first millennium C.E. the Germanic tribes overran large parts of the area. It is the Germanic tribes that eventually overran the western part of the Roman Empire, causing a new Rome in the east, Constantinople, to be built.

Roman Trade

The diffusion of Roman culture is tied intimately to the economics of empire and the trade system that sustained it. The vast amounts of building were funded by a self-sustaining singular imperial economic system that was self-sufficient in all essential commodities. Geographic factors like the Mediterranean and river systems flowing into it tied the system together. Since amber was in great demand and available in the Baltic area, the **Amber Road** developed, following the valleys of the Rhine, Danube, Vistula, and Elbe to Rome. Luxuries came from long-distance trade with India and China. Animals and grain came across the Mediterranean from North Africa. Stone for Roman building schemes and animals for the shows came from afar. The Roman Empire created a vast area with a single currency and low customs barriers. Commerce was not hindered by pirates or frontiers and was aided by an elaborate network of roads and protected harbors. Wealth accumulated through war and taxation was concentrated in Rome. All areas used papyrus as a writing material. Armies staged on the frontiers created their own demand, stimulating the economy in outlying areas.

Roman Economy

The fantastic outward wealth of the empire obscured some of its economic weaknesses. Rome depended on a system of agriculture that required the land to lie fallow in alternate years. Land transport was slow and expensive, depending on donkeys, mules, and oxen rather than horses. As a result, it was cheaper to ship grain across the Mediterranean than to cart it 70 miles. The commercial classes were weak both in capital and social esteem. The shop, not the factory, was the standard unit of production. This was in some measure due to slavery, which, by historical standards, was a very high proportion of the population in many areas. The wealth-consuming rather than wealth-creating nature of the empire, and the fact that it relied to such a high degree on trade, made it vulnerable. The Emperor **Hadrian**, who ruled from 117–138 C.E. withdrew eastern Roman troops to the Euphrates River and built a 73-mile wall across Britain near the border of modern Scotland to protect the empire from attack. From the time of Marcus Aurelius, the Romans were continually involved with repelling the Persians in the east and the Germans in the west. The constant threat of invasion or civil war made trade difficult. Decreasing trade made for decreasing tax revenue, which was often consumed with supporting the army. Emperor **Diocletian** (284–305 C.E.) tried to deal with these problems by issuing an edict establishing price and wage controls. He also divided the empire into East and West and appointed two more caesars for each half of the empire. He attempted to reestablish the authority of the emperor by claiming divine status complete with elaborate court ritual. This all needed a vast new bureaucracy to implement, further adding to the demands on the already diminishing treasury.

Eastern Roman Expansion

While Roman imperial expansion to the west was finite, geographically, expansion to the east opened up possibilities far across Eurasia. Roman military expansion to the east coincided with Chinese expansion to the west and the result was a period in history when two mighty classical civilizations came in touch with each other.

On the road east, Romans came in contact with Parthia. Parthians had entered Iran during the time of the Persian Achaemenid kings, and when Alexander's eastern holdings disintegrated, Parthians became the heir to the Persian empire. They tried to replicate the classical age by dividing the empire into satrapies, but they lacked a sophisticated bureaucracy. They fell to the Romans in 226 C.E., but their place was immediately taken by the **Sassanids**, a people indigenous to southern Iran.

Sassanid Empire

In 227 C.E. a Persian noble, **Ardashir**, killed the Parthian king, seized the capital of Ctesiphon, and proclaimed the Sassanid empire. Sassanian kings not only wore traditional Persian dress and built great palaces in the classical Achaemenid style, but they successfully allied the throne with Zoroastrianism. The priesthood, trained in judicial and administrative functions, and drawn from the ranks of the nobility, allied with the Sassanid monarch. Though Zoroastrianism was the state religion of the Sassanids, other religions competed within the empire. One was a reformist sect called **Manicheism**, but others included Christianity and Judaism. **Shapur II** (309–379 C.E.), Sassanian Persia's greatest monarch, made gains against the Romans, and moved and extended Persian influence as far east as China. With him went western religions as well as Sassanian culture. Sassanid Persia sustained itself against the eastern Roman Empire, Byzantium, the Kushans to the north, and dissolved only when the Arabs slew the last king in 651 C.E.

Silk Road

Despite this warfare, and in fact because of it, the Roman and Chinese empires came in contact with each other. Persia was the link between the two wealthiest and most commercially active realms in the classical world. Parthia tried to become the go-between in this trade, learning a great deal in the process from both cultures. An elaborate network of roads linked Parthia to China in the east, India in the south, and Rome in the west. The most important of the overland routes was the **Silk Road** (see also page 79). Rarely did a merchant travel the entire distance so this relay trade fostered the growth of cities and towns all along the route. Direct maritime trade was established in the second century C.E. Han Emperor Wudi (Wu Ti) took the momentous step of opening the Silk Road to Parthia and a later Han emperor sent an ambassador, **Kan Ying**, directly to the Roman empire by sea (96–98 C.E.). In the province of Syria, Kan Ying left a fascinating firsthand look at the Greco-Roman world, noting that the commercial traffic between Parthia and India made tenfold profits. More than goods passed along these routes. Technology, ideas, religion, and art also spread. Greek art based on the Greek model, portraying Buddha in realistic terms, grew up in northern India. The West developed a taste for silk and spices, a taste that years later drove Europeans across the Atlantic. The trade routes also became the vehicle for diffusion of religious ideas.

Judea

Like all the classical civilizations, belief systems heavily influenced cultural development. Hellenic and Hellenistic gods and rationalist beliefs enveloped the Roman state until the coming of Christianity. After that, both in the eastern and western Roman empire, Christianity became an integral part of Roman culture. Like many religions, Christianity grew up in troubled times, both within the empire and within the state of Judaea. It was the time when Rome moved from republic to empire, and in the civil wars that were fought in this transition, Judaea suffered its share of ravages and military confiscations. Also, the political autonomy that the Jews had long enjoyed under the Romans was shattered when **Pontius Pilate** was appointed prefect. This meant Rome now had direct control over the area rather than indirect, as occurred in the republican system. Besides war, there were also crop failures, famine, and plague. Among the Jews, two movements began to spread. One were the **Zealots**, extremists who worked to rid Judea of the Romans. The other were the **Apocalyptics**, who believed that the coming of a Messiah was near. A crisis in Roman paganism also played a part in the rise of Christianity. Essentially there were three kinds of Roman paganism—the official state religion of Rome, Roman cults, and the mystery religions of the Hellenistic world. All three lacked personal, emotional, and spiritual succor in a rapidly changing political world. In a cosmopolitan social world, where the meeting of many cultures demanded relativistic thinking to promote harmony, people lacked but sought moral anchors.

Judaism

The Christian religion has its roots in Judaism, the basis of which were the Ten Commandments and the belief in one god, Yahweh, often called Jehovah. Among the beliefs of Jews were the concept of sin and the original fall of man, accountability, the promise of redemption through a coming Messiah, the day of last judgment, and the idea that Jews were Yahweh's chosen people, These beliefs began to take shape in 539 B.C.E. when Cyrus the Great of Persia defeated the Babylonians, thereby ending the captivity of the Jews. Under Achaemenid Persian rule, the Jews were allowed to return to Palestine. There they wrote down the core of Judaism, the Law, which can be found in the **Torah**. Acknowledged masters of the law, or **rabbis**, interpreted the law much as Roman praetors interpreted the Twelve Tables. These writings and interpretations were later collected and along with other writings, formed the **Talmud**, the second great source of Judaism.

The Jews of the last century B.C.E. did not live exclusively in Palestine. Many of the **Diaspora** (dispersion of Jewish peoples outside of Palestine) remained in Persia and others settled in Hellenistic cities like Alexandria or in the cities of North Africa, Spain, and Gaul. A large community was established in Rome. Everywhere the Jews lived, they familiarized the non-Jews, or **Gentiles**, with their concept of monotheism, the moral principles of the Law and the hopes for the coming of the Messiah.

The political turmoil between the republic and the empire touched the Jews as well as the Christians. A Jewish revolt in 70 C.E. led to the destruction of the Temple to Yahweh during the reign of Emperor Titus. The final conquest of the rebels and expulsion of the Jews from their homeland occurred during the rule of Hadrian. Like the coming Christian religion, the Jews were persecuted. Because the religion was so tied to the concept of a state, its survival under Roman rule was in great jeopardy. After the Temple was destroyed in 135 C.E. Jews no longer were able to look to Jerusalem as the focus of their spiritual and political hopes. Henceforth, their life centered on their religious devotion and the study of the Law.

Jesus of Nazareth

Jesus of Nazareth (ca. 5 B.C.E.–29 C.E.) was himself a Jew who followed the Judaic message, but he emphasized the importance of brotherly love and the love of God, and of a kingdom in heaven not on earth. He also insisted that he taught in his own name, not that of Yahweh. Twelve men, know as the Apostles, became his followers. Whereas Hammurabi's Code had taught an "eye for an eye," and the Judaic Law emphasized a set of rules of conduct, Jesus's message was one of forgiveness: "Bless your persecutors . . .Never repay injury with injury . . . Do not be conquered by evil but conquer evil with good." (See p. 98.) Jesus incited mistrust, not just among the Romans, but among the Jewish Zealots who were disappointed that he refused to preach rebellion against Rome. The crucifixion of Jesus, while cruel, was not unusual for the time. Rumors of his resurrection, however, promised the faithful immortality. Soon, the rituals like **Baptism** and the **Eucharist** (communal celebration of the Lord's Supper) developed. The evangelical work carried on by the disciples and the establishment of a church turned a belief system into an institutionalized religion. Also, largely due to the travels and work of **Paul of Tarsus** (ca. 5–57 C.E.), an essentially Hebrew religion was turned into a religion for all believers. Paul traveled the length and breadth of the eastern Roman world teaching that Jesus's message was proclaimed for all.

The reasons for the popularity of Christianity are many:

- It embraced both men and women;
- it was less exclusive than the mystery religions;
- it appealed to common people and the poor in its communal celebrations;
- it gave a cause to many in an indifferent world of materialism and pleasure;
- its literature, like the **epistles** (Paul's letters to various Christian communities), and **gospels** (accounts of Jesus's life), and teaching provided an artistic framework for elaboration.

Soon the religion also had a priesthood and ecclesiastical administration, including **priests** who met the local needs of parishioners, **bishops** who headed communities of believers, and, by the fifth century, a successor to the Apostle Saint Peter, founder of the church in Rome, was designated the **Pope**. Using the framework of Roman law, the church began organizing its own body of law called **canon law**. All of this helped to ensure continuity within the church.

Christian Martyrs

Initially, the Roman government persecuted Christians because, with the establishment of the empire, Augustus incorporated the Eastern idea of god-kings to strengthen his rule. The refusal of Christians to offer sacrifices to the emperor opened them to charges of disloyalty and treason. As a result, Christianity was declared illegal, and for three centuries Christians were persecuted. Paradoxically, these persecutions and the **martyrdoms** they elicited made the religion even more popular.

Christian Roman Empire

By the fourth century there were Christians in every class and Christian communities scattered throughout the Hellenistic world and in Europe. This and the deteriorating situation on the frontiers, caused Emperor **Constantine** to issue the **Edict of Milan** in 313 C.E. This edict made Christianity a legal religion throughout the empire. Constantine also encouraged the building of churches and upheld the authority of Christian bishops in religious matters. He is most famous for building a new Roman capital in the east, **Constantinople**. His desire to create a new Christian capital for the empire coincided with his belief that the new capital would be safer from Germanic invasions and at the center of trade that had shifted more to the east. In building his new city, he combined classicism with Christianity. The crowning building was the Church of the Holy Wisdom, better known as the **Cathedral of the Hagia Sophia**. Shortly before his death, Constantine converted to the new faith and every emperor afterward, with the exception of Julian, was a Christian. Finally, by edicts issued in 391 and 392, Christianity was made the official religion of the empire and worship of the old Roman gods was outlawed. Thus, Rome became the Christian Roman Empire, putting in place the third of the classical legacies to Europe.

Roman Catholics

The Roman acceptance of Christianity benefited both the church and the state. The relationship, however, immediately revealed perplexing problems of rule, in some ways not settled to this day. One of the early doctrinal disputes of Christianity was over the question of the divinity of Christ. **Aryan Christians** believed that because God by definition was uncreated and unchangeable, Christ could not have been created and be his coequal. Orthodox Christians branded this **heresy**, or denial of a doctrine of faith. A church council was summoned that produced the **Nicene Creed** (321 C.E.), determining that Christ was the "eternally begotten son of the Father." Emperor Constantine participated in the debate, paving the way for future emperors to claim they could do the same. The move of the Roman capital east to Constantinople and the fall of Rome to the Germans, however, made the pope, not the emperor, the supreme ruler of the land in the West. The emperor, however, was the ruler in the East.

Calling themselves **Catholic**, a word derived from the Greek meaning universal, Christians and their leadership claimed one world of belief united in the person of the pope. This set the stage for another dispute (besides that of secular religious rule) between the Christian church in the West and that in the East.

At first, Christians were against Greco-Roman culture, but gradually they assimilated it into their church organization and art. **Saint Jerome** (340–429 C.E.) translated the Old and New Testaments from Hebrew and Greek into vernacular Latin, producing the **Vulgate** edition of the Bible. The blending of Christian and classical culture is most evident in the work of **Saint Augustine** of Hippo (354–430 C.E.). His *Confessions* combines the Greco-Roman belief that knowledge and virtue are the same with the Christian idea that even knowledgeable people sin. According to Augustine, history is the account of God acting in time. Thus, as the Roman state in the West came under increasing attack by the barbarians, the church remained the repository of the Greco-Roman heritage.

Invasions

Beginning in the late 300s C.E., large numbers of Germans were moving into the Roman Empire in the West. German movements south have a variety of explanations—Germans were pushed by the **Huns** advancing from Central Asia, they were seeking warmer climates and new grazing lands, or they envied the wealth of Rome. For whatever reason, one group, the **Visigoths**, rebelled against Roman rule in 378 C.E. and finally, in 410 C.E. their leader **Alaric** invaded and sacked Rome. In 476 C.E. a German general, **Odoacer**, seized power in Rome and overthrew the emperor. The invasion of the Germans and the collapse of Rome did not end Roman history, for the empire that had already moved east to Constantinople and continued on for another 1000 years. In Europe a new form of culture arose, shaping the Greco-Roman-Christian heritage in a new way.

Roman civilization began as an outpost of Hellenism. In the beginning it adopted its forms and values, but it added to it significant new contributions, principally Roman law and Christianity. Law was to Rome what Greek culture was to the Hellenistic world—the glue of classical civilization. Christianity in the West replaced Greek cultural glue when the Roman political structure fell to the Germans.

CHAPTER 8

Classical Chinese Imperial Civilization

(500 B.C.E.–500 C.E.)

CHRONOLOGY	Zhou (Chou) Dynasty (ca. 1027–256 B.C.E.)	Qin (Ch'in) Period (256–206 B.C.E.)	Age of Disunity (220–589 C.E.)
	Warring States Period (402–332 B.C.E.)	Han Dynasty (207 B.C.E.–210 C.E.)	

TERMS	ancestor worship	Mandate of Heaven	Han Dynasty
	Yin	Dynastic Cycle	civil service bureaucracy
	Yang	Tao Te Ching	ridge-and-furrow
	Daoism (Taoism)	Legalism	paper
	Confucianism	I Ching	Silk Road
	Zhou (Chou) Dynasty	well-field system	tributary relations
	Analects	shi	The Romance of the
	filial peity	Qin (Ch'in) Dynasty	Three Kingdoms
	li	Great Wall	

PEOPLE	Confucius (Kung Fu-tzu)	Shi Huangdi	Wudi (Wu Ti)
	Mencius	(Shi Huang-ti)	Ts'ai Lun (Cai Lun)
	Lao Zi (Lao-tzu)	Xiongnu (Hsiung-nu)	Ban Qao (Pan Chao)
	Han Fei Zi (Han Fei-tzu)	Sima Qian (Ssu-ma	Sima Qian (Ssu-ma
	Li Si (Li Ssu)	Ch'ien)	Ch'ien)
	Zhou (Chou)	Liu Bang (Liu Pang) or	Ching Chi (Ching Chih)
	King Wu	Han Gao Zi (Kao-tsu)	Chang Heng (Ch'ang
	Sun Zi (sun-tzu)	mandarins	Heng)
	Qin (Ch'in)	Sons of Han	

PLACES	Wei Valley	Changan (Ch'ang An)	Dunhuang (Tun-huang)

Classical Chinese Imperial Civilization (500 B.C.E.–500 C.E.)

CHINESE RELIGIOUS TRADITION—CONFUCIANISM, TAOISM, AND LEGALISM

As the western world was being shaped by the classical ideas of humanism, law, and Christianity, China was developing its classical culture. The richness of Chinese belief systems has often been interpreted as a response to the complexity of man. Confucianism appealed to the mind and Daoism (Taoism) to the soul, Buddhism to the heart, and folk religions to the emotions.

Not unlike the West, where nature gods at first predominated, the origins of Chinese beliefs can be found in attitudes regarding man's relationship to nature. In earliest times the Chinese sought, through varied rites like burning paper images or proffering food, to appease the nature spirits. **Ancestors** were worshipped by the family because they provided the communication link to these gods. These rituals, embedded in folk religions, are still apparent in festivals and Chinese astrology. Whereas, in western thought man was viewed as the prime object of the natural order, and in Hindu thought the world of nature was viewed as transitory, the Chinese regard the relationship between man and nature as deep and reciprocal. To them, heaven, earth, and man constitute a single unity governed by the cosmic law or Dao (Tao). Within the Dao (Tao), two interacting forces were recognized—**Yin** and **Yang**. Each represent a constellation of qualities. Yin is negative, feminine, and passive; Yang is positive, masculine, and active. The essential difference between classical Chinese dualism and classical western philosophy, the struggle between light and dark, hot and cold, is that the two forces are complementary rather than opposing. According to the Chinese, the aspiration of man is harmony of sources rather than victory of one over the other. In a sense, the two major philosophies of China themselves reflect Chinese dualistic thought. **Daoism**, or **Taoism**, seeks harmony between man and nature while **Confucianism** seeks harmony among men.

The emergence of formal philosophies—Confucianism, Taoism, and Legalism—based on earlier belief systems occurred during the Zhou (Chou) Dynasty (ca. 1027–256 B.C.E.). The Zhou (Chou) period was a time of turmoil and transition. Not unlike the Greeks, who were struggling at the same time to achieve political harmony within the city-state system, the Chinese were being challenged to create a framework of thought and action for harmonious state rule.

Confucius

Confucius, or Kung Fu-tzu, was born about 551 B.C.E. (ca. 551–479 B.C.E.), less than a century before Socrates and about the same time as Buddha. He was appointed court official by the prince of Lu and from that position reflected on the confused state of society. After he left that position, he became the center of a group of admiring disciples who wrote down his sayings and stories that later became a book, the *Analects*. The thoughts of Confucius centered on the duties and proper behavior of the individual within society. He taught that there was a universal natural law and that human beings should live according to this law. Within that law, he considered the family the basic unit of society. Proper family relationships should replicate those of society at large. In society at large, he identified five relationships that were to be ordered on the basis of **filial piety** or respect for one's parents or elders:

- the ruler should be just and the ruled loyal;
- the father should be loving and the son respectful;
- the husband should be righteous and the wife obedient;
- the older brother should be genteel and the younger humble;
- the older friend should be considerate, the younger deferent.

Confucius also emphasized moderation and proper conduct, or *li*. A Confucian gentleman was a man of integrity, education and culture, and proper conduct. Because gentlemen were made, not born, a man of poor birth could become one without aristocratic birth.

Mencius

Confucius, like Socrates, wrote nothing down. Confucius's most famous follower **Mencius** (372–289 B.C.E.) recorded Confucian thought and added to it. Mencius developed the idea of self-perfection and through self-perfection the society would be ordered. This idea first appeared in the *Record of Rites* (*Li Ji, Li Chi*) which states that

> . . .when the personal life is cultivated, the family will be regulated; when the family is regulated, the state will be in order; and when the state is in order, there will be peace throughout the world. From the Son of Heaven (Emperor) down to the common people, all must regard cultivation of the personal life as the root or foundation (Schirokaur 41).

Mencius taught that a moral leader must enjoy the respect and support of his subjects. A good ruler was thought to possess the **Mandate of Heaven** or a divine right to govern. If a ruler governed badly or was immoral, the people would rise up in revolt. The idea did not originate with Mencius, rather, it was used by the Zhou (Chou) to justify overthrow of the Shang dynasty, but, in tying it to the wider philosophy of cosmic order, the idea of divine rule was legitimized. As a corollary to the Mandate of Heaven, the **Dynastic Cycle** was developed by later Chinese scholars as an interpretation of the past to predict the future. The theory asserted that Chinese civilizations repeat themselves, going through the stages of warring states, unification, barbarian invasions and conquest, absorption into the Chinese system, and finally, creation of a new dynasty based on the Mandate of Heaven. Because it lacks a priesthood, prescribed rituals, temples, and a concept of divinity, Confucianism is closer to a philosophy like humanism than a religion like Christianity. Yet, it is a creed that millions of East Asians follow as an ethical guide.

Taoism

Whereas Confucianism sought to order the proper relationships among men, Taoism sought order between man and nature. Though little is known for certain, the assumed founder of Taoism, **Lao Zi (Lao-tzu)**, lived in the sixth century B.C.E. The book attributed to him, the *Tao Te Ching* (Book of the Way and Its Power), was probably the work of several people and dates only from the fourth century B.C.E. According to Lao Zi (Lao-tzu), the tao, or way, was not a common code of social conduct, but a set of values that would allow a person to live in harmony with nature. This involved knowing the laws of nature and flowing with them rather than reordering them. Thus, the best ruler for a Taoist was the one who governed least. Taoist influence was greatest in the area of art and science due to the seclusion and observation of nature, which were preoccupations of its followers. A person could be both a Taoist and a Confucian—a Taoist when reflective and alone, and a Confucian when a member of the body politic.

Legalism

More pragmatic than Confucianism and less rooted in ancient Chinese thought was **Legalism**, a philosophy gained from many related schools of political thought that flourished during the late Zhou (Chou) primarily led by **Han Fei Zi (Han**

Fei-tzu d. 233 B.C.E.) and **Li Si** (**Li Ssu** d. 208 B.C.E.). The ideal legalist state was authoritarian because human nature was evil. Laws should replace morality. The ruler must provide discipline to maintain order. Education was looked on as unnecessary and impractical as people must work and produce. Legalism as a political philosphy triumphed under the Qin (Ch'in) dynasty.

I Ching

Because of the philosophical nature of Confucianism, Taoism, and Legalism, Chinese people continued to cling to folk religions that provided an avenue for emotional and spiritual activities and thought. The *I Ching* or Book of Changes fulfilled some of the same purpose as the Shang oracle bones; that is, they were used to learn the will of the gods and predict the future. It is essentially a book of oracles the contents of which are read by using randomly tossed coins. Chinese belief systems and philosophical thought provided a number of important underpinnings for the classical age, among them the importance of nature as reflected in art and science, the high esteem in which peasants were held, the importance of the family and elders, filial piety that is reflected in the hierarchical nature of social and political relationships, and the theories of the Mandate of Heaven and Dynastic Cycle that legitimized government.

THE ZHOU (CHOU), QIN (CH'IN), AND HAN DYNASTIES

The **Zhou** (**Chou**) are believed to have been Turkic-speaking peoples from Central Asia as they referred to the subjugated Chinese as "black-haired people." When the Zhou (Chou) under **King Wu** (ca. 1027–221 B.C.E.) overthrew the Shang, they adopted much of Shang culture but extended Chinese rule beyond the boundaries of the Shang. Confronted with the challenge of ruling a large territory of people unlike themselves, they built a second capital in the **Wei Valley** west of the Huang Ho (Yellow River). They gave huge tracts of land to members of the royal family and

to others who had talent and were loyal. Not unlike feudalism in Europe, in formal ceremonies using written records the lord pledged loyalty to the king in return for grants of lands. On these grants of lands were enserfed peasants who lived in villages and tilled the land in the **well-field system**. (It resembled the Chinese character for well.) In this system each of eight households cultivated one of eight plots that were arranged around a central plot and a well. The middle plot was tilled by all the families to provide the produce that would be given to the lord as tribute. In effect, the Zhou (Chou) king was political overlord of the land and supreme religious leader. The role of males at the head of the family, clan, and dynasty increased as the patriarch played the key role in the celebration of religious ceremonies designed to win the blessings of the ancestors or heaven. In the central core regions, Zhou (Chou) kings began to use regular, educated, salaried officials called **shi** to help them administer the kingdom. At first, the Zhou (Chou) kings were in strong control, but, because most of the lands given to lords were on the frontiers where expansion was possible, lords were able to become absolute rulers in their own right. China gradually became a land of independent kingdoms. During the period of the **Warring States** (402–332 B.C.E.) the entire political organization of the Zhou (Chou) collapsed.

Dreary as the warfare was, the Zhou (Chou) period had a lasting impact on Chinese society. During this period, Confucian and Taoist philosophies were born. In overthrowing the Shang, the Zhou (Chou) used the Mandate of Heaven to justify their rule. As the central administration of the Zhou (Chou) collapsed, the impoverished aristocrats gravitated to the border states, bringing their much needed talents to help renegade kings rule. This period saw the origins of a trained and able civil service based on talent. It also produced one of the most important martial classics of world history, one that has become the handbook for twentieth century guerrilla warfare. *The Art of War* by **Sun Zi** (**Sun-tzu** ca. fourth century B.C.E.), who was very likely a contemporary of Confucius, is about how to win wars and battles with superior strategies and tactics rather than weaponry. Its central premise is that successful warfare is based on deception. Despite warfare, cities grew up around forts and roads were built to supply the cities. Trade increased and was made easier with the invention of coined money. Iron technology blossomed during the Zhou (Chou). Chinese metalsmiths produced both wrought (shaped) and cast (poured) iron, an achievement not matched in Europe until the fourteenth century. Iron was used for weapons and for farming. Plows and iron shares broke the ground more easily. Continuing raids in the north drove the peasantry south and east so that by the end of the Zhou (Chou), the two great river systems of China, the Huang Ho (Yellow) and Yangtzi (Yangtse), had been settled. Rice growing in the southern parts began.

Qin Dynasty

In 256 B.C.E. the man who proclaimed himself **Shi Huangdi (Shi Huang-Ti)**, or First Emperor of the **Qin (Ch'in) Dynasty**, deposed the last Zhou (Chou) king. Although his rule lasted only 15 years, Shi Huangdi united China and from him the western word **China** is derived. The Qin (Ch'in), of nomadic origin, were one of many rebel states in Zhou (Chou) China. Their power increased due to a number of factors. They conscripted into military service peasants they had freed in battle with other states. Their superior bureaucracy ensured well-supplied and well-organized forces and they were receptive to military innovation. They were, for instance, one of the first states to use massed cavalry. Soon the Qin (Ch'in) had extended their sway as far south as modern Hong Kong and they even invaded Vietnam.

The First Emperor of the Qin (Ch'in) considered a highly centralized state necessary for a united China. His prime minister Li Si (Li Ssu), a founder of Legalism, helped shape his centralization program. First, he crippled the nobility by ordering them to leave their lands and live at court. Then he took over their land and organized China into provinces subdivided into smaller units. These were ruled by governors and officials who were appointed by the emperor and unable to claim hereditary rights to their positions.

To harness the human population to facilitate tax collection, building projects, and military service, Emperor Qin (Ch'in) ordered a census. Then he centralized trade practices by standardizing the Chinese script, weights, measures, and axle lengths of carts. He furthered irrigation and land reclamation projects, and promoted the production of textiles, especially silk. To protect his empire from northern nomads, primarily the **Xiongnu (Hsiung-nu)**, he linked together existing walls and added sections to form one great wall, extending from the sea some 1400 miles west. The **Great Wall**, rebuilt during the Ming Dynasty, is still regarded as one of the greatest structures of ancient times, visible from outer space.

Among the other remarkable building projects of the First Emperor of the Qin (Ch'in), were a royal tomb and a guardian army of 6000 life-size pottery men and horses to protect the tomb. The royal tomb called Mount Li, located near present-day Xian (Sian), was discovered in 1974 and has yet to be opened due to fears that exposure to the atmosphere will ruin the delicate artifacts. In a quest for immortality, the First Emperor of the Qin (Ch'in) ordered the building of the tomb in 208 B.C.E., two years before his death according to **Sima Qian (Ssu-ma Ch'ien**, ca. 145–ca. 90 B.C.E.), China's Herodotus. Using over 700,000 conscripts, the tomb chamber is said to have reproduced in minute detail the universe over which he ruled. It included mechanically triggered crossbows set to shoot intruders and the various rivers of the empire were reproduced in quicksilver and made to flow mechanically. Heavenly constellations were depicted on the ceiling. The army of terra cotta figures surrounding the tomb are presently being unearthed from their underground chambers. Their lifelike individualized demeanors suggest that actual soldiers and horses served as models. Portrayed in graceful, realistic style, complete with weapons and horse gear, the entombed army has left an authentic record of hairstyles, weapons, armor, and horsemanship of the period.

Despite his achievements the First Emperor of the Qin (Ch'in) was an unpopular ruler. As a Legalist, he distrusted Confucian scholars. They were purged and their literary heritage destroyed in a massive book burning. Heavy taxation and forced labor alienated the peasants. His death in 206 B.C.E. sparked massive revolts. Then **Liu Bang (Liu Pang**, 247–195 B.C.E.), a petty official of the Qin (Ch'in), defeated the Qin (Ch'in) successor and established the **Han Dynasty** (207 B.C.E.–210 C.E.). Liu Bang (Liu Pang) is one of only two commoners in Chinese history to establish a major dynasty. He is often referred to by his posthumous imperial title, **Han Gao Zi (Kao-tsu**). The Han era, which lasted for over 400 years, saw the consolidation of Chinese civilization. Whereas the Zhou (Chou) gave China its philosophy of statecraft, and the Qin (Ch'in) united China and gave it its name, the Han gave it its distinctly classical character by institutionalizing the largest, most effective and enduring **civil service bureaucracy** in the preindustrial world. Chosen by examination, these scholar-bureaucrats, the **mandarins**, not only ran the state, but provided its creative genius and a reverence for education that endures to this day. Dynasties came and went, but the mandarins and their Confucian philosophy shaped the political, economic, social, and cultural framework of China. So closely do the Chinese identify themselves with this tradition that they refer to themselves as "**sons of Han**."

It appeared that China might return to a feudal order under Liu Bang (Liu Pang) because he rewarded his followers with grants of land. His successor, **Wudi (Wu Ti**, 140–87 B.C.E.), however, moved toward bureaucratic centralization by requiring that domains of vassals be divided among heirs and not passed on in perpetuity. This began an ongoing struggle in Chinese history between aristocrats and scholars. Liu Bang (Liu Pang) and Wudi (Wu Ti) also replaced Legalism with Confucianism. Some dedicated scholars had hidden their books or memorized them during the Qin (Ch'in) purges. In the Han Confucian revival, they elaborated on the theories of the Mandate of Heaven and dynastic cycle. According to Han Confucianism, the emperor by mandate had divine powers and was responsible for protecting the empire from invasion and internal disruption. A thorough knowledge of Confucian teaching also became essential for employment and promotion in the Han adminis-

trative hierarchy. This was institutionalized in the establishment of an imperial university at the capital in **Changan (Ch'ang An**) in 124 B.C.E. At the end of the Han era, there were more than 30,000 students concentrating on memorization and interpretation of the Confucian classics. When formal examination for government positions began in the last century B.C.E., the first professional civil service was established. Theoretically, any Chinese citizen could take the exam, but because preparation required education, upper class candidates had a decided advantage. Exams were scored strictly on merit with the scores and the difficulty of the exam determining the scholar's rank at court.

Han Class System

The growing influence of the mandarins affected the class system. Mandarins gained position at the expense of aristocratic families. Gradually, in hierarchical style reflective of Confucian concepts of filial piety, the mandarin class ranked at the top of the social scale, below which were the peasants who were revered for the vital connection they had with the land. Beneath them were the artisans, and lowest in rank were the merchants. Merchants were disdained because they produced nothing and merely made money by transferring produce. Outside the class system altogether were the military who, in Confucian thought, were symbolic of failure to maintain order.

Arts, Sciences, and Technology

The wealth of the Han era led to classical achievements in the arts and sciences. Wealth was driven by improvements in agriculture and trade. During this period, the **ridge-and-furrow** system of planting was developed, with seeds planted in lines along the furrows. To maintain fertility, manure and crushed bones were used. Excellent metallurgy led to more effective plows. New harnesses were developed that, instead of choking the animals, allowed them to pull heavier loads. Tea and sugar cane were still luxuries of the south, but silk was a large item of produce. Porcelain was invented. Unlike Rome, roads remained undeveloped and difficult to travel, but canals and dikes were extensive and facilitated trade. Merchants were encouraged because they brought in tax revenue but were regulated. State monopolies also kept essential commodities under the control of the state as a lucrative source of income. City life reflected the splendid lifestyle of the rich as well as the poverty of the poor. Elements of Taoism developed into a popular religion. Entertainment for the rich included private musical troupes, while gambling and cockfighting entertained the poor.

Wealth and literacy combined to create lasting contributions to the sciences. Key to education, government, and the sciences was **Ts'ai Lun**'s (**Cai Lun**) invention of **paper** (105 C.E.) which was cheaper than silk. In the Han period, the study of history flourished. The Chinese, like the Greeks, began to conceive of history as a discipline where artifacts are examined and data analyzed. **Sima Qian** (**Ssu-ma Ch'ien** ca. 145–86 B.C.E.), who can be seen as the Chinese Thucydidies, wrote a classic study of Chinese history using eyewitnesses and written documents called *Records of the Grand Historian*. **Ban Qao** (**Pan Chao**), China's first woman historian and scholar wrote poems and essays, notably *Lessons for Women*. In medicine, China produced its own Hippocrates, **Ching Chi** (**Ching Chih**), whose *Treatise on Fevers* became a standard work. The career of **Chang Heng** (**Ch'ang Heng**, 78–139 C.E.) was strikingly similar to that of Eratosthenes. Both concluded the earth was round and both built models to test their theories.

Much of China's intellectual life during the Han took place in the Han capital at **Changan** (**Ch'ang An**). Liu Bang (Liu Pang) built the city not far from the Shang/Qin (Ch'in) capital. Whereas Rome sprawled over seven hills, Changan was a picture of mathematically planned discipline, symbolic of the symmetry of the cosmos. The city itself was constructed in square blocks, each of which was walled and had only one gate with a watchtower that was closed at curfew. It did resemble Rome in its massive public works—walls, roads, and canals. Most spectacular was not the Forum and Colisseum, but the Imperial Palace with its awe-inspiring audience halls, pavilions, granaries, arsenals, and artificial lakes. The city was also a hub of commerce and the eastern terminus of the Silk Road.

THE SILK ROAD

The Han period was one of great imperial expansion despite nomads north of the Great Wall who were a repeated threat to the Chinese throughout their imperial history. The nomad could simply apply the skills he used daily, those of horsemanship and archery, to attack the Chinese frontier; while the Chinese peasant farmer had to interrupt his agricultural life and train as a soldier to defend the imperial boundary stretching some 1400 miles. From the Han to the Ching Dynasty, the Chinese generally followed one of two patterns of dealing with the nomads. One was to use military force against the nomads and defend the Great Wall as Qin (Ch'in) had done. The first Han Emperor Gao Zi (Liu Bang or Liu Pang) pursued a different policy. He presented Xiongnu (Hsiung-nu) leaders with elaborate gifts, treated them as equals, and arranged marriages for them with imperial princesses. Later, the Emperor Wudi (Wu Ti) reversed this policy, using military force instead. Military colonies were established in strategic locations along the frontier to prevent nomadic invasions from the north. Nomads were required to enter into **tributary relations** with the Han court, which meant that the nomadic rulers had to travel to the imperial court with gifts as tribute in recognition of Chinese suzerainty. In exchange, they received elaborate gifts that were symbols of the dynasty's wealth and power. The Emperor Wudi (Wu Ti) also required them to send their sons to the capital to receive a "Chinese education." This enabled him to use them as hostages.

In 133 B.C.E. the Han drove the Xiongnu (Hsiung-nu) tribes north and then advanced into western Turkestan where they opened up direct relations with India. Chinese armies also conquered western Korea where they took over trade with Japan. They extended their rule to modern-day Hong Kong, and by 111 B.C.E. they had conquered northern Vietnam. The military conquests brought the Chinese into closer contact with distant peoples. This resulted in a dramatic increase in trade. Chinese merchants opened up a new route from southwestern China via the rivers of Vietnam and Burma to ports on the Bay of Bengal. At first the Chinese left trade in the hands of foreigners, but later Chinese merchants gained control.

Origins of the Silk Road

The origins of the Silk Road can be found in the fact that during the Han a continuous network of advanced societies stretched across the southern half of the continents of Europe and Asia. In the west was Rome, in the east was Han China; in between were the Kushan empire of northern India and Afghanistan, and the Parthians who ruled Persia and Mesopotamia. The coexistence of these great empires meant that vast areas enjoyed internal peace and efficient government, conditions that made possible the growth of large-scale trade. The geography of Asia also made such a transEurasian route possible. There are no major seas or mountains to prohibit east-west movement, and the desert barriers can be circumvented.

Long-distance trade between East and West Asia was also possible by sea because of the monsoon wind cycle. The broad expanse of warm ocean (Indian Ocean), the South Eurasian landmass, and a major mountain barrier (Himalayas) create unique climatological wind conditions. Monsoon winds are created by warming differentials between water and land. From June until September, the summer moisture-laden winds blow from the southwest until they hit the Himalayas, and from October to May they blow the other way from the northeast. Ships could catch the winds going west in the winter and east on the return voyage in the summer. Long-distance trade was also spurred by product specialization and an appetite for luxury goods that rich and stable empires could afford. China was famous for its silk, Southeast Asia for spices, India for textiles (calico, muslin, linen, and cotton), and Rome for glass, gold, and silver. By the second century C.E. trade routes covered Eurasia and sea routes ran from China to Africa.

The Silk Road itself stretched 2500 miles across Central Asia. From the Han capital at Changan, the route proceeded northwest to the frontier town of **Dunhuang (Tun-huang)**. A series of caravanseries dotted the arid deserts and windswept mountains until the convoys reached Merv in the Kushan Empire. From there, the Silk Road ran south of the Caspian Sea, through Parthia and the Roman empire to the shores of the Mediterranean. As the name implies, Chinese silk, which probably comprised 90 percent of China's exports of the time, was much prized in Rome where its manufacture was still unknown. The Romans became aware, even at this early date, that the educated Chinese were supremely confident of their civilization and had little need of the products of other cultures. Wrote Ammianus Marcellinus in 380 C.E., "There Seres (Chinese) . . . , study to pass their lives in peace . . . and so free are they from wants that, though ready to dispose of their own products, they purchase none from abroad." The sea route, while less known, was probably even more important and more durable. This was because land transport was more rudimentary and thus expensive (mules, camels, oxen), and because it was more vulnerable to political disruption. Instead of hugging the coast, merchant marine ships could sail rapidly and directly from India to Arabia and back in four months, some of them with the carrying capacity of 500 tons.

Cultural Interaction

The effects of such long-distance trade were not just commercial. Significant cultural interaction occurred as well. Thousands of people—sailors, camel drivers, merchants, and porters mixed. One of the most important cultural interactions was religious. Zoroasterianism, Judaism, and Christianity were implanted in India and in Central Asia. Especially important for China was the spread of Buddhism, which penetrated China with the fall of the Han Empire. Peasant unrest due to heavy taxation and corvee labor culminated in a great revolutionary effort led by the Daoists (Taoists) in 184 C.E. After years of struggle, the last Han emperor was deposed in 220 C.E. and China was divided into three kingdoms.

Like the Romans, the Chinese had incorporated nomadic peoples in their armies, but as government deteriorated, the nomads began to invade. During the period between the fall of the Han and rise of the Sui, called the **Age of Disunity** (220–589 C.E.), great commanders and warriors were transformed into legendary heroes. Their daring deeds were told over and over and finally written down in *The Romance of the Three Kingdoms*, a novel not unlike the stories of King Arthur and his knights.

Buddhism

In the midst of this economic distress and political stability, Buddhism arrived from India, disseminated by silk merchants and missionaries. Not unlike Christianity in Europe, Buddhism offered spiritual solace and cultural cohesion in a time of political fragmentation. Chinese Buddhists blended practices from many Indian Buddhist sects and included some of their own values like family lineage in Buddhist teachings. Typically, therefore, second sons became Buddhist monks while the first sons maintained family responsibilities. Buddhism often competed with Taoism for the affection of the common people. Buddhism offered a clearer doctrine of personal salvation, but Taoist faith healing, implications for political protest, and connection with nature continued to win Chinese support. Confucianism, with its secular concerns, lost ground during this period but it reappeared when strong rulers in the north drove out nomadic intruders and reestablished the Mandate of Heaven under the Sui and Tang Dynasties beginning in 589 C.E.

Summary

The Chinese classical period established the major patterns of Chinese government, culture, and thought. Legitimization for rule, the Mandate of Heaven and Dynastic Cycle, begun in the Zhou (Chou) period, were formalized by Confucian scholars under the Han. This system of changing dynasties but continuous imperial rule lasted until 1911. The idea of a state run by Confucian scholar-bureaucrats, selected by merit, matured under the Han and is, perhaps, Chinese civilization's most important and enduring legacy. Dynasties came and went, but Confucian values of filial piety, proper conduct, and education gave hierarchical and civil order to the state. It was also the basis for invention, literacy, scholarship, and technological advance. Legalism, at odds with the Chinese cosmic ideas of harmony, shaped the Qin (Ch'in) era of centralization, but it otherwise remained unpopular during the Han Dynasty. The long and stable rule of the Han nourished trade that for the first time in world history linked China to Europe along the Silk Road. Along that Road came foreign ideas, especially Buddhism.

CHAPTER 9

Classical Indian Civilization
(300 B.C.E.–500 C.E.)

CHRONOLOGY	Mauryan Empire (ca. 322–232 B.C.E.) Siddharta Gautama (Buddha) (ca. 563–483 B.C.E.) Age of Invasions (250 B.C.E.–200 C.E.) Gupta Empire (320–467 C.E.)		

TERMS	Brahmanism	Buddha	benevolent paternalism
	Vedas	Enlightened One	stupa
	Code of Manu	Four Noble Truths	Tamil
	dharma	Eightfold Path	Indian (Arabic) numerals
	karma	Nirvana	rock-cut temples
	moksha	Theravada	Chaitya
	Shiva	Mahayana	frescoes
	Vishnu	bodhisvatta	Lakshmi
	nonviolence	mudras	Kali
	Bhagavad Gita	Gupta Empre	mandalas
	Arjuna	Mauryan Empire	satee
	Krishna	Arthashastra	
	Jainism	centralized despotism	

PEOPLE	Mahavira	Kautilya	Dravidians
	Siddharta Gautama	Ashoka	Kalidasa
	(Buddha)	King Demetrius	Caraka
	Sangha	Kushan	gurus
	Chandragupta Mauryan	Kanishka	White Huns
	Megasthenes	Chandra Gupta I	

PLACES	Magadha	Pataliputra	Sanchi
	Bay of Bengal	Kalinga	Ajanta and Ellora
	Hindu Kush	Gandhara	
	Deccan Plateau	Nalanda	

Classical Indian Civilization (300 B.C.E.–500 C.E.)

INDIAN RELIGIOUS TRADITION—HINDUISM, JAINISM, AND BUDDHISM

As in the West and China, Indian classicism was closely connected with the thought and belief systems of India. India's spiritual traditions blossomed in the sixth and fifth centuries B.C.E., about the same time as the Greek and Chinese religious and philosophical leaders. Indian religious thought gave the world three powerful moral and philosophical belief systems—Hinduism, Jainism, and Buddhism.

Hinduism

The most basic and enduring of the Indian religions is Hinduism, a religion that matured and triumphed during the classical age. The origins of Hinduism can be found in Aryan religious traditions, or **Brahmanism**, as revealed in the **Vedas** or hymns to the gods. Hinduism is both the oldest and most diverse of the world's religions, easily mutable and readily able to incorporate new ideas. The bedrock of Hinduistic belief is a sacred division of society into castes, written in the *Code of Manu*, and that all Hindu gods are aspects of Brahma, the supreme, indefinable principle of life. The various deities are both aspects of Brahma and ritual vehicles to help reach Brahma, which is the goal of all Hindus.

The broad outlines of Hindu thought that had evolved during the Aryan period of Indian history matured during the classical era. The Brahman caste gradually worked out the basic outlines of their theology that encompassed both moral and spiritual ideas. According to the dogma, or religious teachings, to reach Brahma, people must follow a proscribed path. First, they must observe **dharma**, the moral duties of their caste. The degree to which dharma is observed determines one's **karma**, or the accumulation of good and bad deeds during life. Those who observed dharma could hope to be reincarnated in a higher caste in the next life. Those with bad karma would be reborn in a lower caste. The law outlines the proper human pursuits such as material gain as long as it is honest, and pleasure and love for perpetuation of the family. When the moral law is observed, the endless cycle of birth, death, and reincarnation will end. **Moksha** is the release from the wheel of life and unity with Brahma. In the long epic poem the *Mahabharata*, an ideal state based on dharma is personified in King Dharma's law.

After the third century B.C.E. Hinduism began to emphasize the role of powerful gods like **Shiva**, the cosmic dancer who creates and destroys, and **Vishnu**, the preserver of creation, in reaching the ideal state of Brahma or god-force. From the emphasis on a god-force of all life, not just human life, came the tradition of **nonviolence** toward all living creatures, which was lifted to new heights in Jainist beliefs. The *Bhagavad Gita*, the best-loved hymn of Hindus and not unlike the Christian parables, is a spiritual guide to life's problems. In it, a warrior, **Arjuna**, struggles with the decision of whether to go to battle against his own kinsmen. **Krishna**, who is a manifestation of the god Vishnu, instructs him to carry out his duties as a warrior because "The eternal in man cannot kill; the Eternal in man cannot die." Thus, Hinduism emphasizes the everlasting nature of Brahma within each person even in death and the duty to one's caste (in this case the warrior caste).

Caste

Not unlike the yin and yang of Chinese cosmic thought, the caste system and the concept of Brahma are two sides of the same core of Hindu classical thought. Religion justifies caste and the stability of the social system proves the validity of the religious teachings. And, not unlike Confucian thought, the hierarchical order established by religious thought, in this case caste, provided the framework for the orderly structure of the state. The Brahmans were the upper caste of priests and scholars. The ruling caste, the Kshatriya, were second. Beneath them were the peasants (Vaishya) and serfs (Shudra). Outide the caste were various groups of outcasts and slaves.

Caste hierarchy was reflected in the life of every village, which became a microcosm of the Hindu order and religious bond. Within the village each caste or subcaste was a community that shared religious duties, working in similar occupations and helping each other in times of calamity. In daily life, social functions as informal as sharing a meal or as formal as a wedding took place within the context of one's own caste. Hindu stability, as opposed to the volatility and feudal nature of Indian political life, made the Hindu castes and religion the glue of classical Indian civilization. As with Confucianism, the vast literature of Hinduism as preserved in Sanskrit (Hindu script) and other regional languages, encouraged and elevated scholarship and united the peoples of India.

Jainism

Around the sixth century B.C.E. two reformers of Hinduism appeared. In part, this was a response to the pessimism of an endless cycle of death and reincarnation prior to reaching unity with Brahma. It was also a protest against Brahman ritual and the power and privilege of the Brahman caste. The founder and most influential thinker of **Jainism** was **Mahavira** (ca. 540–468 B.C.E.). Mahavira thought that the whole of the universe is composed of souls and matter. The only way for any soul to achieve the eternal one-

ness with Brahma was to rid itself of matter and rise to the top of the universe as a soul. Jains considered all life to be composed of souls so they believed that no life, either plant or animal, should be destroyed. Since this would logically lead to starvation and death, Jains devised a hierarchy of life, with human beings at the apex, followed by animals, plants, and inanimate objects. To do the least violence, therefore, one must be a vegetarian and shun material ways. In this way, nonviolence, which was already part of Hindu thought, became a cardinal principle of Jainism. It has influenced many from Emerson to Gandhi and Martin Luther King. The extreme asceticism of the Jains, however, made it a fringe religion.

Buddhism

More influential was **Siddharta Gautama** (ca. 563–483 B.C.E.), better known as **Buddha**, meaning **Enlightened One**. Both Buddha and Mahavira were Kshatryiya, the class below the top and most likely to resent Brahman privilege. Buddha was also distressed by the pessimism of the endless cycle of life and the inability to change one's karma or place in this life until death. Saddened by this human suffering, he tried a life of asceticism and fasting but found it led nowhere. His contemplation then led him to the conclusion that happiness in this life could be found not in changing one's karma but in changing one's thoughts and attitudes. According to the **Four Noble Truths**,

1. life is suffering,
2. suffering is caused by desire,
3. one can be released from desire by following the **Eightfold Path**, after which
4. a state of grace when desire is extinguished (**Nirvana**) could be reached, releasing one from karma.

At the heart of the Eightfold Path (symbolized by a chariot wheel with eight spokes) was self-knowledge, a willingness to be free of suffering and desire, and a decision to adopt "right conduct" and "right speech." In this way of life, one practiced love and compassion, joy and serenity. Buddha also recognized that all things change with time, including death, at which time the combination of physical and mental parts becomes rearranged in a new form of life. In that way, there is life everlasting, not the extinguishing of life in oneness with Brahma.

The appeal of Buddhism, like Christianity, is that the Eightfold Path could be followed by anyone—noble or peasant, educated or ignorant. Anyone could attain enlightenment. Its emphasis on love, the life of the spirit, and an attainable Heaven was, like Christianity, equalizing and humanizing. It opposed the rigid hierarchy of Hinduism and released people from the endless cycle of life. Its success was also related to Buddhist proselytizing and institutionalization. A circle of disciples, the **Sangha**, systematized the faith and spread it far and wide, using the Asian trade routes. Temples, statues of Buddha, and rituals made active participation possible.

Upon Buddha's death, Buddhism split into two sects—**Theravada** (Lesser Vehicle) and **Mahayana** (Larger Vehicle). The Theravada branch, which was popular in Southeast Asia, asserted that the tenets of Buddhism rested on the life and teachings of Buddha. It is called "lesser" because of its strict, conservative doctrines. The Mahayana branch, popular in China, Japan, Korea, and Vietnam, was more liberal, recognizing that beliefs could evolve and go beyond Buddhist scriptures. It emphasized compassion and was called the "larger" because it held that there were many ways to salvation. Mahayana Buddhism maintained that Buddha in his previous lives had been a **bodhisavatta**—a wise being, a buddha. Bodhisvattas had achieved enlightenment but had declined nirvana in order to help others. Around this sect grew a pantheon of heavenly buddhas and bodhisavattas to whom people could pray for enlightenment, becoming much like the saints of Christendom. The Buddha is usually represented as looking like the inhabitants of the country in which he is revered, although all the images hold certain features in common like the hand positions (**mudras**), which are used to show whether the Buddha is meditating, giving blessing, teaching, and so on. In India, Buddhism made a dramatic appearance under King Ashoka. Eventually, Buddha was worshipped as one of the many Hindu gods and Buddhism was folded into Hinduism. But it was from India that Buddhism spread over a wide area of East Asia.

MAURYAN AND GUPTA CIVILIZATION

The strong village social fabric based on caste and the Aryan legacy of local princes (rajes) made political centralization difficult and even irrelevant in India. However, during the classical period two great empires rose, the **Mauryan** (ca. 322–232 B.C.E.) and the **Gupta** (320–467 C.E.). Hindu and Buddhist thought and culture were interwoven through the contours of both empires, influencing art, scholarship, and architecture. Prior to the rise of the Mauryan, India was in turmoil caused both by external invasion and internal unrest. Around 572 B.C.E. the Achaemenid Persians controlled the Indus Valley region. In the northeast around the Ganges Valley, a strong Aryan kingdom, **Magadha**, with the support of the Brahmans, ruled and formed alliances to rebuff the Persians. Unity was fragile, however, always susceptible to inter-Aryan rivalries and outside invasion. It was during this unsettled time, as in Zhou (Chou) China, that Buddha was born, setting off yet another conflict—between Buddhists and Hindus. This turmoil opened the door to yet another invasion, this time by Alexander the Great in 327 B.C.E. After Alexander's brief appearance in India, a number of Greek rulers controlled India's northwest territory, indirectly spreading Greek influence. Of particular importance was the flow into India of Greek astronomical and mathematical ideas and Greek artistic styles.

Mauryan

The Greek invasion also left a political vacuum once Hellenistic kingdoms in the area weakened. The ruler of a small state in the Ganges Valley, **Chandragupta Mauryan** defeated the Greek general Seleucus and made himself king in 322 B.C.E. Chandragupta then created the largest empire yet seen in Indian history, including the whole of northern India from the **Bay of Bengal** in the east, to the **Hindu Kush** Mountains in the west, and south across the **Deccan Plateau**. In the heart of the empire in the Ganges Valley, Chandragupta then proceeded to build a capital city, **Pataliputra**, to which ambassadors came from all over the world. The city boasted a moat and walls surrounding it with 570 watchtowers. Court style became elaborate and the palace rich in jewels and courtiers. The palace hall was similar to the palace hall at Persepolis. It was lined with carved sandstone columns decorated with vines of gold and buds of silver. Roads were built and trade flourished. Indian merchants exported elephants, silk, spices, cotton, and perfume to China and the Hellenistic cities. Chandragupta even requested of the Hellenistic kings that a sophist philosopher be sent. **Megasthenes**, a Greek ambassador to the imperial court of Chandragupta at Pataliputra in 302 B.C.E., found the splendor of India even greater than that of the Persian cities of the Seleucid Empire.

In statecraft, Chandragupta adopted the Persian style of administration by dividing the empire into provinces, each of which was governed by someone linked to Chandragupta's family. He also established a bureaucracy to oversee taxation and the financing and building of public works. He created a standing army of 500,000 and relied on the advice of his chief minister **Kautilya** in matters of statecraft. Kautilya's book, the *Arthashastra* is not unlike Machiavelli's *The Prince* and Sun Tzu's *Art of War* in its advice to rulers about how to amass power and use it by whatever means as long as the ruler pleased his subjects. Wise administration of justice is another subject Kautilya addresses. "Government," according to the *Arthashastra,* is the science of punishment." On Kautilya's advice, Chandragupta sent spies throughout his empire to report on the honesty of officials. Homing pigeons were used to bring messages to the capital. His secular-type rule alienated the Brahmans and reduced their power.

Ashoka

The state reached even greater heights, however, under Chandragupta's grandson, **Ashoka**. In his reign (268–232 B.C.E.) India experienced unprecedented unity, peace, prosperity, and cultural splendor. While Chandragupta's rule was **centralized despotism**, Ashoka's was **benevolent paternalism**. He continued the efficient and centralized rule of Chandragupta, but he is most famous for his embrace of Buddhism, an act that had important intellectual and religious consequences for India and for world history. Ashoka's conversion came in the wake of a bloody struggle for the throne in which Ashoka killed several of his brothers, and after a brutal battle for control of the eastern Indian state of **Kalinga**. Ashoka was filled with revulsion for his own responsibility in the wholesale slaughter of over 150,000 men. It is for this reason that he purportedly converted to Buddhism as it emphasized compassion, nonviolence, and dharma that he viewed as a civic guide to behavior. He spread the religion throughout the empire and erected stone pillars along the roads on which were written edicts from Buddhist teachings. He built many beautiful **stupas**, or domelike structures that contained the remains of saintly monks, often at the crossroads of trade routes. He encouraged pilgrimages to shrines, repairing roads and digging wells along the way to make the journey easier. He also sent missionaries to Ceylon (Sri Lanka), Pagan (Burma), and Southeast Asia, where Buddhism and the stupa design were adopted. He did not force conversion on his subjects. In fact, he honored India's other religions by building shrines for worshippers of Hinduism and Jainism. Because of this, Buddhism did not become an alien religion as Islam later did. Ashoka is regarded in history as one of the world's remarkable leaders.

The rule of Ashoka coincided with the expansion of the Roman Empire in the West and Han China in the East. Indian merchants, especially those exporting cotton that was much in demand throughout Eurasia, benefited from Ashoka's regime. Women also benefited because they could become Buddhist monks and thus engage in scholastic and artistic endeavors. Their place in the family was also strengthened under Buddhist law. Brahmans, however, resented their displacement as political advisers, as did warrior families who lost control of their small states under imperial centralization. Upon Ashoka's death, the empire was divided among rival family members and finally torn apart by internal warfare between local rajes. Shattered unity opened the door to outside invasion.

Kushan Invaders

Between 180 B.C.E. and 300 C.E. numerous invaders crossed into India, but most were ultimately absorbed into Indian society. Two foreign conquerors, however, did have an impact on India. One was the Hellenistic Bactrian Greeks who pushed deep into northwestern India in the second century B.C.E. Under **King Demetrius**, Indian and Greek culture blended. Demetrius transformed his capital at **Gandhara** into a Hellenistic city. Indian scholars studied Hellenistic medicine and astronomy. After that, a new wave of invaders, the **Kushan**, entered India ca. 100 B.C.E. Like the Bactrian Greeks before them, these invaders were gradually folded into Indian society and became the Kshatriya caste. Although the Kushan were Buddhists, they were acquainted with Greek ideas and employed Hellenistic sculptors and artists. A new art, known as the Gandaran school, developed, using Greek styles to portray Buddhist subjects. Buddhist art, in turn, influenced the West. The use of halos, for instance, is reminiscent of earlier Buddhist work. Under the leadership of **Kanishka**, who converted to Buddhism, a great council of Buddhist monks, much like the Council of Nicea, was held to regulate Buddhist teaching. Out of this convocation came Mahayana Buddhism, which was then carried along trade routes to China opened by the Kushan.

Gupta Empire

The Gupta Empire (320–467 C.E.) is considered the Golden Age of Indian culture because of its considerable output in literature, art, and science. In 320 C.E. **Chandra Gupta I** (unrelated to Chandragupta Mauryan) came to power and, by alliance and conquest, created an empire in the Ganges Valley, making his capital again at Pataliputra (the ruins are under present-day Patna). Later Gupta rulers extended the empire as far west as Arabia, but it never attained the size of the Mauryan Empire because it did not include the Deccan Plateau. There, a strong state of **Dravidians** ruled. Dark-skinned and speaking **Tamil**, they grew rich and powerful by becoming the hub of the maritime trade route that stretched by sea from China, to Southeast Asia, India, Arabia, Africa, and Europe. Under Chandra Gupta I's rule, religious tolerance, economic prosperity, and intellectual achievement reached its zenith. Chinese Buddhist monk Fa-hsien, who came to India in search of Buddhist texts, wrote that he was never molested, in danger, or in need of a passport.

Gupta Arts, Sciences, and Technology

The Gupta rulers were patrons of the arts and encouraged scholarship. Using the ancient Sanskrit language, the Indo-European tongue of the Vedic classics, the most famous of all India's poets and dramatists was **Kalidasa**. He wrote stories in complete contrast to the Greek tragedies in which humans wrestled with imperfection and fate. His works created an atmosphere of romance and tranquility in which happy endings abound. Advances in the sciences were encouraged by the founding of many universities. Perhaps the most important was a Buddhist monastery at **Nalanda** where over 5000 students were housed in small, austere cells. Indian scholarship of the period made important contributions to astronomy and math, among them quadratic equations and the use of the square root of two in algebra. **Indian numbers** (known in the West as Arabic numerals), decimals, and the concept of zero were developed as early as the third century B.C.E. and since have been adopted worldwide. Technology advanced, especially in the making of fine iron. One 23-foot column cast in the fifth century still stands rust-free despite monsoon rains. Using fine steel with sharpened edges, the scalpel was developed for surgery. Medicine made great strides. Hospital care was free, doctors knew how to set bones and developed plastic surgery, and **Caraka**, a great Indian doctor like Hippocrates, developed a code of ethics for all doctors to follow.

Gupta Architecture

Most of the buildings that have survived from the Gupta period were religious rather than secular because religious structures were usually built of stone rather than wood and brick, which disintegrated. Three forms of architecture dominated the period. The first was the stupa, which became more elaborate in decoration, often with scenes of the Buddha's life, and higher at the central pinnacle. The 56-foot-high stupa at **Sanchi** was surrounded by a walkway, around which worshippers followed the course of the sun through the heavens. The style reached its zenith in the great temples of Burma and Thailand. The second form was the **rock-cut temple**. Carved into a solid cliff of rock, the principal chamber was the **Chaitya**, designed like a Roman basilica. The two most impressive groups of rock-cut temples are at **Ajanta** (29 chambers) and **Ellora** (34 chambers). The temples were decorated with statues and **frescoes** (pictures painted in stucco), which brought to life the whole universe in which Hindus, Buddhists, and Jains believed they moved. By the end of the Gupta period, the free-standing temple emerged as an architectural form of great import. These temples reflect the reemergence of Hinduism between the sixth and fourteenth centuries and like the stupa form, reached their most sublime expression outside of India, at Borobudur, Indonesia, and at Angkor Wat, Cambodia. Central to the temple was a small room housing the image of the god, like Shiva or Vishnu, to whom the temple was dedicated. This was joined to a hall for worshippers, which then led to a veranda. Above the shrine was an elaborately sculpted tower. Indian architecture, unlike Islamic and Christian, hugs the ground instead of soaring to the heavens. In part, this was due to limitations of architecture, but it also reflects the Hindu view that divinity is related to the earth and encompasses all of the earth's life forms. Indian architecture is also much more symbolic and representational rather than realistic like the Greek. Statuary of Brahma symbolizes creation, Shiva destruction, **Lakshmi** fertility, and **Kali** death. Temple complexes were massive **mandalas** or cosmic designs.

Hindu Reform

The change in architecture reflects basic social change that occurred during the Gupta. The Brahman class, which had been under attack for its worldly excesses by the Buddhist appeal to the masses, gradually made a comeback. This was due to Buddhist weakness and Hindu reform. Gradually, Buddhist monks became concentrated in huge monasteries, obsessed with fine points of philosophy and isolated from urban and village life. The Hindu leaders, meanwhile, began to stress the importance of personal worship and participation, to build shrines and offer participation in cults to all castes and to women, and to otherwise bring Hinduism into the daily life of the people. Special gods were allotted to special occupations and to family rites of passage. As Hinduism's hold on the population strengthened, the Brahmans regained their role as **gurus**, or teachers, of local notables. Castes became more complex with additional subcastes formed. Buddhism was weakened when a major class that supported it, the merchants, weakened once the Silk Road trade slowed, due to the collapse of Rome and Han China. Buddhism was then absorbed by Hinduism.

Hindu Society

Hinduism, in its reemergence, was in many ways more pervasive and soon more conservative than before. Life for the upper class could be luxurious, but it also emphasized a sequence of development infused with religious meaning. Men were to progress through four stages—student, family provider, hermit, and finally, holy man. Under Hindu law, women were legally minors subject to the protection of fathers, husbands, and brothers. The traditions of **satee**, or the widow's self-emolation at her husband's funeral, developed. Despite these ritualized deaths of widows, in no society is love and particularly, that of a woman, so openly enjoyed. Lives of lower castes were harsher. Untouchables were restricted, divisions among the castes became more pronounced. Since India at this time was, perhaps, the most fertile and productive region in the world, the untouchables at times may have lived relatively well with access to such foods as milk, eggs from domesticated chickens, rice, and sugar.

The rule of the Gupta ended with invasion by the **White Huns** of Asia, 480–500 C.E. They took control but were ultimately absorbed into Hindu society. Soon India fell into a patchwork of warring princedoms or rajdoms. Not until the Moslem invasion and establishment of the Delhi Sultantate in the early thirteenth century did India reconstruct itself politically. This was of somewhat unimportant consequence since religion rather than politics was the basis of Indian identity.

Summary

The classical characteristics of India can more likely be found in the village than in the polis as in Greece, the bureaucracy as in China, the empire as in Rome, or the rule of diverse peoples as in Persia. The social fabric of India, the caste, fundamental to Hinduism, served as a measure of both political and social order. The upper caste, or Brahmans, essentially provided the leadership through influence over the local lords. Hinduism's relationship to a broader universe made Indians connect themselves closely with the earth and life rather than with nature and the universe. Buddhism infused a needed measure of compassion into Hindu thought, and it inspired art and architecture, but it ultimately was absorbed by Hinduism. The rise of the two great empires, the Mauryan and Gupta, can be closely related to wealth built up by overland and sea trade with the other contemporaneous empires that flourished at the same time in Rome, Persia, and China. In the contest between trade which nourished Buddhism, and agriculture that nourished Hinduism, agriculture triumphed. Buddhism found a home elsewhere, primarily in Southeast Asia, Japan, and Korea due to its diffusion from India. One of the great missionary religions, Buddhism, reached Sri Lanka (Ceylon) and Burma under the reign of Ashoka, China by the first and second centuries C.E., Korea in the fourth century, Vietnam and Cambodia in the fifth century, and Japan in the sixth century. It triumphed in places where it met weak indigenous cultures and was less successful in places like India and China where strong classical cultures existed. Where it triumphed, it created classical civilizations of its own, as in Cambodia and Japan.

CHAPTER 10
Classical American Civilizations
(100 C.E.–900 C.E.)

CHRONOLOGY			
	Teotihuacan (100–900 C.E.)		
	Time of Troubles (800–1000 C.E.)		
	Maya (300–900 C.E.)		
	Moche (200–700 C.E.)		

TERMS			
	barios	milpa	verticality
	Zamna	steles	ayllus
	ritual ball games	corbeled arch	reciprocity
	ridged field system	codices	

PEOPLE			
	Olmec	Toltec	Pacal of Palenque
	Oaxaca Zapotecan	Maya	Chimu

PLACES			
	Mesoamerica	Yucatan	Huari
	Teotihuacan	Chichen Itza	
	Tikal	Tihuanaco	

Classical American Civilizations (100 C.E.–900 C.E.)

PEOPLES AND CULTURES OF THE AMERICAS

The peoples and cultures of the Americas remained isolated from Eurasia. The result was that invention was indigenous and later than in the Old World. Farming, pottery, writing, time-keeping, and working of copper and gold developed independently. Iron and steel, gunpowder, glass, the plow, and practical applications of the wheel came later when the Old and New Worlds met. The Americas also suffered from a scarcity of animals suitable for domestication. Apart from the turkey, llama, alpaca, dog, and guinea pig, the early peoples of the Americas continued to rely on hunting and fishing for meat and physical labor for drought. Over the vast area of the Americas, hunting and gathering continued longer. In some areas, chiefdoms and farming peoples emerged and only in a few areas did civilized states arise. In the three places where agriculture developed and could sustain large populations—the Teotihuacan Valley in Mexico, in the Yucatan Peninsula, and the Central Andes of Peru and Bolivia—brilliant classical civilizations arose whose splendor, achievements, and legacy makes them worthy of the word classical. There is much more conjecture on the part of historians regarding these three civilizations because of the complexities of a hieroglyphic language and because archeological evidence is in its infant stage. New evidence is being uncovered and decoded daily.

Teotihuacan (Mexico) (100 C.E.–900 C.E.)

As the classical Greek civilization rested on the Minoans, Rome on the Etruscans, India on the Aryans, and China on the Shang, classical **Mesoamerican** (Middle America or Mexico and Central America) civilization rested on the agricultural **Olmec** who had preceded them 1200 B.C.E.–600 B.C.E.). At its centers in San Lorenzo and La Venta, the "Mother of American civilizations," the Olmec built in stone and farmed (without the wheel, metal, or draft animals), developed hieroglyphic writing and a number system with zero. They governed by means of a religious hierarchical elite and believed in a feathered serpent god. About 150 B.C.E. a new group of people, the **Oaxaca Zapotecan**, established a large urban center near modern Mexico City at **Teotihuacan**. Population estimates of the city, which covered nine square miles, reach as high as 200,000, making it greater than the cities of ancient Egypt or Mesopotamia and second to Rome. Prosperity rested on complex intensive agriculture that inspired trade. Within the residential districts of the city, there is evidence of both social and ethnic mix.

Besides being a commercial center, Teotihuacan was also a religious and political center. Laid out in a grid pattern, streets paralleled two great avenues that intersected each other in the heart of the city. Pyramids to the sun and moon, 700 feet long and 200 feet high, dominated either end of the central avenue. The Pyramid of the Sun is about four times the size of the Great Pyramid of Cheops in Egypt. The many gods of Mesoamerica, the god of rain (feathered serpent), the goddess of corn, and the goddess of water, adorned palaces and temples. In fact, all art seems to have been religious in nature. Religion did not progress from the polytheistic to the human-based ethical religion as it did in Eurasia. These enormous pyramids, rivaling those in ancient Egypt, suggest a state apparatus able to plan such works and mobilize large numbers of workers. The upper class seems to have been composed of priests and nobles, and the lower classes of peasants and workers. The rich and powerful lived in large and lavish homes, while working people lived in apartment compounds or **barrios** at the edge of the city.

Teotihuacan's influence extended far south into Guatemala, making some historians look at Teotihuacan as a precursor or appendage of the **Maya**. Whether Teotihuacan was a separate political entity or a dominant cultural and ideological style that spread over much of Mexico is unclear. Teotihuacan probably exacted tribute from many regions as pottery and finely worked obsidian in Teotihuacan style are found in many areas. Regardless, Teotihuacan has many of the hallmarks of classical civilization—an enduring style, urban splendor, a culture with heavy religious overtones, and legacies for succeeding civilizations of Mexico like the Toltec and Aztec. It continued to flourish during the Maya period until about 700 C.E. Then it was burned by hordes from the southwest. A **Time of Troubles** followed (800–1000 C.E.), characterized by militarism and rule by priests in great cities and by warriors in small states. One of the states, the **Toltec** confederation, admired and absorbed Teotihuacan culture.

The Maya (300 C.E.–900 C.E.)

Postdating the classical civilizations of Eurasia but contemporaneous with the Tang in China, Charlemagne in Europe, and Islamic classicism, the Maya of southern Mexico and Central America created a Golden Age of American classicism. The Maya are often called the "Greeks of the New World" because they developed a sophisticated political system, a flourishing trade, a written language, superior textiles, and elegant art. The Maya world included a number of different languages and art styles, but it shared statecraft, a common written language, a calendar, and a mathematical system. Maya seems to have derived from the word **Zamna**, the early Maya culture god. Politically, it appears that families ruled the major Maya city-states and surrounding territories. These included Tikal, Copan, Quirigua, Palenque, and Chichen Itza. Inscriptions on monuments record constant warfare and the deeds of rulers such as **Pacal of Palenque** (d. 683 C.E.), who conquered nearby territory and was buried in a lavish tomb inside a pyramid at Palenque. The leaders had considerable civic and religious power, and a group of elite scribes and priests helped administer the state. The rulers and scribes organized and participated in rituals of self-mutilation and human sacrifice. **Ritual ball games** in which players moved a rubber ball with their hips and elbows through a ring 20 feet in the air were forms of worship and sport.

Agricultural Systems and Urban Centers

Some Maya cities had populations of between 30,000 and 80,000, and the total Maya population was probably about five million. To support such a population, the Maya developed a number of innovative intensive agricultural systems. Besides irrigation and swamp drainage, they used a **ridged field system**. In this system, raised fields were built above low-lying, seasonally flooded lands bordering rivers. Another system, **milpa**, was particularly useful in areas with heavy rainfall and scorching sun. Farmers cut down patches of forest, burned the wood, and planted maize seed in the resulting ash. Besides maize, cotton was a crop in great demand. Rich Maya textiles appear all over Mesoamerica.

In the cities can be found great noble palaces, pyramids where the elite were buried, **steles** (stone slab monuments), temples, altars, and ball courts. The pyramids were impressive with sloping walls and flat tops on which stood temples using a **corbeled arch** (stone blocks placed like steps in reverse to span an opening). While evidence for trade and artisanry within the city is scant, the urban centers were very likely centers of exchange and there is considerable evidence that the Maya carried on extensive long-distance trade. Maya products are found over a large area. Wealth seems to have been concentrated in the hands of a few based on lineage that was traced both through the mother and father. Most other people were free workers, serfs, or slaves taken in battle.

Mathematics and the Sciences

The needs of agriculture and rule seem closely connected to religion, making the religious intellectual class vital and powerful. It is from this class that the many cultural achievements of the Maya emerged. One was a system of hieroglyphic writing in which phonograms were added to a pictographic system. There were 850 hieroglyphic characters developed to record chronology, religion, astronomy, and dynastic lineage. Mayan hieroglyphs were written in **codices** (books) made of bark paper and deerskin or were inscribed on steles. One of the world's most exact methods of measuring and recording time was developed from systematic observations of the planet Venus. Using complex calculations, perseverance, and teamwork spanning several centuries, Mayan priest-astronomers developed a calendar with 365$\frac{1}{4}$ days divided into 18 months of 20 days accurate to within one day in slightly over 6000 years. The Maya also accurately predicted solar eclipses. They were advanced in mathematics, using a system (vigesimal) based on 20 and incorporating the concept of zero. Writing and timekeeping made the Maya recorders of history. While keen astronomical observers, they nevertheless viewed the universe as flat, above which extended 13 levels of heaven and below which were 9 underworlds. The Maya, like the Chinese, had a concept of dualism—male-female, good-bad—which emphasized the unity of all things rather than conflict and choices.

Decline of the Maya

The collapse of the Maya is connected with the general cataclysmic decline in the whole Mesoamerican area between 700 and 900 C.E. During the eighth century the Maya stopped erecting commemorative stelae and by 900 C.E. most major cities were deserted. Agricultural exhaustion is one of the explanations for Mayan collapse. The very success of intensive agriculture led to a population density around **Tikal** of over 300 people per square mile. Increasing population may have led to warfare among the Maya city-states and revolt among the peasantry in the face of increasing tax burdens. Another theory of decline suggests epidemic disease. Whatever the

cause, the center of Maya culture began to move from the southern lowlands and highlands around Tikal to the Yucatan peninsula where Mexicanized families established themselves at **Chichen Itza** carrying on Maya cultural tradition. By 1000 C.E. the militaristic Toltec overtook the Maya as well.

The Moche (200 C.E.–700 C.E.)

While the classical Mesoamerican cultures flourished, another was being established in the Andean world. The Mochica state in the Moche valley developed along the Peruvian coast just north of the agricultural settlement of Chavin. It appears that the Moche expanded by means of conquest. Archaeological evidence reveals hilltop forts and military posts, and the artistic output is filled with representation of war, prisoners, and head taking. Warrior priests, buried with retainers, servants, and dogs, were covered with gold, silver, copper, and fine cloth. Some of the textiles, blends of alpaca and cotton, combined over 100 colors into woven patterns. The spread of the Moche resulted in the development of two large cities at **Tihuanaco** on the shores of Lake Titicaca in Bolivia and **Huari** in southern Peru. In turn, Tihuanaco extended its political control through colonies as far away as Chile. It is unclear what the relationship was between the two cities, whether Huari began as a colony of Tihuanaco and gradually exercised wide control over other areas, or whether it was independent. Tihuanaco was an urban ceremonial center of about 40,000 inhabitants supported by intensive agriculture using raised fields, irrigation, and canals. Tihuanacan stone structures resembling great arches were carved out of single blocks of stone. Decoration often involved a feline motif.

The classical culture that emerged in Andean society seemed to have had certain common characteristics. One is **verticality**, which means that the social and political objective of families and communities was to find economic niches at different altitudes. Thus, along the irrigated coast, maize could be grown, in the altiplano area between the two major mountain chains of the Andes, potatoes and grazing flourished, and on the eastern Andean slopes where tropical rain forests were concentrated, fruits and coca leaf were cultivated. Another characteristic is the idea of kinship units or **ayllus** based on descent from a common mythical ancestor. Ayllus shared the same dialect, dress, and customs. The ayllus assigned households land, water, herds, and rights. Ayllu chiefs mobilized the community for labor and war. Cooperative relationships were based on the concept of **reciprocity** that was infused with religious beliefs. Reciprocity existed within families as between men and women, or within states. For labor and tribute, citizens gained access to resources and irrigation from the state. Reciprocity extended to relationships between states as well, frameworking diplomatic relationships much as the Chinese concept of tribute did.

While knowledge of the Moche is still being unearthed, they appear not to have developed a writing system, though they were highly devel-

oped in metallurgy and textiles. Contact between American peoples from the Andes to Mesoamerica and the southern United States seems to have existed. The ritual ball game, for instance, can be found as far away as the American Southwest and the Caribbean. The end of the Moche coincided with the collapse of the Maya. About 800 C.E. Tihuanaco and Huari fell to the **Chimu** state that eventually controlled over 600 miles of the Peruvian and Chilean coast. It was still expanding when it fell to the Incas in 1465.

The classical period of the Americas exhibits characteristics of classical periods everywhere. Urban centers, religious creativity and influence, advances in scholarship, arts, methods of rule and social organization, and wealth based in sophisticated agriculture and trade created long-lasting traditions and imprints on the area.

UNIT REVIEW

Cross-Regional Developments

The classical civilizations that rose in Greece, Rome, Persia, India, China, and the Americas, touched people far beyond their borders and facilitated long-distance trade. Among the important cross-regional developments of the classical period are:

- the spread of Greek culture during the Hellenistic period;
- the spread of Roman culture to western Europe;
- the expansion of Christianity beyond the Mediterranean to western Europe, eastern Europe, and Southwest Asia;
- the expansion of Buddhism to China, Southeast Asia, Korea, and Japan;
- the development of Eurasian trade along the Silk Road;
- the development of sea routes from East Asia to India, Arabia, and Africa; and
- developing connections among Mesoamerican peoples and between Mesoamerica and the Andean area.

Legacies

The legacies of the classical period are important not just to the history of the West, Persia, India, China, and Mesoamerica, but to world history. The agricultural revolution caused people to live and work more closely together. The classical period ordered these relationships in a way that made greater civil order and cooperative action possible. The belief systems that were born during this period were often created in times of turmoil. In their emphasis on human relationships, they either transformed older systems into human based systems or created new belief systems that emphasized human ethics and meaning.

Among the legacies of the period are:

- the rise of the world's major religions and belief systems including humanism, Judaism, Christianity, Zoroastrianism, Hinduism, Buddhism, Confucianism, and Taoism;
- the rise of great empires like Greece, Rome, Achaemenid Persia, Mauryan and Gupta India, Ch'in and Han China, and Teotihuacan, the Maya, and Moche;
- the rise of cities in both classically indigenous and cosmopolitan forms where human interaction elicited great thought and building;
- great literature of human joy, ethics, and fate;
- art using frescoes, mosaics, and statues;
- the architecture of palaces, temples, stupas, pyramids, and rock-cut temples with architectural features like columns, corbel, and Roman arches and domes;
- the development of important technologies such as steel, paper, the compass, porcelain, and the ridged-field system, and infrastructures such as canals, sewers, irrigation systems, piped water, roads, postal systems, hospitals, and universities;
- systems of social order such as the Indian caste system, the Moche kinship associations and the Chinese belief in filial piety, political order such as Roman law, Persian provincial system, Athenian democracy, Indian nonviolence, and the Chinese civil service, and economic change with the use of money, paper, printing, Arabic numerals, and the zero.

In the next phase of world history, these great traditions and advances are spread over large areas where they are intertwined with local cultures, destroyed and forgotten for periods only to experience periods of renaissance, crucial for the development of new classical systems.

Documents

PERICLES FUNERAL ORATION

Our form of government does not enter into rivalry with the institutions of others. We do not copy our neighbors, but are an example to them. It is true that we are called a democracy, for the administration is in the hands of the many not of the few. But while the law secures equal justice to all alike in their private disputes, the claim of excellence is also recognized; and when a citizen is in any way distinguished, he is preferred to the public service not as a matter of priviledge, but as the reward of merit. Neither is poverty a bar, but a man may benefit his country whatever be the obscurity of his condition.

. . . For we are lovers of beauty, yet with economy, and we cultivate the mind without loss of manliness.

. . . To sum up: I say that Athens is the school of Hellas, and that the individual Athenian in his own person seems to have the power of adapting himself to the most varied forms of action and the upmost versatility and grace. . .

This speech can be compared to the Gettysburg Address in the sense that it was given while a great civil war was being waged among Greeks (the Peloponnesian Wars). It is the most eloquent statement of Athenian political and civic ideals. Pericles (ca. 494–429 B.C.E.) was the leading Athenian statesman when war broke out with Sparta in 431 B.C.E. His speech demonstrates the fundamental values and attitudes of Athenians—reverence for democracy, excellence, individualism, beauty, and love of Athens.

CLASSICAL CHINESE SCHOOLS OF THOUGHT

1. The master said, In serving his father and mother a man may gently remonstrate with them. But if he sees that he has failed to change their opinion, he should resume an attitude of deference and not thwart them; he may feel discouraged, but not resentful.

2. There is a thing confusedly formed,
   Born before heaven and earth.
   Silent and void
   It stands alone and does not change,
   Goes round and does not weary.
   It is capable of being the mother of the world.
   I know not its name
   So I style it "the way."

3. The nature of man is evil; his goodness is acquired.
   His nature being what it is, man is born, first, with a desire for gain.
   If this desire is followed, strife will result and courtesy will disappear.

4. There are two extremes which he who has given up the world ought to avoid.
   A life given to pleasures. . . and a life given to mortifications.

By avoiding these two extremes, the seeker of Truth has gained the knowledge of the Middle Path which leads to insight, which leads to wisdom which conduces to calm, to knowledge, to enlightenment, to Nirvana.

Document 1 is Confucianist, 2 is Taoist, 3 is Legalist, and 4 is Buddhist. In Document 1 the emphasis is on the cardinal Confucian principles of proper conduct and filial piety. Document 2 reflects the Taoist emphasis on nature and discovering "the way" or Tao. Document 3 illustrates the cardinal principle of Legalism, which is that man is basically evil and, therefore, needs a dictatorial political system to order society. Document 4 illustrates the Buddhist emphasis on finding Heaven or Nirvana through enlightenment, self-knowledge, and a middle path. The Chinese found they could live with all these positions except Legalism because Confucianism appeals to the mind, Taoism to the soul, and Buddhism to the heart. Legalism rejects the basic proposition of Chinese thought, which is the harmony of the universe. Legalism is more western in its view that man is basically evil and political systems must be found to balance, for instance, contending and opposing forces.

THE LAWS OF MANU—THE STATUS OF WOMEN

Women must be honored and adorned by their father, brothers, husbands, and brothers-in-law, who desire their own welfare.

Where women are honored, there the gods are pleased; but where they are not honored, no sacred rite yields rewards. . . .

In that family, where the husband is pleased with his wife and the wife with her husband, happiness will assuredly be lasting.

Day and night women must be kept in dependence. . . .

Her father protects her in childhood, her husband protects her in youth, and her sons protect her in old age; a woman is never fit for independence. . .

The Laws of Manu are a collection of social codes based on early Indian customs from about 1000 B.C.E. Probably written by teachers of the Vedas (hymns and prayers to the Aryan gods that, along with the Upanishads or lessons of the nature of the universe, form the basis of Hinduism), the Laws of Manu reflect the Hindu idea that meaning in life can be found in fulfillment of one's caste duties. Women in Hindu society have a special and revered place because the pleasure of love is sanctified within the bonds of the family. Yet, women are subordinate. Large dowries that were to accompany women in marriage made girls a liability in an essentially patriarchal society.

THE SERMON ON THE MOUNT

Blessed are the poor in spirit: for theirs is the kingdom of heaven.

Blessed are they that mourn: for they shall be comforted.

Blessed are the meek: for they shall inherit the earth.

Blessed are they which do hunger and thirst after righteousness: for they shall be filled.

Blessed are the merciful: for they shall obtain mercy.

Blessed are the pure in heart: for they shall see God.

Blessed are the peacemakers: for they shall be called the children of God.

Blessed are they which are persecuted for righteousness's sake: for theirs is the kingdom of heaven.

The Sermon on the Mount is the essence of Jesus's teaching that stresses the importance of love, the avoidance of anger or violence, and the promise of a kingdom of Heaven especially for the downtrodden. Virtually all that is known about Jesus (born ca. 4 B.C.E.), his life and ideas, is contained in the Gospels (histories) of Matthew, Mark, Luke, and John. Near the age of 30, Jesus was baptized by a religious ascetic in the style of the earlier prophets. The virtual creator of Christian theology was Paul (d. 67 C.E.) who refined Christian doctrine in the face of Gnostic Christian refusal to acknowledge the Old Testament. Christian theology was further defined by the Nicene Creed (325 C.E.), which asserted that the Father and Son were fully equal, sharing one being and, together with the Holy Spirit, constitute the Trinity.

Recall Questions

1. The single most important classical characteristic of the Greek polis that altered other societies and remains influential today is
   (A) literature.
   (B) art.
   (C) architecture.
   (D) political thought.
   (E) economic system.

2. All of the following circumstances led to the development of democracy in Athens EXCEPT
   (A) the unusual role of the king who farmed his own land and was advised by a council.
   (B) the success of traders, craftsmen, manufacturers, and farmers who challenged the power of the oligarchs.
   (C) the need for continued support of the common people to fill the ranks of the phalanx.
   (D) the demands by foreign-born residents of Athens to be made citizens and included in the political process.
   (E) the reforms by Solon that abolished debt slavery and limited the amount of land an individual could own.

3. Which of the following is incorrectly linked?
   (A) Herodotus—*History of the Peloponnesian Wars*
   (B) Plato—*The Republic*
   (C) Aristophanes—*Clouds*
   (D) Sappho—*Love Poetry*
   (E) Sophocles—*Oedipus Rex*

4. The Achaemenid Dynasty of the Persians established the world's largest empire. Means of rule included all EXCEPT
   (A) granting a large measure of local autonomy.
   (B) offering all subjects respect, toleration, and protection.
   (C) establishing a comprehensive law code, a stable currency, and an efficient postal system.
   (D) building a network of roads with stations, food, water, and horses.
   (E) requiring all subjects to convert to Zoroastrianism.

5. Which of the following examples of Hellenistic beliefs advocated a universal state ordered by natural law where the citizen's duty was to strengthen society for others?
   (A) The Cult of Serapis
   (B) The Cult of Isis
   (C) Cynicism
   (D) Epicureanism
   (E) Stoicism

6. In the days of the early Roman Republic, Patricians dominated the government but Plebeians were represented through
   (A) elected consuls.
   (B) the commanders of the army.
   (C) the judges.
   (D) the Senate.
   (E) the Assembly of Centuries.

7. The birthplace of Christianity was in the
   (A) Roman Empire.
   (B) independent kingdom of Palestine.
   (C) Ptolemaic kingdom of Egypt.
   (D) Byzantine Empire.
   (E) Persian Empire.

8. Jesus was born
   (A) a Roman.
   (B) a Greek.
   (C) a Jew.
   (D) an Egyptian.
   (E) a Persian.

9. Romans persecuted Christians because they
   (A) refused to pay taxes.
   (B) refused to serve in the Roman army.
   (C) were mostly slaves and criminals who had revolted against Roman rule.
   (D) refused to worship the emperor as a god.
   (E) insisted that Christianity be the sole, official religion of the Roman Empire.

10. The first Bishop of Rome was
    (A) Saint Paul.
    (B) Saint Peter.
    (C) Saint Mark.
    (D) Saint Augustine.
    (E) Saint Jerome.

11. Diocletian tried to strengthen Roman rule by
    (A) dividing the empire between the East and West and appointing two Caesars to rule.
    (B) increasing taxes to pay for a larger army.
    (C) sending representatives to kingdoms along the Silk and Amber Roads to encourage trade.
    (D) building a series of forts and walls along the Roman borders.
    (E) issuing edicts to increase production of essential products with the promise of lucrative payments

12. Which of the following was responsible for uniting China, linking existing frontier walls into the Great Wall and standardizing Chinese script, weights, and measures?
    (A) Sun Zi (Sun Tzu)
    (B) Shi Huangdi (Shi Huang-Ti)
    (C) Wu
    (D) Liu Bang (Liu Pang)
    (E) Wudi (Wu Ti)

13. The "Mandate of Heaven" was a belief held by Chinese that
    (A) ancestral worship was an essential element of religious ritual.
    (B) the ruler and nobles were selected to rule through the will of heaven.
    (C) if a ruler governed badly, the people had the right to revolt.
    (D) the ruler represented a divine presence on earth.
    (E) none of the above.

14. According to believers, all Hindu gods are thought to be aspects of
    (A) Vishnu.
    (B) Krishna.
    (C) Shiva.
    (D) Brahma.
    (E) Lakshmi.

15. Buddha believed that a state of grace or Nirvana could be reached by
    (A) changing one's karma.
    (B) following the moral duties of one's caste.
    (C) being reincarnated as a Brahman.
    (D) following the eight-fold path.
    (E) none of the above.

To check your answers, see page 393.

South American Classical States 850 B.C.E.–1532 C.E. *The classical civilizations of South America, including Ecuador, Peru, and Chile, were situated on the western coast of the continent. The Chavin and Moche states along the northwestern coast were succeeded by the Inca of Peru.*

The Colosseum. *The massive Colosseum in Rome seated 50,000 people. Completed in 80 C.E. its concrete walls were 160 feet (49 m) high with four tiers of seating inside. The emperor and honored guests sat in box seats at the lowest level near the arena, but even from the least expensive seats in the top row, Romans had a clear view of the action below. An awning attached to the outside wall was rolled out to shield the spectators from rain or bright sunshine. Mock naval battles were staged at the Colosseum because the arena was watertight and could be converted into a small lake. After a day of gladiatorial contests, it is thought that the entire crowd of 50,000 could exit the Colosseum in less than ten minutes, using separate stairways from each section that led to one of the Colosseum's 80 entrances.*

The Main African-Eurasian Trade Routes in the Classical Age ca. 200 B.C.E.–200 C.E. *During the Classical Age of great empires, Europe, Asia, and Africa were linked on land and sea by vast trade networks. The Romans called the route linking China with the Roman world, the Silk Road.*

Mi-Le Buddha-Chinese, Tang Dynasty. *Buddhism, a religion of Indian origin, was introduced to China by pilgrims and merchants during the Han dynasty. According to the inscription at the base of this limestone image, the sculpture was dedicated in 705 during the period of the Tang dynasty when Buddhist art developed into an international style. This Buddha represents the Mi-le or the Maitreya Buddha. Mi-le or Maitreya is regarded by believers as the Buddha who will descend to initiate a new heaven and a new earth as the Buddha of the Future. In a natural, observant pose, the figure of the Buddha appears in contrast to the repeating design behind the figure representing Mi-le's radiance. A second, inner halo is formed of lotus petals behind Buddha's head. The Buddha's right hand gesture symbolizes the message, "Fear Not." The ushnisha or knot of hair on top of Buddha's head indicates enlightenment.*

Parthenon. *No architectural masterpiece represents the Athenian Greek sense of beauty and values more than the Parthenon. During the fifth century B.C.E., after the destruction of Athens by the Persians, Pericles appropriated Delian League funds to pay for a huge construction program of temples and other buildings on the Acropolis to honor Athena, the patron goddess of Athens. The dazzling white marbled Parthenon is its chief monument. The Doric columns that support the building are tapered; to the naked eye, they appear harmonious and even. Phidias, considered the greatest sculptor of his day, carved the frieze atop the columns and the huge statue of Athena that stood inside the temple. The building exhibits the rational side of the Greeks. There is no violent emotion in the art, only quiet intensity, balance, and restraint. This captured what Greeks considered the essential aspects of human beings: reason, dignity, and promise.*

The Empire of Alexander the Great 336–323 B.C.E. *In twelve short years, Alexander the Great created a huge empire, and in so doing, spread Greek culture far and wide.*

Pottery Army. *When the grave of the first emperor, Qin, was discovered recently, an army of ceramic soldiers came to light. Six thousand lifelike statues, horses, and militia, armed with spears, swords, bows, and crossbows meant to protect the emperor in the afterlife were unearthed. The statues give a vivid idea of the army that unified China, the power of the emperor, and beliefs in immortality.*

Stupa. The embrace of Buddhism by Ashoka (ca. 269–232 B.C.E.) ushered in a period of Buddhist conversion in India. The practical results led to a more humane governance of India. The architectural results were the building of stupas. Stupa architecture evidently originated in Nepal where the remains of kings were buried in mounds. Ashoka adopted the style to enshrine Buddha's remains. Buddha's remains were divided and dispersed throughout the realm to serve as focal points for Buddhist pilgrimages. The same Buddhist practice evolved in China too, but it used the pagoda style of architecture, which was adopted by the Tang from the old Han watch-tower style. This pagoda style spread to Japan where it was also used in castle building. The common feature of both the pagoda and stupa is the central pole or post in the middle of the shrine, which emanates from the interned remains to the heavens.

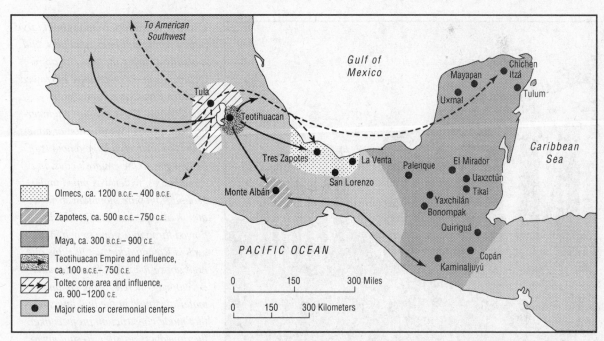

The Mesoamerican Classical States 1200 B.C.E.–1200 C.E. The classical Mesoamerican states were the Maya in the Yucatan and Central America and Teotihuacan in Mexico. Both owed their existence to earlier civilizations, the Olmec and Zapotec, and both succumbed to military invasion, first at the hands of the Toltec and then the Aztecs.

HINDUISM	JUDAISM	JAINISM	ISLAM
TAOISM	ZOROASTRIAN	CHRISTIANITY	BUDDHISM

Religious Symbols. *The religions of the world have always used symbolism to reflect and reinforce major ideas. The Hindu symbol represents all the sounds of the universe. The Hebrew 6-pointed star represents the six books of law or the Torah. The Jainist open palm represents peace. The Islamic crescent and star reflect the divine light of Muhammad. The circle of dark and light represents the Taoist view that the cosmic forces are dualistic but complementary. The Zoroastrian symbol is the chief god Ahuramazda on wings in a boat representing the journey of good. The Christian cross symbolizes Christ's sacrifice in the name of human love and forgiveness. The Buddhist wheel represents the cycle of life, and the spokes the eight-fold path to enlightenment.*

Roman Aqueducts. *Romans built large public baths, buildings, stadiums, and monuments using the arch, an architectural form they may have borrowed from the Etruscans, Persians, or Babylonians. Their greatest engineering feat was the construction of aqueducts that delivered huge amounts of fresh water to the empire's cites. In some places, water was piped underground from pure mountain springs and in others, the water gradually flowed through a stone trench in an arched Roman aqueduct like this one high above the valley floor. Romans developed concrete, using common materials found at the building site that made construction projects like the aqueducts possible. Testimony to the strength and endurance of these aqueducts is that some are still standing and in use today.*

UNIT

IV

EXPANDING CLASSICAL SYSTEMS OF SOCIETY AND CULTURE
(100 C.E.–1200 C.E.)

HISTORICAL PROCESSES: MIGRATIONS, RISE AND FALL, DIFFUSION, INTERACTION, SYNTHESIS, AND SYSTEMS OF EXCHANGE

During the period 100 C.E. to 1200 C.E., ideas and institutions of the classical civilizations of the Mediterranean, India, China, and Mesoamerica spread far and wide. In so doing, they brought to many more parts of the globe the knowledge, ideas, and benefits of civilized society. The transfer of ideas did not always go one way, however, from civilized to uncivilized. Often, when the classical civilizations came into contact with the indigenous peoples of outlying areas, the ways and habits of the indigenous peoples mixed with, influenced, and transformed traditional classicism, producing a new **synthesis** (joining together of the two cultures) or a distinctive new classical civilization.

The Process of Classical Expansionism

The expansion of classical civilization occurred as the result of a number of historical processes. One was **migration**. Often caused by ecological factors like climate changes, land hunger, and overpopulation, migrations caused peoples like the Polynesians to spread their culture over vast new areas of the globe. Another was the rise and fall of classical civilizations. When classical civilizations like the Maya, Rome, Mauryan and Gupta India, and Han China weakened, outside peoples attacked, took over, and mixed with the classical civilizations. In doing so, they learned the ways of classicism. Another method of classical expansion was through **cultural diffusion** (spreading of culture). Through the spread of law, religion, and writing systems, western Europe and Japan were introduced to classicism. Another method of classical expansion was through trade. **Trade systems** (trade patterns that became complex, organized, and stable over broad areas), which arose in the South China, Indian, Arabian, and Mediterranean Seas, across the Sahara Desert, and along land and gulf routes in the southern United States and Mesoamerica, spread religion, culture, and technology across larger areas. The result was the expansion of classical culture.

Feudalism

The collapse of classical civilizations sometimes led to feudal interregna, or feudal breaks, in the patterns of classicism. **Feudalism** is characterized by decentralized political rule, and a political, economic, social, and cultural system oriented toward defense and warfare. In some places, as in Japan, medieval western Europe, and Russia, the feudal period left imprints on classical patterns as important as the classical patterns. Sometimes, completely new civilizations emerged to fill the vacuums left by receding and collapsing classical civilizations. Such is the case with the rise of Islam, which emerged as a new classical civilization in Southwest Asia and North Africa.

CHAPTER 11

Expansion of Systems of Society and Culture in East and Southeast Asia

CHRONOLOGY

Polynesian Migration (2500 B.C.E.–900 C.E.)	Tang (618–907)	Nara (710–794)
China	Song (Sung) (960–1279)	Heian (794–1185)
Sui (589–618)	Golden Age (580–1400)	Khmer (802–1219)
	Yamato (ca. 200–710)	

TERMS

synthesis	pagodas	kowtows
migration	block printing	Neo-Confucianism
cultural diffusion	Sinification	Shinto
trade systems	moveable type	kami
feudalism	meritocracy	Seventeen Article
Austronesian	mandarins	Constitution
ali'i	Bureau of Censors	Taika Reforms
kapu	paper currency	Kana
moa	vernacular	Indianization of
hapu	gentry	Southeast Asia
ahu	tributary system	baray

PEOPLE

Polynesians	Empress Wu	samurai
Maori	Song Dynasty	Thais
Sui Dynasty	Zhu Xi (Chu Hsi)	Burmese
Yangdi (Yang-ti)	Yamato clan	Khmer
Tang Dynasty	Prince Shotoku	Srivijaya
Taizong (T'ai Tsung)	Fujiwara clan	Bodhisattvas
Li Bo (Li Po)	Lady Murasaki	
Du Fu (Tu Fu)	Daimyo	

PLACES

Melanesia	Grand Canal	Kyoto (Heian)
Polynesia	Hangzhou (Hangchou)	Siam (Thailand)
Madagascar	Beijing (Peking)	Pagan
Society Islands	Talas River	Kampuchea (Cambodia)
Easter Island	Kaifeng	Sumatra
Wei Valley	Kyushu	Borobodur
Sinking	Honshu	Angkor Thom
Loyang	Nara	Angkor Wat

CHAPTER 11

Expansion of Systems of Society and Culture in East and Southeast Asia

POLYNESIAN MIGRATIONS
(2500 B.C.E.–900 B.C.E.)

One of the great migrations in history is the Polynesian maritime spread across the 20,000-mile area of the Pacific Ocean from Southeast Asia to Central America. This was not a case of the spread from a great center of civilization to outlying areas, but it was the spread of a culture and its adaptation to new challenges in relative isolation.

Polynesian Culture

The **Polynesians** are a group of linguistically related peoples. Their language group, called **Austronesian**, can be found also in the Philippines, Indonesia, and Southeast Asia. However, they are not linguistically related to the peoples of New Guinea and Australia where the land masses were linked during the last Ice Age and settled earlier, probably since 38,000 B.C.E. Polynesians were root farmers, not rice farmers. In many places their agriculture was complex and intensive leading to highly stratified societies with powerful chiefdoms based on lineage. Through ritual and religion, these chiefs ordered many aspects of life from the building of ceremonial and public architecture to warfare. The commoners tilled taro and sweet potatoes, raised pigs and chickens, and fished. In Hawaii, for example, the high chiefs, or **ali'i**, rested claims on their ability to recite in great detail their genealogical lineages, while the commoners lived lives constrained by sets of **kapu**, or taboo.

Outrigger Canoe

Lacking a written language and using neolithic technology, the Polynesians became expert seamen. The key invention that allowed them to move across the Pacific was the outrigger canoe. The long-distance double outrigger canoe was a canoe hollowed from two single tree trunks joined together by a platform that gave shelter to passengers, animals, and plants. It was driven by large triangular sails and guided by a steering paddle. The buoyant outriggers attached to the gunwales completed a sailing vessel that could travel over 124 miles a day, and could sail windward or against the winds and tides of the Pacific.

Polynesian Migrations

While it is unclear what initially drove the Polynesian migrations, once underway it was no doubt ecological fragility that sustained them. Once reaching new islands, the Polynesians exploited the available resources and then, either had to develop new resources through their own ingenuity or emigrate, colonize, or begin anew on another island. About 4000 years ago, the Austronesians began to expand eastward from **Melanesia** (a group of islands to the east of New Guinea and Australia extending from the Admiralty to the Fiji Islands) to Tonga and Samoa and then to **Polynesia** proper. Polynesia includes the islands contained in a rough imaginary triangle whose points lie at Hawaii to the north, New Zealand to the south, and Easter Island far to the east. Another group of these people seems to have moved westward, eventually settling on the island of **Madagascar** off the African coast. The fact that plants native to the Americas were growing in Hawaii and other islands when Europeans first visited them suggests that the Polynesians arrived on the shores of the Americas as well.

Maori

About the eighth century C.E. still another group, probably from the **Society Islands**, sailed to New Zealand. There they established the **Maori** culture, which at its height in the late eighteenth century C.E. had the highest concentration of Polynesian people anywhere in the world, about 200,000. The Polynesians who emigrated to New Zealand faced a colder and harsher climate than their home islands. There were no native land mammals except bats and various kinds of **moa**, or large wingless birds. Overhunting led to their extinction, but by the introduction of the staple crops of Polynesia supplemented with fishing, a large and complex society was created. Then, overpopulation and scarcity of resources created a society oriented toward war. The building of fortresses, training of males in the martial arts, and fierce combat in which the priest-leader, or **hapu** could cut out the heart of the first enemy killed in battle, illustrates the nature of Maori society in war. In woodworking and decoration they surpassed the Polynesian societies from which their ancestors came and they had a rich and complex spirit world in which gods and goddesses intervened in human affairs.

Easter Island

The history of **Easter Island** followed a somewhat similar pattern of settlement, exploitation of resources, scarcity, and depopulation. Probably no more than 20 or 30 Polynesian people from Tonga and Samoa reached Easter Island about 300 C.E. Due to successful exploitation of the fragile environment, by 1550 there were 7000. A sophisticated culture emerged in which large stone statues called **ahu** were built, but the ecological strain, particularly the deforestation of the island, led to war and the ultimate demise of

this society's culture. The expanding Polynesians inhabited the Pacific. They spread their culture, foodstuffs, and technology to hitherto uninhabited areas of the globe.

THE CHINESE GOLDEN AGE: SUI, TANG, AND SONG (SUNG) DYNASTIES

Chinese classicism did not end with the fall of the Han. Rather it reached great heights under the Sui, Tang, and Song Dynasties, inspired in part by Buddhism. The Golden Age was so vibrant that its cultural effervescence spilled over into many nearby countries.

Buddhism

With the fall of the Han Dynasty in 210 C.E. China became divided into many separate kingdoms. In a society troubled by disorder and disintegration, Buddhism began to appeal to the Chinese. Indian Buddhist monks came to China and Chinese pilgrims traveled west to India. Silk merchants also helped to diffuse this new tradition. The introduction of Buddhism is the only instance until modern times of the Chinese borrowing a major idea from abroad. The long, slow process of translating Indian concepts like Nirvana into Chinese words, understandable as Buddhist terms, began about 200 C.E. Indian Buddhism was somewhat tempered by the imposition of Chinese values like the importance of the family and loyalty to the state. In the interim between the Han and Sui, many kingdoms like the Northern Wei supported Buddhism. The Wei built a number of cave temples with statues of Buddha in Chinese style and **pagodas**, structures reminiscent of the Han watchtowers. The most important legacy of Buddhism for China was the increased use of paper and the development of **block printing**. Buddhist monks spread their message by use of the printed word, a tradition that the Tang later used to regularize the bureaucracy. It also led to the outpouring of literature during the Tang dynasty.

The Sui and the Grand Canal

The period of disunity lasted until 589 C.E., when the Sui Dynasty welded the contending Chinese states together by conquest. Like the Ch'in, the center of Sui dynasty power was in the **Wei Valley**, with their capital at Changan, and like the Ch'in, the Sui built roads and canals to connect the empire. The second Sui emperor, **Yangdi (Yang-ti**, 604–618 C.E.) began a campaign of expansion. He rebuilt the Great Wall, reconquered northern Vietnam and much of **Sinking** and Mongolia, but his campaign in Korea met with resistance. Following the model of the Chou and Han, he built a magnificent new capital at **Loyang**, but his most enduring achievement was the building of the **Grand Canal** from **Hangzhou (Hangchou)** in the south to **Beijing (Peking)** in the north. It cemented the unity of north and south China by bringing rice from the productive Yangzi (Yangtse) delta for troops and officials in the semiarid north. Heavy taxes and spending, corvee labor, and tyrannical officials caused rebellion, and in 618 C.E., after only 14 years on the throne, Yangdi (Yang-ti) was assassinated by a courtier.

Tang Expansionism

Just as the Han benefited from the changes made by the Ch'in, so too did the new Tang dynasty under the leadership of Emperor **Taizong** (T'ai-Tsung) profit from Sui initiatives. Under the Tang most of the Han-ruled territories were reclaimed by conquest. Chinese influence expanded along the Silk Road into Central Asia into what is today modern Afganistan. The Chinese defeated the eastern and western Turks in Central Asia and extended their influence into North Vietnam, Tibet, and Manchuria. Korea became a protectorate. Members of the Tang Dynasty were to rule for 300 years.

The gradual immigration and **Sinification** (becoming part of Chinese culture) of the south below the Yangzi continued. China became the world's leading agricultural empire. Cotton and sugar, introduced from India, fostered new industries. By the late Tang, most of the imperial revenue came from the more productive south where double cropping in some areas became a common practice. In fact, the Tang Chinese found no other civilization that could rival the Celestial Empire. Rome was gone, and the Umayyad Caliphate was no match for Tang.

Diffusion of Printing

Territorial expansion reached its limit in 751 when a coalition of Arabs and western Turks repulsed the Chinese at the Battle of **Talas River** near Samarkand. The battle is, perhaps, more significant because Chinese captives taught the technology of paper making and printing to the Arabs. Printing, which had begun ca. 600s C.E., was first developed by Buddhists using carved wooden blocks and ink to reproduce a whole page. Much later, by 1050 C.E., the Chinese had **moveable type** made of wood or clay. The Koreans produced the first moveable iron type in 1234, 200 years before the process was developed in Europe (or perhaps diffused into Europe by the Mongols).

Tang Golden Age

The recentralization of China under the Sui, growing prosperity as a result of Tang expansion and extension of agriculture, new trade via the Grand Canal and Silk Road, and the challenge and inspiration of an outside influence like Buddhism, resulted in a resurgence and flowering of the classical Chinese tradition under the Tang. Known as the **Golden Age**, or cultural high point, learning and arts flourished. The Tang is still seen as the greatest period of Chinese poetry especially in the works of **Li Bo (Li Po**, 701–762) and **Du Fu (Tu Fu**, 712–770). Over 1800 samples of Li Bo (Li Po)'s poetry survive. His lines are full of nature images and the mood is similar to that of Omar Khayyam's *Rubaiyat* in its passion for life. "Why should one toil away one's life?/ That is why I spend my days drinking . . ./Lustily singing, I wait for the bright moon." Du Fu (Tu Fu)'s poems are more somber, reflecting the human troubles connected with the empire building and expansion that took place under the Tang. The horse became a popular subject for figurines full of life and movement.

Buddhism was still in vogue and in official favor so the Tang became the golden age of temple architecture and the artistic model for much of East Asia.

Porcelain, Silk, and Tea

Other achievements also mark the Tang Golden Age. Porcelain, which had appeared by the Tang period, was made into objects of exquisite beauty. Silk, which had been supposedly smuggled out of China by two monks at the time of the Eastern Roman emperor Justinian (527–565 C.E.) in the form of cocoons concealed in hollow walking sticks, in production and form had no rival outside of China. Tea, largely unknown in Han times, was introduced from southern Asia as a medicine, and during the Tang dynasty became the basic Chinese drink. Thus, the three great export items of China—porcelain, silk, and tea—gained stature during this period.

Cosmopolitan Chang-an

The splendor of the Tang was symbolized by its capital, Changan (where the Ch'in and Han also ruled), the eastern terminus of the overland trade routes (the Silk Road) linking China with Central Asia. It was very likely the largest, wholly planned city ever built, covering some 30 square miles and including about one million people with another million living outside the walls. Laid out in a grid pattern, there were open spaces, theaters, vast supervised markets, polo fields (a game imported from Persia), and a palace that was designed to impress. The palace faced south down a 500-foot-wide central thoroughfare to the south gate of the city. Exotic Zoroastrians, acrobats, horse traders, musicians, and story tellers from Central Asia mingled in the streets with artists and sculptors.

Crucial for restoration of Chinese unity were efforts undertaken by the Tang to rebuild and expand the imperial bureaucracy. To offset the power of the independent aristocracy, the Tang opened to all male Chinese subjects the Confucian-based examination system begun by the Han. Education was the prerequisite for an official career. While in theory, merit and ambition were conditions for success, in practice established bureaucrats and the sons of fathers in positions of power and influence more often rose to upper levels. Still, a **meritocracy** of sorts was established and lasted until the imperial system ended in 1912. The scholar bureaucrats, or **mandarins**, touched the lives of people at all levels, national, district, and local. They drafted decrees, monitored local affairs, and served as heads of departments. The **Bureau of Censors** kept track of officials at all levels and the Commission of Fiscal Census carried out a tax reform including taxes based on wealth.

The Demise of Buddhism

The Confucian-based mandarin revival threatened not only the old aristocracy but also the Buddhists. Buddhism was also threatened by the very weight of dynastic support that produced a backlash. The Tang **Empress Wu** (690–705), for instance, gave vast sums to build and improve monasteries, and at one point she sought to make Buddhism a state religion. She commissioned large statues of Buddha, some two and three stories high, carved in stone or cast in bronze. By the middle of the ninth century there were nearly 50,000 monasteries in China. Monasteries acquired extensive land holdings and accumulated large gold reserves through donations and deposits for safekeeping. Monasteries served as banks, lending money and collecting interest. Buddhist success aroused animosity on the part of Daoists (Taoists) and Confucianists, and it was clear that the growing monastic orders were a major drain on the empire's resources. Measures to limit the monasteries gave way in the 840s to open persecution of Buddhism from which Chinese Buddhism never recovered.

Rise of the Song

The attack on Buddhism reflected a weakening of the Tang dynasty. The demand for more taxes to pay for an extravagant court and an expanding army, a great drought in the north, and spreading dissatisfaction led to a series of rebellions beginning in 755, which eventually led to the dissolution of the Tang Dynasty in 907. In 960 a young general proclaimed a new dynasty, the **Song (Sung)**, which was to last more than three centuries. During the Song (Sung), economic growth, innovation, and cultural flowering continued. The Song (Sung) capital at **Kaifeng**, a city of over one million located near the great bend in the Huang Ho (Yellow River), became a huge commercial entrepot and center of manufacturing. There was a boom in iron and steel production and metal industries, using coal as fuel. Paper promissory notes and letters of credit followed by government issuance of **paper currency**, served the growth of commerce. Government-distributed printed pamphlets in the **vernacular** (everyday language of the common people) promoted improved techniques in agriculture. A new class of educated elite, the **gentry**, established themselves at the local level. The position of women declined, although, in wealthy households, women indicated the status of the family. To demonstrate to society that women were no longer needed for labor, their feet were bound until the arches broke and the foot was reduced by half.

The Tributary System

One of the reasons the Song (Sung) was a golden age of good government, prosperity, and creativity was Song (Sung) foreign policy. Instead of continuing the Han and Tang policy of holding on to outlying areas like Sinking, Tibet, Mongolia, Manchuria, Vietnam, and some fringes of northern China, the Song (Sung) policy was to defend the essential territory and appease neighboring barbarian groups in a complex **tributary system** based on money, bribes, and arranged marriages. The tribute system that had its beginnings during the Han Dynasty matured into a sophisticated foreign policy. In many ways it mirrored the Chinese philosophical view of Sinocentrism and Confucian distaste for the warrior conflict. As the planets revolved around the sun, so states revolved around China in orbits of descending order further from China's borders. States furthest away paid less tribute and made fewer **kowtows** (bowing before the emperor). States closest paid more obeisance but received gifts in return, often of greater value

than the tribute in order to show the power and largesse of the Chinese emperor. Harmonious relationships between China and foreigners insured peace within the Chinese state since war required recruits and taxes that could upset the balance between the emperor and his people leading to his deposition.

The Southern Song

The policy failed, however, in 1122 when the Song (Sung) made an alliance with the Jurchen barbarians in Manchuria against another barbarian group. Following a successful military campaign, the Jurchen betrayed the dynasty and invaded northern China. Kaifeng was besieged, starved, and finally sacked. The Song (Sung) then moved south and established a new capital at **Hangzhou (Hangchou)**. Cut off from the northern land routes, the Southern Song (Sung) turned in earnest to developing sea routes to Southeast Asia and India. This spurred a whole new commercial age and technological revolution, and helped to spread Chinese classical culture in Southeast Asia.

Maritime Trade

Permanent colonies of Chinese merchants grew in Southeast Asia and parts of the southern China coast. These colonies included large numbers of foreign residents. Foreign accounts agree that these were the world's largest port cities at the time. Maritime trade provided a fifth of the imperial revenue. Advances in ship size and design created oceangoing ships, some of which could carry over 600 people plus cargo. The earlier Chinese invention of the compass, use of multiple masts, separate watertight compartments, and the stern-post rudder all predated the modern ships that carried Europeans to the Americas and beyond. Arabs carried Chinese goods to the Mediterranean. Domestically, trade flourished too, aided by an immense network of canals and navigable creeks. Hangzhou (Hangchou) was later visited by Marco Polo and Ibn Battuta, and both marveled at its size, wealth, cosmopolitanism, and ethnic diversity.

Confucian Renaissance

Not unlike the European Renaissance, innovation and technological development also marked the Southern Song (Sung) period. The philosopher **Zhu Xi** (Chu Hsi) (1130–1200) founded **Neo-Confucianism**, a mixture of Confucian, Buddhist, and Daoist thought. Neo-Confucianism was a movement that emphasized self-perfection that supported state and society and provided a framework for understanding the world. Zhu Xi (Chu Hsi)'s "investigation of things" meant the study of moral conduct and the timeless lessons contained in the classics of importance in Korea and Japan as well as China. Like Leonardo da Vinci, but three centuries earlier, Zhu Xi (Chu Hsi)'s journals recorded observations and theories like that of geomorphological uplift.

In addition to Neo-Confucianism, there were rapid developments in agriculture, manufacturing, and transport like tools and machines for cultivation and threshing for water lifting (pumps), for carding, spinning, and weaving fibers, for windlasses, inclined planes, and canal locks. Water clocks and water-powered mills were widespread. The earlier invention of gunpowder led to the development of explosives fired from bamboo or bronze tubes. In some ways, China resembled later eighteenth-century Europe undergoing early industrialization with its characteristics of commercialization, urbanization, and invention.

The Golden Ages

In 1234 North China was overrun by the Mongols and by 1239 the Mongols triumphed over the Southern Song (Sung). The vibrancy of the Chinese Golden Age under the Sui, Tang, and Song (Sung) was carried by the Mongols far beyond its borders to Europe. Chinese classicism was brought to its height under the Sui, Tang, and Song (Sung) dynasties. The arts and technology flourished, nourished by a strong economy and good rule. The Mandate of Heaven was solidified and strengthened by means of a liberalized civil service examination system that infused merit into its selection process. The introduction of Buddhism brought enhanced use of paper, and then printing with it, and inspired the arts and architecture. It was adapted to the Chinese culture and later overcome by Confucianism and Taoism. Expansion of Chinese classicism occurred within China as the population moved south and it expanded outside of China with the rise of maritime trade, especially in Southeast Asia. By the tribute system Chinese diplomatic relations replaced the need to rule vast areas. Nowhere during the Golden Age did the Chinese classical system have more impact though than on Japan during the Nara and Heian periods.

NARA AND HEIAN JAPAN (700 C.E.–1200 C.E.)

Early Japanese history is cloudy, largely because written records do not begin until the eighth century C.E., after Japan adopted the Chinese art of writing from the Koreans. The Japanese spoken language, which is in the same linguistic group as Korean, indicates that the Japanese originally came from mainland Asia via Korea sometime between the second century B.C.E. and the second century C.E. The migrants slowly displaced the indigenous inhabitants. Earlier peoples migrated to Japan from China, Manchuria, Malaysia, and Indonesia, as well as Korea, to settle on the Japanese archipelago of four main islands, as well as thousands of smaller ones. Bronze tools and weapons from China entered via Korea about the first century C.E. and iron around 200 C.E. By 400 C.E. the Japanese had moved north from **Kyushu**, the closest island to Korea, and onto the main island of **Honshu**.

The Yamato

By the third century C.E. the **Yamato clan** seized the narrow coastal plain south of Kyoto, near Osaka Bay. The clan, which traced its descent from the sun-goddess, subordinated other clans to create the Yamato state. Under the authority of their sun-goddess, the Yamato established a chief shrine giving rise to a religion known as **Shinto**, the way of the gods. Shinto was a unifying force. The chief deity of Shinto, the sun-goddess, became the nation's protector. According to the ancient teachings, the emperor descended from Shinto. Shinto also stressed the worship of ancestors and its rituals celebrated the beauty of nature rather than the wrath of gods. Those rituals emphasized cleanliness and respect for **kami**, the spirits of nature. During this period, Japanese and Korean contact was extensive, enriching Japan economically and culturally. According to tradition, the Korean King Song of the Paekche kingdom sent the Yamato court Buddhist images and scriptures in 552. Pro-Buddhists in the Yamato court used the religion to strengthen Yamato rule and to introduce Chinese political and bureaucratic concepts. The architect of this effort was **Prince Shotoku** (547–622), the author of the **Seventeen Article Constitution**. It was not really a constitution but a Buddhist blueprint that stressed the proper goals of government and ethical conduct.

Because Japan lacked trained personnel to build a bureaucracy of professional administrators, Prince Shotoku sent groups of Japanese to Tang China beginning in 607 to learn Chinese culture and Buddhism. The death of Shotoku in 622 set off political chaos, but finally, in 645, supporters of these policies overthrew the government and proclaimed the **Taika Reforms**, a bold effort to create a complete imperial and bureaucratic system like that of Tang China. The symbol of this new system was the establishment in 710 of Japan's first true capital and first city, modeled on the Tang capital, at **Nara** just north of modern Osaka. Reflecting Chinese influence, monasteries, pagodas, and Buddhist art flourished. The statue of the great Buddha, the focal point of Nara, was completed by a Buddhist monk from India at a ceremony in Nara in 752. Nara gave its name to the period that lasted from 710 to 794, an era characterized by the continuing importation of Chinese ideas, an imperial court, and Buddhism.

Some aspects of Japanese culture as it evolved continued to be distinctly Japanese. Shintoism, the animistic, nature-centered, indigenous religion, continued in importance. Beautiful woodcarved Shinto shrines were built. Shintoism was practiced together with Buddhism. Unlike China, but like Korea, feudal-style lords and hereditary nobles retained power. Despite the introduction of the Chinese examination system, hereditary aristocrats reserved most official positions for themselves. The Japanese emperor, unlike the Chinese emperor, was considered divine. After a Buddhist monk tried to usurp the throne, the emperor moved the capital from Nara to **Kyoto** (then called **Heian**), which was to remain the capital for 1000 years. Japanese study groups to China stopped after 838. Japanese leaders began to move even further away from the Chinese model as an expression of cultural independence. A phonetic system known as **Kana**, in which most of the symbols combine a consonant and a vowel, made it possible to transcribe spoken Japanese accurately. Kana replaced Chinese characters in popular writing. Art and architecture began to reflect the Japanese concern with texture and natural materials.

The Chinese meritocracy was largely given up for rule by the **Fujiwara clan** (858–1086) who increased their influence at court through intermarriage with the emperor's family. At court, aristocratic ladies and gentlemen devoted themselves to aesthetic endeavors. The *Kokinshu*, for example, was an anthology of 1100 poems written during the period. The best-known work of the Heian period is **Lady Murasaki**'s *Tale of Genji*, considered the world's first psychological novel because of its insight into human behavior. The tale describes the refined and colorful life at court and its rivalries and intrigues. It is a romantic tale about the life of a prince and his many affairs, told with charm, candor, and attention to detail. It also reveals something about the life of women during the Heian period, suggesting that their lives were less conventional than those of men and that they were freer to express themselves.

The Fujiwara absorption with life at court made them blind to the rise of new families, the **Daimyo**, who expanded their estates and used their private armies to become *de facto* rulers over the lands they formerly had guarded for noble families. Peasants continued to work small plots of land but the Daimyo profited from their labor. Also, as Japanese settlement spread slowly northeastward beyond the Yamato area after the ninth century, a new group of frontier warriors, or **samurai**, emerged as powerful factions that began to interfere with conflicts at court. In 1185 the Heian Era gave way to the Kamakura period, marked by the rise of feudalism in Japan.

Summary

During the Nara period, Chinese classical culture spread to Japan. The Japanese adopted and then adapted it. During the Heian period they developed a distinct Japanese classical style that was then spread to other areas of Japan. While the Chinese classical civilization dominated in East Asia, it was Indian classical civilization that began to dominate in Southeast Asia.

KHMER CAMBODIA
(800 C.E.–1200 C.E.)

Between 650 and 1250 Indian merchants and monks disseminated Indian classical culture along trade routes throughout Southeast Asia. The impact was so pervasive that historians often refer to this phenomenon as the **Indianization of Southeast Asia**, though in reality it was an intermarriage between Indian culture and the indigenous cultures. In Java, for instance, the indigenous peoples adopted the general narrative of the Indian epic, the *Ramayana,* but added to it native Javanese legends.

The Indian Impact

When the Indians entered Southeast Asia, they encountered both indigenous peoples and newcomers. There were three groups of newcomers: the Vietnamese, who established themselves on the eastern coast of the mainland and in 939 became independent of China; the **Thais**, who lived to the west in **Siam** (Thailand) and in the eighth century united in a confederacy and expanded northward against Tang China; and the **Burmese**, who migrated in the eighth century where they established **Pagan**, their capital, in the area of modern Myanmar (Burma). All three spoken languages are distantly related to Chinese, but the Burmese and Thais wrote in Indian-derived script. The two indigenous peoples were the **Khmer** in **Kampuchea (Cambodia)** and the **Srivijaya** on the island of Sumatra. Srivijaya, which originated as a city-state, became a maritime empire. Rulers created a strong navy to protect their seaborne trade and rule the waters around Sumatra, Java, and Borneo, but, in 1025 Srivijaya suffered a stunning blow when a commercial rival in southern India launched a naval raid that succeeded in capturing the king and capital of the empire. In the wake of this incursion, Indian mythology took hold as did Indian architecture and sculpture. Sculptures often depicted **Bodhisattvas** or saints who delayed their acceptance into Nirvana to help others seeking enlightenment. Exquisite Buddhist monuments as at **Borobodur** bespeak the influence of Indian Buddhist culture.

Perhaps the greatest reflection of Indian influence can be seen in the 40-square-mile ruins of temples in Kampuchea (Cambodia). As Indian merchants and monks began to penetrate into Kampuchea, the common people tended to adopt Buddhism because of its emphasis on compassion and equality, and the upper class, Hinduism because of its emphasis on social order. In the ninth century Khmer king Yasovarman began building a new capital and temple complex at **Angkor Thom**. Designed with the help of Brahmans invited from India to legitimate his claim to divine kingship, the plan of the city reflected the structure of the world according to Hindu cosmology. Less than a mile to the south, Suryavarman II (1113–1150) built another major temple complex known as **Angkor Wat** (*wat* meaning temple), which replicated the arrangement and style of those at Angkor Thom. At both sites Buddhist temples and sculptures, often of Bodhisattvas, were added beginning in the thirteenth century when Khmer rulers adopted Mahayana Buddhism.

Such enormous building projects were sustained by the wealth created by a complex and technologically sophisticated agricultural system. The Mekong floodplain's fertile alluvial soil was made still more productive by a system of hydraulic networks of canals, dams, and dikes. The monsoon rains were controlled by a system of **barays**, or reservoirs, which collected water during heavy rains and provided irrigation during dry times. In this way, three harvests a year were possible. Canals were often used to transport stone to building sites. A highly organized bureaucracy directed these works that required enormous amounts of planning and controlled labor, the latter often obtained from raids on outlying areas. As the authority of the Khmer kings weakened due to heavy spending and invasion, the extensive hydraulic systems could not be maintained and the kingdom's economic base declined.

Arab traders had been active in interAsian trade well before the time of Muhammed, but with the rise of Islam a new cultural overlay spread out over Southeast Asia. To the expansion of Chinese civilization and Indian civilization, another was added in the eighth century C.E., that of Islam.

KEY TERMS

CHAPTER 12
The Rise of Islamic Civilization
(600 C.E.–1200 C.E.)

CHRONOLOGY

Revelation (610)	Seljuk Turks (956)	Kingdom of Mali
Hejira (622)	Crusader States	(ca. 1200–1450)
Arab Conquest (632–661)	(1096–1099)	East African States
Abu Bakr (628–634)	Mongols (1258)	(ca. 1300–1400)
Umayyad (661–750)	Kingdom of Ghana	Great Zimbabwe
High Abbasid (750–945)	(ca. 900–1100)	(ca. 1000–1400)
Late Abbasid (945–1258)		

TERMS

Islam	Hadith	Arabian Nights
Kaaba	Sharia	Delhi Sultanate
Semitic	Jihad	stateless societies
Bedouin	Sufism	camel
Archangel Gabriel	Hegira	monetization
Allah	Battle of Tours	manumission
Qur'an (Koran)	Uli	diwan
pillars of faith	mosque	Mande
zakat	confessional community	mediums of exchange
Ramadan	dhow	Swahili
Hajj	lateen sail	
Seal of the Prophets	caravanserai	

PEOPLE

Bedouin	Muawiya	Berbers
Umayyad	amir	Soninke
Muhammad	Abdullah al-Mansur	al-Bakri
Muslim	visier (wazir)	Almoravids
Muezzen	Huran al-Rashid	Sundiata
Abraham	Omar Khayyam	Uli
Ishmael	Ibn Sina (Avicenna)	Mansa Musa
Abu Bakr	Averroës (Ibn Rushd)	sultan
caliph	Fatamid	Sonni Ali
Sunnis	Samanid	Askia Muhammad
Shi'ites	Seljuk Turks	Shona
Ulema	Mahmud of Ghazni	sheik
Imam	Ibn Battuta	Karl Mauch
Abbasids	Slavic	

PLACES

Mecca	Sahil	Ethiopia (Abyssinia)
Yemen	Sudan	Mogadishu
Hadramaut	Ghana	Kilwa
Damascus	Mali	Madagascar
Dome of the Rock	Senegal River	Great Zimbabwe
Mosque	Niger River	Zambezi River
Baghdad	Timbuktu	Sofala
Sumatra	Songhay	
Bali	Gao	

The Rise of Islamic Civilization (600 C.E.–1200 C.E.)

THE ISLAMIC CULTURAL SYNTHESIS

With the rise of **Islam**, Southwest Asia (Middle East), at the confluence of three continents, again became the focus of a rising civilization that expanded over large areas and was the precursor to the Global Age. In Islam can be found strains of earlier cultural and civilizational heritages.

Bedouin Culture

First, it is the product of a synthesis in its own cultural heritage, that is, a wedding together of two Arab cultures—the nomadic herder, the **Bedouin**, and the settled oasis dweller. Competition for water and pasture caused pastoral Arabs to divide into clans. Clans identified members as individuals descended from a common male ancestor, resulting in clan loyalties that crossed the division of interests between sedentary villagers and their nomadic cousins. For instance, the same Bedouin nomad clan that controlled trade of one village controlled the flocks around the village market. Some clans, like the **Umayyad**, dominated the politics and commercial economy of towns like **Mecca**. In a transcontinental trading system that stretched from the Mediterranean to Southeast Asia, Mecca was a vital entrepot. This city was also the site of the most revered religious shrine in Pre-Islamic Arabia, the **Kaaba**. A tribal truce suspending interclan feuds inside Mecca resulted in pilgrims, merchants, and Bedouin nomads flocking to the town to worship and trade in an atmosphere of peace. In the south of Arabia, a third indigenous Arab culture existed, that of the agriculturalist. On the **Yemen** and **Hadramaut** coasts, sizable cities and regional kingdoms arose, producing notable art and architecture, but these were destroyed by marauding Bedouin clans and outsiders well before the time of Muhammad. The main focus of Bedouin cultural creativity in the pre-Islamic era was poetry, which was composed and recited orally. The poems were usually about heroics in war, lovers in passion and conflict, and great deeds of loyalty and generosity. Bedouin religion was a blend of animism and polytheism. Some tribes recognized a supreme God named Allah but ethics were founded in tribal codes of behavior rather than religion.

Islamic Culture and Beliefs

In the century before Muhammad, trade routes through Southwest Asia were seriously disrupted by the growing conflict between Byzantium, which bridged Asia and Europe, and Sassanid Persia with its routes to East Asia. Unable to use the traditional land routes through Southwest Asia, merchants began traveling through the Arabian Peninsula. This contact acquainted the Arabs with all the cultural traditions of the area. Even earlier, the unfertile nature of the Arabian Peninsula had led to a series of migrations to the north in the third millennium B.C.E., resulting in people as diverse as the Babylonians, Assyrians, Hebrews (Jews), and Arabs, all speaking **Semitic** languages. Into the Southwest Asian area between the third and seventh centuries C.E. came successive cultural traditions: the Egyptians under Ramses II, the Greeks during the Hellenistic Age, the Judeo-Christians under the

Romans, and the Persian, Zoroastrian, and Mithraian cultures of the Sassanid empire. Prior to the birth of Muhammad, the Arabs became acquainted with all of these traditions. In this way, the new religion and culture of Islam reflects a synthesis of Arab lifestyles, Semitic ethnicity, and the cultural traditions of Southwest Asia.

Muhammad

Muhammad was born about 570 C.E. into a branch of one of Mecca's leading families. A devout man, he described visions from the **Archangel Gabriel** in 610 C.E. who delivered the word of **Allah**, the Arabic word for God. The revelations Muhammad recited became the basis of Islam found in the verses of the Muslim holy book, the *Qur'an (Koran)*.

The most fundamental belief of Muhammad's new religion was the supremacy of Allah. **Islam** itself means submission to the will of God (Allah). As in Christianity, Muhammad believed in the resurrection of the physical body in the afterlife and an eventual Last Judgment. Unlike Christianity, which emphasized God's love, Islam stressed the "wrath of God to come." A **Muslim** is thus one who submits to the will of God and wins forgiveness by living by the **pillars of faith** which are five fold:

1. profession of the creed, "There is no God but Allah, Muhammad is His prophet."
2. prayer five times a day called by a **muezzin** or reciter;
3. almsgiving or **zakat**;
4. fasting during the holy month of **Ramadan**;
5. a pilgrimage to Mecca (**hajj**).

Another fundamental doctrine is that Allah has sent many prophets to preach and warn of the Last Judgment including **Abraham**, of the Old Testament, who was the first to accept monotheism. His son **Ishmael** is recognized by Arabs as their first leader. Muslims accept Christians and Jews as people who worship the same God. Moses, Alexander the Great, and Jesus were also recognized as Islamic prophets. Followers believe that these prophets, however, had possession of only part of God's message, but with

Muhammad as the last prophet, the full and perfect religion was revealed. Muhammad was thus the "**Seal of the Prophets**." Devout followers believe the teachings and revelations preached by Muhammad are the sacred word of Allah recorded in the Qur'an (Koran). Islamic social teachings can be found in the *Hadith*, a collection of traditional sayings and acts of Muhammad. Both the Hadith and the Qur'an (Koran) written in Arabic form the basis of Islamic Law, which defines ethical behavior and is codified in the *Sharia*.

One of the appeals of Islam is its simplicity, instruction, and guidance in social affairs and its message of equality. Women are equal to men in the sight of Allah. Laws for dowries, divorce, and inheritance are given in detail. Women, for example, are entitled to half their dowry if they are divorced, and they keep control of the property they bring to a marriage. Women are assured of rights, but, in continuance of Arab tradition, fathers and husbands have superior rights. Slavery is allowed but controlled by fair treatment. Fraud, slander, and perjury are condemned, and gambling and money lending forbidden, as is the consumption of alcohol or pork. Muslims believe that Islam will establish justice on earth. As Muslims they must lead a holy life and spread the Islamic faith through **Jihad**, or holy war. Jihad is waged by four means: the heart, the tongue, the hand, and the sword. Through Jihad, defenders of the faith are assured of paradise. Because a Muslim was required to read and recite the Qur'an (Koran) in Arabic, the spread of Islam provided a unifying cultural element and language and an emphasis on literacy in all countries in which it was established.

In the eighth and ninth centuries a mystic movement within Islam known as **Sufism** developed in Baghdad. Like Christian monks, men and women wore a coarse wool robe called a *suf* from which the movement gets its name. Sufism, like the Christian monastic movement, taught that individuals could find salvation through fasting, prayer, and meditation outside the realm of daily life. Sufism played a considerable role in spreading the faith in Africa, India, and Southeast Asia where the practice of meditation was already part of religious custom.

THE SPREAD OF ISLAM

Islam spread rapidly and afar for a number of reasons besides the Sufi movement. First, the weakness of the Byzantine and Sassanid Empires in Southwest Asia, which made them vulnerable to outside attack. Second, Islam as a religion was appealing because of its inspiring and clear message, daily responsibilities and rituals, and element of familiarity to people of the area. Third, when united, the Arabs became a formidable military force.

Arab Adoption of Islam

When Muhammad announced his revelations in Mecca, he found few supporters, especially among the Umayyad clan who feared the new religion would cause pilgrimages to the Kaaba to decline, and with it, their income. In 622 Muhammad fled to Medina, a journey that is known as the **Hegira** (emigration) and was soon recognized as the first year of the Muslim era. Between 622 and 628, when Muhammad returned to Mecca, Muhammad had won over 1000 converts. The appeal of Islam to the Arabs was twofold. Belief in one God provided a unifying element to the deeply divided and contentious clans, and it provided a social system that helped heal deep social rifts within Arabian society, as, for example, between clans. By the time of the death of Muhammad in 632, much of the Arabian peninsula had been unified under Muhammad who, in effect, had become both a political and religious leader.

When loyal clans met to choose a **caliph** or successor to Muhammad, a division of opinion arose that was to have longlasting effects. One choice was a relative of Muhammad's, Ali, a cousin and son-in-law. The other was a political follower and close friend, **Abu Bakr**. The succession question led to the development of sects. The **Sunnis** believed that the caliphs should be elected by the community of believers, and the **Shi'ites** believed that the caliphs should be a relative of Muhammad. Sunnis believed that the political and military power was the responsibility of the Caliph. Religious matters such as the interpretation of the Qur'an and the Hadith was reached through study, discussion, and consensus of religious scholars known as the **Ulema**. The Shi'ite, on the other hand, believed that the successor of Muhammad, or **Imam**, is inspired by Allah. The Imam, therefore, is the political and religious leader of the community of believers.

The Umayyad Clan

In the first phase of Islamic history, the Sunnis triumphed. Abu Bakr was elected successor and the Umayyad clan ruled until 750 when the **Abbasids** and their Shi'ite allies established a new caliphate. The Umayyad unified the Bedouin forces and in rapid succession took Syria, western Iraq, and Palestine. In the early 640s Egypt was occupied, followed by Libya. By the mid-640s the desert Bedouins were also putting together war fleets, making further inroads into the Byzantine Empire by way of the sea. An Arab advance in the west crossed North Africa into the Iberian peninsula and was finally halted in France by Charles Martel at the **Battle of Tours** in 732. In the last half of the seventh century Muslim armies broke into Central Asia. By the early eighth century an advance had been made to northwest India, inaugurating a contest with Buddhism and Hinduism that continues to this day. There is evidence that before he died Muhammad envisioned such conquest, though the immediate motive was probably a yearning for booty. This in part helps to explain why the Muslims did not force conversion on those they conquered, requiring only tribute and obedience.

The Umayyads moved the political capital to a more central point in their new empire, at **Damascus**, Syria. During the reign of the first caliph, **Muawiya** (661–680), a system of government and rule based on the Roman model was established. Regions were encouraged to develop agricultural and industrial projects, providing a solid base for prosperity and taxation. The Umayyads also pioneered important cultural developments. In the early years of Islam the faithful gathered in **mosques**, or places of worship, which were usually simple courtyards with roofed porticoes. Borrowing from the Byzantine dome design, the mosques became more elaborate. In 691 the Muslims built the **Dome of the Rock Mosque** in Jerusalem as a sacred shrine at the site where Muslims believe that Muhammad ascended into heaven. In 705 they built the Mosque of the Umayyads in Damascus. Because idolatry was forbidden in the Islamic faith, mosques were decorated with beautiful calligraphy and mosaics. As court life grew more elaborate, elegant poetry and song blended the old oral traditions with the new.

In terms of society, the Umayyads attempted to create a society in which a small Arab and Muslim aristocracy ruled over people who were neither Arab nor Muslim. Following Byzantine and Sassanid examples, Arab **emirs** were appointed as governors to maintain order and collect taxes. Local officials retained their positions. The Muslim warrior elite was concentrated in garrison towns and separated from the local population. It was hoped separation would prevent intermarriage and conversion and thus loss of taxable subjects. In reality, there was extensive interaction and conversion. The Umayyad elite, therefore, developed a policy in which converts continued to be taxed and non-converts were allowed to live in their **confessional communities** with their legal systems intact and to worship as they pleased. This policy made it easier to accept Arab rule since many had been previously oppressed, but it led to lasting fragmentation in Southwest Asia that bedevils unity to this day.

The other social aspect of Umayyad rule of import was the declining position of women. Historians of social history generally find that women had greater position in precivilized societies than in civilized societies. This seems true in the case of Islamic history. Bedouin women had considerable freedom in terms of marriage partners, occupational choice, and clan decisions. This tradition was continued by Muhammad who proclaimed the equality of men and women. However, under the Umayyads, seclusion and loss of rights occurred, especially among upper class women. The harem and veil became twin symbols of the woman's status.

The Abbasids

Social unrest between Arab Muslims and converts who were treated as second-class citizens, clan rivalries, and elaborate court spending brought down Umayyad rule. By the middle of the eighth century more than 50,000 warriors had settled in the eastern Iranian borderlands of the empire. They were angered by the fact that they were rarely given their share of booty. These opponents allied with another venerable family, the Abbasids, one of whose ancestors had been a cousin of Muhammad. The Abbasids defeated the Umayyads, and then slaughtered the remaining family members, except for the grandson of the former caliph who fled to Spain and established the Caliphate of Cordoba.

The shift from Umayyad to Abbasid rule reflects a fundamental transformation in evolving Islamic civilization. One transformation was the growing regional identities and divisions. Umayyad rule was dominated by Arabs, the Abbasid rule increasingly by Persians. Another transformation was that the second-class converts became full members of the Islamic community, converting it into a cosmopolitan and universal faith embracing millions of converts as equals from Spain to the Philippines.

The rule of the Abbasids was firmly established in the reign of **Abdullah al-Mansur** (754–775). Al-Mansur moved the capital from Damascus to **Baghdad** where he built mosques and palaces within great walls, further isolating the caliphs and engendering a fortress mentality among the rulers. He ruled from jewel-encrusted thrones like those of ancient Persian emperors. Once in a position of power, the Abbasids moved quickly to eliminate all dissenting groups, including the Shi'ites who had supported them in their takeover against the Umayyads. A vast bureaucracy headed by a **vizier** (wazir), or chief administrator, was created. Sometimes the administration was abused by the vizier (wazir) to extend his own personal wealth and power, even though the punishment for such corruption was death. The Abbasids became absolutists but stopped short of calling themselves divine, saying rather that they were the "shadow of God on earth."

The luxurious lifestyle of the Abbasid rulers reflected the tremendous growth in wealth and social status of the commercial and landlord class. This was linked to the expanding Afro-Eurasian trading network that was revived in East Asia under the Tang and Song (Sung) empires. From the western Mediterranean to the South China Seas, Arab **dhows,** or sailing vessels, with triangular or **lateen sails** carried goods from one civilization to another. Land routes were kept in good condition with stopping places along the way at **caravanserais**, a kind of camel motel. Long-distance trade was facilitated by the development of a banking system. Banks exchanged money, set exchange rates, issued letters of credit, and used checks three centuries before Europe did.

Besides commerce, artisan handicraft production increased. Much of the unskilled labor was left to slaves, many of whom were captured during slave raids in East Africa. In the countryside, a wealthy and entrenched landed elite emerged. Troops under the supervision of the emir were garrisoned in strategic towns. The majority of peasants did not own land and were tenant farmers, sharecroppers, or migrants. Agriculture thrived in part because of careful water management.

The Golden Age of Islam

It was during the rule of Abassid caliph **Harun al-Rashid** that the Golden Age of Islam took place. Within the confines of the Islamic Abbasid empire were located centers of Hellenistic, Egyptian, Mesopotamian, Christian, Jewish, Persian, and Indian civilizations. The Arab tradition, by contrast, was meager. During the first phase of Abbasid rule (High Abbasid, 750–945), the main task was recovering and preserving the learning of ancient civilizations. Classics were preserved, translated into Arabic, and distributed throughout the Empire. For example, Indian numerals were learned by Muslim traders and carried to centers of Islamic civilization. Later they were known as Arabic numerals and transmitted to Europe. In the second phase (Late Abbasid, 945–1258), Muslim scholars and artists themselves made significant contributions. Literary examples include the *Thousand and*

One Nights, a Series of Tales, and *Rubaiyat of Omar Khayyam.* Meanwhile, Muslim scientists absorbed and ultimately passed on the many inventions of the East like the magnetic compass, gunpowder, and paper. The use of glass lenses for magnification was an Arab discovery. Since Islam forbade the dissection of corpses, medical advances were made more in the area of infectious diseases. **Ibn Sina (Avicenna,** 980–1037) published the *Canon of Medicine,* in which he identified diseases and their causes. In the field of philosophy, the Spanish-born **Averroës (Ibn Rushd,** 1126–1198), who had studied the writings of Aristotle, taught that religious beliefs could not be reconciled with philosophy.

The unity of the Islamic world was based on religion, the Arab language, and trade. But under the Abbasids a united political empire failed to be established. Spain never accepted Baghdad's rule and returned to Umayyad rule in 756. Egypt was taken in 969 by the **Fatamid** clan. Parts of Persia and territories east of the Oxus in Central Asia fell under control of the **Samanids.** By the eleventh century, the **Seljuk Turks**, originally from Asia, swept through Persia, Syria, Iraq, and most of western Asia. In 1055 they conquered Baghdad, and in 1071 they won a commanding victory over the Byzantines. Soon, however, other invaders appeared, first the Christian Crusaders in 1099 and then the Mongols in the early decades of the thirteenth century.

Islam in India and Southeast Asia

Islamic religion and culture spread to India and Southeast Asia. The first Muslim intrusion into India came during Umayyad and Abbasid rule by way of trade contacts and cultural exchanges. Traders brought Muslim culture to India and Hindu mathematicians and astronomers traveled to Baghdad. The Indian game of chess became a favorite in the Muslim world and some of the tales in the *Arabian Nights* are Indian stories. Arabs established trading colonies in coastal areas such as Malabar to the south and Bengal in the east.

Peaceful contacts, however, turned to military invasions during the eleventh century when Turkish Muslims led by **Mahmud of Ghazni**

(971–1030) invaded northern India. Known as the "Sword of Islam," Mahmud mounted 17 plundering expeditions. Pillage and slaughter in the name of Allah did not make Islam popular among Indians, but the simplicity and promise of equality did. Islam replaced Hinduism and Buddhism in the Indus Valley (now Pakistan) and at the mouth of the Ganges (now Bangladesh). These incursions established Muslim rule in the Gangetic plain, creating the **Delhi Sultanate**.

The Muslim incursion led to longlasting enmity between Hindus and Muslims, especially in the Delhi area. Many Hindus were willing to take positions as administrators in the bureaucracies of Muslim overlords, or as soldiers, but they remained socially aloof. Often, Muslims were regarded by Hindus as just another caste, but at the top. In other regions of India, forced conversion was rare, and those conversions that occurred were voluntary and mostly as the result of trade contacts or among low caste Hindus. Sufis, the Islamic mystics, acquired recognition within villages or cities as holy men or individual saints in the tradition of Indian ascetics. For the most part, Indians maintained their caste identities and remained devoted Hindus. The spread of Islam into India set the stage for expansion to Island Southeast Asia.

The spread of Islam to Southeast Asia also occurred primarily at the hands of traders and sailors. The first areas to be won to Islam in the last decades of the thirteenth century were the small port centers on the northern coast of **Sumatra**. From these ports, the religion spread across the Straits of Malacca to Malaya, Borneo, Java, and the Philippines. The island of **Bali**, where Hinduism had taken deep root at the popular level, remained largely impervious to Islam, as did the interior of the islands where Hindu-Buddhist dynasties remained strong. In Southeast Asia, local law and indigenous cultural staples endured. Javanese shadow plays, for instance, which were based on Indian epics, remained popular. Women retained their strong place in society as small-scale traders and matriarchal lineage patterns continued.

THE AFRICAN KINGDOMS AND CITY-STATES

Besides India and Southeast Asia, Islamic civilization penetrated sub-Saharan Africa, giving rise to important kingdoms and city-states in African history. Prior to this development, African societies were what scholars call **stateless societies**, that is, culturally and ethnically homogeneous societies without a central government. Ethnic and blood ties bound family members together and ordered political relationships. Some societies were small nomadic clans, others were large agricultural and herding kinship groups involving thousands of people. Between 800 and 1450 Islamic trade led to change and the rise of powerful African kingdoms.

The Camel Caravan

The **camel** had an impact on African trade comparable to that of the horse in Europe and Asia. Sometime before 200 C.E. the camel was introduced into North Africa and in the fifth century nomads adopted a saddle for its use. This gave them a powerful political and military advantage in the area. Between 700 and 900 C.E. they developed a network of caravan routes from the Mediterranean to the Sudan. Camels are efficient and economical beasts of burden. A thousand or more camels can be strung together in a caravan. They can carry 500 pounds as far as 25 miles a day for as much as ten days without water or forage. Their large, splayed feet allowed caravans to traverse the soft shifting sands of the Sahara. The transSaharan trip took about three months. **Ibn Battuta**, the Arab traveler often likened to Marco Polo, traveled by caravan throughout the Islamic world perhaps as far east as China. He noted the indomitable spirit of the traders who traveled at night to avoid 110 degree daytime temperatures, endured marauder attacks, blinding sandstorms, and thirst at the hands of nomadic raiders who poisoned wells. South of the Sahara the caravans reached safety in the **Sahil**, Arabic for the boundary between sand and grassland.

Salt, Slaves, and Gold

Trade stimulated salt and gold mining and the search for slaves. Thick deposits of salt in the western Sahara were cut into slabs and strapped to camels for transport to the salt-scarce lands south of the Sahara where there was gold to trade. The rich gold veins were exploited by men hacking out the gold as women washed it, in a system not unlike American gold panning. North African Islamic states sought more gold to mint coins in the ninth and tenth centuries. Scholars estimate that by the eleventh century nine tons of gold were exported to Europe annually, which facilitated expanding trade in and between Christian Europe, North Africa, and Southwest Asia as the medium of exchange. Even with modern machinery from the same region, in 1937 only 21 tons were exported. West African gold was crucial to the **monetization** of European commerce in the late Middle Ages and to the balance of payments in South Asia. Slaves, the second great export item, helped fill the armed forces of the Islamic regimes in Morocco and Egypt, and provided household workers for Muslim cities everywhere. Slaves in Muslim societies were not all black; in fact, the word slave comes from the word **Slavic** and refers to Caucasian Slavs from the area around the Black Sea. Demand for slaves remained high due to death by disease, **manumission** (freedom), or conversion of Africans to Islam. It is estimated that four million people were enslaved over an 850-year period, 650–1500 C.E.

TransSaharan trade caused settlements and cities like Jenne, Goa, and Timbutktu to grow. In the twelfth century, Kumbi had between 15,000 and 20,000 inhabitants, a size achieved by London and Paris only in the late thirteenth century. The most influential consequence of the transSaharan trade was the introduction of Islam. Islamic cultural and literary tradition, government, statecraft, architecture, science, and theology shaped the history of the great West African kingdoms of Ghana, Mali, and Songhay.

Ghana

Islamization began in 753 when Muslims first crossed the Sahara Desert into the **Sudan**. There they found a number of kingdoms, particularly the **Berbers**, who were indigenous Caucasoid nomads of Northwest Africa, originally Phoenician colonists. They also found a number of settled agricultural communities and remnants of a horse culture that had come from East Africa. (Horses cannot survive south of the Sudan due to the tsetse fly.) But it was the riches of **Ghana**, known as "the land of gold," which further enticed Muslim traders across the Sahara.

The nucleus of the territory that was to become the kingdom of Ghana was inhabited by the **Soninke** people by the fifth century C.E. The Soninke, who called their ruler Ghana or war chief, had acquired iron technology and horses. The area they occupied was located north of the **Senegal** and **Niger** Rivers. (The kingdom of Ghana should not be confused with the location of the modern state of Ghana.) Its southern areas received enough rainfall so that, with skillful farming and efficient irrigation systems, crops supported a population of as many as 200,000. The rise of Ghana began in 992 when a Berber town situated on the transSaharan trade route was captured by the Ghanaians. This allowed Ghanaian leaders to reap the rewards of the transSaharan trade rather than the Berbers, and it led to the spread of Muslim culture into Ghana. Ghanaians were agriculturalists and herders, but trade was based on salt and gold.

According to Muslim geographer **al-Bakri**, Ghana claimed 22 kings prior to the arrival of the Muslims, and a kingdom of such wealth that 20,000 gold coins could be traded in a single contract. Besides the royal monopoly in gold, wealth came from royal estates and tribute from subordinate chiefs to support an extravagant royal court. Rule passed from the king to his sister's son. Social classes consisted of the aristocracy at the top—king, court, and Muslim administrators—next the merchants, then the farmers and craftsmen, and, at the bottom, slaves. The army stood apart from these but, according to al-Bakri, "the king of Ghana can put 200,000 warriors on the field," perhaps an exaggeration though the force was likely formidable. The king of Ghana adopted the Muslim **diwan**, or agency for record keeping. All justice derived from the king who held court and assigned judgment based on the supernatural, much like the European tradition of trial by ordeal. Ghanaian leaders did not officially convert to Islam but local merchants did. Rulers used Islamic traditions and culture to improve rule and embellish upper class lifestyles.

Al-Bakri described how the religion of Ghana remained pagan and how foreign enclaves were built six miles from the capital. Ghana's independence ended in 1076–1077 when the **Almoravids**, Saharan tribesmen who had been converted to Islam, swept into Ghana and imposed on the Ghanaians a Muslim king. Overgrazing and the deterioration of agricultural lands may have hastened the kingdom's disintegration. Subsequent struggles between Ghanaians and Almoravids so disrupted trade that Ghana broke up into tribal units and power passed to Mali.

Mali

The collapse of Ghana caused many people to flee south. They found safety from Saharan marauders in more productive land with other **Mande**-speaking clans. This became the empire of **Mali**, which reigned as the most powerful West African state for 200 years (ca. 1250–ca. 1460 C.E.). The founder of the empire was **Sundiata** (ca. 1230–ca. 1255 C.E.) who put together a federal state of subservient governors, combining the southern half of Ghana, Mali, and parts of what is now Guinea. He thereby controlled a major gold-producing area and a communications network provided by the upper Niger River and its tributaries. The major sources of income were tribute and a tax on trade, although the economic basis of Mali was agriculture.

Sundiata claimed to be both tribal and Muslim, thus satisfying both Muslim merchants and non-Muslim rural populations. His son, **Uli**, however, was a pious Muslim and the wholesale conversion that followed had numerous benefits. It helped establish good trade relations with Arab states north of the Sahara and it helped politically. Rule of a large empire demanded an efficient, stable central administration with control over the governors. With the spread of Muslim education, a class of scholars who could serve as

public servants was created. Gold and salt served as **mediums of exchange** though the government introduced cowrie shells as a medium of exchange in western Sudan to improve internal trade. A central currency system and systems of weights and measures added to the success of merchants and the growing prosperity of Mali. Mali's products were widely prized including ivory, animal skins, slaves, and, especially, gold. The wealth allowed Mali leaders to purchase an army and arms from abroad.

Mali's zenith came under the rule of **Mansa Musa** (1312–1337). (In the Mandinke language, Mansa means emperor.) Mansa Musa extended Malian territory to a size roughly double that of Ghana, from Lake Chad to the Atlantic and from Morocco to southern Nigeria. Mali contained a population of eight million and controlled fabulous wealth. Mansa Musa further systematized government, appointing members of the royal family to be governors. He became a devout Muslim, leading to the most celebrated event of his reign, an event that was immortalized in a medieval European map. In 1324–1325 he embarked on a pilgrimage to Mecca during which he paid a state visit to the **sultan** (ruler of an Islamic state, Turkish in derivation rather than caliph, which is Arabic) of Egypt. On his entrance into Cairo, he was preceded by 500 slaves, each carrying a six-pound staff of gold, and he was followed by a host of retainers including 100 elephants, each bearing 100 pounds of gold. He lavished the wealth on the citizens of the city, leading an Egyptian official to record that Mansa Musa's gold brought terrible inflation throughout Egypt. Mansa Musa brought back with him the distinguished Muslim architect al-Saheli whom he commissioned to build new mosques.

Timbuktu

Timbuktu, the capital of Mali, which began as a campsite for desert nomads, became a thriving commercial entrepot and great intellectual center with its famed mosque and university. Timbuktu's 150 schools were devoted to the study of the Qur'an (Koran) and trade in books was the greatest in the world at that time. Muslim intellectuals and Arab traders married native women, leading to a racially mixed and culturally diverse cosmopolitan atmosphere.

Shortly after Ibn Battuta's visit in 1352–1353, the Mali empire began to crumble. Around 1375 **Songhay** fishermen refused to pay tribute and the Songhay leader, **Sonni Ali** (ca. 1464–1492) conquered Mali itself. Like Mali, Songhay was a Muslim kingdom that grew wealthy by control of the gold trade. The empire Sonni Ali assembled had its capital at **Gao** and was larger even than Mali. **Askia Muhammad**, who followed Sonni Ali as ruler, expanded Songhai territory with a professional army of slaves and prisoners of war until it became the largest kingdom in West African history. By 1591 Arab rulers in Morocco were strong enough to regain control over the West African gold trade and the whole area south of the Sahara fragmented into tribal kingdoms that Europeans found on their arrival at the end of the eighteenth century.

Islam and East Africa

The Islamic world trade system also had an impact on East Africa, leading to the rise of **Swahili** city-states. Even in Roman times, East Africa had strong commercial links with India and the Mediterranean. Greco-Roman ships traveled down the East African coast carrying manufactured goods and exchanged them for cinnamon, myrrh and frankincense, slaves, and ivory. Somewhere along the Horn of Africa, they caught the monsoon winds to India. After the death of Muhammad, a great emigration from Arabia accelerated Muslim penetration of the area. Although **Ethiopia (Abyssinia)** remained Coptic Christian, trading colonies were established along the coast and people converted. Beginning in the twelfth century, fresh waves of Arabs and Persians came down the coast and settled at **Mogadishu** and then pressed southward to **Kilwa**. Similarly, Indonesians crossed the Indian Ocean and settled in **Madagascar**.

The East African coastal culture that emerged on the heels of Islamic trade penetration was called Swahili after the Bantu language whose poetry and vocabulary exhibit Arabic influence. Much of our knowledge of this area again rests on the account of Ibn Battuta who observed the Muslim mosques at Mogadishu, the stone buildings in cities like Kilwa, and the life of the rich coastal, monopolistic, mercantile families. Leaders of these families took the Arabic title **sheik** (which by this time meant sultan) and ruled the small city-states. The Portuguese, who arrived in the late fifteenth century, were astounded by the wealth and prosperity of the area. Wealth rested on control of sought after products and the import taxes that sometimes reached 80 percent of value. Slaves also were part of the trade complex, but their sale was never as valuable as ivory. Some slaves became soldiers in the armies of rulers in India. Others worked on docks and dhows.

Great Zimbabwe

The Islamic trade complex seems also to have touched South Africa and was a component in creating an empire called **Great Zimbabwe** (ca. 1000–1400). While North, East, and West Africa had contacts with Arabia, Persia, and traders across the Indian Ocean, South Africa seemed far removed until the Islamic period. The earliest inhabitants were hunter-gatherers. In the eighth century, Bantu-speaking people reached there bringing iron working and farming skills. Sometime before 1000, inhabitants of the area, the **Shona**, began panning the alluvial gold in the **Zambezi River** tributaries. Traders shipped the gold east to **Sofala** where it met up with the East African coastal trade complex. The wealth and power of Great Zimbabwe rested on this trade. Originally, the Shona panned gold, but by 1000 C.E. they were mining as far as 100 feet below the surface. They cracked the veins of ore using fire and water to heat the rock and rapidly cool it. Iron picks were used to split the ore from the surrounding rock and remove it. Skeletal remains of small females found at the bottom of these mining shafts indicate that mining accidents occurred as girls, working as miners, squeezed through the minuscule openings of these shafts to mine the ore.

In 1871 **Karl Mauch**, a German explorer, discovered ruins of the great city of Zimbabwe southeast of modern Fort Victoria. Zimbabwe comes from a Shona term "dzimba dzamabwe," meaning stone buildings. Stone buildings without mortar were not all that unusual in southern Africa but a wall 32 feet high and 17 feet thick using 900,000 granite blocks to enclose 60 acres is. The wall encloses the ruins of two building complexes that appear to demonstrate the power and wealth of the ruler. Although the ruins were looted many times, evidence indicates extensive weaving of locally produced cotton but the wealthy appeared to favor Indian cotton imported from the coast. Birds carved of soapstone, fine gold jewelry and copper ornaments, a wide variety of iron tools, and Persian and Chinese ceramics indicate that Zimbabwe was a center of manufacture and trade.

Summary

Great West, East, and South African states arose as a result of the growth and spread of Islamic trade and culture. The Africans supplied gold to the Islamic world, and from those profits built kingdoms and city-states of considerable wealth. With trade came a new culture, giving these kingdoms not just a new religion but Islamic literacy, methods of statecraft, and artistic modes of expression. The history of Islamic civilizations is one of the first in history to illustrate what is a common modern phenomena, that is, cultural and commercial hegemony that can wield power equal to that of political hegemony. In the case of Islam, a fragmented political state, whose cultural traditions and commercial networks ranged over large areas of the globe, touched and changed the lives of many across the Afro-Eurasian continent. It probably would have penetrated into Europe had it not been for the Christian outpost of Byzantium that provided a bulwark against the spread of Islam for 1000 years.

CHAPTER 13

The Byzantine Empire and Kievan State

CHRONOLOGY Byzantine Empire (527–1453 C.E.)

TERMS			
	Eastern Roman Empire	Trinity	Greek fire
	Byzantium	Nicene Creed	byzantine
	Greek or Eastern	Hagia Sophia	mosaics
	Orthodoxy	Corpus Juris Civilis	Russian Primary
	schism	(Justinian's Code)	Chronicle
	monasticism	Battle of Manzikerk	veche
	iconoclasm	themes	Cyrillic Alphabet
	icons	stirrups	liturgy

PEOPLE			
	pope	Procopius	Prince Rurik of
	patriarch	Slavic peoples	Scandinavia
	Justinian	Varangians	Saint Cyril
	Theodora	Rus	Vladimir
	Mehmet II		

PLACES			
	Constantinople	Golden Horn	Kievan Russia
	Bosporus	Dnepr River	

The Byzantine Empire and Kievan State

THE BYZANTINE EMPIRE

The Roman Empire did not collapse completely in the late fifth century C.E. While the western part disintegrated into feudalism, the eastern part continued on for another thousand years. The **Eastern Roman Empire** was Greek in language, Roman in jurisprudence, and Christian in culture. Politically, it was distinguished by the twin rule of church and state, and culturally, it observed a form of Christianity called **Greek or Eastern Orthodoxy**. These traditions it spread into Southeastern Europe and Russia until it was overwhelmed in 1453 by the Ottoman Muslims. Along with the Muslims, the Byzantines became preservers of the wisdom of the ancient world.

The Origins

During the reign of Roman emperor Constantine (306–337 C.E.), Christianity was legalized. Constantine also took the bold step of building a new capital for the empire. **Constantinople**, the new Rome, was constructed on the site of **Byzantium**, an old Greek city on the **Bosporus** (the narrow straits between the Black Sea and the Sea of Marmora) because it was easier to defend from the devastating German raids than Rome, because it was a commercial entrepot in the lucrative Eurasian trade and thus wealthy and urbane, and because there Christianity was widespread. When Rome fell to the Germanic invaders in the fifth century C.E., Constantinople effectively became politically independent.

Christian Church Split

The final separation or **schism** between the Eastern and Western Roman Empires occurred in 1054 when the two churches split. There were a number of theological issues that divided the Latin Christian or Roman Catholic church from the Eastern Orthodox church. One was the relationship of church and state. In the West, the **pope**, or head of the Catholic church based in Rome, had control over bishops, monks, and doctrine. By contrast, in the East, the leader of the church, the **patriarch**, had no such comparable authority. The Byzantine emperors recognized no papal directives from Rome and the emperors themselves regulated church structure. Thus, church and state ruled cooperatively in the East as was the tradition in eastern countries like Persia. Another factor that separated the eastern and western churches was **monasticism**. Monasticism developed earlier in the East than in the West. No doubt influenced by ascetic aspects of eastern religions, such as Buddhism, holy men and monks sought to follow Christ in a complete way by fasting, celibacy, prayer, and separation from the world. In the West, the monastic movements had more to do with active missionary work than asceticism and denial. In the 700s and 800s, yet another controversy emerged over **iconoclasm** or prohibition of veneration of sacred pictures or images called **icons**. In 726 C.E. Byzantine emperor Leo III issued a decree that all images and painting be removed from the churches. He was opposed by many in his own empire and by the pope in Rome. A church council at Nicaea in 787 C.E. declared iconoclasm a heresy. While Byzantine leaders finally agreed to this, the controversy acerbated already strained relations. In 954 the two churches finally split over the issue of the nature of the **Trinity**, or the concept of God the Father, God the Son, and God the Holy Ghost, which had been established in 325 by a church council in the **Nicene Creed**.

Emperor Justinian

The Byzantine Empire reached its greatest height under Emperor **Justinian** (527–565 C.E.) and his wife **Theodora**. Theodora took an active part in the political life of the empire. She worked to improve the social standing of women by having Justinian issue a decree allowing a wife to own land. At one point, she helped save Justinian's throne by persuading him to stay and fight against rebels when they threatened the government. During the rule of Justinian, the Byzantine Empire reached its largest extent. Justinian helped to stave off the Persians and he reconquered territory in the west lost to the Vandals in North Africa, the Visigoths in southern Spain, and the Ostrogoths in Italy. He also was a great builder. He ordered construction of new roads, fortresses, aqueducts, monasteries, and churches, the most beautiful of which was the **Hagia Sophia**. Its enormous dome is anchored by four piers making it seem to float overhead. Justinian's fame, however, rests mostly on the *Corpus Juris Civilis* or *Justinian's Code*. This monumental work preserved the Roman legal heritage and integrated the numerous and conflicting laws that had been observed in the Roman Empire. This body of civil law is the legal foundation for nearly every modern European country.

Under Attack

From the time of Justinian until Constantinople finally fell to the Ottoman Turks in 1453, the Byzantine Empire was under almost constant attack. Persians invaded Syria, Palestine, and Egypt and in 626 C.E. reached the walls of Constantinople. From 674 to 678 C.E., the Arab Muslims lay siege to the capital and then gained former Byzantine territories in North Africa and Southwest Italy and the Seljuk Turks defeated the Byzantines in the **Battle of Manzikerk**, gaining control of Syria, Palestine, and Turkey. Then, in 1204 Christian crusaders attacked. By the late 1300s the empire consisted only of Constantinople and part of mainland Greece. It wasn't until **1453**, when the Ottoman sultan, Mehmet II, lay siege to the city with cannons, that the capital finally succumbed. On May 29 Mehmet II entered the city, converted the Hagia Sophia into a mosque, and promised protection to the Greek Christians. The 1000-year-old Byzantine Empire passed into history.

Byzantine Defenses

That Constantinople survived so long under siege, is probably due to its impregnable defenses. It is, in essence, a fortress city, surrounded on three sides by water and on the fourth or landward side, by a series of walls and gates. At the gateway to the **Golden Horn**, or waterway, on the northern side, a chain was hung in the water to prevent entrance of foreign ships. A system of cisterns freed the city from dependence on water pipelines that could be cut off in times of attack. Besides these physical attributes, the Byzantine military was small but well trained and equipped. Soldiering was hereditary and the officers appointed by the emperor. The empire was divided into districts called **themes** where the district commander acted also as governor. The cavalry was equipped with **stirrups**, a Eurasian invention borrowed from the Persians but unknown to the Romans. This gave horsemen a steady seat while they used the bow and arrow, lance and sword. The Byzantine navy was less efficient than the army but it possessed a super weapon called **Greek fire**, possibly a mixture of petroleum sulfur and pitch, which ignited when sent in projectile form onto another ship, turning it into a fiery inferno.

The other defense weapon the Byzantines possessed, was intelligence. The Bureau of Barbarians was probably the first Central Intelligence Agency in world history. Spies fed information to the emperors who then used sophisticated diplomacy to play one group of frontier people against another. The origins of much of today's diplomatic language and ranking comes from the Byzantines. As in the Chinese court, Byzantine emperors invested officials in silken robes and bestowed titles such as Excellency (used by ambassadors, governors, and Roman Catholic bishops today) and Magnificence (adopted by popes); England's monarch adopted his orb and scepter, protocol officers, the order of precedence at imperial banquets. Ceremony and splendor to outside officials was meant to dazzle and thereby intimidate enemies into submission.

Byzantine Society

Byzantine society was highly regulated and hierarchical. Trades were organized in guilds that controlled prices, quality, output, and surplus. The emperor had monopolies in minting, armaments, and silk (an industry Justinian started with silkworm eggs smuggled from China.) Unlike in the West, money lending was legal but also regulated. There was an eight percent ceiling on interest. Idleness was a crime and taverns closed at eight to prevent drunkenness. The church and government provided free medical and hospital care. Organizations took care of the poor, helpless, and blind. Women lived partly in seclusion in their own separate rooms, and when in public, they sometimes veiled their faces. The historian **Procopius** had to reserve his personal opinions for his *Secret History* in which he revealed the cruelty of an autocratic system where the emperor ruled by divine providence. Lacking an order of succession, usurpations and assassinations line the pages of Byzantine history. Of the 88 emperors from Constantine I to XI, 13 took to a monastery and 30 others died violently. The intricate court intrigue that characterized Byzantine imperial government comes to the English language in the word **byzantine**, which means extremely entangled and complicated politics.

The wealth and splendor of Byzantium was derived from trade and manufacturing. Constantinople's location gave it control of the trade routes between Russia and the Mediterranean, and between Europe, Asia, and Africa. Trade stimulated manufacturing and the Byzantines became master craftsmen. In the twelfth and thirteenth centuries craftsmen from all parts of Europe went to Constantinople to learn how to work with marble, enamel, precious metals, and gems, how to make chalices, decorate manuscripts, and make **mosaics** (pictures made by fitting small, flat pieces of stone or colored glass in mortar), an art form the Romans developed. For this reason, the decreasing size of the empire meant little to the survival of the empire as agriculture was a small part of Byzantine economy. Boats and ships plied Byzantine ports and the city itself was a bustle of shops and markets. Feeding into this trade system were Russians, and it is in these links that one of Byzantium's most profound impacts can be found. From Byzantium, classical Roman culture spread to Russia.

THE KIEVAN STATE

Origins

The Russians are part of the Eastern **Slavic peoples** (Russians, White Russians, and Ukrainians) who migrated into the Baltic and Black Sea areas sometime during the Roman era. They lived in tribes and hunted, farmed, and fished. As Muslim power increased in the Mediterranean and Southwest Asia in the eighth century C.E., Byzantine Christians increasingly looked north into Southeast Europe and Russia for allies and trade routes to Europe. The **Dnepr River** formed the basis of an important trade network that went from Constantinople to the Baltic and then to Europe. Along this river road, the Russians contributed honey, furs, and wax, The Scandinavians or **Varangians** provided boats in the summer and sleighs in the winter as well as protection up and down this route. As the *Russian Primary Chronicle* (first Russian history) relates, the 12 Russian tribes who were called **Rus** decided they needed a leader to unite them so they called on the Varangians to send a prince. **Prince Rurik of Scandinavia** became the first Russian prince and the founder of the Russian state and dynasty in 862 C.E.

This first Russian state, called **Kievan Russia,** was really a confederation of about 300 city-states. Each city-state like Suzdal, Pskov, and Novgorod, had a council or **veche** that hired a prince for protection but limited his powers. At the core of each city-state was a town, usually walled, with shops that sold manufactured goods and agricultural products from outlying areas. What united these city-states was the Grand

Prince of Kiev, a law code, and Christianity. When Prince Sviatoslav, a descendant of Rurik's, won victories over Asiatic tribes to the east and west, Kiev became the strongest state in eastern Europe. In 955 Olga, the first ruling princess, was converted to Orthodox Christianity by Byzantine missionaries who had been sent to convert the Slavs in the wake of Muslim gains in Southwest Asia and increasing hostilities with Rome. The most famous of these missionaries was **Saint Cyril** who fashioned an alphabet for the Russian-speaking peoples, called the **Cyrillic Alphabet**, which has many Greek letters.

Adoption of Christianity

In 988 Olga's grandson, **Vladimir**, officially adopted the Orthodox faith for all Kiev. As the story goes, Vladimir sent ten men to observe Muslim Bulgarians, Catholic Germans, Jewish Khazars, and Orthodox Byzantines. It was the brilliance of the Byzantine court and church that persuaded them toward Orthodoxy. Inspired by the resplendent **liturgy** (Christian ceremony and rituals) in Hagia Sophia, the delegation knew not whether we were in heaven or on earth. For on earth there is no such splendor . . ." Whereupon, Vladimir had his people, on pain of the sword, baptized in the Dnepr River. No doubt, in his decision, Vladimir considered economic and political relationships with Byzantium that were at the center of Kiev's prosperity. The adoption of Orthodox Christianity was the most important event in Russia's history. As in Byzantium, it made the church subservient to the state and thus set the pattern of political rule in which autocracy flourished for centuries to come. It influenced literature and art, especially the painting of icons in which Russian masters like Andrew Rublev excelled. During the rule of Yaroslav the Wise,

1019–1054, schools and libraries were founded and the first Russian code of laws was written. Yaroslav the Wise also had a copy of the cathedral of Hagia Sophia built in Kiev.

Fall of Kiev

The fall of Kiev coincided with the changing trade patterns of Byzantium. In the eleventh century, the city-state of Venice offered serious competition to Byzantine trade in the eastern Mediterranean, making the "river road" to Europe no longer necessary. Then, in 1071, when the Seljuk Turks defeated a Byzantine army at Manzikert, the Byzantines lost the trade through Turkey to Asia. The Russians reacted by moving slowly to the northeast, founding new city-states like Moscow. In 1240 C.E. the Mongols invaded, sacked Kiev, and destroyed all but about 30 of the city-states of the Kievan Confederation.

Summary

While Chinese classical systems of society and culture were spreading in East Asia, a new civilization based on earlier classical models was emerging in Southwest Asia. This Islamic civilization developed and then spread its culture throughout Southwest Asia, North Africa, Africa south of the Sahara, and by trade to East Africa and Southeast Asia. Along the way, this culture absorbed and preserved the classical heritage that had preceded it. Classical systems of Christian western Europe escaped Islamic conversion because of the Eastern Christian center at Byzantium, which became a bulwark against Islam for more than 1000 years. Byzantine culture, meanwhile, spread north into Russia, converting it to its own unique form of classical western culture.

CHAPTER 14

The Rise of Feudal States
(500 C.E.–1870 C.E.)

CHRONOLOGY	medieval western Europe (476–1200)	Ashikaga Shogunate (1338–1573)	Toltec (1000–1300)
	Kamakura Shogunate (1192–1333)	Tokugawa Shogunate (1600–1867)	Anasazi (300–1200) Mississippian (800–1300)

TERMS	medieval	Gothic	Amida
	Dark Ages	flying buttresses	shiki rights
	Age of Faith	Scholasticism	Bushido (Way of the
	castle	monarchies	Warrior)
	fief (feudum)	Treaty of Verdun	seppuku
	manor	Estates General	Zen Buddhism
	open field system	parlement	Noh Theatre
	charter	Battle of Hastings	White Heron Castle
	guilds	Domesday Book	shogun
	university system	common law	Kamakura Shogunate
	Unam sanctam	Magna Carta	bakufu
	lay investiture	Parliament	Ashikaga Shogunate
	heresy	House of Lords	Tokugawa Shogunate
	Inquistion	House of Commons	Holy Roman Empire
	Crusades	Concordat of Worms	Kabuki Theater
	canon	Golden Bull	appanages
	sacraments	shoen	"Third Rome"
	excommunication	mappo	kiva
	chivalry	JoDo or Pure Land	
	Romanesque	Buddhism	

PEOPLE	Ibn Khaldun	Vikings	Hojo
	Edward Gibbon	Varangians	Ashikaga Takauji
	Arnold Toynbee	Danes	Nobunaga
	Oswald Spengler	Norwegians	Hideyoshi
	lords	Normans	geishas
	vassal	Capetians	Ieyasu
	serf/villein	William I	Tarters
	Pope Urban II	Henry II	Prince Alexander Nevsky
	Moors	Thomas à Becket	boyars
	Teutonic Knights	Geoffrey Chaucer	Toltec
	Knights Templars	King John	Anasazi
	Thomas Aquinas	Frederick the Great	Mississippians
	Charlemagne	Minamoto	Adena culture
	Holy Roman Emperor	Yoritomo	Hopewell culture

PLACES	Norsemanland (Normandy)	Galicia/Volynia	Chaco Canyon
	Novgorod/Pskov	Rostov/Suzdal/Moscow Tula	

CHAPTER 14

The Rise of Feudal States
(500 C.E.–1870 C.E.)

REASONS FOR FEUDAL INTERRUPTIONS

Change and continuity are the warp and weave of history. Historians, when examining the past, are always trying to detect what occurred, what changed, and what stayed the same. The attempt to examine the past scientifically began with Thucydides (455–400 B.C.E.), the Athenian historian, who strove to write impartial history that separated fact from legend. Other civilizations have also tried to establish a framework for legitimate history. Sima Qian (Ssu-ma Ch'ien ca. 145–93 B.C.E.) established the tradition of Chinese history by writing the official history of the early dynasties. In his *Historical Records* he sought objectivity by extensively quoting original documents and by separating the narrative from his own editorial comments. He related change to the dynastic cycle and morality in the following observation that

> . . . government of the Hsia dynasty was marked by good faith, which in time deteriorated until mean men had turned it into rusticity. Wherefore the men of Shang who succeeded to the Hsia reformed this defect through the virtue of piety. But piety degenerated . . . Therefore what was needed to reform this hollow show was a return to good faith, for the way of the Three Dynasties of old is like a cycle which, when it ends, must begin over again (Stearns 47).

Islamic historian **Ibn Khaldun** (1332–1406) urged those who studied history to analyze the

similarities and differences between the present and past, and to learn "the origins of dynasties and communities, the reasons for their coming into existence, the circumstances of the persons involved in them and their history." Some historians have gone to great lengths to try to create paradigms which not only explain the past but are capable of predicting the future. This has been especially popular in modern history when the physical sciences discovered rules of the universe that it was thought could be applied to the story of the human past as well. Historians, like **Edward Gibbon** (1737–1794), who wrote about the *Rise and Fall of the Roman Empire*, **Arnold Toynbee** (1889–1975), who studied the vast diversity of civilizations that he believed rose and fell as a recurring pattern, and **Oswald Spengler** (1880–1936), who produced a cyclical theory of history in which he predicted the eclipse of western civilization, have tried to rationalize the study of history. Marxist historians have also tried to make history scientific and thus predict the future on the basis of class struggle over materialism.

In examining the past, historians are fascinated by the reasons for collapse of civilizations. Throughout history, civilizations have risen and fallen, and besides describing these events, historians ask why they occurred.

All the great classical civilizations and cultures that have been examined collapsed. The reasons vary, from outside attack to internal disorder, interaction with other peoples, ecological disasters, theological change, mass migrations, or the spread of infectious diseases. What happens in the interim between collapse and a new civilization is rarely the subject of historical investigation. Sometimes the interims are simply periods between dynasties, as in China or Egypt, so that with new leadership the collapsed civilization merely reappears with a few minor changes. Sometimes the interims are between the ancient period and the growth of classical civilization as in the case of Zhou China. Sometimes the collapse is so total that the civilization never appears again, instead becoming a part of another's history as is the case of Egypt, which became subsumed into the history of the Islamic world.

Feudalism

Somewhere in the middle are the feudal states, which carry remnants of the old but create new states that have considerable impact on succeeding history. Such are the cases with feudal Europe, Japan, and Russia. Feudalism as a system usually has the following characteristics:

- a decentralized political system oriented to defense;
- an agrarian economy;
- a hierarchical social system;
- a culture permeated with military overtones and a religious preoccupation with death.

Princes, towns, manors, castles, religion, and cults of honor are reminiscent of such systems. While the feudal periods in western Europe, Japan, and Russia exhibit many of these characteristics in common, there were also differences between them that make each a distinct culture. The system itself expanded and then united ever larger areas, leading to the end of decentralization and feudalism.

MEDIEVAL WESTERN EUROPE

The word **medieval**, or between eras, portrays the interim nature of this period in western European history—after the collapse of classical Greece and Rome and before the modern period. Its culture was a combination of Judeo-Christian values, classical ideals and concepts, and Germanic traditions. The period has also been known in history as the **Dark Ages** because it

was an age darkened by war and illiteracy, or the **Age of Faith** because Christianity was the most powerful unifying force of the time. It began with the nomadic invasions of the fifth century, invasions that struck again in the ninth century. Much of Europe and Asia was threatened by the wanderings of the nomads, but the impact was perhaps greatest in the West because the nomads tended to migrate westward where land was more fertile and water plentiful, and because the cultures of China and India were more capable of resistance both militarily and culturally.

Feudal System

The feudal system in part grew out of traditions of the Germanic tribes that attacked the Roman Empire. German tribes elected their chiefs, who led their warriors into battle. In return for military service, the warriors received weapons, subsistence, and a share of the spoils. As the feudal system evolved, the same kind of exchange, military service for land, became regularized and institutionalized. **Lords** (chiefs) or nobles ruled districts with miniature governments of their own, dispensing justice, collecting fees, raising troops, and sometimes minting money. The **castle** was the seat of this political and military jurisdiction. Those needing land or seeking protection, the **vassals**, pledged personal loyalty, military service, and other duties to the lord in exchange for grants of land, or **fiefs** (**feudums**). The land grant was the means by which the vassal could outfit himself for battle.

On a fief could be one or many **manors**. A manor consisted of one or several villages in which lived peasants who farmed the land and made the implements of farming and war. Peasants entered into personal relationships with vassals, not unlike those between lords and vassals. In return for protection and use of mills, common pasture, and woodlands, the peasants gave the lords the product of the land, usually one-third of the agricultural output. While the peasants who were **serfs** or **villeins** inherited their position and were bound to the land in exchange for protection, peasants who were free paid rent and could move, but they lacked any assurance of protection from the vassal. Serfs differed from slaves who could be separated from the land they worked to be bought and sold.

Life for peasants was insular and fraught with dangers from disease to famine. For this reason both religion and superstition played a large role in their lives. Strangely, many peasants were healthier than the nobility because their diet consisted of grains rather than meat. Much of the success of feudalism in Europe can be attributed to the peasant who cleared European land using the **open field system** (leaving half fallow) as a means of refertilization, and adoption of the breast-strap harness (which was developed in North Africa for camels between the second and fourth centuries C.E.) and collar harness (which had its origns in China ca. the third century C.E.), allowing use of the horse rather than oxen (horses were stronger and ate less) to till the fields.

Historians emphasize the contractual nature of agreements between lords and vassals and vassals and peasants because they were often written down as well as endowed with the honor of one's word. Contractualism led to the carefully worked out systems of rights and responsibilities as well as perpetuating the Roman concept of law and justice. Towns also entered into agreements with lords. The towns that existed were small, self-contained, and highly organized. Townsmen often received **charters** or documents of self-government from the vassals. The townsmen regulated their affairs within the framework of **guilds**. These organizations regulated price, quality, and quantity of goods produced. Guilds also spawned the **university system** where students were taught by masters, hence "master of arts." Trade was generally dangerous due to wars between lords, pillaging nomads, and outside invaders. Therefore, roads, cities, luxury goods, and wealth was rare.

The Catholic Christian Church

Surrounding this whole system was the Catholic Christian Church headed by the pope in Rome. The Church provided the only extensive organization in an otherwise unorganized time. With the collapse of the Roman emperors, the popes, unlike the patriarchs in Constantinople, not only achieved independence from the state but

claimed superiority over lords and monarchs. The papal bull **Unam sanctam** issued by Pope Boniface VIII in 1302 is the classic statement of the medieval church's claim to spiritual and temporal supremacy. "Submission on the part of every man to bishop or Rome is altogether necessary for his salvation." When **heresy**, or unorthodox views, appeared as they did in the thirteenth century by the Albigensians, the pope created the **Inquisition**, or interrogation to convert, convict, and prevent the spread of these ideas. While the church claimed superiority, in reality many kings and lords claimed the right to appoint local prelates (called **lay investiture**). This situation led to many conflicts and was never completely settled even to this day, as the tradition of separation of church and state indicates.

One vanguard of Roman Christian authority, power, and conversion was the monastic movements. Groups like the Cluniacs, Carthusians, Benedictines, Dominicans, and Franciscans cleared land, produced prayer books, ministered to the poor and sick, preserved learning, preached, and spread the faith. Another vanguard was the **Crusades**, or military campaigns of conversion. The most famous were the expeditions to free the Holy Land from the hands of the Muslim Turks. In 1095 **Pope Urban II** called the first of what turned out to be seven or eight Crusades. During the Fourth Crusade the Christian warriors even attacked fellow Christians in Byzantium. From time to time, crusader states were established, but by 1270 the area was once again in the hands of the Muslims. Crusades were also directed against Islamic infidels (**Moors**) in Spain and against pagans in northern Europe by the **Teutonic Knights** and **Knights Templars**.

Christian Culture

In an age of warfare and uncertainty, the Catholic Christian Church provided a civilization and cultural basis for society. The church was regulated by **canon** or church law, carrying forward the Roman legal traditions. Village life and holidays centered around the church. The church **sacraments**, or ceremonies, necessary to salvation, including baptism, confirmation, penance, the Holy Eucharist, extreme unction, matrimony, and the holy orders, were observed under threat of **excommunication** (expulsion from the church and thus condemnation to an afterlife in hell). Nobility and warfare were regulated by the church. "The Peace of God" declared that feudal warfare could not take place on church property and the "Truce of God" forbade fighting from Wednesday evening until Monday morning, on holidays, and during the religious seasons.

The knightly code of behavior called **chivalry** was influenced by religion. The knight was expected to be courteous, treat prisoners well, be honorable and generous, and treat women as if they were the embodiment of the Virgin Mary. Much of the literature produced in this era, such as the King Arthur stories, revolved around religion, in this case the search for the Holy Grail, the cup from which Christ drank at the Last Supper.

The greatest architectural achievements of the age were churches. The **Romanesque** style was an adaptation of the Roman basilica and barrel arch form. It was characterized by heavy thick walls and small windows. To add height and light, the **Gothic** style was developed in the late twelfth century. It had **flying buttresses** to brace high walls and exquisite stained glass windows. The most sublime example of this type is the cathedral at Chartres, France. Religion also dominated thought and learning. Monks studied and copied church manuscripts. The major philosophy of the period was **Scholasticism**, which was an attempt to wed religious beliefs to rational thought. The most famous of the scholastics was **Thomas Aquinas** who, in his book *Summa Theologia* attempted to unify all knowledge of the world and describe the nature and destiny of Christian man.

Charlemagne

Gradually in Europe certain lords became masters over large tracts of land and many vassals. This led to the formation of **monarchies** (a state headed by a hereditary king). Three monarchies began to take shape as early as the sixth century

C.E.—the Frankish monarchy in France, the Anglo-Saxon monarchy in England, and the Holy Roman monarchy in Germany. The most famous of the early French Kings was **Charlemagne**. Charlemagne, who ruled from 768–814, conquered a large area in France, western Germany, and northern Italy, took steps to rule the territory efficiently, convert the heathen, and reunite the western territories of the Roman Empire. On Christmas Day, 800, he was crowned by the pope as the **Holy Roman Emperor** or Christian successor to the Roman emperors. His efforts to reunite the Western Roman Empire failed, however, and in 843, by the **Treaty of Verdun**, the empire was divided among his three grandsons.

Western Europe Under Attack

Then, in the middle of the ninth century, a second wave of Asiatic barbarians, the Magyars, Vikings, and Bulgars, swept across western Europe, plunging it back into feudalism. In the north another group of warriors, the **Vikings**, raided coastal villages and traveled by river far inland to loot and destroy poorly defended monasteries and isolated churches. Possible reasons for this sudden Viking expansion have been attributed to overpopulation, changes in climate, improved shipbuilding, or the desire for trade and booty. Viking ships, made of oak, weighed over 20 tons. They were designed with sails and oars for speed and maneuverability and could carry an attack force of 40 to 60 men and horses. Vikings overran and later colonized northwestern France, which was known as **Norsemanland (Normandy)**. Besides their trade in Russia, the **Varangians (Swedes)** crossed the Black Sea to Constantinople and farther east they made their way into the Caspian where they encountered the Persians. **Danes** raided the coasts of Germany, France, and Spain, and were responsible for invasions of England. The **Norwegians** reached North America ca. 1000 and established lasting colonies—Greenland and Iceland. Later, in the eleventh and twelfth centuries, **Norman** invaders moved south into the Mediterranean to establish kingdoms in Italy and Sicily.

Unification of France

Early in the twelfth century, however, a line of **Capetian** monarchs (987–1328) centered around Paris, began to unite and extend their power. To strengthen their hands against the pope, Philip IV, "The Fair" (1285–1314) called a meeting of the **Estates General**, an assembly of the clergy, nobility, and commoners, because he needed money above and beyond the feudal dues. Philip got his money and France held the first **parlement** in its history. Philip also began to handpick officials whom he paid directly, to maintain a regular army, and to make the language of Paris the common tongue. Literature in the vernacular of the common people like *The Song of Roland* helped create a common literary heritage.

Unification of England

Strong kings began to emerge in England in 1066 when, at the **Battle of Hastings**, Norman duke William I of France crossed the English Channel at the head of 5000 warriors and defeated the Saxon army under Harold. By means of an oath of loyalty, the "Salisbury Oath," a record of taxable property, the *Domesday Book*, and a Great Council, William began to centralize the English state. In 1166, by the "assize of Clarendon," **Henry II** brought the court system under royal control. Thereafter, English law became a **common law** for all Englishmen. Trial by a jury of 12 peers gradually replaced trial by sworn inquest or trial by ordeal. Then, in an attempt to bring the church under his control, he had his friend **Thomas à Becket** elected archbishop, but, once in office, a Becket refused to be a royal puppet. He was murdered sometime after in the Canterbury Cathedral, allegedly by Henry's knights. This episode has been somewhat immortalized in **Geoffrey Chaucer**'s *Canterbury Tales*, a literary masterpiece written in the vernacular in which pilgrims were going to worship the shrine of Thomas a Becket at Canterbury. During this period, English nobles often held large tracts of land in France. Their absorption with properties in France led to one of the peculiarly English customs of law and government. Englishmen began to limit the power of the monarchy and to establish a Parliament. This came under **King John**, who had irritated his vassals by losing English possessions in France, surrendering England as a fief to the pope, and making the vassals pay undue taxes. In 1215 these lords met King John on the meadow at Runnymede and made him sign a constitutional document called the **Magna Carta**. In it, John promised to respect the specific rights and privileges of the nobles, accept the principle of the rule of law, and promise that no tax shall be imposed except by the common council of the kingdom. Under successive kings Henry III and Edward I, the idea of **Parliament** as a permanent institution with powers of the purse came into being. Parliament was divided into two assemblies, the **House of Lords** and the **House of Commons**, which represented different constituencies.

Germany

In Germany, Otto I (king 936–973) brought all of Germany under his control by allying with the church in Rome. Later rulers like Henry III, however, weakened the monarchy when they tried to overstep their bounds and appoint the pope. This brought the question of lay investiture to a head, and in a compromise called the **Concordat of Worms** in 1122 Henry V surrendered his claim to invest bishops and the pope gave up his right to govern religious estates. In 1125, when the dynasty died out, Germany disintegrated into warring factions. In 1152, however, a new Holy Roman emperor was chosen. Frederick Babarossa or **Frederick the Great** (emperor 1152–1190) reunited Germany and Italy, but by 1250 his line had died out and in 1278 another emperor, Rudolph of Habsburg, was elected. In 1356 the German princes, in effect, cemented the power of the lords over monarchs in the **Golden Bull**, which allowed seven "electors" authority over their own territories and to choose the emperor. In this way, feudalism continued in Germany while in the rest of western Europe monarchs recentralized the state. Because of this, Germany and Italy were the last states in Europe to unite and did not do so until the nineteenth century. Portugal united under King John I (king 1385–1433) and Spain united under King Ferdinand and Queen Isabella in 1453.

Summary

The feudal period left a lasting imprint on the history of western Europe. Politically, it cemented the present-day, divided Europe. It gave rise to longlasting political traditions like parliaments, charters of rights, and constitutions. Culturally, it gave western Europe some of its greatest architectural monuments, cathedrals, castles, and walled towns. It endowed Europe with a concept of chivalry or honor, attitudes toward women, and a Christian order of life. The system itself helped western Europe survive repeated nomadic attacks, clear the land, and give rise to a new concept of nation-state, commerce, and social flexibility.

FEUDAL JAPAN

Origins

Internal conflicts rather than external invasion led to the rise of feudalism in Japan. During the Heian period, emperors tried to centralize their authority while aristocrats were striving to free themselves from it. The aristocrats won, leading to the rise of strong family groups like the Fujiwaras. It was the emperors' land laws that unwittingly contributed to their demise. The imperial government had tried to appropriate land and redistribute it among peasants in order to weaken powerful families. The opposite resulted because the government was too weak to overcome resistance and evasion of laws. Provincial warriors, high government officials, and Buddhist monasteries became great landlords. In 1156 civil war erupted among the great families. It was during this period that the institutions of feudalism took shape.

In both Europe and Shogunate Japan, the military aristocracy held local power, a system of vassalage developed, and land was the source of wealth. To keep order on the **shoen**, or private domain, outside imperial control, feudal lords organized private armies of professional soldiers, the samurai. The shoen had its origins in the ninth century when local lords began escaping imperial taxes and control by giving their land to Buddhist monasteries that were exempt from taxes. The local lord then received his land back as a tenant who paid nominal fees, free of imperial taxes, and owned specific fields, or as dependent farmers, or both. In many cases the peasants were reduced to serfdom and treated as property of the lord. Artisans were also accorded little status and paid poorly. Peasants and artisans were separated by rigid class barriers from the warrior elite. They wore different styles of clothing, could not carry swords, or ride horseback. As in Europe, they turned to religion for salvation. Disorder within the society led to widespread belief that history had entered its final stage, **mappo**, or decline, in Buddha's law. A popular form of Buddhism called the **JoDo**, or **Pure Land**, sect, offered the promise of bliss in heaven or the pure land for those who lived upright lives on earth. Central to this faith was belief in **Amida**, the Buddha of Infinite Light, who was thought to preside over the Western Paradise and was reminiscent of the Shinto sun-goddess. Like the miracle plays and traveling minstrels in Europe, colorful figures like evangelists Kuya (903–972) and later Ippen (1239–1289) outlined in great detail the pleasure of Paradise and the tortures of Hell that were painted by Buddhist monks in vivid narrative picture scrolls for all to see.

Samurai Culture

The samurai originally only received **shiki rights**, or a certain portion of an estate's produce, but later they began receiving a grant of land for their service in a formal ceremony that included a religious element much like the knighting ceremony in Europe. The samurai had their own code of honor called **Bushido**, or **Way of the Warrior**, the bedrock of which was complete loyalty to the lord. The demands upon the warrior were harsh. A defeated warror expected to be decapitated rather than held for ransom as was the European practice. To avoid dishonor, to demonstrate loyalty, or to display a protest, warriors committed **seppuku**, or ritual suicide by self-disembowelment. The code of conduct of the samurai emphasized self-discipline in order to face death, swordsmanship, respect for the gods, generosity to others and sympathy for the weak and helpless. Physical hardship was routine, and soft living despised. Life of a samurai was symbolized in art by the cherry blossom that falls from the tree at the height of its beauty. Unlike the European warrior, Japanese samurai were expected to be graced in the arts. **Zen Buddhism** was the popular religion among the samurai because it emphasized meditation giving the warrior the courage to face death. The tea ceremony and rock gardens ritualized methods of encouraging meditation. **Noh Theatre**, performed by two masked actors who were accompanied by music and chorus to create an aura of ritualized, poetic mystery, became the classical theater of Japan. Samurai went into battle in armor, often on horseback wearing elaborate helmets that themselves became an art form. Castles were built as in Europe, the most famous being the **White Heron Castle**. In Europe, contractual and personal relationships were emphasized. In Japan, group values predominated.

The Kamakura Shogunate

During the feudal period, one family after another rose to power and at times united Japan. Unlike Europe, this did not lead to the end of feudalism largely because the Japanese **shoguns** were generals-in-chief rather than hereditary administrators or kings. Emperors retained their title but possessed little power beyond the court. The military class was more pervasive in Japan. While in Europe only two to three percent of the population belonged to the noble class, in Japan it was as high as ten percent. In 1192 civil wars and feuds abated when the **Minamoto** family and their leader **Yoritomo** (1147–1199) became shogun and began the **Kamakura Shogunate** (1192–1333). The Kyoto nobility and Buddhist institutions managed to retain a measure of their wealth and influence as Yoritomo built his **bakufu** (which, literally translated, means tent government). In an attempt to centralize rule, Yoritomo granted land rights but not the land to his vassals. He appointed military land stewards who collected taxes and military governors who maintained law and order. Before the end of the twelfth century, however, these officials had

become hereditary officials and local officials in their own right. During the course of his rule, Yoritomo killed everyone within his own family who might challenge his rule. When he died in 1199 his wife's father became the defacto shogun. Rule passed to her family, who were known as the **Hojo** regents.

Hojo

During Hojo rule, warrior law was codified while the nobility retained their own laws and peasants' matters were left to local officials. One of the code's purposes was to establish rules for land tenure and ensure the impartial administration of justice in disputes between warriors. Decisions were based on precedent and common sense. It was under this code that divorced women were allowed to keep the land they brought to a marriage. The simplicity and effectiveness of the code became a symbol of justice and a legacy to later shogunates. During Hojo rule, the samurai were called on to defend Japan against the Mongols, but there were no rewards for them as there was little booty. By the fourteenth century the numbers of samurai grew and there was little wealth to support them. This created discontent among the samurai leading to an uprising, unseating the Kamakura Shogunate.

The Ashikaga Shogunate

In 1338 another military leader, **Ashikaga Takauji** established the **Ashikaga Shogunate**, which lasted until 1573. This was a victory for the samurai who took over civil authority throughout Japan but left Japan far from united. Rival heirs to the Ashikaga Shogunate battled and more than 300 small states emerged with warlord rulers called daimyos. During this era, warlords became virtual owners and rulers in their domain. For this reason, they began to try to build up the wealth of their areas by encouraging peasants to produce items such as silk, hemp, paper, dyes and other marketable items. This growing producer and commercial class began to resemble in their activities the medieval guild system in Europe.

The Tokugawa Shogunate

The pattern of recurring civil war was so entrenched in Japanese society that it took a succession of three remarkable military leaders and the use of gunpowder to restore order and unity. Japanese children are taught that "Ieyasu ate the pie that Nobunaga made and Hideyoshi baked." **Nobunaga**, the first of these leaders, defeated a powerful daimyo in 1560 and seized Kyoto eight years later. He then went on to subdue the rest of Japan and unite it by standardizing currency, eliminating customs barriers and encouraging trade and industry. Where Nobunaga had subdued by force, **Hideyoshi** centralized institutions. He soothed the vanquished daimyos with lands and military positions but made them swear loyalty to him.   His agents collected detailed information about taxable property much like the English *Domesday Book*. Finally, **Ieyasu**, who owned vast estates around Tokyo, followed by obtaining from the emperor the title of shogun and establishing the **Tokugawa Shogunate** (1600–1867). The Tokugawa isolated the emperor and nobility from the military class. The main aim of the Tokugawa was to establish control over (not abolish) the feudal lords. They did this by requiring all daimyo to reside in Edo in alternate years, and by their monopoly over gunpowder. The Portuguese introduced gunpowder to Japan in 1543.

Gunpowder

In 1575, at the battle of Nagashino, 3000 foot soldiers equipped with muskets were stationed behind high wooden palisades under the command of Oda Nobunaga. As waves of mounted warriors attacked, Nobunaga's men fired continual volleys as they rotated their postions, firing and reloading. The resulting heavy losses demonstrated the significance of the new weapon. In 1584 Hideyoshi's victorious army included both a gun-carrying infantry and samurai with swords.

Once the Tokugawa Shogunate was firmly established, however, gunmaking was reserved as a government monopoly and the peasants were disarmed. Japanese Christians who rebelled against the shogun in 1637 were the last in Japan to use guns until the arrival of the American warships in 1853. See Chapter 21, the Shimabara Rebellion. The gunpowder that had helped the Tokugawa come to power now became the privy possession of the Tokugawa who built up a modern military under their control. The Tokugawa brought peace and prosperity to Japan, and, more importantly, isolationism that protected them from European imperialism. Isolation was accompanied by anti-Christian decrees derived from the fear that Spain and Portugal were using Christianity to facilitate colonization of the country. Gunpowder also called into question the importance of individual bravery and the skillful swordsmanship of the samurai.

Prosperity and a subdued nobility with little to do led to a proliferation of spending by this increasingly superfluous class of samurai. The samurai spent heavily on **geishas**, or girls accomplished in the arts, and **Kabuki Theater**, which consisted of bawdy skits dealing with adventure, love, and romance. Conspicuous consumption of the upper classes led to taxation and deterioration of peasant life. Peasant rebellions became a chronic problem. On the positive side, peace led to trade and commerce, the growth of urban life, and an expanding merchant class, as occurred in Europe during the Renaissance. Japan became centralized but feudal culture continued.

Summary

The feudal period in Japanese history left lasting imprints as it did in Europe. Politically, while Japan was ultimately united, it was under the leadership of a shogun or military dictator more powerful than the emperor. The samurai remained a powerful class as did the land owners. The samurai tradition left lasting cultural traditions like the tea ceremony, gardens, Zen and JoDo Buddhism, and attitudes toward honor, death, civil authority, and outsiders.

OTHER SOCIETIES IN COLLAPSE—RUSSIA AND THE AMERICAS

Origins of Russian Feudalism

Other societies of this period also experienced the effects of collapse and exhibit one or more features of feudal orders. One was in Russia. The Kievan Russian state that had grown up on the fringes of the Byzantine Empire created a Russian consciousness and concept of Russian land. Its legacy was a uniform religion, a common language and literature, and a historical memory. But the twin terrors of Kievan Russia, internal division and invasion from abroad, caused the collapse of the Russian state and its division into **appanages** or separate holdings by individual princes. The appanage period lasted from 1240 when the Mongols invaded to 1462 when Czar Ivan the Great declared Russia independent of Mongol rule.

The Mongols, or **Tartars** as they are cited in Russian sources, refer to mostly Turkic peoples who suddenly appeared in 1223 and again in 1237–1240. The inability of the Russian princes to unite in their own defense allowed the Mongols to attack with impunity. The princes on the frontiers tended to give in to the Mongols rather than fight, allowing the other city-states to be easily overcome. After conquest the Mongols settled down to rule indirectly through Russian princes. These princes became virtual autocrats in their domains, delivering to the Mongols only taxes and recruits.

Appanages

There were three variations on the appanage theme: To the northwest were small city-states like **Novgorod and Pskov**; To the southwest were appanages like Volynia and Galicia; and to the northeast princely domains like Moscow and Iaroslavl. Pskov and Novgorod essentially escaped Mongol pillage. They became independent trading states. The towns were walled, formulated their municipal affairs in a way not unlike the European medieval town councils, and produced and sold under strong groups not unlike guilds. In the outlying areas, peasants farmed, bringing their produce to market in the towns. The greatest moment in Novgorodian history was the repulsion of the Swedes and Teutonic knights under **Prince Alexander Nevsky** in 1240 and 1242 respectively. These victories delimited the movement of Germans into Russia, which had already occurred in Estonia, Lithuania, and Latvia. It preserved Orthodoxy and halted a likely conversion to Catholicism.

By 1250 **Galicia** and **Volynia**, west of Kiev and at the foothills of the Carpathian Mountains, grew independent as the strength of Kiev waned. In this area, **boyars**, or aristocratic families, ruled. In 1197 Prince Roman united the two appanages and successfully defended them from incursions by the Poles, Hungarians, Lithuanians, and Polovtsy. Roman's son Daniel ruled the area that became an emporium of East-West trade. He even accepted the king's crown from the pope, thus delivering this area of Kievan Russia to the Catholic West. In 1253 the Mongols lay waste to the area, and by 1387 Galicia had been absorbed into the Polish state and Volynia into Lithuania. In the northeast appanages like **Rostov**, **Suzdal**, and **Moscow** began to gather strength against the Mongols. These states had suffered staggering blows by the Mongols, but their distance from the Mongol heartland allowed them to move toward independence more rapidly than in the Kievan heartland.

Whereas the evolution of Novgorod emphasized the role of the veche, and in Galicia and Volynia that of the boyars, in the northeast the prince predominated. One reason for this is that in this area there were many frontier lands into which the princes could expand. In so doing, they could pay off their warriors with land. Control of agriculture and the peasants on it became part of the Russian feudal system. By the rule of primogeniture, long lives, advantageous marriages, and the power of warfare, the Moscow princes were eventually able to free Russia from the Mongol yoke, claim independence from the Orthodox Church in Constantinople (because it had fallen to the

Ottoman Turks in 1453), and reunite Russia much as the kings in Europe had been able to do.

Summary

Appanage Russia resembles other feudal periods under examination. A united state was shattered and decentralized. Small trade towns were apparent in some places, agrarian states in others. Warriors and nobles predominated as the upper class. Religion played a role in preserving and identifying a cultural being. In the end, the state was partially reunited with remnants of the warrior culture to influence the history to come.

Mesoamerica

Between 700 and 900 C.E. the Mesoamerican classical societies were in decline. Teotihuacan in the valley of Mexico was destroyed around 700 C.E. by nomadic hunters from the north, perhaps aided by groups restless under Teotihuacan rule. The collapse and abandonment of Maya cities, which began around the eighth century C.E., was more gradual. Scholars disagree on the reasons for collapse. Some suggest ecological problems and agricultural exhaustion; others cite internal revolt or foreign pressure.

Toltec

Around 1000 C.E. a new group of peoples called the **Toltec** (1000–1300) began to occupy Mexico. As in other feudal societies, the Toltec were militaristic, though they derived much of their culture from their classical predecessors. On the other hand, they succeeded by political control and trade in uniting much of Mexico and former Maya territory and ruling it from their capital at **Tula**. Toltec influence and trade spread as far as the American Southwest where cliff-dwelling and maize growing **Anasazi** (300–1200) people lived. The Anasazi were noted for their beautiful ceramic work and their **kivas**, or circular pits, which were used for religious meetings by men of the community. Another type of Anasazi settlement can be found in the **Chaco Canyon** area of New Mexico. Here about 125 planned towns built of stone and adobe can be found. Many were connected by roads. Ball courts and temple mounds suggest influence by the classical Mesoamerican cultures.

Mississipians

Another group of people, the **Mississippians**, located in the southcentral part of the United States, flourished about 800–1300 C.E. This culture exhibited both classical expansionism and feudal decentralization. Prior to the Mississippian culture, around 2000 B.C.E., the area around the Mississippi and Ohio Rivers was inhabited by agricultural people called the **Adena culture**. They constructed great earthen mounds, some defensive and some for burial. Around 200–500 C.E. the **Hopewell culture** rose in the Ohio valley. These people built more elaborate mounds and extended Adena culture trade networks as far as the Gulf of Mexico and the Rocky Mountains. Then, around 800 C.E. new sites such as Moundville (Alabama) and Cahokia (Illinois) were built. Moundville and Cahokia, in turn, much like a feudal web, seem to have had communities around them. The Mississisippians were organized around a powerful chiefdom under a ruler known as the Great Sun. The large towns, temple complexes, pyramid mounds, religious symbols, and crops reflect a strong Mesoamerican influence. Thus, as more is discovered about the Amerindian cultures, scholars are beginning to see in the Americas trends that occurred in other parts of the world as well. Those that have been the subject of this chapter include classical cultural expansion and feudal interruptions due to collapse.

UNIT REVIEW

Cross-Regional Developments

Across the globe from 100 C.E. to 1200 C.E. classical civilizations collapsed. These included Han China, Gupta India, Imperial Rome, and Teotihuacan and Mayan Mesoamerica. In China and eastern Europe, the classical civilizations reemerged under new leadership (Byzantium and Sui/Tang/Song (Sung) China) and created a Golden Age. During the Golden Age, the classical civilizations spread to new parts of the globe, like Japan (Nara and Heian periods), Southeast Asia (Khmer Cambodia), and Russia (Kievan Russia). In other instances, the collapse led to decentralization and creation of a feudal culture blending classical and barbarian ways. This occurred in western Europe and Japan primarily, but also to some extent in Russia and the Americas. In the Southwest Asian cradle of civilization, where a vacuum was left by the collapse of Rome, a brilliant new Islamic civilization emerged that developed and spread its culture far and wide, often blending with other cultures as in Southeast Asia, or creating new states like the African kingdom. In other parts of the world, as in Polynesia, the migration of people led to the expansion of culture. The historical processes of change like migration, rise and fall, cultural diffusion, interaction, synthesis, and systems of exchange are evident in this period of history leading to expansion of civilization and creation of new cultures.

Legacies

The legacies of this period are of great import to world history:

- the populating of the Pacific islands extended humankind over an area three times that of Eurasia;
- the spread of Mesoamerican culture advanced civilization in North America;
- Chinese culture spread to Korea, Japan, and Southeast Asia and set the stage for its advance across Asia to Europe;
- the spread of classical Indian culture led to the rise of a brilliant society in Cambodia at Angkor Wat;
- Islam completely transformed the culture of Southwest Asia and spread to India, Southeast Asia, and Africa south of the Sahara;
- the Byzantine empire created a bulwark against Islamic advance into Europe and formed the basis of the first Russian civilization at Kiev;
- Islam and Byzantium preserved the knowledge of the western world;
- the collapse of civilization in western Europe spawned the creation of a new type of culture based on defensive needs;
- a decentralized feudal Europe united under the banner of Christendom, creating a new kind of culture bearing the seeds of and empowering a new western Europe;
- technological advances like the outrigger canoe, dhow, compass, cartography, gunpowder, horse collar, paper currency, and printing, to name a few, soon spread for all the world to use and possess;
- efficient transportation systems like the camel caravanserais and large ships led to long-distance trade networks other than those across central Asia;

- Golden Ages in China and Southwest Asia led to an outpouring of literature and art still enjoyed throughout the world.

Overall, expansion and interaction in world history has been a stimulating and creative force.

Documents

THE BANTU MYTH OF MIGRATION

In the country of the east, on the right bank of the Lualaba River, there once was a man and a woman. Their names mean respectively "he who builds many houses," and "she who makes much pottery." They live in ignorance of each other. Guided by the sound of chopping, the man discovered the woman who was preparing firewood. . . They brought forth twins of opposite sex, who became inseparable companions. One day the twins found a locality that was exceptionally rich in fish. They finally obtained permission from their parents to leave the village and devote themselves entirely to fishing. In their turn, they brought forth twins, who lived in the same incestuous manner, far from their parents. This new generation took up trapping. So pairs of twins, moving each generation a little farther westward, populated the country.

The Bantu migrations, which took place ca. 100 C.E. to 900 C.E., spread agriculture and ironmaking throughout Africa. These Bantu peoples probably originated in eastern Nigeria and moved first to central Sudan and then along the Congo into the forests of West and Central Africa, East Africa, and south along the Zambezi River into Zimbabwe and South Africa. About 90 percent of the languages south of a line from the Bight of Benin to Somalia are part of the Bantu family. The migration was probably set in motion by an increase in population due to farming and the desiccation of the Sahara. The early Bantu depended on agriculture and fishing, and were village dwellers who organized their societies around kinship. The history of the Bantu migrations is not well known, but the epic tales among the Luba peoples collected in the twentieth century explain this occurrence in their own way. The emphasis on fishing and trapping is probably due to the fact the migration patterns followed the rivers.

THE POETRY OF LI BO

A girl picking lotuses beside the stream—
At the sound of my oars she turns;
She vanishes giggling among the flowers,
And, all pretense, declines to come out.
Amid the flowers with a jug of wine
The world is like a great empty dream.
Why should one toil away one's life?
That is why I spend my days drinking. . . .
Lustily singing, I wait for the bright moon.

I drink alone with no one to share
Raising up my cup, I welcome the moon. . . .
We frolic in revels suited to the spring.

Li Bo (701–762 C.E.) was the titan of Chinese poetry during the Tang Golden Age. Some 1800 samples of his 20,000 poems survive. The legend regarding this excerpt, almost certainly untrue, is that Li Bo drunkenly leaned out of a boat to embrace the reflection of the moon and drowned, happy in his illusion. Tang poetry reflects Chinese love of nature, attention to form, meter, and rhythm, genuine emotion frequently sprinkled with light humor, and a songlike quality. It reflects an urbane, elegant, and brilliant culture at its height. The tone and essence of this poem reminds the reader of the poems of Omar Khayyam (*Rubaiyat*) written during the Golden Age of Islam.

THE TALE OF GENJI

Though it seemed a shame to put so lovely a child into man's dress, he was now twelve years old and the time for his Initiation was come. The Emperor directed the preparations with tireless zeal and insisted upon a magnificence beyond what was prescribed. . . . The ceremony took place in the eastern wing of the Emperor's own apartments, and the Throne was placed facing toward the east, with the seats of the Initiate-to-be and his Sponsor in front.

Genji arrived at the hour of the Monkey (3 pm). He looked very handsome with his long childish locks and the Sponsor, whose duty it had just been to bind them with the purple ribbon, was sorry to think that all this would soon be changed, and even the Clerk of the Treasury seemed reluctant to sever those lovely tresses with the ritual knife. . . .

Duly crowned, Genji went to his chamber and changing into man's dress went down into the courtyard and performed the Dance of Homage, which he did with such grace that tears stood in every eye. . .

During the seventh and eighth centuries C.E., the Japanese court at Nara borrowed heavily from the Chinese. Later periods like the Heian (794–857 C.E.) reaped the benefits. During the Heian period Chinese and Japanese ideas were blended. One family, the Fujiwara, acquired power, and they and their followers followed an elaborate court style. Many court women kept diaries and composed poetry written in Japanese (the men wrote in Chinese). *The Tale of Genji* was written by Lady Murasaki Shikibu and is not only a Japanese masterpiece, but one of the world's first novels. The novel, probably written about 1004 C.E., describes the many adventures of a legendary Prince Genji.

THE QUR'AN (KORAN)

Set no other god beside Allah . . .
Who hath ordered that you worship none but Him.
Show kindness to your parents, and to your kindred,
And to the poor, and to the wayfaring stranger.
Commit no adultery, for this is taboo and sinful.
Slay none whom Allah hath forbidden you to slay.
Rob not the orphan.
Keep your promises.
Cheat not when you sell.
Walk humbly on the earth.
Other than this is evil, a stench before the Lord.

Muslims believe the Qur'an (Koran) contains the words of Allah or God as spoken through Muhammad (570–632), the last of the great prophets. The central belief of

Islam, meaning submission to God, is that Allah is worshipped as the only deity. Besides that, the faithful are called upon to live in accordance with the teachings of the *Koran* by performing mandatory observances called the "Pillars of Faith." Belief in the prophets, the Last Judgment, and that the good will enter paradise are key concepts of Islam as in Christianity. Muslims enjoy the *Koran,* not only as a holy book, but as a work of literature that, in the Arabic language, has rhythm and balance.

Recall Questions

1. Which of the following choices is arranged in the correct chronological order?
   (A) Song (Sung), Tang, Sui, Han
   (B) Sui, Han, Song (Sung), Tang
   (C) Han, Sui, Tang, Song (Sung)
   (D) Sui, Song (Sung), Han, Tang
   (E) Han, Tang, Sui, Song (Sung)

2. On which of the following islands was the society destroyed through ecological degradation and war?
   (A) Easter
   (B) New Guinea
   (C) Fiji
   (D) Madagascar
   (E) Hawaii

3. Built to replicate the Tang imperial center, the site of Japan's first capital was
   (A) Changan
   (B) Nara
   (C) Kyoto
   (D) Angkor Wat
   (E) Loyang

4. Which of the following is incorrectly linked?
   (A) Prince Shotoku stressed the proper goals of government and ethical
       conduct in the 17-Article Constitution.
   (B) Li Bo (Li Po) was the Chinese Buddhist monk who discovered gunpowder.
   (C) Empress Wu gave vast sums of money to support Buddhist monasteries.
   (D) Lady Murasaki wrote the world's first psychological novel, the *Tale of Genji.*
   (E) Emperor Taizong (T'ai-Tsung) defeated the eastern and western Turks to gain control of the
       Silk Road trade.

5. Who is recognized by Muslims as their first leader?
   (A) Abraham
   (B) Ishmael
   (C) Abu Bakr
   (D) Muhammad
   (E) Moses

6. All of the following are pillars of the Islamic faith EXCEPT
   (A) belief in the creed that "There is no God but Alla, Muhammad is His prophet."
   (B) prayer five times a day.
   (C) almsgiving.
   (D) fasting during the holy month of Ramadan.
   (E) pilgrimage to Medina.

7. All of the following Muslim societies are Sunni EXCEPT
   (A) Syria.
   (B) Libya.
   (C) Egypt.
   (D) Iran.
   (E) Morocco.

8. Shi'ites believe their leader, who fulfills both political and religious functions, is inspired by Allah as successor of Muhammad and recognize him as
   (A) Caliph.
   (B) Imam.
   (C) Emir.
   (D) Sheik.
   (E) Muezzin.

9. Within Jerusalem, there are holy sites sacred to
   (1) Jews.
   (2) Buddhists.
   (3) Zoroastrians.
   (4) Christians.
   (5) Muslims.

   (A) 1, 2, and 3
   (B) 2, 3, and 4
   (C) 3, 4, and 5
   (D) 1, 3, and 5
   (E) 1, 4, and 5

10. Like Christians, Muslims profess all of the following beliefs EXCEPT
    (A) monotheism.
    (B) resurrection.
    (C) the Last Judgment.
    (D) the teachings of Moses.
    (E) the Trinity.

11. The nomadic peoples indigenous to North Africa were the
    (A) Seljuk Turks.
    (B) Bedouins.
    (C) Berbers.
    (D) Mande.
    (E) Slavs.

12. Which of the following enhanced long distance trade from 100 to 1200 C.E.?
    (A) dhows
    (B) domestication of the camel
    (C) monetization of trade and letters of credit
    (D) West African gold
    (E) All of the above

13. The leader of Mali who, as a devout Muslim, embarked on an Islamic pilgrimage to Arabia was
    (A) Sundiata.
    (B) Mansa Musa.
    (C) Uli.
    (D) Sonni Ali.
    (E) Askia Mohammed.

14. Cultural characteristics of the Byzantine Empire included all EXCEPT
    (A) Greek.
    (B) Orthodox Christian.
    (C) Roman.
    (D) Muslim.
    (E) none of the above.

15. The wealth and independence of the Byzantine Empire resulted from
    (A) a carefully designed defense system for Constantinople that included cisterns, walls, a chain
        across the harbor, and a small well-trained army.
    (B) the skillful use of intelligence and diplomacy to establish a system of military alliances with
        Catholic popes and European kings.
    (C) Constantinople developing as a western entrepot of the Silk Road.
    (D) stimulating the production of luxury products by master craftsmen.
    (E) all of the above.

To check your answers, see page 393.

The Gothic Cathedral at Amiens. *Built in the twelfth century in France, this cathedral exhibits the basic features of Gothic architecture—the pointed arch, the ribbed vault, and the flying buttresses. The inspiration for Gothic architecture was the Christian desire to reach to the heavens by adding height and light to the Romanesque church style. The cathedral, like those at Chartres and elsewhere, reflects the essence of medieval western Europe—the power and unity of the Christian church, the centrality of Christian spirituality to everyday life, the quest for beauty in perilous times, and the ability of even feudal societies to mount massive projects requiring complex human interaction.*

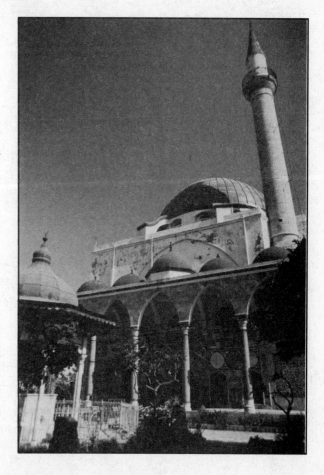

The Ahmed El-Jazzar Mosque in Akko (on the Mediterranean coast). *A mosque is the Muslim equivalent of a Christian church, a Jewish temple, or a Buddhist pagoda or stupa. It is the church of Islam. Its architectural style reflects the influence of the Romans and Christians as well as the Muslims. A mosque, which uses the dome of the Byzantine Christian style of church, is usually surrounded by a rectangular courtyard in the Roman style containing a fountain for ritual ablutions (religious rites of washing) as well as a minaret or lofty tower that is not unlike Christian bell towers. From the minaret an official, the muezzin, summons the faithful to prayer.*

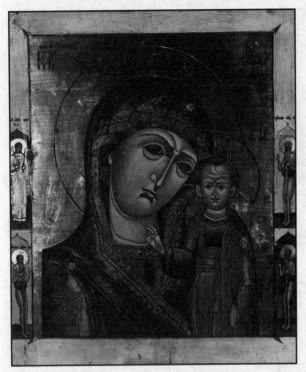

Icon. *An icon is an image or representation in painting, bas-relief, or mosaic of God, Jesus, the Virgin, or a saint venerated in Christian religious devotion. Since the third century, the Church allowed people to venerate icons. They later became a matter of controversy that provoked violent conflict. When their removal was ordered by the iconoclastic emperor in 730 C.E., the Byzantine Church split and the Roman papacy severed relations. In 843 icons were restored in the Eastern Orthodox Church, and the art form was carried into Russia where it reached its height. Andrew Rublev (ca. 1370–1430) of the Russian Novgorodian School of icon painting is the most celebrated icon painter of all time. This Russian icon is an eighteenth-century tempera on wood depicting the Madonna and Child with Saints. The entire area behind the figures is gold, as are the thin lines accentuating the contours of the garments and the jewels around the neckline. Islamic influence can be seen on the borders in the pointed architectural canope over the heads of the saints. The static stylized figures and penetrating glances evoke the passion of death and the eternity of life after death.*

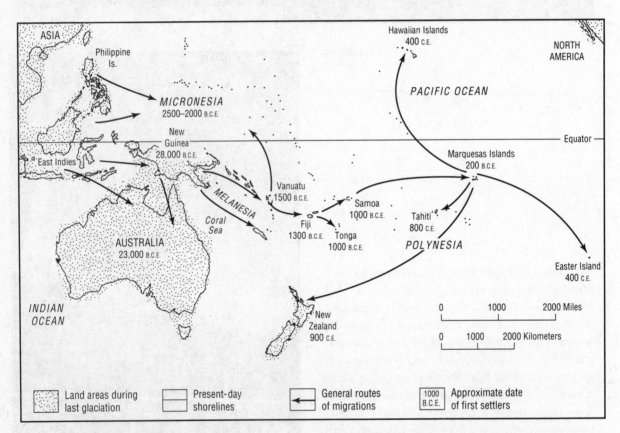

The Spread of Polynesian Culture 2500 B.C.E.***–900*** C.E. *The greatest migration in world history was the Polynesian maritime migration, which took place across the vast distances of the Pacific Ocean, one-third of the globe.*

Angkor Wat. *The great artistic achievement of the Khmer Empire of Kampuchea (Cambodia) 802–1219 C.E. was the planning and building of Angkor Wat, the enormous and lavishly decorated temple complex that spreads over 40 square miles. While the temple is designed to replicate Hindu cosmology and honors the Hindu god Vishnu, the style (as in the cone domes, for instance) and decoration reflects much Buddhist influence as well. It is the outward expression of the Hindu-Buddhist synthesis that can be found in much of Southeast Asia.*

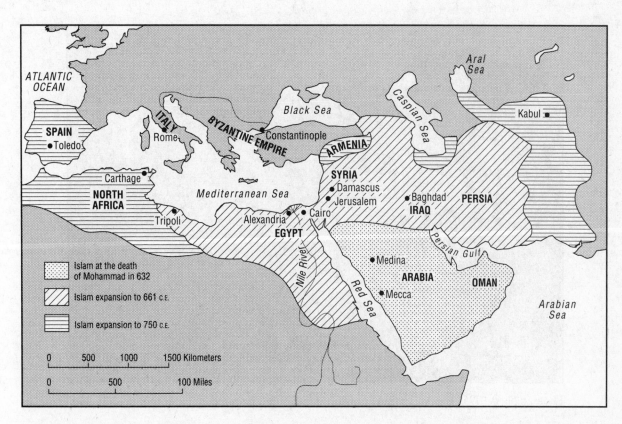

The Spread of Islam 632–750 C.E. *In a little more than a century, Islam spread across North Africa and into Spain, throughout Southwest Asia, and as far east as China. Soon after Islamic traders crossed the Sahara into Africa and controlled the Indian Ocean trade as far east as Indonesia.*

The Post Classical World ca. 900 C.E. *By 900* C.E. *all the great classical states of Eurasia had fallen and the Maya empire in the Americas was coming to an end. This political fragmentation made it easier for the Mongols to sweep across Eurasia and for the Toltec to sweep across Mesoamerica.*

Hokusai **The Tatsuta River in Autumn.** *In this woodblock print by Katsushika Hokusai (1760–1849), three couples are crossing the Tatsuta River in autumn. The subjects of these prints, known as ukiyo-e, are common, ordinary people. This print illustrates a poem written by a ninth-century Japanese poet. It celebrates the beauty of the blue Tatsuta waves that carry the red, star-shaped maple leaves of fall.*

Mansa Musa Map. *This important map depicts the pilgrimage to Mecca and fantastic wealth of the famous ruler of Mali, Mansu Musa (r. 1312–1337). Mansa Musa is holding a gold nugget as he barters with an Arab trader. The journey across the Sahara took over a year. The king assembled over 60,000 people to guard and serve the mansa and his household. Each of the 500 slaves carried heavy gold bars. When he returned, Mansa Musa brought a Muslim architect to design new mosques and palaces. This map, drawn in 1375, was the first European map of western Africa. When news of Mansa Musa's extraordinary wealth spread across the Mediterranean Sea to Europe, a Spanish mapmaker drew a map of a then "unknown continent," for the first time showing Europeans where western Africa was located.*

Japanese Rock Garden at Ryoan-Ji. *The Ryoan-ji Temple in Kyoto, Japan was founded in 1450 by a powerful feudal lord, Katsumoto Kosokawa. The rock garden has no plants and is simply an arrangement of five rocks on snow white grit. The arrangement of the rocks has many meanings. For some, the rocks represent a tiger taking its cub from one island to another. Others say the rocks show the Five Temples of the Zen Sect of Buddhism in China. Visitors are instructed to "Please sit down quietly and try to talk with the rock garden. The gardener shows us the philosophy of the Zen Buddhism by means of only rock and grit." Someone said, "Zen is the religion without any god or Buddha, it is a religion to read one's own heart and mind." The rock garden reflects the Japanese love of nature and the power of nature to invoke for the samurai the calm and peace that is necessary to face death.*

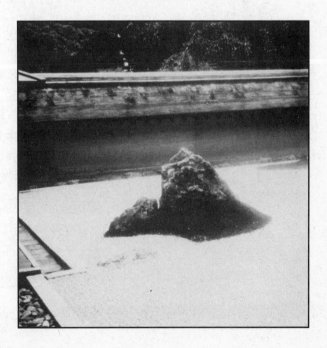

UNIT
V

EMERGENCE OF A GLOBAL AGE
(1200 C.E.–1600 C.E.)

CHAPTER 15

The Eurasian Highway

CHRONOLOGY	Mongol Empire (1206–1259)	Delhi Sultanate (1206–1526)	Ottoman Empire (1299–1918)
	Yuan Dynasty (1271–1368)	Mughal Empire (1526–1858)	Crusades (1071–1270)
	Muscovy (1463–1533)	Safavid Persia (1501–1736)	Black Plague (1348–1350)
	Time of Troubles (1598–1613)		

TERMS	pastoral nomadism	Sudebnik	Peacock Throne
	Shamanism	serfdom	Taj Mahal
	tumen	boyar	gazi
	horde	lamissaries	Battle of Mohacs
	Pax Mongolica	Urdu	Battle of Lepanto
	kamikaze	Bhakti	trimars
	Golden Horde	gunpowder empire	devshirme
	Battle of Kulikovo	syncretic	harem
	autocracy	diwan	Battle of Manzikert
	Russian Orthodox Church	mansabdars	indulgence
	czar	Red Fort	Crusader states

PEOPLE	Khan	Tamerlane	Mustafa Naima
	Temujin (Genghiz Khan)	Babur	janissaries
	Ogedei	Akbar	pasha
	Batu Khan	Aurangzeb	vizir
	Monke	shah	Pasha Sinan
	Hulagu	Ismail	Pope Urban II
	Mamluk	Shah Abbas	Saladin
	Kublai Khan	Seljuk Turk	Moors
	Hung We	sultan	el Cid
	Tartars	Osman	Teutonic Knights
	Ivan III (Great)	Mehmed II	heretics
	Ivan IV (Terrible)	Suleiman the Magnificent	Marco Polo

PLACES	Mongolia	Sarai	Chaldiran
	Khwarizm	Samarkand	Isfahan
	Karakorum	Delhi	

From 1200 to 1475 the world was on the threshold of a Global Age when all the continents would be linked. The Mongols played a vital part in setting the stage for this. As they swept across Asia, they reopened the highway along which passed to Europe Asian technology that was vital to the Atlantic voyages and that awakened in Europeans a taste for East Asian goods. The Mongols also preoccupied the states of Asia with their presence, leaving Europe free to transform itself in a way that prepared it for these new adventures, a way that became a precursor of the modern age.

CHAPTER 15

The Eurasian Highway

THE RISE OF THE MONGOLS

Pastoral Nomadism

The Mongols were classic pastoral nomads whose lifestyles had evolved, along with that of the agriculturalists, into well-defined forms. **Pastoral nomadism** probably originated when people with herds were driven from the fertile valleys of civilization. It was widely distributed across Eurasia about 800 B.C.E., displacing hunter-gatherers. The pastoral lifestyle was nomadic because herdsmen followed their flocks. Indo-European and Turkic-speaking peoples dominated the Eurasian steppes as horse nomads, but some people followed reindeer herds, others, as in Arabia, followed camels. In East and South Africa cattle were herded, and in the Andean Americas herders followed llama and alpaca. The land over which the pastoralists roamed was climatically harsh, marginally productive, and vulnerable to droughts and wind. The relationship between nomadic cultures and settled societies was mostly symbiotic, the nomads trading animals for foodstuffs. When civilizations became disordered, so too were the nomads. Nomads often became the carriers of long-distance trade. However, during times of population increase and land hunger, nomads often raided settled areas and then either retreated or settled down and became absorbed into civilization.

Competition for land between nomadic societies bred a military culture where courage, physical strength, and the ability to forge a personal following led to leadership in societies that had no clearly established rules for succession. In the Asian steppes, rulers were often called **khans**. By the time of the Mongols, the Eurasian steppe people had adopted the horse stirrup, bow, and bridle. As horse archers, they were formidable cavalrymen and guerrilla fighters able to live off the land and cover vast distances. Social stratification was less complex and more egalitarian than among settled societies. The classes were usually divided between an aristocratic upper leadership class and common people. Women acted as shamans, settled questions of succession, and even could become warriors. The tribe and clan were the basic social and political structures. Art and culture was connected with animals and most was carried or worn, as for example in bridles, saddles, tent tapestries, and ornate weaponry. The **Shamanist** religion, found in Central Asia, Siberia, Korea, and Japan, predominated among nomads in Central Asia. It is based on the belief that certain people (shamans) could serve as intermediaries between humans and deities. Since nomads were basically illiterate, their image has been shaped by writers in civilized societies who have tended to see them as "barbarian" (uncivilized) and cruel. This should not obscure the fact that in world history pastoral nomads have provided an essential role as herders, mercenaries, empire builders, long-distance traders, and agents of change.

The Mongols were one of many Eurasian steppe nomad groups who had attacked settled populations through the ages. So constant were the nomadic attacks on the northern Chinese frontiers that the Qin (Ch'in) dynasty had constructed the Great Wall. Elsewhere, the Middle Egyptian kingdom had fallen to the Hyksos, Rome to Germanic tribes, and Gupta India to the Huns. The Mongol attacks became important in world history because of their breadth, the amount of change they elicited, and because they were the last of the great Eurasian steppe movements. From then on, the settled way of life became predominant and pastoralism limited to small and isolated areas.

Genghiz Khan

Periodically, a leader of unusual ability would be able to unite a number of tribes. Such was **Temujin** (1162–1227), who later became known as **Genghiz Khan**, "Prince of all between the Oceans." Temujin was born around 1167 C.E. in **Mongolia**, north of China. He was the son of the Mongkhal tribe from which the Mongols got their name. The Great Khan set out to conquer the sedentary societies and his avowed aim was to conquer the world. He began with China, which was vulnerable due to its division between the Chin with their capital at Beijing (Peking) in the north, and the Song (Sung) with their capital at Hangzhou in the south. In 1215 Beijing (Peking) fell, after which Genghiz turned west where he attacked the Islamic state of **Khwarizm** (between the Caspian Sea and Pamir Mountains). In 1220 he razed the city of Bukhara, slaughtering 30,000 of its defenders including women and children. In a sermon to the surviving population he said, "Oh people, know that you have committed great sins. . . If you ask me what proof I have. . . I say it is because I am the punishment of God." He returned and invaded China again in 1226 and died the next year.

Genghiz Khan ranks as one of the great empire builders of world history. In fact his was the largest empire in world history. In 20 years he extended rule from the Pacific Ocean to the Caspian Sea, and he died undefeated. Such conquest was possible for many reasons. Genghiz Khan forged the loyalty of different ethnic clans and tribes of steppe nomads such as the Turks into a well led fighting force by disregarding family ties or social rank. The Mongol war machine was well organized. The army was made up of fighting units called **tumens** consisting of 10,000 cavalrymen. These were divided into 1000, 100, and 10 units with commanders at each level responsible for discipline and training. Commanders were personally chosen by Genghiz Khan and promoted based on their ability. Lightly equipped, fast moving, and agile, the army could cover 200 miles a day and hit an enemy from 400 yards. They intimidated many into surrender. Heads of their enemies were used to build columns as gruesome beacons to warn of further attacks. They were masters of deception, feigning attack in order to draw the enemy in closer and putting dummy soldiers on horseback to make the size of the army appear larger. As one chronicler wrote, "Detachment after detachment arrived, each like a billowing sea." Once conquered, Genghiz Khan took keen interest in the arts and learning of the new subjects of his empire, but he continued to live in the steppes, establishing a new capital at **Karakorum**, south of Lake Baikal. He consulted Confucian scholars on how to rule China, Muslim engineers on how to improve trade, and he welcomed Muslim mullahs, Buddhist and Taoist monks, and Christian missionaries. All religions were tolerated, a script was devised for the Mongol language, and a law code put an end to tribal squabbles. In this way, cultural diffusion and exchange were nourished.

The Mongol Empire

After Genghiz's death, his third son **Ogedei** was elected Great Khan. During his reign, the Mongol attack was extended against China, Persia, and Europe. In 1234 Ogedei overthrew the Northern Song (Sung) Dynasty of China and in 1237–1240, **Batu Khan**, a grandson of

Genghiz's, launched the only successful winter attack on Russia, laying waste to the Kievan Confederation. Then Batu Khan proceeded into eastern Europe, nearly reaching Vienna and the Adriatic. Had the Mongols continued westward, the entire history of the European continent might have been different. As it was, disputes over succession after the death of Ogedei in 1241 caused Batu Khan to return to Mongolia. Eventually, Ogedei's nephew **Monke** was elected the Great Khan and he undertook a campaign against the Song (Sung) Empire in southern China. Meanwhile, Monke's younger brother, **Hulagu**, struck a decisive blow against the Islamic world by capturing Baghdad in 1253. Much of the world cultural heritage of five centuries, which had been accumulated by the Muslims, was thereby destroyed. Just as Ogedei's death in 1241 had saved Europe, Monke's death in 1259 saved the Muslim world. Rival claimants for succession caused Hulagu to withdraw leaving a remnant force. The Muslims rallied under the leadership of the Egyptian **Mamluk** sultans and in 1259, near Nazareth, defeated the Mongols. This defeat shattered the spell of Mongol invincibility and stopped the Mongol spread west. The death of Monke ended the unity of the Mongol Empire. From then on, the empire was divided into "**hordes**" and ruled independently. The younger brother of Monke, **Kublai Khan**, though proclaimed the fifth Great Khan, had direct authority only over China, which fell under his control in the 1270s. Descendants of Hulagu ruled Persia, Batu Khan Russia, and Chagatai, the Mongol heartland.

Because the illiterate Mongols left no written record, it is through the eyes of others that these events have been chronicled. The Arab historian, Abn al-Athir, said he waited many years to record events too horrible to recall. The Great Chronicler of Europe, Matthew Paris said, "Mongols are inhuman, beastly, rather monsters than men. . ." Papal legate, Plano Carpini, who crossed into southern Russia in 1245–1246, wrote that "they besieged Kiev. . . barely two hundred houses stand there, and those people are held in the harshest slavery." By contrast, Marco Polo, a Venetian merchant who spent 17 years at the court of Kublai Khan, described the Mongol

rule of China as brilliant, especially as reflected in the bustling trade and wealth of Hangzhou. The variation in viewpoint can be seen in the differences in impact left on each society.

Pax Mongolica

As a whole, the Mongols destroyed, but they also built new empires, reopened the land and maritime highways from east to west and established an imperial peace, the **Pax Mongolica**. As one Muslim historian wrote, the peoples of the khanate "enjoy such peace that a man might have journeyed from the land of sunrise to the land of sunset with a golden platter upon his head without suffering the least violence from anyone." This peace allowed the spread not just of goods, but of foodstuffs like sugar and citrus fruits, inventions like printing, gunpowder, windmills, and papermaking, as well as disease. The Europeans especially seemed to have benefited. From the 1240s on, European churchmen were allowed to travel eastward and the pope appointed a succession of archbishops to Beijing (Peking) to minister to the growing flock of believers. European merchants, chiefly from Genoa and Venice, also moved east in search of the goods they had formerly purchased in Southwest Asia (often called the Levant during this period). The total number of European merchants who traveled to Asia must have been substantial for detailed guidebooks were prepared to help with the journey. The most comprehensive was written in 1340 by Francesco Balducchi Pegolotti, manager of a Cyprus branch of a large Italian banking firm. He gave merchants invaluable insights into routes and where in convoy they "would be as safe as if they were in their own home." Better known were the reports of Marco Polo (ca. 1254–1324), the Venetian merchant who left a detailed account of life at the court of Kublai Khan.

As a rule, the Mongols had less impact the more advanced the society they attacked, as for example in China and the Muslim world where they eventually became absorbed. Mongol conquests and empires represented the most formidable but last of the Asian nomadic challenges to the growing global dominance of the sedentary people of the civilized world. This was due to ever diminishing amounts of land available to them, to the Black Plague (see page 177), to the considerable numeric disadvantage of the nomadic peoples, and to the increasing ability of settled populations to defend themselves once gunpowder empires won control of Eurasia.

THE COMPARATIVE MONGOL IMPACT ON CHINA (YUAN), KOREA, JAPAN, RUSSIA (MOSCOVY), INDIA (DELHI AND MUGHAL), PERSIA (SAFAVID), AND SOUTHWEST ASIA (OTTOMAN TURKS)

China (Yuan)

In 1279 Genghiz Khan's grandson, Kublai Khan (1216–1294) crushed the Southern Song (Sung), proclaimed himself emperor, and in the Chinese tradition founded the Yuan Dynasty (1271–1368). Heeding the words of Genghiz Khan's advisers that "the empire was won on horseback but it will not be governed on horseback," Kublai Khan set about finding a method of rule acceptable to the Chinese but keeping him in control. Distrusting the mandarin class, but needing their expertise and system, Kublai Khan assigned foreigners to the highest administrative posts, allowing Chinese scholars to serve in lower posts. He disarmed the Chinese and forbade them to assemble in large numbers. He divided society into four classes with varying rights and privileges. At the top were Mongols and their Asian allies (mostly Muslim), below them the north Chinese who were more compliant, then the ethnic Chinese, and finally minority peoples of the south. Some Mongol women made a considerable impact as for example Kublai's wife, Chaki, who promoted the interests of Buddhists and pleaded for lenient treatment of prisoners, but the position of common Chinese women improved little. The capital was established at Beijing (Peking) nearer the Mongol homeland.

The Mongol Impact on China

Despite efforts to remain aloof, the Mongols ultimately became Sinified. With 90 million Chinese armed with a venerable cultural tradition, and a few hundred thousand Mongols, this was inevitable. Kublai's capital was laid out in Chinese pattern and decorated with Chinese buildings. Kublai Khan gave his son a Confucian education. He also patronized Muslim scholars. Persian astronomers corrected the Chinese calendar, made accurate maps, and ran hospitals. In this way, the richness of the Muslim world was spread across Asia. Despite Kublai's efforts at enlightened rule, dissatisfaction grew. Many Mongols were alienated because they wanted to preserve Mongol separateness. The Chinese scholar-gentry regarded the Mongols as uncouth barbarians and were threatened by the disappearance of the examination route to administrative office. The Chinese upper class was also threatened by the growing influence of the artisan and merchant classes that Kublai supported. To aid commerce, the Mongols expanded the money supply, and, surprisingly for a landed people, built a war fleet that helped to cut down on privateering. Toward the end of his reign, Kublai Khan began to support overseas expeditions and explorations from southern China west. The peasants also became dissatisfied. Though Kublai Khan restored the granary system for famine relief, reduced peasant taxes and labor demand, and formulated revolutionary plans for educating the peasantry, he also organized peasants into 50-unit cooperatives supervised by state officials that was unpopular.

In the last years of Kublai's long nine-decade reign, his lifestyle became dissolute. This was followed by excesses by other state officials and later rulers. By the 1350s, banditry and privateering escalated, famines hit, and secret societies dedicated to Mongol overthrow proliferated. In 1351 C.E. the rebels struck a decisive blow. Led by a peasant monk, **Hung Wu** and his followers drove the Mongols out of China and established the Ming dynasty (1368–1644).

Korea

The Mongol attack shaped Korea too. Korea, whose civilization grew up in the shadows of China and its tributary system, and had been particularly affected by Chinese Buddhism, was a land of aristocratic rule rather than bureaucratic rule as in China. Periodically, quarrels between aristocratic households and protests by the common people broke out. Then, after a century of conflict triggered by the Mongol invasion in 1231, the Koryo regime (918–1392) collapsed and the Choson or Yi dynasty was established in Korea, ruling until 1910. In this obtuse way, a stronger centralized state was established, much as happened in Japan.

Japan

Even before establishing the Yuan dynasty in China in 1271, Kublai Khan sent a message to Japanese leaders demanding submission. When Japan refused, Kublai Khan, with 15,000 soldiers and 900 ships, attacked Japan in 1274. After one day, storms overtook the fleet and the Mongols withdrew. To protect themselves, the Japanese built a wall around the harbor and prayed to the gods. They were not safe for long. On June 23, 1281, Kublai Khan launched another invasion, this time with 4400 ships, 142,000 disciplined men, and sophisticated weapons including arrows, gunpowder, and projectiles. On August 1, yet another typhoon, the **kamikaze**, or divine wind, hit, destroying all but 200 of the Mongol ships and saving Japan. In this way, the myth of the "divine wind" was born and subsequently revived during World War II when American invasion threatened. There were other indirect effects of the Mongol invasion on Japan as well. The attack weakened the Kamakura Shogunate because no booty was found among the wreckage of Mongol ships. This made it impossible to pay off samurai warriors who were already growing impoverished due to their growing numbers. Soon the Kamakura were deposed, replaced by the Ashikaga Shogunate. Not until 1600 was a centralized state under the Tokugawa established. Isolationist attitudes toward the outside world also grew as a result of the Mongol experience.

Russia (Muscovy)

Compared to China, Russia was poorer, had fewer established traditions and was more vulnerable to social and political destruction and change. For these reasons, the Mongol attack on Russia had a greater impact than it did on China.

Out of the ashes of the Kievan city-state system destroyed by the Mongols grew the autocratic patterns of czarist Russia. The Mongols, **Tartars** as they are called in Russian sources (Tartar referred originally to the Mongol tribe, later to the Mongol-Turkic mix, many of whom had converted to Islam), suddenly came upon Russia. They appeared in 1223 in southeastern Russia, smashing the Russians and their rivals the Polovtsy and then disappearing into the steppe. They returned in 1237–1240 to impose their 200-year rule called the "Tartar Yoke." Many Russians fled north into the forest regions around Moscow, in this way settling new parts of Russia. Around Novgorod, the princes instituted a policy of cooperation with the Mongols because they were at the same time engaged with the Swedes and Germans. Once victory had been achieved, Batu Khan organized peasants into collectives of 100 for census and tax purposes. Then he withdrew from his domain called the **Golden Horde** and established his headquarters far to the south at **Sarai** on the lower Volga. From there, he ruled indirectly through the Russian princes. Most Russian upper classes submitted to Mongol rule as a way to protect their status. Even so, this class was decimated by battle and intermarriage with Mongols. Many Tartar names can be found within the Russian noble ranks from this point forward. The princes that served the Khan had to journey to the Mongol headquarters and pay humble obeisance, hand over the tribute they had collected from the Russian people on behalf of the Khan, and send military detachments on demand. Otherwise, the Mongols interfered little in Russian life.

Growth of Autocracy

The Russian princes who served as intermediaries of the Khan became virtual autocrats (rulers with unlimited authority) over the Russian people. Gradually, one prince, the prince of Moscow, became stronger than the other princes of Russia. This was due to a number of factors, among them long life, the tradition of primogeniture that helped keep their holdings intact, and successful marriage and alliances allowing them to enlarge their territory and power. In 1328 Moscow prince

Ivan I, or Kalita, meaning "Moneybags," received the position of Grand Prince, a commission that allowed him to gather tribute from the other princes for the Khan. He used his increasing revenue to purchase more land. In 1328 he persuaded the Metropolitan of the Eastern Orthodox Church to move its headquarters from Kiev to Moscow, further strengthening the power of Moscow and its prince. The Mongols suffered their first defeat at the hands of Moscow in 1380 at the **Battle of Kulikovo** on the Don River. Under the leadership of Prince Dmitri "Donskoy," the Russians laid to rest the belief in Mongol invincibility. In 1395 Tamerlane invaded Russia and in 1408 the Golden Horde launched a major assault on Moscow to punish the prince for not paying tribute. In neither assault was Moscow captured, lending even more credence to the belief in the liberation powers of the Moscow princedom. From then on, the Mongols slowly lost power in Russia and the Moscow princes to whom all Russians now looked for leadership assumed the position formerly held by the Khan as overlord. During the reign of **Ivan III** or Great (1462–1505), Moscow declared Russian independence from the Mongols.

Two other events made the Moscow princes autocrats rather than rulers. (**Autocracy** refers to power above and beyond political power, that is, power over the church and any other national institutions.) The first was the creation of a state church. In 1453, when the Byzantine Empire fell to the Ottoman Turks, the Russian Church became independent of the Eastern Orthodox Church in Constantinople, creating the **Russian Orthodox Church** with its own patriarch or pope, independent of any power but that of the prince. Soon Moscow was considered the "Third Rome." According to this doctrine, the first Rome in Italy was destroyed by the Germans, and the second in Constantinople by the Turks. This left Russia as the true repository of the Christian faith. The second event was the reincorporation of the former Kievan territories into the new Moscow state. By claiming not just former territory but the former Russian heritage, Ivan III assumed the title of **czar**, or Caesar, Sovereign of all the Russias, and autocrat. Whereas autocrat originally referred to independence from the Mongols, it soon came to be synonymous with czar. To implement such authority, Ivan the Great promulgated a **Sudebnik**, or code of laws. Because all Moscow princes claimed descent from Rurik, the founder of the Russian line of princes, legitimacy for power rested not just on military power, achievement, and the church, but on blood lines as well.

The Mongol Impact on Russia

The attack and subsequent indirect Mongol rule of Russia had a great impact on Russia's history. The destruction and heavy tribute set Russia back economically for centuries, keeping it isolated and prevented participation in the European Renaissance. It brought the Russian princes to power, and because they were essentially liberated khans, they had autocratic power over their Russian subjects. Yet, Russian autocracy cannot be entirely laid at the lap of the Mongols. It was the Russians themselves who made the church subservient to the state and institutionalized **serfdom** (the tying of the peasants to the land). Serfdom began during the reign of **Ivan IV** or Terrible (1533–1584), when the independent land-owning class, the **boyars**, were purged and replaced by a dependent and politically loyal class of landed gentry. Then dynastic legitimacy was put in question when Ivan IV left no heir. He had killed his first son, his second died, and his third had disappeared mysteriously. This crisis led to civil war and Polish invasion, a time period in Russian history known as the **Time of Troubles** (1598–1613). During these years of turmoil, the population was in flight, leaving land barren and people short of food. This led to the passage of the so-called *forbidden years* laws forbidding peasants from leaving their land. These laws were never rescinded and so serfdom became institutionalized. In theories of Russian autocratic statecraft, the czar served God, the nobility served the czar, and the people served the nobility.

Summary

Thus, the Mongols absorbed little of Russian culture (as they did in China) and contributed little of their own culture to Russia (as they did in Southwest Asia where they were carriers of Islam). Through their destructive actions and their indirect rule of Russia, they paved the way for serfdom and autocracy.

India (Delhi and Mughal)

After the end of the Indian classical age (480 c.e.), India experienced wave after wave of foreign invasions. First came the Arab Muslims, then the Turkish Muslims, and finally the Mongol Muslims. The major result of these invasions was the importation of Islam, which, due to the ferocity of its entrance, left a history of religious division that has bloodied the pages of Indian history to this day. In 711 the first and least lasting Muslim intrusion came to India when the Arab Umayyad rulers invaded and later annexed territory in western India (Sind). Cultural interaction resulted and was particularly enriching to Islamic scholars who learned Indian math (Arabic numerals), medicine, and astronomy. The second wave came in 1192 when Turkish Muslims from Afghanistan captured **Delhi** and extended control across northern India. Hindu and Buddhist statues, shrines, and temples were destroyed along the way. Many Buddhists took refuge in Tibet establishing the fine Buddhist **lamsaries** (monasteries) that are so characteristic of the country. In 1206 Qutb-ud-din established a Muslim kingdom in northern India, the **Delhi Sultanate** (1206–1526). Because the Muslims were a minority, Turks and Persians (Iranians) were recruited to run the government. Many of the recruits themselves were Muslim refugees fleeing Mongol devastation of Iran and Southwest Asia. Under the Sultanate, Persian influences deeply affected Hindu art and architecture, especially the introduction of the minaret, arch, and dome. The most stunning effect was the evolution of a new language, **Urdu**, which is a mixture of Persian, Arabic, and Hindi. It is the official language of Pakistan today. While Muslim and Hindu cultural exchange occurred, political, social, and religious separation caused tension. Most Indians looked at the invaders as a new ruling caste capable of taxing and ruling but otherwise irrelevant to their lives. A renaissance of pious devotional

Hinduism or **Bhakti** of the Gupta Brahmans, which emphasized reverence and worship of the gods, captured the religious lives of the people.

Tensions between Muslims and Hindus were based on a number of factors; for example, the Muslim belief in one God was at odds with the Hindu belief in many gods. The Muslim subscription to the idea of social and religious equality ran counter to the Hindu belief in castes. The Muslim belief that the cow was just another source of food conflicted with the Hindu view that it was sacred. Finally, tensions grew between Muslim rulers and Hindu subjects. Unlike Buddhism, which was eventually folded into Hinduism, Islam remained aloof and connected in the Hindu mind with foreign invasion and rule.

Tamerlane

The Mongol period of Indian history begins with the invasion of Tamerlane (Timur) in 1398. By this time the Mongols had intermarried with the Turkish steppe people and many had become Muslim. **Tamerlane** claimed descent from the Mongol Jagatai Khanate (Genghiz Khan's second son), Lord of Central Asia, Iran, and Southwest Asia. From his capital in **Samarkand**, Tamerlane conquered Persia, the Fertile Crescent, and southern Russia. Then he invaded India for booty, and when he had finished his campaign of destruction, he retreated to Samarkand leaving India again politically divided. In this way, Islam was once again swept into India, but in a more hostile way even than during the previous Delhi Sultanate.

The Mughal Empire

Almost a century later, in 1526, **Babur**, who claimed descent from Tamerlane and Genghiz Khan, invaded and established the Mughal Empire (1526–1858). Babur seems to have been driven by the fact that he had lost his original kingdom in central Asia. Though he was outnumbered ten to one, he prevailed, among other reasons because he frightened hundreds of Indian war elephants that trampled warriors sending them into flight. Victory was also due to the employment of guns and movable artillery, weapons that were to prove decisive in battle everywhere on the globe from 1450 to 1800. Those who had guns, like the Muscovite czars, Mughal Indians, Ottoman Turks, Ming Chinese, Tokugawa Japanese, and Spanish, created so-called "**gunpowder empires**." The Mongols were indirectly responsible for this turn of events, for it was along the reopened Silk Road that Chinese technology moved to the West where the Byzantines, Europeans, and steppe people began to devise siege weapons and guns, bringing down castle defenses.

Akbar

Babur was not just a conqueror, but a man of cultivated taste for the arts. He wrote one of the great histories of India, but he was an ineffective administrator and squandered his opportunity to create a politically cohesive Indian state. That was left to his grandson, **Akbar** (1556–1605) who may have been one of India's greatest rulers. Not only was Akbar an able military commander who assembled an empire including Afghanistan, Pakistan, Bangladesh, and all of present-day India north of the Godavari River, he also had a state vision. He staffed an administrative bureaucracy with Muslims and non-Muslims. He brought order to finances by creating a **diwan**, or bureau of finance, to mint money and create budgetary and tax procedures. He appointed 800 **mansabdars**, or imperial officials, who performed military, judicial, and financial functions at the local level. He left intact, however, life in the village communities. He is most famous for his policies of religious toleration, especially toward Hindus. He ended the pilgrimage tax, twice married Hindu princesses, and allowed Hindus to serve in the army and administration. However, the refusal of many Hindus to serve and learn Urdu hampered his efforts. Though Akbar considered himself a devout orthodox Muslim, he invited Jains, Hindus, Jesuits, and Zoroastrians to join Muslim ulema in theological debates. The outcome was a **syncretic** religion (a religion that reconciles different views), called the Din-i-Ilahi or "divine discipline."

Historians are divided on whether Akbar's motives as a philosopher-king were theological or political. Regardless, the new religion of synthesis satisfied neither side and social divisions remained. Akbar was also a patron of the arts, supporting painters of the Indo-Persian style and leaving a library of 24,000 books. The birth of his son, Jahangir, prompted the building of a new capital city (1569), Fatehpur-Sikri. The city included an imperial palace, a mosque, lavish gardens, thousands of houses for ordinary people, and a blend of Hindu architecture (flat stone beams and ornate decoration) and Muslim architecture (domes, arches, and courts.)

The Mughal Impact

It was under the reign of Akbar's grandson, Shah Jahan (r. 1628–1658) that the legacy of the Mughals is most outwardly apparent. The Mongols who had swept Islam into India found the greatest expression of Hindu-Islamic synthesis in the artistic and architectural expression of Shah Jahan's reign. After subduing Muslim revolts and Portuguese resistance in Bengal, Shah Jahan reasserted Mughal control in the Deccan Plateau. He then proceeded to build a new capital city at Delhi, a city that became one of the great cities of the Muslim world, boasting fine boulevards and beautiful mosques. He built the **Red Fort**, named for its red sandstone walls, which housed the imperial palace, administrative treasury, and arsenal, and the Hall of Public Audience, a room of restrained elegance to which only the most privileged came. Inscribed on the walls were the words, "If there is paradise on earth, It is here. It is here. It is here." Shah Jahan also ordered construction of the **Peacock Throne**, which was encrusted with emeralds, diamonds, pearls, and rubies. (In 1739 it was carried off to Persia.) But the most enduring monument was the **Taj Mahal**, a building of such sublime beauty it inspires world admiration. A garden tomb that employed 20,000 workers and took 18 years to build, it was built in memorial for his beloved wife, Mumtaz Mahal, who died giving birth to their fifteenth child. The tomb, of the purest white marble, sits on a vast platform of sandstone and marble overlooking the river

Jumna. The Persian dome, seen in a frame of four soaring minarets, seems to float, especially by moonlight when the white marble exudes a soft blue cast. Shah Jahan intended to build himself a companion tomb in black marble on the opposite bank, but one of his sons, **Aurangzeb**, executed the eldest brother and locked Shah Jahan away until his death.

Aurangzeb's reign was one of religious reaction. He enforced Muslim laws against gambling and drink, forbade Hindu practices like satee, reimposed the tax on non-Muslims, and ordered destruction of some Hindu temples. His expansionist exploits depleted the treasury and brought opposition not just from Hindus, but from other groups as well. From then on, India was again politically vulnerable, open to outside attack, as by the Persians in 1739 and later by the British. The power of the rajes, Brahmans, and caste reasserted itself. British and Portuguese merchants trickled in. The delicate Muslim-Hindu religious synthesis nurtured by early Mughal rulers unraveled, and the dark side of the Mongol impact, religious tension, and political decentralization reemerged.

Persia (Safavid)

When the Mongols invaded India, it was already a weakened and decentralized state. When they invaded Persia, however, the Golden Age of Islam under the Abbasid Caliphate was at its height. The great Mongol invasions of the early thirteenth century and Tamerlane's attack at the end of the fourteenth century, made a shambles of the Muslim world. The result was threefold: first, the conversion of the Mongol nomads and their absorption into Islamic society; second, the growth in power of militant Turkish nomads; and third, the creation of new Islamic empires like the Mughals, Safavids, and Ottomans, which possessed gunpowder and cannons.

Rise of the Safavids

The conquest of the Islamic heartlands had begun under Genghiz Khan's grandson, Hulagu. In 1258 he destroyed Baghdad and murdered the Abbasid caliph and some 800,000 people who resisted. The result was that the Muslim world was left without central authority and its military strength severely eroded. Throughout the fourteenth and fifteenth centuries, rival nomadic groups, infused with Turkish warriors, fought for control of the area. Amidst the chaos, two powerful families emerged, the Ottomans in Turkey and the Safavids in Persia. The Safi al-Din family, which gave the Safavid dynasty its name, gained power, launching a militant campaign to purify and reform Islam and to spread the religion among the Mongol-Turkic tribes of the area. As they began to preach Shi'ite doctrines, Sunni enemies battled back until 1501, when a Safavid commander, **Ismail**, won a string of victories and proclaimed himself **shah** or emperor. Then, in 1514 at **Chaldiran** in northwest Persia, Sunni Ottomans and Shi'ite Safavids battled it out. Ismail's cavalry proved no match for Ottoman musketeers and cannons. The Safavids were defeated, limiting the spread of Shiite Islam westward. The Ottomans, however, could not follow up with an assault, which could have ended the Safavids. The result was the emergence of two empires and two sects of Islam in Southwest Asia.

The strength of the Safavid state (1501–1736) begun by Ismail was due to several factors: the loyalty of nomadic tribesmen who were granted grazing lands especially on the Ottoman frontier; the skill of Persian bureaucrats; and Shi'ite Islam, which was proclaimed the official and compulsory religion of the new empire. Ismail's decision to make Shi'ite Islam the state religion when the majority of the people were Sunni proved crucial to the future of Persia (Iran) and Southwest Asia. It provided the ideological and institutional support for Safavid rulers. It melded with a tradition of ethnic religious kings established during the Achaemenid and Sassanid empires that had shaped the cultural and political identity of Persia. Safavid shahs claimed descent from one of the Shi'ite imams or successors to Ali, cousin and son-in-law to Muhammed. This gave rise to a theocratic state that, even to this day, distinguishes Iran.

Safavid power reached its height under **Shah Abbas** (1587–1629). Shah Abbas built a strong national army based on the Ottoman model using cannons and the engineering skills of an English adventurer, Sir Anthony Sherley. Besides military victories resulting in expansion to the Tigris River, Caspian Sea, and Afghanistan, he improved export trade by building up a cottage industry of carpet weaving and glazed building tiles. He also endowed the arts, much of which appeared in the new capital city of his empire, **Isfahan**. The city boasted a bustling bazaar, 162 mosques, 48 seminaries where ulema studied Muslim science, 273 public baths, a vast imperial palace, wide boulevards, and public parks and pools.

Despite political and religious rivalries that emerged between the Ottoman and Safavids, their social systems had much in common. Both were dominated in the earlier phase by soldier-aristocrats who later retreated to landed estates and had resplendent lifestyles. Here, life was increasingly difficult for the peasants on whom they depended. As expansion slowed, land scarcity squeezed both peasant and aristocrat until banditry and uprisings became common, undermining dynastic power and legitimacy. Women faced legal and social disadvantages though the influx of freer nomadic women during the Mongol assaults tempered this somewhat. Travelers to Isfahan often noted that women wore bright colors, made no effort to hide their faces, and were active in trade and money lending.

Summary

Shah Abbas was succeeded by inept rulers. The monarchy weakened, Shi'ite theologians seized power, and in the eighteenth century Turks, Afghans, and Russians invaded and divided power. Thus, the major impact of the Mongols on Persia was the rise of a new Islamic state dominated by the Shi'ite sect. The inability of either the Ottomans or the Safavids to reunite the Islamic world shattered by the Mongols continued the trend toward political fragmentation in Southwest Asia.

Southwest Asia (Ottomans)

In the mid-tenth century, even before the Mongol attack on Southwest Asia, mobile and militant **Seljuk Turks**, nomads originating in Turkestan

(central Asia), surged westward. They accepted Sunni Islam, swarmed over Persia learning Persian culture, and then pushed into the heart of the Abbasid Caliphate in Iraq and Syria. Baghdad fell to them in 1055 and the caliph became a puppet of the Turkish **sultan** (ruler, literally "he with authority"). The Turks did not control all of the Muslim world, however. By the middle of the eleventh century there were three Muslim centers of power—Cordoba in Spain, Cairo in Egypt, and Baghdad in Iraq. Into this politically divided but culturally united world in the early thirteenth century came the Mongols, crushing Baghdad (1258) and Damascus (1260). Mongol chief Hulagu tried to eradicate Muslim culture but a succession crisis made him return to Mongolia, leaving Egypt, Noth Africa, and Spain free of Mongol control. Hulagu's descendant, Ghazan, embraced Islam in 1295 and worked to revive Muslim culture in the area. Turks and Mongols intermingled with the cosmopolitan Muslim world of Arabs and Persians of the Abbasids. While the Mongols became absorbed by Muslim culture, the disruptions they wrought facilitated the rise of other warrior nomadic groups who could fill the political vacuum.

The Ottoman Turks

Such a group were the Turkish warriors from western Anatolia (Turkey), the Ottomans, who began expansionist moves under their leader **Osman** (r. 1299–1326). Because the Ottomans lived in the borderlands between Islam and Byzantine Christendom, the leader considered himself "border chief" of the **gazis**, or frontier fighters, in the jihad, or holy war. The Islamic religious jihad principle in Ottoman hands turned into a political and economic weapon of expansionism. To use it effectively, they had to move against Christians rather than the fractured Muslim world.

First Osman wrestled northwestern Anatolia from the Byzantines and then crossed over the Dardanelles near Gallipoli in 1352 into the Balkans. Alarmed Christians under the Holy Roman Hapsburg emperor Charles V met the Ottoman force on the Danube in 1396 and on the Black Sea in 1444, only to have their forces wiped out. After centuries of attack, Constantinople was now surrounded. In 1453 Sultan **Mehmed II** (r. 1451–1481) in a six-week siege breached the walls of the Byzantine capital and put a final end to the venerable 2000-year history of Rome. Western technology proved decisive in the battle. Christian Hungarians working for the Ottomans cast a huge bronze cannon on the spot. The cannon shattered a city-gate allowing Mehmed's 100,000 man army to enter and route the 10,000-man army, which defended the circular walls and stone fortifications that had made the city impregnable for 1000 years. On May 28, 1453, Mehmed the Conqueror rode into the city on his white horse. Zealots of Islam removed the cross from atop Hagia Sophia and soon the muezzin's chant rang from minarets. In 1454 the first dated work from Gutenberg's printing press warned Christian Europe of the Turkish peril.

The warning soon became reality. This battle only initiated the expansionist phase of Ottoman history. The Ottomans took control of the Adriatic. In 1480 an Ottoman fleet lay plans for the conquest of the Italian city-states that, if completed as was likely, due to the political instability of the city-state system, might have changed the history of Europe. As it was, Mehmed II died and his successor moved south instead into Syria, Palestine (1516), Egypt (1517) and North Africa. Under Suleiman (r. 1520–1566) the Ottomans reached their widest geographical limit. At the **Battle of Mohacs** (1526) he crushed the Hungarians, and three years later he besieged the Hapsburg capital of Vienna where he was finally stopped. In 1571, at the **Battle of Lepanto**, the Ottomans lost their bid to control the Mediterranean when their fleet was routed by a combined Spanish, Venetian, and Hapsburg force led by Charles V. Each case of Ottoman victory was due to distrust between enemies and superiority of Ottoman military organization and artillery.

Ottoman Rule

The reign of **Suleiman the Magnificent** (r. 1520–1566) brought the Ottoman Empire to its height. Not only did Ottoman expansionism reach its zenith, but the classic form of Ottoman social and administrative system was established. This was heavily influenced by military organization. According to Ottoman historian **Mustafa Naima**, Ottoman society was divided into producers of wealth, Muslim and non-Muslim, and the military. The state responsibility was to supply the justice necessary to produce wealth needed to support the military. The ruling class was all Muslim and mostly descendants of Turkish families related to the Ottomans. In return for bureaucratic service, this class received **trimars,** or landed estates, but only for their lifetime as the Sultan owned all the land and it reverted back to him upon death. For civil and military service, the sultan's agents rounded up boys between the ages of 12 and 20 from poor villages of the empire in a system known as **devshirme**. All were taken as slaves and converted to Islam, and the brightest 10 percent were trained to read and write Arabic, Ottoman Turkish, and Persian in preparation for civil service jobs. Others known as **janissaries** (Turkish for *recruits*) were prepared for military service. The system allowed social mobility for non-Turkish peoples and many Slavs, Greeks, and Armenians rose to high position in the state. It also ensured a talented pool of state servants who were loyal to the sultan for their jobs, their promotions, their income, and even their lives. All authority rested with the sultan and designated state servants like generals and provincial governors or **pashas**. The sultan's closest advisers, or **vizirs**, met together in a diwan, or council, to make important decisions. The Grand Vizir acted as a prime minister.

Under Suleiman I, the Ottoman state witnessed the height of its cultural flowering. Suleiman was known in history as *the Lawgiver* because of his influence on civil law. His image can be found in the United States House of Representatives along with other great lawgivers like Solon, Moses, and Thomas Jefferson. The law regulated penalties for criminal acts, reformed administration, and legal procedures in order to root out corruption, and introduced the idea of a balanced budget. Europeans called Suleiman *the Magnificent* because of the lavishness of his court and his presumptions of power. He began a letter to the European monarchs as "I who am sultan of sultans, the sovereign of sovereigns, the dispenser of crowns to the monarchs of the earth. . ." He adorned the capital of Istanbul (the Ottoman name given to Constantinople) with palaces and mosques, among the most famous the Topkapi Palace and the Suleimanye Mosque. A contemporary of Michelangelo, **Pasha Sinan** (1491–1588), a Christian rounded up in the devshirme, designed 312 public buildings. Poetry dominated literary expression. Written in Turkish, it followed classic Islamic (Arabic) forms and rules. Perhaps the best known Ottoman art form was the beautiful glazed pottery of Iznik, which was influenced by Ming blue and white and Persian craft styles. Books on history and astronomy were written. Of special interest was the *Book of the Sea* (1521) by Piri Reis, which contained 129 chapters, each with a map incorporating Islamic and western knowledge of the seas. Medical scholarship and research advanced in the fields of surgery and disease. The large number of public hospitals in Istanbul attests to Suleiman's interest. Istanbul's great bazaars were filled with merchants and travelers going from England to Malaya. Coffeehouses became popular places for men to gather, debate politics, do business, and play chess. Most businesses were organized into guilds highly regulated by the government.

Decline of the Ottomans

By the seventeenth and eighteenth centuries, weaknesses in the Ottoman system became apparent and irreparable. One was the necessity for expansion to feed the army and bureaucracy. When that stopped, the empire lacked the influx of new manpower that kept the system fluid and merit based. The system also relied heavily on the sultan's ability to rule. Some sultans became lavish and decadent. With no tradition of succession, usurpations of the throne were common. Rival claimants were often confined to the palace and "**harem**" (the place in a Muslim house assigned to women) leading to the exaggerated stories of concubinage and debauchery. Expanding population led to inflation, famine, and revolts. The result was that, during the sixteenth century the Ottomans made no advances in

Europe and, as has already been noted, in 1514 at Chaldiran they were unable to follow up on the defeat they inflicted on the Safavids.

Summary

Nowhere the Mongols touched remained the same after they swept across Eurasia, but the impacts and legacies differed. Though the Mongols never successfully invaded Japan, the attack itself had repercussions. It gave rise to the myth of the divine wind, it promoted a psychology of isolation toward the outside world, and it paved the way for the eventual unification of Japan under the Tokugawa. In China the Mongols overcame the Song (Sung) and established a new dynasty, the Yuan. Ironically, this changed the Mongols more than the Chinese. Kublai Khan, in fact, became another Chinese emperor. The Mandarin bureaucracy remained and Chinese values remained intact. The Mongols were instrumental in reopening the Silk Road and strengthening maritime trade in the South China Seas. This whetted the European appetite for Asian goods, diffused technology necessary for the Atlantic voyages, and gave mariners crucial practice for long-distance open sea voyages. As a result of the Mongols, the use of Chinese gunpowder was spread, initiating an age of gunpowder empires.

Russia too was overcome by the Mongols, but, unlike China, the attack wiped out the political and social system of Kievan Russia. The 200-year Tartar Yoke gave rise to autocracy because the Mongols left Russian princes with supreme authority in Russian lands where they enserfed the peasants. In the fight to liberate Russia from the Mongols, Christian Orthodoxy under state control created legitimization for divine rule of the Grand Prince of Moscow. In India the Mongols brought with them the Islamic faith. The militancy with which Islam was introduced into India made Islam unpopular among Hindus despite the efforts of the Delhi and Mughal rulers to integrate the two religions. The Mongols did what India had been unable to do except on rare occasions and that was to unite politically. The result was that, during the Delhi and Mughal empires, roads, trade, and building reached new heights stimulated by contact with China and Persia.

In Southwest Asia, the ailing Abbasid Caliphate was still the symbol of unity and authority for the majority of Muslims. In 1258, however, when the Mongols sacked Baghdad, a united single, universal Islamic authority never again reasserted itself. Instead, Egypt, North Africa, and Spain became independent and in the Islamic heartland, militant Turkish tribes asserted their authority over the other parts of the Islamic world. After their defeat at Ain Jalut in 1260 the Mongols withdrew to Persia, leaving a power vacuum in Anatolia. Earlier, Byzantium would have taken advantage of it, but the sack of Constantinople by the Crusaders in 1204 weakened Byzantine power. Into this no-man's land came the Ottoman Turks. The Ottomans failed to march east, however, in some measure because Tamerlane, who claimed descent from Genghiz Khan, defeated and captured the Ottoman sultan, Bayezid, in 1402. After the demise of Tamerlane, a group of Turkish warriors, the Safavids, rose in Persia, creating a militarily and ideologically (Shi'ite Muslim) hostile state to the Ottomans. While the Ottomans inflicted a crushing defeat at Caldiran in 1514, largely because they possessed big guns, they turned their attention against the Mameluks of Egypt, regaining the holy places of Islam—Mecca, Medina, and Jerusalem—in 1517. This gave the Safavids rule of Persia and cemented for posterity the ethnic, territorial, and ideological split between Arab and Persian, Sunni and Shi'ite Islam. Meanwhile, the Ottomans built a strong state and finally overcame Byzantium in 1453, giving Islam a pathway into Europe. This set off a titanic struggle between Islam and Christianity, putting in motion the European voyages for trade, conquest, and conversion.

A Legacy of Leadership

In this titanic struggle between the Islamic world led by the Ottomans and the European Christian coalition, there was a star-studded cast of great personalities of world history. Added to the Great Suleiman were Charles V, Hapsburg monarch of imperial Spain and the Holy Roman Empire, Francis I, the Christian king of France, Martin Luther, the reformer who unintentionally shattered the Christian coalition and diverted Christian resources from the struggle with the Ottomans, Henry VIII of England, enemy of Catholics, and Ivan the Terrible, who stamped autocracy on succeeding pages of Russian history. At the same time, around the world other great personalities emerged—Babur, who lay the basis for the Mughal Dynasty, Ismail, who founded the Safavid dynasty, Hideyoshi, shogun of Japan, and Montezuma and Atahualpa, who led great civilizations in the Americas. That such forceful political personalities could converge at this point in world history, at the doorstep of the Global Age, is only partially explainable, and otherwise as mysterious as the rise of great religious leaders 2000 years earlier. In Eurasia, these great leaders stepped in to fill the vacuum left by the Mongols and with new gunpowder technology were able to dominate large areas. In the Americas, political decentralization and chaos also led to the rise of new states.

THE CRUSADES AND THE BLACK PLAGUE

Origins of the Crusades

Besides the Mongols, other forces were at work that markedly changed the course of events. The Crusades and the Black Plague significantly affected large areas of the world at this time and particularly the Europeans. The Crusades reshaped Europe, signaling the end to medieval times. The **Battle of Manzikert** 1071 was the event that initiated the Crusades. Some time prior to this, the Seljuk Turks had established leadership of the Muslim world by sacking Baghdad in 1055, initiating a remarkably successful partnership between "men of the sword," mainly of Turkish origin, and "men of the law," mainly of Arab and Persian origin. At Manzikert, the Seljuk Turks defeated the Byzantines and drove the Christians out of most of Southwest Asia. Byzantine emperor Alexius I, in despair, sent messengers to **Pope Urban II**, regretting past differences between Constantinople and Rome, and pleading for help to save the empire and to preserve Christianity in the East. Pope Urban II, convinced of the need for reuniting the Roman and Orthodox Churches, and hoping to extend his authority over all Christendom and to make Rome once again the capital of the world, called for a Crusade. In doing so, he demanded revenge against the infidel, "an accursed race wholly alienated from God" who had "depopulated them by pillage and fire." He also promised Crusaders that they would find Jerusalem "a paradise of delights" would be "assured of the reward of imperishable glory in the kingdom of heaven." The remission of sin for those who crusaded or gave money was known as an "**indulgence**." He also declared a three-year truce in private war and promised to protect the families and property of Crusaders.

For many reasons, western Christians flocked to join the movement. Pilgrimages to the Holy Land, which had been made since earliest Christian times, were now in jeopardy. Also, the medieval warrior world was in search of a mission since no new outside barbarian threat had appeared since the tenth century. Trade between northern Italian merchants and the Byzantines was now put in danger as well, so the merchant class lent money to Crusaders, and when the warriors died in battle, acquired their land as repayment. Ordinary people went too, for adventure, and younger sons of nobility, for a chance to carve out a feudal fief. Kings were anxious to be rid of these troublesome nobles and therefore supported them. Between 1096 and 1270 eight papally approved expeditions made their way to the Holy Land.

The First Crusade

Priests and monks preached the Crusade all over Europe. Forty thousand people responded. Ten thousand of them were peasants like Walter the Penniless and Peter the Hermit who lived off the land as they marched, quarreled among themselves, and destroyed Byzantine Christian property. Most were massacred by the Turks. About 20,000 to 25,000 were knights who successfully

moved against Jerusalem recapturing it in 1099. Emperor Alexius regained control of parts of Anatolia and Crusaders set up states in a strip of land that extended all the way from the upper Tigris River valley to the boundary of Egypt. The **Crusader states** resembled feudal states of Europe, complete with castles and courts. Italian merchants set up trading posts in their ports. A steady stream of pilgrims, soldiers, settlers, and merchants flowed back and forth between Southwest Asia and western Europe. However, there were differences. While Catholicism was the official religion, Orthodox Christians, Jews, and Muslims were ruled tolerantly. Many Europeans adopted customs of the land they conquered, wearing turbans and flowing robes, taking baths, visiting Arab physicians, intermarrying with local women, and teaching the Koran in their schools.

The Second Crusade

Soon both secular and religious disputes divided the Crusaders, divisions that the Muslims learned to play upon. In 1144 Edessa, the Christian outpost in Syria, fell to the Turks, leaving the three remaining states threatened by a new infidel invasion. This set the Second Crusade into motion. Led by Bernard of Clairvaux, leader of a branch of the Benedictine monks, the Cistercians, kings like Louis VII of France took up the cross. Distrusting each other, French and Germans traveled separately and both looted Byzantine cities on their way. The Byzantines retaliated by mixing chalk with their flour and rushing the crusaders, still divided, into the arms of the Turks. The Second Crusade resulted in the loss of thousands of lives.

The Third Crusade

A quarter of a century later, the Turks found an able leader in **Saladin** (1138–1193). He reunited the Muslim world from Egypt to Mesopotamia, surrounding the Crusader states on three sides. He refrained from attacking the Crusader states until a petty Christian lord attacked a caravan in which his sister was traveling. Then, in 1187 he destroyed a Christian army and seized Jerusalem, finally conquering all of the Crusader states except Tyre. Three of Europe's greatest kings led the Third Crusade to recapture the Holy Land: Frederick Barbarossa, the Holy Roman Emperor, Richard the Lion-Hearted of England, and Philip Augustus of France. They captured the city of Acre in 1191 after a siege of a year and a half. When Frederick Barbarossa was drowned and Philip returned to France, Richard and Saladin carried on a religious war that became part of legend. In 1192 Richard and Saladin signed a truce that left the Crusaders with a foothold in the Holy Land and little else.

Later Crusades

Later Crusades deteriorated into campaigns of greed, gore, glory, and loot. In 1198, Pope Innocent III called the Fourth Crusade. The crusaders assembled in Venice but lacked the money to pay for their journey. The Venetians persuaded them to attack Zara, their rival on the Adriatic Sea, to pay for the trip, and then convinced the Crusaders to join in an attack on Constantinople. In Easter week of 1204 they tore apart the altar of the Hagia Sophia for its gold and jewels, ransacked the libraries, seized many of the greatest Byzantine art treasures, and ousted the Byzantine ruler. They then established a "Latin Empire of Byzantium," which lasted half a century. In 1261 the native Byzantines recaptured Constantinople and restored Orthodox Christianity. The Fourth Crusade discredited the crusading movement and so intensified the hatred between Catholic and Orthodox Christians that the two groups never again joined to fight the Muslims. The winners were the Muslims and northern Italian cities who gained commercial concessions from the Byzantines.

There were other Crusades later but they were pathetic efforts. The "Children's Crusade" was noteworthy only because little Crusaders were sold into slavery. The saintly King Louis IX of France later led two Crusades; he was captured on the first and died during the second in 1270.

More successful from the European Christian point of view were the Crusades against the **Moors** (Muslims) on the Iberian peninsula that was part of Islam since the Umayyads estab-

lished themselves as rulers in the eighth century. By 1034 the old Caliphate of Cordoba had broken up into quarreling kingdoms. Taking advantage of this, the Christian knights by 1055 had occupied Toledo and central Spain, but Berber warriors from North Africa came to the aid of their Muslim neighbors. During this struggle, one of the great heroes of Spanish history, immortalized by Cervantes, was **"el Cid"** ("Master") who fought first for his native Castile, then for the Moors, and finally for himself as ruler of Valencia. Cruel, self-seeking, and haughty, but fearless and daring, he became a model for later Spanish noblemen. Gradually, during the twelfth and thirteenth centuries, the effort to oust the Moors was successful. Sargossa, key to eastern Spain fell in 1118, the king of Portugal conquered Lisbon in 1147, and in 1212 the combined armies of the Christian states drove the Moors from all but the southern coast and city of Granada. The rest of the peninsula was divided between the kingdoms of Portugal, Castile, and Aragon. Other successful Crusades occurred in Northeast Europe where **Teutonic Knights** conquered and controlled lands on the southern coast of the Baltic, now Estonia, Latvia, and Lithuania, and converting the inhabitants to Latin Christendom. A number of other crusades were called by popes mainly against "**heretics**" (a person who believes other than the official doctrine), but because the Holy War was against fellow Christians, the attempt at creating a political weapon out of the crusading spirit only succeeded in discrediting the church.

Effects of the Crusades on Europe

While the Crusades failed to accomplish their stated mission against the Muslims, they had dramatic effects nonetheless. Some historians argue that later events would still have happened, but it is generally agreed the Crusades hastened developments. One effect was the increasing power of royal authority at the expense of the popes. Papal taxes that were imposed to pay for Crusades were later misused and led to increasing secularization and the Reformation. Royal authority grew because many powerful lords died in the Crusades, because kings used the Crusades as an excuse to impose new taxes, and because the increased cost of living hurt nobles on limited cash incomes, forcing them to sell feudal rights to peasants and towns who wanted to increase their rights. The Crusades revolutionized warfare, introducing Europeans to new weapons like the crossbow and techniques of building fortifications. Merchants and townsmen copied Muslim weavers, gold- and silversmiths, and architecture. Returning Crusaders introduced Arabic numerals, algebra, Greek philosophy, and Arab medicine to Europe.

Trade with the East grew. Silks, spices, and sugar, when first brought back, were upper class luxuries and later necessities. Even common Europeans were introduced to dates, yogurt, and coffee. Trade in these and other products led to new trade routes and commercial towns all over Europe. The greatness of Venice can be traced directly to the Crusades. The Crusades helped Europeans discover Asia. A few went eastward to Persia and some all the way to China. The journals of **Marco Polo** and the fictional adventures of Sir John de Mandeville were widely read, stimulating interest in travel and geography. When the Portuguese started down the western coast of Africa, they hoped, among other things, they were starting a Crusade to attack the western flank of Islam. The date of the fall of the last Crusader stronghold at Acre in 1291 is as good a date as any to mark the beginning of the change in Europe from medieval to modern times.

Effects of The Crusades on The Muslims

While in the chronicles compiled by Muslims the Crusades are scarcely mentioned, they had an effect on them too. The Crusades weakened the Byzantine empire and thereby empowered the Turks in their impending successful assault against Byzantium in 1453. Bitterness between Christians and Muslims grew while trade between Muslims and Europeans strengthened. Pockets of Christians like the Maronites remained in Southwest Asia. On the whole, however, the "exchange" was largely a one-way process. While Muslims imported weapons and horses from Christian Italy and Byzantium, and beeswax, slaves, and timber from Russia, Muslim people were only marginally affected politically and militarily, and culturally, even less.

The Black Plague

Like the Crusades, the Black Plague (1348–1350), while affecting many parts of Asia, seems to have had an unusual effect on Europe. The Black Plague was really a form of bubonic plague that was spread by deadly parasites carried in the stomach of a flea that was attracted to house rats and to humans. The best defense was to kill the rats. Instead, people killed dogs and cats, believing they were the source of infection, and the rats multiplied even more. The Black Plague was never known as such during its time, but the name was given, some argue, because "blackness" became a metaphor for the magnitude of the epidemic, one utterly without hope or light. It might also have become known as such because the disease causes black nodules to form on the skin. Still other explanations describe the endless days of funeral processions and black-robed gravediggers. The mortality rate was probably high wherever it struck and there is some evidence of plagues in China at this time, which helped bring down the Ming, and of its presence among the Mongols decimating their ranks. The plague weakened Mamluk rule in Egypt, but records from Europe are better known and suggest losses of close to 40 to 45 percent there. Rural areas were hit as hard as cities but the rich who could flee to the safety of hills survived somewhat better. Otherwise, death was indiscriminate—merchants, one-third of the College of Cardinals, and three archbishops of Canterbury within a year.

The plague's passage replicates the paths of "international trade." The plague spread faster by sea and river than by land. Thus, London, which exported great quantities of wool to Italian ports, was affected before Paris, and remote inland areas of Europe were not affected until 1350. Its origins are still obscure, but a group of Genoese who returned to the West after the seizure of the fortress at Kaffa in the Crimea, reported that Mongol besiegers began to die of a strange disease that gave the victims "black swellings that oozed blood." In desperation, the Mongols hurled the rotting corpses over the city walls by catapult, so when the Genoese survivors escaped from Kaffa, the plague had consumed them. Most died when they reached Sicily. Having traveled remorselessly across Asia, the Black Plague arrived in Europe first at Pisa and Genoa, and then Marseilles. In 1348 it moved north into France and east into Spain and the rest of the continent. Only a handful of places escaped—central Poland, Silesia, and Milan.

The effects of the Plague were many. One was a long period of economic recession as death ate into the labor force of harvesting and production. On the other hand, the shortage of labor pushed wages up and caused many peasants to assert their rights, move to wage labor, and acquire land from dying nobles. The power of the church declined, not just because many high officials died, but because the best priests went out to minister to the sick, only to then meet their own death. People also lost faith in spiritual powers as they observed that the pious died along with the heathen.

The Plague crept into literature and art. One of the greatest literary works was the *Decameron* by Giovanni Boccaccio. In it, seven young women and three young men escape the sights and smells of the plague to the hills around Florence where each day one of the young people tells ten stories. Another literary master, Francesco Petrarch, left 366 love poems to Laura who died of the plague 21 years to the day after he met her in 1348. One of the most vivid pictorial images is the "Dance of Death," a series of 24 sketches in which men and women in all stations of life are shown. Each had recently died and each was forced to dance around the graveyard with moldering corpses. In popular culture, perhaps, there was a children's game, "Ring Around the Rosie," the "rosie" being the place where the flea bit.

Summary

Thus, while the Crusades introduced Europeans to the culture, technology, and learning of the East, the Black Plague changed the internal complexion of Europe. Both signaled the end of medieval times and set the stage for a European awakening that led to the Global Age.

CHAPTER 16
Maritime Trade Complexes

CHRONOLOGY	Ming Dynasty (1368–1644)
	Qing Dynasty (1644–1912)

TERMS			
	dhows	Tamil	Hanseatic League
	lateen sail	Chola	Nordic
	junk	Flanders Fleet	

PEOPLE			
	Youngle (Yung-lo)	Henry the Navigator	Pedro Alvares Cabral
	Zheng He (Cheng Ho)	Bartholomew Dias	Yoruba
	Ibn Majid	Vasco da Gama	Oba

PLACES			
	Forbidden City	Malaba	Ile-Ife
	Cape of Good Hope	Calicut	Benin
	Gujarat	Flanders	Lubeck
	Cambay	Levant	

Maritime Trade Complexes

On the eve of the Global Age, the increased tempo, breadth, and sophistication of maritime trade paved the way for the Atlantic voyages. Maritime trade gave seamen increasing experience in sailing the open oceans, spawned new technologies necessary for long-distance voyages, and introduced Europeans to the products and cultures of the East. Three trade routes in particular gained status during this time period: those in the Indian Ocean carried on by the Ming and Muslim traders, Nordic routes in Europe, and Mediterranean and African routes by the Italian and Portuguese traders.

THE INDIAN OCEAN—MING AND MUSLIM TRADERS

The Ming

The spread of Chinese civilization south during the Song (Sung) and then encouragement of both overland and sea trade during the Yuan, set the stage for the spectacular sea voyages of the Ming. There had been many coups and counter-coups as rival claimants for the Chinese throne tried to overthrow the foreign rule by the Mongols. Then, during the 1340s and 1350s, when Europe was convulsed by the Black Plague, China too was afflicted by floods, droughts, and epidemics. This touched off uprisings, the most powerful of which was led by Zhu Yuan-chang (Chu Yuan-chang), a southern rebel who in 1368 proclaimed a new dynasty, the **Ming** (1368–1644). After Zhu's death in 1398 the fourth son, **Yongle** (Yung-lo, 1405–1433) assumed the throne. He moved the capital back to the former Mongol capital of Beijing (Peking) and, employing 200,000 workmen, built the famous "**Forbidden City**" in the center. The buildings themselves established the physical setting for the lofty despotism that governed China throughout the Ming and **Qing** (Ch'ing) **Dynasty** (1644–1912). It was designed like a series of Chinese boxes, one walled city inside another. At the core was the Imperial Palace, or Forbidden City, surrounded by a red brick wall and moat. Around it was the Imperial City itself surrounded by a wall 14 miles long. The architects of the Forbidden City constructed one of the most exciting architectural progressions ever made. Passing through the Meridian Gate, the visitors crossed a river, through an imperial gate into the largest courtyard of the palace, where great drama was achieved by the play of roof lines of golden tiles and upswinging eves decorated with golden dragons that symbolized the power and wisdom of the emperor. Dominating the view was the marble platform and red-columned Hall of Supreme Harmony in which the emperor held audience.

Reinvigorating its strong maritime history stretching back to the eleventh century, China became the greatest maritime power in the world, but the purpose was more political and military than commercial. Yung-lo had two motives in launching the expeditions. First, he sent them in search of Chien Wen, a serious contender for the throne, who, it was rumored, had escaped to Southeast Asia. Second, he sent them to explore, expand trade, and provide the imperial court with luxury objects. Led by Muslim admiral **Zheng He** (Cheng Ho), the expeditions crossed the Indian Ocean to Ceylon, the Persian coast, and the east coast of Africa. Navigating by compass, the first expedition carried 27,800 men, and involved 62 major ships. The voyages greatly extended the prestige of the Ming in Asia. Trade, however, was more in the form of tribute than exchange. Nineteen states, including Java, Sumatra, Malacca, and the west coast of India, participated. Just before Zheng He (Cheng Ho) left on his seventh and final voyage, he carved the following inscription into stone: "The Imperial Ming Dynasty, in unifying seas and continents. . . The countries beyond the horizon at the ends of the earth have all become subjects. . . the barbarians beyond the sea. . . have come. . . bearing precious objects and presents." The voyages led to publication of geographical works such as the *Treatise on the Barbarian Kingdoms on the Western Oceans* (1434), putting China considerably ahead of Portugal whose seafaring began a half-century later. The expeditions also led to Chinese emigration to Southeast Asia and parts of southern India. The voyages were suddenly terminated in 1435 due to the pressures from Confucian court intellectuals who found the new wealth and knowledge of the merchants a threat, and because the voyages were primarily political rather than economic and became a drain on the treasury. There is no doubt world history would have been different if the Chinese thrust had continued, for the European expeditions making their way down the west coast of Africa were no match for the Chinese in military and merchant organization. After these voyages, financial pressures from supporting an elaborate court style and barbarian pressures on the northern frontier weakened the Ming. Coastal raids attributed to Japanese pirates were common. Vietnam liberated itself from China in 1427, and the mass refusals to pay taxes weakened the Chinese government and army.

Arab Trade Routes

While the Chinese maritime activity was primarily political, Muslim activity followed the Islamic sanctification of commerce. Arab merchants generally sailed in **dhows**, vessels with two or three masts, triangular or **lateen sails**, and built in India of teakwood. They were less sturdy than Chinese **junks**, which were large—

some able to carry 1500 tons—and used a square sail. The Indian Ocean trade was driven by monsoon wind patterns well described in Arab sea manuals like those of **Ibn Majid** written toward the end of the fifteenth century. He described one complex that circulated between West India, Arabia, and the east coast of Africa, and another that circulated from East India through the Bay of Bengal and the Straits of Malacca and back. Ibn Majid's manual also described in detail sailing directions going down the east coast of Africa, rounding the **Cape of Good Hope**, and sailing up the west coast of Africa to the Mediterranean, the reverse route Vasco da Gama was later to take. Majid's account does not include any notations of Arabs sailing to China, which they had done earlier. This was because, by this time, after Zheng He's (Cheng Ho) voyages, Chinese ports were closed and Chinese fleets had withdrawn from the Persian Gulf, leaving an enormous vacuum for the Portuguese to fill 70 years later.

Indian Traders

The geography of the Indian peninsula naturally divided Indian Ocean trade between West and East India. In the west, a major area of trade grew up on the **Gujarat** peninsula. Horses were especially important because the Indian military used horses but needed to import them from Arabia and Persia where they could be bred and raised. Other items of trade included foodstuffs like grain and sugar, weapons, cotton, silk, and spices. The presence of Gujaratis in East Africa was typical, cotton cloth being a major item of export. By the thirteenth century, expansion in Mediterranean trade fed into Indian Ocean trade, and in 1303–1304, when Gujarat was absorbed into the Delhi Sultanate, trade vitality in the area increased even more to meet the conspicuous consumption of the Delhi elite. Ibn Battuta described **Cambay**, the major port of Gujarat, as "one of the most beautiful cities. . . the majority of its inhabitants are foreign merchants." Further down the West Indian coast was another area of trade centered at **Malaba** and its major city of **Calicut**. On the east coast, Indian **Tamil** traders organized into commercial corporations supported by the **Chola** state, dominated the trade. In this area, wealthy merchants controlled supply by "putting out" raw material into the homes of spinners and weavers. Indian textile technology at this time included the vertical loom, block printing, and the spinning wheel, which was introduced into India from Turkey in the fourteenth century. (It was not introduced into Europe until the sixteenth century.) In the twelfth century the Tamils lost ground as Muslim merchants from the West took over these roles.

Summary

While the Arabs dominated the Indian Ocean trade, Persian, Indian, Malaysian, and Chinese ships (the latter until the 1430s) all participated, mostly peacefully. Merchants did not depend, as did the Italians, on state armed convoys to guard passage as ships tended to travel together for mutual assistance due to the limited sailing times of the monsoon winds. This multiethnic, laissez-faire system was unprepared for the armed Portuguese, especially when the Chinese withdrew.

ITALIAN AND PORTUGUESE TRADERS

Feeding into the growing Indian Ocean and South China Sea trade between 1120 and 1475, were the Italian mariners. In 1368, when the overland Silk Road was closed by the Ming, trade swung back to older sea routes. Venice and her rival Genoa nourished good relations with the Muslims and, as a result, began to exploit the opportunities of Southwest Asia or the Levant, exporting to the West caviar from Russia, sugar from their colonies, and wine from Greece. The most competitive and callous item of trade that neither the popes nor the Venetian senate could stop, was slaves from the shores of the Black Sea. Men were sent to serve in the armies of the sultans of Egypt and girls, especially the blond Circassians, were sold into domestic servitude and prostitution in both Muslim and Christian cities.

In some measure, growth in Italian trade was the result also of changing conditions in Europe. At first, Italian and Flemish (**Flanders**—where the North Sea meets the English Channel) traders had little contact with each other, for ships were too primitive to brave the Atlantic and robbers and barons subjected overland trade to attack and tolls. In the twelfth century, however, lords in central France established fairs where Flemish and Italian merchants met. The riverine systems that crisscross Europe also helped promote trade as they were easier to navigate than roads. The principal European route began in the **Levant** (the eastern shore of the Mediterranean), where Italian ships took on cargoes of luxury goods from the Islamic-dominated eastern trade and delivered them to the ports of Venice, Pisa, and Genoa. Here, merchants shipped them either by sea to the harbors of southern France up the river valleys or overland. Early in the fourteenth century the first "**Flanders Fleets**" made the 2500-mile voyage from their home port of Venice around southern Italy and the coast of Spain to the Atlantic ports carrying cargoes of sugar, wine, spices, and armor in exchange for leather, hides, and primary wool cloth. As in India, merchants near wool-growing regions in England and Germany developed a "putting out" system in which raw wool was put out to workers who made it into cloth for set fees. In the Flanders Fleets were great galleys, sometimes as long as 150 feet, manned by crews of 200 sailors who could transport large amounts of bulky goods relatively inexpensively.

Italian Commercial Cities

A few Italian cities dominated the sea lanes of the Mediterranean and the overland routes to Europe. Milan became a center of silk, wool, and armor industries. Venice controlled most of the trade with the Mediterranean. Florence was the richest of all because its merchants sailed to all parts of the world and it was home to some 80 banking houses. Venice, as a maritime community overwhelmingly dependent on trade in spices and exotic goods from the East, tried to maintain a neutral policy between Christendom and the Islamic world. For a time, the precarious policy worked but the Turkish advance continued and eventually overwhelmed Venetian trade. Venice's traditional rival with the Orient, Genoa, reacted completely differently to the rise of Ottoman power. Its merchants shifted wealth into opportunities presented by Spain and Portugal. They lent money to kings, ran lucrative monopolies, and, most important, backed voyages of exploration.

Henry the Navigator

The Portuguese discovery of a sea route from Europe to India began with a Crusade rather than a voyage of exploration. In 1415 the king of Portugal led an army to conquer the Moorish pirate base at Ceuta, just across the Straits of Gibraltar. Among those present at the successful capture was one of the king's sons, **Henry the Navigator**. As the younger son, Henry was excluded from politics and chronically short of money. Nevertheless, within a few years of the capture of Ceuta, seamen in his service began to sail along the Atlantic coast of Africa. To aid in these endeavors, he established a school in Portugal where the best mapmakers, sailors, and seamen exchanged information about the winds, currents, reefs, and harbors. Soon, islands to the west of the African landmass were discovered when ships were obliged to stand out to sea by prevailing winds or as the sailors searched for realms of medieval imagination.

Portuguese Voyages

The Portuguese discovered the uninhabited Madeira, Azores, and Cape Verde islands ca. 1420. They were soon populated, and brought under cultivation with the help of Genoese capital, becoming profitable producers of sugar. Other islands that were populated required greater effort to claim. The Spanish finally subjugated the Guanches of the Canary Islands, following unsuccessful attempts by the Portuguese. The process took from 1385, when European slavers began to appear, until 1496. This served as a prelude to the European imperialism to come. The Guanches, suffering from defeat and

exposure to new European diseases, were extinct by the mid-sixteenth century.

As Henry inched down the African coast, gold and slaves in Guinea promised new wealth. The pace and scale of Portugal's endeavors then increased and by the 1460s Henry's captains had traveled 2000 miles down the West African coast. Now the motive was no longer religious or exploratory but commercial. In 1445 the first great slave auction in Europe to involve West Africans was held at Lagos. In the words of the chronicler Azurara, "Some held their heads low with their faces bathed in tears. . . They parted husbands from wives, fathers from sons, brothers from brothers. . . It was a terrible scene of misery and disorder. . . ." Yet slavery was a universal fact of life in the fifteenth century. There were European slaves in Southwest Asia, Moorish slaves in Europe, and a well-established system in Africa where servitude was the normal punishment for crime.

The profits from this activity were so substantial that the voyages continued even after the death of Prince Henry in 1460. Patronized by the Portuguese government, the explorers discovered the "Gold Coast," "Ivory Coast," and "Slave Coast," whose names reflect their primary products. In 1488 **Bartholomew Dias** rounded the Cape of Good Hope, named because the Portuguese hoped now to find the water route to India. Dias's voyage had finally settled the geographical question proving wrong Ptolemy's theory of an extended African continent. In 1490 cartographer Henricus Martellus accurately depicted the sea route prompting the Portuguese to outfit a new fleet in 1497 commanded by **Vasco da Gama**. He rounded the Cape of Good Hope and then arrived at the port of Mozambique where the crew was amazed at the sight of Muslim dhows loaded with cloves, pepper, coconuts, gold, silver, and pearls.

From Mozambique, da Gama sailed to Mombasa, where the king provided him with experienced Muslim pilots for the trip across the Indian Ocean. In 1498 da Gama and his crew reached Calicut. When he returned to Portugal in 1499, his cargo of pepper and cinnamon was worth 60 times the cost of the voyage. The Portuguese were among the first to use knowledge and experience of Muslim and Chinese sailors to sail the seas and innovations developed by the Venetians to construct stronger hulls. In 1500 they mounted heavy cannons on their ships, giving them a tremendous military advantage by being able to destroy ships at a distance rather than by ramming. The Portuguese understood that the Indian Ocean trade was firmly in control of the Muslims, and so the contest for wealth also became a religious contest to divert wealth into Christian hands. Therefore, in 1500 a fleet of 14 vessels under **Pedro Alvares Cabral**, having accidentally discovered Brazil on the way, entered the Indian Ocean to destroy the Muslim seaborne commerce.

The Portuguese misunderstood much of what they saw along the way, taking, for instance, the Hindus for errant Christians. In the 1480s along the west coast of Africa, they came in contact with a remarkable African people who lived in the forest of central Nigeria, probably descendants of the ancient Nok (500 B.C.E.–200 C.E.), who practiced agriculture, used iron tools, and produced Nok sculpture.

Around 1000 C.E. another group of people, the **Yoruba**, whose major city was **Ile-Ife**, produced some of the greatest achievements of African art in wood and ivory. The Yoruba were organized in a small number of city-states under the authority of regional kings who were considered divine. Much of the art is centered around the kings. A similar pattern to the Yoruba city-states could be found among the Edo people to the east. A large state called **Benin** was formed sometime in the fourteenth century under Ewuare the Great (1440–1473). Benin City was described by early Europeans as a city of great population and broad avenues. The **Oba**, or ruler, lived in a large royal compound surrounded by a sizable entourage. His authority was the theme of the magnificent artistic output in ivory and caste bronze. Soon the bronzes and ivories began to include representations of Portuguese soldiers and themes reflected contact with outsiders.

NORDIC ROUTES

Besides growing maritime activity in the Indian Ocean, around Europe and Africa, the **Nordic** (North European) countries began active trade and exploration. From the ninth to the eleventh centuries, at the same time the second wave of Asiatic barbarians hit Europe, barbarians from Scandinavia, known variously as Vikings, Northmen, Norsemen, Norwegians, Danes, and Varangians, sallied out from their fiords in small war parties, attacking and settling in England (Anglo-Saxons), the Baltic, Iceland, Greenland, Ireland, and France (Normans). After this wave of invasions, population increased, causing people to push up along the Northeast European coast. Towns developed everywhere, many with circuits of walls to protect against further Viking raids. **Lubeck**, on the Baltic, was rebuilt and fortified in 1143 by the local count who sent messengers to every country inviting anyone desiring land to come and settle. The multitudes of peoples who responded provided the economic base for prosperity of towns of the area. The damming of the river Wakenitz in Lubeck permitted construction of powerful watermills, assuring future prosperity for the town as a processing and trade center.

Wealth was also due to a series of treaties reducing conflict and facilitating access to each others' markets. In time, these alliances grew into the **Hanseatic League** under Lubeck's leadership, linking over 200 towns and cities from London to Novgorod, and from Bergen to Cologne. Hanseatic counting houses held ready stocks of metals, fish, textiles, and Russian furs. Across regular, well-defined trade routes along the Baltic and North Seas, the ships of league cities carried goods that were exchanged for finished products like cloth. Hanseatic merchants established foreign trading centers called "factories." The most famous of these was the London Steelyard, a walled community with warehouses, offices, a church, and residential quarters for company representatives. Their meetings in Flanders joined two huge zones of commercial activity, the Nordic and Mediterranean, which, in turn, fed into the Indian Ocean trade.

Summary

Both the Eurasian highway and the maritime trade complexes formed the background for the emergence of the Global Age. The Eurasian highway introduced Europeans to the goods of the East, and the maritime trade complexes gave mariners considerable experience in open sea sailing. Compared to overland travel, sea trade was fast, efficient, and cheap. Unlike the camel caravans, there were few political barriers to surmount, and wind was a cheap if not a free source of fuel. The Portuguese were the first to explore the route to India and East Asia. The unexpected discovery of America by the Spanish introduced Europeans to yet other sources of wealth and prospects for conversion. Had the Americas been poor, it is unlikely this new continent would have transformed the history of the world as it did.

```
┌─────────────────────┐
│     KEY TERMS       │
└─────────────────────┘
```

CHAPTER 17
The Americas

| **CHRONOLOGY** | Aztec (1224–1520) | | |
| | Inca (1438–1525) | | |

TERMS	Quetzalcoatl	calpulli	pochteca
	chinampas	macana	Quechua
	Codex Mendoza	Huitzilopochtli	quipu

| **PEOPLE** | Moctezuma I | Bernardino de Sahagun | Pachacuti |
| | Moctezuma II | metate | |

| **PLACES** | Tenochtitlan | Cuzco | Machu Picchu |
| | Tlatelolco | | |

The Americas

In the several centuries before Columbus, the Americas continued to display significant diversity in cultural systems, but there were significant changes also, particularly in the increasingly extensive organization of agriculture and in the ability to form larger political units. Two of these states dazzled the Europeans on their arrival—the Aztec in Mexico and the Inca in Peru.

THE AZTECS

The **Aztec** (1224–1520) empire grew up on the heels of the Toltec state, which collapsed in 1224 when the Chichimec captured Tula. The last of the Chichimec to arrive in central Mexico were the Aztec, who spoke the same Nahuatl language as the Toltec. They absorbed the cultural achievements of predecessors of the area including the Olmec, Maya, Teotihuacan, and Toltec. One of these traditions was the legend of **Quetzalcoatl**. The legend describes a powerful struggle between the Toltec tribal god Tezcatlipoca, who required human sacrifice, and Quetzalcoatl who gave his people bumper crops and fostered learning and the arts. Tezcatlipoca won the battle, continuing the tradition of human sacrifice, and Quetzalcoatl was driven into exile, promising to return. By a remarkable coincidence, the year Quetzalcoatl had promised to return happened to be the year the Spaniard Hernando Cortes landed in Mexico.

The Aztecs settled on a few swampy islands in Lake Texcoco where they founded the city of **Tenochtitlan** (Mexico City) in 1325. In 1428 they embarked on a policy of territorial expansion. **Moctezuma I** (1440–1469) conquered the area around the central plateau and by the time of **Moctezuma II** (1502–1520) all of central Mexico from the Gulf to the Pacific and south to Guatemala had been conquered.

Thirty-eight subordinate provinces paid tribute to the Aztec state. Aztec strategy was to ally with neighboring states, defeat common enemies, and then turn on their allies. The professional army was maintained by the food produced on the fertile floating gardens called **chinampas** and by the heavy tribute paid to the Aztecs from all conquered people. The *Codex Mendoza*, one of the few surviving manuscripts concerning pre-Columbian America, contains a copy of the register of tribute paid annually to the Aztec emperors. Meticulously noted were clothes, armor, maize, and even a live eagle. There was another more important form of tribute too, that is, captives who could be sacrificed to the bloodthirsty gods of the tribe. Tens of thousands of victims were sacrificed each year by having their hearts ripped out of their bodies. During certain occasions, like the consecration of the great new temple at Tenochtitlan in 1487, 20,000 men and women were ritually murdered. The rationale for such human destruction can only partially be understood in terms of a pessimistic theology that believed that sacrifices, however numerous, were not enough to avert ultimate destruction. Population pressures as indicated by frequent famines and revolts might also have played a part. Or, ritual human sacrifice could have been an instrument of state terror to crush dissent.

Aztec Society

Early Aztec society lacked sharp social distinctions, but soon it became complex, stratified, and ordered. At the top of the social and political pyramid was the emperor, who ruled by right, not just of inheritance, but by election. The monarchy passed from the emperor to the ablest son, chosen by a small oligarchy of chief priests, warriors, and state officials. The emperor was chief warrior but also chief benefactor and judge. Records show Aztec emperors were serious public servants. The emperor Moctezuma I distributed 20,000 loads of grain when a flood hit the city. Below the emperor were the temple priests. Aztecs looked to priests for divination, omens, and signs of upcoming events. Because the emperor and wealthy gave generously, the temples possessed enormous wealth. Along with the priests, the upper class was composed of high military officials and governors. The upper class had its origins in the heads of the original clans, or **calpulli**, plus those who rose to the top through service or great deeds. In local affairs the calpulli still regulated social and political life. The great lords lived grandly and luxuriously in palaces and only they could wear jewelry and embroidered cloaks.

Beneath the upper class were the warriors. All freemen could become warriors if they passed through a grueling military training that included capture of prisoners for ritual sacrifice and skill with the use of a **macana**, a paddle-shaped wooden club edged with bits of obsidian. This weapon was so ferocious it could slash the head off a horse in one blow. If a young man failed to become a warrior, he joined the plebeian or working class. These people performed all sorts of agricultural, military, and domestic services. Unlike nobles, priests, orphans, and slaves, this class paid taxes, but they also had rights and could own land and share in tribute. Beneath the worker class were the landless workers who were bound to the soil like serfs. Slaves were the lowest class, usually prisoners of war or criminals. Female slaves often became concubines. However, unlike European slaves, they could possess goods, save money, buy land and houses, and even have slaves in their service and buy freedom. Much of what is known about Aztec

life comes from **Bernardino de Sahagun**, a Spanish missionary priest who in the sixteenth century prepared an extraordinary encyclopedia called *The General History of Things of New Spain*. Among the aspects of Aztec culture he noted was the position of women who could own and inherit property but were subordinate in political and social life. The technology of the Americas to some extent limited social development. Women in Mesoamerica spent six hours a day grinding corn by hand on stone slabs or **metates**, whereas in Egypt, similar technology had been replaced by animal and water power wheels.

Tenochtitlan

Among the outstanding features of Aztec society were its cities and sophisticated agricultural and trade systems. When the Spanish entered Tenochtitlan in 1519, they could not believe their eyes. This island city, often compared to Venice, was approached by four great highways that connected it with the mainland. Wide, straight streets and canals crisscrossed the city, and boats and canoes plied the canals. Thousands of one-story stucco houses lined the roads and a large sophisticated aqueduct carried pure water from distant springs to parks and marketplaces. Crowning the central square was the great temple of **Huitzilopochtli**, the Aztec war god. Built as a pyramid and approached by three flights of 120 steps each, the 100-foot-high temple dominated the skyline.

Tlatelolco

Tenochtitlan's sister city was **Tlatelolco**, the site of a cornucopian market offering a profusion of products as well as order and efficiency. Fixed places in the market sold certain items from gold, silver, and precious stones, to feathers, mantles, and embroidered goods, tobacco, cloves, pottery, amatle (bark) paper, and axes of copper, brass, and tin. The variety of goods illustrates the long-distance trade networks that sent the hereditary class of merchants (**pochteca**) as far north as the pueblos and as far south as Central America. Most trade was barter but cocoa beans and gold dust were sometimes used as currency. Pochteca became wealthy and some of the trade was state supported and had political overtones whereby merchants served as spies, ambassadors, and government agents. The other remarkable aspect of Aztec economic life was its sophisticated agricultural system. Vast quantities of maize, beans, and other food were brought into Tenochtitlan, but in and around the lake the Aztecs developed an ingenious system of chinampas or floating islands. The yield from these was high, as many as four corn crops a year.

The Aztec Empire was in many ways never really integrated as local rulers often acted as surrogates and tribute collectors. Because of this, the century of Aztec expansion left local areas relatively unchanged. In the long run, this and the system of terror tribute weakened the empire and led to its collapse at the hands of the Spanish.

THE INCA

The Inca empire existed for less than a century and played only a minor role in Andean history, but it was spectacular in its political and social organization and sophisticated building. Inca was originally the name of a governing family of Amerindian people who settled in the basin of Cuzco. In 1438 **Pachacuti** Inca came to the throne and he and his successors in a period of 40 years extended Inca control for 2000 miles along the Andes, including Lake Titicaca, Peru, Ecuador, much of present-day Chile, and parts of Argentina. Some authorities rank Pachacuti and Topa Inca, his son, with Alexander the Great and Napoleon. By 1532, 16 million people owed allegiance to the Inca ruler. This astounding growth was due to the emperor's rigid control by means of a highly trained bureaucracy, a state religion, a powerful conscripted army, and, most remarkably, an advanced communication network. An elaborate system of roads linked every part of the empire. Professional architects, engineers, and administrators supervised a work force and materials needed to build these paved roads, bridges, and tunnels that linked **Cuzco**, the capital, with the distant fringes of the empire. The reason for

the empire seems to be found not just in economic gain, but in religion. The Inca believed that all a ruler's wealth should go to his male descendants to be used to support the cult of the dead Inca's mummy for eternity. Thus, each new emperor had to carve out new lands and tribute to support him in his afterlife.

Whereas the Aztecs controlled people by terror, Inca civilization was consolidated by a number of means, among them imposition of a common language on the various Amerindian cultures of the Andes valley. Pachacuti made **Quechua** the official language of his people and administration, sending colonists to subject regions and forcing them to adopt the language. The Incas also imposed their pantheon of gods— the sun-god, divine ancestor of the royal family, his wife, the moon-god, and the god of rain. The Incas held the sun to be the highest deity and the magnificent Temple of the Sun in Cuzco was the center of the state religion. Within it, all the mummies of past Incas resided. Other magnificent temples are scattered throughout the empire. One of the most beautiful is the citadel at **Machu Picchu**, which clings to a crag on the mountain surrounded by clouds. Priests led prayers and, on special occasions or disaster, human beings were sacrificed. Imperial unity was also achieved by forced participation of local chieftains in the bureaucracy and by transfers of inhabitants to other parts of the empire. Sometimes emperors gave newly acquired lands to victorious generals and distinguished civil servants.

Inca Society

Just as in medieval Europe, peasants worked several days each week on their lord's lands, state lands, or construction projects. The state required everyone to marry and sometimes decided when and to whom. As is common in states where there are high male death rates, polygamy was practiced. One of the outstanding features of Inca society was its socialistic approach to paternalism. Common people were denied choice and were regimented, but the Incas took care of the poor and aged, distributed grain in periods of shortage, and assisted in natural disasters. On the other hand, the socialism did not mean equality of class. The nobles were called "Big Ears" because they pierced their ears and distended the lobes with heavy jewelry. Nobles were exempt from agricultural work and other kinds of public service. The economy of the Inca was essentially based on agriculture wherein complex irrigation systems permitted the farming of steep hillsides. Llamas were used as beasts of burden and alpacas were raised for their long fine wool.

Inca Culture

Inca cultural achievements include the making of beautiful pottery and cloth, and the working of gold, silver, and copper. The Inca had no system of writing but they did make use of a system of knotted strings or **quipu**, which functioned something like an abacus. Inca stone cutting was remarkably accurate as a result and the best buildings were constructed with stones fitted so perfectly that they did not require mortar. Large irrigation projects, agricultural terraces, and systems of roads display a technical ability unsurpassed in the Americas.

Summary

The history of the world would have been quite different had the Spanish explorers found nothing in the Americas comparable to the riches of India, or no subjects for conversion, for they would very likely have passed over it and moved on. Instead, they found a brilliant and wealthy culture that rivaled India and the East. And so it was that this newly discovered hemisphere became part of the world system.

UNIT REVIEW

Cross-Regional Developments

In the period 1200–1600 the expanding classical systems were fundamentally over-whelmed and changed by large overarching forces. The first of these was the Mongols who destroyed old systems, but out of the wreckage emerged new and larger states, among them Yuan China, Muscovy Russia, Mughal India, Safavid Persia, and Ottoman Turkey. The Mongols, by both land and sea, facilitated large Eurasian exchange systems whereby goods, technologies, and learning fundamental to the Global Age passed. From this exchange also came gunpowder, which transformed the military, destroyed medieval structures, and created "gunpowder empires." The Mongols continued the spread of Islam, which particularly affected India. Another development of great con-sequence was the rise of the Ottoman Turks in Southwest Asia. They altered the nature of the Islamic world and finally overcame Byzantium, placing pressure on Christian Europe. Maritime trade complexes in the Indian Ocean, Atlantic Ocean, and North Sea gained strength, giving mariners experience in long-distance sailing and illustrating the superiority in terms of speed and cost of sea trade. The Crusades and the Black Plague, which engaged many Eurasian countries, particularly affected Europe. Europeans became acquainted with a larger world and its internal structures changed to accom-modate this. In the Americas large and sophisticated states in Mexico and Peru emerged at the same time Europeans began looking for a passage east.

Legacies

Among the legacies of this period are:

- the rise of great new empires and states like Tokugawa Japan, Yuan and Ming China, Delhi and Mughal India, Muscovy Russia, Safavid Persia, Ottoman Turkey, Aztec Mexico, and Inca Peru;
- the cementing of the national and religious divisions between Shi'ite Persia and Sunni Ottoman;
- the end of European medievalism by means of the Crusades and the Black Plague;
- increased maritime trade;
- emergence of gunpowder empires;
- the end of the Byzantine Empire and the consequent march of Islam into Europe
- the rise of great American civilizations—the Aztec and Inca;
- a Eurasian exchange of technology, foodstuffs, arts, and knowledge; and
- monuments of architecture like the Forbidden City, Taj Mahal, Tenochtitlan, and Machu Picchu.

Documents

LONG-DISTANCE TRAVEL
THE TRAVELS OF MARCO POLO

The coinage of this paper money is authenticated with as much form and ceremony as if it were actually of pure gold or silver. To each note a number of officers, specially appointed, not only subscribe their names, but affix their seals also . . .When thus coined in large quantities, this paper currency is circulated in every part of the grand khan's dominions; no person, at the peril of his life, dares refuse to accept it in payment. All his subjects receive it without hestitation, because, wherever their business may call them, they can dispose of it again in the purchase of merchandise . . . such as pearls, jewels, gold, or silver. With it, in short, every article may be procured.

In 1272 a Venetian merchant, Marco Polo, set out for China. Polo served the great Kublai Khan for 17 years. On his return to Europe, he left a book detailing his travels and observations of the Tartars in Asia, lifestyle in India, and the fabulous life at the Chinese court. Marco Polo was awed by the luxury and advances of the Chinese, among them great cities, burning "black stones" (coal), paved roads, and paper money. Thus began the European enchantment with East Asia that ultimately led to great voyages of discovery and a world European empire.

THE TRAVELS OF IBN BATTUTA

So when he held a session at the beginning of Ramadan and I stood before him and said: "I have journeyed to the countries of the world and met their kings. I have been four months in your country without your giving me a reception gift and anything else. What shall I say of you in the presence of other sultans?" He replied: "I have not seen you nor known about you." The qadi and Ibn al-Faqih rose and replied to him saying: "He greeted you and you sent to him some food." Thereupon he ordered that a house be provided for me to stay in and an allowance to be allotted to me. Then, on the night of 27 Ramadan, he distributed among the qadi and the khatib and the faqihs a sum of money which they call zakah (alms distributed at the end of Ramadan) and gave to me with them 33 1/3 mithquals. (standard weight of gold, about 4.72 grams) When I departed he bestowed on me 100 mithqals of gold. . . .

Ibn Battuta (1304–1369) was the Muslim world's Marco Polo. In 1325 he left his home in Tangier and for the next 30 years he covered 75,000 miles within the Dar al Islam ("the abode of Islam") where the sacred law of the Koran prevailed. He is a major source of our knowledge of African kingdoms of the time period, in this case, Mali. In this passage, Ibn Battuta meets Mansa Sulayman. The gold bestowed on Ibn Battuta is at the heart of the story as to why Islamic trades crossed the Sahara, why great African kingdoms arose at this time, and why they were Islamic.

THE VOYAGES OF CHENG HO

The country of Ku-li (Calicut) (a city on India's southwest coast) is the great country of the Western Ocean.

In the fifth year of the Yung-lo (period) the court ordered the principal envoy, the grand eunuch Cheng Ho, and others to deliver an imperial mandate to the king of this country and to bestow on him a patent conferring a title of honor, and the grant of a silver seal, (also) to promote all the chiefs and award them hats and girdles of various grades.

(So Cheng Ho) went there in command of a large fleet of treasure-ships, and he erected a tablet with a pavilion over it and set up a stone which said "Though the journey from this country to the Central Country is more than a hundred thousand li (one-third of a mile), yet the people are very similar, happy and prosperous, with identical customs. We have here engraved a stone, a perpetual declaration for ten thousand ages."

The king of the country is a Nan-k'un (upper class) man; he is a firm believer in the Buddhist (probably Hindu) religion; (and) he venerates the elephant and the ox.

Under the reign of Ming emperor Yung-lo (1402–1424), six great fleets were sent through the waters of Southeast Asia and the Indian Ocean as far as Arabia under the command of China's most famous admiral, a Muslim eunuch of Mongolian ancestry named Cheng Ho (1371–1435). These ships were commissioned to accept the "submission" of various "barbarian" rulers and to stimulate Chinese trade as a result of the severing of the Silk Road by Tamerlane. The expeditions were huge. On the first voyage (1405–1407) there were probably 317 vessels, including 62 massive "treasure ships." The reason the expeditions were stopped after Yung-Lo seems unclear. It could be the cost was too high, or that the traditional Chinese contempt for trade and foreigners reasserted itself. Whatever the case, China never dominated the Indian Ocean trade and isolationism set in. The record of these voyages was made by Ma Huan (ca. 1380), a Chinese Muslim who joined the expeditions as an Arab translator. The reading illustrates China's view of themselves and others.

THE DANCE OF DEATH

Pope: I was, while alive, called holy.
        I feared no one.
        Now I am led wretchedly to death:
        in vain do I resist.

Corpse: Lord Pope, pay attention to the piper's tune!
        You have got to hope to it!
        Dispensations do not help
        When Death wishes to dance with you!

        Ring around the rosies
        Pocket full of posies
        Ashes, ashes
        We all fall down.

The legend of the Dance of Death, which came to the fore during the Black Plague, tells of an encounter between three living and three dead men in which the corpses speak. From this legend were drawn a series of 24 pictures in which men and women from all stations in life who had recently died were forced to dance around a graveyard of moldering corpses. The series begins and ends with a caution that life is brief, that death may come at any moment, and that sin is to be avoided. In this reading, even the pope must abide by the Dance of Death. In the posie rhyme, the ring around the rosies describes the red rash that followed the plague victim's jawline, and the posies tell how people put flowers in their pockets to fend off the disease. Ashes to ashes is when they die and fall down.

THE GENERAL HISTORY OF THINGS OF NEW SPAIN

Montezuma came later. In front of the messengers, the captives were killed—their hearts torn out, their blood sprinkled over the messengers; for they had gone into great danger; they had looked into the very faces of the gods; they had even spoken to them.

After this they reported to Montezuma all the wonder they had seen, and they showed him samples of the food the Spaniards ate.

Montezuma was shocked, terrified by what he heard. He was much puzzled by their food, but what made him almost faint away was the telling of how the great lombard gun, at the Spaniards' command, expelled the shot which thundered as it went off. The noise weakened one, dizzied one. . . .

As as to their gear, it was all iron. They were iron. Their head pieces were of iron. . . .

Their animals they rode—they looked like deer—were as high as roof tops.

They were very white. Their eyes were like chalk. . . .

Their dogs were huge. . . .

When Montezuma was told all this, he was terror-struck. He felt faint. His heart failed him.

Most of the Aztec written sources were destroyed by the Spanish when they arrived in Mexico in the early sixteenth century. One surviving manuscript, the *Codex Mendoza*, which is written in pictographic script, has yet to be translated. As a result, we have few sources for Amerindian culture before the arrival of the Europeans. One exception is the *General History of the Things of New Spain* by Bernardino de Sahagun (ca. 1499–1590). A Franciscan missionary who arrived in New Spain in 1529, he possessed a thorough knowledge of the Aztec language and a scientific curiosity. Relying on the tales of the people and narratives of elderly storytellers, as well as observations, he produced a 12-volume ethnographic work on Amerindian society. This remains today the principal source for the study of Mexican culture at the time of the Spanish conquest. In his own day, Sahagun's work was confiscated by royal decree (1578) because it was seen as an effort to preserve native culture and bloc transformation of society into a Spanish Christian state. It was only rediscovered in the nineteenth century.

Recall Questions

1. Which of the following was the original faith of the Mongols?
   (A) Islam
   (B) Shamanism
   (C) Buddhism
   (D) Christianity
   (E) Sufism

2. Which of the following societies continued into the twentieth century?
   (A) Muscovy
   (B) Ottoman Empire
   (C) Delhi Sultanate
   (D) Mughal Empire
   (E) Safavid Persia

3. The Mongol leader of the Yuan dynasty who was responsible for the unsuccessful attack on Japan was
   (A) Timujin (Genghiz Khan).
   (B) Ogedei.
   (C) Batu Khan.
   (D) Hulagu.
   (E) Kublai Khan.

4. The emerging rulers who gained control of Russian society in the 1500s were
   (A) the Tartars.
   (B) the boyars.
   (C) the serfs.
   (D) the czars.
   (E) the veche.

5. All of the following were gunpowder empires EXCEPT
   (A) Inca.
   (B) Muscovy.
   (C) Ottoman Turkey.
   (D) Spain.
   (E) Mughal India.

6. Which leader encouraged a syncretic Indian religion, organized a diwan, and appointed mansab-dars to represent the government at the local level?
   (A) Tamerlane.
   (B) Akbar.
   (C) Babur.
   (D) Aurangzeb.
   (E) Shah Jahan.

7. Of the following, which language emerged as a new language of trade and became the official language of Pakistan?
   (A) Persian
   (B) Arabic
   (C) Hindi
   (D) Turkic
   (E) Urdu

8. Iran developed a separate identity from other Islamic states of Southwest Asia because
   (1) the Ottoman Turks who conquered Iran were Shi'ite.
   (2) the Safavid leaders claimed to be successors to Ali, cousin and son-in-law of Muhammad.
   (3) the ruler of Iran, Shah Abbas, built a strong, independent national army with the assistance of Sir Anthony Sherley.
   (4) the Safavid leaders established a theocracy.

   (A) 1, 2, and 3
   (B) 1, 2, and 4
   (C) 1, 3, and 4
   (D) 2, 3, and 4
   (E) all of the above

9. The Ottoman Turk who conquered Constantinople was
   (A) Shah Abbas.
   (B) Osman.
   (C) Mehmed II.
   (D) Suleiman.
   (E) Saladin.

10. The janissaries served as
    (A) ambassadors.
    (B) managers of landed estates.
    (C) the sultan's closest advisers.
    (D) provincial governors.
    (E) none of these

11. Among the causes that initiated the Crusades were
    (A) the arrival of the Seljuk Turks in Baghdad.
    (B) the promise of Pope Urban II to defeat the Moors.
    (C) the promise of indulgences for all of those in the Holy Land.
    (D) the desire of Richard the Lion-Hearted to capture Jerusalem.
    (E) the hope of reuniting the Roman and Orthodox Churches.

12. Effects of the plague included
    (A) population losses in Europe of 40 to 45 percent.
    (B) decline of the power of the church.
    (C) increase in wages.
    (D) economic recession.
    (E) all of the above.

13. Which of the following choices appears in the correct chronological order?
    (A) Inca, Aztec, Olmec, Maya
    (B) Aztec, Maya, Inca, Olmec
    (C) Maya, Inca, Olmec, Aztec
    (D) Maya, Olmec, Inca, Aztec
    (E) Olmec, Maya, Aztec, Inca

14. The first maritime power to navigate the Indian Ocean in order to extend political and military power, as well as trade in luxury products, was
    (A) Portugal.
    (B) Spain.
    (C) England.
    (D) France.
    (E) China.

15. Which of the following peoples built Ile-Ife, a city noted for its art in wood and ivory?
    (A) Nok
    (B) Yoruba
    (C) Edo
    (D) Soninke
    (E) Abyssinian

16. What advantages did sea trade offer?
    (A) few political barriers
    (B) wind was a free source of fuel
    (C) shipping was more efficient
    (D) new sources of wealth
    (E) all of the above

To check your answers, see page 393.

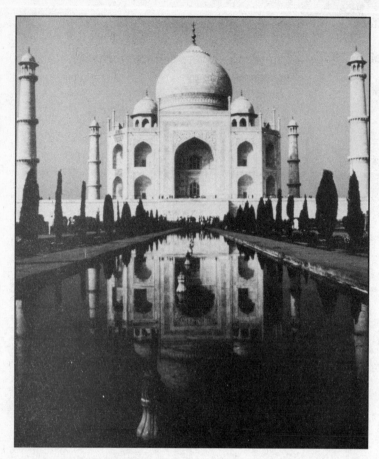

Taj Mahal. *Besides being one of the most beautiful buildings of the world, the Taj Mahal is the best reflection of the synthesis of Muslim, Roman/Byzantine, and Indian architectural styles. The minarets and calligraphy exhibit Islamic forms and the dome the Roman/Byzantine style. The general disposition of the building and its reflection in the water asserts the power of the Mughal dynasty and Hindu artistic styles. Its white marble exterior is inlaid with semi-precious stones in Arabic inscription and floral designs. Built by Shah Jahan (r. 1628–1558) as a memorial tomb for his beloved wife, the Taj Mahal was just one of many buildings like the Red Fort constructed during Shah Jahan's reign that made it the Golden Age of the Mughal Dynasty.*

The Mongol Empire 1294 C.E. *Between 1218 and 1227 C.E. Genghis Khan created the world's greatest empire. At his death, as was Mongol custom, the empire was divided among his four sons.*

The Voyages of Cheng Ho 1405–1433. *At the same time the Chinese were exploring the South China Sea and the Indian Ocean as far west as Africa, Prince Henry of Portugal was inching down the west coast of Africa. Both set the stage and amassed some of the necessary technological knowledge and experience for the voyages of Columbus.*

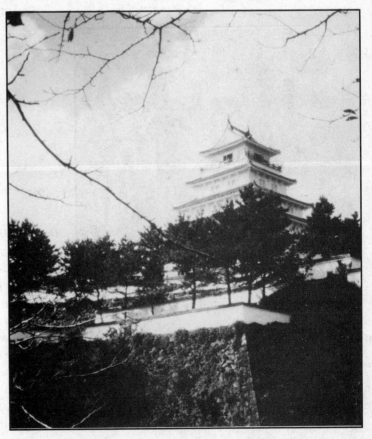

Japanese Gunpowder Castle. This is a Japanese gunpowder castle of the Tokugawa period. In the foreground are the defensive walls and moats typical of feudal castles worldwide. In Europe when gunpowder began to be used, the medieval castles fell into disuse because the walls simply collapsed under canon bombardment. In Japan, however, the greatest castles were built during the Tokugawa regime because only the emperor possessed gunpowder technology. This enabled the samurai warriors to continue their feudal traditions including castle building.

European Trade Routes in the 15th and 16th Centuries. *Increasing trade within Europe by land and sea ended medieval times and created the commercial capital and mentality necessary for launching long distance trade voyages.*

Dance of Death. *The Black Death, or Bubonic Plague, which swept across Asia reaching its zenith in Europe between 1348 and 1350 C.E., was one of the worst pandemics in world history. It killed an estimated one-third of Europe's population and caused long-lasting changes in the political, social, economic, and cultural life of western Europe. The psychological effects of the plague are best seen in the art and literature of the period. One powerful set of visuals is called the* Dance of Death, *a series of 24 sketches in which dead men and women in all stations of life are shown dancing around a graveyard of corpses.*

*Wall Plaque of a Warrior-Kingdom of Benin. In this plaque
from the fifteenth or sixteenth century, a Benin warrior wears
symbols of royal status—a kilt bordered with the woven
pattern of royalty and the high choker, a symbol of the Oda.
The armlet and the leopard-tooth collar are other indicators
of his high status. To the left of the warrior's sword is a
horseshoe-shaped object (a brass manilla) used as currency
and symbolizes in this wall plaque the wealth and power
of Benin.*

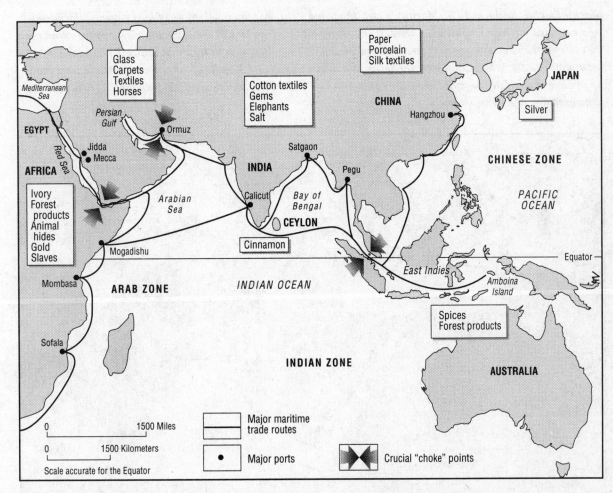

*Indian Ocean Trade Before the Europeans 1500 c.e. Before the arrival of the Europeans, Indian Ocean trade
was extensive and largely in the hands of the Indian and Muslim traders. These traders used the monsoon winds
to travel back and forth across the ocean rather than hugging the coast lines. Once the Portuguese appeared,
the Muslim traders could no longer compete because the Portuguese mounted guns on their ships.*

Machu Picchu. *Begun in 1450, Machu Picchu, in upland Peru, was the royal estate of Inca emperor Pachacuti who extended the Inca Empire to its greatest size. It reflects the Inca love of the mountain view and the reverence they felt for the mountain gods, or* apus. *Machu Picchu was supplied with water by an intricate and extensive system of aqueducts. So skillful were the Incas as builders that the thick walls of the emperor's palace were made up of huge stones fitted together without mortar. Machu Picchu contained courtyards, fountains, agricultural and urban sectors, and living quarters.*

Ottoman, Safavid, and Mughal Empires ca. 1629–1707 c.e. *At the same time that strong absolutist European states were emerging, strong empires stretched across Asia. The common element in the rise of these states was gunpowder, giving rise to the term Gunpowder Empires.*

UNIT
VI

FORCES THAT SHAPED THE MODERN WORLD
(1450–1750)

CHAPTER 18

The Transformation of Europe

CHRONOLOGY	European Renaissance (fourteenth–sixteenth centuries)
	Reformation (1517–1600)
	Commercial Revolution (1300–1700)
	Age of Absolutism (1500–1795)

TERMS

states	humanism	partnerships
nations	secularism	joint stock companies
universities	indulgences	banking system
Salisbury Oath	Lateran Council	mercantilism
Domesday Book	Ninety-Five Theses	Dutch East India
Assize of Clarendon	Edict of Worms	Company
common law	Protestant	absolutism
rights	Confessions of Augsburg	intendants
Magna Carta	Peace of Augsburg	Fronde
parliament	Calvinism	baroque
parlement	Anglican Church	bastion
Estates General	Council of Trent	field army
Babylonian Captivity	Society of Jesus	War of the Spanish
fabliaux	Inquisition	Succession
chansons de geste	Edict of Nantes	Spanish Armada
Hundred Years' War	Thirty Years' War	Great Northern War
Jacquerie	Treaty of Westphalia	Puritanism
Investiture Controversy	"putting out"	The Long Parliament
Golden Bull	("domestic") system	Civil War
Cortes	capitalism	commonwealth
renaissance	insurance	Glorious Revolution

PEOPLE

Niccolo Machiavelli	Leonardo da Vinci	Ignatius of Loyola
Peter Abelard	Julius II	entrepreneurs
Saint Thomas Aquinas	Michelangelo	Huguenots
William I "Conqueror"	Raphael	Johann Fugger
Geoffrey Chaucer	Johann Gutenberg	Louis XIV
William Shakespeare	Desiderius Erasmus	Cardinal Richelieu
Capetian	Thomas More	Cardinal Jules Mazarin
Louis IX	Albrecht Dürer	Jean-Baptiste Colbert
Philip IV "Fair"	Jerome Bosch	Bourbon
Joan of Arc	Nicolaus Copernicus	Philip II
Maximilian I	Galileo Galilei	Peter the Great
condottieri	Descartes	Hapsburgs
Ferdinand and Isabella	Pascal	Hohenzollerns
Castiglione	Isaac Newton	Elizabeth I
Francesco Petrarch	Martin Luther	Oliver Cromwell
Lorenzo "the Magnificent"	Charles V	
Dante	Henry VIII	

PLACES

Holy Roman Empire	Granada	Escorial
Iberian peninsula	Holland	St. Petersburg
Castile and Aragon	Versailles	

The modern world is characterized by global exchange and by notions of government, society, and culture, which differ markably from those of the classical world. Secularism, liberalism, and science and technology are its hallmarks. All emerged in the period when Europe was transformed and then launched the maritime voyages that finally linked the separate continents into one world.

CHAPTER 18

The Transformation of Europe

THE RISE OF THE NATION-STATE

Until this period in history, there had been no such political entity as a nation-state. Up to this point, **states**, defined as sovereign entities, had been based on conquest and control (empires), dynastic heritage and lineage (kingdoms), cultural and religious bonds (theocracies, tribes) or civic cohesion (polis). **Nations** imply another bond—that of people who share a common language, geography, history, and culture. The strength of the nation-state is that it is a sovereignty of people rather than leadership. **Niccolo Machiavelli** (1409–1527), author of *The Prince*, is recognized as one of the first writers to note this new relationship in which the prince must be cognizant of the people. Born in Florence surrounded by a competitive state system, Machiavelli was exiled by the ruling Medicis, causing him to address the question of political power—how a ruler should gain, maintain, and increase it. Instead of suggesting conquest, conversion, or coercion, he suggested that the prince must know the people he ruled, that they are often fickle and ungrateful and are loyal only as benefits are bestowed on them. While maintaining it is better to be feared than loved, the prince would find it desirable "to be both the one and the other."

The nation-state became a unique European political entity growing out of the struggles of kings to diminish the power of the nobility and church by allying with the power of the people.

In putting together a nation-state, all kings did certain things in common: they regularized a common language, gathered together a geographically separate territory, passed laws common for all, developed institutions like parliaments where people other than nobility could have a voice, and raised and paid for standing armies by nourishing a commercial money economy. Some even used religion as a bond. Many nations became conglomerates, joining and homogenizing different ethnic groups. In some cases, certain ethnic groups remained outside the dominant nation as minorities.

Secular Education

At the same time that nation-states began to form in the thirteenth century, secular **universities** appeared. This was in response to the needs of the new bureaucratic states and the increasingly political churches. During medieval times, schools were overwhelmingly connected with churches or monasteries. By the eleventh century, wealthy businessmen in Italian cities like Bologna established municipal schools. By the twelfth century cathedral schools in France and schools in Italy developed into universities. University faculties grouped themselves into schools of law, medicine, arts, and theology. The teachers were known as "**scholastics**" who, in lectures, tried to use faith and reason to arrive at truth. They explored Roman law and Greek and Arabic medical texts. Examinations were oral and difficult. Passage testified to competence in a given subject and were technically licenses to teach. One of the most inspirational teachers of the day was **Peter Abelard** (1079–1142) because he did not merely repeat what was orthodox philosophy, but questioned accepted dogma by systematic doubting. **Saint Thomas Aquinas**, (1225–1274), meanwhile, devoted his time to collecting and organizing knowledge on all topics. These collections were published as summa, or reference books, the most famous of which was *Summa Theologica,* which dealt with a vast number of theological questions.

Formation of the English Nation-State

England, France, Germany, and Spain provide classic studies of how nation-states were formed, some more successfully than others. English nation-state building began with **William I "Conqueror"** (1066–1087). After he had subdued the Saxons in 1066 he set about creating a cohesive state. First, he created a Great Council of lords to help him rule and required that every feudal lord take the **Salisbury Oath** recognizing him as supreme ruler. At the same time, to make sure everyone paid his full taxes, he compiled a **Domesday Book** of taxable property. He also attempted to tame the church by appointing an Archbishop of Canterbury as the highest ranking church official. In 1166 Henry II brought the courts under royal control when he issued the **Assize of Clarendon**. Among other things, this created a system of grand and petit juries, the processes of indictment, and English law as the **common law** of the land. To maintain control over the church, Henry II appointed his friend Thomas à Becket archbishop. When Becket insisted that the church be free of temporal control, Henry's knights assassinated him. Institutionalization of **rights** came in 1215 when English king John found himself needing money to pay for wars. Meeting the barons on the field of Runnymede, John received his money in return for signing the **Magna Carta** (Great Charter), wherein he gave basic liberties to the church, nobles, and city of London, and promised each freeman protection from imprisonment except by "legal judgment of his peers." In addition, taxes could not be imposed except by common council

of the kingdom. Besides the principles of laws and rights, the English nation-state established the principle of **parliament**, or lawmaking, in the hands of the people. During the reign of Edward I (king 1272–1307), an assembly of four powerful groups of the realm were called—bishops, barons, knights, and towns. This served as a model for later parliaments.

The development of a common language and culture also played a part in nation building. For three centuries after the Norman conquest, the ruling classes of England retained their French Norman customs and language while the Anglo-Saxons spoke German dialects. Gradually, however, the two races and languages merged. Some writers like **Geoffrey Chaucer** (ca. 1340–1400) were writing their stories (*Canterbury Tales*) in the vernacular, or everyday language. By the sixteenth century, **William Shakespeare** (1564–1616) was writing plays not only in the national language, but with national themes such as stories about English kings. England also began to develop its own distinct form of Gothic architecture as at Westminster Abbey and Winchester Cathedral, which retained more Romanesque features than those in France. Over the centuries, common political institutions, language, history, and culture created a people tied to a concept of state rather than to the nobility or church. Implicit was the inclusion of the people or nation.

Formation of the French Nation-State

The French, meanwhile, were building their new nation-state. Under the **Capetian** kings (987–1328) in the Ile de France, a well organized centralized government took shape. During the reign of **Louis IX**, a uniform coinage, standard system of law, a **parlement**, or high court of trained lawyers, nobles, and clergymen, developed. A money tax was introduced and a court of commoners so that appeals could be made over the heads of nobles. Having brought the nobility under control, **Philip IV "Fair"** challenged the power of the church and called the first **Estates General** (the three estates were the clergy, nobility, and commoners from the towns) to strengthen his hand against the pope. The result was the **Babylonian Captivity** (1305–1377), transferring the papacy from Rome to Avignon, France. Before he died, Philip governed most of France and the language of the Ile de France supplanted many local dialects. Then, a vernacular literature in the form of **fabliaux** (little songs about animals) and **chansons de geste,** or heroic tales, became popular, giving Frenchmen a common literary heritage.

The Hundred Years' War

The **Hundred Years' War** (1337–1453) between England and France added the last element to the nation-state building process, for it finally delimited the French and English territory and forced inhabitants to identify themselves as either English or French. Up to this time, many nobles owned parcels of land in both countries. In the first phase of the war (1337–1360), the English won battles both on land and sea probably due to the use of artillery for the first time. In the second phase of the war, France received most of the French lands lost to the English, only to lose them again in the third phase. The final phase of the war (1429–1453) began with a miracle when a French peasant girl, **Joan of Arc,** claimed to hear mysterious voices directing her to lead an army to free France of the English. She led French troops to victory and finally drove the English from most of France. By the war's end, the kings with their standing armies financed by a growing commercial class had been strengthened at the expense of the nobles. The loyalty of the middle class had been gained, the rights of the popes to appoint bishops and abbots and hear local appeals had been challenged, and the peasants, in some measure because of the Black Plague, had agitated for higher pay and greater freedom in a great revolt or **Jacquerie** in 1358.

Failure of the German Nation-State Building

The German effort at nation-state building failed and localism triumphed. The reason, perhaps, lay in the goal of its leader, which was to create a **Holy Roman Empire** rather than a German state. The continued reliance and ties with the church, and imperial acquisition rather than state consolidation, caused power to remain in

Germany in the hands of the local princes. The tie between church and state began with Saxon Otto I "Great" (king 936–973). In alliance with the church, he subdued the nobles, moved eastward and created an empire that stretched from the North and Baltic Seas on the Mediterranean and from the Meuse River in France to the Oder River in eastern Germany. Later German emperors also neglected Germany, this time for interests in Italy. The close relationship with the church, however, led to the **Investiture Controversy.** At issue was who had power to appoint bishops and abbots—the church or state. By the Concordat of Worms (1122) the Germany emperors surrendered their claim to invest bishops, and the popes gave up their demand to govern religious estates. The compromise was threatened by German emperor Frederick Barbarossa (emperor 1152–1190) when he reasserted authority over the popes and reunited Germany and Italy. Governing such a large empire, however, allowed the local lords and bishops to reassert their power once more.

When the House of Hapsburg won control of Germany in 1278, the princes were powerful enough to enact the **Golden Bull** (1356), which granted them seven electors sovereign in their own territory and the right to choose the emperor. After 1438 the head of the Hapsburgs was always elected emperor, but he did so by promising not to interfere with the sovereignty of 300 independent governments. National feeling led some Germans to want to restore a central government. This, Hapsburg emperor **Maximilian I** (emperor 1493–1519) tried to do, but he succeeded, not in tying Germany together, but in creating a multinational empire when he added the Netherlands and then, by marriage, Spain to his domain. German emperors from time to time claimed territory in Italy too, especially because of the close relationship with popes.

Failure of the Italian Nation-State Building

Italy was divided into a number of governments. In the north towns became independent, fighting each other bitterly with hired soldiers, or **condottieri,** and in the south, Italy was divided between the kingdoms of Naples and Sicily. Thus, in Germany and Italy, no nation-states were formed because both church and nobility maintained control.

Formation of the Portuguese and Spanish Nation-State

On the **Iberian peninsula**, except for Portugal, the nation-state of Spain took shape. One of the peculiarities of this process was that Catholicism rather than secularism became a cardinal principle of national identity. For centuries the crusading against the Islamic Spanish Moors had failed to unite the Iberian peninsula. Portugal achieved independence under John I (1385–1433) who was elected king by the parliament of **Cortes**. In alliance with England, he drove the Spanish and Arabs from his boundaries. Later monarchs crushed the nobility, made rich commercial entities royal monopolies, and, as already discussed, created a commercial empire. During this period, the rest of the Iberian peninsula was divided also among the Christian kingdoms of **Castile** and **Aragon**, and the Moorish state of **Granada**. The kings in Aragon and Castile tried to create a national spirit by winning the support of the towns. This they did by granting liberal charts and creating local parliaments (Cortes), and by allowing free worship by Moorish and Jewish artisans and merchants. However, they were unable to bring the church under their control. In 1469 **Ferdinand**, heir to the throne of Aragon, married **Isabella**, heiress to Castile. This paved the way for a single Spanish monarchy. Ferdinand and Isabella reorganized the central government, codified laws, sent royal officials to every part of the country to perform tasks once performed by the nobles, and supported the middle class. They depended on the church, however, to help drive out the Moors from Spain. Granada fell in 1492. After winning control of Spain, they turned their attentions to sponsoring the voyages to the East.

Summary

The diminution in power of the nobility and church, and elevation of power of kings aided by the moneyed middle class, was the basic nation-state building mechanism of this period. In exchange for winning the hearts and pocketbooks of the growing commercial class, institutions like Parliaments, Estates Generals, and Cortes were established, giving more people a voice in the government. England, France, Portugal, and Spain succeeded in this process while Germany and Italy did not. This had long-lasting consequences for the history of Europe.

THE SCIENTIFIC AND SECULAR SPIRIT OF THE RENAISSANCE AND REFORMATION

Another aspect of the transformation of Europe besides nation-state building was the transformation in culture from one based in religion to one infused with the scientific and secular spirit. The European Crusaders brought back more than goods from their forays in Southwest Asia. They also became acquainted with the world's scientific and scholarly heritage that had been preserved by Muslim and Byzantine institutions of learning. In 1453, when Byzantium fell to the Ottoman Turks, many Byzantine artists fled to Italy where they passed on their knowledge of paint, color, and technique to Renaissance painters and artists. The worldliness of the church and popes who engaged extensively in wars and politics, secularized much of the Christian mission. In addition, increased commercialization brought the wealth necessary to finance a flourishing of the arts. Finally, the competitive nature of the Italian city-states ruled by despots or oligarchs created an atmosphere conducive to change and innovation.

Renaissance Characteristics

The Renaissance (fourteenth to sixteenth centuries) was first and foremost a cultural movement that began in Florence, Italy, and then moved into northern Europe where commerce also flourished. The world renaissance technically means "rebirth," referring to the rebirth of classical Greek and Roman civilization that had stressed science and secularism. The scientific part of the equation led to experimentation and exploration. The intellectual hallmarks of the Renaissance include individualism, humanism, and secularism. Individualism stressed uniqueness, creativity, genius, and personality. Typical of the spirit was Leon Battista Alberti, architect, artist, mathematician, educator, musician, and poet, who remarked, "Men can do all things if they will." Three types of Renaissance individuals seemed to emerge:

- the gentleman's gentleman as represented by **Castiglione** who wrote *The Book of the Courtier*, the Renaissance man's guide to proper behavior;
- the scholar who, like **Francesco Petrarch**, studied and admired the classics; and
- the "tyrant" who ruled an Italian city state like **Lorenzo "the Magnificent"** of the Medici banking family.

The second hallmark of the Renaissance was **humanism** derived ultimately from the Latin *humanitas* meaning the literary culture needed by anyone who would be considered educated and civilized. It stressed the relearning of antiquity and the classics and copied the classical authors' concern with man's problems and possibilities on this earth rather than remote issues of God. A good example of humanist writing is **Dante**'s *The Divine Comedy*. This long poem is filled with medieval symbolism but it also discusses Homer, Hector, Plato, and other classical figures. Humanism also stressed the classical interest in science. **Leonardo da Vinci**, who is remembered for his artistic masterpieces, the *Mona Lisa* and *The Last Supper*, tinkered with inventions ranging from a flying machine to a water pump.

The third hallmark of the Renaissance was **secularism**. Secularism is a basic concern with the material world instead of with eternal and spiritual considerations. The economic changes and rising prosperity of the Italian cities worked to shift peoples' thoughts toward money and what it could buy. Church leaders did little to combat this new spirit because they participated in it as well. Pope **Julius II** (r. 1503–1513) patronized artists like **Michelangelo** who endowed him with tombs and the great Saint Peter's Basilica.

Renaissance Art

The artistic output of Rome and Florence is the most distinguishing legacy of the Renaissance. While the subject matter of the early Renaissance was overwhelmingly religious, the techniques were classical, illustrating balance, harmony, and restraint. Painter, sculptor, and architect, Michelangelo Buonarroti whose statues of *David*, *Moses,* and the *Pietà* and his frescoes of scenes from the Bible covering the ceiling of the Sistine Chapel remain monuments to his mastery of the human form. Italian Renaissance painters like Giotto used shadings of dark and light and later artists like Tommaso Masaccio and Brunelleschi developed the rules of perspective. When Flemish painters (from Belgium and the Netherlands) began using paints with an oil base rather than a tempera base, artists could make changes on the canvas and develop subtle blends of colors. The brilliance of Italian **Raphael** Santi's colors inspired others, including Leonardo and Michelangelo.

Artists during the Renaissance were revered as free intellectual workers who, because of their genius, were sometimes considered divine. Increasingly art symbolized power. Wealthy merchants and oligarchs commissioned artists to glorify themselves and their families in the form of frescoes, religious panels, and tombs. Steadily the art became more secular in content and realistic in style, reflective of the culture of a small mercantile elite.

The Northern Renaissance

The Renaissance in the north was oriented more toward writing than visual arts, but it also occurred in a milieu of commercial activity around Flanders. The literary emphasis may have been due to European development of movable type by **Johann Gutenberg** around 1450. Paper had been invented by the Chinese in the second century; the Muslims learned it in the eighth century and began exporting it to France and England around 1300. Just as the Koreans had done previously, Gutenberg used blocks of metal, each with an engraved letter, to form pages of words that could be printed using a printing press. Presses began to appear in Italy and northern Europe. Where a medieval copier could only produce two books a year, the publisher Froben printed 24,000 copies of a book by Erasmus.

The Northern Renaissance was also more religious in character perhaps because of its distance from the worldly popes of Rome. Northern humanists had a profound faith in the power of the human intellect. According to the Scholastic Renaissance philosophy, classical ideals of broadmindedness and stoic patience were joined with Christian virtues of love, faith, and hope. Probably the most famous of the Scholastics was **Desiderius Erasmus**. In his book *In Praise of Folly* (1511), he launched a humorous attack on the problems of the Catholic Church. Another northern humanist, **Thomas More** (1478–1535), explored the idea of an ideal socialistic community in Utopia (which literally means "nowhere"). The fine arts in the north were more influenced by medieval traditions, using engraving and religious themes, for example. But they adopted the Italian style of depicting the world realistically and accurately. Painters like Pietr Bruegel, Jan van Eyck, and **Albrecht Dürer**, the "Leonardo of Germany," painted everyday subjects as well as religious subjects with attention to perspective and proportion. Flemish painter, **Jerome Bosch** (ca. 1450–1516) created a masterpiece in *Death and the Miser*. In his treatment of the "dance of death" theme, evil rats control the miser's usurious gold and his guardian angel urges the miser to choose the crucifix, not worldly wealth.

Origins of Modern Science

Science had played important roles in other civilizations like China, classical Greece, and Islam. In the West, science was unique in that it combined observation with the idea of general laws of nature. The origins of modern science can be found in the Renaissance, but not at the hands of the humanist who believed and accepted classical scientific theories like those of Ptolemy (his

geocentric theory of the universe). The scientific tradition that emphasized empirical research, skepticism, and proof grew out of the medieval traditions of careful scholarship and experimental science as established by Roger Bacon (1214–1294) and expanded upon by Francis Bacon (1561–1626) who concluded that the true scientific method was inductive (facts lead to conclusions). Aided by Arab ideas in math, science advanced toward ideas that directly challenged humanists and theologians alike. **Nicolaus Copernicus** (1473–1543), in his book *On the Revolution of Heavenly Bodies*, maintained that the universe was heliocentric. Then Johannes Kepler (1571–1630) and **Galileo Galilei** (1564–1642) supported it with telescopic observations and mathematical proof. Building on the introduction of numerals and algebra to Europe, Dutch engineer Simon Stevin (1584) explained the use of the decimal system, John Napier published the *Marvelous Rule of Logarythms* (1585) making the slide rule possible, **Descartes** (1596–1650) introduced analytical geometry, and **Pascal** (1623–1662) the law of probabilities. The crowning scientific achievement came with **Isaac Newton** (1642–1727). With mathematical evidence, Newton explained the "law of gravitation" as a governing principle of the universe. In marvelous simplicity, he showed a universe operated by unchanging laws that, when discovered, could reach into other areas of life. His book *Principia* inspired a new way of thinking and looking at the world for he insisted that ideas must meet the test of reason and observation. Science became a religion in itself for many, but for others such as Descartes, there remained separate religious and physical worlds. **Pascal**, however, in a remarkable book called *Pensées*, said there was no separation. One must "wager" that God exists and that the whole world is infused with meaning, a tenet of contemporary science.

The Reformation

The Renaissance spirit of individualism and reason met head on with growing secularism and corruption in the church, producing a serious challenge, not just to its power, which had already been under attack by the kings, but its theology. Christian humanists like Erasmus were already satirizing church corruption, which took several forms—immorality and illiteracy of priests, pluralism, and absenteeism (clerics holding many benefices and collecting taxes but never visiting the parishes), ostentatious wealth, and military involvement of popes, and **indulgences** (payment for the remission of sin). Not unaware of the situation, Pope Julius II called a **Lateran Council** to Rome from 1512 to 1517 to discuss issues. Before reform could be instituted, **Martin Luther** in 1517 forced the issue when he attached to the door of the Wittenburg church the Ninety-Five Theses, or propositions, on indulgences. At the heart of Luther's attack was the question of where authority in Christianity lay— with the church or the individual. Luther argued that salvation could be attained by faith alone, that religious authority resided in the individual conscience, that the church was the entire Christian community, not just the clergy, and that all vocations were of equal merit. **Charles V** of the Holy Roman Empire reacted by declaring Luther an outlaw in the **Edict of Worms**. In 1529 German princes met to "protest" lending the name **Protestant** to a movement that was formally defined in the **Confessions of Augsburg** in 1530.

The Triumph of Lutheranism

Luther ignited not just religious but political and social unrest as well. Townspeople were attracted because they resented the fact that ecclesiastics were exempt from taxes and civic responsibilities. Peasants were attracted because, in his treatise *On Christian Liberty*, Luther wrote, "A Christian man is the most free lord of all and subject to none." This the peasants interpreted as license to rebel against the local lords, which they did in 1525, even though Luther disassociated himself from it. As Lutheran theology developed, it exalted the state and subordinated the church to the state, positions crucial to the development of nation-states. Charles V's preoccupation with his territories in Flanders, Spain, Italy, and the Americas, and the besieging of

Vienna by the Turks in 1529 prevented him from taking strong measures against the Protestants. The result was that Germany was torn apart politically. Between 1521 and 1555 the Hapsburg-Valois wars between Germany and France advanced the cause of Protestantism. In this contest the ironic situation occurred where Catholic French kings were supporting Protestant German nobles. Finally, in 1555 Charles V agreed to the **Peace of Augsburg**, accepting the status quo and officially recognizing Lutheranism.

Calvinism

Soon the Protestant Reformation spread to other areas of Europe. By 1555 much of northern Europe had broken with the Roman Catholic Church. All of Scandinavia, England, Scotland, and cities like Geneva and Zurich rejected the authority of Rome and adopted new faiths. **Calvinism**, with its belief in predestination and the value of work, became the most dynamic force in sixteenth-century Protestantism because it had a strong and well-organized church and a systematic theology. It also promoted education so people could read the Bible. Calvinism was accepted, not only in Switzerland, but in portions of Germany, France, the Netherlands, England, and Scotland. In England, **Henry VIII** set up the **Anglican Church** initially to challenge papal attempts to enforce his first marriage.

Catholic Counter-Reformation

The Catholic Church soon set about reform and hopes of a Counter-Reformation. Between 1545 and 1563 the **Council of Trent** met to work on reconciliation and reform. Reconciliation became impossible when Lutherans and Calvinists who had been invited insisted that the sole basis for discussion was the Scriptures, but the Council corrected many of the abuses that had previously plagued the church. New religious orders also rose to play powerful reform roles. The **Society of Jesus**, or Jesuits, founded by **Ignatius of Loyola** (1491–1556) was one of them. They played a powerful role in converting Asians, Latin American Indians, and others to Catholicism and in spreading Christian education all over Europe. Another instrument of the Counter-Reformation was the **Inquisition**, which ferreted out heretics and during which was published an *Index of Prohibited Books*.

Religious Wars

Despite these efforts, religious wars erupted everywhere. In most cases they were intertwined with nation-state and colonial rivalries. France was the scene of bitter battles between French Protestants or **Huguenots** and Catholics, as well as new rebellions by landed nobles against royal authority. These ended only with the granting of tolerance to Protestants in the **Edict of Nantes** in 1598. In 1618 the **Thirty Years' War** raged in Germany. German Protestants and their allies, such as Lutheran Sweden, were pitted against the Holy Roman Emperor backed by Spain. It was ended only by the **Treaty of Westphalia** in 1648, in which princely states and cities chose one religion or another. This treaty also reduced Spanish power in favor of France. Religious wars broke out in England also. These too were often intertwined with questions of royal power. During the sixteenth century Elizabeth I and Catholic Mary Queen of Scots quarreled, and in the 1640s civil war broke out, resulting in limited religious toleration in 1688.

The wars promoted growing literacy, concentration on family life, and secularism as people became disillusioned with the power of religion to maintain peace. Martin Luther's anxieties about salvation illustrated that the religious convulsions had one foot in past medieval times. But they also opened the door to the modern secular world. The Renaissance humanist spirit favored individual salvation over church dictate. The political complexion of Europe changed as well. Part of the religious conflict was intertwined, not only with the creation of nation-states, but with commercial rivalries and changes in class structure.

THE COMMERCIAL REVOLUTION— THE CAPITALIST SYSTEM AND MIDDLE CLASS CULTURE

The commercial revolution can be compared to the agricultural revolution in importance in world history. It affected political, social, and cultural institutions and was the impetus for the Industrial Revolution. Nations that have experienced the commercial revolution have, in a sense, become "modern." Those that have not remain stultified in their ability to distribute efficiently the products of industry, produce capital, assess profitability, meet consumer demand, and efficiently handle currency transactions. Like the agricultural revolution, the commercial revolution did not occur overnight. Trade and barter had been a fact of life for as long as there was a surplus. What changed and made it a so-called "revolution," was the amount of people engaged in trade, the distances and range of items that were included in trade, the change in society and culture that took place, particularly the growth of the middle class, and the system under which trade was carried out, called capitalism. Aspects of the commercial revolution have already been noted in the rise of maritime trade complexes, and the nation-state and the scientific and secular spirit. While only ten percent of the population engaged in trade in the sixteenth century, merchants exerted influence far beyond their numbers.

The origins of the commercial revolution were in the late Middle Ages when there was a great increase in trade in luxury items from the East and staple items like wool in Flanders. Some merchants operated between the countryside and the towns, while others operated on an international scale. For example, merchants might buy raw wool in sheep-grazing countries of Spain and England. They would then sell it to cloth manufacturers in the Netherlands and Italy in a **"putting out"** or **"domestic" system**. In this system, the merchants would distribute or "put out" wool to individual cottage weavers and then collect the finished cloth product to sell in the marketplace. This system greatly undermined the medieval guild system and was the precursor to the factory.

Capitalism

The capitalist system under which commerce was practiced greatly aided its development. Under **capitalism**, ownership of private property gave traders the impetus to take great risks in return for great profits. This profit or "capital" they often reinvested in their own businesses or held in banks to lend to others. Out of this free exchange pattern came a free market where supply and demand regulated price and became a way of reckoning cost and profit. Private ownership, profit, or capital reinvestment and a free market are the hallmarks of the capitalist system.

Reasons for Commercialization

Greater commercialization occurred for three reasons:

1. In the sixteenth century massive imports of gold and silver from Spain's colonies in Latin America provided both species for an expanding economy and forced prices up. New wealth, in turn, heightened demand. Inflation, in turn, hurt landlords with fixed rent and encouraged merchants to take new risks, for borrowing was cheap when money was losing value.
2. The population grew 20 percent between 1500 and 1650, causing an increase in demand, production, and exchange in items from pewter tableware to feather beds.
3. Colonial markets increased trade and stimulated manufacturing.

The hopes for high profits lured many merchants into overseas ventures that were risky due to the cost of outfitting ships, the dangers in the voyage, and the uncertainty of market price. Merchants who were willing to take great risks were called **entrepreneurs**. Entrepreneurs developed new ways of doing business to reduce the financial risks. They developed a system of **insurance** and formed **partnerships** or **joint stock companies**. To protect markets and create monopolies, they formed trading leagues like the Hanseatic League, or in partnership with government, were granted regional monopolies as, for instance, the English East India Company, the Dutch East India Company, and so on, which increasingly pushed out Arab and Indian traders in East Asia and the Indian Ocean.

Banking

Not only did merchants need to reduce risk, they needed vast amounts of capital. This gave rise to the **banking system**. The Muslim inventions of banking, letters of credit, and checks were copied by Italian merchants. At first, banks were private firms. The Medici bank in Florence made loans to entrepreneurs and monarchs who were also generally cash poor. **Johann Fugger** founded another influential bank in Germany in the late 1300s. Since monarchs felt no obligation to repay a predecessor's debt, many private banks either went bankrupt or charged exorbitantly high interest rates. Soon public banks backed by the state like Banco di San Giorgio in Genoa (1584) and the Bank of England (1694) came into existence. Government revenues from taxes and tariffs as well as individuals and other countries were deposited in national banks. To increase state wealth, governments began instituting a policy of **mercantilism**. This policy attempted to create a favorable balance of trade by increasing exports over imports by means of tariffs, trade monopolies, and increased foreign trade. European monarchs saw the advantages of increased trade and production for they could tax the wealth of merchants and of imports. They often used this for military hardware and overseas empire to create even more wealth.

The Rise of the Middle Class

The rise of the merchant class completely reshaped the culture of the period and laid the basis for the middle class. Dietary habits changed as tastes became more sophisticated. Contact with the eastern civilizations introduced Europeans to eating with forks and knives and using napkins. Many serfs improved their social position by moving from the countryside. One historian estimates that by 1600 the average western peasant or artisan owned five times as many "things" as his southeastern European counterpart. Better furnishings prompted people to stay at home. Women became regulators of the domestic social routine. The changes in values and destruction of old ways contributed to the witchcraft hysteria that arose in various parts of western Europe and New England in the seventeenth and eighteenth centuries, in which 100,000 suspected witches were accused and killed. The hysteria reflected new tensions in the family and the role of women, resentments against the poor by communities unwilling to accept their poverty, and uncertainties about religion. The rich merchants, meanwhile, spent conspicuously and attempted to move into the aristocracy by buying up land and becoming landed gentry. The idea of "upward mobility" began with the commercial revolution.

The Commercial Revolution in Holland

A classic study of the commercial revolution as it occurred in **Holland** is instructive. By the Peace of Westphalia (1648), the seven northern provinces of the Netherlands (Holland being one and the most important) became independent of Spain. Within each province, an oligarchy of wealthy merchants called "regents" held power and a federal assembly met at The Hague to handle foreign affairs. Holland, because of its navy and wealth, dominated the republic. The merchants and financiers who controlled the government were not aristocratic but middle class, emphasizing the value of thrift, hard work, and moderation. They also divorced the state and religion, welcoming people of all faiths. This, in turn, attracted foreign capital and investment and made Holland a financial clearinghouse. The fishing industry gave Holland its start. Profits from herring stimulated the largest merchant marine, estimated at 16,000 ships, and the lowest shipping rates in Europe. Because all the wood for ships had to be imported, Holland bought whole forests from Norway. They controlled the Baltic grain trade, and, because they dealt in bulk, they could not be undersold. Soon they became known for precision lenses (for the newly invented telescope for muskets) and diamonds. In 1602 a group of regents formed the **Dutch East India Company** as a joint stock company. Within half a century, the Dutch were competing with the Portuguese seizing the Cape of Good Hope, Ceylon, and Malacca, giving stockholders a 30 percent annual return on investment. The Dutch West India Company, founded in 1621, traded with Latin America and Africa. Trade and commerce brought tremendous wealth and the highest standard of living in Europe. Wealth, however, also brought war in the 1670s with England and France and the long war of the Spanish Succession.

Summary

Views on why the commercial revolution occurred in western Europe vary. Some historians believe the rise of the nation-state with the political alliance of king and merchants was the reason. Others find a link between capitalism and Protestantism. The Protestant work ethic and frugality underpinned the accumulation of capital. Still others find the answer in Europe's maritime adventures, which brought spectacular wealth and specie to fund commerce. Yet others see the spirit of the Renaissance, of secularism, science, and adventure as the reason. Whatever the reason, western Europe became the seat of a vibrant new wealth that completely changed the world economy.

ABSOLUTISM AND EMPIRE

The rise in power of kings as heads of nation-states, the secular spirit, and commercialism began to give European heads of state unprecedented power. This was especially so because a money economy combined with taxing abilities gave kings the means to build and maintain large state military and bureaucratic systems. This led to war. In fact, there were only five years of complete peace in Europe during the sixteenth century.

Absolutism

Absolutism means the unlimited power to govern. The absolutist state is one in which sovereignty is embodied in the person of the ruler as exemplified in Louis XIV's statement, "L'etat c'est moi!" (I am the state.) Absolutist kings often claimed to rule by "divine right," that is, they were responsible to God alone. They tried to control all important institutions of state including the church, the bureaucracy, and the military, and they often set court style. Instead of being dependent on the nobility and church as medieval kings were, absolutist monarchs freed themselves from this by gaining financial support from the nobility in return for freedom from taxation, by the creation of bureaucracies that, in some countries like France, utilized the middle class and in others an aristocratic elite, and by the right to maintain permanent standing armies. Underpinning absolutist power was the power to raise revenue by forcing taxes higher, devising alternative methods of raising revenue or gaining empire.

Absolutist France

The best example of an absolute monarchy of this period is France under **Louis XIV** who became an inspiration for rulers across Europe. Henry IV and his minister Maximilian de Bethune, duke of Sully (1560–1641) laid the basis for absolutism by reducing government debt and taxes on the overburdened peasantry and by appreciating the significance of overseas trade in their subsidization of the Company for Trade with the Indies. After his death, **Cardinal Richelieu**, as first minister of state, set in place the cornerstone of French absolutism by subordinating all groups and institutions to the monarchy. He leveled castles to crush the nobility, and never called a session of the Estates General. He introduced agents of the central government called **intendants** into the provinces, regulated economic activity, collected taxes, recruited for the army, and put down a Huguenot revolt. The strength of the government, however, was in some measure related to the government's ability to tax and this was limited by hereditary exemptions of the wealthy and rights of provincial assemblies. Richelieu's successor, **Cardinal Jules Mazarin**'s attempt to increase royal revenue led to the **Fronde**, or uprising, between 1648 and 1653. The result was certain that factions of French society remained beyond the pale

of taxes. This convinced Louis XIV (1643–1715) that as much power as possible must be concentrated in his hands to prevent anarchy. Among other ways, he did this by building a magnificent palace at **Versailles**, which became a symbol of order and the king's power. It is decorated in a style called **baroque** that is characterized by religious emotionalism, drama, and lavish decoration and frescoes.

Under foreign minister **Jean-Baptiste Colbert** (1619–1683), France followed a rigorous mercantilist policy. The state supported new and old industries in order to make France self-sufficient and avoid imports. He also built a formidable merchant marine. The commercial classes prospered from 1660 to 1700 as a result but the brunt of taxes still fell on the poor French peasants, many of whom emigrated. To unify the state religiously, Louis XIV revoked the Edict of Nantes, causing many skilled craftsmen to flee also.

The Modern Military

As with all absolute monarchs, the military consumed a great amount of time and money. The growing power of the state coincided with great changes in warfare. The crucial development both by land and sea was the use of artillery. Cannons became larger and more powerful. Starting with the Portuguese, ships were designed with side-mounted guns that destroyed by gunfire rather than ramming. This technique was used in European naval warfare until the twentieth century. By 1714 the British navy possessed 247 of these "capital" ships. The key to land warfare of the period was the **bastion** with its low walls, vast moats, and outworks, with defensive cannons to protect it from artillery. Blockades became a major offensive strategy to counteract this, causing sieges to be the most common form of warfare. During the Spanish struggle to suppress the Dutch revolt, the seizure of Haarlem (1572–1573) took seven months; that of Ostend, three years. This led to the great "military revolution" of the age—the **field army**. In the early sixteenth century the field army consisted of about 10,000 men armed with lances and archers. From the late sixteenth century, most of the infantry was armed with muskets. In the 1590s, starting with the Dutch, field training and firing drills were developed. Army size grew. The major battles of Louis XIV's war in the 1700s involved as many as 100,000 per army. The cost involved meant that small countries could only go to war in alliance with large countries.

France led the way in changing the character of warfare. Secretary of War Le Tellier, created a professional army, employing soldiers rather than nobles, standardizing weapons, and utilizing training, discipline, drill, promotions, and so on. With this, France was able to dominate the politics of Europe. In 1667 it invaded Flanders; in 1681 it sent armies into Germany. Then, an alliance led by Britain countered and halted France temporarily. After five years, however, Louis XIV prepared for the **War of the Spanish Succession** (1701–1713). Provoked by dynastic and territorial questions, the Dutch and English countered the French acquisition of the Spanish Netherlands and rich trade with Spanish colonies. The wars ended with the Treaty of Utrecht in 1713 where balance of power and partition principles prevailed. Louis XIV's grandson Philip remained the first **Bourbon** (French) king of Spain but France surrendered Newfoundland, Nova Scotia, and Hudson Bay territory to England. England acquired Gibraltar, Minorca, and control of Spanish African slave trade. The very concentration of French power caused enemies to attack at the periphery and, to some extent, the conflicts of European powers were "world wars" that were fought as much for overseas empire as for territory in Europe. These rivalries, in their way, led to the West's domination of the world.

Spanish Absolutism

Spanish absolutism preceded that of the French and had a more international flavor to it. As with all absolutist states, the Spanish in the sixteenth century developed a permanent bureaucracy, a standing army, and national taxes. Spain also had monarchs whose claims to divine right were connected with a state religion, Roman Catholicism, and whose monarchs ruled as defenders of the faith. While France's absolutism was confined to its borders, Spain's developed on the basis of silver bullion from Peru. Spanish gold, silver, and armies dominated Europe and much of the world in the sixteenth century. Unlike France, Spanish wealth was based on specie from the New World rather than commerce and the middle class, largely as a result of expulsion of the Jews and Moors. As in France, wars became an artifice of absolutism and empire. **Philip II** believed England under the rule of Elizabeth I was the major factor in his inability to regain control of the Netherlands and restore Catholicism. From behind the walls of the beautiful **Escorial** palace, the Versailles of Spain, he plotted his holy war. Pouring millions of Spanish ducats into a vast fleet, the **Spanish Armada** sailed for England in 1588 only to be decisively defeated by the British. From then on, Spain went into decline. Between 1610 and 1650 Spanish trade with the colonies fell 60 percent as the Dutch and English began trading with the colonies. Epidemics among miners and exhaustion of veins left the Spanish with no revenue, high debt and no middle class to rescue it. By the seventeenth century, Spain's grandeur was a memory of cherished Spanish ideals—military glory and strong Roman Catholic faith.

Russian Absolutism

Peter the Great (1682–1725) of Russia was yet another example of an absolutist monarch. He completely revamped the Russian government, dividing the state into provinces and appointing governors, creating a senate, making the church a state agency, and creating a merit-based, military-civilian bureaucracy in which nobles and non-nobles alike had to work their way up the ranks. Instead of building a palace like Versailles or the Escorial, he built a new city, **St. Petersburg**, from which to rule. He set the style for Russia, including the cutting of beards. Like other absolutist states, he waged war incessantly from 1700 to 1721 against Sweden in the **Great Northern War**, giving Russia much of Estonia and Latvia. He established a regular service army, infantry, special forces of Cossacks (frontier horsemen) and an elite sharp shooter corps of "streltsy."

Other absolutist states were created in Austria under the **Hapsburgs** and in Prussia under the **Hohenzollerns**. In neither of these states were the nobility and serfdom sufficiently extinguished and the forces of nationalism sufficiently inspired to create absolutist nation-states.

The Failure of Absolutism in England

In England limited monarchical power and constitutionalism (or limitation of government by law) emerged. In 1588 **Elizabeth I** exercised great personal power, manipulating, as her father Henry VIII had done, the House of Commons to pass legislation. But debt by Elizabeth I, the last of the Tudor royal family, and James I, the first of the Stuart royal family, soon became an issue, as did religion. Many in England wanted to inject middle class values and ethics into the Church of England and "purify" it (**Puritanism**). When Scotland revolted, Charles I was compelled to call Parliament. The **Long Parliament** as it was called (1640–1660), to his dismay, enacted legislation limiting the power of the monarch. Soon **Civil War** broke out (1642–1649) between Parliament and its supporters the Roundheads, and the king and his supporters, the Cavaliers. When parliamentary forces prevailed, Charles I was beheaded (1649) and kingship abolished. A **commonwealth**, or republican, form of

government was formed but, in fact, **Oliver Cromwell** (1599–1658), who had controlled the parliamentary army, controlled the government. He instituted a Puritan military dictatorship of sorts, which collapsed on his death. In 1660 the Stuart monarchy and Parliament were reestablished, but distrust between king and Parliament grew during the reigns of Charles II and James II. The king suspended the Parliament at will, reviving the absolutism of his father, Charles I. This caused the **Glorious Revolution** (1688–1689) in which, without bloodshed, William and Mary accepted the English throne from Parliament, recognizing its supremacy once and for all.

Summary

The internal transformation of Europe, including the growth of the nation-state, the rise of secularism and science, the commercial revolution, and absolutism, produced the spectacular changes that made the West Europeans launch the Atlantic voyages and introduced the Global Age. The nation-state was the political framework necessary to launch the voyages, science gave them the means, the commercial revolution the reason, and absolutism the military wherewithal to dominate the seas and lands touched by the adventurers.

KEY TERMS

CHAPTER 19
The World Exchange

CHRONOLOGY   *Voyages of Discovery and Conquest of the Americas (1450–1650)*
Christopher Columbus—Discovery of America (1492)
Columbian Exchange (1500–1850)

TERMS

Treaty of Tordesillas	chattel slavery	Company of New France
Line of Demarcation	metis	Dutch West India
caravel	British East India	Company
Reconquista	Company	corporate colony
encomienda	Treaty of Paris	Virginia Company
Council of the Indies	India Act	indentures
audiencia	Shimabara Rebellion	Mayflower Compact
New Laws	galleons	Russian American
diaspora	presidios	Company
Middle Passage	missions	Treaty of Nerchinsk
factories	Northwest Passage	

PEOPLE

Prestor John	mestizo	Manchus
Bartholomew Diaz	mulatto	Ch'ing
Vasco da Gama	zambo	Miguel Lopez de Legazpi
Pedro Alvares Cabral	castizo	Francisco de Coronado
Alfonso de Albuquerque	casta	Hernando de Soto
Christopher Columbus	peninsulares	Junipero Sera
Ferdinand Magellan	Creoles	Samuel de Champlain
Hernando Cortes	Osei Tutu	Jacques Marquette
Francisco Pizarro	Agaja	Louis Joliet
Atahualpa	Boer	Henry Hudson
John Cabot	sepoys	Puritans
Jacques Cartier	Francis Xavier	Old Believers
viceroys	Robert de Nobili	Anika Stroganov
Bartolome de las Casas	Matteo Ricci	Yermak

PLACES

Hispaniola	Songhay	Nagasaki
Azore Islands	Kanem-Borneo	Manila
Cape Horn	Hausaland	New Amsterdam
Malay Archipelago	Mauritius	Jamestown Colony
Potosi	Zanzibar	Siberia
Roanoke	Goa	Lena River
Jamestown	Madras	Okhotsk
St. Lawrence	Bombay	Kamchatka
Ashanti	Calcutta	Kuriles
Dahomey	Malacca	
Bight of Benin	Macao	

The World Exchange

The transformation of Europe prompted the voyages of discovery and an Atlantic exchange that soon became worldwide. With their worldly appetites and concerns, nation-states became the vehicle of spectacular voyages west. The discoveries, conversely, enriched the nation-states of Europe and their monarchs, fueling even more competitive adventures and commercial enterprise. The Americas, Africa, and Europe were changed in the process.

The process of change across the Atlantic is often called the Columbian Exchange. The exchange refers to the process of hemispheric transfer of people, disease, plants and animals, and traditions. Between 1500 and 1850 perhaps 10 to 15 million Africans and five million Europeans crossed the Atlantic. In terms of disease, Amerindians, long isolated, suffered more than the Europeans. Measles and smallpox devastated Indian populations. The Indian population of the Caribbean was almost totally wiped out, and in Mexico there were 25 million Indians in 1519 and one million in 1605. In Peru the population is estimated to have fallen from 1.3 million in 1570 to 600,000 in 1620. Disease went the other way too, as syphilis seems to have had an American origin. In terms of animals, the Spanish introduced horses, cattle, sheep, chickens, and domestic goats and pigs. The arrival of horses gave the plains Indians like the Apaches the mobility to hold off the Europeans for 300 years and cattle soon replaced Indians in Mexico. So receptive was the American environment to cattle that, when, in 1587, 100 head of cattle were abandoned in the Rio de la Plata, 20 years later their numbers had swelled to 100,000. To Europe from the Americas went parrots and other exotic animals. In terms of foodstuffs, Europeans brought wheat, melons, olives, and most important, sugar cane, which became the basis of plantation economies. Subsequently, bananas, coffee, and coconuts were introduced from other parts of the world encountered by Europeans. From the Americas went corn, potatoes, tomatoes, tobacco, and chocolate. The potato became a staple of Russia and Ireland, and manioc (tapioca) and casava spread to tropical regions in Asia and Africa. Finally, traditions crossed the Atlantic, from Europe came Christianity, capitalism, and nationalism. To Europe went a spirit of pioneering, freedom, change, and adaptation.

THE VOYAGES OF DISCOVERY AND CONQUEST OF THE AMERICAS

The period from 1450 to 1650, when Europeans discovered, explored and then migrated to the Americas, launched a Global Age in world history. The Portuguese started the process when, in 1415 they took Ceuta (an Arab city in northern Morocco) in search of gold, an overseas route to the spice markets of India, the Christian conversion of the Muslims, and search for the mythical Christian ruler of Ethiopia, **Prestor John**. Between 1394 and 1460 the Portuguese explored the coast of West Africa, then, between 1481 and 1495 established trading posts on the Guinea coast where gold from Timbuktu was brought back to Lisbon. In 1487 **Bartholomew Diaz** rounded the Cape of Good Hope and between

1497 and 1499, **Vasco da Gama** reached India. He returned with Indian wares, prompting King Manuel to dispatch 13 ships under **Pedro Alvares Cabral** to set up trading posts in India. On April 22, 1500, during the voyage, the coast of South America was sighted and claimed for Portugal. Returning from India, half of Cabral's fleet was lost, but the six spice-laden ships that did return more than paid for the whole expedition. Thereafter, regular expeditions were sent, pitting Muslims against Christians for control of the Indian Ocean trade. From 1509 to 1515 **Alfonso de Albuquerque** destroyed the Muslim coastal forts with cannons at Calicut, Ormuz, Goa, and Malacca, the vital centers that controlled South Asian trade.

Spanish Exploration

Spanish exploration began with the fall of Granada in 1492, signaling the end of Muslim kingdoms in Spain. Then Isabella ordered the Jews to convert or leave the country (200,000 may have left), severely disrupting some aspects of the economy. With religious unification established, Isabella and Ferdinand were willing to support Genoese merchant, **Christopher Columbus**'s (1451–1507) project to reach the Indies by going west. On August 3, 1492, Columbus, with three small vessels—the Santa Maria, Nina, and Pinta—sailed from Palos, Spain, landing in the Bahamas in October. Reconnoitering around Cuba and Haiti, Columbus found some gold and some unfamiliar plants, but no grand Asian civilization with spices, silks, or pearls. Columbus returned to Spain in January, 1493, having left a crew in **Hispaniola** (Haiti). Between 1492 and 1502 Columbus made three more voyages, discovering San Salvador, Puerto Rico, Jamaica, Cuba, Trinidad, and Honduras.

Columbus' voyages fueled rivalry between Spain and Portugal. Both, for instance, lay claim to new lands and to the Caribbean. To keep peace between his two Christian subjects, the pope facilitated the **Treaty of Tordesillas** in 1494. The Treaty drew a **Line of Demarcation** that ran 1100 miles north and south of the **Azore Islands** in the Atlantic around the globe. This gave Portugal trading rights in India, China, the East Indies and eastern Brazil, and the Spanish Americas. The search for precious metals not found in the Caribbean caused Charles V of Spain in 1519 to commission **Ferdinand Magellan** (1480–1521) to find a direct route to Southeast Asia. He found his way around **Cape Horn** to the Pacific, sailing to the **Malay Archipelago**. Though Magellan was killed, the expedition returned to Spain by way of the Indian Ocean and the Atlantic, proving the earth was round and bigger than once thought.

Spanish Conquest

Soon after, conquest began. Spanish adventurer, **Hernando Cortes** (1485–1547) crossed from Hispaniola to Mexico in 1519. With 600 men, 17 horses, and 10 cannons, he subdued the Aztec Empire and took the Aztec emperor Montezuma captive. This remarkable feat was due to help received by Cortes along the way from disgruntled Aztec subjects, who believed that Cortes might be the fabled Quetzocoatl, who was supposed to return that very year. European disease and superior European weaponry also aided the conquest. Between 1531 and 1550 the Spanish gained control of rich silver veins in northern Mexico. The story of Mexican conquest was repeated in Peru. **Francisco Pizarro** (1470–1541), another conquistador (explorer, conqueror) crushed the Inca empire in Peru when he imprisoned and then killed Inca leader **Atahualpa**. As in Mexico, disease greatly aided Spanish conquest. In 1545 Pizarro opened the richest silver mine in the New World at **Potosi** in the Peruvian highlands. Once the Spanish found bullion in the New World, they lost interest in the spice trade in the Malaccas.

Explorers from Other Countries

There were explorers from other countries as well. In 1497 a Genoese merchant living in London, **John Cabot**, discovered Newfoundland, and in 1498 the New England coast. Between 1534 and 1541 a Frenchman, **Jacques Cartier**, explored the Saint Lawrence region of

Canada. Since neither expedition found spices or gold, the English and French lost interest in exploration for the time being.

Reasons for Discovery and Conquest

Reasons for exploration and conquest vary. Some historians stress technology, noting the Portuguese development of the **caravel**, a light, three-masted sailing ship that, though slower than a galley, could hold more cargo. When fitted with cannons and powered by the wind, it gave Europeans navigational and military superiority. Another reason was spices. Europeans had become used to spices like nutmeg, mace, ginger, cinnamon, and pepper to add flavor to their diet and for medicinal purposes. When the Ming expelled foreigners and the Ottomans captured the eastern Mediterranean trade, Europeans were forced to find a new route to the spice market. Yet another reason for exploration was, no doubt, the Renaissance spirit of curiosity. Also, government sponsorship and national rivalries assisted in the explorations, for, until the likelihood of riches was found, investors were reluctant to expend the massive sums necessary for the expeditions. Social conditions in Spain and Portugal were also a cause. After the **Reconquista** (reconquest of Spain from Muslims), young upper class Spanish found economic and political opportunities limited as the aristocracy controlled the land and administrative positions and Spanish law forbade noble participation in economic ventures. Ambitious young men, therefore, sought their fortunes in the New World. Religion also played a part. The desire to convert Muslims and pagans was real and of deep conviction. There is no greater testament to this than the 70,000 churches and 20,000 missions that the Spanish built in the New World. The final reason for exploration and conquest was wealth. As Cortes announced on his conquest of Mexico, "I have come to win gold, not plow the fields like a peasant." Indeed, between 1503 and 1650, 16 million kilograms of silver and 185,000 kilograms of gold from mines at Zacatecas and Guanajuato in Mexico and Potosi in Peru entered Seville's port.

THE EMERGING "ATLANTIC WORLD"—THE AFRICAN DIASPORA AND THE PLANTATION SYSTEM

Spanish Rule in the Americas

The Caribbean experience laid the framework for Spanish economic and political control in the Americas. The West African model of African-European relationships based on trade forts, trade in gold and slaves, and private investment by royal contract proved unworkable in the Caribbean where there was no gold. Therefore, more extensive colonialization began to take place. The surplus product in the Caribbean proved to be the agricultural Taino Indians, so that the **encomienda** systems or grants of Indians to individuals in a kind of serfdom grew. The Spanish began to build towns according to a grand plan form with the town hall, major church, and governor's palace in the central plaza. In 1570 Spain issued a basic set of instructions for setting up towns. Then, administrative institutions were created. The Spanish king ruled through the **Council of the Indies**, which made policy and appointed governors or **viceroys**, oversaw the treasury office, and the royal court of appeals or **audiencia**. Spanish legal tradition transferred as did the Catholic Church represented by contingents of missionaries such as the Dominicans, Franciscans, and Jesuits. Holders of ecclesiastical powers were nominated by the Spanish crown. The Catholic Church profoundly influenced the intellectual and cultural life of the Americas. Construction of baroque cathedrals, publication of religious books, and education was dominated by the Catholic clergy, creating an ideological as well as political and cultural framework for society.

Disease, dislocation of traditional ways that came when Indian labor was used in the mines, and the rigors of mine work led to Indian extermination. The Spanish government did its best to protect the Indians. In 1542, in legislation called the **New Laws**, exploitation and enslavement of Indians was prohibited. In Mexico the decree was ignored and in Peru there was revolt. This led to a public debate about how the colonies should be run, the polemics of which were often printed. Bishop **Bartolome de las Casas** argued that Indians were like children who needed protection and care. Others argued they were slaves. Eventually, the government retreated from the New Laws. On ranches, in mines, and on private estates like Cortes' which had 23,000 Indian vassals, forced labor was permitted though the government and missionaries tried to improve local conditions and temper the worst of the abuses. To address this problem and prevent the growth of a new nobility, the Crown moved to end the encomienda system in the 1540s. Thereafter, colonists and descendants increasingly sought grants of land creating rural estates or haciendas that produced agricultural products mostly for the local market.

The African Diaspora

The depopulation of Indians and the end of gold hunting led to the establishment of ranches and sugar plantations. By the mid 1500s Indian numbers had fallen to the point where an alternative source of labor was necessary. The African slave **diaspora** (dispersion of peoples) began. The Portuguese had engaged in slaving to help pay for their voyages, and in 1455 a papal bull recognized the "right" to enslave any non-Christian in the course of exploration. Then, from the 1540s the Spanish Crown began to sell licenses to the Portuguese slave traders so that by the 1650s there were some 40,000 Africans in Mexico and perhaps 30,000 in Peru. In Brazil and the Caribbean, the figures were much higher. In the 1550s the Portuguese began to settle Brazil's coastal plains and cultivate sugar in large amounts. This labor-intensive industry between 1550 and 1800 brought, perhaps, 2.5 million black slaves to Brazil. The picture was repeated in the Caribbean where sugar production brought about two million from Africa.

The Plantation System

Based on a single crop produced by slave labor, Brazil was the first great plantation colony and a model for others. The hierarchy of the plantation became the hierarchy of society with the white planter family as the aristocracy controlling local social and political life. Below them were the bureaucrats, officials, and merchants often linked to the plantation owner by marriage. At the bottom were slaves distinguished by their color. The scarcity of European women led to a mixing of the three major ethnic groups—Indian, European, and African, and the creation of a multiracial society, one in which distinctions of race and place of birth were crucial. From the three original groups, many combinations of ethnic and racial categories grew—**mestizo** (European-Indian), **mulatto** (Negro-European), **zambo** (Indian-African), **castizo** (Mestizo-European), etc. The people of mixed origin, called **castas**, were an increasingly large population relegated to secondary status. Over time, even whites were categorized between **peninsulares**, or those born in Spain, and **Creoles**, those born in the New World. Like the old Roman family, women were in a subordinate position as the father had legal authority over children, though women could inherit property. The intermingling of racial groups and trade patterns between Africa, the Americas, and Europe created an "Atlantic World."

North America

The Atlantic World soon spread to North America but with less success. The first French settlement in Florida was destroyed in 1565 by the Spanish who established a settlement at St. Augustine. The first English attempt at **Roanoke** (1587) was abandoned. Sustained colonialization began only in the seventeenth century at **Jamestown** (1607) by the English and on the **St. Lawrence** in Quebec (1608) by the French. Gradually, by supplying tribes with weapons and then aiding allies against the less well-armed people west, the Europeans colonized—the Pilgrim Fathers in Massachusetts, the Puritans in Connecticut and Rhode Island, and the Catholics and Protestants in Maryland. Soon there were one-crop plantations in Virginia, first tobacco and then cotton, and the importation of Africans reached there as well. The movement and mix of peoples, cultures, crops, and bullion between Africa, the New World, and Europe created an Atlantic World and the African diaspora in the Americas.

NEW AFRICAN KINGDOMS AND EMPIRES

The African Slave Trade

The slave trade made many African leaders wealthy, giving rise to new kingdoms and empires in Africa. Slaving ships sailed out of European ports, such as Nantes in France and Liverpool in England. When they reached Africa, they sold or bartered textiles, beads, iron bars, alcohol, and firearms for slaves, gold, and timber. They then set sail for the Americas on an often horrifying two-month voyage called the **Middle Passage**. Most of the Africans sent to America were first enslaved as prisoners of war. African states often fought over territory, in the course of which captors were taken and sold into slavery. Africans were also sold into slavery if they were rebels, enemies of the king, criminals, or refugees. European trading companies and governments founded settlements called **factories** along the West African coast. Europeans did not conquer, raid, or even travel into the interior to collect slaves. Rather, African kingdoms and merchants groups controlled the interior trade and used military power, if necessary, to prevent Europeans from interfering in the trade business.

New African States

One of the kingdoms that profited from the slave trade was **Ashanti** located in the Gold Coast (present-day Ghana). Its first great political leader was **Osei Tutu** (d. 1717), who built a powerful army using guns purchased from Europeans. With these weapons he conquered weaker neighbors and sold prisoners into slavery. This "guns-for-slave" exchange was repeated all over Africa. In the 1720s, under king Agaja (1708–1740) **Dahomey**, inland from the **Bight of Benin** (present–day Lagos, Benin, and Togo) increasingly turned to this exchange that was controlled by the royal court whose armies (including a regiment of women) were used to raid for more captives. Over 1.8 million slaves were exported from the Bight of Benin between 1640 and 1890.

Slaves also played a role in the rise of **Songhay**, **Kanem-Borneo**, and **Hausaland** in the Niger region of western and central Sudan, though, as Muslim states, the slave trade was somewhat reduced because the Koran forbade Muslims to enslave fellow Muslims. Under the reign of Muhammed Toure (1492–1528), the expansionist consolidation of Songhay was completed, greatly increasing the number of slaves on royal lands. Slaves were also sold at the large market in Goa where traders from North Africa bought them for sale in Cairo, Istanbul, Lisbon, and Naples, and for sugar plantations in Sicily and domestic servants in Portugal and northern Italy.

The slave trade also affected the East Coast of Africa. Slaves from the interior along the Zambezi River were shipped to Arabia and Southwest Asia, while on islands like **Mauritius** (in the Indian Ocean) and **Zanzibar**, Swahili, Indian, and Arabian merchants followed the European model and set up plantations producing cloves and other items, using African slave labor. In 1652 the Dutch East India Company established a colony on the Cape of Good Hope. Large farms developed that depended on slave labor from Asia and Africa. The labor needs of the expanding colony led to a series of wars with the San and Hottentot populations who, as a result, were pushed further north and west across the Orange River in 1760 by Dutch (**Boer**) farmers. Around 1800 the Cape colony had 17,000 settlers and 26,000 slaves.

Changes in African Society

The arrival of the Europeans caused basic social changes in West African societies. One was **chattel slavery** in which slaves were used as craftsmen, sailors, and farm workers, uses unknown until the Europeans came. Another was a new class of **metis**, or mulattos, resulting from intermarriage of Africans and Europeans, primarily French. This class adopted the French language and Catholic religion, and gained economic and political power. The political consequences varied. In the Congo, the perpetual search for slaves undermined the monarchy and destroyed political unity. In Dahomey, however, the slave trade became a royal monopoly, gaining economic strength for the state. The king of Dahomey, for instance, made a gross income of 250,000 pounds (English) from the export of slaves, a portion of which was used to improve the living standard of its people. The European introduction of corn, pineapple, cassava, and sweet potato to West Africa improved the African diet to the degree that population increased. In the long run, this did not cause the demographic catastrophe it could have because of the forced migration of Africans to the Americas. The new African societies that arose were often influenced by European culture—French in Senegambia, English in the Gold Coast, and Portuguese in Angola. Yet, European influence did not penetrate the interior, despite the export of 12 million slaves—three percent from 1450 to 1600, 16 percent from 1601 to 1700, 52 percent from 1701 to 1800, and 28 percent from 1801 to 1900. When nineteenth-century European empire builders arrived, the interior of Africa was still a mystery.

EUROPEAN TRADE IN INDIA AND EAST ASIA

India

The Portuguese were the first to establish trade with India. In 1510 they established the port of **Goa** on the Arabian Sea and during the next century swept the Muslims out of Indian Ocean trade. Then, early in the seventeenth century, with a charter signed by Queen Elizabeth, 80 London merchants organized the **British East India Company** to compete with the Portuguese for control of the Indian spice and cotton trade. In 1619 Mughal emperor Jahangir granted important commercial concessions at the port of Surat on the west coast. Subsequent British gifts, bribes, and medical supplies enabled the British to set up 27 other trading ports or "factories" along the coasts. The lynchpins of British trade were at three centers—**Madras, Bombay** (acquired by marriage from the Portuguese), and **Calcutta**. The "factories" themselves were

walled compounds containing warehouses, residences, gardens, and offices of the British East India Company. The Company president had political authority over all residents. The British East India Company sold silver, copper, zinc, lead, and fabrics to the Indians and bought cotton goods, silks, pepper and other spices, sugar, and opium. Substantial profits were made by both Indian and English merchants. Since profit was the main motive of the company, interference in Indian politics and missionary activities was discouraged.

Disorder and violence, which wracked the Indian countryside in the early eighteenth century, forced company officials to man their small trade garrison with native troops, and, because of political instability, factories gradually began to gain some political control in the surrounding areas. Indian political weakness also encouraged the development of the French East Indian Company in Bengal and elsewhere. Both the French and English then began to employ native troops called **sepoys**. From 1740 to 1763 Britain and France were continually struggling around the world to define their respective spheres, and India became one of the battlegrounds. The French won many land battles but English seapower decided the contest when French reinforcements were prevented from entering India. In the **Treaty of Paris**, 1763, France recognized British control in India. In this way the British government became involved in Indian politics and in the **India Act** of 1784, the governors were to be picked from outside the Company. From then on, India was ruled from London through puppet Indian princes, sepoys, and effective British-trained civil service.

Commerce and Conversion

Everywhere European traders went, Christian missionaries were soon to go. In India, from the 1540s on, **Francis Xavier** and his Jesuit order converted thousands of low-caste fisherfolk and outcastes through their care of the poor. In the early 1600s Italian Jesuit **Robert di Nobili** tried a new approach by attempting to convert the elite class, a strategy the Jesuits tried elsewhere in Asia but without much success. Most often, it was the lower classes who were converted as in the Philippines where, after conquistadors had established control, administration was turned over to the friars and priests. In 1582 Jesuit **Matteo Ricci** (1552–1610) settled in Macao on the mouth of the Canton River. Ricci sought first to convert the emperor and elite groups. This he did by presenting Christianity on Chinese terms (emphasizing education) and by presents of western technology like clocks and astronomical equipment. But the Chinese ultimately rejected Christianity because it ran counter to Chinese traditions of ancestor worship and public order (Christ was executed as a criminal). The Chinese story of merchant and missionary was repeated in Japan. In 1542 Portuguese traders arrived in Japan. The Dutch and English quickly followed suit. In 1547 Francis Xavier landed in Japan and won many converts. The Japanese feared a repeat of the wholesale conversion and control of the Philippines, and so, in 1635 the Japanese expelled the Spanish and Portuguese. The shogun Tokugawa Ieyasu suppressed a revolt by Christian peasants known as the **Shimabara Rebellion** in 1637–1638. Thereafter, the Japanese banned all western books on science and religion.

China

After Ming cessation of the long-distance Indian Ocean voyages, trade did not cease in China. Rather, as in India, European commerce stimulated the local economy. In fact, southern China enjoyed considerable prosperity in the late sixteenth and early seventeenth centuries because Japanese, Portuguese, and Dutch merchants paid in silver for Chinese silks and ceramics. The steady flow of specie into China devalued Chinese paper currency and the Ming emperor had to recognize the triumph of silver as a medium of exchange. The blue and white porcelain so typical of the Ming was imitated by Muslim craftsmen in Baghdad and Isfahan, and soon copied by westerners, such as the Wedgewoods in England. The word "china," meaning porcelain, entered the English language in 1579.

In the southern maritime provinces, where there was active trade with Japan, the Philippines and Indonesia, merchants invested surplus capital in town ventures, causing an influx of workers, many of whom were women, to work in cotton and silk mills and porcelain factories. The Ming merchant marine transported these products to the Philippines and brought back sweet potatoes, tobacco, firearms, and silver from the Spanish fleet at Manila. The Dutch transported tea in boatloads to the Europeans.

Soon, as in Europe, Chinese merchants began to invest large amounts of capital in commercial and craft industries like silk making, cotton weaving, porcelain manufacture, printing, and steel production. As a result, there were great technological advances from looms to new machines for working the soil, sowing seed, and irrigation. Population went from 70 million in 1368 to 130 million in 1600, making China the world's most populated country. This and other problems, like ostentatious living by the imperial court, a large, expensive army to protect against the **Manchus** in the north, a recalcitrant bureaucracy, and famine, brought down the Ming dynasty in 1644. The Manchus (from Manchuria) invaded from the north and established a new dynasty, the **Ch'ing**. The Ch'ing purged the old bureaucracy and replaced it with new and honest officials. In its heyday in the eighteenth century, the empire covered much of Asia—China Proper, Manchuria, Mongolia, Tibet, and Sinking—with tribute trade from Burma, Nepal, Laos, Siam, Annam, and Korea. Imperial factories produced porcelain masterpieces that were shipped all over the world.

THE DEVELOPING WORLD SYSTEM— THE MANILA GALLEONS

By 1550 European overseas exploration and conquest had given rise to successive commercial empires—the Portuguese, Spanish, Dutch, and English. The Spanish dominated in the Americas, the Portuguese, Dutch, and English in Asia. Eventually, the Manila Galleons tied the whole system together.

Portuguese Trade

In the sixteenth century the Portuguese were the predominant sea power establishing control over Asian and then world commerce. So dominant were they that Portuguese was the language of Asian maritime trade. From Africa to Lisbon went gold and ivory, and from India to Lisbon went textiles that were exchanged for Asian spices. From bases at Goa (western India) and **Malacca** (Malay peninsula), Portuguese ships carried goods to the Portuguese settlement at **Macao** on the South China Sea. From Macao, loaded with Chinese silks and porcelains, Portuguese ships sailed to the Japanese port of **Nagasaki** and the Philippine port of **Manila** where they were exchanged for Spanish silver. Throughout Asia, the Portuguese merchants, traded slaves—Africans, Chinese, and Japanese. Across the Atlantic the Portuguese provided most of the sugar consumed in Europe in the sixteenth century and most of the slaves for the plantations.

Dutch Trade

In the latter half of the seventeenth century, the Dutch had hegemony over Asian trade. In 1599 a Dutch fleet returned to Holland with spices and a 100 percent profit return, prompting the establishment in 1602 of the Dutch East India Company, whose stated aim was to wrest the spice trade from the Portuguese. By sailing directly to Indonesia, thereby avoiding India, and by helping local princes against the Portuguese, the Dutch won rich commercial concessions and, ultimately, control of the Indonesian archipelago. Trading armor, firearms, and linens, the Dutch gained a monopoly over the spice trade. Dutch profits whetted the appetite of the English who went on to establish the British East India Company and dominate trade in India.

The Manila Galleons

The Spanish, meanwhile, took the Philippines, and, with their **galleons** (a trade warship with three or four decks at the stern and one or more at the bow), created a world exchange. Galleons were a synthesis of Europe and the Orient. Designed in Spain, they were built of durable tropical wood cut by laborers on outlying islands. Anchor lines and rigging were of Manila hemp and fasteners forged by Spanish, Chinese, or Malay smiths. The galleons carried quantities of Spanish terra cotta and Chinese porcelain. Magellan had made contact with the Philippines on his voyage, and in 1565 a fleet sent from America under **Miguel Lopez de Legazpi** claimed the islands for Philip II of Spain, hence the name of "Philippines." The Spanish established Manila in 1572 at the best natural harbor in Asia and, due to developing trade, the city grew to 80,000 in 1640.

The galleon system evolved out of the need to protect Spanish ships sailing for Spain full of precious metals. To discourage pirates and foreign ships, the Spanish developed a convoy system. Two great galleons a year sailed from Manila in the Philippines to Acapulco loaded with Chinese silks, porcelain, and lacquer. These were then transshipped on the convoy to Spain along with American silver. From Spain, ships went to India, Malaya, and China where they were loaded with eastern treasure. In Manila, the world entrepot, eastern goods met American specie. The trips in overloaded galleons often became epics of suffering and endurance that took as long as a year to complete. On more than 40 occasions between 1565 and 1815 ships did not arrive, either wrecked or lost at sea.

Transfer Specie

This trade and American precious metals should have made Spain rich. Instead, as Sancho de Moncada wrote in 1619, "The poverty of Spain resulted from the discovery of the Indies." Between 1500 and 1650, 181 tons of gold and 17,000 tons of silver went to Europe. Much stayed in the Americas to build churches and missions. Other bullion paid for Spanish debt and wars. American treasure also led to European inflation during the sixteenth century, eating up more wealth. Nor did the windfall of specie stay in Europe. Most ended up in the treasuries of China, India, and Southeast Asia because, before the industrial revolution, few products produced in Europe could be sold at a profit in the East. Thus, imports had to be paid for with bullion. In this way, the output of America paid for the riches of Asia. Scholars estimate that over half went to China.

COLONIZATION AND THE END OF THE FRONTIER

After the European explorers, traders, and missionaries came the colonists. In some places in the world, colonization was sparse. In Africa, for instance, the forbidding interior wracked with malaria and difficult travel prevented penetration until the nineteenth century. In other areas that were heavily populated like India and China, opportunities for colonization were limited by land scarcity and politics. In Australia, the Americas, and Russia, however, empty spaces and resources beckoned Europeans. Slowly, around the world, the peopling of the earth reached its final stages and the frontier came to an end.

European colonization of the Americas was tied to European maritime expertise, missionary impulses, access to resources, and dissatisfied social and religious groups. Mercantilism generally tied colonies to the mother country, who saw partial political control as a way to ensure access to cheap supplies of precious metals, cash crops, timber, and markets. Not only the Spanish colonized in South America for those reasons. In 1530 the king of Portugal offered large land grants to nobles who would set up colonies there. By about 1550 the Portuguese controlled 15 towns up and down the Brazilian coast. Then came the Dutch, establishing themselves in Guiana north of the Amazon and on the eastern tip northeast of the Brazilian highlands.

Spanish Colonization in North America

In North America, the Spanish, French, and English carved out colonies. The Spanish settled as far east as the Mississippi and as far north as New Mexico and southern California. **Francisco de Coronado** in the 1540s moved across Texas to Kansas in search of gold, while **Hernando de Soto** with a like vision advanced into Florida.

The Catholic Church, however, was the primary force in colonizing New Spain north of the Rio Grande. Missionaries spread the gospel among the Indians, and in 1769 the Spanish began to consolidate their holdings by building the first of several **presidios** (military garrisons) in San Diego. Simultaneously, **Junipero Serra** and other Franciscan monks established a series of **missions**. Indians were sometimes persuaded and sometimes coerced into living and working at the missions in a Spanish effort to create permanent agricultural communities.

French Colonization in North America

France also sent explorers and missionaries to claim vast tracts and they staked out territory in the St. Lawrence in an effort to find a **Northwest Passage** to Asia. In 1628 **Samuel de Champlain** founded the royal colony of Quebec, and in 1627 the king chartered the **Company of New France** to encourage emigration. This proved a failure, however, for several reasons. First, population pressures were not as great in France as in England and French peasants were discouraged by reports of cold weather. Also, the French government refused to let French Huguenots (Protestants) emigrate for fear of political revolt. Instead, French Canada became a fur trading enterprise and fertile ground for Jesuit Catholic conversion. **Jacques Marquette**, a French Jesuit priest, and **Louis Joliet,** a fur trader, reached the Mississippi, and in 1681 the French claimed sovereignty over the whole Mississippi River system in the name of Louis XIV (Louisiana).

Dutch Colonization in North America

Meanwhile, the Dutch had little interest in conversion or territory. They sought commerce. **Henry Hudson** of the Dutch East India Company named the Hudson River and established fur trading posts on Manhattan Island. In 1621 the Dutch government gave a trade monopoly to the **Dutch West India Company** in America. Soon thereafter, the Company "purchased" Manhattan Island from the Indians and founded **New Amsterdam** as its capital of the New Netherlands colony. The growing threat of

New England and New France caused the Dutch government to encourage migration by granting huge estates along the Hudson River to wealthy Dutchmen, but the lure of profitable slave trade and plantations in Brazil outweighed the appeal of North America. Therefore, after a series of Anglo-Dutch wars, New Amsterdam went into British hands.

English Colonization in North America

Like New Netherland, the first English settlement in North America was a **corporate colony**, an enterprise of ambitious merchants. In 1606 the merchant stockholders of the **Virginia Company** of London received a charter from James I giving them the right to exploit the riches of North America and incidentally to "propagate the Christian religion." The **Jamestown Colony** barely survived its first winter, but once it was clear tobacco would grow in the area, the plantation system was underway. The colony also attracted settlers without grants of land. Maryland was settled as a proprietary colony and as a refuge for Catholics. Both Virginia and Maryland used contracts called indentures to attract settlers. **Indentures** bound migrants to labor for a period from four to seven years in exchange for passage. Plymouth, meanwhile, was settled by **Puritans**, that is, by those trying to preserve the "pure" Christian faith. Sailing on the Mayflower and lacking a charter from James I, they created their own constitution, the **Mayflower Compact**. Other Puritans followed to the Massachusetts Bay Colony. Everywhere Europeans pushed the frontier, Amerindian societies fought, were destroyed or forced to fashion a new life.

Russian Colonization in North America

In the sixteenth century when Europeans were making their way across the vast oceans, Russians were moving into the regions east of the Ural Mountains. Many were runaway serfs seeking escape. Others were **Old Believers**, religious traditionalists like the Puritans fleeing in order to continue forbidden rites and practices. The most fearless pioneers were the fur traders and trappers. One such trader was **Anika Stroganov**, whose agents in the early 1500s crossed the Urals in search of furs that they exchanged for drink. In the course of the forays, the Stroganovs mapped much of **Siberia** and by 1594 they had a monopoly of the region's fur trade. Then, in 1581 **Yermak**, a Cossack (horseman) chieftain in the czar's employ, swept across Siberia in search of gold, claiming territory for Russia as he went. Subsequently, fortresses were built in such places as Tobolsk, Sunger, and Yakutsk on the **Lena River**. Finally, in 1639 a small band of Cossacks reached the Pacific coast at **Okhotsk**. Later in the century the Russians explored **Kamchatka**, the **Kuriles** (1711), and finally crossed the Bering Straits into Alaska, establishing the **Russian American Company** and founding permanent settlements. By 1812 the Russians had established a trading post at Fort Ross, just a few miles from San Francisco. Also during the seventeenth century, the Russians moved into the Amur Valley on the Chinese border, finally defining the Sino-Russian demarcation in the **Treaty of Nerchinsk**. Subsequently, Siberia became not a haven for free farmers, but a place of exile.

Summary

The Portuguese, Dutch, and English dominated the Asian exchange, but they met up with the Spanish in Manila, creating a world market. From the East went luxury goods paid for with American bullion extracted by Indian and African slaves. From the plantations went sugar. After European explorers went merchants, missionaries, and then colonists to all parts of the globe. In places with sparse population, as in the Americas and Russia, the end of the world's frontier was in sight.

UNIT REVIEW

Cross-Regional Developments

There were important cross-regional developments between 1450 and 1750 that helped shape the modern world. These include the development of a new type of political unit, the nation-state, growing European exploration, conquest of the Americas and Russian conquest of Siberia, an African exodus that created an Atlantic diaspora, a world exchange of peoples, specie, plants, and animals, transformation of the military due to artillery, conquest of the oceans by means of ships like the caravel and galleon, plantation economies, and a world exchange based on American bullion.

Legacies

This period brought the world into modern times. Thus, many of its legacies are apparent in the contemporary world.

- Political legacies include the rise of the nation-state and, as a consequence, divided Europe reinforced by religious separations;
- parliaments, constitutions, national literature and national identities emerged;
- the tremendous artistic, literary, and scientific output of the Renaissance, some of the world's greatest contributors being Michelangelo, Erasmus, and Newton;
- a secular spirit, Protestantism, mechanisms of exchange and the capitalist system, and a middle class;
- standing armies and navies and drills developed, as did warfare based on artillery;
- absolutist states grew strong because of this state military.

In the Americas are the legacies of vanished Indian populations, multiracial societies, and states of differing national character based on language, as well as a treasure house of Spanish-American art.

Documents

THE MAGNA CARTA

John, by the grace of God king of England, Lord of Ireland, duke of Normandy and Aquitaine, count of Anjou: to the archbishops, bishops, abbots, earls, barons, justices, foresters, sheriffs, provosts, serving men, and to all his bailiffs and faithful subjects, greeting . . .

1. First of all . . . the English church shall be free and shall have its rights intact and its liberties uninfringed upon . . .

8. No widow shall be forced to marry when she prefers to live without a husband . . .

12. No scutage or aid shall be imposed in our realm unless by the common counsel of our realm. . .

14. And, in order to have the common counsel of the realm in the matter of assessing an aid . . . we shall cause, under seal through our letters, the archbishops, bishops, abbots, earls and great barons to be summoned for a fixed day—for a term, namely, at least forty days distant, —and for a fixed place. . .

39. No freeman shall be taken, or imprisoned, or disseized, or outlawed, or exiled, or in any way harmed—nor will we go upon or send upon him— save by the lawful judgment of his peers or by the law of the land . . .

. . . Given through our hand, in the plain called Runnimede, between Windsor and Stanes, on the fifteenth day of June, in the seventeenth year of our reign.

King John of England was in disfavor among his lords in 1215 for two reasons: first, he had lost some of England's sovereignty by becoming a vassal to the pope, and he had used extreme measures to raise money for his wars in France. The barons objected and made him accept a charter—the Magna Carta— affirming their rights. The document became the basis for limiting power of the monarchs, giving rights to the people, securing due process and the right of representation for those being taxed.

MACHIAVELLI'S *THE PRINCE*

. . . One ought to be both feared and loved, but as it is difficult for the two to go together, it is much safer to be feared than loved, if one of the two has to be wanting. For it may be said of men in general that they are ungrateful, voluble, dissemblers, anxious to avoid danger, and covetous of gain; as long as you benefit them, they are entirely yours, they offer you their blood, their goods, their life, and their children as I have before said, when the necessity is remote; but when it approaches, they revolt. And the prince who has relied solely on their words, without making other preparations, is ruined; for the friendship which is gained by purchase and not through grandeur and nobility of spirit is bought but not secured, and at a pinch is not to be expended in your service.

Niccolo Machiavelli (1469–1527) was a diplomat for the republican Florentine government until the Medici returned to power in Florence and sent him into exile. In his isolation, he reflected on the political problems of Italy. *The Prince* is dedicated to Lorenzo de' Medici who reflects the primary theme of the book, which is how to acquire and keep power. Machiavelli ransacked classical history and used his own observations to argue that a successful prince must recognize that power, not virtue, is the cardinal principle of princely conduct. The realism of his analysis is often heralded as the beginning of the modern age of politics.

THE NINETY-FIVE THESES

6. The Pope has no power to remit any guilt, except by declaring and warranting it to have been remitted by God. . .

21. Thus those preachers of indulgences are in error who say that by the indulgences of the Pope a man is freed and saved from all punishment.

28. It is certain that, when the money rattles in the chest, avarice and gain may be increased, but the effect of the intercession of the Church depends on the will of God alone . . .

37. Every true Christian, whether living or dead, has a share in all the benefits of Christ and the Church, given him by God, even without letters of pardon. . .

On October 31, 1517, Martin Luther, an Augustinian monk, as was the medieval custom, pinned on the church door of Wittenburg, his 95 principles with regard to the misuse of indulgences. In effect, the theses challenged the pope in matters of faith. Thus began the Protestant Revolt, which split the Christian church, the Christian faith, and the political and social landscape of Europe. It also played a part in the voyages of discovery, the commercial revolution, and growing spirit of individualism.

LAS CASAS AND THE BLACK LEGEND

This infinite multitude of people (the Indians) was . . . without fraud, without subtlety or malice. . . toward the Spaniards whom they serve, patient, meek and peaceful. . .

To these quiet Lambs . . . came the Spaniards like most cruel Tygres, Wolves and Lions, enrag'd with a sharp and tedious hunger; for these forty years past, minding nothing else but the slaughter of these unfortunate wretches, whom with divers kinds of torments neither seen nor heard of before, they have so cruelly and inhumanely butchered, that three millions of people which Hispaniola itself did contain, there are left remaining alive scarce three hundred persons. . .

Bartolome de las Casas took part in the Spanish conquest of Cuba in 1513. He was shocked by the Spanish treatment of the American Indians and argued aggressively with the king of Spain that such treatment was not worthy of a Christian monarch. The Spanish king, Charles V, tried to implement Las Casas's ideas, but resistance from Spanish settlers meant they only partly succeeded. The ideas of Las Casas, which can be found in his *General History of the Indies,* led to the so-called "black legend," which theorized that American Indians had souls and that Amerindian genocide was due to the Spanish maliciously killing them. In fact, disease was a greater factor in Amerindian deaths than mass murder, though enslavement and work on plantations and in mines made many vulnerable to foreign illnesses.

MATTEO RICCI

The Chinese are the most industrious people, and most of the mechanical arts flourish among them. They have all sorts of raw material and they are endowed by nature with a talent for trading, both of which are potent factors in bringing about a high development of the mechanical arts. . . Their skill in the manufacture of fireworks is really extraordinary and there is scarcely anything which they cannot cleverly imitate with them.. . . Their method of making printing books is quite ingenious. . . . The simplicity of Chinese printing is what accounts for the exceedingly large number of books in circulation here and the ridiculously low prices at which they are sold. Such facts as these would scarcely be believed by anyone who has not witnessed them.

Matteo Ricci was the first Jesuit to enter China (1583). The document illustrates the continuing admiration westerners had for the Chinese who seemed more advanced in every way. Though Gutenberg had already invented moveable type, to Ricci China was still far ahead of the West. To win over and convert the Chinese, Ricci developed a phenomenal memory, a talent the Chinese admired because it helped them pass the civil service examination. Ricci also brought western trinkets and mechanical devices like watches, which intrigued the Chinese. His efforts at conversion were negligible, largely because the Pope refused to permit a softening of Catholic doctrine or the acceptance of Confucian rites. Ricci is a reflection of his times both as a Jesuit of the Catholic reformation spirit, and as a western traveler to East Asia.

Recall Questions

1. Which of the following occurred first?
   (A) the Renaissance
   (B) the Commercial Revolution
   (C) the Magna Carta
   (D) the Crusades
   (E) the Reformation

2. Who was the author of *The Prince,* an analysis of how the prince should gain, maintain and increase power?
   (A) Peter Abelard
   (B) Thomas Aquinas
   (C) Petrarch
   (D) Niccolo Machiavelli
   (E) Thomas More

3. All of the following were hallmarks of the Renaissance EXCEPT
   (A) secular experimentation in the sciences.
   (B) rebirth of Greek and Roman classics.
   (C) individualism.
   (D) humanism.
   (E) scholasticism.

4. Which of the following artists was responsible for the frescoes of the Sistine Chapel?
   (A) Michelangelo
   (B) Raphael
   (C) Albrecht Dürer
   (D) Leonardo da Vinci
   (E) Pietr Brueghel

5. Who was responsible for uniting Spain?
   (A) Castiglione
   (B) Ignatius of Loyola
   (C) Maximilian I
   (D) Capetian kings
   (E) Ferdinand and Isabella

6. Who was responsible for uniting the French in successful resistance to the English during the Hundred Years' War?
   (A) Capetian kings
   (B) Louis IX
   (C) Charles V
   (D) Huguenots
   (E) Joan of Arc

7. Who initiated the Reformation?
   (A) Ignatius of Loyola
   (B) Martin Luther
   (C) Thomas More
   (D) Thomas à Becket
   (E) Erasmus

8. Which of the following scientists, in *On the Revolution of Heavenly Bodies,* reasserted the Greek and Chinese theories that the universe was heliocentric?
   (A) Nicolaus Copernicus
   (B) Johannes Kepler
   (C) Galileo
   (D) Descartes
   (E) Isaac Newton

9. Which were causes of the Reformation in Germany?
   (A) the ostentatious wealth and military involvement of popes
   (B) the sale of indulgences in exchange for the remission of sins
   (C) the opportunity of peasants to rebel against the nobility
   (D) the preoccupation of Charles V with secular affairs
   (E) all of the above

10. A counter-reformation of Catholics in the sixteenth century led to
    (A) the Peace of Augsburg.
    (B) the formation of new religious orders like the Jesuits.
    (C) reconciliation between Catholics and Protestants.
    (D) religious toleration of Protestants.
    (E) the Treaty of Westphalia.

11. Greater commercialization occurred in the sixteenth century because of
    (A) a larger population.
    (B) the introduction of new products.
    (C) expanding markets.
    (D) "cheap" money.
    (E) all of the above.

12. Joint stock companies proved to be popular because they
    (A) monopolized trade within a specific market.
    (B) utilized letters of credit and checks for trading purposes.
    (C) encouraged "putting out" or the "domestic system" for textiles in Italy and the Netherlands.
    (D) gained access to an expanding system of credit.
    (E) reduced financial risks for the investor.

13. Which of the following occasions permanently established constitutionalism and the supremacy of the English Parliament over the monarchy?
    (A) the Glorious Revolution
    (B) the Long Parliament
    (C) Oliver Cromwell's Puritan commonwealth
    (D) signing the Magna Carta
    (E) expansion of legislative power during the reign of Elizabeth I

14. The site of the first sugar plantations in the New World was in
    (A) Mexico.
    (B) Virginia.
    (C) Brazil.
    (D) Peru.
    (E) the Caribbean.

15. Which of the following Jesuit priests sought to convert the Ming court on Chinese terms through western education and presents of western technology?
    (A) Francis Xavier
    (B) Robert de Nobili
    (C) Matteo Ricci
    (D) Junipero Serra
    (E) Jacques Marquette

To check your answers, see page 393.

Colonial Empires of the New World 1776 C.E. *The Spanish and Portuguese were the major imperial powers in Latin America, while the English and French dominated the North American continent. Both Spain and Portugal created New World administrations based on the concept of vice-royalties or secondary royal states.*

End of the Frontier, Russia 1598–1801 C.E. The European explorations marked the last chapter in the human story of the peopling of the globe. Pristine frontiers vanished, especially in Russia and the United States, where sparsely populated areas were soon occupied by sedentary civilizations.

French, British, and Dutch World Holdings in 1700 C.E. After exploration came conquest, trade, and settlement. The Spanish and Portuguese were gradually eclipsed by the French, British, and Dutch, especially in the lucrative trade areas of the world in East Asia.

World Boundaries in 1453 and 1700 C.E. *In 1453 world civilizations were confined to middle Eurasia and small parts of the Americas and Africa. By 1700 civilization had pushed deep into Africa, across Russia, and into larger parts of the Americas. The spread of civilization took a great leap forward due to the ability of humans to traverse the oceans.*

Versailles Palace. *Louis XIII of France, in the mid-seventeenth century, began Versailles as a hunting lodge, a retreat from the queen he did not like. Louis XIV turned it into one of the greatest palaces of Europe and the world. He required all the great nobility of France, at the peril of social, political, and sometimes economic disaster, to live at Versailles for part of the year. Versailles set the trend in everything from dress to dance. It is the most important monument to absolutism. Its size and grandeur bespeak the power of absolutist monarchs, its symmetry reflects absolutism's belief in a rational order, and its splendor for the few reveals the great gulf between classes that existed in absolutist Europe.*

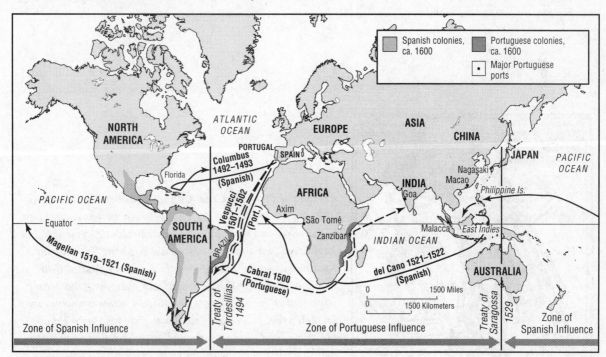

European Explorations and the Treaty of Torsedillas 1492–1529 C.E. *The initial European voyages of discovery were led by the Spanish and Portuguese. In the early sixteenth century, the two countries virtually divided the world into two spheres of oceanic influence.*

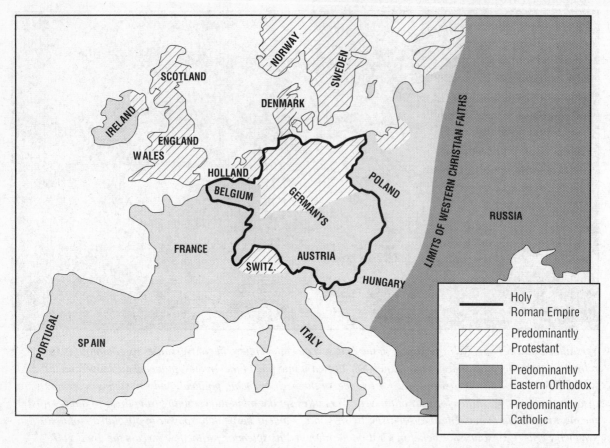

Religious Divisions in Europe 1600 C.E. *The Protestant Revolt divided Europe. Germany was most affected by the division, a factor in the inability of Germany to become a nation-state until the late nineteenth century.*

Cartoon of Peter the Great Cutting Beards. *Peter the Great of Russia (r. 1689–1725 C.E.) not only built a new capital city in the north and named it after himself (Saint Petersburg), but he decreed that mens' beards should be shorn. To Peter, the Russian custom of wearing beards, a custom equated with manhood and Christianity, symbolized everything that was backward about his country. Supposedly, when his nobles fell on their knees to welcome him home from his trip to Europe, the czar raised them up, whipped out a long European razor, and shaved off their beards. To make sure his decree was obeyed, he posted barbers at Moscow's gates. Noblemen who wished to keep their beards had to pay an annual beard tax and hang a medal from their necks as proof of payment.*

***Michelangelo's* David.** *Michelangelo's* David *illustrates another aspect of Renaissance art, art inspired by humanism. This heroic, 16 foot statue of* David, *one of Michelangelo's masterpieces, was completed in Florence in 1504. Unlike medieval artists who carved only the side facing the viewer, Michelangelo designed this work to be free standing like ancient Greek and Roman statues. Using marble as the medium, Michelangelo demonstrated a clear understanding of structure, in this case the human anatomy.*

The tension of the moment is portrayed in David's expression of independence and resolution. His gaze indicates the conflict which is to come. This sculpture exemplifies the Renaissance quote by Leon Battista Alberti that man can do all things if he will.

***Correggio's* Virgin and Child with the Young Saint John the Baptist.** *Correggio's* Virgin and Child with the Young Saint John the Baptist *illustrates one facet of Italian art of the High Renaissance—religious themes portrayed in realistic terms. With a distant landscape as a background, the three figures of the painting form a pyramidal composition. Line is modulated by shadow. The artist appeals to the spectator's eye using bright, contrasting reds, blues, and greens. The soft, full figures with the suggestion of halos appear in a delicate light creating an image of serenity.*

Middle Passage. *The voyage of slave ships from Africa to America was called the Middle Passage. The trip took an average of two months. Slaves were crammed below deck into small, stifling spaces. The diagram shows how a ship was filled. Approximately 17 percent of the slaves died, due to disease, bad food, mistreatment, overcrowding, or despair. Most slaves were prisoners of war. Their sale enriched African rulers, merchants, shippers, and plantation owners. The slave trade ended in 1870.*

UNIT
VII

PATTERNS OF MODERNITY IN THE NINETEENTH CENTURY
(1750–1900)

CHAPTER 20
Liberal Democratic Movements

CHRONOLOGY	American Revolution (1776–1789)	Napoleonic Era (1799–1818)	Latin American Revolutions (1810–1825)
	French Revolution (1789–1799)	Haitian Revolution (1804)	Revolutions of 1848
	Reign of Terror (1793–1794)		

TERMS	liberalism	bourgeois	Declaration of the Rights of Man
	inductive method	Declaration of Independence	Directory
	deductive method	National Assembly	Civil Code of 1804
	scientific revolution	Tennis Court Oath	Congress of Vienna
	Enlightenment	liberty, equality, and fraternity	balance of power
	natural rights		romanticism
	civil rights		
	separation of power		

PEOPLE	Francis Bacon	third estate	Alexander Ypsilanti
	René Descartes	sans culottes	Victor Hugo
	Isaac Newton	Marie Antoinette	Delacroix
	Thomas Hobbes	Maximilien Robespierre	Johann Wolfgang von Goethe
	John Locke	Napoleon Bonaparte	William Wordsworth
	Voltaire	Klemens von Metternich	J. M. W. Turner
	Baron de Montesquieu	Toussaint L'Overture	John Constable
	Voltaire	juntas	Ludwig von Beethoven
	Jean-Jacques Rousseau	Father Miguel de Hidalgo	Tchaikovsky
	Thomas Jefferson	Simon Bolivar	
	Louis XVI	Jose de San Martin	
	first and second estates	caudillos	

PLACES	Bastille	Moscow	Haiti
	Trafalgar	Waterloo	

Between 1750 and 1900 most of the characteristics that we call "modern" emerged in the world. Ideologies like liberalism, socialism, and nationalism, revolutions both democratic and industrial, and a new class of workers and their culture made their appearances. Thus began the quest by many countries to become "modern" meaning being secular, scientific, liberal, industrial and materialistic.

CHAPTER 20

Liberal Democratic Movements

Liberalism is generally understood as a political viewpoint that originated in western Europe during the eighteenth and nineteenth centuries. It stressed limited state interference in individual life and representation of people in government, and it urged the importance of constitutional rule and parliaments. Liberty and political (not economic) equality were its hallmarks. When democratic, liberalism meant rule by the majority. Liberalism developed during this period and has since become a beacon for freedom of the common man the world over. The concept of liberalism as the foundation of social and political order and harmony was rooted, in part, in the theories of Enlightenment science.

SCIENCE AND POLITICS—THE ENLIGHTENMENT

Enlightenment Science

The scientific view that the natural world is regulated by laws of nature that maintain order and harmony in the universe influenced politics. The scientific revolution that began during the sixteenth century Renaissance used the scientific method to discover the laws of nature. It was born in the medieval university system when science began to develop as a distinct branch of philosophy. Using rationalism, the scientific method involved experimentation and observation, reason to interpret the results, and math to prove and predict. The giants of the revolution included Nicolaus Copernicus (1473–1543), Tycho Brahe (1546–1601), Johannes Kepler (1571–1630), Galileo Galilei (1564–1642), **Francis Bacon** (1561–1626), **René Descartes** (1596–1642), and **Isaac Newton** (1642–1727). The two giants of methodology were Bacon and Descartes. Bacon formalized the empirical or **inductive method**, which called for observations, measurement, experiment, hypothesis, and verification, while Descartes championed the **deductive method**, a mathematical approach that began with simple, self-evident truths and advanced to more complex truths. Copernicus, using astronomy and observation, in a startling publication *On the Revolution of Heavenly Bodies*, postulated the axial theory of the universe, that is, that the planets revolve around the sun. Brahe went on to build one of the most sophisticated observatories of the day and to amass volumes of data that helped Kepler formulate the laws of planetary motion.

Where Copernicus had speculated, Kepler proved his theories mathematically. While Kepler was unraveling the secrets of planetary motion, Galileo, using experimentation, showed that a uniform force like gravity produces a uniform acceleration, and formulated the law of inertia—an object continues in motion forever unless stopped by some external force. The accomplishments of Kepler, Galileo, and others put the old astronomy and physics in ruins, but it was left to Isaac Newton to create a new synthesis of theory and observation. His contribution was in proving mathematically the basic laws of physics. In his immortal *Principia* he outlined the universal laws of gravitation—that every body in the universe attracts every other body in a precise mathematical relationship. From Kepler's elliptical orbits and Galileo's objects in motion, Newton unified the whole universe in one constant system.

Various reasons have been given for the **scientific revolution**, among them the Renaissance, which stimulated investigation into classical science, the development of new instruments like the telescope, barometer, thermometer, pendulum clock, microscope, and air pump, new methods of thought, and Protestantism, which made scientific inquiry a question of individual conscience and not of religious doctrine.

Enlightenment

The impact of the scientific revolution was more on how people thought than on technology, which did not occur until the nineteenth century. It was the most important fact in the eighteenth-century **Enlightenment**. The Enlightenment was the intellectual movement centered in France that advocated using scientific methods to study human society and that rational laws could describe social behavior. The Enlightenment had a profound impact on the politics and culture of the urban middle class and upper classes. Basically, it believed that, as there are scientific laws of nature, so are there laws of society. It also introduced the idea of progress or the belief that the discovery of the laws of nature and man could produce a steadily improved human condition. The Enlightenment tried to find new truths in a period of chaos and confusion. Religious truths were being challenged by the new science, and the rapidly growing travel literature on non-European lands and cultures served to challenge absolute morality and truth. Much of the new thinking was developed by a group of intellectuals in France called the *philosophes*.

Natural Rights

Essentially the "laws of society" as worked out by the philosophes, supported the view that all men have **natural rights** including life, liberty, and property, that government is a contract between ruler and ruled and, if violated by the ruler, there is a license to rebel, and that, properly aligned, government is a balance of power. **Thomas Hobbes** (1588–1679) was the first English philosopher to apply natural laws to those of society. After observing the chaos and conflict of the English Civil War, he observed in his book *Leviathan* that a state without laws is brutish. To avoid such a state of affairs, people must enter in a contract with the ruler in which they give up some of their freedom and thereby forfeit their right to rebel. **John Locke** (1632–1704) went a step further, writing that all people have **natural rights** to life, liberty, and property, which the government is responsible for protecting. Since the purpose of government is to establish order, the ruler, to stay in power, must have the consent of the governed. If the ruler is a tyrant and, therefore, has broken the contract, the people have the right to rebel. **Baron de Montesquieu** (1689–1755), meanwhile, focused on the question of how to promote liberty and prevent tyranny. He argued that despotism could be avoided if the power of the state were divided so that neither one person nor one governing body had unlimited power. Montesquieu envisioned **separation of power** with distinct branches of government (legislative, judicial, executive) responsible for specific functions of government, each with power to check the other branches.

The most famous, perhaps most representative, philosophe was François Marie Arouet, known by his pen name **Voltaire** (1694–1778). Unlike Montesquieu, he concluded that since human beings "are very rarely worthy to govern themselves," the best government was one with a good monarch. He also disputed the idea of equality between the classes, but he did advocate equality before the law. He expanded the idea of rights to include **civil rights**, especially of religion and culture. He wrote, "I do not agree with the word you say, but I will defend to the death your right to say it." His view of a deistic God, a great clockmaker who built an orderly universe and then stepped aside and let it run, embodies the core of the philosophe spirit.

The last of the great philosophes was **Jean-Jacques Rousseau** (1712–1778). Passionately committed to individual freedom, Rousseau argued in *The Social Contract* (1762) that sovereign power is vested in the people not the monarch, and that the "general will" (democracy) reflecting the common interests of the people, is sacred and absolute. Rousseau believed that if the ruler ignored the will of the people, the social contract was broken and the people had the right to demand their freedom. The concept of the "general will" has been used by dictators (Hitler) and democrats (Jefferson) alike. (Dictators espouse the belief that they represent and embody the true interest of the sovereign masses.) Rousseau, while a typical Enlightenment thinker, also had one foot in the oncoming romantic period, as he did not agree that rationalism and civilization were liberating. Rather, he believed feeling should complement intellect, and he argued in *Emile* that education in the form of natural, unspoiled development could avoid the corrupting influences of civilization.

Summary

Enlightenment thought was used to justify absolutism and the bougeois revolution (Hobbes, Locke), blueprint future governments in terms of natural rights (Locke), civil rights (Voltaire), separation of power (Montesquieu), and the social contract (Rousseau), and to create a myth of human progress along which all human beings should travel. It especially provided the intellectual framework for the bourgeois revolutions in France and the Americas.

REVOLUTIONS IN FRANCE AND THE AMERICAS

The American Revolution of 1776, the French Revolution of 1789, and the revolutions in Latin America during the first part of the nineteenth century, were, to varying degrees, wars of national liberation, social revolutions, and political revolutions. In a social sense they can be bulked together under the term **"bourgeois"** (middle class) because they reflect the growing power and culture of the middle class whose money economy gave them the power and motivation to gain political ability and social status in the name of liberty and equality.

The American Revolution

The **American Revolution** (1776–1789) has been regarded both as a conservative war of independence and a radical political revolution. In a conservative sense it was only asserting traditional liberties of English citizens, but in a radical sense it achieved goals that went way beyond those of independence. Both views are probably correct as in the American context, liberal ideas took a much more democratic flavor.

The immediate issue in the revolution was taxes. The high cost of the Seven Years' War caused Britain to try to raise money in the colonies by means of a Stamp Act in 1765 (on documents, newspapers, cards, etc.) The Americans protested, in part because they regarded themselves as Englishmen who could not be taxed without representation. They also protested because they were used to greater religious and political freedom as the colonial assemblies made most of the important laws. They considered themselves distinct because of their greater social and economic equality. Most were independent farmers, not landed gentry, indentured servants, or slaves. By September, 1774, colonial assemblies began to meet to protest other perceived abuses including the Coercive Acts, which curtailed local elections and town meetings. In April, 1775, fighting began in Lexington and Concord, and on July 4, 1776, the Second Continental Congress adopted **Thomas Jefferson**'s draft of the **Declaration of Independence**, which listed tyrannical acts and then proclaimed rights for all humanity, not just Americans: "All men are created equal. . .they are endowed by their Creator with certain inalienable rights. . ." The documents stirred hearts in America and abroad.

In America the conflict often took the form of civil war pitting loyalists, who were politically conservative, wealthy, and loyal to Britain against liberals like Benjamin Franklin, John and Samuel Adams, and Patrick Henry, often wealthy too but infected with Enlightenment thought and self-rule. As the war progressed, with George Washington leading the rebel troops, liberalism advanced, causing state governments to extend the right to vote to many people.

The war also became internationalized. France sent volunteers, in 1779 and 1780 the Spanish and Dutch declared war on Britain, and Catherine the Great of Russia helped organize a League of Armed Neutrality. Faced with an imperial war and with reverses at Yorktown, in India, and in the West Indies, Britain offered independence and territory between the Appalachians and Mississippi to Americans, mostly to keep them out of French and Spanish hands (Treaty of Paris 1783). Many Americans who remained loyal to Britain emigrated to Canada.

Gathering in Philadelphia in the summer of 1787, delegates to the Constitutional Convention framed a government based on liberal principles of constitution, rights, and a national republic. Equality, as it existed in the document, meant before the law, not equality of political participation or material well-being. The Revolution ignited the world's imagination in terms of progress, liberalism, and changing international conflicts. Soon it spilled over into France.

The French Revolution

Taxes were also at the heart of the French Revolution. Expenditures in the American War caused the French government to look for new sources of taxes. In general, the **first and second estates** (clergy and nobility) had been exempt from taxes, but, facing bankruptcy in 1788, **Louis XVI** imposed a general tax on all landed property by decree. The decree met such resistance that he was forced to call the Estates General into session. Included in the 1200 delegates who arrived in May, 1789, were numbers of the growing **third estate**, or middle class, mostly lawyers and government officials, not merchants, and there were no delegates from the laboring poor. When the first and second estate refused to meet with the third estate, the third estate renamed itself the **National Assembly** and withdrew to a large indoor tennis court, swearing in the famous **Tennis Court Oath** not to disband until a constitution was written. Meanwhile, the lower classes, or **sans culottes**, who had suffered inflation and food shortages, took to the streets. On July 14, 1789 they stormed the medieval fortress where prisoners were held, the **Bastille**, under the banner of "**liberty, equality, and fraternity**." In the countryside peasants revolted, causing the so-called Great Fear (fear of vagabonds and outlaws). The result was that on August 4 all feudal dues paid by peasants were ended, and on August 27 the National Assembly issued the **Declaration of the Rights of Man**. This document closely followed the American Declaration of Independence, and guaranteed liberal ideas like equality before the law, representative government for a sovereign people, and individual freedom based on the idea of natural rights. During the next two years, in the spirit of the Enlightenment, a constitutional monarchy was established, wherein all lawmaking power was placed in the hands of the National Assembly, the nobility as a legal order was abolished, and the property of the church nationalized.

Domestic and International Aspects

Changes brought debate on both sides. Edmund Burke (1729–1797) wrote the classic conservative view in *Reflections on the Revolution* in France arguing for inherited privilege and against the chaos and tyranny revolution inspired. Mary Wollstonecraft (1757–1797) wrote a blistering rebuttal, *A Vindication of the Rights of Man* (1790) in which she argued for the elimination of economic and sexual inequality. Amidst this debate, the kings and nobility of Europe felt threatened as did Louis XVI and **Marie Antionette**, his unpopular Austrian wife, who tried unsuccessfully to flee France. Meanwhile, the Legislative Assembly, elected in 1791, was decidedly more liberal than the National Assembly. The majority, loosely allied as **Jacobins** and led by **Maximilien Robespierre** (1758–1794), enlarged the republican crusade outside Europe. France declared war on Austria and Prussia in order to "incite a war of people against kings . . ." Rumors of treason and threats from outside French borders led to the fall of the monarchy and rapid radicalization of the Revolution.

The French Republic

In September, 1792, the National Convention, elected under expanded franchise by universal male suffrage, proclaimed a republic and sentenced Louis XVI to death. The National Convention then declared war against Britain, Holland, and Spain as well. In an atmosphere of French defeats, food shortages, and inflation, Robespierre created the Committee of Public Safety, which carried out a campaign of terror, and, for the first time in history, a total war effort with a planned economy, revolutionary terror, and modern nationalism. Rationing, nationalized workshops, requisitioning, weapons manufacture, and imprisonment and execution of political enemies under the **Reign of Terror (1793–1794)** seemed to many to pervert the ideals of the revolution. But French national feeling, the sense of life and death struggle against outside enemies and those hostile to the revolution, and a forced draft of French young men for the army, made French armies victorious in 1794. At this point, the National Convention on 9 Thermidor (July 27, 1794) led the "Thermidorian Reaction" against the excesses of the National Convention. Robespierre was executed, and yet another constitution was written, this time with a five-man executive, the **Directory**. In 1799 **Napoleon Bonaparte**, who had gained fame defeating Italian armies in Austria, ended the Directory in a coup d'etat and substituted a strong dictatorship, thus ending the revolution.

Napoleonic Era

During the **Napoleonic Era (1799–1815)** France created an empire and then lost it, enshrined many of the revolutionary ideals, both at home and in other countries it occupied, and in the end

returned to a semimonarchy. Napoleon's greatest civil achievement was the **Civil Code (1804)** based on Roman law in which two fundamental principles of revolution were reasserted—equality of all citizens before the law, and security of wealth and private property. But the Code, as in Roman law, recognized men as the head of the family and made women dependent. Because France was at war during most of Napoleon's reign, basic political freedoms like freedom of the press and security from political imprisonment were violated. In 1802 Napoleon controlled Holland, the Austrian Netherlands, and most of Italy. When he made plans to invade England, he was soundly defeated by Lord Nelson at the Battle of Trafalgar. Napoleon then turned his attention to the east, decisively beating a combination Austrian/Russian force at the Battle of Austerlitz in 1805. He moved into Prussia and, when defeat was certain, Russia sued for peace at Tilsit in 1807.

The Grand Empire considerably impacted the people of Europe by abolishing feudal dues and serfdom, but Napoleon's conquest and heavy taxation turned many against him and the revolution. France itself began to experience shortages due to the British counter-blockade to France's Continental System, which was designed to keep British goods from Europe. When Russia resumed trade with Britain, Napoleon invaded in June, 1812. This was a disaster because, when Alexander I of Russia ordered the evacuation of **Moscow**, Napoleon occupied a burned-out city. As winter came, retreat began. Only 30,000 men out of an army of 600,000 returned to France. In April, 1814, Napoleon abdicated his throne and the Bourbon dynasty was restored. The new monarch, Louis XVIII (1814–1824) restored rights and accepted a constitutional monarchy. At this point, Napoleon staged a comeback but was decisively defeated at **Waterloo** in 1815.

Congress of Vienna

At the **Congress of Vienna**, composed of representatives of Russia, Prussia, Austria, and Great Britain, construction of a peace settlement based on balance of power principles was undertaken. Led by **Klemens von Metternich** of Austria,

balance of power meant an international equilibrium of political and military forces that would preserve the freedom and independence of the great powers. To do this, France was returned to its pre-war size, territories were balanced elsewhere, and there was agreement that the members would meet periodically to settle international crises, a system called the "Congress System." This lasted well into the nineteenth century and kept the peace in Europe.

Summary

Views of the French Revolution differ. Some historians emphasize the importance of the conflict between the growing middle class, or bourgeoisie, which made up eight percent of France's population, and the upper classes. Revisionist historians see the middle class and upper classes as much more fluid and disunited, and thus not so important to the conflict as the outdated medieval bureaucratic monarchy. Other debates have to do with whether or not the French Revolution was really a bourgeois revolution since it returned to a dictatorship with Napoleon and a partial monarchy with Louis XVIII. Most historians agree that France and Europe were forever changed and that liberal ideas made a considerable impact on France and Europe as a result of the French Revolution.

Latin American Revolutions

The revolutions in Latin America were closely connected with those in America and France. From the American Revolution came the ideas. Particularly appealing to Creole (American-born Spaniards) leaders was the Declaration of Independence, which served as reasons for their own revolution. The slogan of the French Revolution, "liberty, equality, and fraternity," appealed to other sectors of the population, but as revolution became more radical, it was rejected by the Creole elites. As an extension of the French Revolution, the revolt in Haiti, France's great island sugar colony in the Caribbean, was a prelude to the Latin American revolutions. Slaves, under the leadership of **Toussaint L'Overture**, seized the moment and staged a rebellion that resulted in the proclamation of the independent republic of Haiti in 1804. To the Creole elites of Latin America, such a lower class revolt was to be avoided, but to the lower classes, it was a symbol of hope. Independence, when it did come, lacked social transformation.

What sparked the Latin American revolts was the confused Iberian situation caused by the French Revolution. Portugal was invaded by France in 1807, and in 1808 Napoleon's brother Joseph sought to replace Ferdinand VII and rule Spain. Since everything in Spanish America was done in the name of the king, the Creoles argued that the removal of the legitimate king shifted sovereignty to the people. In the colonies, in places like Caracas, Bogota, and Mexico, Creoles set up **juntas** (groups of people controlling the government after a revolution) to rule in place of Ferdinand VII. Independence movements followed. In Mexico, Creoles led by **Father Miguel de Hidalgo** won a number of early victories in 1810, but when Hidalgo called for Indian and mestizo help, he lost the support of the Creoles who feared social rebellion. He was executed, but, in 1820 Augustin de Iturbide, a Creole officer, linked up with insurgents and the combined forces occupied Mexico City. Iturbide was named emperor and briefly included Central America in the Mexican Empire. However, the Central American states established their own independence and Mexico became a republic in 1838.

In northern Latin America, a movement for independence centered in Caracas began in 1810 under the leadership of a wealthy Creole officer, **Simon Bolivar**. In 1822 his victories in Venezuela, Colombia, and Ecuador led to a new nation called Grand Colombia. However, political and regional differences led to its breakup. Bolivar rejected all efforts to crown him king and in 1830 he left Colombia republican and independent.

In South America, another movement coalesced under **Jose de San Martin** around Buenos Aires. A booming commercial center, its residents resented Spanish trade restriction. Jose de San Martin's forces ranged across the Andes to Chile and Peru. Brazil's quest for independence occurred without upheaval. When Napoleon's troops entered Portugal, the royal family fled to Brazil and, under popular pressure, declared independence in 1822.

By 1825 all of Spanish Latin America had gained political independence and, despite plans to create some form of monarchy in the new 18 states, all emerged as independent republics with representative governments, fullfilling Enlightenment ideas. In none, though, was there a radical redistribution of property or reconstruction of society.

Results

The Latin American revolutions produced political fragmentation and independence, but not revolutionary change. Political stability proved elusive as Creole leaders, who led the revolutions, had no experience in government. In practice, generals or **caudillos** ruled. Independence brought economic problems due to destruction of land and mines and dislocation of the colonial market system. The three-tiered socioracial structure composed of whites, mixed, and blacks persisted. Large immigration in the second half of the nineteenth century complicated the picture for immigrants, who were usually at the bottom though they could move up more quickly than blacks. The church remained strong, but was continually vulnerable to liberal reformers who wanted to secularize the state. In terms of culture, the dominant role of the Creoles tended to Europeanize life in Latin America. During the romantic era of the 1830s, however, local customs became idealized. The appearance of secular education created some opportunities for women, though for the upper class, women's lives changed little. Lower class women, however, often controlled the local market. Born of Enlightenment liberalism, many questions of government and society remained unresolved by independence and appear similar to those in the twentieth century in the experience of emerging nations. The colonial heritage left little tradition of participatory government, and the highly centralized colonial state created dependence and resentment of government. Class and regional differences divided the new nations and wealth was unequally distributed. The rise of industrial

capitalism then placed the new nation in an economically dependent position.

Summary

The middle class revolutions based on Enlightenment thought produced varying degrees of social and political change. In North America the most complete revolution took place, gaining independence, republican government, and social leveling. In France, significant political change took place, but social change was minimal. In Latin America, independence was achieved, but political and social change was minimal.

In all places, nationalism based on liberalism played a significant role in the political process.

The Enlightenment, with its ideals of liberty, equality, and fraternity contrasted with the ownership and sale of slaves. The French philosophes called for an end to slavery, but it was the English Protestants, such as the Quakers, Baptists, and Anglicans, who began an active political campaign to abolish slavery. In 1795 the Dutch ended their shipments of slaves, followed by most other countries by the end of the Napoleonic Wars. Africans freed in the Americas or freed by the British navy en route to slave markets were returned to settlements in Sierra Leone, Liberia, and the Gold Coast. In 1833 slavery was declared illegal in the British Empire. Gradually, slavery was abolished in one country after another as slavery became less profitable. In the United States, however, slaves were not freed until the conclusion of the American Civil War. In the 1880s Cuba and Brazil were the last major countries to abolish slavery.

NEW NATIONALISM IN EUROPE

Besides the Americas, Latin America, and France, liberal movements occurred in other parts of Europe as well, particularly in Greece, Italy, Germany, and the decaying Ottoman Empire. Infused into these movements was a heightened spirit of nationalism that combined ideas of national liberation, nation-state building, and republicanism.

Greece

Since the fifteenth century, Greece had lived under the domination of the Ottoman Turks. In 1812, led by **Alexander Ypsilanti**, Greeks revolted. The Great Powers, who had pledged to preserve the balance of power status quo at the Congress of Vienna, were against such revolution, but Americans, Europeans, and Russians responded enthusiastically, especially after Turkish atrocities fanned outrage. In 1827 a combined British, French, and Russian fleet destroyed the Turkish fleet at Navarino, after which Russia gained a protectorate over Romania, and Greece declared its independence (1830).

France

Meanwhile, in France, the 1789 liberal revolution experienced setbacks during the reigns of Louis XVIII and Charles X. When Charles X stripped much of the middle class of its voting rights and censored the press, the streets of Paris once again erupted. The 1830 French revolution is immortalized in **Victor Hugo**'s *Les Miserables* and by the great romantic painter **Delacroix** in *Liberty Leading the People,* in which Liberty unites the worker, bourgeois, and street child in a righteous crusade against privilege and oppression. This revolution produced a new leader, Louis Philippe (r. 1830–1848), but republicans, democrats, social reformers, and the poor of Paris were bitterly disappointed as the elite actually tightened its control.

Revolutions of 1848

The **Revolutions of 1848** again broke out, this time over much of Europe. Only liberal Britain and immobile Russia escaped. Behind this were hard economic times and the growing power of the working class. The potato famine in Ireland had echoes on the continent in 1846 when poor harvests led to higher food prices. Workers, meanwhile, were infected with the ideas of socialism. Once again revolution started in Paris when the government refused to consider electoral reform (only the rich could vote for deputies and many were docile bureaucrats). The people were enraged and called for the abdication of Louis Philippe and the drafting of a constitution for France's Second Republic. Yet there were profound differences in the revolutionary coalition in Paris. One group, representing the workers, wanted a republican socialist government, while another, representing the middle class and owners of land (the bulk of the peasantry), were frightened by the socialists. In an attempt to pacify the workers, "national workshops," or public works programs, were established, but when the workers invaded the newly elected Constituent Assembly, the workshops were suspended. Barricades went up on the streets of Paris and three days of class war ensued, the so-called "June Days," in which 10,000 were killed. The Republican army triumphed and France returned to a constitution with a strong executive led by Louis Napoleon, a nephew of Napoleon Bonaparte.

Central Europe

News of the upheaval in France led to demands all over Europe for written constitutions, representative government, and greater civil liberties. In the beginning, urban workers united with middle class liberals, peasants, and nationalists. In the Austrian Empire, for instance, Hungarian nationalists led by Louis Kossuth demanded national autonomy, civil liberties, and universal suffrage. Students, workers, and peasants joined the protests. Soon the coalition fell apart, however. When the monarchy abolished serfdom, the peasants lost interest in other social and political questions. Then national questions superseded social and political ones. When Hungarian nationalists tried to recreate the ancient Hungary of Saint Stephen out of a mosaic of nationalities, the minorities went over to the monarchy. In Prague, Czech nationalists came in conflict with German nationalists. Then the middle class recoiled when the urban poor presented their own demands for suffrage and socialist workshops. The result was that the conservative aristocratic forces reasserted their strength and crushed the revolution.

Germany 1848

A similar course of events happened in Germany with the additional problem of unifying the 38 states of the German Confederation. The middle class Prussian liberals wanted to take the lead in establishing a liberal constitutional monarchy that would then merge with the other German states. Following the fall of Louis Philippe in France, the workers and artisans joined the middle class in revolt on the streets of Berlin. On March 21, 1848, King Frederick William IV gave in to demands to grant Prussia a liberal constitution merging the other German states into it. Immediately, two problems emerged. One was that the workers wanted a more radical program of universal voting rights, a minimum wage, and a 10-hour work day. The other was that the German states called for a national constituent assembly to write a federal constitution instead of a Prussian constitution to which others would accede. As the Constituent Assembly debated, it got bogged down in a battle with Denmark over control of Schleswig and Holstein. By 1849 the stalemate caused Frederick William to reassert his royal authority and grant a conservative constitution, but this too failed when Austria refused to join. Germany returned to a confederation, having failed to unite first in a liberal national state and then a conservative German Empire.

Summary

The European peace that had been established at the Congress of Vienna in 1814 turned into an arrangement that supported the status quo and thus conservatism in Europe. One reason this occurred was because of a growing worker class whose interests went beyond the middle class liberal political agenda to embrace a liberal social and economic program as well. Therefore, in central Europe in 1848 the liberal, national, and social revolution failed. In Greece, however, and Belgium, independence was achieved. Worldwide, liberal democratic movements based on a growing and powerful middle class, suc-

cessfully challenged the power of aristocratic privilege and monarchy. Revolution in America, France, and Latin America gave the world models of democratic liberalism that remain beacons of political liberty in the world today. Infused into these movements was a sense of optimism and progress well reflected in the romantic movement.

ROMANTICISM

The artistic and cultural movement that accompanied liberalism in the first half of the nineteenth century was **romanticism**. It was kindled in part by the spirit of the French Revolution that believed radical reconstruction was possible in all segments of society. Romanticism was a reaction to the enforced rules of classicism and of the Enlightenment. It stressed emotionalism, imagination, yearning for the unattainable, and nature. In its dethronement of tradition and the quest for the new, it put emphasis on the role of the individual. Thus, the solitary inventor like Edison, the great political figure like Napoleon, the starving artist, the misunderstood, and the man ready to die in a duel, were its heros. What emerged was a confidence in the collective destiny of western culture. Most romantics saw the growth of modern industry as ugly. Thus, much of the artistic and literary works had motifs rooted in nature.

The Arts

The greatest of the romantics was German poet and dramatist **Johann Wolfgang von Goethe** (1749–1832). Goethe began with one foot in Enlightenment thought as he was a keen observer of nature and a scientist. His conception of nature was highly romantic, though, because he saw the cosmos as the ultimate living organism composed of innumerable individual elements, a notion that was easy to apply to the relationship of the individual to the state. The notion of the state as a living organism influenced German nationalism thereafter, infusing it with a special sense of uniqueness and destiny. The leading

English romanticist was **William Wordsworth** (1775–1850), whose works are filled with fantasies of the glory of the English countryside. In France, Victor Hugo's (1802– 1885) famous *Les Misérables* depicted the hero, Jean Valjean, as a romantic hero of goodness and justice. The most famous English artists, **J. M. W. Turner** (1775–1857) and **John Constable** (1776–1837) painted wild storms, sinking ships, and the unspoiled English countryside in emotional terms. Hector Berlioz (1803–1869) exemplified the romantic tradition in music with the rich orchestral coloration of *Symphonie fantastique*. The greatest romantic composer, **Ludwig von Beethoven** (1770–1827) wrote symphonies that inspired not just emotional heroics but patriotic sentiment as well. In Russia, the romantic movement was reflected in the Slavophile movement, which idealized the Russian land and agrarianism, and in the music of composers like **Tchaikovsky**. Women in romantic attire came to stand allegorically for revolution itself as Delacroix's famous painting *Liberty on the Barricades* illustrates.

Summary

With the Industrial Revolution and its problems, the optimism of liberals and romantics gave way to social comment and realistic portrayals of society's ills, but with the strong western liberal belief that utopian solutions could be found to even the most vexing of them.

CHAPTER 21

Revolution in Energy, Industry, and Transportation

CHRONOLOGY	Franco-Prussian War (1870–1871)	The Opium War (1839–1842)	Boxer Rebellion (1900)
	Boer War (1899–1902)	Taiping Rebellion (1850–1864)	Spanish American War (1898)
	Sepoy Rebellion (1857)		

TERMS	modernization	free capitalist economy	Second Reich
	enclosed fields	socialism	Trans-Siberian Railroad
	Industrial Revolution	dialectical materialism	Great Trek
	Crédit Mobilier of France	communism	lapse
	socialism	realism	Indian National Congress
	laissez-fiare	Social Darwinism	
	classical liberalism	manifest destiny	

PEOPLE	Charles Townsend	Cound Henri de Saint-Simon	Sigmund Freud
	Jethro Tull		Feodor Dostoevsky
	James Hargreaves	Charles Fourier	nationalists
	Richard Arkwright	Louis Blanc	Count Camillo Cavour
	James Watt	Pierre Joseph Proudhon	Giuseppe Garibaldi
	George Stephenson	Robert Owen	Otto von Bismark
	Alfred Krupp	John Stewart Mill	Cecil John Rhodes
	proletariat	utopian socialist	John Livingston
	Edwin Chadwick	George Hegel	Rudyard Kipling
	Jeremy Bentham	Karl Marx	J. A. Hobson
	Georges Haussmann	Frederick Engels	Joseph Conrad
	Louis Pasteur	Emile Zola	Horatio Kitchener
	Joseph Lister	George Eliot	modernizers
	Adam Smith	Edgar Degas	traditionalist
	Thomas Malthus	determinist	antiimperialist
	David Ricardo	Charles Darwin	

PLACES	Sardinia	Piedmont	Suez Canal

Revolution in Energy, Industry, and Transportation

TECHNOLOGY AND THE INDUSTRIAL SYSTEM

The coming of industry transformed western Europe and then world society, a process that historians call **modernization**, meaning the development of new forms of economic and institutional life, large state apparatus, better education, urbanization, empire, and new ideologies. The Industrial Revolution began at about the same time as the political revolutions in France and America, but its impact was more profound, second only, perhaps, to the agricultural revolution. While it seemed to happen in a more evolutionary manner, in terms of world history, it was sudden and abrupt, occurring in the course of only 100 years.

The **Industrial Revolution** began in England due to a number of factors, among them a stable government that had avoided the liberal political revolutions of the period, an experienced business class, a central bank, a class of wage-earning peasants, a large domestic market due to cheap goods made possible by navigable rivers, and an agricultural revolution that produced enough surplus to free agricultural laborers for industry. This agricultural revolution started in the Low Countries (Belgium and Holland) and was adopted by the British. It revolved around intensive agriculture associated with innovations like **enclosed fields** (causing common grazing lands to be put into cultivation), continual crop rotation, heavy manuring rather than letting lands lie fallow, and a wide variety of crops. Many of these were put in practice by **Charles Townsend** (1674–1738) who had learned them in the Low Countries, and copied by others. **Jethro Tull** (1674–1741) made another advance—that is, the sowing of seed with a drill rather than scattering by hand. The enclosure movement, meanwhile, changed farming into a capitalist market venture in which all sorts of improvements were made to increase profits. Even before the Parliament passed the hundreds of enclosure acts of the eighteenth century, peasants had voluntarily been fencing off field for sheep grazing, producing for the lucrative wool market. By 1870 the English farmer produced 300 percent more food than he had produced in 1700. Other reasons for English industrial pioneering are related to the increased demand for goods and English control of commercial networks supplying them. Between 1700 and 1774 England's North American colonies absorbed 2.2 million surplus population from England, Scotland, and Northern Ireland. This population, through agricultural and resource development of vast lands in the Americas, achieved a standard of living high enough to create increased demand for goods. Meanwhile, England, in its competition with France, in effect became master of the seas after the War of the Spanish Succcession. By this war, Britain obtained territory in North America and control of the lucrative West African slave trade. Then, after the Seven Years' War (1756–1763) and the Treaty of Paris (1763), France lost all its mainland possessions in North America and in India. Britain's colonial empire became a stimulus for many branches of English manufacturing.

Industrial Technology

The pressure to produce more cotton, which had first been imported into England by the East India Company, created the world's first large factories. Before machines, four or five spinners were necessary to keep one weaver steadily employed. Thus, there was great impetus to find ways of improving spinning. In 1765 **James Hargreaves** invented his cotton spinning jenny (a wheel turned by hand supplied the power) and **Richard Arkwright** invented the water frame, in which water supplied the power. By 1790 the machines produced ten times as much cotton yarn as in 1770. The Arkwright invention used water to power several hundred spindles and thus required large specialized factories that employed hundreds of people. By 1831 the cotton textile industry was largely mechanized and factories dotted the river banks of England.

Industrial Revolution

The next breakthrough came in the age-old problem of energy and power. In fact, the energy revolution that replaced human and then animal and wind power with other energy sources was a monumental transformation in world history that permitted the gradual generalization of the factory system, a revolution in transportation, and the fulfillment of the Industrial Revolution. Coal, which had been used to heat homes since the 1640s, was first employed by **James Watt** (1736–1819) to power a steam engine. The steam engine was employed in many industries. It was used to power steam-driven bellows in the iron industry, to power flour, malt, and sugar mills, and to pump water out of coal mines. The steam engine was applied to sailing ships and then overland transportation. In 1825 **George Stephenson** built an effective locomotive. The railroad companies in England had to get permission to build and had to pay for rights of way, but otherwise were free to build railroads all over England.

The significance of the railroad was tremendous because it reduced the cost of shipping overland and integrated both internal markets and world markets. In 1860 Britain produced about 20 percent of the world's output of industrial goods. This, in turn, increased wealth and population, which grew from 9 million in 1780 to 21 million in 1851, and average consumption per person increased by 75 percent between 1780 and 1851. Another aspect of industrialism was that science was used not only to improve technology, but to find new products like dyes (William Perkins), batteries (Volta), generators (Faraday), and photography (Daguerre).

European Industrialization

The new technologies that developed in England soon spread to the continent where they developed in a somewhat different way and made advances of their own. Government throughout Europe believed industrial power equaled international power so industrialization took place with full government backing. In addition, the instability of the French Revolution set the continent back, necessitating more government action to catch up. In some cases, English technology arrived on the continent surreptitiously. Until 1825 it was illegal for artisans and skilled mechanics to leave Britain, and until 1843 to export textile machinery and other equipment. Many talented and ambitious workers slipped out, however, like William and John Cockerill of Lancaster, who built a factory that produced steam engines, machinery, and locomotives in France. One way the German government played a much larger role in industry was by setting high external tariffs and creating an internal customs union among the German states, the Zollverein (1834). Also, big stockholder or industrial banks were created to support industrial development. The most famous was the **Crédit Mobilier of France**, founded in 1852 by two young Jewish journalists, Isaac and Emile Pereire. The result was that all European states as well as the United States, Canada, and Japan, raised industrial levels in the nineteenth century, and by 1913, the United States had passed Britain, and Germany was rapidly closing in. This was in contrast to the non-western countries, where cottage industry decreased due to western mechanical industrialization that flooded the world markets.

URBANIZATION

Above all, industrialization meant urbanization. By 1914 a mere 10 percent of England's population was rural. A similar, if not so dramatic, shift occurred in Germany and the United States between 1870 and 1914. An example of abrupt and large-scale urbanization occurred in Germany when **Alfred Krupp** set up his armaments works in the Ruhr in the 1840s transforming the whole valley into a European industrial powerhouse. City life bred new classes of urban workers (**proletariat**) and entrepreneurial middle class (bourgeoisie), and a whole new urban culture. Education became more important as the demand for a literate work force and trained bureaucracy increased. In most countries, compulsory education for young children was introduced by law (Britain, 1870, France, 1882). Methods of work and play changed too. At first, destitute people and orphans filled the ranks of factory workers, but the outlawing of pauper apprentices in 1802, and the use of steam power rather than water power attracted whole families to the cities to work. While much has been written about poor working and living conditions in the cities, for the first time the standard of living improved to the point that people could feed themselves adequately and still have enough money left for amusements. This can be seen through the popularity of daily newspapers, bicycles, the rise of the popular theater and revues, and movies. Industrial and urban growth ushered in the age of mass consumption and culture.

Industrial Cities

At first, cities grew like topsy-turvy. This created more problems in old medieval towns than in new ones. There, the typical city was a "walking city" without public transport. Parks and open space were nonexistent. The hasty erection of small, closely packed houses in already congested areas led to slum conditions, while the incursions of new roads and railways added to pollution. Infectious disease spread rapidly and filth lay underfoot everywhere due to lack of plumbing and sewage facilities. The question

was, who was responsible for the plight of the city? Soon it became a matter of public concern and responsibility. **Edwin Chadwick** (1748–1832), following the philosopher **Jeremy Bentham**, who taught that public problems could be solved on a rational basis according to the dictum the "greatest good for the greatest number," advocated a public health movement that included clean, piped water, public parks, and transportation. Under the leadership of **Georges Haussmann**, Paris was completely transformed with broad boulevards and parks and streetcars. Meanwhile, **Louis Pasteur**'s (1822–1895) germ theory of diseases, which replaced the miasmatic theory (that bad odors cause disease), allowed identification of the organisms that caused them and vaccines to protect against them. **Joseph Lister**'s (1827–1912) "antiseptic principle," which led to the use of disinfectants, improved the surgical and public hospital environment. Gradually, cities became modern complexes using the machines and science that had bred industrialism to solved the problems of industrialism. Industrialization and urbanization also spawned some ways of thinking about the world.

Architecture

The architecture of the 1800s also exhibited both liberalism and industrialism. When European architects set out to design important public buildings, they harkened back to two traditions—the Greco-Roman, as embodied in the Paris Opera (1861–75), and the Gothic, as embodied in the British House of Parliament, completed in 1857. These structures architecturally reflect the pride Europeans felt in their culture and the political advances in a time of liberalism and national self-confidence. New industrial age materials like iron girders and glass also found their way into the period's architectural construction. Joseph Paxton explored these new principles and materials in the construction of the Crystal Palace, which housed the great Exhibition of 1851 in London's Hyde Park. The steel frame allowed construction of large windows to let in light, but in exterior decoration, the older ideas of architectural grandeur remained.

The technical possibilities of steel frame construction allowed American architects in the late 1800s to build upward in the form of skyscrapers like the Wainwright Building in St. Louis (1891) and the Woolworth Building in New York (1913). In decoration, however, traditional conceptions of magnificence remained. The skyscraper reflects the genius of the modern metropolis where people, by means of elaborate transportation systems, work in offices piled one on top of another, creating a collective creation that epitomizes the entire structure of modern civilization, a whole artificial landscape.

IDEOLOGIES—SOCIALISM AND REALISM

Classical Liberalism

With industrialization, the Enlightenment ideas of scientific order that so transformed politics gave way to the romantic belief in progress in the human condition. **Socialism** resulted from a romantic and utopian view of how this would be achieved for workers. Socialism had its roots in the classical liberalism that seemed to favor the middle class over the worker. The principal ideas of liberalism—equality and liberty—continued to be important during the early nineteenth century, but their propensity to espouse **laissez-faire,** or opposition to government interference, a form of liberalism that is often called **classical liberalism,** left a gap in the social and economic needs of the industrial age. The idea of a free economy was outlined by **Adam Smith** (1723–1790), whose *Inquiry into the Nature and Causes of the Wealth of Nations* (1776) founded modern economics. In this treatise, Smith argued against mercantilism on the basis that free trade creates wealth through specialization. He outlined the characteristics of a **free capitalist economy**—private property, profit, and a free market whose "Invisible Hand" guides and regulates supply and demand. The classical liberal idea that government should not interfere often became a doctrine used by businessmen to outlaw labor unions (as it restricted free labor com-

petition) and other government interference in the workplace. Other thinkers added to Smith's view that government should not interfere in the economy. **Thomas Malthus** (1766–1834) argued that population always tends to rise faster than the food supply. If the government were to interfere with emergency welfare, it would make matters worse as the population would rise even further, whereas a hands-off policy would return population to equilibrium levels. **David Ricardo** (1772–1823) in his *Iron Law of Wages* postulated that population could be controlled by wage rates. If wages rose, population would rise, as families would have more children, whereas if wages were just high enough to keep workers from starving, population growth would equal the supply of food.

French Utopian Socialists

It was against these classical liberal ideas, which seemed to represent the interests of the middle class capitalist factory owners, that socialism developed. To socialists, the liberal practices in politics and economics appeared selfish, individualistic, and lacking in community spirit. Socialist thought, which originated in France, began to challenge classical liberal ideas. Socialists argued that government should rationally organize the economy and not depend on competition, that the poor should be protected, that wealth should be more equally distributed between rich and poor, and that private property should be abolished in favor of state ownership. There were four giants of French utopian socialist thought:

1. One of the earliest socialist thinkers was **Count Henri de Saint-Simon** (1760–1825). He believed that the "doers" in society—the scientists, engineers, and industrialists—should plan the economy, create public works projects, and create national banks.
2. **Charles Fourier** (1772–1837) envisioned a social utopia in which self-sufficient communities lived communally, and in which women were totally emancipated.
3. **Louis Blanc** (1811–1882), advocated universal voting rights and government-

backed workshops and factories guaranteeing full employment.

4. **Pierre Joseph Proudhon** (1809–1865), in a pamphlet *What is Property?* wrote that property was theft as it was profit stolen from the worker, but Proudhon also feared the state as a solution to the problem.

English Utopian Socialists

In England, meanwhile, other utopian thinkers were addressing the plight of the workers. There, however, the result was that socialist thought found its way into legislation and government action that significantly improved the lot of the worker. **Robert Owen** (1771–1858), a successful Scottish cotton manufacturer, testified before a parliamentary committee about the poor working conditions in factories, especially for women and children. He suggested that, if people were healthy, they would be better producers. He advocated that the fruits of labor should be shared by philanthropy, and that owners should follow a paternalistic attitude by setting up ideal communities in which the focus was not the factory but the community. Jeremy Bentham (1748–1832) taught that the government should follow a policy of the "greatest good for the greatest number and, therefore, should be actively involved in solving problems like urban blight and the right to vote, unionization, and education." **John Stewart Mill** (1806–1873) in his famous *Essay on Liberty* argued that, to protect the rights of individuals and minorities, voting rights should be extended. These voices on behalf of the working man resulted in a series of legislative acts on behalf of workers that altered the classical liberal laissez-faire position. In 1833, the Factory Act limited the workday for children and required that factories establish schools for children under nine. Reformers published a shocking picture of children in mines leading to the Mines Act of 1842, prohibiting work for all women as well as boys younger than 10 underground. In 1884, in the Third Reform Bill, the right to vote was given to almost every adult male. By 1900 the Labour Party had formed, advocating redistribution of wealth by means of an income tax. In this way, the **utopian socialist program** was fulfilled in England by means of a democratic system.

Marxian Socialists

In Germany, a new kind of socialism, scientific or Marxian socialism, developed. Marxian socialism had its origins in the scientific rationality of the Enlightenment and in **George Hegel**'s (1770–1831) theory of change, which emphasized dialectics. Dialectics described a process of being or "thesis" that produced non-being or "antithesis," resulting in a state of becoming or "synthesis." In the *Communist Manifesto*, **Karl Marx** (1818–1883) and **Frederick Engels** (1820–1895) applied Hegel's theory to economic relationships between classes. According to the Manifesto, "the history of all previously existing societies is the history of class struggle" and a state of conflict between the bourgeoisie, or capitalist factory owners, and the workers of proletariat over material things, hence, **dialectical materialism**." Based on history, Marx predicted that, just as the bourgeoisie had triumphed over feudal aristocracy, the proletariat would conquer the bourgeoisie in revolution. This revolution would produce **communism**, a utopia in which the state would wither away, there would be freedom from want, and the world would be united in an international worker world without national boundaries. The book concludes with the line, "Working Men of All Countries, Unite." Marxian socialism failed in its bid to influence world history during the Revolution of 1848, the year the Manifesto was published, but it steadily gained converts in Germany and Russia during the last half of the nineteenth century and became a dominant force in the twentieth century, ironically in the non-industrialized countries.

Realism

In the second half of the nineteenth century, as industrialism and the worker class gained strength, the artistic and cultural movements moved from a romantic view of liberty and progress to social comment and a realistic depiction of life experiences. This included an application of science to society and its problems. **Realism** reflected life as it was, recorded and observed and used scientific objectivity rather than emotional intuition. **Emile Zola** (1840– 1902) was the literary giant of the realistic movement. Zola wrote carefully researched stories about urban slums, coal strikes, and the stock exchange. He sympathized with socialism and his concern was inequality. In England, Mary Ann Evans (1819–1880), who wrote under the pen name **George Eliot**, in her great novel *Middlemarch* examined the way people are shaped by their society. In the visual arts, painters like **Edgar Degas** in *Women Ironing* captured the hard work of the laboring classes.

Determinists

The realists were also **determinists**. Unlike the romantics who glorified individual freedom, the realists believed human beings were governed by unalterable natural laws of heredity and environment. In particular, science began to be used to study society giving rise to "social science." One of the most famous determinists was **Charles Darwin** (1809–1882), who concluded in *On the Origin of Species by Means of Natural Selection* (1859) that life had evolved or changed on the basis of a struggle for survival. Darwin's theory was applied to society by **Herbert Spenser** (1820–1903), a **Social Darwinist**, who argued that social progress occurred as a result of human survival of the fittest. Meanwhile, scientists begain delving into the mind. **Sigmund Freud** (1856–1939) founder of psychoanalysis, theorized that much of human behavior was motivated by unconscious emotional needs. The exploration of the mind was reflected in literature too, especially in the works of Russian author **Feodor Dostoevsky**, whose works are filled with elements of conscience, guilt, and resentment. Realism reflected both the problems of urban industrial society and the faith in science to expose, understand, and correct the weaknesses in the social and economic fabric of late nineteenth-century western society.

EMPIRE

The European race for world empire, which occurred in the second half of the nineteenth century, was the industrial counterpart to the European search for markets during the commercial revolution. In 1800 the Europeans and North Americans dominated 35 percent of the world's land surface, by 1914 they controlled 84 percent. During the period European money, migrants, and manufactured goods streamed particularly into Africa and Asia, resulting in tensions between European powers and putting millions of black and brown people under the control of whites.

Nationalism

The new scramble for empire was caused by nationalism and industrialism. European nationalism inspired competition between states for markets, wealth, and power. Inflamed by the French Revolution, the idea of nation and liberty became linked. **Nationalists** believed that every nation, like every citizen, should have the right to exist in freedom, a freedom that was threatened when Napoleon's shadow spread over Europe. After the Napoleonic era, national citizens began to identify themselves as "we" or "they," to adopt a sense of national mission, and to see imperial conquest as crucial to national security, military power, and international prestige. In the Americas, this national mission began to be reflected in the idea of **manifest destiny**, a phrase coined by John L. Sullivan in 1845 to mean that God had ordained the nation to cover the continent. Often this meant moving the Indians off the land into reservations in the name of "civilization and progress." In 1789, the new nation controlled the land east of the Appalachians. In 1803, with the Louisiana Purchase, the United States lay claim to most of the land between the Mississippi and Rocky Mountains. After a bloody war with Mexico, U.S. territory reached the Pacific (1848) and, in 1867 Alaska was purchased from the Russians.

Unification of Germany and Italy

Nationalism of a different sort occurred in Italy and Germany, which finally coalesced into nation-states. This served to step up the competition for empire among the European states, adding two new contestants. Unification of Italy took place between 1858 and 1870. Two leaders instrumental in this were **Count Camillo Cavour**, who united **Sardinia** and the **Piedmont** (northwest Italy), and **Giuseppe Garibaldi**, who rallied the people of Sicily. The two then supported King Victor Emmanuel II in his election bid in 1861. The Parliament proclaimed him king of Italy "by grace of God and will of the nation."

German unification, meanwhile, came at the hands of **Otto von Bismark**. In his position as prime minister, Bismark hoped to unite Germany "not with speeches. . .but with blood and iron." Bismark's plan, supported by Wilhelm I, was to unite the German states under Prussia. To do this, he fought three wars. In the war with Denmark, he obtained Schleswig Holstein. In the war with Austria, the Seven Weeks' War (1866), Austria approved the dissolution of the confederation of German states, and in 1867 the northern states were joined with Prussia. In 1870, Prussia fought France (the **Franco-Prussian War**), ending in German victory and French cession of Alsace-Lorraine. In 1871 delegates wrote a constitution for a new German Empire made up of all the German states except Austria. The Germans called their Empire the **Second Reich** (*reich* meaning empire, the first Reich being the Holy Roman Empire).

German Industrialization

Once united, Germany rapidly industrialized and began to challenge Britain's industrial supremacy. Germany was able to do this for several reasons:

1. Germany was able to import technology invented and perfected by others;
2. Britain's traditional power sources—water and coal—were soon eclipsed by a German internal combustion engine that ran on petroleum and could drive machines, automobiles, and ships;
3. tariffs were introduced to protect infant industry.

Germany was not the only area, where industrial output advanced. While in Britain it doubled between 1870 and 1914 and in Germany it quadrupled, in the United States it trebled, and in Russia it increased ninefold. Thus began the scramble for raw materials and commodities overseas and a race to control and monopolize the areas from which supplies came. The scramble occurred mostly in Africa and Asia, areas rich in mineral and human resources and unable to defend against European military might.

Causes of Imperialism

There were other reasons for empire. One was demographic. In the nineteenth century, Europe's population soared from 190 million to 423 million. Thus, empire became a place for excess population and a full 40 million people emigrated. Another was the transportation revolution. Large ocean-going steamships allowed fast transport across the world's seas, and the opening of the **Suez Canal** in 1869 cut the sea journey from Europe to India by almost half. Likewise, on land the railroad allowed penetration of central Africa, and the **Trans-Siberian Railroad**, begun in 1891 and completed in 1905, linked Europe and Asia. Railroads and irrigation allowed development of unpromising terraine in Kenya and Nigeria, where land was transformed into plantation colonies that grew tea, coffee, cotton, tobacco, and cocoa at great profit. Motor cars and airplanes completed the transportation revolution. Empire in Africa was also made possible by the mass-production of quinine in 1830, providing defense against the tropical disease, malaria. Finally, empire became a focus of national adventure and missionary zeal. Explorers like **Cecil John Rhodes** (1853–1902) discovered diamonds, made a fortune, and then became prime minister of the Cape Colony. Missionaries like **John Livingston** spread Christianity. Europeans justified their intrusion in terms of bringing enlightenment and civilization to native people. Indeed, schools, hospitals, and churches were established and roads built.

The notion of white racial superiority was rarely questioned. Nowhere is the sentiment more clearly delineated than in **Rudyard Kipling**'s poem *The White Man's Burden*. Imperialism had its critics too, like economist **J. A. Hobson** (1858–1940) whose work *Imperialism* influenced Lenin and others. He contended that imperialism was an outgrowth of capitalism's need for labor, raw materials, and markets. **Joseph Conrad** (1857–1924) also castigated Europeans for pure selfishness in "civilizing" Africa.

Imperialism in Africa

In 1880 European nations controlled about 10 percent of Africa, but by 1914 they had gobbled up almost the entire continent. Only Ethiopia in Northeast Africa and Liberia on the West African coast remained independent. Before 1880 the French had conquered Algeria and the British had taken over the Dutch possessions in Cape Town. This had caused the Dutch settlers (Afrikaners or Boers) to make their **Great Trek** into the interior (1835) where they fought the Zulu people. In 1853 the Dutch proclaimed their independence, creating the Afrikaner states, the Orange Free State and the Transvaal. Between 1880 and 1900, however, Britain, France, Germany, and Italy created empires in Africa. Even the Afrikaner states were conquered by the British in the **Boer War** (1899–1902). In 1884 Leopold II of Belgium took over the entire Congo Basin, which he ruled directly and exploited mercilessly. Leopold's foray into Africa caused Bismark of Germany to arrange an international conference establishing principles for European claims in Africa. The Berlin Conference (1884–1885) declared "effective occupation" the determining factor in laying claim. This set off another relentless push to the interior. Shortly thereafter, Germany claimed Togoland, the Cameroons, Southwest Africa, and East Africa. France, meanwhile, extended its control over much of West and North Africa. Then, Britain claimed Zanzibar and thrust southward from Egypt into Sudan where it was stopped by a Muslim army that decimated the British forces at Khartoum (1885). Britain retrieved its position when General **Horatio**

Kitchener built a railroad to supply arms and reinforcements. Then, at Omduran in 1898 Britain soundly defeated the Sudanese forces and pushed on to Fashoda on the upper Nile. There Britain came in conflict with France, a contest that ended with France capitulating. This illustrated the explosive nature of European competition.

Imperialism in Asia

In Asia, the imperialist competition was no less fierce. Czsarist Russia began in the 1820s to push against the steppe Muslim Khanates and one by one they fell—Tashkent in 1865, Samarkand and Bukhara in 1868, Merv in 1884, and finally, to the borders of India, where they met the British who had expanded by war and the doctrine of **lapse** (native states without a clear successor fell under British rule) into the Punjab, Afghanistan, and Burma.

The British, meanwhile, acquired India, the "jewel" in the crown of the British empire. This occurred as a result of the **Sepoy Rebellion** in 1857. This mutiny, which began among native regiments of the British army in India, involved princes and landowners as well as peasants. It resulted in the transfer of India from the British East India Company to the crown. A British viceroy was responsible for enacting the government policy in India. The British began educating Indians for jobs in the Indian civil service and building railroads to open Indian markets to British goods. The British encouraged the production of cotton rather than food crops and discouraged local industries that might compete with British factories. During the 1880s famines led to the deaths of millions of Indians and fostered sporadic revolts by poorly armed peasants. Although British telegraph lines, new railroads, and the Suez Canal increased communication and trade between India and Europe, British-educated, middle class Indians organized the **Indian National Congress** in 1885. This new political party was demanding an end to British rule by the early twentieth century.

In China in the early nineteenth century the Europeans were confined to the coast. By then they had persuaded Chinese merchants to accept Indian opium instead of silver for purchases. In

1839 the imperial court decided to use force to halt the trade, but were defeated (**The Opium War**). In the Treaty of Nanking in 1842, China was forced to cede Hong Kong to Britain, to open five cities to foreign trade, and to accept low tariffs. The economic dislocation caused by the loss of silver resulted in widespread discontent and brought on the **Taiping Rebellion** in 1853. Leaders of the revolt capitalized on ancient Chinese traditions and ideas taken from Christian missionaries. They favored a redistribution of land, equality between men and women, and a reduction in taxes. The rebellion took 14 years to suppress and cost 20 million lives, further weakening Ch'ing rule and leading to another round of European incursions and trading concessions.

Chinese weakness also led to Russian occupation of the Amur basin and Vladivostock and loss of the Chinese tribute states. Britain acquired Burma; France, Indochina; and Japan, Korea. This string of defeats led to the **Boxer Rebellion** (1900), aimed at ousting foreigners. The Ch'ing, in desperation, had to call in the western powers to restore order. In return, China was divided into spheres of influence by the western powers. Meanwhile, the Dutch extended their rule from Java throughout the East Indian Archipelago (Indonesia) and the United States, as a result of the **Spanish American War** (1898), gained Cuba and the Philippines.

Results

The people of Africa and Asia initially tried to drive out the unwelcome foreigners, but, overpowered by superior weaponry, they responded in various ways. Some **modernizers** tried to adapt, while **traditionalists** tried to maintain the old ways. For some, on both ends of the spectrum, social and economic advancement was the result. Inevitably there were **anti-imperialists** as well, who resented foreign domination. Learning about liberalism and nationalism from their masters, eventually they used such theories to overthrow the Europeans in twentieth-century wars of liberation.

CHAPTER 22

Modernization Movements

CHRONOLOGY	Meiji Restoration (1868) Russo-Japanese War (1904)	Tanzimat Reforms (1839–1876) Suez Canal (1869) Crimean War (1853)	Revolution of 1905 Great Potato Famine (1846–1851)
TERMS	modernization Japanese Diet zaibatsus State Shintoism decolonialization	capitulations Emancipation Proclamation zemstvos Bloody Sunday	October Manifesto Duma pogroms
PEOPLE	Commodore Matthew Perry Tokugawa shoguns	Emperor Meiji Young Turks Ataturk	Muhammad Ali Khedive Ismail Sergei Witte
PLACES	Edo Bay Taiwan	Karlowitz	Serbia

Modernization Movements

In the areas of the world that were not overcome by European imperialism, governments took note of the power Europeans had assumed as a result of **modernization**. They began to copy industrialism and tinker with their political systems to accommodate the economic changes. In most cases, liberalism was introduced only in a limited way, industrialism came from the top down, and nationalism became a potent rationale for change. Japan, the Ottoman Empire and Russia all attempted to modernize with varying results.

MEIJI JAPAN (1868)

Japan's ability to change in the face of the western challenge contrasted sharply with Chinese impotence. Perhaps this was possible for Japan because Japan had a history of imitation and fewer goods that the West wanted. At first, however, it seemed that Japan would be laid open for western exploitation like China, India, and Africa. In 1853 American **Commodore Matthew Perry** arrived with a fleet in **Edo Bay** near Tokyo and threatened bombardment if Americans were not allowed to trade. The Japanese were forced into concessions, and in 1858 other European nations followed suit. Then Japan changed course. Unlike China and India, who were ruled by foreign dynasties, Japanese political authority was exercised by a dynasty of military autocrats, the **Tokugawa shoguns**. Their failure to stand up to the westerners caused unrest so serious that in 1868 **Emperor Meiji** threw out the shogun system and reclaimed the right of emperor to rule in the **Meiji Restoration**. Immediately, both political and economic restructuring took place.

Meiji Restoration

Ironically, the Tokugawa period, which had created a centralized Japanese state, also set in place much of the framework for Meiji modernization plans. By requiring all daimyo to reside in Edo and Osaka on alternative years, these cities exploded in population. Edo had a population of over one million in the eighteenth century, making it a leading world city. Thus grew up a middle class of providers of goods and services. It also shifted the position of the samurai, or privileged ruling class, which made up five percent of the population. Samurai became educated and moved into the bureaucracy. Removing the samurai from agriculture also had the effect of creating an agricultural sector that began producing for the market. The Tokugawa also built roads and political infrastructure, ports, and fleets.

The new Meiji government abolished feudalism, replacing the domains of the daimyos with a system of nationally appointed prefects. From this centralized base, Emperor Meiji and his advisers were able to effect change. They sent samurai officials abroad to study economic and political institutions and technology. A national education system and a conscript army financed by a new tax system were established in 1872. The army introduced peasants to the discipline of the military and educated them to be both a modern work force and the foundation of a modern army. Feudal fighting tradition was put aside in favor of formal officer training and upgraded armaments. Stipends to the samurai class were abolished, impoverishing many, but becoming the impetus for the samurai to enter new areas of activity in politics and business.

The bureaucracy was reorganized and opened to talent on the basis of civil service examinations, a bureaucracy that would grow from 29,000 officials in 1890 to 72,000 in 1908. A constitution was issued based on the German model, giving the emperor control over the military and the ability to appoint ministers and the parliament or **Diet** the ability to pass laws and approve the budget. Only about five percent of adult male population could vote, however, due to high property qualifications. Political parties arose but they had limited power and the most liberal of them was suppressed. To avoid becoming a colony, Japan sought to exploit rivalries of the colonial powers abroad. The structure that evolved was highly centralized and gave power to an oligarchy of wealthy businessmen and former nobles.

Japanese Industrialization

The Meiji government then set about the process of industrialization. Scarce capital, unfamiliarity with new technology, and fear of foreigners forced government control. The Ministry of Industry, created in 1870, oversaw economic policy and operation. State banks were created to fund trade and provide industrial capital. State-built railroads spread across the country and rapid steamers connected the islands. Guilds and internal tariffs were abolished to create a national market. Land reform, giving individual ownership to farmers, raised agricultural output by introduction of fertilizers and equipment. Private enterprise also grew in Japan. Older merchant families and some newcomers established factories producing textiles, chemicals, and food products. By the 1890s, as in the United States, where corporations were being formed, large new industrial combines, called *zaibatsus,* emerged as a result of accumulations of capital and far-flung merchant and industrial operations. Japan, unlike other industrializing countries, depended on exports and had no prior capital built on foreign trade to rely on. Thus, the burden of production and capital accumulation fell on poorly paid workers at home and in sweatshops, who turned out silk destined for foreign markets. A few big corporations provided benefits and social organizations, but maintained low wage policies and prohibited labor organizations.

Social Change

There were many social ramifications of industrialization. One was demographic. Population grew from 35 million in 1873 to 55 million in 1918. This strained resources and maintained low wages. Education stressed science and technical subjects. The Japanese copied western fashions, learned western standards of hygiene, and adopted the western calendar and metric system, but they did not adopt Christianity and retained many of their traditional emphases, especially the inferior position of women. Industrialization did affect the family as men moved to the cities leaving women behind; in 1900 Japan had the highest divorce rate in the world. Buddhism lost ground but **State Shintoism**, which appealed to the new nationalist concern with Japan's distinctive mission and the religious functions of the emperor, found favor. Modernization also caused many tensions in Japanese life—tensions between generations, between old and new, and between the traditional and foreign. The response of the government was to urge national loyalty and devotion to the government, resulting in a rise in nationalist sentiment.

As Japanese industrial power grew, in imitation of the West and in self-defense, it joined the ranks of the imperialist powers. Japan also needed markets and raw materials. In 1879 Japan annexed the Ryukus, and in 1895, after war with China, it acquired **Taiwan** and a claim to the Liaotung peninsula (vetoed by Russia). In 1904 Russian influence in Manchuria and Japanese influence in Korea led to the **Russo-Japanese War**. Japan won handily and in 1910 annexed Korea. This war is often seen as a turning point in world history because it marked the first major defeat of an industrial European empire by a non-western power, setting in motion a process of **decolonialization** that was to dominate twentieth-century history. It also illustrated an alternative route to modernization from that followed by the West. Meiji modernization was unusual in that it avoided the revolutionary pressures that afflicted Russia and China, while maintaining rule from above. This is, perhaps, due to its nationalist bent.

OTTOMAN REFORM

The Ottoman attempts at modernization and reform were less successful than those of the Japanese in safeguarding the Ottoman state from western imperialism. Yet they did have a profound impact on the course Turkey would take in modern times. In the seventeenth and eighteenth centuries, the Ottoman Empire appeared to be in decline. Questions of dynastic succession, a series of incompetent rulers, rising population, corruption, competition from abroad that deprived artisans of their livelihood, and impoverishment of the peasantry at the hands of tax collectors, all served to weaken the Ottoman state. The result was incursions by both the Austrian Habsburgs and the Russians. In 1683, in an Ottoman attack on Vienna, a strong allied Christian force and Habsburg heavy artillery gave the Europeans victory. The peace treaty signed at **Karlowitz** (1699) proved a turning point as, by it, the Ottomans lost to Austria the vast and wealthy provinces of Hungary and Transylvania.

Meanwhile, after Russian westernization under Peter the Great, the Russians advanced across the steppes, taking control of the Caucasus and Crimean areas. In 1804 a Christian uprising in **Serbia** was brought under control at great cost. In 1830 Greece gained independence, and in 1867, Serbia. In addition, the Ottomans signed a series of agreements with the Europeans called **capitulations**. Not unlike the treaty ports given by China to the western powers, the capitulations allowed French, English, and Habsburg merchants to travel, buy, and sell throughout Ottoman dominions, pay low customs duties, and be exempt from Ottoman law. At the beginning of the nineteenth century, loss of territory, pressures of European capitalist imperialism, and unresolved internal problems caused the Ottoman Empire to be called "the sick man of Europe."

Modernization of Ottoman Turkey

Ottoman survival rested on European inaction due to fears among themselves that others would gain more from dismemberment, and on Ottoman internal reform. But internal reform was dangerous business because of vested interests among strong groups like the *ulema*. There were deep divisions among the ruling elite as to how this could be done. Some argued for far-reading change based on the European model. Others backed reforms based on precedents, and it was in the interests of some to forestall any change at all. A first series of reforms were carried out under Sultan Selim (1789–1807). These were aimed at improving administration and building a new army and navy. The Janissary corps was so threatened by this that they revolted and killed him in 1807. A more skillful sultan, Mahmud II, in 1826 secretly built a small professional army with European help, and then subdued the Janissaries, threatened provincial notables into submission, and launched a series of reforms based on the western model, despite protestations by the religious experts. He established a diplomatic corps and an army and navy on western models. In succeeding decades, particularly during the **Tanzimat reforms**, (1839–1876), a state-run postal and telegraph service was introduced, universal education that emphasized science and technology, legal reforms, newspapers, and a constitution. The reforms helped religious minorities, but did little to improve the role of women or artisans. The reforms did not settle the tensions between conservative elites and the western-educated bureaucrats who favored the end to the sultantate. In 1908, in resistance against the despotism reintroduced by Sultan Abdul Hamid (r. 1878– 1908) the westernized officers and civilians united in an organization called the **Young Turks** and staged a bloodless coup in 1908. This led to the rise of Mustafa Kemal or **Ataturk** (1881–1938) after World War I and the emergence of a westernized Turkey.

An even more astounding modernization program was undertaken by **Muhammad Ali** (1769–1849) in Egypt. In 1798 French armies under Napoleon invaded the Egyptian part of the Ottoman Empire. When they left, the Albanian-born Ottoman general Muhammad Ali stepped in to fill the vacuum. He immediately set about building a new state and military based on western lines. His policies of modernization attracted large numbers of European fortune seekers, including engineers, doctors, policemen, financiers, shippers and high government officials. One of the most important changes Muhammad Ali made, and one that was duplicated in many modernizing countries with the same deleterious effects, was the development of commercial agriculture geared to the European market. Peasants had been poor but self-sufficient, growing food for their own use on state-allotted lands, but to pay for a modern army, high ranking officials and members of Ali's family began carving out large private holdings on which were grown crops like cotton for export, and on which labored peasant tenants. These landlords often borrowed heavily from abroad, but still made fortunes. Thus, modernization and accumulation of capital came on the backs of the peasants.

Egyptian Modernization

The trend was continued under Muhammad Ali's grandson, **Khedive** (prince) **Ismail** (r. 1863–1879), especially in Egypt. He promoted a large irrigation network that furthered estate building. He borrowed large sums to install modern communications, and with his support the **Suez Canal** was completed by a French company in 1869. In addition, young Egyptians were educated in Europe; Arabic instead of Turkish became the official language; and Cairo acquired modern boulevards and hospitals. The cost of modernization had another detrimental effect typical of many modernizing countries. Incurring colossal debt to European countries, they could not pay interest on the debt. This caused the governments of France and England to intervene financially and politically to avoid Egyptian bankruptcy. When violent nationalist reaction occurred, a British expeditionary force occupied Egypt. While British rule resulted in somewhat better conditions for peasants, as well as tax

reforms necessary to ensure revenues to repay foreign bondholders, they did not encourage education in fear of inciting political unrest. The Egyptian experience provided a new model for European expansion based on military and political domination justified by civil stability and good administration. It was a model repeated in many places, as in the Caribbean by Theodore Roosevelt, and in China by the European powers under the guise of the Ching Rule.

RUSSIA

The modernization of Russia had many of the hallmarks of the Egyptian experience—heavy financial and technological borrowing from abroad and capital formation on the backs of the peasants, but, unlike Egypt and like Japan, Russia maintained its independence and became a substantial industrial power. In the nineteenth century Russia was a large multinational empire. For this reason, liberalism and nationalism were dangerous and subversive ideologies that the czarist leadership tried to repress, especially after they were introduced into Russia during Napoleon's invasion. In fact, much of the great outpouring of literature of nineteenth-century Russia had as its backdrop the struggles for liberal reform. When the Russians lost the **Crimean War** in 1853 to England and France because they lacked a modern military, the urgency for reform was apparent to all. In the 1850s almost 90 percent of Russia's population lived on the land, bound to their lords in hereditary serfdom and working the land with old-fashioned techniques. The Crimean War caused hardship on them too and raised the spector of revolt. To avoid this and to free the peasantry to be able to provide a labor force for industry, the **Emancipation Proclamation** was issued in 1861. Along with emancipation were other reforms. **Zemstvos**, or institutions of local government, marked a first though limited step toward popular participation in government. Political modernization was scant next to economic modernization, however.

Russian Industrialization

With the peasantry freed, Russia embarked on a program of industrialization. The first step came with the creation of an extensive railroad network in the 1870s. The government encouraged and subsidized this effort. In the 1880s the railroad lines had almost quintupled compared to 1860. This had the effect of stimulating Russia's coal and iron sectors and linking Russia with the Pacific. It also stimulated the grain export market to Europe, which helped pay for western machinery and technology. In this way, the peasantry in Russia, too, underwrote industrial capitalization. Under **Sergei Witte**, Minister of Finance from 1892 to 1903, the government enacted high tariffs to protect Russian industry, improved the banking system, and encouraged western investors to build great factories with advanced technology. By 1900 half of Russian industry was owned by foreigners. On the positive side, this did not lead to foreign political influence and it helped Russia to surge to fourth place in world steel production and second to the United States in petroleum production. On the negative side, Russia did not create a class of entrepreneurs nor was the agricultural sector modernized.

The Revolution of 1905

This was partially remedied after the **Revolution of 1905**, when more economic and political liberalization took place. Russia's defeat in the Russo-Japanese War led to an explosion of grievances by the peasants, factory workers, and ethnic minorities, which made up 55 percent of the population in 1900. On **Bloody Sunday**, January, 1905, a peaceful demonstration of factory workers marched to the Winter Palace in St. Petersburg, carrying icons and singing "God Save the Czar." Suddenly, troops opened fire, killing and wounding workers in the crowd. During the summer, there were more protests across the country, including the sailors on the battleship *Potemkin* in the Black Sea, a mutiny immortalized in Sergei Eisenstein's classic movie *The Potemkin*. In October massive strikes paralyzed the country leading to the **October Manifesto**, which granted civil rights and a popularly elected legislative branch, the **Duma**.

While the czar backtracked somewhat when he issued the Fundamental Laws limiting the powers of the legislature, the reforms proved the impetus for Peter Stolypin, Chief Minister, to push through land reforms. These broke down collective village ownership of land and encouraged the most enterprising peasants to produce for the market. Thus, on the eve of World War I, Russia was partially modernized, with a conservative constitutional monarchy and a peasant-based but industrialized economy free of foreign political control.

Summary

The liberalism and industrialism of western Europe provided a mystique of power and success attractive to many countries. Japan, the Ottoman Empire, and Russia all followed different paths to modernization but the impetus for all was military strengthening and the process for all was from the top down, because of this, liberalism was less apparent. In all cases, money for the capitalization of industry came from abroad or from agriculture at the expense of the peasantry. Because of this, none of the attempts followed the western path, which was capitalized by merchant profit and investment within the framework of nationalism and liberalism. In the Japanese case, industrialism occurred without liberalism or foreign control, but with ample nationalism. In the Russian case, industrialism proceeded with some liberalism and nationalism but heavy foreign borrowing. In the Ottoman Empire, heavy borrowing led to growing foreign control despite attempts to liberalize and modernize.

CULTURE AND SOCIETY

The New Class of Factory Owners and Workers

The Industrial Revolution brought two new classes to the fore—a strengthened middle class with factory owners and industrial capitalists added to the ranks of merchants and professional people, and a much larger group of factory workers. In terms of social structure based on wealth, there remained a great disparity between rich and poor, despite the fact that real wages for British workers between 1850 and 1906 doubled. In almost every advanced country around 1900, the richest five percent received one-third of the national income and the richest one-fifth received between 50 and 60 percent. The middle class was smaller than today, about 20 percent of the population.

Social Change

The new class of factory owners came from a variety of backgrounds and exhibited great class mobility. Some were from merchant families; others were from religious minorities previously discriminated against; and still others, from the artisan and skilled worker ranks. Competition was fierce and profits uncertain. By the 1860s many more industrialists inherited their businesses and advancement became more based on education. The nineteenth century was the golden age of the middle class because their culture and habits became the aspirations for many. While there was much diversity within this class, they were distinguished by occupations that required mental rather than physical skill. The upper middle class, composed of business families from banking and industry and large-scale commerce, aspired to the aristocratic lifestyle. They bought houses in the country, had servants and private carriages, and attempted favorable marriages with the upper classes. The middle class was composed of successful industrialists and merchants and professionals. The lower middle class was composed of shopkeepers, traders, and small manufacturers. Many other professions joined the middle class also, including engineers, architects, chemists, accountants, white collar office workers, teachers, and nurses. While occupationally diverse, the middle classes could be united by a certain style of life. They were clothes-conscious and they rented, rather than owned, their own homes, which usually included tiny rooms for the servants under the eves. Education was a growing expense and the middle classes observed a code of morality and behavior that stressed hard work, self-discipline and personal achievement. People who fell into poverty were looked on as irresponsible. The largest part of the family budget and time was devoted to food. Middle class families ate three substantial meals, spent lavishly on dinner parties, and employed an array of help to serve guests.

About four out of five people belonged to the working classes, meaning people who depended on physical labor and did not employ domestic servants. Many were landowning peasants, especially in eastern Europe, though in England only eight percent worked in agriculture. The rest worked in factories.

The condition of the working class has been controversial in history. Marx and Engels tended to portray them as exploited, and William Blake called early factories "satanic mills." Others saw improvement in the life of the masses because they were increasingly able to buy more of the necessities and a few luxuries. Statistics seem to show that during the years before 1850 prices rose faster than wages, but after that time there was considerable improvement. Generally speaking, food and clothing became cheaper and more plentiful, but housing worsened. The same sort of improvement occurred in working conditions. Cottage workers who were used to working as a family, hard and long but at their own pace, had difficulty getting used to the monotony and discipline of factory life. Furthermore, the presence of the whole family in the factory kept the family together but meant that young children were working with dangerous equipment and mothers did not have time to tend to their needs. Although large numbers of women worked in factories, female working patterns did not change. Studies of the year 1851 in Britain and France indicate that 40 percent of the women working in Britain were employed as domestic servants, and in France, 40 percent worked in agriculture. The number of women factory workers in Britain was 20 percent and 10 percent in France. Gradually, however, a sexual division of labor occurred— men worked in the factory and women stayed home and tended the children. Ties of blood and kinship were important in getting jobs as manufacturers often used subcontractors to hire and fire, many of whom became known to subcontractors through acquaintanceship.

Like the middle class, the working class had several levels. The highly skilled working classes were construction bosses, makers of scientific equipment, and highly skilled workers such as metalworkers and locomotive engineers. They comprised about 15 percent of the working classes and earned twice as much as the unskilled workers. They maintained puritanical behavior not unlike the middle class though they did not aspire to become middle class. They were the leaders of the working class. Below the skilled workers were the semiskilled or unskilled urban workers. This group worked as carpenters and bricklayers, factory workers, wagon drivers, and domestic servants, many of whom were young girls from the countryside. Rather than giving dinner parties, the favorite leisure activities of the working class were drinking, sports, and going to music halls. In fact, this was the era when mass leisure began. As factories turned out massive quantities of goods, they had to be mass advertised in order to be sold. Middle class families flocked to buy bicycles, a fad of the 1880s. Popular newspapers and organized sports like soccer and baseball emerged. Religion, however, was still an important component in families values and traditions, though church attendance declined.

Women and the Family

The tremendous changes wrought by the commercial and industrial revolutions are no more evident than in the family and life of women. One of the most startling changes was the emergence of adolescence as a distinct stage of life, a habit that continued longer for the middle classes because the necessity to train for mental occupations took longer. With couples increasingly coming from different towns, romantic sentiments triumphed, and with girls and boys away from home, illegitimacy exploded between 1750 and 1850. By the end of the century, however, marriage and pregnancy went hand in hand, thus strengthening the urban family. Because welfare services were limited before the twentieth century, kinship ties remained strong and people depended on family in times of disaster, death, and crisis.

The biggest change for women in this era came from the strict division of labor. The ideal was the wife as mother and homemaker, the husband as provider. The result was that men were hostile to women in the workplace and in education and women were subordinated to their husbands financially and legally. Thus began the struggle for women's rights. On the other hand, women had considerable power within the family, often controlling the purse strings and managing the home, providing emotional warmth and stability. One of the most important signs of change in family life was in child-rearing. Loving care was lavished on infants and greater concern was given to adolescents who entered the workplace at increasingly older ages. Declining birth rates also contributed to the reduction of family size. Greater individual attention and expenditures on children demonstrated a hope of improved economic and social status for them. Children became financial liabilities rather than assets. Despite the increasingly stable and redefined family and social life of many in the industrial world, for many others, it was a time of great upheaval caused by mass migrations.

Population and Migration

Liberalism and industrialism gave rise to one of the great migrations in world history. People fled Europe in great numbers to find political freedom and economic opportunities in the Americas. It was part of the West's global expansion and growing power and was a poignant human drama in which millions of people left their ancestral lands and planted stakes in a new land.

Causes

There were several reasons for the great migration, one of which was population pressures. The population of Europe, including European Russia, more than doubled between 1800 and 1900, from approximately 188 million to 432 million, not including the 60 million who left Europe. Since population grew more slowly in Africa and Asia than in Europe, people of

European origin jumped from 22 percent of the world's total to about 38 percent. The reason was rising birth rates and declining death rates due to a better standard of living and improved medical care. In the twentieth century this same phenomena has led to rising population and migration on the part of Asiatic populations. Europeans migrated primarily to the United States (slightly less than half), Canada, Argentina, Brazil, Austrialia, and Asiatic Russia. Much of the movement was migration rather than immigration. One of three immigrants to the United States, one in two to Argentina, and seven out of eight from the Balkans returned to their homeland. At the other extreme, one in ten from Ireland and one in twenty of East European Jews returned. Other reasons for movement were land hunger and the hope of land ownership, social mobility, and political freedom.

European Migrations

The sequence of migration was determined by the circumstances in the European countries. People left Britain and Ireland in large numbers from the 1840s on. In fact, fully one-third of all Europeans who migrated between 1840 and 1920 came from the British Isles. This was due to rural poverty, the thirst for skilled industrial technicians in the new lands, and preferences shown to British migrants in the British Empire. In the case of Ireland, the **Great Potato Famine** was a major reason. Once potatoes were introduced into Ireland from the Americas, Irish peasants became dependent on them and population grew because of them. In 1846, 1848, and 1851 the potato crop failed as blight attacked the single strain plants. Widespread starvation and mass epidemic followed. One million emigrants fled between 1845 and 1851 and at least 1.5 million died. British relief, when it did come, was too late and hampered by a poor distributional infrastructure.

Another wave of immigrants left Europe after the 1848 revolutions for political reasons. In the 1880s a wave of five million Russian Jews left their homes due to the **pogroms** (organized

persecutions or massacres) and discrimination that occurred beginning in 1881 under Czar Alexander II. In the 1880s Italians began to migrate due to deteriorating agricultural conditions in Italy after the influx of cheap North American wheat and the lack of industrial opportunities. Many Italians went to the United States but more went to Argentina and Brazil.

Not all migration was to the Americas from Europe. At least three million Asians, primarily Chinese, Japanese, Indians, and Filipinos (as opposed to 60 million Europeans, a situation reversed in the twentieth century) moved abroad before 1920. Most were indentured laborers used in plantations and gold fields to supplant African labor in Latin America, California, Hawaii, and Australia. Between 1853 and 1873, 130,000 Chinese laborers went to Cuba. More would have come except for the fact that Asian migrants often fled to the cities where they came in competition with natives who began to demand a halt to Asian immigration. This was another reason why Europeans and peoples of European ancestry reaped the main benefits from migration and monopolized the best overseas opportunities.

After the American Revolution, the English colonized Australia with convicts from British prisons. Other English pioneers followed. When gold was discovered in 1851, prospectors flooded in from all over the world. New Zealand also attracted English settlers. Chinese began moving into Southeast Asia in the 1870s, where unskilled workers were employed as plantation laborers and miners. There, educated Chinese became traders, money lenders, and commercial agents. By the time of World War II, 15 million Chinese had settled in Southeast Asia and Africa as laborers and merchants.

Canada was split between the French-speaking Canadians and English-speaking subjects. Canadians moved west to claim new land for agriculture. Following several small protests, the British government sent Lord Durham to investigate the causes of the civil unrest. This was the first step that eventually led to Home Rule and Canadian independence, granted through the British North America Act in 1867.

Summary

Thus, industrialism and liberalism significantly altered world culture and society. Industrialism created a larger middle class and a burgeoning laboring class, both of which infiltrated liberal governments to the point of passage of legislation in their interests. The habits and values of the middle class—good food, leisure, family, hard work, social advancement—became the prototype for industrializing societies everywhere. As women's roles became more connected with the home, opportunities in the workplace declined causing the rise of emancipation movments. Rising standards of living caused a population explosion, a circumstance that served as the impetus for migration alongside a quest for economic opportunities, social mobility, and political freedom.

UNIT REVIEW

Cross-Regional Developments

This period in history is the beginning of world westernization. European liberal thought based on the enlightenment ideas of liberty, rights, and equality ignited revolutions in the Americas and France. Napoleon's advance over Europe helped spread them further across Europe. Meanwhile, an agricultural revolution that began in the Low Countries spread to England, where it created the necessary environment for the Industrial Revolution. The development of machines, new energy sources, and transportation networks allowed Europeans to travel far and wide, and improve their military capabilities. Soon such innovations spread to North America. Wherever westerners went, especially in Asia and Africa, they overwhelmed the native populations, creating empires that delivered to them markets and resources. Empire itself helped to spread western ideas. Meanwhile, industrialism created tremendous social change across Europe and in North America. Factory owners and professions that fed industrialism joined the middle class, swelling its ranks. The lower classes increasingly became dominated by factory workers. The workers and the conditions of industry became the basis for new ideologies, especially socialism, which advocated an end to laissez-faire policies and the active role of government in the economy. This impacted the revolutions of 1848, but negatively, causing liberalism to fail due to middle class fears of the workers and their new agenda. During the 1800s, middle class values and culture set the style of life. This style included a sexual division of labor, leisure, consumerism, self-discipline, hard work, a get-ahead mentality, and infatuation with the metropolis. Industrialism caused a population explosion and migration of Europeans around the world, especially to the Americas. The attractiveness of modern ways caused other countries to attempt to carve out their owns paths to modernity. Along this road, industrialism usually triumphed over liberalism and, thus, industrial change came from the top down. Industrialism and liberalism also fed the flames of national pride and power, causing new countries like Germany and Italy to coalesce. Nations became highly competitive especially in contests over empire. This set the stage for the explosions among European states of the twentieth century.

Legacies

Many of the legacies of this period endure and cast their brilliance and shadow over today's world. These include:

- enlightenment thought;
- bourgeois revolutions in North America and France;
- political fragmentation and independence but not social revolution in Latin America;
- the balance of power concept for Europe;
- failed liberalism in eastern Europe;
- romantic art, literature, and music;
- the machine, energy, and transportation revolutions;
- modern cities and architecture;
- socialist thought and realism;
- European empire in Africa and Asia;
- adaptations to the western model of modernization;

- middle class culture and the rise of the worker
- European mass migration; and
- sexual division of labor and women's rights movements.

Documents

THE WEALTH OF NATIONS

The annual revenue of every society is always precisely equal to the exchangeable value of the whole annual produce of its industry, or rather is precisely the same thing with that exchangeable value. As every individual, therefore, endeavours as much as he can both to employ his capital in the support of domestic industry, and so to direct that industry that its produce may be of the greatest value; every individual necessarily labours to render the annual revenue of the society as great as he can. He generally, indeed, neither intends to promote the public interest, nor knows how much he is promoting it. By preferring the support of domestic to that of foreign industry, he intends only his own security; and by directing that industry in such a manner as its produce may be of the greatest value, he intends only his own gain, and he is in this, as in many other cases, led by an invisible hand to promote an end which was no part of his intention. Nor is it always the worse for the society that it was no part of it. By pursuing his own interest he frequently promotes that of society more effectually than when he really intends to promote it. I have never known much good done by those who affected to trade for the public good.

Adam Smith (1723–1790) became the "father of economics" by brilliantly analyzing how the capitalist free market works. His discoveries include the law of supply and demand, the law of competition, and the law of self-interest. In his famous book *The Wealth of Nations,* he tried to explain that trade brings wealth and, therefore, the policy of mercantilism should be abandoned in favor of free trade. As a classical economist, he argued that the economy would prosper if it was left alone, a policy that became known as laissez-faire. His ideas have again found favor in the latter part of the twentieth century as socialist systems failed to create wealth. In this excerpt he explains the individual profit motive leads to the good of all when guided by the invisible hand of the free market.

ROUSSEAU AND THE SOCIAL CONTRACT

Man is born free but is everywhere in chains. One thinks himself master of others, but is himself the greater slave. How did this change take place? I do not know. What can render it legitimate? I believe I can answer this question. . . .

If, therefore, we take from the social compact everything that is not essential to it, we shall find it reduced to the following terms: "We, the contracting parties, do jointly and severally submit our persons and abilities, to the supreme direction of the general will of all, and, in a collective body, receive each member into that body, as an indivisible part of the whole."

Jean-Jacques Rousseau (1712–1778) was the most radical of the philosophes. While John Locke emphasized natural rights and representative government, Voltaire, constitutionalism and the rule of law, and Montesquieu a balance of power, Rousseau advocated democracy and social equality. In Rousseau's view, true liberty can only be obtained when men retain all rights except those given to the general will or majority of the people. To him, liberal government was a social compact as well as a political contract, one in which social as well as legal relationships are based on equality and rule of the majority. Rousseau's ideas were important for shaping liberal ideas in the nineteenth century, but they have been used also in the twentieth century by dictators like Hitler who see themselves, not as chosen by the "general will," but as the embodiment of the "general will."

THE DECLARATION OF THE RIGHTS OF MAN

1. The aim of society is the common welfare. Government is established to guarantee to man the enjoyment of his natural and inalienable rights.

2. These rights are equality, liberty, security, and property.

3. All men are equal by nature and before law.

4. Law is the free and solemn expression of the general will. . . .

5. All citizens are equally eligible for public office. . . .

9. The law must protect both public and individual liberty against the oppression of those who govern.

13. All men are presumed innocent until proved guilty . . .

16. The right of property is the right which belongs to every citizen to enjoy, and at will to dispose of, his goods, his revenues, and the fruit of his labor and industry.

The Declaration of the Rights of Man was issued August 27, 1789 by the French National Assembly, which had taken control after the Bastille Revolution on July 14. This French liberal document had an American flavor to it. In fact, American Ambassador Thomas Jefferson helped in its drafting. It became the French Revolutionary credo. Only two pages long, it was propagandized throughout France, Europe, and around the world. The results of the French Revolution did not enshrine its values completely. Instead, the Napoleonic Code became the legal basis for much of twentieth-century French and European law.

THE COMMUNIST MANIFESTO

The history of all hitherto existing societies is the history of class struggles. . . .

In short, the Communists everywhere support every revolutionary movement against the existing social and political order of things.

In all these movements they bring to the front, as the leading question in each, the property question, no matter what its degree of development at the time.

Finally, they labor everywhere for the union and agreement of the democratic parties of all countries.

The Communists disdain to conceal their views and aims. They openly declare that their ends can be attained only by the forcible overthrow of all existing social conditions. Let the ruling classes tremble at a Communist revolution. The proletarians have nothing to lose but their chains. They have a world to win.

WORKING MEN OF ALL COUNTRIES, UNITE!

The *Manifesto* was published in 1848 as the platform of the "Communist League," a workingmen's underground association in Europe. Marx and Engels were commissioned to prepare for publication a complete theoretical and practical program. When the 1848 revolutions failed, the document lingered until Russian theorists picked it up to use as a guide for their revolution. In most industrialized countries in Europe, legislation had improved the lot of the worker to the point that the *Communist Manifesto* seemed irrelevant. In countries like Russia, however, where neither social nor political revolution had taken place, and industrialization was on the march, the theories of Marx and Engels became a Bible for political and social change. The *Communist Manifesto* advocates not just socialist programs like nationalization of industry, but revolution to overthrow existing states.

THE WHITE MAN'S BURDEN

Take up the White Man's burden—
  Send forth the best ye breed—
Go bind your sons to exile
  To serve your captives' need;
To wait in heavy harness,
  On fluttered folk and wild—
Your new-caught, sullen peoples,
  Half-devil and half-child.

Take up the White Man's burden—
  In patience to abide,
To veil the threat of terror
  And check the show of pride;
By open speech and simple,
  An hundred times made plain,
To seek another's profit,
  And work another's gain.

This poem by Rudyard Kipling, written in the latter half of the nineteenth century, expresses a typical rationale for European imperialism in Africa. Kipling believed that Europeans had a duty to spread their civilization throughout the world in order to bring progress to native peoples. It was the beginning of racial overtones because many of the areas of the earth imperialized by Europeans had populations with dark skins.

Recall Questions

1. The site of the liberal revolution led by Toussaint L'Overture was
   (A) Paris.
   (B) Moscow.
   (C) Colombia.
   (D) Haiti.
   (E) Venezuela.

2. In which of the following choices are events arranged in the correct chronological order?
   (A) Napoleonic Era, Latin American Revolutions, American Revolution, French Revolution, Reign of Terror
   (B) Latin American Revolutions, Napoleonic Era, American Revolution, French Revolution, Reign of Terror
   (C) American Revolution, Napoleonic Era, Latin American Revolutions, French Revolution, Reign of Terror
   (D) American Revolution, French Revolution, Reign of Terror, Napoleonic Era, Latin American Revolutions
   (E) American Revolution, Reign of Terror, Napoleonic Era, French Revolution, Latin American Revolutions

3. All of the following are considered reasons for the scientific revolution EXCEPT
   (A) the Renaissance with its investigation of classical science.
   (B) the acceptance of faith and reason as the source of the universal laws of science.
   (C) the development of the inductive and deductive methods of investigation.
   (D) the separation of scientific inquiry and religious doctrine.
   (E) the invention of new scientific instruments such as the telescope, barometer, and microscope.

4. Basic beliefs of the Enlightenment include all of the following beliefs EXCEPT
   (A) the belief that rulers govern only in accordance with God's will.
   (B) the belief in progress.
   (C) the belief that the discovery of the laws of nature and man will improve the human condition.
   (D) the belief that there are rational laws that describe social behavior.
   (E) the belief that all men have natural rights including life, liberty, and property.

5. During the French Revolution, July 14, 1789, marked the
   (A) call for a National Assembly.
   (B) fall of the Bastille.
   (C) execution of Louis XVI and Marie Antoinette.
   (D) acceptance of universal male suffrage.
   (E) presentation of the Declaration of the Rights of Man.

6. The only Napoleonic battlefield victory of those sites listed below was
   (A) Trafalgar.
   (B) Austerlitz.
   (C) Moscow.
   (D) Waterloo.
   (E) Tilsit.

7. In Latin America, a group of people controlling the government following a revolution were known as
   (A) a coup d'etat.
   (B) a junta.
   (C) the first estate.
   (D) a committee of public safety.
   (E) none of the above.

8. Those instrumental in Europeanizing life in Latin America were
   (A) the caudillos.
   (B) women who controlled the local markets.
   (C) mestizos.
   (D) Creoles.
   (E) church officials.

9. Of those listed below, who were the first to initiate a political campaign to abolish slavery?
   (A) French philosophes
   (B) the British navy
   (C) Quakers, Baptists, and Anglicans
   (D) Dutch merchants
   (E) Cubans

10. Between 1814 and 1850 revolutions occurred in all of the following countries EXCEPT
    (A) Greece.
    (B) France.
    (C) Russia.
    (D) Belgium.
    (E) Prussia.

11. The romantic hero of goodness and justice, Jean Valjean, in *Les Miserables* was the creation of
    (A) Victor Hugo.
    (B) William Wordsworth.
    (C) Joseph Conrad.
    (D) Rudyard Kipling.
    (E) Feodor Dostoevsky.

12. Which of the following events occurred first?
    (A) Taiping Rebellion
    (B) Sino-Japanese War
    (C) Opium War
    (D) Boxer Rebellion
    (E) the end of dynastic rule in China

13. The greatest of the Romantic composers was
    (A) Bach.
    (B) Mozart.
    (C) Beethoven.
    (D) Tchaikovsky.
    (E) Berlioz.

14. The Industrial Revolution had its beginnings in
    (A) France.
    (B) Spain.
    (C) England.
    (D) the United States.
    (E) Germany.

15. The English economy benefited from
    (A) a stable government.
    (B) a central bank.
    (C) a strong domestic market supplied by navigable rivers.
    (D) an expanding colonial market.
    (E) all of the above.

16. Which of the following inventors developed the steam engine, the source of power for the Industrial Revolution?
    (A) George Stephenson
    (B) Richard Arkwright
    (C) James Hargreaves
    (D) James Watt
    (E) Jethro Tull

17. Which of the following men is incorrectly linked with his work?
    (A) Adam Smith—*Inquiry into the Nature and Causes of the Wealth of Nations*
    (B) Pierre Joseph Proudhon—*What Is Property?*
    (C) David Ricardo—*Essay on Liberty*
    (D) Karl Marx and Frederick Engels—*Communist Manifesto*
    (E) Charles Darwin—*On the Origin of Species by Means of Natural Selection*

To check your answers, see page 393.

Spheres of Influence in China ca. 1910 C.E. *The Europeans were another in a long list of outsiders in world history who penetrated China. Russia, Britain, France, Japan, and Germany all sought trade privileges, and to secure them, they carved out spheres. In an ironic way, this competition saved China from conquest by any one of them, but it led to the end of Chinese Imperial rule.*

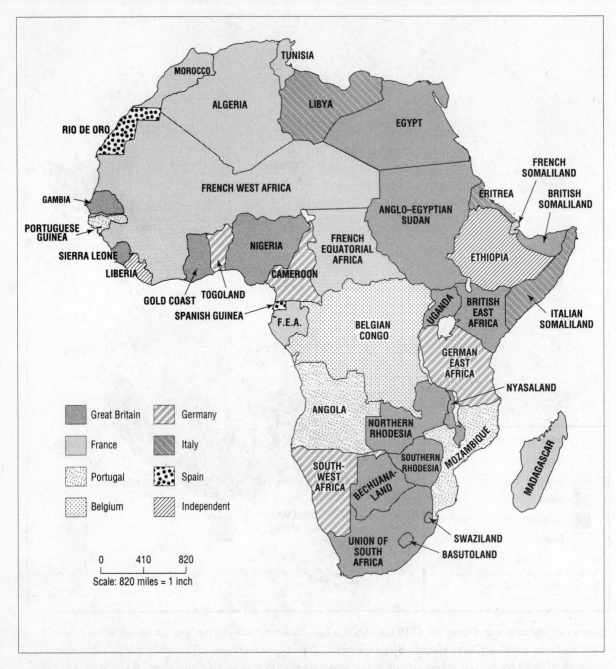

European Imperialism in Africa 1914 C.E. *Unlike in China, where the European powers claimed only spheres of interest, European powers carved up the African continent. The imperialization of Africa was often more costly than productive, but raw materials, the western predisposition to civilize, and, most of all, the desire to keep African territory out of rival European hands resulted in the partition of Africa.*

Industrial Development and Foreign Investment about 1900 C.E. *World industrial development in 1900 was confined to a few places on the globe, primarily western Europe and the northeast coast of the United States. However, European countries made substantial investments in many places around the globe primarily in infrastructure projects like railroads and resource development like mines and agriculture. These investments paid handsome returns to European investors and provided the necessary groundwork for later industrialization.*

Europe in 1815 C.E. *After the French Revolution and defeat of Napoleon, the map of Europe was significantly altered. A balance of power principle was established at the Congress of Vienna in the hope of maintaining European peace. Germany and Italy remained divided and the Europeans' attention toward expansion turned abroad.*

***Claude Monet's* Arrival of the Normandy Train, Saint-Lazare Station, 1877.** *The excitement of the new industrial age is illustrated in* Arrival of the Normandy Train, Saint-Lazare Station, 1877 *by Claude Monet (1840–1926). Monet broke with the realism of past European artists to paint a fleeting impression of the train and passengers engulfed in what today might be considered air pollution but at the time portrayed as shimmering billows of cloudlike steam. Monet used dabs of color on canvas to suggest structures, shapes, and light. He often painted the same subject at different times to spontaneously capture the subject in a new play of light with new atmospheric conditions.*

***Delacroix Painting of* The Combat of the Giaour and Hassan, 1826.** *Eugene Delacroix is one of the greatest romantic artists of the nineteenth century. Romanticism emphasized emotion, individual expression, nature, and the glories of the past. In art, romantics often showed their country as a human figure. In this picture, Delacroix is portraying the struggle for Greek independence from the Turks. The painting was inspired by* The Giaour, *a poem by England's most famous Romantic poet, Lord Byron. The scene shows the poem's dramatic climax when a Venetian Giaour (a Christian infidel), his eyes bloodshot, avenges his lover's death at the hands of a Turk named Hassan. The painting's exotic costumes, intense drama, and high-keyed colors and forms, typify romantic artistic style and subject matter.*

***Paul Gaugin's* Ancestors of Tehamana.** *Paul Gaugin (1848–1903) created exotic art of the Pacific dring the age of European imperialism, an age of transformation and change. In 1891 he left France for what he hoped was a less materialistic, more spiritually pure society in Tahiti. His work, characterized by flat, decorative color, marks a break with European tradition, a change represented by a new art form, postimpressionism. In this oil entitled* Ancestors of Tehamana, *Gauguin's young wife sits in front of a wall painting of a mysterious figure in traditional Tahitian dress. The fan in Tehamana's right hand points toward the shadowy figure indicating a tie between the two, a link between past tradition and the present, while her European dress demonstrates her presence in a society undergoing transformation.*

Mug, Turkish (Ottoman Empire). *The floral decoration of this earthenware mug represents one of a combination of designs popular during the sixteenth and seventeenth centuries as the subject of paintings, illustrations, and textile designs sold in international markets. Some of the finest pottery and tiles like this example were produced in Ottoman, Turkey at a royal kiln south of Istanbul. This pattern of tulips, roses, and hyacinths is reminiscent of Chinese porcelain designs of the fourteenth and fifteenth centuries.*

Children in the Coal Mines. *Child labor was one of the most shocking abuses of the Industrial Revolution. Because they could fit into small spaces, boys and girls dragged coal through dark, cramped passages. In 1831, Parliament set up a committee to investigate abuses of child labor. This illustration was appended to a British Parliamentary Commission Report on work in the mines. In 1833 the Factory Act made it illegal to hire children under nine years old and restricted the work day for young people under 18. The propensity of democratic nations to find answers to industrial problems through legislation dulled the radical spirit of socialism that, instead of appeasing workers, called for complete change in the economic and political structures of state and revolution, and even a rejection of industrialism itself.*

UNIT

VIII

THE CONTEMPORARY WORLD

CHAPTER 23

The End of European Hegemony

CHRONOLOGY	World War I (1914–1918)	World War II (1939–1945)	Sputnik I (1957)
	Wall Street Crash (1929)	United Nations Charter (1945)	Cuban Missile Crisis (1962)
	Great Depression (1929–1942)	Berlin Wall (1949)	U.S. Man on the Moon (1969)
		Korean War (1950–1953)	

TERMS	blitzkrieg	mandate system	United Nations
	sonar	League of Nations	Atlantic charter
	radar	Great Depression	Iron Curtain
	mutually assured destruction	National Socialist (Nazi)	containment
		Twenty-one Demands	Truman Doctrine
	Sputnik I	Kuomintang	Marshall Plan
	welfare state	May Fourth Movement	NATO
	Triple Entente	Three Principles of the People	Warsaw Pact
	Triple Alliance		European Economic Community
	Powder Keg	Government of India Act	Comecon
	Schlieffin Plan	Amritsar Massacre	SEATO
	Battle of the Marne	Dawes Plan	Sino-Soviet Alliance
	trench warfare	Long March	Berlin Wall
	U-Boat	appeasement	Korean War
	Trench Warfare	Nuremburg Laws	Cuban Missile Crisis
	Peace of Brest-Litovsk	Final Solution	peaceful coexistence
	Weimar Republic	Anschluss	Test Ban Treaty
	Wilson's Fourteen Points	Munich Agreements	Detente
	Treaty of Versailles	NonAggression Pact	
	national self-determination	Arsenal of Democracy	
		D-Day	

PEOPLE	Yuri Gagarin	Sun Yat-sen	Franklin Roosevelt
	Neil Armstrong	Chiang Kai-shek	Erwin Rommel
	John Maynard Keynes	Mao Tse-tung	Hirohito
	Archduke Franz Ferdinand	Mohandas Ghandi	Harry Truman
		Jawaharlal Nehru	Tito
	Eric Remarque	Gestapo	Douglas MacArthur
	Albert Schweitzer	Francisco Franco	Syngman Rhee
	Benito Mussolini	Pablo Picasso	Kim Il Sung
	Fascists	Joseph Stalin	Gamal Abdel Nasser
	Adolf Hitler	Winston Churchill	

PLACES	Balkans	Vichy	Nagasaki
	Gallipoli	Pearl Harbor	Nuremburg
	Manchuria	El Alamein	Yalta
	Dachau	Stalingrad	
	Auschwitz	Hiroshima	

A person living in 1900, driving a horse drawn buggy to visit with friends and relatives living within a few miles, would be astounded at life at the end of the twentieth century. During this period the world went from a few nations to a world of nation-states, from telegraph to E-mail, from western industrialization to world industrialization, from travel within countries to travel between countries and into outer space, and from local foods and handmade clothes to those of international design and manufacture. Ironically, world wars are partially responsible for this dramatic shift. War produced new technologies and inventions, and troop movements on a global scale introduced people to different cultures. As in all world history, times of great interaction stimulate new ways of doing things and new habits of thought.

CHAPTER 23

The End of European Hegemony

During the first half of the twentieth century, explosive intraEuropean conflict ended Europe's world political hegemony. Decolonialization, national liberation movements, communist revolutions, and alternative routes to modernization followed. The West's decline is exhibited by the decline in its population as a percentage of the world's total, the end of European empire and monopoly over advanced weapons systems, and the end to its unchallenged preeminent position as the world's leading trader and manufacturer. Yet, not unlike Greek and Islamic history, the end of global political power did not mean the end of global influence. Western culture and especially American culture continued to set world trends.

The second characteristic of the twentieth century is world modernization. Not only has industrialism spread throughout the world, second and third industrial revolutions—the communications and computer revolutions—have completely transformed world political, economic, social, and cultural life. Modernization has challenged the earth's people to deal with problems like population pressures, resource depletion, and environmental disequilibrium. The tempo of change, chaos, scientific theories, and uncertainties of a nuclear age have led to angst and protest as well as optimism and opportunity. At the least, humans have extended their vision beyond the planet Earth to the colonialization of space. Instead of a global world, on the horizon is an intergalactic world, a continuation of the story of humankind's dispersal and conquest.

MODERN WARFARE

Industrialism and its technology led to new weapons and methods of warfare. Liberalism caused whole nations and peoples to be involved, leading to total war and the blurring of lines between civilian and military. The Crimean War in Europe and the Civil War in the United States were two of the last wars to be fought in the style developed during the preceding centuries. In these wars, armies lined up on the open fields and with cavalry and artillery, engaged in man-to-man combat. Increasingly in the twentieth century, war became mechanized combat and political systems were co-opted into the effort, greatly expanding the powers of government.

Weaponry

Twentieth-century weaponry completely changed the face of war, from a war of men to a war of weapons. Nations that were modern and wealthy won in this contest because they could support the science, innovation, and technology necessary to gain the edge. When World War I began, countries that possessed the telegraph and railroad were greatly aided in their systems of organization for war. Also, artillery capability had advanced considerably. In 1870–1877 the average Prussian cannon dispensed 200 rounds a minute, and in 1914, 600. The only defense against this was the trench. From 1914 to 1917, trench warfare led to a stalemate, which was ended, in large part, by the introduction of new military technology. The tremendous power of artillery caused the role of cavalry to decline, though its use in transport increased. The stalemate that occurred on World War I battlefields led to a technological change that ended the war. In 1916 tanks, airplanes, poison gas, and submarines were all introduced.

Aviation history actually began in 1783 when hot air balloons were used during the Napoleonic Wars to drop propaganda leaflets. In 1914 all the belligerents together only had 500 aircraft, used mainly for reconnaissance. By 1918, 300,000 British officers were engaged in aircraft and there were 50,000 flying machines, some used in aerial combat. On the seas, the great advance was the iron-clad steamship and then the battleship, fueled by petroleum rather than coal, greatly extending its range and flexibility. The submarine was actually invented in the 1890s by John Holland and used two machines, one for above water and one below. When put to use at sea in 1916, there was no defense against it.

All the weapons introduced in World War I were perfected in the interwar period and put to battle in a systematic barrage, or **blitzkrieg**, in World War II. In a typical blitzkrieg, airplanes moved forward first to establish air superiority, followed by parachutists, ground force movement, and then armored divisions. On sea, it was a contest of carrier and submarine. The fact that pilots who dropped tremendous payloads never saw their victims, and submarines sunk ships they never saw, added to war's impersonality.

Defenses against this were few, but acoustic **sonar** and **radar** made dramatic differences in defense capabilities against the blitz. As with many inventions, radar was developed in the private sector and taken over by the military, which had vast resources to develop it. By the end of World War II, the sentiment prevailed that "weapons, if only the right ones can be found, constitute ninety-nine percent of victory."

After 1945 atomic and nuclear weapons and cruise missiles, and automation in the form of computers, transformed the battlefield once again. In 1945 the Americans had a monopoly on atomic weapons, but by 1949 the Soviet Union, by efficient espionage, had caught up, and then both engaged in nuclear research development producing an even more fearsome collection of weapons—hydrogen bombs in the 1950s, intercontinental ballistic missiles (ICBM) and nuclear powered and armed Polaris submarines in the 1960s, neutron bombs and a prolific range of intermediate and short-range ballistic missiles (Cruise and Trident) in the 1970s. By 1985 there were some 20,000 thermonuclear weapons in existence, 90 percent of which were in two countries. The effect of these nuclear devices was to suspend war rather than to contribute to it because of the fear of MAD, "**mutually assured destruction**." Paradoxically, the sheer expense of it all ensured that nuclear weaponry would be confined to countries with large economies. Consequently, wars of traditional and guerrilla nature, often supplied from the post-World War II stockpiles of large nations, continued around the world among those who did not possess such advanced weapons capability. By the 1990s, however, nuclear proliferation among many other countries destabilized world power politics.

Economy

Modern warfare had traumatic effects on the economies of countries. The cost of World War II alone was four trillion dollars, counting lost employment, consumption of resources, and destruction. For post-World War II weaponry, Britain spent four billion pounds more than on education and two billion pounds more than on social expenditures, while the Soviet Union devoted almost a fifth of its resources and the United States almost one tenth to it. Perhaps a third of American industry depended on defense contracts. With little to show for this, the Soviet Union and the United States embarked on a complicated space exploration program. In 1957 the Russians put the first satellite into space, **Sputnik I**, and in 1961 they put the first man, **Yuri Gagarin**, in space. The United States then devoted more to space research and won the "Space Race" by putting a man, **Neil Armstrong**, on the moon in 1969.

To meet the cost of these vast spending programs, economies were completely revamped. All economies—capitalist and socialist alike—came under greater government control. Organization for war included not only massive, compulsory recruitment, the draft, but also government control of the economy via obligatory planning, rationing, altered management policy, controlled labor relations, and personal consumption patterns. A good example of total planning in World War I was the German economy developed by Walter Rathenau. Under his direction, every conceivable raw material was inventoried, rationed, and distributed. Moreover, attempts to produce substitutes, like synthetic rubber, were undertaken. In England, 90 percent of all imports were bought and allocated by the state. In most countries during World War II, gas, women's stockings, liquor, tobacco, and rubber were all rationed.

Economic and Social Consequences of World War I

At the end of World War I, the withdrawal of government involvement was a severe shock to the economy and, in some measure, led to the Great Depression. Economic theories were postulated, like those by **John Maynard Keynes** that stressed the importance of government spending to compensate for loss of purchasing power during the Depression.

War also added to the growth of the **welfare state**. Wartime planning in Britain had pointed to the need for new programs to reduce the impact of economic inequality and to reward the lower classes for their loyalty. The welfare state elabo-

rated a host of social insurance measures from medical care to housing, retirement insurance, and child care. In dictatorial states like Germany and Russia, government control was even greater. After World War II, the western and communist countries remained highly militarized, thereby avoiding the post-war economic shock experienced after World War I.

Total war also affected the social aspects of life. Both in democracies and dictatorships it included unprecedented control of the media through censorship and jailing of dissidents, and through powerful propaganda to incite passionate, all-out commitment to the national cause. Vivid posters, movies, and flaming speeches combined in the mobilization effort. Direct bombings of civilian populations, internment, forced labor, and poison gas caused great psychological suffering. The position of women drastically changed as a result of war. With so many men at the front, women increasingly joined the work force. By 1916, 1.6 million women were working, half in engineering plants. As they did so, they gained the right to vote (the 1920s), began to smoke and drink in public, enjoy leisure activities, and be active in politics. The importance of workers also gave greater power and prestige to labor unions. All in all, total mechanized warfare transformed governments, economies, and societies into war machines where personal liberties and individual actions mattered for little.

THE CAUSES AND RESULTS OF WORLD WAR I

The long-range causes of World War I are nationalism, imperialism, militarism, and the alliance system. There were several ways nationalism became a factor. First, the liberal aspects of nationalism began to assert themselves in the Austro-Hungarian empire as minorities like the Bosnians, encouraged by outside powers like the Russians, maneuvered to declare their independence. Second, the formation of the new nations of Italy and Germany in the late 1800s threatened to upset the European balance of power so carefully worked out at the Congress of Vienna in 1815. The European states were also prey to imperialist contests around the world that damaged European relationships. Russia and Austria-Hungary sparred in the **Balkans**, Germany's plans for a Berlin to Baghdad railroad threatened British control of the Suez Canal, and Germany and France competed for territory in North Africa. Militarism also played a part. Industrial power led to a great buildup of weapons and elaborate plans for their use. This was particularly true of Germany, which built up an army of 95 divisions, twice the size of the French army, and its navy, with 20 modern battleships, was large enough to rival Britain's. Countries also began formulating carefully worked-out mobilization and attack plans that dictated irrevocable courses of action should war become imminent. Finally, by 1914 two opposing alliances had developed. The growing power of Germany on land threatened France and Russia, and at sea, Britain, bringing France, Russia, and Britain together in the **Triple Entente**. To Germany this seemed like encirclement causing her to draw closer to Austria and Italy in the **Triple Alliance**.

The Balkans

The chief bone of contention among the European powers was in their own backyard, the Balkans, the **Powder Keg** of Europe. During the 1800s Greece (1830), Bulgaria, Serbia, Montenegro, and Romania (1878) had secured their independence. The Ottomans, Austria, and Russia all desired to extend their influence in the area. In 1908, for example, Austria annexed Turkish provinces of Bosnia and Herzegovina, and then, in 1911–1913, the Balkan states fought against Turkey and then among themselves, resulting in gains for Austria's enemy Serbia. When Austrian **Archduke Franz Ferdinand** was assassinated on June 28, 1914 by Serbian-backed terrorists, Austria soon got revenge. Austria, which had received a "blank check" or free hand from Germany, sent an ultimatum to Serbia and, when it was rejected, declared war on Serbia. Russia mobilized, causing Germany to call up its forces and then to declare war on Russia. Instead of invading Russia, however, Germany moved

west against France, according to the **Schlieffin Plan** that advocated a swift knock-out blow against France before turning on Russia. On August 3 Germany declared war on France and the next day invaded Belgium. Then the alliances came into play. Britain declared war on Germany, and Austria declared war on Russia. World War I began with enthusiasm and the high expectation that it would "be over by Christmas."

The Fighting

At the **Battle of the Marne**, German troops were stopped by French and British forces. For the rest of the year, outflanking maneuvers failed. Along a 400-mile western front, **trench warfare** began. Losses were appalling due to artillery, poison gas, and the horrors of the trenches. At Verdun, half a million Frenchmen were killed in 1916. At Ypres, the Menin Gate war memorial records the names of no less than 70,000 British officers and men who died with no known grave. As war poet Siegfried Sassoon wrote, "Who will remember, passing through this gate, The unheroic dead who fed the guns?" The stalemate in the west caused Germany to launch a campaign against Russia in 1915. By the end of the year, Russia had lost two million men and most of Poland, a blow it never recovered from. Meanwhile, the Turks, who entered on Germany's side, repulsed an Allied attempt to invade via the Dardanelles at **Gallipoli**. Italy, who entered on the Allied side, was bogged down in Austria.

The stalemate ended in 1917 when Germany initiated two new lines of attack. The first was the equipping of a submarine fleet to destroy shipping to the allies, and the second was a new offensive against Russia. Unrestricted **U-boat** activity succeeded in destroying 25 percent of all shipping leaving British ports but it brought the United States into the war (April 1917). On the eastern front, the Russian revolution began even before German troops arrived. Russia left the war in early 1918 by the **Peace of Brest-Litovsk**, whereby it lost much of its industrial and resource capacity in western Russia. Germany then launched an all-out attack in the west. On March 21 the British stood "with their backs to the wall" and the Germans were within 40 miles of Paris. By then, however, the Americans had arrived, over one million by November. In August the Germans fell back; in September Bulgaria and Turkey surrendered, and in October Austria gave in. Emperor William abdicated on November 9 and the **Weimar Republic**, which replaced him, authorized a cease-fire.

War's End

At war's end, there were 30 million casualties and 8 million dead. The best of Europe's youth was sacrificed and the land ravaged. The spirit of liberalism and faith in progress were shattered, to be replaced by pessimism and existentialism that proclaimed God is dead. The classic statement of disillusionment with war was German author **Eric Remarque**'s *All Quiet on the Western Front*, a novel that documented life in the trenches for young Germans. At the other end of the spectrum was the giddiness of the Roaring Twenties in the United States and the revival of Christianity. **Albert Schweitzer**, a theologian who saw in Christian revival the return to sanity and the moral path. A sentiment for disarmament also prevailed, as in the Washington Naval Agreements.

The peace treaties, one with each of the belligerents, which were signed, were influenced by American President **Wilson's Fourteen Points** and by the interests of the victors. The **Treaty of Versailles**, negotiated by 30 sovereign states with Germany, blamed Germany for the war and invoked reparations and demilitarization of Germany. In redrawing the map of Europe, the principle of "**national self-determination**," meaning the joining together of historic peoples and ethnic groups in their own nation-state, was applied. Out of the former German, Austrian, and Russian empires, new nation-states like Czechoslovakia, Poland, Austria, Hungary, Latvia, Lithuania, Estonia, and Yugoslavia were created. This principle was not applied to colonies as politicians determined that these areas were inhabited "by peoples not yet able to stand by themselves under the strenuous conditions of the modern world." Instead, the former colonies of the defeated powers in Africa and Southwest Asia were transferred under the **mandate system** (theoretically, "nations on the road to independence") to the "tutelage" of one of the victors. Out of the former Ottoman Empire, Lebanon and Syria went to France, and Palestine and Mesopotamia to Britain. Most former German colonies were transferred to Australia, New Zealand, and Britain. The mandate system was administered by the **League of Nations**, the first world-wide association of governments in world history dedicated to the resolution of disputes by peaceful means, or, as President Wilson asserted, "to make the world safe for democracy," as well as to improve general social and economic conditions the world over.

World realities did not match the idealistic hopes of the World War I victors. The United States never joined the League of Nations, took an interventionist course in the Mexican Revolution (1910–1920), and then withdrew into political isolationism when it came to European affairs. Russia became communist, isolated, xenophobic, and adversarial in world affairs. Economic and political instability in Italy led to the fascist regime of Mussolini. Bulgaria (1923), Poland (1926), Greece (1926), and Yugoslavia (1929) fell to military coups. Meanwhile, China and Germany struggled to make new democratic republics work while India made strides toward self-rule. World stability might have returned had it not been for the Great Depression, which started in the United States in 1929 and spread throughout the world in the early 1930s. In its wake came extremist governments in Japan, Germany, Italy, and Russia, and in the West, pacifism, isolationism, and appeasement.

THE CAUSES AND RESULTS OF WORLD WAR II

France and England in the 1920s

All participants of World War I suffered severe dislocation at war's end, but most recovered by the late 1920s. In France, communists and socialists battled for support of the workers, and the franc fell to 10 percent of its prewar value, but under the careful leadership of Raymond

Poincaré, democratic government and financial stability returned by 1930. Britain faced severe unemployment (two million were unemployed in 1920) because it had lost its best markets during the war. This labour government responded with creation of a welfare state. This led to a strengthened Labour Party, which was able to elect its leader, Ramsay MacDonald, to the prime ministership in the 1924 and 1929 election.

Italy and Germany in the 1920s

In Italy there was chaos. Communist insurrections led to numerous right wing groups that broke up strikes and protected capital assets. **Mussolini** and his party, the **Fascists** (after the *fasces* used as a symbol of authority in the Roman Republic), seized power in 1922 and ruled Italy thereafter as a one-party state. The Fascist program was both antidemocratic and anticommunist, extolling instead nationalism, authoritarianism, totalitarianism, militarism, and idealism. Fascist rhetoric and hyperbole viewed liberty as a "putrefying corpse," strife as ennobling and exalting, internationalism as a gross perversion of human progress, the state as effecting the highest loyalty, and the Mediterranean as an Italian lake.

A similar seesaw between leftist and rightist groups occurred in Germany after the war. In 1918 Karl Liebnecht announced the creation of a Soviet state, soon suppressed by the army, and in 1923 **Adolf Hitler** and his fascist **National Socialist** or **Nazi** party attempted a takeover in Munich. By 1924, the German mark was virtually worthless, 1.5 trillion to the dollar.

China in the 1920s

In China, meanwhile, the fragile new national republic established by **Sun Yat-sen** after the fall of the Manchu dynasty in 1911 was put on the defensive. This was due to revelations at war's end that the Allies had signed the **Twenty-One Demands** giving Japan control of Shantung and southern **Manchuria**. During the **May Fourth Movement** in 1919, Chinese students protested betrayal by both the allies and the republican government. This led Sun to ally his Nationalist party, or **Kuomintang** with the communists. For the Russian communists, this was the first of many "national liberation fronts," but for Sun, it was a helpful blueprint for party reorganization and a campaign against the warlords who threatened Chinese republican unification. In his **Three Principles of the People**—nationalism, democracy, and people's livelihood, nationalism remained of prime importance. When Sun died in 1925, the task of uniting China fell to **Chiang Kai-shek** (1887–1975). Fearful of communist subversion, Chiang purged the communists in 1927. This led the communists, under their leader **Mao Tse-tung**, to shift the focus of their activities to the countryside.

India in the 1920s

In India, the 1920s saw the beginnings of independence. During World War I, 1.2 million Indian soldiers and laborers volunteered for duty in Europe, Africa, and Southwest Asia. In return, Indians pressed for self-governing status as a British dominion, especially after the Lucknow Pact in 1916 in which Muslims and Hindus joined together in this goal. The British capitulated to the extent that, in 1919, the **Government of India Act** established dual administration, part Indian and elected, part British and authoritarian. Bipartisan rule was rolled back, however, in 1919 and the repressive Rowlatt Acts indefinitely extended "wartime emergency measures." Protest erupted at a Hindu religious festival leading to the **Amritsar Massacre** in which 379 were killed and 1137 Indians were wounded by British troops. India was on the verge of violence when national liberation took a different path under the leadership of **Mohandas Gandhi** (1869–1948). Gandhi's vision of nonviolent protest or Satyagraha (*satya*—"spiritual truth," *agraha*—"strength") was formed during his early years as a lawyer in South Africa where he was treated as a second class citizen due to his dark skin color. In 1915 Gandhi returned to India, and in 1920 launched a national campaign of nonviolent resistance to British rule. Throughout the 1920s radical nationalists led by **Jawaharlal Nehru** called for outright independence. Gandhi tempered this and for the first time involved the general population. Reminiscent of the American colonists dumping the tea in Boston Harbor, Gandhi defied British rule. He led 50,000 people in a spectacular march to the sea to make salt rather than pay the British salt tax. For this he was jailed, but with the Depression bringing the industrialized world to its knees, he was released in 1931. In 1935 the British negotiated a new constitution, a virtual blueprint of independence.

The Depression

The quest for economic and political stability and colonial independence that took place in the 1920s was severely undermined by the Depression. World War I reparations and war debt set the stage for the Depression. According to the **Dawes Plan** worked out in 1924, German reparations to Britain and France would pass on to the United States in repayment of war debt. This led to a massive imbalance in the international economy as more and more resources of Europe were diverted to debt payment, thereby reducing the market for American industrial goods.

The Great Depression began as a spectacular fall in share prices on the New York Stock Exchange in 1929, followed by the collapse of banks. When American banks called in their foreign loans, the effects of the Wall Street Crash reverberated around the world. In 1931 the largest Austrian bank declared bankruptcy, followed by many others. International trade decreased 60 percent and world industrial production (except in the Soviet Union) fell 40 percent, leading to unemployment everywhere. In the democracies like the United States, Britain, and France, governments spent massively on welfare and public works projects.

Results in Germany

In weak democracies like Germany, Italy, and Japan, dictatorships came to power that put people back to work with military spending. In the 1930 German elections, the Nazis polled 18 percent of the vote, but by 1932 they gained 37 percent, enough to bring Adolf Hitler to power in 1933. In 1934 the Enabling Act abolished the Reichstag or parliament. Hitler immediately began a program of Nazification. Trade unions, news media, and schools were brought under control. Economic affairs were closely regulated and public works like the autobahn system brought people back to work.

Results in Japan

Japan, meanwhile, suffered a drastic decline in trade as a result of the Depression. Between 1929 and 1931 Japanese foreign trade halved, a trade that had grown during and after World War I and had compensated for the fact that Japan had gained little in terms of territory from World War I. Besides that, there were natural disasters—an earthquake in 1923 that destroyed three-quarters of Tokyo—and population increases of 1.5 percent per year. Empire, particularly in Manchuria, seemed a solution to the problem of Japanese economic independence of the rest of the world. In 1931, just as the Nationalists under Chiang Kai-shek were poised to reunite China, Japan invaded Manchuria and took control of the province with its rich industrial resources. Chinese protests to the League of Nations failed to mobilize international action. In 1933 Japan annexed Manchuria, after which Chiang Kai-shek made a final desperate effort to rid China of the communists. He chased Mao and his followers, on what became the legendary "**Long March,**" from their southern bases in Kiangsi and Hunan to a new base in the northwest. When an unsatisfactory truce was forged between the communists and nationalists, Japan launched a full-scale invasion of northern China. For China, World War II had begun. The other powers, uncertain of which way Japan would next move, began to secure their positions. Russia initiated hostilities along the Manchurian border to deter the Japanese in the summer of 1939. The United States, fearing an attack to the south on the Philippines, restricted iron and steel exports to Japan, threatened to cut off oil supplies, froze Japanese credit in America, and stepped up aid to Chiang Kai-shek. On April 13, 1941, the Japanese signed a nonaggression pact with the Soviet government, saving Russia but paving the way for the Japanese move southward.

German-Italian Aggression

Meanwhile, in Europe, both Italy and Germany embarked on unimpeded paths of aggression because Britain and France followed policies of appeasement (giving in for the sake of peace). Hitler's domestic and foreign policy goals, which he quickly began to realize, were outlined in his book *Mein Kampf* (*My Struggle*). Domestically, Hitler began to enforce his idea of German racial superiority by instituting the **Nuremburg Laws** of 1935, which deprived Jews of their civil and commercial rights. By 1941 the Nazi state proceeded to what became known as the **Final Solution** of the Jewish problem, the deliberate extermination of Jewish communities throughout Europe. Many of the estimated six million killed were transported by rail to concentration camps like **Dachau** and **Auschwitz** where they were systematically gassed. Germany turned into a police state run by the **Gestapo** (secret police) and SS, Hitler's private army.

On the foreign front, Hitler began by rearming Germany in defiance of the Versailles Treaty. In 1938 he annexed Austria (**Anschluss**) and large areas of Czechoslovakia, a move sanctioned by Great Britain and France in the **Munich Agreements**.

Meanwhile, Italy attacked Ethiopia and both Germany and Italy aided the Fascist leader General **Francisco Franco** during the Spanish Civil War, a war whose horrific cruelties for civilian populations were immortalized in artist **Pablo Picasso**'s *Guernica*. The painting commemorates the bombing of the ancient Spanish town by Fascist planes, an attack that took the lives of one of every eight inhabitants in a single night of terror. This was a prelude of what was to come in World War II.

By March, 1939, Hitler proceeded to occupy the rest of Czechoslovakia and seized the port of Memel from Lithuania. In April, Mussolini overran Albania. On August 23 Germany and Russia signed a **NonAggression Pact** that allowed Hitler to attack Poland on September 1 from the west while **Joseph Stalin** ordered Soviet troops to invade Poland from the east. At this point, Great Britain and France ended their appeasement and declared war.

The Course of the War

Hitler's shadow spread quickly over Europe. In April 1940, his forces overran Denmark and Norway. On May 10 he initiated successful attacks on Holland, Belgium, and France. France surrendered on June 22. The northern half of France was occupied by Germans and the southern half ruled from **Vichy** with a puppet government. Now Britain stood virtually alone, but under the dogged leadership of **Winston Churchill**, England withstood massive German bombings without capitulating. This caused Hitler to turn in the other direction against Russia in June. In 1941 the brilliant German general **Erwin Rommel** advanced across North Africa toward the Suez Canal.

The Japanese Attack

Meanwhile, the Japanese, certain now that they had nothing to fear from Russia, attacked **Pearl Harbor** on December 7, bringing the United States into the war. Shortly thereafter, Japan took the Philippines, Malaya, Singapore, and Hong Kong.

At the height of Fascist power, the tide turned. The United States, through the Lend-Lease program, became the "**Arsenal of Democracy**" by supplying huge amounts of weapons and war materiel to Britain and Russia. Gradually, the Axis powers were stopped. The Germans suffered two crucial defeats in 1942—one in North Africa at **El Alamein** and one in Russia at **Stalingrad**. Stalingrad became the turning point of the war. From then on, Germany and Italy were beaten back and defeated. In 1943 the Allies invaded Italy. Rome fell in June 1944, the same month Operation Overlord (the **D-Day** landings) across the English Channel started. On June 6 the largest amphibious operation in history began, involving 100,000 assault troops, 5000 ships, and 14,000 aircraft. In the spring of 1945 Allied strategic bombing against German industrial cities culminated in the destruction of Dresden, the counterpart of the German bombardment of London. On May 7, 1945, the Nazi leadership finally surrendered.

By this time, in the Pacific, only Burma and the Philippines had been recovered. There were one million undefeated Japanese troops in China and another half million in Malaya, Thailand, Indonesia, and Indochina. The American strategy of island hopping proved costly and aerial bombardment of Japanese cities failed to make the Japanese submit. In hopes of ending the war without invading Japan, President **Harry Truman** ordered atomic bombs dropped on **Hiroshima** on August 6 and **Nagasaki** on August 9. On August 8 Russia declared war on Japan, and on August 14 Japanese emperor **Hirohito** accepted the terms for Japan's surrender.

Results

The world lay in ruins. Europe's hegemony had ended and the Pacific rim was a political vacuum. While Russia lay exhausted, it survived as a power ready to take advantage of its position as the only Eurasian power. Only the United States, whose borders had seen no direct action, emerged with any sort of power position. Americans, however, were weary of war and its costs. The surrender and the mushroom cloud set the stage for a new age in world history.

THE COLD WAR

At war's end, all who had been involved were appalled at the death and destruction. As after World War I, the answers to establishing a new and peaceful world seemed to lie in punishment of the perpetrators of war and founding of representative world organizations to keep the peace. The Fascist regimes were blamed for the war, Nazis were put on trial for "crimes against humanity" at the **Nuremburg** military tribunals, and all the defeated were made to establish democratic governments with civil liberties ensured.

The United Nations

The League of Nations was dissolved and the **United Nations** chartered in June 1945, with 50 nations signed on. Main power in the United Nations rested with the Security Council, whose permanent members—the United States, Soviet Union, Britain, France, and China—could veto any decisions. Subsidiary agencies like the World Health Organization and Food and Agricultural Organization made important contributions to combating disease and starvation, and to promoting social and cultural understanding. The United Nations became involved in many political disputes worldwide, but was often hampered by Cold War power politics. The real mechanism of peace was fear of the atomic bomb.

The Cold War

The paradoxical effect of atomic weaponry was to promote peace. After the dawn of the Atomic Age the two countries that possessed atomic, and then nuclear, capability—the United States and the Soviet Union—faced off in a "Balance of Terror." Enemies politically, economically, and ideologically, these two combatants carried on a war of words, a contest for allies, and a policy of expansionism—all short of outright war. Both feared unforeseen consequences if the new weapons were to be used. The Cold War was a face-off between the United States and its allies and the Soviet Union and its allies. It had many manifestations—an arms buildup of colossal and frightening proportions, support for small wars as in Korea, Southwest Asia, Africa, and East Asia, and the quest for the minds and hearts of people through propaganda, political infiltration, and cultural exchanges.

Origins

The origins of the Cold War can be found in World War II wartime aims and agreements. During the war, despite differing aims, the United States and Soviet Union made victory over Germany the highest priority. Lurking beneath this shared aim were differences. Stalin's territorial gains in Poland ran counter to the **"Atlantic Charter"** of August 1941, an expression of war aims by Great Britain and the United States. It called for peace without territorial expansion or secret agreements, and for free elections and self-determination for liberated nations. At Tehran in 1943, however, it was agreed that Soviet troops could liberate eastern Europe. In February 1945 at **Yalta**, the Red Army was already in eastern Europe but Britain and France were yet to cross the Rhine into Germany. Meanwhile the United States was fighting alone against Japan in the Pacific. Therefore, Roosevelt agreed to divide Germany, pay reparations to the Soviet Union in the form of agricultural and industrial goods confiscated in the occupied areas, and welcome Soviet help in the war against Japan. After Roosevelt's death in 1945, President Truman demanded free elections in eastern Europe at a meeting in Potsdam. Stalin refused. Instead, elections were held under the aegis of communism and the Soviets delivered power to communist officials.

Containment

This was the beginning of the Cold War and the implementation by both sides of their differing war aims. The American response to Soviet occupation and the co-opting of elections was to "get tough." In May 1945, Truman cut off all aid to Russia, and in October he declared the United States would never recognize any government formed against the will of the people. In March 1946, Winston Churchill informed an American audience that an "**Iron Curtain**" had fallen across the continent, dividing Europe into two camps. Only Yugoslavia in eastern Europe remained outside the Soviet sphere, mainly because communist leader **Tito** had his own army and had not been dependent on Soviet troops to liberate Yugoslavia from the Nazis. The foreign policy that guided the United States through the Cold War was called "**containment**," that is, taking action where necessary to stop the spread of Soviet and communist influence. The policy the Soviet Union followed was expansionism under the banner "the ideological struggle against capitalist imperialism." When the Soviet Union put pressure on Iran and Turkey, and civil war raged in Greece and China between communists and loyalists, the United States announced the **Truman Doctrine**. "I believe it must be the policy of the United States to support free people who are resisting attempted subjugation by armed minorities or by outside pressure." Truman asked for military aid to Greece and Turkey and Secretary of State George Marshall offered economic aid to rebuild Europe. This **Marshall Plan** was a huge success. A similar plan was undertaken in Japan.

Occupied by the United States under the direction of General **Douglas MacArthur**, the Japanese military establishment was dismantled, a democratic constitution adopted, and large amounts of American aid restored the economy. Thus, nations like West Germany, a former enemy, became an ally. The Soviet Union, meanwhile, supplied aid to communist parties in China, resulting in the fall of the republic of China to communism in 1949.

Cold War Alliances

The Cold War manifested itself in a series of alliances and wars. The United States formed a European defensive alliance called **NATO**, the North Atlantic Treaty Organization. This was countered by the **Warsaw Pact**, a military alliance between the Soviet Union and eastern European allies. The western European economic union, the **European Economic Community** (EEC), was opposed in eastern Europe by **Comecon**, a trade union between the Soviet Union and its allies. In Asia, the United States signed **SEATO**, the Southeast Asia Treaty Organization, countered by Russia in the **Sino-Soviet Alliance**.

Cold War Conflicts

Soon the alliances were tested. When the Soviet Union closed the highway in July, 1948 from West Germany to West Berlin, the United States responded with a massive airlift for over a year, supplying West Berliners with everything needed from coal to food. In May 1949, the Soviets backed down. Massive desertions from East Germany to the West resulted, until the Soviets built the **Berlin Wall**, sealing off East Berlin from West Berlin.

The Korean War

The next confrontation was in Korea. From 1910 to 1945 Korea had been a colony of Japan. Stalin's troops entered North Korea two days before the atomic bomb was dropped on Hiroshima. By war' end they had driven to the 38th parallel. The Soviet Union occupied the north and the United States the south. In 1948 elections in the south established a republic under **Syngman Rhee**. In the north the communists set up a Democratic Peoples Republic led by Moscow-trained **Kim Il Sung.** In June 1950, North Korea, heavily armed by the Russians, invaded the south. This began the **Korean War**, which lasted from 1950 until an armistice was signed at Panmunjom in 1953. The United States and South Korea, with the support of the United Nations troops, drove the North Koreans to the Yalu River at the border of China. The Chinese, with massive troop reinforcements, pushed U.N. forces back to the 38th parallel. There the division has remained to this day.

There were other confrontations as well. In 1962 the Soviet Union placed missiles in Cuba. The **Cuban Missile Crisis** began when the United States issued an ultimatum to end further shipments and demanded the missiles dismantled. The Soviets backed down.

Peaceful Coexistence

Between 1955 and 1965, however, the outright hostilities between the United States and Soviet Union began to subside. This period is known as **peaceful coexistence**, a time when both countries accepted the existence of an antagonistic relationship between the superpowers but began to work together where possible. An example of peaceful coexistence occurred when the United States and Soviet Union joined the United Nations in an effort to end the Suez Crisis in 1956. During this crisis, Russian-backed Egyptian President **Gamal Abdel Nasser** seized the Suez Canal from Great Britain, bringing Egypt to the brink of war with Great Britain and France. Since such a war might have expanded into a superpower war, both the United States

and the Soviet Union worked to end the crisis. Another example of peaceful coexistence was the **Test Ban Treaty** signed between the two superpowers in 1962. This treaty prohibited nuclear tests in the atmosphere, outer space, and underwater.

Detente

Between 1965 and 1975 the Cold War relationship went a step further in its amelioration, entering a period of **detente** or understanding. Reasons for more amicable relations have to do with the fragmenting of the Soviet bloc and, similar to American problems in its hemisphere, the uncertainties as to China's position after the Sino-Soviet split, the acquisition by other powers of nuclear capability, and the growing economic power of other parts of the world like Japan and Europe.

End of the Cold War

By the 1980s, the Cold War was over. It was no longer a bipolar political world. Other countries had obtained nuclear capability and the world had other economic superpowers, like Japan and Germany. While the Cold War between the United States and the Soviet Union never resulted in outright confrontation, military conflict between their proxies did occur. Decolonialization and revolutions in the Third World countries were peripheral aspects of the Cold War because they were often engineered and orchestrated by the superpowers in their quest for allies. Both the United States and the Soviet Union tried to woo countries to their side with economic aid, ideological propaganda, and military materiel. This fanned the flames of decolonialization and nationalist wars.

CHAPTER 24

Revolution, Decolonization, and Wars of National Liberation

CHRONOLOGY

Russian Revolution
(1917)
Mexican Revolution
(1917)
Partition of India (1947)

Arab-Israeli War (1948)
Chinese Communist
Revolution (1949)
Bandung Conference
(1955)

Cultural Revolution (1965)
Vietnam War
(1954–1969)
Persian Gulf War (1991)

TERMS

Social Democratic Party
soviet
Communist International
Marxism-Leninism
communism
Comintern
Provisional Government
New Economic Policy
PRI
Third World

Alliance for Progress
North American Free
Trade Agreement
Congress party
Balfour Declaration
OPEC
Arab League
Arab Israeli War
Palestine Liberation
Organization

Six-Day War
neocolonialism
wars of national
liberation
guerrilla warfare
Great Proletarian
Cultural Revolution
negritude
apartheid

PEOPLE

Mensheviks
Bolsheviks
V. I. Lenin
Alexander Kerensky
Whites
Reds
Leon Trotsky
kulaks
Porfirio Diaz
Mohammad Ali Jinnah
Indira Gandhi
Sikhs
Reza Shah Pahlavi
Ayatollah Khomeini

Saddam Hussein
Anwar el-Sadat
Golda Meir
Henry Kissinger
Menachem Begin
Yasir Arafat
Jian Qing
Deng Xiaoping
Ho Chi Minh
Viet Minh
Ngo Din Diem
Viet Cong
Richard Nixon
Pol Pot

Sukarno
Kwame Nkrumah
Joseph Mobuto
Jomo Kenyatta
Mau Mau
Nelson Mandela
F. W. de Klerk
Fidel Castro
Fulgencio Batista
Salvador Allende
Sandinistas
Anastasio Somoza

PLACES

Pakistan
Kashmir
Bangladesh
Syria
Lebanon
Israel
Taiwan
People's Republic of
China

Tiananmen Square
Indochina
Vietnam
Laos
Cambodia
Dien Bien Phu
Malaysia
Indonesia

Nigeria
Biafra
Zaire
Namibia
Angola
Mozambique
Guantanamo Bay

Revolution, Decolonization, and Wars of National Liberation

As liberal bourgeois revolutions dominated the 19th century, communist revolutions dominated the twentieth century. The Russian Revolution was the first of these, and it provided the blueprint for all subsequent communist revolutions. None of these occurred until after World War II, when countries in search of national independence found a rationale for revolution and a structure for a new state in communist ideology and Russian experience. These wars of national liberation were anticapitalist and procommunist, turning independence movements into anti-western revolts. Decolonization, on the other hand, occurred largely within the western liberal context. In many Third World countries, the inability of liberalism to meld with local traditions, and the impatience of these countries with the slow pace of western modernization, caused them to turn to communism. This too failed, leaving many newly formed countries with dictatorships and engaged in incessant civil wars.

THE RUSSIAN REVOLUTION

Marxism in Russia

Marxian ideology came to Russia at the hands of intellectuals who formed the **Social Democratic Party** in 1898. In 1903 the party split into two factions, the **Mensheviks**, who argued that Russia was not yet ready for a Marxist revolution because it was not industrialized, and the **Bolsheviks**, who believed in the inevitability of the proletarian revolution in Russia. Bolsheviks like **V. I. Lenin** were disappointed by the bourgeois nature of the 1905 Russian Revolution because it resulted in the beginning of a liberal government on the western model instead of a Marxist government. During the 1905 Revolution, Social Democrats refused to have anything to do with the Duma, or Parliament, and instead formed a **soviet**, or workers' council. When the czar restored order, many like Lenin were forced to go abroad. In England and Switzerland Lenin worked out the necessary adaptations to

Marxism to make it fit the Russian situation. This was the beginning of the ironic situation wherein Marxist revolutions have tended to be successful only in nonindustrialized nations instead of in industrialized nations as envisioned by Marx.

Marxism-Leninism

Noting that in Russia 80 to 90 percent of the population were peasants, Lenin called for a revolution of workers (symbolized by the hammer) and peasants (symbolized by the sickle). In view of the failure of the 1905 Revolution, Lenin also disregarded the spontaneous nature of revolution and instead called for a planned and directed revolution that would end in the "Dictatorship of the Proletariat," instead of in communism in which the state withers away.

The third adaptation Lenin made to classical Marxism was to link capitalism with imperialism. In classical Marxism, the capitalist was the enemy of the worker. In Marxism-Leninism, capitalists are by nature imperialists, broadening the enemy to include all those oppressed under the colonial yoke. Stalin added the last tenet to Marxism-Leninism and that was to reinsert the nation, in this case Russia, as the vanguard of the revolution world-wide. Thus began the notion of the "**Communist International**," or the exporting of Soviet brand communism to other places in the world. These tenets—a revolution of worker and peasant, a planned revolution ending in dictatorship of one class over another, imperialists as well as capitalists as the enemy, and the power of a state to carry out socialism became known as **Marxism-Leninism**, or what is generally thought of today as **communism**.

The February-March Revolution, 1917

Lenin and bolshevism were of little threat to Russia until Russian war losses, terrible conditions in the cities, and finally the toppling of the czar left Russia vulnerable to a new ideology and strong leadership. During the war, workers had become highly politicized due to close working conditions and public subscription to government bonds. On March 8, 1917, in protest against military defeats at the front and lack of fuel and food in the cities, workers in St. Petersburg called for a general strike. The streets filled with demonstrators, but, unlike in 1905, the troops were sympathetic and did not fire on the workers. In fact, the army's rank and file joined the workers. The czar was away at the front, and when he started out for St. Petersburg in person to direct the repression, his train was held up by striking railway workers. With the government in collapse, the Duma asked for the czar's abdication on March 15.

The Provisional Government

Power now fell to two groups—the Duma, which called itself the **Provisional Government**, and the Soviet of Workers' and Soldiers' Deputies. The Duma knew how to run the machinery of state and the Soviets controlled the streets. Disregarding the Duma, the Soviet issued Order No. 1 (dated March 14, 1917), depriving all officers of authority and placing military affairs under the control of committees elected by officers and men. Immediately, the situation at the

front became chaotic with desertions and fraternizations across enemies lines. Seizing the opportunity to end Russian involvement in World War I, Germany sent Lenin in a sealed train back to Russia to foment a Marxist revolution in the hope that it would lead to Russian withdrawal from the war as called for in Marxist doctrine. Lenin arrived in Russia on April 17 with radical aims—"All power to the Soviets" and "Land, Peace, and Bread." This extreme position did not immediately find any support, but the failure of the July offensive at the front discredited the Provisional Government.

The Duma became more radical. Menshevik **Alexander Kerensky** became prime minister, and to restore order, he exiled Lenin once again, this time to Finland. From there, Lenin orchestrated the Bolshevik takeover of the St. Petersburg and Moscow soldiers' and workers' soviets.

The October-November Revolution, 1917

Lenin returned, and on November 7 the Bolsheviks seized strategic points in St. Petersburg, arrested the Provisional Government, and assumed power. The next day, Lenin issued a Land Decree that ordered immediate redistribution of all large landed estates among the peasants, nationalization of banks, worker control of the factories (but they lost the power to strike), the repudiation of the national debt, and confiscation of church property. The timing of Lenin's move was determined by his control of the soviets and the coming constituent elections, the first all-Russian elections to elect delegates to a constitutional convention. Lenin feared if he did not control the elections, the vote would not be for him. He was right. The vote was taken and the majority went to the Socialist Revolutionaries who represented the peasants. Lenin immediately dispersed the Constituent Assembly, putting an end to liberalism in Russia. In 1919 the "**Comintern**" or Communist International, was formed to export communism abroad.

Civil War, 1918–1921

Immediately, Lenin called for an end to Russia's participation in World War I. The reason was both ideological and practical. Ideologically, socialists were opposed to participation in what they considered a capitalist war. More important, however, was the disintegration of Russia. Scarcely a month after the Bolshevik revolution, many groups mobilized against it. There were revolts by the Don Cossacks, separatist movements in the Ukraine, Azerbaijan, Armenia, and the Baltic provinces, and rebellions in eastern Siberia and White Russia. A civil war (1918–1921) began, pitting separatists, former officers, and Provisional Government proponents (**Whites**), against the **Reds,** or communists. Soon the civil war internationalized as Japanese, Polish and western armies assisted the Whites, some because they opposed communism and others in order to take advantage of Russian weakness. At this point, Lenin appointed a brilliant Bolshevik orator and strategist, **Leon Trotsky**, to organize a Red Army. Because the Bolsheviks controlled the central part of Russia and the railroads, and because they had superb organization and ruthless fanaticism, the Reds were able to pick off one White enemy after another. By 1921 victory was in Bolshevik hands, but the cost was enormous. Russia was in shambles and a remnant of its old self. Lenin went out immediately to meet the situation. He instituted the **New Economic Policy** (NEP), which injected some capitalism at the consumer level, but Lenin kept control of finance and industry. The wheels of the economy slowly began to move again. By the time of Lenin's death in 1924, Russia had reorganized as the Union of Soviet Socialist Republics (U.S.S.R.), having reintegrated the Ukraine, White Russia, and Transcaucasia into the new state. By 1929 industrial production had reached pre-war levels largely independent of the world community.

By 1928 Lenin's successor, Joseph Stalin, had assumed power. In order to fully implement communism, he embarked on a program of forced industrialization and collectivization. The class of capitalist peasant landowners, the "**kulaks**," was purged. As the threat from Nazi Germany increased in 1936–1937, Stalin purged the military ranks as well in a series of show trials. In 1936 the Stalin constitution outlined a democratic framework for government but gave all power to the communist party and its politburo leaders. Historians are divided on whether Stalin's reign of terror prepared Russia for war against Germany or weakened the effort. The signing of the Nazi-Soviet NonAggression Pact in 1939 could be interpreted as a sign of weakness on Stalin's part or an attempt to turn the war west. Whatever the case, the Russian effort during World War II was effective enough to hold Hitler at bay in Leningrad, Moscow, and Stalingrad. Russia emerged from World War II weakened internally but enlarged territorially. The Russian model of revolution, creation of the socialist welfare state, and military strength became a model for many Third World countries in their quest for national liberation, modernization, and an end to poverty.

REVOLUTION AND DECOLONIZATION IN MEXICO, INDIA, AND SOUTHWEST ASIA (THE MIDDLE EAST)

Nationalism was a potent and popular force in the twentieth century despite its tragic manifestations in World War I and World War II. People outside Europe often equated it with liberty, civil rights, and economic empowerment. As the imperial hold of western countries weakened after World War I, and completely collapsed after World War II, national independence movements gained strength. In Mexico, India, and Southwest Asia, western powers managed and oversaw decolonization efforts, trying to steer them in the direction of liberal democracies. This became particularly important during the Cold War as a strategy for keeping these countries from falling into communist hands.

The Third World

Attempts at independence and liberal democracy did not always meet with initial success. This was because western ideas often ran counter to local traditions and because these experiments were being attempted in **Third World** countries. "Third World" was a term used during the Cold

War to refer to Asia, Africa, and Latin America. This distinguished it from the "First" and "Second" worlds—the capitalist and communist industrialized nations respectively. The term was taken from a French scholar who likened these countries to the Third Estate during the French Revolution. Third World countries as a whole lacked the literacy, national cohesiveness, and economic wealth necessary to make liberal democracies work. Many, as a result, ended with nations that were free of colonial dictate but ruled by dictators of the right or left.

Mexico

Mexico was one of the first Third World countries to engage in decolonialist struggles. Decolonization for Mexico meant removing itself from the economic and political sphere of the United States. This struggle was also a revolution that attempted to complete the social and political revolution begun by Latin American independence movements in the 1820s. Mexico had been ruled by a dictator, **Porfirio Diaz**, from 1881 to 1910. Despite his dictatorial regime, Mexican economic development made great strides. Railroad mileage increased more than fortyfold, but the price was heavy U.S. investment. By 1910 U.S. companies controlled three-fourths of Mexico's mines and almost three-fifths of its oil production. Mexico became a powder keg of political, social, and antiforeign discontent. From 1910 on, Diaz was challenged by an array of rival politicians producing a decade of violent revolution. By 1920 two Mexican presidents had been murdered and about one of every eight Mexicans had died.

Revolution

In 1917 a radical constitution was written that guaranteed universal suffrage, gave Mexican workers the right to organize and strike, authorized eight-hour work days, and called for the redistribution of land to peasants. Rival claimants to power, including Pancho Villa and Emiliano Zapata, however, challenged the "constitutionalist" politicians. In 1920 the Institutional Revolutionary Party (**PRI**) was organized and came to represent all factions of Mexican politics, but politicians in Mexico City gained the upper hand. By 1923 President Alvaro Obregon had reneged on most of the constitutional promises. American companies continued to control Mexico's oil and little land changed hands.

Thus Mexico, like Africa, fell into a neocolonialist position, becoming a producer of foodstuffs and raw materials, exporter to Europe and the United States. This had devastating effects during the Depression of the 1930s when the Mexican export market collapsed. The Mexican response was to gain control over industry by means of huge tariffs and expropriation of foreign-owned oil properties. During World War II, Mexican prosperity increased though much of it went into the hands of the upper classes and the rest was wiped out by population increases.

Decolonization

Floundering Latin American economies and the Cold War fears of the growth of leftists government like those in Cuba caused the United States to pledge $10 billion in economic assistance through the **Alliance for Progress** (1961). Unfortunately, the aid often propped up authoritarian governments at the expense of democratic social reforms. National political and economic independence has not led to prosperity or equality. This is no more evident than in the propensity of Mexicans to flow across the border into the United States. The fragile line between national independence and economic partnerships with American neighbors as exhibited in the **North American Free Trade Agreement** (NAFTA) signed in 1994 between the United States, Canada, and Mexico, continues to challenge Mexico in its quest for independence.

India

Decolonization and then national independence in India was closely connected with the religious traditions of Hinduism and Islam. By the 1930s, the populist nationalist movement, which had coalesced around Gandhi and Hindu nonviolence, began to disturb the Muslim minority. The leaders of the Muslim League began calling for a Muslim nation, a "**Pakistan**" or "land of the pure." These conflicting nationalisms were to lead to tragedy. By 1937 Gandhi's movement had matured into the Congress party. In the face of this, the British gave in to limited self-rule, but when Britain declared war on Germany in India's behalf without consultation, Gandhi called on Britain to "Quit India." He and other Congress party rulers were quickly arrested and remained jailed for the rest of the war. This allowed the rival Moslem League led by English-educated **Muhammad Ali Jinnah** (1876–1948) to assert the right of Muslims to separate independence areas.

Gandhi was appalled at the notion of a two-nation India, but murderous clashes between Hindus and Muslims after World War II led to the partition of India in 1947. Since most Muslims lived in the western and eastern parts of northern India, the new nation was split into West and East Pakistan. It proved to be only the beginning of tragedy. An estimated 100,000 Hindus and Muslims were slaughtered and about five million refugees fled in opposite directions. Gandhi himself was gunned down by a Hindu fanatic in 1948.

Partition

Mutual hostility between Muslims and Hindus has remained to this day. Fighting over the disputed area of **Kashmir** broke out in 1965 and 1971. Even Pakistani national unity failed. East and West Pakistan, separated by 1000 miles of territory, shared only the Muslim religion. In ethnicity and custom, the Bengalis of East Pakistan are closer to Indian Hindus than to Pakistanis. They revolted and created a new nation, **Bangladesh** (1978), the world's eighth most populous country but one of its poorest. In India, therefore, decolonization led to national fragmentation.

Democratic Independent India

India, meanwhile, was ruled for a generation by Jawaharlal Nehru and the **Congress Party**, which introduced a string of reforms—abolition of the untouchable caste, legal and social rights for women, economic advancement under democratic socialism, and a neutral stance in the Cold War. But population growth of 2.4 percent per year inhibited India's ability to progress and strained the fragile democracy. Nehru's daughter, **Indira Gandhi** (her deceased husband was no relation to Mahatma Gandhi) in 1975 subverted parliamentary democracy in order to attack corruption and carry on a campaign of mass sterilization. Despite the unpopularity of her campaign, both she and democracy survived.

Sikh Nationalism

Other political problems rooted in the diversity of ethnicity and religion became the next challenge to Indian democracy. **Sikhs** with their own religion, which is a blend of Islam and Hinduism, and a military culture marked by wearing coiled turbans had long been a dominant force in the Punjab. In 1984 militant Sikhs occupied the Golden Temple of Amritsar, sacred to all Sikhs, and used it as a base for armed attacks against the anti-Sikh government. In June of 1984 the Indian army, in the process of occupying the temple, killed hundreds of militants. In response, Indira Gandhi was assassinated and hundreds of Sikhs were killed in revenge. As her son Rajiv campaigned for office, he also was assassinated by a Tamil militant from an ethnic minority in the south. Despite violence, population pressures, ethnic and religious diversity, and corruption, India remains dedicated to elected representative government based on the English model. It is the world's largest democracy.

The Middle East

In the Middle East religious tradition also played a crucial role in establishing a national framework for independence. In Persia, Russia and Britain struggled continually during the nineteenth century for imperial control. In 1906 a nationalist coalition of merchants, religious leaders, and intellectuals revolted against the puppet shah forcing a constitution and national assembly, the Majlis. This was crushed by Britain and Russia who divided the country into spheres. After World War I and the Bolshevik Revolution, Great Britain in 1919 negotiated a treaty installing British "advisers" in every government department, a move that aroused deep nationalist sentiment.

Persia/Iran

Following the Turkish example, in 1921 a strong military dictator, **Reza Shah Pahlavi** (1877–1944) came to power, ousting the British. He reigned until 1921 and tried, as in Turkey, to build a modern secular nation. However, his increasingly brutal rule and support of Nazi Germany during World War II led to his overthrow and the installation of his son, Muhammad Reza Pahlavi (r. 1941–1979). He also angered Iranian nationalists by courting western powers and western oil companies. With oil revenues, the shah undermined large landowners and religious leaders in order to carry out his modernization program of land reform, secular education, and centralized government. The result was violent reaction in 1978. A spellbinding religious leader, **Ayatollah Khomeini**, seized power and forced the shah to flee abroad. In order to establish national independence, the Ayatollah set up a radical Shi'ite Muslim government isolating Iran and irritating neighbors, mostly Sunni Muslim states. In 1980 Iran and Iraq fought a bloody war with both Soviet and American weapons. The economic consequences of that war and the drive for power by Iraq's leader, **Saddam Hussein**, led to the Iraqi invasion of Kuwait in 1990 (the Persian Gulf War). Swift action on the part of the United States and other Arab states, foiled the invasion.

Afghanistan

Afghanistan followed a similar route to national independence. Under a religious banner of anti-British sentiment, Amir Amanullah (1892–1960) declared a holy war on Britain and in 1919 won complete independence. Like the shah, his radical attempts at modernization led to religious revolt, tribal civil war, and retreat from reform. This weakness led to external intervention on the part of the Soviets (1979) and a protracted war. The Soviets began to retreat only during the restructuring under Mikhail Gorbachev in the mid-1980s. In the case of Iran and Afghanistan, the Islamic religion formed the basis of national sentiment and the nexus around which decolonization occurred. However, religious sentiment also stymied secular modernization efforts in these countries and served to divide the new nations.

Independence from the Ottoman Empire

The course of Arab independence in the former Ottoman Empire was colored by religion but also by wartime agreements primarily involving the Jews. During World War I, Arabs, led by Hussein Ibn-Ali (1856–1931), a direct descendant of Muhammad, allied with the British against the Ottoman Turks with the vague promise of independence after the war. However, in the secret Sykes-Picot treaties of 1916, Britain and France agreed that France would receive modern-day **Syria** and Lebanon after the war and Britain would receive Palestine, Jordan, and Iraq. A related source of irritation was the **Balfour Declaration** of November 17, which said, "His Majesty views with favor the establishment in Palestine of a National Home for the Jewish people . . . ."

Iraq, Egypt, Syria, and Lebanon

After World War I, the establishment of British (Palestine, Jordan, and Iraq) and French (Syria and Lebanon) mandates forced Arab nationalists to seek independence gradually after 1920. Because western taxpayers wanted cheap administration, the Arabs gained considerable control over local affairs. By 1932 Iraq had gained independence in exchange for a long-term military alliance with Britain. Egypt followed a similar course. A protectorate since 1914, it gained independence in 1922. The French held on longer, playing ethnic and religious groups against each other in Syria. They carved out a second mandate, **Lebanon**, which became a republic dominated by Christians, a situation that never found favor among Muslims, resulting in the collapse of the state in 1990. In 1936 Syria became independent in return for a treaty of friendship.

Israel

Meanwhile, the Jewish population in Palestine leaped from 10 percent to 30 percent in the interwar period. The reasons were twofold. First, the isolationist sentiment of the United States limited Jewish immigration in the 1930s. Second, the increasing persecution of Jews in Germany and Poland made them flee to Palestine. Resentment between Jews and Arabs grew, especially over land, so that by 1939 Britain proposed an independent Palestine and a limit on Jewish immigrants. Technically, sovereignty had been attained in the Middle East, but these former mandates were still under the economic and political influence of the West. This was especially true as World War II approached.

During World War II, the western nations maintained their hegemony in the Middle East despite German efforts to capture the Suez Canal. After the war, Arab nationalism intensified. One strand of sentiment envisioned a Pan Arab group of nations united under the banner of Islam and in alliances like the Arab League (in opposition to Jewish immigration) and **OPEC** (Organization of Petroleum Exporting Countries). The other strand concentrated on the growth of nationalism within countries. National independence proved greater than Arab solidarity, fragmenting the nations of the Middle East. Divisions occurred along ethnic lines (Persians and Arabs), religious lines (Sunni and Shi'ite Muslims), and economic lines (oil-producing and nonoil-producing states). Only the overriding problem of the Jewish question, which grew explosive, united them. Jews demanded that all survivors of Hitler's death camps could settle in Palestine, but Palestine and the **Arab League** (Egypt, Iraq, Jordan, Lebanon, Saudi Arabia, Syria, and Yemen) were opposed. The question went to the United Nations, which partitioned Palestine between Jews and Arabs. When the British mandate in Palestine ended in 1948, the Jews created the Jewish state of **Israel** out of the former Palestine.

Palestine

The Arab countries united in attack, but the Israelis defeated them decisively with modern weaponry they had acquired with U.S. help. Almost one million Arabs fled Palestine. This 1948 **Arab-Israeli War** left a legacy of bitterness between Israel and its political allies, the United States and Great Britain on the one hand, and the Arab states and its growing ties with the Soviet Union on the other. It also gave rise to a virulent Palestinian independence organization called the **Palestine Liberation Organization** (PLO). This organization remained the nerve center for anti-Israeli and pro-Palestinian nationalist sentiment. Terrorism became the major Palestinian weapon of retaliation. After persistent Palestinian raids, Israel invaded the Egyptian Sinai in 1956, and in 1967, the "**Six-Day War**" between Israel and the Arab states resulted in Israeli occupation of Gaza, Sinai, Old Jerusalem, the Golan Heights, and the West Bank. This expansion at the expense of Egypt, Jordan, Syria, and Lebanon made the Middle East a tinderbox. In the Yom Kippur War of 1973 Egyptian forces under **Anwar el-Sadat** demonstrated new fighting ability against the Israelis, led by the surprised coalition government of **Golda Meir**. As the war ground to a halt, U.S. secretary of state Henry Kissinger began efforts to find a diplomatic solution. In 1982, bowing to economic pressures caused by anti-Israeli defense spending, Egypt broke ranks with the Arab countries and recognized Israel in return for the Sinai. This historic agreement between Egyptian president Anwar Sadat and Israeli prime minister **Menachem Begin**, frustrated, the PLO and its flamboyant leader **Yasir Arafat**, who then moved into Lebanon instigating its dismemberment among Arab states. Not until the Cold War ended did the United States and the Soviet Union come together to sanctify a settlement in the area. Gradually taking place in the 1990s is Arab acceptance of Israel's right to exist and the Israeli acceptance of a homeland for the Palestinians, and Arab national independence.

REVOLUTION AND NATIONAL LIBERATION IN CHINA, SOUTHEAST ASIA, AFRICA, AND LATIN AMERICA

In China, Southeast Asia, Africa, and Latin America, independence movements took another path. In these areas, decolonization led initially to new liberal nations, but for one reason or another, they failed. A period of **neocolonialism** (economic or political dependence) followed. This was the context within which **wars of national liberation** occurred. Wars of national liberation freed countries from western imperialism under the banner of communism. The net result of national liberation and decolonization for world history has been an explosion of fragile new nations susceptible to dictatorships of all types, the dilution of western and communist influence, the rise of religious fundamentalism, and modernization programs. The rise of the "Third World" has changed the economic and political balance of the twentieth-century world.

China

The Chinese war of national liberation began in the 1920s and culminated in the **Chinese Communist Revolution** of 1949. As in Russia, when the Chinese imperial system fell (1911), two strands of thought competed for the new government. One followed western-style liberal democracy as represented by the Chinese Nationalists (Guomintang) led by Sun Yat-sen and then Chiang Kai-shek, and those who followed the Marxist-style communist model led by Mao Tse-tung. As in Russia, the first phase of change was dominated by western liberalism. In the 1920s Nationalists attempted to set up a western-style government and to modernize along capitalist lines. Throughout this period, however, the Nationalists struggled with the communists. Mao converted to Marxian socialism in 1918 but his lack of success in leading the country to communism led him to make major changes in the doctrine. After the Long March pushed Mao and his followers to the northwest of China, Mao mapped out a new course for his Chinese revolution. While Marx had envisioned the workers as the engine of revolution and Lenin, the workers and peasants, Mao envisioned the peasants as the engine of change. This was because they were the majority of the population and because they were the most oppressed, now not by the old regime, but by the Nationalist Guomintang. Mao also shifted the locus of the revolution from the city to the countryside where, in a campaign among peasants, his communist cadres preached communist doctrines. Countryside warfare demanded a different kind of war, **guerrilla warfare**, so Mao went back to the ancient Chinese martial expert, Sun Tzu, to find inspiration. "The enemy advances, we retreat; the enemy halts, we harass; the enemy slackens, we attack; the enemy retreats, we pursue." Finally, Mao defined the enemy as the imperialist rather than capitalist. These ideas can be found in the *Little Red Book*, a collection of Mao's sayings that became a bible of Chinese communism. A peasant revolution carried on in the countryside with guerrilla tactics against imperialists instead of capitalists became the model for Third World peasant revolution.

Chinese Communist Revolution

Like Lenin, Mao used war and its tragic effects to bring his vision of revolution to reality. In fact, as one historian has noted, "Japanese aggression was... the most important single factor in Mao's rise to power." When Japanese armies advanced rapidly into China in 1938, the Nationalist Government of Chiang Kai-shek was forced to form a "united front" with the communists. This allowed Mao to build up strength in guerrilla bases in the countryside behind Japanese lines where his forces avoided pitched battles and concentrated on winning peasant support. The communists began to appear in peasant eyes as genuine nationalists and true patriots, especially because they promised radical land redistribution. Meanwhile, the Nationalists took the brunt of the fighting. A staggering three million Chinese were killed and Chinese deficits and runaway inflation discredited the Nationalist government. When the Japanese collapsed in 1945, both communists and Nationalists rushed to seize evacuated territory. Civil war began in which the United States aided the Nationalists and the Soviet Union the communists. By 1948 the Nationalist forces were in disarray and demoralized. The following year, Chiang Kai-shek and a million mainland Chinese fled to **Taiwan**, and in October 1949, Mao proclaimed the **People's Republic of China** and laid claim to a new Mandate of Heaven.

Immediately, Mao liquidated over 800,000 "class enemies" and carried on a relentless campaign of "reeducation." In the mid-1950's, China followed the Soviet Union closely and seemed to be firmly in the Marxist-Leninist mold. In 1958, however, China began to go its own way both politically and economically. When Russian leader Nikita Khrushchev criticized Chinese policy, Mao condemned the Russians as "modern revisionists." This led to the Sino-Soviet split in the early 1960s.

The Cultural Revolution

Apprehensive that China was becoming bureaucratic, capitalistic and "revisionist," Mao launched the **Great Proletarian Cultural Revolution**. Its object was to purge the party of time-serving bureaucrats and recapture the revolutionary fervor. To do this, he dispatched the "Red Guards." young people who denounced their teachers and parents. Party officials, professors, and intellectuals were exiled to remote villages to "purify" themselves with heavy peasant labor.

Women's Liberation

Among those who gained during the Cultural Revolution were radical Maoists like Mao's wife **Jian Qing**, a character not unlike Lenin's wife Krupskaya who was a communist presence and advocate in her own right. In fact, in revolutions of the twentieth century, women have been drawn in large numbers to the revolutionary struggles, particularly in China and Vietnam. The reason is that during the revolutionary struggles, the political, social, and family structures that had subordinated women were broken down and, in some cases, the brutality of the conflicts forced women to take an active role just for survival. Jian Qing's position of power did not outlast the Cultural Revolution, however. When the campaign was called off by Mao in 1968, Jian Qing and her three allies, known as the "Gang of Four," were arrested, tried for crimes against the people, purged from the party, and imprisoned for life.

Chinese Liberalization

The chaos and senseless persecutions of the Cultural Revolution caused a counterattack. This liberal shift in China, coupled with actual fighting between China and the Soviet Union on the northern border in 1969, led to reconciliation with the United States in 1972. The moderates were led by **Deng Xiaoping**. After Mao's death in 1976, Deng and his supporters began to free the economy from socialism. Economic liberalization, however, led to demands for political liberalization. Deng, witnessing how such a program had gotten out of hand in Russia, quickly crushed the liberal student revolt in **Tiananmen Square** on May 17, 1989, the year the Berlin Wall fell in Europe.

Southeast Asia

The Chinese war of national liberation based on the Marxist and Soviet model, became the guide for the wars of national liberation in Southeast Asia. The national liberation struggles in Southeast Asia were first against the French, then against the United States. **Indochina**, including **Vietnam, Laos**, and **Cambodia**, had been a French colony since the 1880s scramble for empire. The French had been interested in the area as early as the seventeenth century when Christian missionaries successfully entered the region and won converts. As in China, the failure of Vietnam's Confucian emperor and bureaucracy to repel outside invasion, discredited it and made French colonization easier. The French were more reluctant than the British to decolonize after the war because French civilization was more universalist, claiming that all natives were entitled to be considered French, and because Indochina was a much valued colony with its plantations and rubber. French presence completely disrupted local agriculture and forced impoverished peasants into work in mines.

Ho Chi Minh

As in the history of other revolutions of this era, the new western-educated middle class, children of the former elite, became the backbone of the nationalist revolutions. While the French were embroiled in World War I, they lost control of the clandestine Nationalist party, but in 1929 they were still strong enough to repress and severely weaken a Nationalist uprising. The demise of the Nationalist party, however, only served to empower the nascent communist party, which had been formed in the 1920s by **Ho Chi Minh**, a converted Marxist who had studied in France and Russia during World War I. In the 1930s, Ho followed Mao's lead and switched the emphasis of revolution from worker to peasant.

Liberation from France

When the French were weakened by the Japanese invasion of Indochina in 1941, the communists used France's setback to advance their struggle for national liberation. Calling themselves **Viet Minh**, they established bases in south China and from there, by 1945 they advanced into the Red River delta as the Japanese withdrew. The Vietnamese communists reached Hanoi in August 1945. There they proclaimed the independent state of Vietnam. Along the way, they had gained support of rural regions much as Mao had, by a system of reeducation, building programs, and assistance, particularly during the famine of 1944–1945. After World War II, the French, with British aid, regained control of territory in the south, reoccupying Saigon and attempting to regain the rest of Vietnam. For almost ten years, the communist Vietnamese carried on a guerrilla war against them. In 1954 the Viet Minh decisively defeated the French at **Dien Bien Phu** despite American aid, which was part of the Cold War effort to contain the spread of communism. Their victory at Dien Bien Phu won for the Viet Minh control of the north at an international conference at Geneva.

Southeast Asia Becomes Communist

The second phase of national liberation came with U.S. involvement. Despite cooperation between the Viet Minh and the United States during the war against Japan, the anticommunist sentiment of the Cold War turned the Viet Minh into enemies. The United States feared that if one country fell in Southeast Asia others would fall in a "domino effect." The United States began to back **Ngo Dinh Diem** as leader of South Vietnam. From the beginning he was discredited in the eyes of the Vietnamese people because he was Catholic and had lived in exile in the United States in the 1940s. To counter U.S.-supported Diem, the Viet Minh began supplying weapons to communists in the south, the **Viet Cong**. When Diem proved unable to stem the tide of communism in the south, the U.S. gave the go-ahead for the military to overthrow him. Then the United States stepped up military intervention so that by 1968 there were 500,000 Americans in Vietnam. Their very presence served to add to the popularity of the national liberation sentiment. Meanwhile, popular sentiment in the United States against involvement mounted. By 1969 the new president, **Richard Nixon**, withdrew U.S. troops (1973). In 1975 the South Vietnamese state was overrun by the communists. Within a few years, many who supported the South were in prison camps and another substantial proportion fled by sea in leaky boats, many coming eventually to the United States in a "boat people" migration. The American fear of the domino effect was partly realized when Laos and Cambodia also fell to the communists. Cambodia became a "killing field." First Chinese-backed communists led by **Pol Pot** ravaged the country and then the Vietnamese communists invaded. The beleaguered nation has yet to awaken fully from a holocaust in which over one-third of the population was killed or died.

Malaysia and Indonesia

The national independence movements in Malaysia and Indonesia illustrate that many newly emerging nations wished to maintain independence and neutrality in the Cold War. In order to avoid becoming the Cold War battleground that Vietnam, Cambodia, and Laos had become, both national liberation and decolonization rhetoric was toned down.

Making a nation of the East Indies was a challenge, due to geography and diversity. The Malay peninsula and the 3000 islands that make up the East Indies are an amalgam of Indian, Chinese, Buddhist, and Islamic religious, artistic, cultural, and political concepts. These peoples do not share racial, national, linguistic, or social unity and, therefore, became fertile ground for European traders. First the Portuguese came in 1511 and then the Dutch and English. The Dutch took control of the East Indies in the mid-seventeenth century and the British took over the Malay peninsula during the Napoleonic Wars. During World War II, the Japanese conquered these colonial areas. Before the colonial rulers could reestablish their control, the native leaders took over and declared independence.

In 1950 the Dutch East Indies were united as the Republic of Indonesia under the leadership of President **Sukarno**. He feared American and European neocolonialist efforts to exploit Indonesian natural resources. To address this challenge, Sukarno sponsored the **Bandung Conference** in 1955, which represented 29 Asian and African countries and nearly one and a half billion people. The Bandung Conference called on these newly independent states to form a Neutral Bloc in the Cold War. Prime Minister Nehru of India became the leading spokesman for the "neutralists." However, the threat of old-style colonialism was soon overshadowed by the new threat of communism or "super-colonialism." Communist China occupied Tibet in 1959 and later invaded the northern borders of India. As a result, Nehru turned to the United States and Britain for assistance. Meanwhile, Sukarno, who had moved closer to communist China and had become more dictatorial, was toppled in a government coup led by General Suharto. Suharto then began to court western capital to develop Indonesia's great natural resources. Malaysia, meanwhile, continued a steady course of neutrality and economic development, also relying on the West.

Africa

The first phase of African national independence was dominated by African relationships with Europe; the second with the United States and Soviet Union. The African road to national independence began with political decolonization, but most African countries remained economically dependent on the West. Democracy and constitutionalism had a fragile hold on African countries, which had neither the political experience nor the national identity and unity to make a liberal political government work. This became the context within which Marxist ideas of the Soviet and Chinese brand began to take hold. Many African countries found in communism a program for fast economic development, a legitimization for dictatorship and banner under which they could become economically and politically independent. But Marxism, too, often failed in Africa, leading to civil wars and repressive dictatorships. In this search for national independence, first on the liberal model and then on the Marxist, the

Cold War played its part. The Soviet Union and China supported Marxist governments, and the United States supported the opposite, often putting the United States in the uncomfortable position of backing dictatorships.

African Decolonization

Between 1947 and 1962, almost every African country was decolonized and gained formal independence. Most occurred peacefully except in Algeria where there was a long bloody struggle for independence from the French. After independence, both the British and French offered the new nations association in their commonwealths. Most former colonies accepted because they identified with French and British culture. Also, the close association buoyed up their economies, and the British and French and their European Market partners helped foot the bill for programs of economic development and political recovery, an African Marshall Plan of sorts. The European states did this in part as a Cold War strategy to prevent Africa from falling under Soviet or Chinese influence. The close political and economic ties that developed led many leaders and scholars to charge that western Europe and the United States had imposed a system of neocolonialism on them. According to this view, neocolonialism was a system designed to undermine political independence and perpetuate economic dependence. It was often likened to the subordination that the United States had established in Latin America in the early nineteenth century, but it also often had racial overtones. Racial neoimperialism became the rationale for wars of national independence. These wars of national liberation were infused with an anticapitalist and prosocialist rhetoric and ideology.

Ghana

Like other wars of national liberation, the seeds of leadership had been planted after World War I by educated Africans who studied in western countries and became acquainted with both Marxist and liberal thought. The Senegalese poet and political leader Leopol Senghor is an excellent example. In the 1920s and 1930s he and other black and white intellectuals formulated the idea of **negritude** or blackness, meaning racial pride, self-confidence, and black creativity. When the Depression hit, many of these intellectuals lost their jobs to whites, while the masses suffered no less as their labors depended on foreign markets that also deteriorated. This radicalized them into calling for outright independence. World War II both interrupted and strengthened the movement. African mines and plantations burgeoned with wartime production, and the attentions of colonial masters were focused elsewhere. The new leadership was now of humbler origin—former schoolteachers, union leaders, and government clerks—and, thus, was more radical. These leaders accepted the existing boundaries to avoid border disputes and focused instead on solidifying their own power positions much as Lenin had. A good example of this was **Kwame Nkrumah** (1909–1972), who led the Gold Coast to independence. Nkrumah built a mass party, injecting it with a religious revival sentiment and indigenous historical forms (the country was renamed Ghana), and staging strikes and riots. In 1957, under Nkrumah's influence, Ghana became the first African state to emerge from colonial rule. Nkrumah soon fell under the spell of Marxism, however. In 1964, with the help of Chinese and East German technicians, he set up a one-party socialist state, claimed dictatorial powers, and went heavily into debt building hospitals, schools, and development projects like the Volta River hydroelectric and aluminum plants. In 1966 he was overthrown by a police-army coup, and coups have continued in 1972, 1978, 1979, and 1981.

Nigeria

The same sequence of events was played out in other countries in Africa like **Nigeria**. Nigeria encompassed an ethnic mix of Yorubas in the west, who had strong military traditions, and Ibos in the east, who had a tradition of business and independent villages. There was also a religious mix—Muslims in the north and Christians and Animists in the south. In response to these divisions, Nigeria adopted a federal system after independence, but by 1965 ethnic rivalries caused law and order to break down. An Ibo-led army group seized power. When a counter-group

overtook them, Ibos were massacred. Then they seceded, much as the South had done in the United States leading to the Civil War, and created an independent state of **Biafra** in the east. Biafra lasted only three years and then became the site of genocide and starvation. During the 1970s and 1980s, there were more coups and continued military dictatorships, reinforced with Soviet and American weaponry on both sides.

Zaire

The Congo, Kenya, and South Africa illustrate the same kinds of problems in their struggles for national independence. Belgian rule in the Congo had been so dictatorial that, when the Belgians retreated, there were only 16 African college graduates. No organized national movements and no mechanisms for rule existed. When independence came to the Congo in 1960 (now called **Zaire**), a series of rulers came to power, one after another. In 1964 leftist rebels set up a People's Republic causing U.S. paratroopers to get involved rescuing thousands of whites and hostages. In 1971 the "republic" of Zaire was formed by General **Joseph Mobuto**, who created a military rule.

Kenya

In Kenya, the independence movement was led by **Jomo Kenyatta**. In 1956 the British crushed the rebel movement, called **Mau Mau**, but by 1963 a multiracial Kenya had won independence from Britain under Kenyatta's leadership. Kenyatta sought the broad support of both blacks and whites. He encouraged Europeans and Asians to remain in Kenya as long as they accepted African rule. However, Kenyatta's leadership became increasingly repressive and autocratic. His successor, Daniel arap Moi, has maintained political power despite debt, inflation, and disputes with neighbors.

South Africa

In South Africa, the Afrikans (Dutch) won control from the British in 1948, and to cement their rule, instituted a policy of **apartheid**, or racial separation. The legislature gave certain tribes "homelands" (much like the American Indian reservations) but reserved the best jobs and lands for whites and made political participation impossible for blacks. Key nationalist leaders like **Nelson Mandela** were jailed. In general, Soviet arms went to the blacks and U.S. arms to whites. Only after the Berlin Wall fell in 1989, ending the Cold War, did the white president of South Africa, **F. W. de Klerk**, begin discussion with Nelson Mandela, paving the way for an end to apartheid and the beginning of rule based on racial equality.

Southwest Africa

In Southwest Africa, national independence also became wrapped up with Cold War ideologies and involvement. **Namibia**, or Southwest Africa, was a German colony mandated to South Africa after World War I. In 1966 the Marxist Southwest Africa People's Organization (SWAPO) launched guerrilla warfare involving both superpowers. Namibia finally gained independence in 1990 after the end of the Cold War.

Angola and Mozambique

No states in Africa showed the international Cold War aspects of African liberation movements better than **Angola** and **Mozambique**, former Portuguese colonies. In 1974 Portugal offered independence. Immediately, violence between the National Front based in Zaire, the Soviet-backed Popular movement using Cuban troops, and the National Union, backed by the United States and South Africa, led to bloody civil war. This 16-year conflict ended in 1991 when Jonas Savimbi, leader of UNITA (National Union for Total Independence of Angola), negotiated Cuban and South African troop removal. In Mozambique, a ten-year war of independence ended in 1974 when Maoist President Samora Machel promised gradual transition to a communist system. Many emigrated, especially whites, with the result that Mozambique became economically dependent on South Africa and riddled with debt.

The Cold War and National Liberation in Cuba, Chile, and Nicaragua

The story of African national liberation movements illustrates how European withdrawal led to struggles for power in African states, which were both civil wars and international Cold War contests. This was true also in Latin America, particularly in Cuba, Chile, and Nicaragua. Under agreements in 1903 and 1934, the United States leased a naval base at **Guantanamo Bay** and gained a dominant role in the Cuban economy. In 1952 **Fulgencio Batista** assumed dictatorial control. Immediately, guerrillas, led by communist-trained **Fidel Castro**, who was backed by the Soviet Union, led a successful overthrow of Batista and instituted a communist government in Cuba. From then on, Cuba became a Soviet satellite and a U.S. nemesis. In Chile, Marxist **Salvador Allende** took over in 1970 and nationalized the country's economy on the Soviet model. By 1973 there was a backlash against this regime and a military junta took over vowing to "exterminate Marxism." Repression followed and only in 1989 did Chile rid itself of military dictatorship. In Nicaragua, Marxist **Sandinista** guerrillas battled the U.S.-backed "elected" president General **Anastasio Somoza**. In 1979 Somoza fled, leading to increased U.S. intervention to prevent Marxist control of the country. Only in 1989 did national elections lead to the democratic election of Violeta Chamorro.

Summary

The end of European world hegemony occasioned by World Wars I and II led to national independence movements worldwide. Begun in World War I and completed after World War II, these movements took two forms. Decolonization movements were aimed at removing European rule and setting up independent states based on western models. National wars of liberation were aimed at removing European and U.S. rule and economic domination and setting up communist states. Both movements became intertwined with Cold War politics and social and political revolutions. In many cases, they failed to establish stable sovereign states or to fulfill revolutionary social and political aims.

The results of decolonization and wars of national liberation for world history have been an explosion of new nations, the dilution of western and communist influence, the rise of religious fundamentalism, and economic power blocs able to challenge western and communist political and economic hegemony. One of the quests of all new nations has been economic modernization because it is equated with power, wealth, and inclusion in the world system on an independent rather than dependent basis. Modernization has taken may forms in the twentieth century, some more successful than others in terms of economic prosperity and social and political justice.

CHAPTER 25
Modernization

CHRONOLOGY	Soviet Five-Year Plan and Collectivization of Agriculture (1928)	Privatization (1974)	Fourth World Conference on Women, China (1995)
	Great Leap Forward in China (1958)	Fall of the Berlin Wall (1989)	

TERMS	Less Developed Countries (LDCs)	multinational corporation	Sputnik I
	Five Year Plans	newly industrializing countries	glasnost
	collectivized	privatization	perestroika
	communizied	Green Revolution	Breshnev Doctrine
	Geat Leap Forward	deforestation	Solidarity
	Four Modernizations	Earth Summit	Bauhaus
	World Bank	sustainable development	AIDS
	International Monetary Fund	relativity	genocide
		quantum physics	

PEOPLE	Nikita Khrushchev	Nicolae Ceausescu	Henri Matisse
	Mikhail Gorbachev	Guglielmo Marconi	Pablo Picasso
	Max Planck	Sergei Eisenstein	Marc Chagall
	Albert Einstein	Leni Riefenstahl	Salvador Dali
	Ernest Rutherford	Louis Sullivan	Arnold Schoenberg
	Niels Bohr	Claude Monet	Frantz Fanon
	James Watson	Pierre-Auguste Renoir	Chinua Achebe
	F. H. C. Crick	Camille Pissarro	Alexander Solzhenitsyn
	Boris Yeltsin	Vincent van Gogh	Djilas
	Lech Walesa	Paul Cezanne	Rachel Carson

PLACES	Tanzania	South Korea	Chernobyl
	Mozambique	Singapore	Rio de Janeiro
	Taiwan		

CHAPTER 25

Modernization

Before the twentieth century, modernization was closely linked with the western concepts of secularism, industrialism, and liberalism. For many of the world's nations, however, the western model, which had taken centuries, seemed impossible, if not too slow, to follow. Increasingly, the road to modernization encompassed other models including the socialist and communist and variants in between. The drive to modernize ignored the costs. The nineteenth century costs seemed mostly to be social in nature, like poor living and working conditions. In the twentieth century, ecological costs, in the form of resource depletion and pollution predominate, particularly as more and more countries join the ranks of industrialized nations. In the twentieth century, secularism seems to have led to base materialism, and liberalism to unchecked behavior. By the end of the century, therefore, there has been a resurgence of religious fundamentalism and a call for moral responsibility as well as rights. For some, the answers to the modernization dilemma can be found in the very science and technology that had given birth to industrialism. For others, the answers are in conservation, preservation, and deindustrialization. Despite the problems, modernization has made the twentieth-century world wealthier, more highly educated, and more culturally integrated.

PATTERNS OF DEVELOPMENT—THE CAPITALIST AND SOCIALIST MODERNIZATION MODELS

The western model of modernization was capitalistic. According to this model, the nation-state with its constitutional and republican forms protected private property. This, in turn, spawned the commercial revolution. This revolution set in place the structures for material distribution, its profits created the capital for the Industrial Revolution, and its appetite for goods urged invention onward. However, many countries entering the industrial age had neither the political structures, commercial infrastructure, or capital for such a revolution. In fact, 80 percent of the world's population lives in "**less developed countries**" (LDCs). These LDCs are characterized by subsistence agriculture, shortage of capital, poor infrastructure, poor technology, an illiterate work force, and dependence on primary products. To remedy this situation, many LDCs began to imitate western political structures while borrowing heavily from abroad. The result was, in many cases, failure, as has been seen in the histories of Iran and others where modernization turned into reactionary revolution. In addition, huge debts were incurred destabilizing the monetary health of both industrialized and non-industrialized countries alike. These obstacles caused many countries to look for another model of modernization—a socialist or collective model in which the state owned the property and the capital earned from the agricultural sector became the capital used for industrialization. Often, in this model, the commercial stage was bypassed causing distribution and cost problems for socialist and communist systems.

The method of industrialization also became a question of philosophy and morality. Collective structures put the group ahead of the individual, while the western model continued to rely on individual participation and motive. The U.S.S.R. and China provide good models of the communist/socialist model, and Germany and Japan of the capitalist model. The attempts by the Third World or LDCs illustrate the difficulty of either the socialist or capitalist models to provide successful blueprints for modernization.

U.S.S.R.

In 1927, when Stalin came to power, he abandoned the NEP (New Economic Policy), which, in the consumer sectors, had allowed private trade and property. Unlike the czarist government that had borrowed heavily from abroad, racking up debts to build railroads and factories, debts that were later repudiated by the Bolsheviks, Stalin pressed for rapid industrialization in 1931 without western aid, which was, in any case, impossible, due to the Depression. He structured development on **Five-Year Plans**, in which all parts of the economy were owned, planned, and controlled by the state and communist bureaucrats. Food rationing was introduced, production of consumer goods curtailed and all private enterprise abolished. Heavy industry like steel and hydroelectric power took precedence. Beginning in 1929 Stalin **collectivized** agriculture in order to earn capital for industrialization. Farms were gathered into huge collectives in which peasants used their own implements and seed, but were provided with state tractors. Each collective was required to meet production quotas, and the profits after the state took its share were divided among peasants in the collective. At first, the peasants resisted, slaughtering their animals and burning their crops, creating a man-made famine of epic proportions. Grain output from 1928 to 1938 was identical to that in 1913. Instead of agricultural profit, the state had to invest heavily in agriculture. Collectivization was an economic failure but a political success as it created a subservient peasant class and assured grain for urban workers.

The industrial side of the planned economy was more successful. Soviet industry produced four times as much in 1937 as in 1928. The great industrial drive did not lead to a better living standard, however, because over one-third of the net income went to investment, bureaucracy, and the military. The communist model of modernization used state ownership and a planned economy. To this was added the idea of social paternalism—improved free education, health care, and pension provision. On the other hand, poor housing (in 1926 there were 2.7 per room and in 1940, 4.04 per room), a lack of motivation, and a climate of fear and terror accompanied the communist/socialist model. In order to make spectacular industrial gains, Russian women went to work, giving them opportunities, especially for education, but adding to their home responsibilities that men refused to share.

During World War II, all the trends put in place in the 1930s continued. In 1956, however, after Stalin's death, **Nikita Khrushchev** (1894–1974) at the Twentieth Party Congress denounced Stalin and promised liberalization or "destalinization." He pressed for increased agricultural output by opening up vast areas in Central Asia for cotton ("white gold") production, but the need for vast irrigation projects meant that only three out of five crops were productive. Meanwhile, the consumer sector, despite increased production, failed due to an underdeveloped distribution system.

China

China followed the same pattern as the U.S.S.R. except that, in the initial stages of modernization on the communist model, emphasis was on agricultural rather than industrial development. Chinese leaders realized that in a country of one billion people, the failure of agriculture would mean the failure of the state. Thus, all land in China was collectivized and then "**communized**," meaning farms worked like factories. Peasants became agricultural workers who received wages. State farms in which peasants worked in state fields and lived in barrack conditions were common in the 1950s. Family ties were destroyed. This co-called economic utopia turned out to be not only a social disaster but an economic disaster. Only efficient rationing prevented starvation. To mitigate agricultural failures, Mao in 1958 launched a program of industrialization called the **Great Leap Forward**. This program emphasized development of heavy industry, but on a small-scale model rather than in the big factories, as in Russia. Iron, for instance, was produced in backyard furnaces. As in Russia, the five-year plan system of development displayed spectacular statistical gains, mostly because, as in the U.S.S.R., the country had been so destroyed by the war that any gain was a leap forward. As in the U.S.S.R., heavy industry made spectacular gains at the expense of the consumer economy and was built on agricultural profits. Per capita consumption in the 1950s was only slightly higher than in 1937.

By the time Deng Xioping came to power in 1976, the clamor for a better standard of living forced him to liberalize the consumer economy. Deng and his supporters initiated a series of new policies embodied in a campaign called the **"Four Modernizations"**—agriculture, industry, science and technology, and national defense. Not unlike NEP in the U.S.S.R., Deng introduced capitalism into the consumer and agricultural economies. Peasants were encouraged to produce and "dare to the rich." The results were spectacular. Food production increased 50 percent between 1978 and 1982. Because the Chinese had historically had a strong commercial expertise and tradition, the Chinese economy grew at an annual rate of ten percent between 1978 and 1987, and the per capita income doubled in those years. Still, only three percent of the urban work force was employed by private enterprise in 1986 and industry remains largely state owned. As in the U.S.S.R., the people's economy basically runs on the black market. In both examples military expenditures are a heavy drain on the ability of the socialist model to make gains, and the concept of a planned economy has fallen short of the ideal as an efficient way to allocate resources and produce efficiently.

Japan

While the communist/socialist model made spectacular industrial gains and provided a safety net for old age, health, and educational services, it floundered in both the agricultural and consumer sectors, it failed to provide investment capital, and it created a police state. By contrast, Japan and West Germany rebuilt their economies on the capitalist model, paying attention to the consumer sector, building a commercial infrastructure of banks, law, and highways to facilitate it, allowing private property and profit, and obtaining investment capital from abroad. After Japan's surrender in 1945, American occupation

forces under General Douglas MacArthur introduced political reforms including democratization and demilitarization. With this in gear, American antitrust laws were introduced (later rescinded) to break up the zaibatsu firms, and Japan carved out, perhaps the most successful agricultural development program in twentieth-century history. The Japanese Diet bought up the land of absentee landlords who were generally well-educated elite. The elite were then forced to become managers of new factories. In this way, industrial production utilized a highly educated managerial workforce. Meanwhile, instead of redistributing land to peasants, the land was sold on generous terms creating a new class of entrepreneurial peasant farmers. The United States provided investment capital both in the form of grants and loans and by the creation of a stock market enticing private world investment.

The Japanese, meanwhile, blended their own traditions like family and state direction, with American-style capitalism. State policymakers and factory enterprises worked together. In 1952 U.S. occupation ended and between 1950 and 1970 real growth averaged 10 percent a year. The measures that aided the recovery in Japan were the same as in Europe—cheap labor, a freer international market, investment capital, an alliance between government and business, a respect for education, a disciplined family, and the loyalty of workers to factories because of job security, pensions, and so on. Only women failed to advance under these changes.

West Germany

West Germany's economic miracle was not unlike Japan's. Under the Marshall Plan, investment capital by the United States helped rebuild factories. Under Minister of Economy Ludwig Erhard, West Germany bet on the free market while maintaining the welfare network of Nazi Germany. West Germany also reformed its currency, became part of the international investment and consumer economy, and participated in the European Free Market. Freed from military expenditures, West Germany was soon supplying automobiles and electronics to the West, and its prosperity next to the communist East German backward economy was one of the major reasons why the Berlin Wall fell in 1989.

Third World Countries

Most Third World leaders saw rapid industrialization and "modernization" as the answer to their triple challenges of poverty, malnutrition, and disease, as well as legitimization for their rule. At first they chose the communist model of the "plan" as their approach in order to avoid dependence on the West for capital and markets, and to avoid the class conflict that capitalism seemed to engender. Socialism also seemed more compatible with village culture and historical conditions that emphasized communal sharing and equality. Following the communist model, land was taken from large landowners and divided among the peasantry, but the peasantry continued to farm it the old way and divided it among their families. Increasingly smaller plots producing smaller amounts of food kept agriculture at subsistence levels. Poverty was the result, not because they consumed too much but because they produced too little. Industry fared little better under the socialist model, floundering because of an inadequacy of statistics on which to base the plan and scarcity of knowledgeable personnel to implement it.

Tanzania

Tanzania under the leadership of Julius Nyerere provides an excellent example of the experience of LDCs with socialism. Tanzania began independence with a "mixed economy," part socialist, part capitalist; there was, for instance, an important private sector. By the mid-1970s, however, the state controlled 80 percent of medium and large-scale economic activity. In addition, the government sought to relocate by persuasion or coercion a scattered peasantry into compact villages (*ujaamas*) to which modern services could be more readily provided. While there have been some impressive results, the socioeconomic results have been dismal. By 1985 the country had a literacy rate of 85 percent (up from 15 percent at independence in 1961) and health care has improved. On the other hand, inefficiency, corruption, and lack of a commercial

infrastructure have created many unprofitable enterprises, some of which have been returned to private hands. In the countryside, peasants resisted the experiment in rural socialism because it disrupted traditional economic patterns that were rooted in family farms rather than communal enterprises. In the decade of 1974–1984 the country suffered a negative rate of per capita GNP growth. A recent assessment of experiments in African socialism by historian John Iliffe is as follows: "African governments have shown that they can prevent capitalism; they have not yet shown that they can replace it with anything else that will release their people's energies."

The Capitalist and Afro-Marxist Model

The failures of socialist experiments have caused many LDCs to either return to capitalism or move to rigorous Marxism-Leninism or "Afro-Marxism." Each approach has had problems. The western model encouraged borrowing investment capital from private sources, the **World Bank** (a U.N. agency whose purpose is to provide economic and technical assistance for development) or from the **International Monetary Fund** (an international bank funded by industrialized countries to make money available to countries having difficulty securing loans). This floundered too because sometimes as little as five cents of every dollar was used for development, the rest being eaten up by government bureaucracies and military spending. The other problem was massive foreign debt that reached crisis proportions after the OPEC oil cartel in 1973–1974 reduced supply, causing prices to soar. In 1982 Mexico, Brazil, and Argentina owed foreign banks and governments $600 billion and could not make the interest payments. Debt repudiation was avoided only when industrialized countries rewrote the debt. The other problem for Third World countries following the capitalist model, was the rise of the **multinational corporation**. While these corporations invested on behalf of the American or European corporations in third world countries, their profits flowed back to Europe and the United States. Their products cornered the local markets and they employed local people at low wages. In this way, local development was stunted. Soon LDCs were again tied to the international market only by the production of raw materials.

Mozambique

The Afro-Marxist experiments fared little better. In **Mozambique**, for instance, the government created a series of large state farms from abandoned Portuguese estates, and gave priority to the purchase of machinery for them. The result was the disruption of millions of family farms and the lack of incentives to produce for the market because there were few goods for consumption to buy like sugar, salt, soap, cloth, and bicycles. Thus, production for export and the ability to import ceased. Mozambique, like Cuba, became hostage to economic subsidization and political control of communists. Since the end of the Cold War, Mozambique has made adjustments to its plan, like courting western investment, including a contract with Exxon for oil exploration and signing a security pact with South Africa in order to regain valuable economic connections with its wealthy neighbor.

Rich and Poor Nations

Less developed countries continue to search for an effective method of modernization. The failures of both socialist and capitalist models to date have led many to the conclusion that there are "rich" countries and "poor" countries in the world and that they are divided geographically between "North and South." According to this theory, the rich industrialized countries of the United States, Europe, and Japan, all located in the Northern Hemisphere, gobble up most of the world's resources and produce most of the pollution, while the Third World countries suffer increasing poverty and famine, as in Ethiopia. In turn, this has led to the rise of drug trafficking as drugs are one of the few ways LDCs can create capital.

Others contend that this is a simplistic view and that, in fact, there are many different levels of modernization going on in the world. While two out of three of the world's desperately poor are women, women's banks, now in 50 countries, make small loans to women starting businesses. Scrap paper collectors, embroiderers, and sheep raisers borrow as little as $10 with 10 percent collateral. These banks are copied after the Grameen Bank, which has lent small sums to three million women in the villages of Bangladesh. Half of the Grameen loan recipients are now out of poverty. Countries like Brazil and South Africa, both in the Southern Hemisphere, are economic dynamos who have found their own paths to successful modernization.

Newly Industrializing Countries

In between the "less developed countries" and the industrialized countries are a group of states called "**newly industrializing countries**." These are countries like **Taiwan**, **South Korea**, and **Singapore**, which have made spectacular industrial gains by integrating their own traditions with aspects of both the communist and capitalist models. Newly industrializing countries are distinguished by their emphasis on education and their cohesive social and political structures. Education is regarded as a must, an important capital investment ensuring modernization process success. South Korea's literacy rate (99 percent) is the highest in the world. After the Korean War, huge industrial firms were created by a combination of government and active entrepreneurship. Exports were encouraged and the capital earned from these was fed into technology, technical training, and worker housing. Workers, as at Hyundai, responded in kind, putting in six-day work weeks and participating in almost worshipful ceremonies when a fleet of cars is shipped abroad. Taiwan has followed a similar course—rapid industrialization and high capital investment. Singapore, meanwhile has become not just a production center, but a center of merchant and individual capital for Southeast Asia. While Singapore has been ruled by a strong political leader, South Korea and Taiwan are also "newly democratizing countries" with naissant political parties and open elections.

Privatization

In general, in the last quarter of the twentieth century, world economic policies have veered away from state welfare programs and planned economies, and toward **privatization**. Privatization means relying less on government to meet people's needs and more on private institutions like the markerplace, family, and voluntary organizations. Privatization can take many forms, from "denationalization" (when a government divests itself of a company it owns), to delegation of some functions by contracting them out to private companies. While privatization is not new in world history (in 1492 Queen Isabella and King Ferdinand hired a private contractor to seek an alternative route to India!), it has exploded in the present era because of disillusionment with the inefficiences and economic and ecological costs associated with socialist economies and big government, and the renewed popularity of liberalism and freedom as enshrined in the concept of private property and ownership. In 1974 an unlikely leader, General Augusto Pinochet of Chile, launched privatization when he unilaterally freed prices, gutted labor laws, and auctioned off hundreds of companies. Then, in 1979 Margaret Thatcher, prime minister of England, privatized the British aviation and telecommunications industries. France, Japan, and New Zealand followed with their own large-scale privatization programs. When the Berlin Wall fell in 1989, an avalanche of privatization rolled across East Europe and the former Soviet Union. Even in the United States, the growth, inefficiencies, and inequities of state entitlement programs like social security and medicare as a proportion of state income, had led to calls for privatization of the health care and pensions systems. Privatization has become the one economic beacon around which hopes for improved standards of living and increased levels of freedom have rallied worldwide.

All in all, the twentieth century has seen an increasing drive on the part of all countries on the globe to modernize, largely because modernization equals a higher living standard and greater world power. A patchwork of approaches has emerged, and for many parts of the globe, has resulted in increasing prosperity rather than poverty. The greatest testament to this is the rise in world population. The drive to modernize, however, has put great stress on planet Earth in terms of resource utilization, environmental balance, and waste disposal.

ECOLOGICAL RESULTS—THE GREEN REVOLUTION, POLLUTION, AND RESOURCE DEPLETION

The Green Revolution

National elites in Third World countries had neglected agriculture in the 1950s and 1960s for a variety of reasons—their desire to industrialize, the need to squeeze agriculture to provide investment for industry, neglect by absentee landlords, ignorance and reluctance by peasants to change ways of farming, the food surplus of the United States, allowing importation of cheap grain (in 1967 the United States gave India one-fifth of its crop), and the political volatility of land reform. Population increase and famine, however, led to alarm and the **Green Revolution** (higher yields and more land in cultivation). In the United States and Europe, scientists developed new strains of corn and rice that enabled farmers to double their yields. The positive effects were most evident in China and Mexico. The negative effects were that the new strains needed more water and fertilizers, putting increased pressure on resources and the environment. Also, the new strains failed to be adopted in countries where there were large numbers of landless peasants and tenant farmers, as in the Philippines and Latin America. Furthermore, the increased population due to the new strains has meant land hunger and the chopping down of rain forests and the move into virgin lands by farmers. In Africa, the strain is evident in the constant pressure exerted by the population to limit game park land. The drive for more land has meant a gobbling up of the globe by farmers.

Deforestation and Pollution

Likewise, industrialism has produced unprecedented amounts and dangerous kinds of pollution and resource depletion. In rural areas, **deforestation** has become a major problem. India was all but denuded of trees. Industrialism, with its huge urban landscape has created mountains of garbage and waste material. Landfills have run out of space. Threats of nuclear pollution, as evidenced in the 1980s when the nuclear reactor at **Chernobyl** in the Ukraine experienced a meltdown, devastated immediate regions with radiation. In the Persian Gulf War in 1991, massive oil spills and oil fires blackened the atmosphere, and in 1989 a series of spills in Alaska, notably the running aground of the *Exxon Valdez,* severely damaged the shoreline and marine life. In Russia, diversion of tributaries to the Aral Sea to irrigate cotton fields has caused the drying up of the sea. In its wake is salt and mineral pollution. Increasing use of hydrocarbons has damaged the ozone layer, exposing planet Earth to dangerous levels of sunrays. World fossil fuel usage may one day lead to oil and gas scarcity.

To address such problems, the **Earth Summit**, or the U.N. Conference on Environment and Development, was held in **Rio de Janeiro**. There, 178 nations reached accords on "**sustainable development**," reconciling economic needs with environmental responsibility. In addition, the capitalist, industrialized world has begun to see resource depletion and pollution as a cost factor of doing business. This has caused it to develop pollution control and resource preservation strategies. The lumber business in the United States, for instance, is dominated by "tree farms," in which forests are replanted as they are depleted. For many, science and technology have been the perpetrator of the very assault on planet Earth. For others, science and technology provide the keys for solving environmental and ecological problems.

SCIENCE AND TECHNOLOGY

Since the Renaissance, the West, and then the world, has tended to equate advancement with the world of science. The liberal view was that the patterns of nature could be discovered, and that their balance and symmetry, once discovered, could be applied to all sorts of human problems from politics to social order. This view of scientific predictability has been shattered in the twentieth century by the new science, primarily chaos theories of the universe and quantum physics. The optimism of the eighteenth and nineteenth centuries has given way to skepticism and pessimism of the twentieth century.

Quantum Physics

To Newton, the world was a billiard ball with everything determined by the initial forces of the universe. These were, in turn, determined by discernible rules of behavior. God was the supreme clockmaker and man ticked right along with the rest of creation. The first challenge to this notion came with the work in radiation of German physicist **Max Planck** (1858–1947). He showed that subatomic energy is emitted in uneven little spurts called "quanta" and not in a steady stream. His discovery called into question the old sharp distinction between matter and energy and the notion that atoms are stable basic building blocks of nature. **Albert Einstein** went a step further, taking Newtonian laws and explaining what happened to them at the speed of light. This led to the idea of **relativity**, the notion that time and space are not absolute. The 1920s opened the "heroic age of physics," a phrase coined by **Ernest Rutherford** (1871–1937), who showed that the atom could be split. Subsequently, physicist **Niels Bohr** held that within the atom properties are "massless" and that particles within this world of **quantum physics** (quantum meaning quantity or discrete amount with the connotation of smaller, rather than subatomic, particles— hence our metaphor, quantum leap, meaning sudden jump from one level to another without the usual process of climbing through the steps) move randomly rather than predictably. There is no quantum world, he wrote, only "an abstract quantum description. . . ." According to this theory, the world changes just by looking at it and the Big Bang was a random event. Besides physics, there have been significant discoveries in the world of biology, the most important being in the field of genetics. In 1953 **James Watson** and **F. H. C. Crick** developed a model for the DNA molecule that carries genetic heritage. Since then, DNA has been used to track diseases, manipulate plant biology, and find remedies for illness.

These scientific theories have spilled over into other aspects of life, giving the modern world a sense of uncertainty and lack of objective reality. Moral certainties have vanished, and in their place is cultural relativity. Historians think about complex systems rather than isolated nations. The theory of evolution appears less linear and more random. Chaos is accepted as the order of things. Randomness, thinglessness, and interconnectedness have become realities. The twenty-first century generation accepts the possibility of many jobs and the uncertainty of employment, and is prepared for constant change. The psychology of flux has become permanent and the business of reeducation constant. The new science has led to technologies which have transformed global communication.

New Technologies

The two most important technologies of the twentieth century are the rocket and the computer. Rocket technology was developed by the Germans during World War II, and in 1957 the Russians put the first satellite in space, **Sputnik I**. In 1961 they put the first man in space. The United States then initiated a crash program devoted to space research, putting the first man on the moon in 1969. While this lacked tangible benefits, it caused breakthroughs, in photography and communications. Satellites have become an everyday occurrence, used for everything from cellular phones to navigation. The space program also led the drive toward miniaturization and computerization. The computer is undoubtedly the greatest technological offshoot of the move into space. The computational needs of the military in World War II led to the construction of the first successful general-purpose computer, "Mark I," in 1944. Subsequently used to guide space travel and keep records, it is the equivalent to the writing revolution of the first millennium B.C.E. and the printing revolution of the first millennium C.E. As an extension of memory and a machine of numeracy, computers have transformed business, education, medicine, electronics, record keeping, vehicle operation, travel, and communications.

The world wars of the first half of the twentieth century tended to discredit liberalism, for the liberal western nations betrayed liberalism when they imperialized and then fought among themselves over their empire. When the world wars ended, the new nations looked for other models. The ideology of communism and the power of the Soviet Union and China to sway these new nations to follow their course of modernization, led to some social successes, but to economic, environmental, and political failures. By the last decade of the twentieth century, liberalism's attention to civil rights and freedom, its ability to provide a rich living style for the common man, and its better record with respect to environmental preservation, caused the collapse of communism and the worldwide shift to liberalism.

THE TRIUMPH OF LIBERALISM

Gorbachev's Reforms

In the face of economic collapse due to decades of heavy defense spending and an inefficient consumer economy, Russian leader Mikhail Gorbachev in 1985 launched a series of reforms. In his program of "**glasnost**," or openness, he attempted to gain new political allies among the intellectual class and to explore new solutions to Soviet problems. In his program of "**perestroika**," or economic restructuring, he encouraged private investment and growth of the consumer economy. In his program of democratization, he hoped to revitalize the Congress of People's Deputies by electing a group of progressive representatives to replace the old class of privileged communist deputies who were resistant to change. In foreign affairs Gorbachev brought "new political thinking" to the field. He withdrew Soviet troops from Afghanistan, encouraged reform movements in Poland and Hungary, and sought to reduce East-West tensions. He denounced the **Breshnev Doctrine**, which had proclaimed the right of the Soviet Union and its allies to intervene at will in eastern Europe.

Fall of Gorbachev

Gorbachev's reform program soon got out of hand. Openness gave way to free speech and expression, restructuring gave way to free enterprise, and democratization to calls for greater national autonomy on the part of the republics that made up the U.S.S.R. In 1990 Russian politicians in the newly elected Parliament, joined by a strong Russian environmental movement, independence-minded republics, and the communist old guard, challenged Gorbachev. At the communist party congress in July, 1990, a group of desperate hardliners tried to seize control, but Gorbachev was rescued by the progressives. Now beholdened to them, he watched while an anticommunist and nationalist revolution swept Russia. The Soviet Union was dissolved and independence of all republics proclaimed. Gorbachev's failure to renounce communism and to follow, rather than to lead the revolution led to his downfall and his replacement by **Boris Yeltsin**. Under Yeltsin, Russian and other republics are in the process of implementing a new political and economic structure for Russia along western liberal lines.

Eastern Europe

In a world of instant communication, events in Russia reverberated worldwide. In 1989 in eastern Europe, liberal revolutions overturned existing communist regimes and led to the formation of new states dedicated to democratic elections, human rights, and national rejuvenation. **Solidarity**, the Polish democratic movement that represented the workers, Catholicism, and nationalists, led the way. Profiting from Gorbachev's lenient attitude, Solidarity pressed for free elections, and in 1989 it won every single contested seat. In August, Solidarity's leader, **Lech Walesa**, was sworn in as the first noncommunist leader in eastern Europe since Stalin. Hungary followed Poland. In 1989 the communist party renounced one-party rule, scheduled free elections, began welcoming western investment, and moved toward multiparty democracy. Hungarians gleefully opened the Iron Curtain separating Hungary, and Austria and East Germany. East German refugees flowed in on the way to prosperous West Germany. Huge candlelight demonstrations brought revolution in East Berlin. People danced for joy on the Berlin Wall as it came tumbling down. In July, 1990, German chancellor Kohl and Gorbachev removed the last obstacles to German reunification. Communism died in Czechoslovakia in December, 1989, when, in ten short days, communist bosses were ousted. In Romania, the revolution was violent and bloody. Communist dictator, **Nicolae Ceausescu**, ordered ruthless security, but his forces were defeated and a coalitions government emerged. With the triumph of liberalism in East Europe and Russia, the Cold War ended.

The Middle East

The events in Russia and East Europe soon affected other parts of the world. With no support from the Soviet Union or the United States, leaders in the Middle East are moving toward a political settlement of the Israeli and Palestinian problems. Cuba holds out against abandonment of communism despite desperate effects of the end of Soviet subsidization. South Africa has moved toward liberal democratic black rule. Unfortunately, liberalism has also unleashed a series of new nationalist clashes as in Yugoslavia and Armenia. Still, as the world moves into the twenty-first century, the demands of people worldwide for more participation in government, increased civil rights, and improved economic conditions have triumphed.

Summary

Global modernization has changed society and culture. The simplicity of the capitalist and socialist models have given way to the complexity of differing routes to secularism, industrialism, and liberalism. Global ecological pressures have fostered protest and countercultures as well-reasoned solutions. Science and technology have facilitated mass movement, necessitated longer and more expensive educational experiences, and changed the population curve. The quest for modernity has both homogenized and particularized global society.

SOCIETY AND CULTURE

Race, Ethnicity, and Gender

In the twentieth century, global mobility and communication has led to a great mixing of races, ethnic groups, and genders. Living, working, and traveling side by side, people have not only become more aware of the differences that separate them, but have had the means at their disposal to unite under a common banner or cause. Striving for justice and equality has involved race, ethnic and gender groups, rather than classes of people, and their struggles have resulted in major advances. Among the racial groups that have been discriminated against are Blacks, Jews, and Asians. All three groups have found increasing acceptance and legal protection in many areas of the world. All groups have increased their economic capabilities.

The twentieth century has also witnessed the increasing power of ethnic groups to promote their rights within nation-states and in many cases to destroy nation-states. The multiplicity of ethnic groups in Yugoslavia, the former Soviet Union, and in Africa has led to bloody wars as in Bosnia, Georgia (in the former Soviet Union), and South Africa. The more homogenized world culture has become, the more virulent has become ethnicity as a means of identity and a safeguard of minority rights.

More than any other event, the twentieth-century wars elevated the position of women especially in the workplace. As more women took the place of men in the factories, they began asserting their rights. Birth control also played a part as women could gain control over their position as mothers and employees. Educational levels for women worldwide have risen as have the appearance of women in political and leadership positions. A simulation study by the World Bank of 72 countries in 1995 shows that, if all factors were held constant, doubling female secondary school enrollments in 1975 would have reduced average fertility rates in 1988 from 5.3 to 3.9 children and lowered births by almost 30 percent. At the Fourth World Conference on Women held in 1995 in Beijing, 45,000 women participants from 189 countries made clear gains by reaching a consensus platform which stated that women's rights are human rights.

Mass Media, Culture, Education, and Metropolis

The radio, movies, and television, all inventions of the twentieth century, have made it possible for people around the globe to interact on a world scale. Radio became possible with the transatlantic "wireless" communication of **Guglielmo Marconi** (1874–1937) in 1901 and the development of the vacuum tube in 1904. Only after 1920 did every major western country establish national broadcasting networks. By the late 1930s, more than three out of every four households in both democratic Great Britain and dictatorial Germany had at least one radio. Roosevelt's "Fireside Chats" and Hitler's speeches informed the masses who sat huddled around them. The transistor radio has penetrated the most isolated hamlets of the Third World and today no automobile is without it. The continued development of the radio in the form of "Walkmans" makes radio listening a worldwide phenomena.

The second communications revolution—the visual one—in the form of movies and television has penetrated the deepest corners of the earth. The camera was invented in the mid-nineteenth century and the movie camera in the early twentieth century. **Sergei Eisenstein** in Russia was the first to use the camera as a device to tell a story rather than record events. His epic film, *Potemkin,* gave all future filmmakers the techniques necessary to turn the camera into an art form. **Leni Riefenstahl**, in her masterpiece documentary, *The Triumph of the Will,* used the camera as an instrument of Nazi propaganda. Movies remain one of the great instruments of mass media. Today, a movie made in any country of the world is apt to be seen around the world. Television, invented during World War II has become the major entertainment and information medium of world society.

The radio, movies, television, travel, and a world market have created a world culture. The popularity of western fads, from blue jeans to

Reeboks, and popular music have created a culture, especially among the younger generation, that is generic. It is possible to travel to most of the world's cities today and buy a McDonald's hamburger or stay in a Hilton Hotel. One of the most important aspects of this culture has been education. The importance of "human capital" and faith in "book learning" has spread rapidly to the world's masses for whom education principally means jobs. Increasingly, knowing English has been the key to economic and social improvement. Students from developing countries studying in the United States are apt to pursue professions like engineering and medicine, giving them skills directly applicable to improving the standard of living in their home countries. Unfortunately, many students studying abroad never return home. Rather, they take jobs in whatever country offers them the best opportunities for professional advancement, education for their children, and better standards of living. This "brain drain" has severely hampered efforts in the less developed countries to improve conditions in their countries.

Megalopolis

Modernization has led to mass movement to cities where job opportunities, urban culture, and social safety networks attract many disadvantaged. The cities of the Third World expanded at an astonishing pace after World War II. Many doubled and some even tripled in size in a single decade. In 1920 three out of every four of the world's urban inhabitants lived in Europe and North America. By 1990, 60 percent of the planet's city dwellers lived in the cities of the Third World. Gigantic "super cities" of two to ten million people arose. Mexico City, for example, grew from 3 million in 1950 to 12 million in 1975 and it could possibly have a staggering 31 million by the year 2000. In the year 2000, the world could have 25 "megalopolises" with more than 10 million people. More than half of all urban growth has been due to rural migration, and more than half of all industrial jobs in Mexico have been concentrated in Mexico City. The attraction of cities has not only been for jobs, but for educational opportunities, medical care,

amenities like a ready water supply (rural women spend much of their time carrying water and grinding grain), and modern cultural amusements. In many cases, men migrated to cities first, leaving women to become unprecedentedly self-reliant and independent. Surging urban population has created overcrowding, shantytowns, crime, unemployment, drug trafficking, and pollution. However bad this life may be, the rush to the cities has continued unabated. In today's world the cultural differences between urban and rural dwellers are greater than between people of different countries. Today's world resembles Hellenistic times when the mixing of cultures in urban settings has produced a world culture.

Art, Protest, and Counterculture

Rapid change, insecurities, the unseen world of the atom, and cross-cultural pollination have been reflected in twentieth-century art. Modernism in art, architecture, and music has been marked by rejection of old forms, and constant experimentation and a search for new kinds of expression.

Architecture

Modern architecture has revolved around the principle of "functionalism." Believing that buildings, like industrial products, should be useful, designers have used less ornamentation and found beauty and esthetics in clean lines and new materials. Steel and concrete allowed for the development of the skyscraper, which was invented by **Louis Sullivan** and his schools of architects. His student, **Frank Lloyd Wright**, built a series of truly modern houses featuring low lines and attentive to the surrounding environment. During the 1920s an interdisciplinary group called the **Bauhaus** worked to merge the schools of fine and applied arts with architecture. Their work culminated in buildings using steel frame and glass walls.

Visual Art

In painting, the realism and social commentary of late nineteenth-century art gave way to impressionism. **Claude Monet, Pierre-Auguste Renoir,** and **Camille Pissarro** tried to capture the momentary overall feeling or impression in their work. Modern art grew out of a revolt against this. The "Postimpressionists" or "Expressionists" experimented with styles that allowed them to depict worlds other than the visible world of fact. **Vincent van Gogh** in *The Starry Night,* for instance, painted the vision of his mind's eye—flaming cypress trees, exploding stars, and a comet-like Milky Way—a great cosmic vision. Fascination with form also was part of the Expressionist experiment. **Paul Cézanne** told a young painter, "You must see in nature the cylinder, the sphere, and the cone." Expressionism in the hands of painters like **Henri Matisse** became increasingly abstract and nonrepresentational. In the hands of **Pablo Picasso**, **Marc Chagal**, and **Salvador Dali**, expressionism turned into surrealism, in which painters depicted the fantastic world of wild dreams and complex symbols where watches melted and giant metronomes beat time in alien landscapes.

Music

The same kind of experimentation also occurred in ballet and music. Led by Viennese composer **Arnold Schoenberg**, traditional harmony and tonality was abandoned in favor of abstract mathematical patterns or "tone rows." The influence of African music turned the music and format of ballet into pulsating rhythms representational of earth rites and mystical religious experience. African music was also the inspiration for popular music forms like jazz and rock.

Literature

The homogenization, westernization, and mechanization of twentieth-century culture repulsed many and led to protest and countercultures. In the Third World, for instance, writers like **Frantz Fanon** in *The Wretched of the Earth,* and **Chinua Achebe** in *Things Fall Apart* argued that real independence would come only with a total rejection of western values. The "wretched," according to Fanon, were the colonized who must purge themselves not only of the colonizers but of the local collaborators, the "white men with black faces." Achebe's message was that African people must rediscover their own culture, its depth, volume, and beauty. In

communist areas of the world, protest literature often went underground to escape totalitarian authorities. In the Soviet Union, for instance, writers like **Alexander Solzhenitsyn** opened up the secrets of the slave labor camps and psychological torture in books like *One Day in the Life of Ivan Denisovitch* and *Cancer Ward.* Yugoslav writer **Djilas** in *The New Class* unmasked the ideological failures of communism like the growth of new bureaucracies and party corruption. Environmental protest also emerged, as in **Rachel Carson**'s *The Silent Spring.* Among the world's youth, protest against violence, war, and dogmatisms of all types is reflected in the 1960s move to long hair, drugs, casual and unkempt dress styles and music, as in that of the "Beatles."

Peace Movements and Religious Fundamentalism

While there has been no nuclear war in the twentieth century, violence has continued. The holocausts in Cambodia, Germany, and other countries, and the myriads of small wars, like the Persian Gulf conflict in which 100,000 Iraqis were killed, has led to a Peace Movement and groups like Amnesty International, the world watchdog of human rights. The reaction to industrialism, consumerism, and moral relativism has spawned a religious revival. Christian evangelicalism and the extensive travels of Pope John Paul II exemplify this in the Christian world. Islamic fundamentalism in the form of strict adherence to Koranic custom and "Islamic Republics," as in Iran, have tried to turn back the clock. Along with religious revivalism has come the search for the mystical experience. The popularity of figures like the Dalai Lama and of eastern religions like Hindusim and Buddhism have replaced faith in endless progress and secularism.

POPULATION AND MIGRATION

Population

For many, the most disturbing trend in twentieth-century world history has been the dramatic increase in world population. While population growth has slowed markedly or even topped out in the industrialized world, it has exploded in the Third World. This is due to better health care, nutrition, foreign aid, and the unpopularity and inaccessibility of birth control programs. In 1985 Africa led the world with a population growth of 3.2 percent per year, enough to double the continent's numbers in only 22 years. The world's population in 1900 was 1.6 billion; in 1987 it was 5 billion, and it is not expected to stabilize until the mid-twenty-first century, when it will have reached 10 to 12 billion. While this puts tremendous stress on the world's resources, it is instructive to realize that, even at 11 billion, the earth would not be as populated as Europe is today. Mandated population control programs have been controversial and in many cases, failures. Indira Gandhi's compulsory sterilization and the objection to the one-child family in China illustrate both cultural and religious resistance to forced family planning. The most promising aspect of population control is the statistical evidence that suggests that industrialization and modernization slows population growth.

Migration

Population pressures, poverty, lack of economic opportunity, and political turmoil have caused major migration movements in the twentieth century. Many of these migrants have been refugees or people seeking sanctuary abroad from wars and civil strife. The number of refugees has grown from 2.5 million in 1970 to 7.5 million in 1980 and 15 million in 1990. The greatest concentration is in Pakistan where more than three million Afghans have taken refuge from the war in that country. The situation in the Horn of Africa is numerically less dramatic but in human terms far worse. There are more than two million refugees as a result of migrations between Ethiopia, Sudan, and Somalia. After the Vietnam War in 1973, over 1.5 million people fled to the West. In addition to people, disease has traveled across borders, most principally **AIDS**, which has now spread from Africa to many other parts of the world.

Genocide

Another aspect of migration is the twentieth-century phenomenon of **genocide**. The word genocide first appeared in a 1944 book by Phael Lemkin, a Polish-born law professor and Jew who lost 49 family members in the Holocaust. He defined genocide as any effort to destroy a national, ethnic, racial, or religious group. Psychologists have found the reason for genocide in the turmoil, change, and uncertainty of the twentieth century. These insecurities and frustrations, they say, have led to the impulse to blame or find scapegoats. Others explain genocide in terms of the quest for fulfillment of political and nationalist aspirations. The early twentieth century witnessed a number of genocides from the Turkish disposal of 1.5 million Armenians in 1915 to Stalin's purges in the 1930s. In 1948 the United Nations approved Lemkin's Genocide Convention, a treaty that has been signed by 120 countries. Still, genocide goes on from China's Cultural Revolution (1966–1976, 1.5 million), Cambodia's killing fields (1975–1979, 1.7 million), Guatemala (1980–1984, 100,000), Iraq's gassing of the Kurds (1987–1988, 100,000), the Serb "ethnic cleansing" in Yugoslavia (1992, 1 million Bosnians), and the Rwandan massacres (1994, 500,000). Such genocide has sent millions of people fleeing their countries in migrations of epic proportions.

Twentieth-century society and culture has been noted for its international character, its rapid tempo of change and propensity for experimentation, and its mass movements of people and communications technologies. Tremendous cultural and social mixing reminds us of other ages in world history like the Hellenistic or age of expanding empires when cultural blending rather than construction of classical forms has provided the major historical narrative. Historians have reflected this in their attention to world history and to its propensity to concentrate on cross-cultural encounter, trade, and world themes.

UNIT REVIEW

Cross-Regional Developments

Almost all developments in the twentieth century have been cross-regional because this century has been characterized above all by being a global age. The communications revolution has made what happens in one area instantly knowable in all other areas of the globe. Thus, this century has seen the development of a global economy, monetary system, trade, and regional economic zones. Migrations have flowed from one country to another, one region to another, one continent to another, and one hemisphere to another. Concern about environmental problems from pollution to disappearance of rain forests are global concerns. Rapid scientific and technological change, from weaponry and nuclear proliferation to television and computers, leapfrog across borders and regions. The twentieth century has seen the emergence of a global culture in which McDonald's hamburgers are as common in China as Chinese food is in America. This century has witnessed the spread of ideologies like communism and the wholescale quest for modernization. Across regions the power of women and youth has risen to unprecedented heights as illustrated by the 1995 International Conference on Women. Decolonization and wars of national liberation occurred over large parts of the globe after World War II, establishing many new nations, but the nation-state has also been weakened in the face of multinational corporations, international organizations, regional economic groupings, and racial and ethnic mixing. The entire twentieth century story has been cross-regional.

Legacies

The legacies of the twentieth century are almost all living history and part of our living experience. They include:

- a half-century or more of world war, which led to the development of fearsome new weapons like the airplane, submarine, atomic and nuclear bomb, poison gas, and guided missiles, and to wars of weapons rather than men and economies over which governments gained increasing control and spent enormous sums;
- a Cold War between ideological and political adversaries which led to a paralyzing arms buildup and support of small conflicts worldwide;
- experiments with totalitarian government, which led to a legacy of terror and human holocaust;
- world economic depression, which led to the accommodation of capitalism with welfare state socialism;
- the end of European colonialism and the rise of a myriad of new nations in Africa and Asia;
- a quest for modernization that has largely disregarded the environment and human spiritual yearnings;
- the triumph of liberalism over communism;
- population increases that have strained planetary resources and environmental health, and created a world of megalopolises;
- homogenization of world culture despite ethnic and national yearnings;
- amazing scientific and technological advances like DNA, space travel, and the computer which have redefined geographical, social, and intellectual frontiers; and

- modern art, architecture, and literature reflective experimentation and the unseen world of math and science.

The twentieth century has completed one of the human narratives addressed in Chapter One—The Peopling of the Globe. The twenty-first century may well see the peopling of the galaxy.

Documents

THE HORRORS OF TRENCH WARFARE

After a few hours we are finished with the barbed wire. But there is still some time before the trucks return for us. Most of us lie down to sleep. . . .
Then it begins in earnest. Bombardment. . . . Green rockets shoot up the sky line. Barrage. The mud flies high, fragments whizz past.. . .
Not a moment too soon. The dark goes mad. The flames of the explosions light up the graveyard. There is no escape anywhere. . . .
The earth bursts before us. It rains clods. My sleeve is torn away by a splinter. Now a crack on the skull. . . .
I open my eyes. My fingers grasp a sleeve, an arm. A wounded man? I yell to him—no answer. A dead man. Now I remember that we are lying in a graveyard. But the shelling is stronger than any other thought so I merely crawl deeper into the coffin. It should protect me. . . .
Cautiously, I breathe through the gas mask. The gas still creeps over the ground and sinks into the hollows. . . .

In 1929 a former German soldier, Erich Maria Remarque, wrote a novel titled *All Quiet on the Western Front.* This book remains the classic description of the horrors of trench warfare on the Western Front during World War I. Written through the eyes of a young German soldier, it has become the story of all soldiers in an age of total war.

THE BALFOUR DECLARATION

His Majesty's Government views with favor the establishment in Palestine of a National Home for the Jewish People, and will use their best endeavors to facilitate the achievement of this object, it being clearly understood that nothing shall be done which may prejudice the civil and religious rights of existing non-Jewish communities in Palestine, or the rights and political status enjoyed by Jews in any other country.

In November, 1917, the British foreign secretary issued the Balfour Declaration stating Britain's intention to provide a homeland for the Jews in Palestine after World War I. As a secret wartime agreement, it was intended to rally as many countries as possible to the Allied side. A careful reading of the document reveals contradictory promises to both Jews and Palestinians. It has been the subject of passionate debate and many wars ever since. Only in 1995 did Jews and Palestinians come to some agreement about rule of this area of the world.

THE BATTLE OF BRITAIN

What General Weygand called the "Battle of France" is over. I expect that the battle of Britain is about to begin. Upon this battle depends the survival of Christian civilization. Upon it depends our own British life and the long continuity of our institutions and our Empire. The whole fury and might of the enemy must very soon be turned on us. Hitler knows that he will have to break us in this island or lose the war. If we can stand up to him all Europe may be free, and the life of the world may move forward into broad, sunlit uplands; but if we fail then the whole world, including the United States, and all that we have known and cared for, will sink into the abyss of a new dark age made more sinister, and perhaps more prolonged, by the lights of perverted science. Let us therefore brace ourselves to our duty and so bear ourselves that if the British Commonwealth and Empire lasts for a thousand years men will say, "This was their finest hour."

Winston Churchill became the prime minister of Great Britain in May, 1940. At this time, Soviet Russia was allied with Hitler, France was about to fall to German invaders, and the United States was not in the war. Britain stood alone against Fascist tyranny, which looked like it might sweep Europe and the world. Churchill's eloquent language and steadfastness helped Britain survive. Britain provided the necessary European bastion of defense prior to United States' entry into the war. After the Battle of Britain was won, Churchill gave another memorable speech in which he saluted the British airmen. He said, "Never in the field of human conflict was so much owed by so many to so few."

THE LAW FOR PROTECTION OF GERMAN BLOOD AND GERMAN HONOR

Clearly realizing that the purity of the German blood is the prerequisite for perpetuating the German people, and inspired by an inflexible determination to secure the existence of the German nation for all time to come, the Reichstag has unanimously passed the following law. . . .

1. Marriage between Jews and citizens of German or kindred stock are prohibited. . . .

3. Jews shall not employ in their household female citizens of German or kindred stock under 45 years of age.

4. Jews shall not hoist the Reich or national flag nor display the Reich colors.

Issued September 15, 1935, this law was the beginning of Jewish genocide at the hands of the Nazis. Based on Hitler's theory of a superior Aryan (German) race, put into practice, it lead to discrimination, then confiscation of property, exploitation of Jewish labor, and finally execution as the "final solution" to the so-called "Jewish Problem."

TRUMAN ANNOUNCES THE BOMBING OF HIROSHIMA

Sixteen hours ago an American airplane dropped one bomb on Hiroshima, an important Japanese Army base. That bomb had more power than 20,000 tons of T.N.T. It had more than two thousand times the blast power of the British "Grand Slam" which is the largest bomb ever yet used in the history of warfare. . . .

It is an atomic bomb. It is a harnessing of the power of the universe. The force from which the sun draws its power has been loosed against those who brought war to the Far East. . . .

Let there be no mistake; we shall completely destroy Japan's power to make war.

It was to spare the Japanese people from utter destruction that the ultimatum of July 26 was issued at Potsdam. Their leaders promptly rejected that ultimatum. If they do not now accept our terms, they may expect a rain of ruin from the air . . .

The fact that we can release atomic energy ushers in a new era in man's understanding of nature's forces. Atomic energy may in the future supplement the power that now comes from coal, oil, and falling water . . .

I shall recommend that the Congress of the United States consider promptly the establishment of an appropriate commission to control the production and use of atomic power within the United States. I shall give further consideration and make further recommendations to the Congress as to how atomic power can become a powerful and forceful influence towards the maintenance of world peace.

On August 6, 1945, the United States dropped an atomic bomb on Hiroshima, obliterating the city and killing over 78,000 civilians. Russia declared war on August 8 and swept into Manchuria. The next day, a second bomb was dropped on Nagasaki. On August 15 Emperor Hirohito announced Japanese surrender. Hiroshima ushered in the Atomic Age and the Cold War. It has been controversial ever since. Some equate it with German atrocities against the Jews; others defend it on the basis that it saved lives by ending the war quickly. Truman seemed well aware of its awesome power if not the historical ramifications.

THE VIETNAM DECLARATION OF INDEPENDENCE

"All men are created equal.". . . This immortal statement was made in the Declaration of Independence of the United States of America in 1776. . . . The Declaration of the French Revolution made in 1791 on the Rights of Man and the Citizen also states: "All men are born free and with equal rights, . . . "

Nevertheless, for more than eighty years, the French imperialists, abusing the standard of Libery, Equality, and Fraternity, have violated our Fatherland and oppressed our fellow-citizens. They have acted contrary to the ideals of humanity and justice.

In the field of politics, they have deprived our people of every democratic liberty. . . .

In the autumn of 1940 when the Japanese Fascists violated Indochina's territory to establish new bases in their fight against the Allies, the French imperialists went down on their bended knees and handed over our country to them.

Thus, from that date, our people were subjected to the double yoke of the French and Japanese. . . .

For these reasons, we, members of the Provisional Government of the Democratic Republic of Vietnam, solemnly declare to the world that Vietnam has the right to be a free and independent country—and in fact is so already. The entire Vietnamese people are determined to mobilize all their physical and mental strength, to sacrifice their lives and property in order to safeguard their independence and liberty.

One of the many results of World War II was the stirring of independence movements in former colonies. The words and aspirations of nationalist leaders echo those of the other great liberal revolutions of modern times. On September 2, 1945, Ho Chi Minh, leader of the Vietminh or Vietnamese Army, issued this declaration of independence. While a trained communist, his words seem more familiar to the world of democracy than to that of communism.

THE IRON CURTAIN

From Stettin in the Baltic to Trieste in the Adriatic, an iron curtain has descended across the continent. Behind that line lie all the captitals of the ancient states of Central and Eastern Europe. Warsaw, Berlin, Prague, Vienna, Budapest, Belgrade, Bucharest, and Sophia. All these famous cities and the populations around them lie in the Soviet sphere, and all are subject, in one form or another, not only to Soviet influence but to a very high and, in many cases, increasing measure of control from Moscow. . . .

Whatever conclusions may be drawn from these facts—and facts they are—this is certainly not the Liberated Europe we fought to build up. Nor is it one which contains the essentials of permanent peace. . . .

Last time I saw it all coming, and cried aloud to my fellow countrymen and to the world, but no one paid any attention. . . .

We surely must not let that happen again.

While on a visit to the United States in 1946, Winston Churchill warned the world of coming dictatorship and war. Unlike before World War II, when he was ignored, this time the world listened. Immediately the West set in place a number of measures to prevent more nations from becoming communist by setting up a bulwark of containment. Thus began the Cold War.

THE SAYINGS OF MAO TSE-TUNG

It is up to us to organize the people. As for the reactionaries in China, it is up to us to organize the people to overthrow them. . . .

Just as there is not a single thing in the world without a dual nature (this is the law of the unity of opposites), so imperialism and all reactionaries have a dual nature—they are real tigers and paper tigers at the same time. . . . On the one hand, they were real tigers; they devoured people, devoured people by the millions and tens of millions. . . before the victory in 1949. Look! Were these not tigers, dead tigers, iron tigers, real tigers? But in the end they changed into paper tigers, dead tigers, bean-curd tigers. . . .

Without a people's army the people have nothing. . . .

We should be modest and prudent, guard against arrogance and rashness, and serve the Chinese people heart and soul. . .

With the increasing bankruptcy of the rural economy in recent years, the basis for men's domination over women has already been undermined. With the rise of the peasant movement, the women in many places have now begun to organize rural women's associations; the opportunity has come for them to lift up their heads, and the authority of the husband is getting shakier every day. In a word, the whole feudal-patriarchal ideology and system is tottering with the growth of the peasants' power. . .

Since the key cities have long been occupied by the powerful imperialists and their reactionary Chinese allies, it is imperative for the revolutionary ranks to turn the backward villages into advanced consolidated base areas, . . . bastions of the revolution from which to fight their vicious enemies.

The leader of the Communist Chinese Revolution in 1949 was Mao Tse-Tung (1893–1976). In his plans for a new China, he used Marxist-Leninst ideas of class struggle, but he adapted them to fit the Chinese situation. For instance, he placed the revolution in the countryside rather than the city, he talked in Chinese terms emphasizing Chinese complementary dualism and proper conduct. At the same time, he envisioned a new world and liberal changes for women. His sayings have been collected in a little handbook widely read in the 1960s and 1970s, *The Little Red Book.*

BLACK POWER

The demand for Africanization is made by the black people and means a replacement by them of those of different origin. Despite the wider meaning than the term African has acquired today, the Blacks are still at the bottom of every ladder and identify themselves completely and practically with the struggle for change. To ask the indigenous Africans to forget the agony of their past is to ask them to ignore the lesson that their experience has taught them. Asians and Europeans are crying in Tanganyika today for non-racial parties, but just how practical is this? Those non-racial parties which have been formed in Tanganyika have never succeeded, for they never aimed at emancipating the African, but only at deluding him into satisfaction with the lowest rung. It is the experience of the present that will constitute African reaction in the future; and the place that the Asian and the European will build for themselves in Africa will be governed by the degree of sacrifice they are prepared to make in the cause of a life in joint advancement and dedication with and amongst the Africans.

The aspirations of African blacks to direct their own destiny was eloquently stated in 1960 by Rashidi Mfaume Kawawa. He succeeded Julius Nyerere as prime minister of Tanganyika. Independence in Africa was intimately tied to race, which became an identifiable banner around which liberation could occur. Once independent, these countries had to find new ideologies of rule. In this case, race proved inadequate as a vision of progress.

PERESTROIKA

We have come to the conclusions that unless we activate the human factor, that is, unless we take into consideration the diverse interests of people, work collectives, public bodies, and various social groups, unless we rely on them, and draw them into active, constructive endeavor, it will be impossible for us to accomplish any of the tasks set, or to change the situation of the country. . .

Perestroika is a word with many meanings. But if we are to choose from its many possible synonyms the key one which expresses its essence most accurately, then we can say thus: perestroika is a revolution. A decisive acceleration of the socioeconomic and cultural development of Soviet society which involves radical changes on the way to a qualitatively new state is undoubtedly a revolutionary task. . . .

In accordance with our theory, revolution means construction, but it also always implies demolition. Revolution requires the demolition of all that is obsolete, stagnant and hinders fast progress. . . . Perestroika also means a resolute and radical elimination of obstacles hindering social and economic development, of outdated methods of managing the economy and of dogmatic stereotype mentality. . . .

**And like revolution, our day-to-day activites must be unparalleled, revolution-
ary. Perestroika requires Party leaders who are very close to Lenin's ideal of a revolutionary Bolshevik. Officialdom, red tape, patronizing attitudes, and careerism
are incompatible with this ideal. . . .**

In April, 1985, party secretary and president of the Soviet Union Mikhail Gorbachev
announced a policy of far-reaching reform. As the reading suggests, he had no intention of abandoning either communism or the party. He was simply attempting to
breathe life into the bureaucracy that typically builds up within communist systems.
This phenomenon was first noted by Yugoslav writer Djilas in *The New Class*. Mao
Tse-Tung attempted to deal with it by means of a cultural revolution; this attempt did
not bring down the communist state. The "restructuring" that Gorbachev set in motion,
however, went on to become a revolution of such proportion, that communism was
repudiated and the Soviet empire collapsed.

THE COMPUTER AND THE FUTURE

**The spread of cheap, universal computer power will result in a gradual loosening
of restraints on the movement of information within society. . . . Characteristically
this favors the kind of open society which most of us in the Western world enjoy
today, and has just the opposite effect on autocracies—both right and left—who
like to make sure that all information is handed very firmly downward. . . .**

   **Another dramatic effect of the Computer Revolution may be to put an end to
war. . . . Today, when the same statistics are fed into the computer's unemotional,
apolitical interior, what comes out is as true and objective an appraisal as can be
made from the facts. Furthermore, whenever the data involves confrontation
between nuclear powers, the unequivocal message that spills out—to both sides—
is: you will lose!. . .**

   **. . . the increased affluence of the computerized world will inevitably spill over
into the less developed quarters. . . .The third factor promoting the rise of the
underdeveloped world concerns the way in which computer power can be
brought directly to bear on its problems.**

   **. . . One of the most intriguing features of the 1990's will be the way in which
the new, freely communicating societies will control their own destinies.**

Christopher Evans in his book *The Micro Millenium* argues that the computer will
have a positive effect on society by preventing war, helping Third World countries
progress, and nourishing freedom. Certainly the information age had a dramatic effect
on the events in the former Soviet Union and eastern Europe. News of the changes out-
paced the ability of the institutions themselves to maintain control of the revolution set
in motion. Around the world, newsviewers saw the Berlin Wall come down before the
leadership in these countries could act.

Recall Questions

1. The first man in space was
   (A) Yuri Gagarin.
   (B) Neil Armstrong.
   (C) James Watson.
   (D) F. H. C. Crick.
   (E) John Holland.

2. The economist who advocated government spending during the Depression to compensate for the loss of purchasing power was
   (A) Walter Rathenau.
   (B) John Maynard Keynes.
   (C) Adam Smith.
   (D) V. I. Lenin.
   (E) none of the above.

3. Indicators of the decline of the West include
   (A) a decline in population as a percentage of the world's total population.
   (B) the end of European empires.
   (C) the end of the West's advanced weapons monopoly.
   (D) a challenge to the West's manufacturing and trading positions in the world market.
   (E) all of the above.

4. The immediate cause of World War I was the
   (A) assassination of Archduke Franz Ferdinand.
   (B) German invasion of Belgium.
   (C) Austrian declaration of war on Russia.
   (D) Serbian rejection of Austria's ultimatum.
   (E) none of the above.

5. In August of 1939 Hitler signed a nonaggression pact with
   (A) Spain.
   (B) Poland.
   (C) Lithuania.
   (D) Italy.
   (E) Russia.

6. The turning point of World War II was
   (A) Gallipoli.
   (B) El Alamein.
   (C) D-Day.
   (D) Stalingrad.
   (E) the Philippines.

7. After both World War I and World War II
   (A) the World Health Organization continued its work.
   (B) the U.N. Food and Agricultural Organization delivered food to the needy.
   (C) world organizations were established to keep the peace.
   (D) less developed countries became protectorates.
   (E) a ban on new weapons development was instituted by the victors.

8. The agreement that recognized and confirmed the Soviet occupation of eastern Europe was
   (A) the Atlantic charter.
   (B) Yalta.
   (C) Tehran.
   (D) Potsdam.
   (E) the Treaty of Versailles.

9. Which of the following conflicts was a United Nations peace-keeping operation?
   (A) the Six-Day War
   (B) the Korean War
   (C) Vietnam
   (D) the Cuban Missile Crisis
   (E) none of the above

10. Which of the following Cold War alliances was between the United States and its allies in Asia?
    (A) NATO
    (B) the Warsaw Pact
    (C) Comecon
    (D) SEATO
    (E) EEC

11. Which of the following is arranged in correct chronological order?
    (A) World War II, Wall Street Crash, United Nations Charter
    (B) World War II, Cuban Missile Crisis, Korean War
    (C) World War II, Berlin Wall, Cuban Missile Crisis
    (D) United Nations Charter, Korean War, Wall Street Crash
    (E) Berlin Wall, Korean War, World War II

12. All of the following countries experienced communist revolutions EXCEPT
    (A) Russia.
    (B) Cuba.
    (C) Vietnam.
    (D) China.
    (E) South Africa.

13. Which of the following countries experienced wars related to decolonialization?
    (A) Mexico
    (B) Pakistan
    (C) Bangladesh
    (D) Iran
    (E) all of the above

14. Decolonization in Mexico has NOT resulted in
    (A) challenges to the established, "constitutionalist" government by revolutionaries like Pancho Villa and Emiliano Zapata from 1910 to 1920.
    (B) the organization of the PRI or Institutional Revolutionary Party that represented all factions of Mexican politics.
    (C) U.S. control of the Mexican oil industry until 1938.
    (D) economic and social reform through the use of tariffs and nationalization of foreign-owned properties.
    (E) a constitution advocating an eight-hour work day and redistribution of land, and guaranteeing universal suffrage and the right for workers to organize.

15. Bangladesh is a society in which the majority of the people are
    (A) Hindus.
    (B) Muslims.
    (C) Sikhs.
    (D) Christian.
    (E) none of the above.

16. The Balfour Declaration
    (A) promised the Arabs independence following World War I.
    (B) pledged France Syria and Lebanon as mandates.
    (C) pledged Palestine would remain under British control.
    (D) guaranteed Palestine as a Jewish homeland.
    (E) none of the above

17. The national wars of liberation in Southeast Asia were first waged against the
    (A) British.
    (B) French.
    (C) Germans.
    (D) Americans.
    (E) Chinese.

18. The South African leader who opposed apartheid in South Africa was
    (A) Jomo Kenyatta.
    (B) Kwame Nkrumah.
    (C) Nelson Mandela.
    (D) Daniel arap Moi.
    (E) Jonas Savimbi.

19. Which of the following artists was not an impressionist?
    (A) Claude Monet
    (B) Pierre-Auguste Renoir
    (C) Edgar Degas
    (D) Camille Pissarro
    (E) Salvador Dali

20. Which statement about the twentieth century is probably NOT accurate given the documentary evidence?
    (A) Truman had no idea of the consequences of using the atomic bomb.
    (B) Discrimination against Jews was legal in Germany after 1935.
    (C) Churchill warned against the increasing threat of communism after World War II, much as he had warned against the increasing threat of Nazism in the 1930s.
    (D) Following decolonization, Africans believed that nonracial political parties would not offer political power to blacks.
    (E) The spread of cheap, computers will result in a gradual loosening of restraints on the movement of information between societies.

To check your answers, see page 393.

Cold War Europe 1955–1957 C.E. *After World War II, Europe once again became divided, this time between Communist and non-Communist blocs led by the Soviet Union and United States respectively. The dividing line bacame known as the Iron Curtain, a line that roughly coincided with the area occupied by Soviet troops when the war ended.*

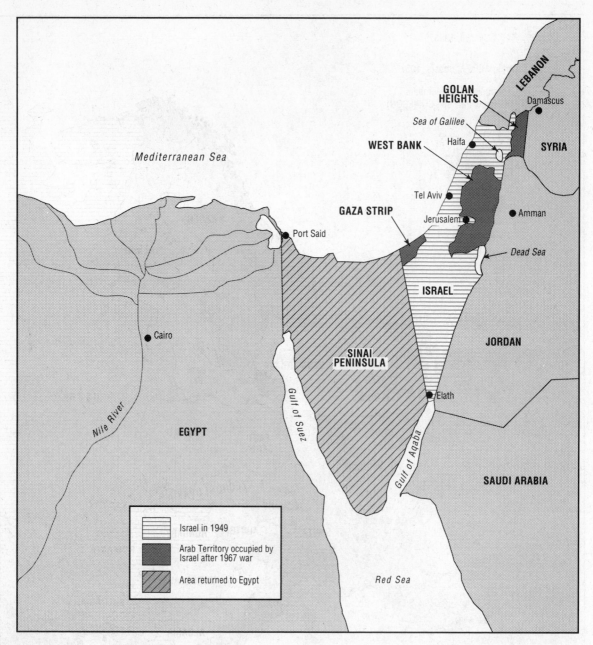

Arab-Israeli Conflict 1949–1973 C.E. *The struggle for Israeli national existence in the face of Arab resistance led to several wars favorable to the Israelis. Complicating the situation was the Cold War, during which both the Soviets and Americans kept the situation volatile by supplying weapons and support. With the end of the Cold War, peace has finally come to the region in the form of both Israeli and Palestinian nation-states.*

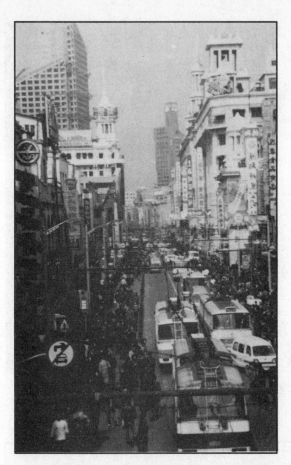

Skyscraper. *Skyscrapers are the most conspicuous reflection of modern urban life. The need to squeeze multitudes of people within a small land space made building up imperative. Steel made that possible. This scene of Shanghai, the largest city in China, illustrates the use of twentieth century glass and steel buildings alongside older buildings and crowded streets.*

Pablo Picasso's Guernica. *Pablo Picasso's art embraced many of the themes and styles of modern art. Guernica expressed his outrage and anguish at the wanton bombing of the village of Guernica in Spain during the Spanish Civil War, which broke out in July 1936. In April, 1937, a squadron of German planes dropped a load of bombs on the small town of Guernica, killing hundreds of villagers, mostly women and children. Picasso ordered that the painting should not go to Spain until democracy was restored there, as it was in the 1970s.*

***Deigo Rivera's* Zapata.** *Diego Rivera is one of the twentieth century's most gifted mural artists. In the early 1920s, Mexican President Obregon's education minister, Jose Vasconcelos, started a program stressing the Indian roots of Mexican culture. This movement, called the Mexican Renaissance, had been one of the themes of the Mexican Revolution. In encouraging it, Vasconcelos named artists like Diego Rivera, Jose Clement Orozco, and David Siqueiros to decorate public buildings. The subject of this mural is the Zapatistas (followers of Zapata), peasant men and women who fought in the Mexican Revolution. After President Diaz was overthrown in 1911, many rival claimants struggled for control of Mexico, among them Pancho Villa in northern Mexico and Emiliano Zapata in southern Mexico. Zapata pressed for land reform and urded peasants to seize some of the hacienda land for themselves.*

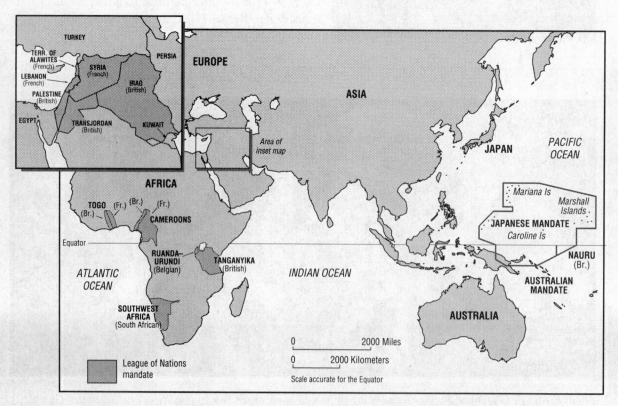

***League of Nations Mandates* 1920 C.E.** *In treaties that ended World War I, imperial territory of the defeated powers was taken and handed over to the League of Nations, which then mandated that winning states oversee them until independence. The mandates in Southwest Asia became the most contentious, primarily because of wartime promises to Jews and Arabs alike.*

Space Exploration. *A new period of exploration was ushered into history when American astronauts Neil Armstrong and Buzz Aldrin stepped onto the moon on July 20, 1969. Neil Armstrong noted to the world below that it was "one small step for a man and one giant step for mankind."*

In this August 1971 picture, James Irwin of the Apollo 15 mission is exploring the lunar surface with the aid of the Lunar Roving Vehicle. In all, there were four lunar landings between 1969 and 1972.

Population (in millions)

Estonia, Latvia, Lithuania 8.0
Georgia 5.5

Armenia	3.3
Turmenistan	3.5
Moldova	4.3
Kyrgyzstan	4.3
Tajikistan	5.1
Azerbaijan	7.0
Belarus	10.2
Kazakhstan	16.5
Uzbekistan	19.9

Russia 147.4
Ukraine 51.7

Ethnic Groups

Other 8.2%

Russian 50.8%

Ukrainian 15.4%

Kyrgz	0.9%
Turkmen	1.0%
Lithuanian	1.1%
Moldovan	1.2%
Georgian	1.4%
Tajik	1.5%
Armenian	1.6%
Azerbaijani	2.4%
Tatar	2.4%
Kazakh	2.8%
Belarusian	3.5%
Uzbek	5.8%

Republics Joining Commonwealth
Not Joining

The Dissolution of the Soviet Union and Commonwealth of Independent States 1989–Present. *In 1989 the Berlin Wall fell and with it came the end of the Soviet empire and comunism. New independent national states emerged, some of which rejoined Russia in a commonwealth grouping of economically interdependent states.*

Europe in 1914 C.E. *The basic framework of World War I was put in place in the first year of the war. Europe was divided into two camps and two fronts. This situation remained until 1917 when new weapons, revolution in Russia, and the entrance of the United States ended the stalemate.*

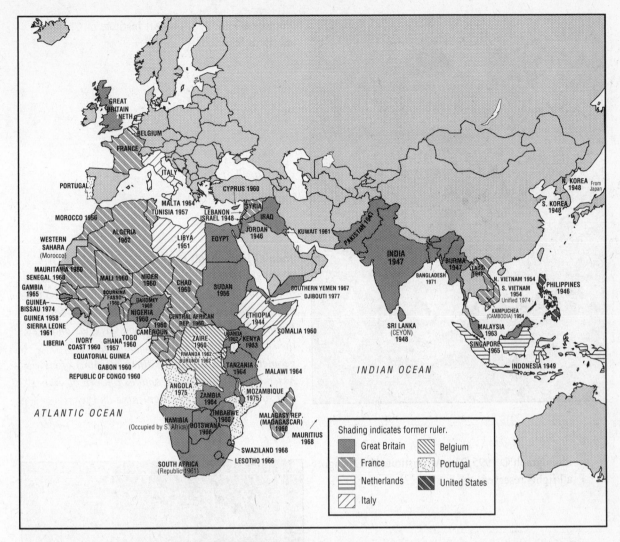

Political Independence in Africa and Asia 1945–1985 C.E. *After World War II, countries in Africa and Asia gained independence either by a process of decolonization of wars of liberation, or both. The predisposition to form new states based on national-liberal principles has been a major world political characteristic of the twentieth century.*

***Juan Gris'* Portrait of Pablo Picasso.** *Juan Gris (Spanish, 1887–1927) developed a distinctive style of cubism in this* Portrait of Pablo Picasso. *Juan Gris honors Picasso who founded cubism with Georges Braque. In this oil painting, Juan Gris has analyzed the surface of his subject's face and torso as geometric forms seen from different points of view. Assembled together, this complex pattern of shapes and surfaces remains recognizable as Picasso.*

***Rene Magritte's* Time Transfixed.** *Rene Magritte French, (1898–1967) creates the impossible in his surrealistic masterpiece,* Time Transfixed. *A locomotive (made of a stovepipe) explodes in midair from a fireplace, not a tunnel, with its billowing smoke drawn into the chimney. The meticulously painted clock, fireplace, mirror, and candlesticks are frozen in a perfectly paneled room. The realism of each detail of the painting coupled with the disturbing impossibility of this picture exemplifies surrealism.*

Earth Seen From the Moon. *The view of earth from space has completely altered the way we think about ourselves and our planet. Among other things, it has reshaped our view of history. It has produced a world history that increasingly finds its narrative threads in themes like global exchange and environment, cross-cultural encounters, and broad patterns of change.*

MODEL
TESTS

HISTORICAL LITERACY

Historical literacy involves knowing content and historical methodology. Increasingly in history, students are being asked not only to have a basic knowledge of the subject matter, but to know how the historian works. Students must know for instance, what constitutes evidence and how to read this evidence. This often involves evaluation of viewpoint, understanding of context, and the testing of conclusions.

This review book has dealt with historical methodology within the text itself, with explanations of causality, discussions of evidence, and representations of viewpoint. The visual, document, and map sections are also designed to engage you in historical methodology.

Listed below are some of the historical thinking skills that you should be acquiring in the study of world history. Following this discussion are a number of sample test questions with explanations that test your ability to deal with historical methodology.

1. Chronological Thinking. Historians attempt to pinpoint evidence in time and space. They then note change over time, trying to find patterns and discontinuities in this change, and what changes have been continuous and enduring, and which have not. In world history, similar changes often occur at different times in different places across the globe. Sometime change seems incidental to only one place or time period. World historians are apt to ask how and why this change occurred. This has made the question of cultural diffusion and of cross-regional exchange crucial for world historical interpretation. Testing for this type of understanding often involves questions that ask the student to order a course of events, pick which is not a logical explanation of change, what cause-and-effect relationship occurred, and how this change occurred over time.

2. Historical Comprehension. Historians learn how to see the past through the eyes of those who lived it at the time. They know how to read various kinds of evidence, such as documents, pictures, data, and literature, with this in mind. For historians of world history, this means being sensitive to and knowledgeable about the cultural framework of different societies. Testing this often asks the student to come to conclusions about an author of a document, or the message of a visual, or the likely interpretation, given the time period and place.

3. Historical Analysis and Interpretation. For purposes of analysis, or the taking apart, of history, historians have tended to divide history into parts—political, economic, social, and cultural. For example, students must be able to identify the military as part of political history, class as part of social history, ideas as part of cultural history, and trade as part of economic history. With respect to interpretation, students should learn that there are often multiple causes, motives, interests, and records of experience that have shaped the past. In world history it is particularly important to be able to make valid comparisons between places and peoples, to see, for instance, that the same outcome (i.e., the agricultural revolution) may have occurred for different reasons in different parts of the world with different consequences. World history test questions will often involve the student's ability to make valid comparisons and to identify interpretations based on faulty analysis.

4. Historical Research Capabilities. Historical research capabilities involve the ability to determine time and context within an artifact, the ability to assess credibility of the artifact, and the ability to construct a sound argument or story from it. In world history this is a particularly important capability because not all societies have used western ideas of evidence. Oral histories, myth histories, and art have become important artifacts where written evidence is lacking. A test question in this regard might ask you to come to some conclusion about a chart, graph, or written fragment.

5. Historical Issues—Analysis and Decision-Making. Historians must identify problems that confronted people in the past and come to some conclusions about the actions that were taken. In world history this is particularly challenging because societies different from our own have identified different problems and come to different decisions with respect to those problems. In evaluating this, historians must be free from bias and educated in the traditions of many societies. On the exam, this skill is often tested with questions that deal with explanations about why certain decisions were made at a certain time and place.

The historical methodological questions that appear on the SAT II: World History exam are apt to test one or more of these skills in any one question. You may test your ability with the Sample Test Questions on the next four pages. Two Model Tests follow the sample questions.

Sample Test Questions

1. Which of the following statements can be supported by the table on the following page?
   - (A) Tokyo will be the largest city in the world in the year 2000.
   - (B) All urban areas will increase in size by the year 2000.
   - (C) In 1991 more than 50 percent of the world's largest urban areas are in Third World countries.
   - (D) Tokyo-Yokohama, Japan is listed first in this chart because it is projected to have the largest urban population by the year 2000.
   - (E) New York City counts suburbs in its 1991 total, whereas Tokyo-Yokohama does not.

The correct answer choice is **C**. To answer this question, you need to look carefully at the information contained in the chart. Answer choice A is incorrect because the third column is a projected estimate of size. Answer choice B is incorrect because some cities will remain the same or decrease in size. One should also be wary of words like *always, never, all,* and *one.* Answer choice D is incorrect because the urban areas are ranked according to 1991 population figures. Answer choice E is incorrect because information concerning suburbs is not included in the chart.

2. Which of the following statements would be the MOST difficult for the historian to prove?
   - (A) The Pacific Ocean is three times as large as the Atlantic Ocean.
   - (B) Although not generally recognized, William Gladstone was more effective as a prime minister than Benjamin Disraeli.
   - (C) The Suez Canal increased trade between India and Britain after its completion.
   - (D) The invention of the airplane changed the way people lived in the twentieth century.
   - (E) There was little opposition in the United States to the dropping of the atomic bomb on Hiroshima.

The correct answer choice is **B**, which expresses an opinion. The other four statements can be proven or disproven using historical evidence.

3. A preponderance of evidence about prehistoric life forms has come from East Africa because
   - (A) the "Out-of-Africa" theory has proved that all humans originated in Africa.
   - (B) archaeologists like the Leakeys have concentrated their efforts in East Africa.
   - (C) when the continents were all united in Pangaea, Africa was at its heart.
   - (D) the humid, tropical areas preserve human bone fossils better.
   - (E) the Olduvai gorge fault system reveals fossils easily .

The correct answer is **E**. The other choices are informationally or logically incorrect. Choice A is incorrect because the "Out-of-Africa" model has not been proven. Choice B is incorrect because of faulty logic. The Leakeys concentrated their efforts in this area because of the possibility of finding such prehistorical fossils. Choice C is incorrect because of chronological inaccuracy, there was no human life until long after the continents were formed. Choice D is incorrect because tropical areas are one of the poorest places to find fossils whereas dry or frozen sites or areas covered by volcanic ash are the best.

Population, by World's Largest Cities: 1992 to 2000

City and Country	Rank	Midyear Population (1,000)			Average Annual Growth Rate (percent)	
		1992	1995	2000	1992–1995	1995–2000
Tokyo-Yokohama, Japan	1	27,540	26,447	29,971	1.1	1.0
Mexico City, Mexico	2	21,615	23,913	27,872	3.4	3.1
Sao Paulo, Brazil	3	19,373	21,539	25,364	3.5	3.3
Seoul, South Korea	4	17,334	19,065	21,976	3.2	2.6
New York, United States	5	14,629	14,638	14,646	(Z)	(Z)
Osaka-Kobe-Kyoto, Japan	6	13,919	14,060	14,267	0.3	0.3
Bombay, India	7	12,450	13,532	15,367	2.8	2.5
Calcutta, India	8	12,137	12,885	14,068	2.0	1.6
Rio de Janeiro, Brazil	9	12,009	12,786	14,169	2.1	2.1
Buenos Aires, Argentina	10	11,743	12,232	12,911	1.4	1.1
Manila, Philippines	11	10,554	11,342	12,846	2.4	2.5
Moscow, Russia	12	10,526	10,769	11,121	0.8	0.6
Cairo, Egypt	13	10,372	11,155	12,612	2.4	2.3
Jakarta, Indonesia	14	10,165	11,151	12,804	3.0	2.8
Tehran, Iran	15	10,102	11,661	14,251	4.6	4.0
Los Angeles, United States	16	10,072	10,414	10,714	1.1	0.6
Paris, France	19	8,589	8,764	8,803	0.7	0.1
Lagos, Nigeria	20	8,487	9,799	12,526	4.8	4.9
Karachi, Pakistan	21	8,174	9,350	11,299	4.5	3.6
Essen, Germany	22	7,506	7,364	7,239	–0.6	–0.3
Lima, Peru	23	7,026	7,653	9,241	3.7	3.3
Shanghai, China	24	7,000	7,194	7,540	0.9	0.9
Istanbul, Turkey	25	6,937	7,624	8,675	3.2	3.0
Taipei, Taiwan	26	6,924	7,477	8,516	2.6	2.6
Chicago, United States	27	6,483	6,541	6,568	0.2	0.1
Bogota, Colombia	28	6,176	6,601	7,935	3.2	3.1
Bangkok, Thailand	29	6,068	6,657	7,587	3.0	2.6
Madras, India	30	5,996	6,650	7,384	2.9	2.4
Beijing, China	31	5,791	5,865	5,993	0.4	0.4
Hong Kong, Hong Kong	32	5,762	5,841	5,956	0.5	0.4
Santiago, Chile	33	5,464	5,812	6,294	1.9	1.6
Pusan, South Korea	34	5,161	5,748	6,700	3.6	3.1
Bangalore, India	35	5,060	5,644	6,764	3.5	3.6
Nagoya, Japan	36	4,909	5,017	5,303	0.7	1.1
Tianjin, China	37	4,857	5,041	5,288	1.2	1.0
Milan, Italy	38	4,718	4,795	4,839	0.5	0.2
St. Petersburg, Russia	39	4,645	4,694	4,738	0.4	0.2
Dhaka, Bangladesh	40	4,640	5,296	5,492	4.4	4.1
Madrid, Spain	41	4,577	4,772	5,104	1.4	1.4
Lahore, Pakistan	42	4,475	4,986	5,564	3.6	3.2

This chart relates to Sample Test Question 1.

4. Which conclusion based on the evidence included is correct?
   (A) The Indus valley civilization with its planned cities, piped water, and public drainage systems had a centralized political power.
   (B) Irrigation systems, bridges, road building, and large temple platforms indicate an increase in population in the Altiplano region of what is now Peru.
   (C) Egyptian trade goods found in Crete and post and lintel construction similar to the system used at Karnak indicate that the Minoans and Egyptians traded and copied aspects of Egyptian culture.
   (D) Montezuma's initial friendly attitude toward Cortes indicates the openness of Aztec society to strangers.
   (E) The continued Muslim use of the camel rather than wagons for transport on the overland trade routes of Eurasia indicates a resistance to change.

The correct answer is **A**. Planned cities, piped water, and public drainage would have been impossible without some centralized mechanisms of organization. Choice B is incorrect because irrigation systems, bridges, roads, and temple platforms would not necessarily indicate increased population though they might indicate substantial population. Choice C is incorrect; while there is evidence of trade, there is no stated evidence to identify who copied from whom. Choice D is incorrect because the occasion is removed from its historical context. Montezuma welcomed Cortes in the belief that he might be the returning Aztec god Quetzalcoatl. Choice E is incorrect because this conclusion fails to consider that resistance to change is often for logical reasons. Camel transport was cheap and efficient while wagon wheels required extensive road building, so there was no reason to change.

5. Estimates of the number who perished with the Black Death in Europe in the thirteenth century would LEAST likely be found in
   (A) church records.
   (B) personal diaries.
   (C) tax records.
   (D) newspapers.
   (E) shiplogs.

The correct answer choice is **D**. This question is asking you to identify the exception among the five options. Since the technology for printing newspapers was not available in Europe at the time of the plague, choice D is incorrect. Questions asking for the exception, posed in the negative, make up one-quarter of the test. Negative questions may also be worded to indicate that all of the following are true— EXCEPT—or may be phrased to include the word NOT. Sometimes it helps in questions like this to read without EXCEPT, to determine which answer is different.

6. Given the rapid rise and spread of Buddhism during the reign of Ashoka, which of the following is the LEAST likely hypothesis about why this change occurred?
   (A) Buddhism was carried by merchants into new areas of India as they exchanged goods along the trade routes.
   (B) Buddhism appealed to the down trodden.
   (C) A powerful secular leader converted to Buddhism and supported it.
   (D) Buddhism offered new forms of rich cultural expression.
   (E) Buddhism acquired many converts through the pilgrimages and sermons of Siddhartha Gautama.

Constructing a hypothesis based on historical data is one of the key skills of a historian. All of the choices above are possible hypotheses that can be supported with evidence from the period except choice **E**. Siddhartha Gautama died in about 485 B.C.E., long before Ashoka ruled India in 250 B.C.E.

Sample Test Questions 7 and 8 are based on this quotation. "The enemy advances, we retreat; the enemy halts, we harass; the enemy slackens, we attack; the enemy retreats, we pursue."

7. The strategies described in this passage can MOST closely be connected with
   (A) medieval warfare.
   (B) trench warfare.
   (C) mechanized warfare.
   (D) guerrilla warfare.
   (E) siege warfare.

8. The author of this passage would MOST likely have supported the strategy of which of the following military leaders?
   (A) Hitler
   (B) Philip II
   (C) Dwight D. Eisenhower
   (D) Napoleon
   (E) Ho Chi Minh

The answer to question 7 is **D**, guerrilla warfare, and to question 8 is **E**, Ho Chi Minh. This quote by Sun Tzu in *The Art of War* provides basic strategies that the reader should infer to be most useful in guerrilla warfare. Knowledge of Sun Tzu's strategies was used by guerrilla leaders like Mao Zedong (Mao Tse-tung) and Ho Chi Minh in the twentieth century.

ANSWER SHEET — MODEL TEST 1

1. Ⓐ Ⓑ Ⓒ Ⓓ Ⓔ
2. Ⓐ Ⓑ Ⓒ Ⓓ Ⓔ
3. Ⓐ Ⓑ Ⓒ Ⓓ Ⓔ
4. Ⓐ Ⓑ Ⓒ Ⓓ Ⓔ
5. Ⓐ Ⓑ Ⓒ Ⓓ Ⓔ
6. Ⓐ Ⓑ Ⓒ Ⓓ Ⓔ
7. Ⓐ Ⓑ Ⓒ Ⓓ Ⓔ
8. Ⓐ Ⓑ Ⓒ Ⓓ Ⓔ
9. Ⓐ Ⓑ Ⓒ Ⓓ Ⓔ
10. Ⓐ Ⓑ Ⓒ Ⓓ Ⓔ
11. Ⓐ Ⓑ Ⓒ Ⓓ Ⓔ
12. Ⓐ Ⓑ Ⓒ Ⓓ Ⓔ
13. Ⓐ Ⓑ Ⓒ Ⓓ Ⓔ
14. Ⓐ Ⓑ Ⓒ Ⓓ Ⓔ
15. Ⓐ Ⓑ Ⓒ Ⓓ Ⓔ
16. Ⓐ Ⓑ Ⓒ Ⓓ Ⓔ
17. Ⓐ Ⓑ Ⓒ Ⓓ Ⓔ
18. Ⓐ Ⓑ Ⓒ Ⓓ Ⓔ
19. Ⓐ Ⓑ Ⓒ Ⓓ Ⓔ
20. Ⓐ Ⓑ Ⓒ Ⓓ Ⓔ
21. Ⓐ Ⓑ Ⓒ Ⓓ Ⓔ
22. Ⓐ Ⓑ Ⓒ Ⓓ Ⓔ
23. Ⓐ Ⓑ Ⓒ Ⓓ Ⓔ
24. Ⓐ Ⓑ Ⓒ Ⓓ Ⓔ
25. Ⓐ Ⓑ Ⓒ Ⓓ Ⓔ
26. Ⓐ Ⓑ Ⓒ Ⓓ Ⓔ
27. Ⓐ Ⓑ Ⓒ Ⓓ Ⓔ
28. Ⓐ Ⓑ Ⓒ Ⓓ Ⓔ
29. Ⓐ Ⓑ Ⓒ Ⓓ Ⓔ
30. Ⓐ Ⓑ Ⓒ Ⓓ Ⓔ
31. Ⓐ Ⓑ Ⓒ Ⓓ Ⓔ
32. Ⓐ Ⓑ Ⓒ Ⓓ Ⓔ
33. Ⓐ Ⓑ Ⓒ Ⓓ Ⓔ
34. Ⓐ Ⓑ Ⓒ Ⓓ Ⓔ

35. Ⓐ Ⓑ Ⓒ Ⓓ Ⓔ
36. Ⓐ Ⓑ Ⓒ Ⓓ Ⓔ
37. Ⓐ Ⓑ Ⓒ Ⓓ Ⓔ
38. Ⓐ Ⓑ Ⓒ Ⓓ Ⓔ
39. Ⓐ Ⓑ Ⓒ Ⓓ Ⓔ
40. Ⓐ Ⓑ Ⓒ Ⓓ Ⓔ
41. Ⓐ Ⓑ Ⓒ Ⓓ Ⓔ
42. Ⓐ Ⓑ Ⓒ Ⓓ Ⓔ
43. Ⓐ Ⓑ Ⓒ Ⓓ Ⓔ
44. Ⓐ Ⓑ Ⓒ Ⓓ Ⓔ
45. Ⓐ Ⓑ Ⓒ Ⓓ Ⓔ
46. Ⓐ Ⓑ Ⓒ Ⓓ Ⓔ
47. Ⓐ Ⓑ Ⓒ Ⓓ Ⓔ
48. Ⓐ Ⓑ Ⓒ Ⓓ Ⓔ
49. Ⓐ Ⓑ Ⓒ Ⓓ Ⓔ
50. Ⓐ Ⓑ Ⓒ Ⓓ Ⓔ
51. Ⓐ Ⓑ Ⓒ Ⓓ Ⓔ
52. Ⓐ Ⓑ Ⓒ Ⓓ Ⓔ
53. Ⓐ Ⓑ Ⓒ Ⓓ Ⓔ
54. Ⓐ Ⓑ Ⓒ Ⓓ Ⓔ
55. Ⓐ Ⓑ Ⓒ Ⓓ Ⓔ
56. Ⓐ Ⓑ Ⓒ Ⓓ Ⓔ
57. Ⓐ Ⓑ Ⓒ Ⓓ Ⓔ
58. Ⓐ Ⓑ Ⓒ Ⓓ Ⓔ
59. Ⓐ Ⓑ Ⓒ Ⓓ Ⓔ
60. Ⓐ Ⓑ Ⓒ Ⓓ Ⓔ
61. Ⓐ Ⓑ Ⓒ Ⓓ Ⓔ
62. Ⓐ Ⓑ Ⓒ Ⓓ Ⓔ
63. Ⓐ Ⓑ Ⓒ Ⓓ Ⓔ
64. Ⓐ Ⓑ Ⓒ Ⓓ Ⓔ
65. Ⓐ Ⓑ Ⓒ Ⓓ Ⓔ
66. Ⓐ Ⓑ Ⓒ Ⓓ Ⓔ
67. Ⓐ Ⓑ Ⓒ Ⓓ Ⓔ
68. Ⓐ Ⓑ Ⓒ Ⓓ Ⓔ

69. Ⓐ Ⓑ Ⓒ Ⓓ Ⓔ
70. Ⓐ Ⓑ Ⓒ Ⓓ Ⓔ
71. Ⓐ Ⓑ Ⓒ Ⓓ Ⓔ
72. Ⓐ Ⓑ Ⓒ Ⓓ Ⓔ
73. Ⓐ Ⓑ Ⓒ Ⓓ Ⓔ
74. Ⓐ Ⓑ Ⓒ Ⓓ Ⓔ
75. Ⓐ Ⓑ Ⓒ Ⓓ Ⓔ
76. Ⓐ Ⓑ Ⓒ Ⓓ Ⓔ
77. Ⓐ Ⓑ Ⓒ Ⓓ Ⓔ
78. Ⓐ Ⓑ Ⓒ Ⓓ Ⓔ
79. Ⓐ Ⓑ Ⓒ Ⓓ Ⓔ
80. Ⓐ Ⓑ Ⓒ Ⓓ Ⓔ
81. Ⓐ Ⓑ Ⓒ Ⓓ Ⓔ
82. Ⓐ Ⓑ Ⓒ Ⓓ Ⓔ
83. Ⓐ Ⓑ Ⓒ Ⓓ Ⓔ
84. Ⓐ Ⓑ Ⓒ Ⓓ Ⓔ
85. Ⓐ Ⓑ Ⓒ Ⓓ Ⓔ
86. Ⓐ Ⓑ Ⓒ Ⓓ Ⓔ
87. Ⓐ Ⓑ Ⓒ Ⓓ Ⓔ
88. Ⓐ Ⓑ Ⓒ Ⓓ Ⓔ
89. Ⓐ Ⓑ Ⓒ Ⓓ Ⓔ
90. Ⓐ Ⓑ Ⓒ Ⓓ Ⓔ
91. Ⓐ Ⓑ Ⓒ Ⓓ Ⓔ
92. Ⓐ Ⓑ Ⓒ Ⓓ Ⓔ
93. Ⓐ Ⓑ Ⓒ Ⓓ Ⓔ
94. Ⓐ Ⓑ Ⓒ Ⓓ Ⓔ
95. Ⓐ Ⓑ Ⓒ Ⓓ Ⓔ
96. Ⓐ Ⓑ Ⓒ Ⓓ Ⓔ
97. Ⓐ Ⓑ Ⓒ Ⓓ Ⓔ
99. Ⓐ Ⓑ Ⓒ Ⓓ Ⓔ
99. Ⓐ Ⓑ Ⓒ Ⓓ Ⓔ
100. Ⓐ Ⓑ Ⓒ Ⓓ Ⓔ
101. Ⓐ Ⓑ Ⓒ Ⓓ Ⓔ

Model Test 1

The actual SAT II: World History examination will contain ninety questions. This Model Test includes more than that, in order to give you a more comprehensive practice exam.

1. "There are four questions essential to royal authority. First, the royal authority is sacred; second, it is paternal; third, it is absolute; fourth, it is submitted to reason . . . ."

   Franklin L. Baumer

   This passage sums up the spirit of
   (A) lay investiture.
   (B) constitutional monarchy.
   (C) divine right of kings.
   (D) absolutism.
   (E) socialism.

2. Mary Leakey's discovery of Zinjanthropus is important not just because it was evidence of a species called *Australopithecus boisei* but because it was found *in situ,* which means that
   (A) bone fragments represented a complete skeleton.
   (B) fragments could be matched chronologically with specie fragments.
   (C) fragments were found in their original place along with other remains including indications of lifestyle.
   (D) surrounding fragments had been washed away.
   (E) fragments, discovered along a river bed, offered evidence of the surrounding geologic formations.

3. Women were important contributors to the agricultural revolution because they were likely the gender who
   (A) owned property.
   (B) wanted more leisure time.
   (C) gathered edible plants and knew where grains grew.
   (D) found carrying children on their backs too burdensome.
   (E) liked farming.

4. In an effort to strengthen his power against the pope, Philip IV of France organized the Estates General of
   (A) Protestant dissenters.
   (B) nobles and clergymen.
   (C) university faculties of law, medicine, and the arts.
   (D) clergy, nobility, and commoners.
   (E) bankers, merchants, and guilds.

5. Which writing system is NOT correctly linked with its evolutionary characteristics?
   (A) Mesopotamian cuneiform began as pictures but changed into wedge-shaped symbols written with a stylus on a wet clay tablet.
   (B) Indus Valley writing was adapted from Mesopotamian cuneiform.
   (C) The Phoenician alphabet combined sound symbols to reproduce the spoken word.
   (D) Chinese hieroglyphics combined pictographs and ideograms into a system first carved into bone and later painted on silk.
   (E) Egyptian hieroglyphics originated as pictures but later included ideograms and phonetic symbols written on papyrus.

6. All of the following were reasons for European emigration in the second half of the nineteenth century EXCEPT
   (A) pogroms in eastern Europe and Russia.
   (B) the Irish potato famine.
   (C) rapid increases in population.
   (D) demand for skilled technicans.
   (E) easy credit to encourage emigration.

7. Art of the Romantic era reflects
   (A) the abstract expression of quantum physics.
   (B) people as opposed to scenery as the preferred subject matter.
   (C) a rationalist approach.
   (D) national consciousness and increasing feelings of nationalism.
   (E) an interest in the working man.

8. One principle of Hammurabi's Code that would probably NOT be considered "just" today is
   (A) less punishment for the first offense.
   (B) the less important the social status, the more severe the punishment.
   (C) the more important the social status, the more severe the punishment.
   (D) the punishment equals the crime.
   (E) all of the above.

9. Which of the following does NOT illustrate socialist thought?
   (A) Minimum wages to control the size of working class families
   (B) Government-backed workshops and factories to guarantee full employment
   (C) Redistribution of wealth by means of an income tax
   (D) "The greatest good for the greatest number of people"
   (E) Universal voting rights

10. Within the United Nations, who has the power to veto any decision made by the organization?
    (A) permanent members of the United Nations Security Council
    (B) World Court
    (C) a majority of the membership of participating nations
    (D) the individual elected to lead the United Nations
    (E) none of the above

11. Egyptian Pharaohs of the Old Kingdom exercised unusual authority over their subjects because
    (A) they served as military commanders of a highly successful army.
    (B) they were respected for developing a lucrative trade with Mesopotamia, Crete, and Palestine.
    (C) they were worshipped as gods who ruled the society through an extensive theocracy.
    (D) they were recognized as the ruler by the royal family and nobility.
    (E) they inherited their position in the dynastic order through their mother's family.

12. Effects of the plague included
    (A) population losses in Europe of 40 to 45 percent.
    (B) loss of productivity.
    (C) increase in wages.
    (D) economic recession.
    (E) all of the above.

13. All of the following are reasons for the end of the West's world political hegemony EXCEPT
    (A) western control of the world economy.
    (B) national liberation movements.
    (C) communist revolutions.
    (D) warfare between western nations.
    (E) decolonization.

14. The Greek epic stories, the *Iliad* and the *Odyssey* are most clearly similar to the
    (A) Torah.
    (B) Ramayana.
    (C) Shariah.
    (D) Codices.
    (E) Meditations.

15. The recent history of which nation displays most successful top-down change without revolt?
    (A) France
    (B) United States
    (C) China
    (D) Japan
    (E) Russia

16. Which of the following terms is used
    INCORRECTLY?
    (A) Japanese, Koreans, and Central Asians
        recognized certain individuals as
        shamans who acted as intermediaries
        between humans and deities.
    (B) A *kamikaze* or divine wind protected
        the Japanese mainland from Mongol
        invasion.
    (C) *Tartars* were Russian pastoral nomads
        who served the princes of Moscow as
        the Golden Horde.
    (D) The Ottoman Turks, Ming Chinese,
        Mughal Indians, and Spanish created
        gunpowder empires with newly devel-
        oped guns and seige weapons.
    (E) In Benin the *Oba* was a ruler who
        lived in a large royal compound sur-
        rounded by an entourage.

17. Roman law changed as society changed
    because
    (A) all Romans were included in the law-
        making process.
    (B) a code of law known as the Twelve
        Tables was established in the early
        days of the Republic.
    (C) an intricate code of civil law was
        devised to be applied equally to all.
    (D) special courts to deal with differences
        between Roman and foreign law in
        trade issues were abolished.
    (E) newly elected judges announced laws
        they intended to enforce and those
        they considered out of date.

18. "Blessed are the poor in spirit; for theirs is
    the kingdom of Heaven."

    This excerpt from the Christian "Sermon
    on the Mount" is closest to the orientation
    of what other world belief system?
    (A) Confucianism
    (B) Taoism
    (C) Buddhism
    (D) Hinduism
    (E) Zoroastrianism

19. The man who argued that population could
    be controlled by wages was
    (A) Thomas Hobbes.
    (B) David Ricardo.
    (C) Thomas Malthus.
    (D) John Stuart Mill.
    (E) John Maynard Keynes.

20. What system of Chinese thought saw the
    world as interacting opposites, *Yin* and
    Yang, which form the harmony of the
    whole?
    (A) Confucianism
    (B) Legalism
    (C) Daoism
    (D) *I Ching*
    (E) Buddhism

21. After Mao Tse-tung's death, what hap-
    pened in China?
    (A) Population declined.
    (B) The Cultural Revolution.
    (C) The Sino-Soviet split intensified.
    (D) The economy was liberalized.
    (E) Per capita income decreased.

22. Which Roman leader is associated with
    the building of a new Roman capital in the
    East?
    (A) Julius Caesar
    (B) Caesar Augustus
    (C) Marcus Aurelius
    (D) Constantine
    (E) Justinian

23. Americans born of African and European
    parents in the New World were known in
    Brazil as
    (A) Mestizo.
    (B) Mulatto.
    (C) Zambo.
    (D) Peninsulare.
    (E) Creole.

24. The founder of psychoanalysis, who theorized that much of human behavior was motivated by unconscious emotional needs, was
(A) Charles Darwin.
(B) Herbert Spenser.
(C) Charles Fourier.
(D) Sigmund Freud.
(E) Joseph Lister.

25. The Mandate of Heaven was a belief held by Chinese that
(A) ancestral worship was an essential element of religious ritual.
(B) the ruler and nobles were selected to rule through the will of heaven.
(C) if a ruler governed badly, he lost the consent of the heavens to rule and the people had the right to revolt.
(D) the ruler was a divine presence on earth.
(E) none of these.

26.

Relative Shares of World Manufacturing Output, 1750–1900

	1750	1800	1830	1860	1880	1900
(Europe as a whole)	23.2	28.1	34.2	53.2	61.3	62.0
United Kingdom	1.9	4.3	9.5	19.9	22.9	18.5
Habsburg Empire	2.9	3.2	3.2	4.2	4.4	4.7
France	4.0	4.2	5.2	7.9	7.8	6.8
German States/ Germany	2.9	3.5	3.5	4.9	8.5	13.2
Italian States/ Italy	2.4	2.5	2.3	2.5	2.5	2.5
Russia	5.0	5.6	5.6	7.0	7.6	8.8
United States	0.1	0.8	2.4	7.2	14.7	23.6
Japan	3.8	3.5	2.8	2.6	2.4	2.4
Third World	73.0	67.7	60.5	36.6	20.9	11.0
China	32.8	33.3	29.8	19.7	12.5	6.2
India/Pakistan	24.5	19.7	17.6	8.6	2.8	1.7

What conclusion can be drawn from the chart of relative shares of world manufacturing output between 1750 and 1900?
(A) Asians increased their share.
(B) Europeans decreased their share.
(C) European countries industrialized.
(D) Literacy rates increased in Asia.
(E) The Chinese developed superior technology.

27. Results of the Crusades included all of the following EXCEPT
(A) freeing the Holy Land from Muslim control.
(B) increasing the sale of feudal rights to the peasants and towns.
(C) introducing new weapons and methods of warfare in Europe.
(D) increasing royal authority at the expense of the popes.
(E) promoting the wealth and influence of commercial towns like Venice.

28. The principles of nonviolence and asceticism taught by Mahavira are central to
(A) Hinduism.
(B) Jainism.
(C) Theravada Buddhism.
(D) Mahayana Buddhism.
(E) Zoroastrianism.

29. Rising population in Third World countries in the 20th century can be best linked to
(A) government incentives for large families.
(B) growth of poverty.
(C) decline in death rates.
(D) industrialization.
(E) the Colombian exchange of foodstuffs.

30. The Mauryan ruler of India noted for renouncing war; advocating civic compassion, duty, and nonviolence; and respecting religions was
(A) Kanishka.
(B) Kautilya.
(C) Chandragupta Mauryan.
(D) Ashoka.
(E) Chandra Gupta I.

31. All of the following were expressions of nationalism EXCEPT the
(A) Manifest Destiny.
(B) Italian unification.
(C) "white man's burden."
(D) Boxer Rebellion.
(E) Franco-Prussian War.

32. The Portuguese profited from their exploration of the west coast of Africa through the trade of
(A) lumber and fish.
(B) slaves and gold.
(C) tobacco and salt.
(D) wool.
(E) cattle.

33. Which of the following is an example of cultural diffusion resulting from Silk Road trade and exchange, circa 300 B.C.E.?
(A) Buddhism in China
(B) paper in Rome
(C) Pagoda architecture in Ceylon (Sri Lanka)
(D) Civil Service examinations in Greece
(E) poured iron tools in Jerusalem

34. All can be said of this painting EXCEPT:
(A) This is one of the most outstanding examples of 20th century abstract expressionism.
(B) The painting depicts the results of the bombing of Guernica during the Spanish Civil War.
(C) This is one of the great masterpieces of Pablo Picasso.
(D) This style of painting was a forerunner to impressionism.
(E) This painting can be interpreted as a protest against war.

35. Which of the following evolutions in warfare occurred last?
(A) the invention of gunpowder
(B) fortress construction with low walls, vast moats, and outworks
(C) ships with side-mounted guns
(D) field armies of 100,000 men
(E) the development of gunpowder weaponry

36. In which sentence is the term incorrectly used?
(A) A *synthesis* of Chinese and Indian cultures occurred with the introduction of Buddhism to China.
(B) An example of *cultural diffusion* is the use of Indian numerals, first by Arab traders and then by others around the globe.
(C) Polynesian maritime *migrations,* facilitated by the outrigger canoe, spread over a 20,000 mile area of the Pacific Ocean.
(D) The gradual *Sinification* of Arabic peoples began two centuries before the birth of Christ and continued into the 1400s.
(E) Kaifeng, capital of China during the Song (Sung) dynasty, became the eastern *entrepot* for both locally manufactured and long distance trade items on the Yellow River.

37. Which was NOT a country occupied by the Soviet army following World War II?
(A) Rumania
(B) Yugoslavia
(C) Bulgaria
(D) Czechoslovakia
(E) Poland

38. The Bantu Myth of Migration emphasizes fishing as the motive for movement. This is probably due to the fact that
(A) the Bantu were hunters and gatherers.
(B) migratory patterns followed the rivers.
(C) the Bantu farmers invented fishing.
(D) myths are always centered around animals.
(E) the word "Bantu" means fish.

39. Pastoral nomads were found in all of the following areas EXCEPT
(A) Eurasian steppes.
(B) Andean America.
(C) Amazonian rainforests.
(D) Arabia.
(E) East and South Africa.

40. Because of the work of the Byzantine missionaries, all of the following became societies where the Orthodox faith predominated EXCEPT
(A) Greece.
(B) Russia.
(C) Rumania.
(D) Poland.
(E) Serbia.

41. World War II in Europe started when
(A) Germany invaded Poland.
(B) Germany annexed Austria.
(C) Germany annexed the Sudetenland.
(D) Germany and Russia signed the Non-Aggression Pact.
(E) the Munich agreements were signed.

42. Which of the following were marks of the feudal period?
(A) The state was decentralized.
(B) Small trade towns and/or agrarian states reorganized.
(C) Warriors and nobles predominated in the ruling class.
(D) Religion played a central role in preserving and identifying the culture.
(E) All of the above.

43. The history of all hitherto existing societies is the history of class struggles . . . The proletarians have nothing to lose but their chains. They have a world to win. WORKING MEN OF ALL COUNTRIES UNITE!

The probable author of this passage was
(A) Vladimir Lenin.
(B) Karl Marx.
(C) Mao Tse Tung.
(D) Ho Chi Minh.
(E) Fidel Castro.

44. Characteristics of pastoral nomads include
(A) their displacement of hunter-gatherers across Eurasia.
(B) a symbiotic relationship with settled societies.
(C) acting as carriers of overland, long distance trade.
(D) herding reindeer in the north, camels in Arabia, llama in the Andes, and cattle in South Africa.
(E) all of the above.

45. All are characteristics of civilization EXCEPT
(A) specialization of jobs.
(B) writing system.
(C) cities.
(D) gender equality.
(E) systems of political order and power.

46. The nation-state differed from earlier political entities in that it was based on all of the following historical means of gaining power, PLUS
(A) conquest and control through leadership.
(B) cultural bonds.
(C) religious bonds through a state religion.
(D) civic cohesion and the rule of law.
(E) sovereignty of the people.

47. Demographically, the history of the Americas since 1492 was shaped by
  I. Europeans.
 II. Africans.
III. Asians.
IV. Amerindians.

(A) 1, 2, 3, and 4
(B) 1 and 3
(C) 1 and 2
(D) 1, 2, and 3
(E) 1, 2, and 4

48. The Great Depression affected western Europe in all of the following ways EXCEPT
(A) welfare programs.
(B) appeasement.
(C) creation of the IMF.
(D) increase in protectionism.
(E) increasing involvement of government in the economy.

49. This figure constructed of bronze using the lost wax process is representative of the art of
(A) Benin.
(B) Timbuktu.
(C) Zimbabwe.
(D) Bantu peoples.
(E) Ghana.

50. Name the European power that established hegemony over the Asian trade in the 16th century.
(A) Dutch
(B) English
(C) Spanish
(D) Portuguese
(E) French

51. By the 18th century, both the French and the Portuguese had lost their bid for controlling trade in India for which of the following reasons?
  I. The Mughal Emperor Jahangir granted trading concessions to the British in 1619.
  II. The British had built the Suez Canal.
  III. The British established 28 trading ports or factories along the Indian coast including Madras, Bombay, and Calcutta.
  IV. Substantial profits were made by both Indian and English merchants.
  V. English seapower prevented reinforcements.

(A) I and II
(B) I, III, IV, and V
(C) I, IV, and V
(D) IV only
(E) all of the above

52. A dividing line drawn by the pope to separate Portuguese and Spanish claims was established through the
(A) Treaty of Tordesillas.
(B) Treaty of Westphalia.
(C) Edict of Nantes.
(D) Treaty of Paris.
(E) Council of Trent.

53. In a SOCIAL sense the American, French, and Latin American revolutions can all be regarded as wars that
(A) protested against taxes.
(B) established religious freedom.
(C) implemented governments that would foster commercial expansion.
(D) protected the populace from growing foreign dominance.
(E) reflected the growing power and culture of the bourgeois.

54. Humanism, the mortar of Greek culture, permeated religion, politics, philosophy, and the arts. Which of the following are examples of humanism?
(A) anthropomorphic examples of Greek gods
(B) Greek tragedies in which fate was shaped by decisions of the hero
(C) rationalism, or the belief that reason is the source of knowledge
(D) the sophist belief that humans were the proper subject of study
(E) all of the above

55. France's financial crisis of the 1780s was due to the
(A) loss of agricultural markets to India.
(B) suppression of the popular revolt in Haiti.
(C) Napoleon's wars in Europe.
(D) French empire abroad.
(E) support for the American Revolution against Britain.

56. The descriptions of Amerindian society by Bernardino de Sahagun in the *General History of the Things of New Spain* are considered authentic because
(A) they are a translation of the Codex Mendoza.
(B) they are translations of written sources later burned by the Spaniards.
(C) they were written by the Aztecs themselves and given to Sahagun to use.
(D) they were the result of Sahagun's research and collection of oral histories at the time of the Spanish conquest.
(E) they are a twentieth century scientific study of the Aztec.

57. Napoleon's greatest achievement as dictator of France was the institution of the Civil Code in 1804, which included all the following EXCEPT
(A) equality of all citizens before the law.
(B) protection of private property.
(C) guaranteed freedom of the press.
(D) the recognition of men as heads of the household.
(E) voting rights for women.

58. A factor that precipitated the Industrial Revolution was
(A) the development of intensive agriculture.
(B) the liberal political revolution in France.
(C) the widespread use of serfs and sharecroppers.
(D) the demand for luxury goods.
(E) none of the above.

59. The man who established the Tokugawa Shogunate was
(A) Ieyasu.
(B) Yoritomo.
(C) Hideyoshi.
(D) Nobunaga.
(E) Ashikaga Takauji.

60. "If therefore, we take from the social compact everything that is not essential to it, we shall find it reduced to the following terms: We, the contracting parties, do jointly and severally submit our persons and abilities to the supreme direction of the general will of all, and, in a part collective body, receive each member into that body, as an indivisible part of the whole."

The author of this passage was probably
(A) Jean Jacques Rousseau.
(B) Baron de Montesquieu.
(C) Adolf Hitler.
(D) Voltaire.
(E) John Locke.

61. "It is true that reason ought to be the torch which lights the conduct of both princes and their states, it is also true that there is nothing in nature less compatible with reason than emotion."

This was most likely written by a political leader in
(A) sixteenth century Italy.
(B) seventeenth century France.
(C) eighteenth century U.S.
(D) nineteenth century Japan.
(E) twentieth century Africa.

62. Where did European colonies become independent in the 19th century?
(A) Latin America
(B) sub-Saharan Africa
(C) Southeast Asia
(D) Southwest Asia
(E) North Africa

63. Romanticism was an artistic and cultural movement infatuated with all EXCEPT
(A) liberalism.
(B) nature.
(C) individualism.
(D) emotionalism.
(E) modern industry.

64. Which of the following 19th-century groups believed the proletariat would conquer the bourgeoisie in revolution?
(A) Chartists
(B) Communists
(C) Social Revolutionaries
(D) Democrats
(E) Anarchists

65. Motivation(s) for empire among industrialized nations was(were)
(A) desire for overseas commodities and raw materials.
(B) opportunity for a rapidly expanding population to emigrate.
(C) profit from the rapid transport of people and products from remote corners of the world.
(D) a focus for national adventure and missionary zeal.
(E) all of the above.

66. All were engineered by Bismark to unite Germany EXCEPT the
(A) Franco-Prussian War.
(B) Austro-Prussian War.
(C) Danish-Prussian War.
(D) Crimean War.
(E) Congress of Berlin.

67. Which great American civilization left these mountain-top palace ruins?
(A) the Aztecs of Mexico
(B) the Olmec of Mesoamerica
(C) the Maya of the Yucatan
(D) the Moche of Peru
(E) the Inca of Peru

68. The Europeans used all of the following tactics to colonize Africa EXCEPT
(A) Christian conversion.
(B) Western education of the elite.
(C) encouraging economic self-sufficiency.
(D) building railroads.
(E) undermining tribal loyalties.

69. The *Bhagavad Gita* is
(A) an excerpt from the *Ramayana*.
(B) one of the longest poems in world literature.
(C) the oldest epic poem in world history.
(D) a story about a Sumerian head of state.
(E) devoid of religious meaning.

70. Which of the following italicized terms is used INCORRECTLY?
(A) The growing *bourgeois* influence led to a National Assembly of lawyers, government officials, and merchants.
(B) *Balance of power* was used by Klemens von Metternich at the Congress of Vienna to preserve the freedom and independence of the great powers.
(C) Liberty, political equality, and representative government are hallmarks of eighteenth and nineteenth century *liberalism.*
(D) The *romantic* movement defended the power of the nobility, aristocratic privilege, and the monarchy.
(E) The *proletariat* developed as a new class of urban workers in the 1800s with industrialization and urbanization.

71. During the Bronze Age, military aristocracies dominated because
(A) weapons and chariot warfare were available only to those who could afford the expensive equipment.
(B) peasants were prohibited from owning bronze weapons.
(C) most people were slaves.
(D) only nobles were permitted to be warriors.
(E) few people possessed the technological skills necessary for producing a chariot.

72. In India, the British imperial policy in the second half of the nineteenth century encouraged
(A) railroad construction.
(B) industrialization.
(C) Asian immigration.
(D) land reform.
(E) universal suffrage.

73. Russia was reunited under the rulers of Moscow because
(A) Russian rulers assumed the title of Czar and claimed descent from Rurik.
(B) Moscow repelled an assult by the Mongols in 1408 and declared Russian independence under Ivan III.
(C) the Russian Orthodox Church with its patriarch recognized the Prince of Moscow as the Autocrat of Russia.
(D) all of the above.
(E) none of the above.

74. All of the following statements are true with regard to twentieth century warfare EXCEPT:
(A) The increased efficiency of the cannon by the time of World War I led to trench warfare.
(B) Battleships using petroleum rather than coal extended their fighting range and their flexibility during World War I.
(C) The blitzkrieg of World War II depended on aircraft carriers and submarines.
(D) Accoustic sonar and radar served as defenses against the rapid deployment of military forces in the 1940s.
(E) Intercontinental Ballistic Missiles (ICBMs) and nuclear-powered Polaris submarines of the 1950s and 1960s increased the ability of nations to accurately target nuclear weapons.

75. By World War I, Britain had formed the Triple Entente with France and
(A) Germany.
(B) Russia.
(C) Italy.
(D) Austria.
(E) Turkey.

76. Which was NOT true of the mandate system instituted after World War I?
(A) Most of Germany's former colonies were transferred to Australia, New Zealand, or Britain.
(B) The principle of "national self-determination," or the joining of historic peoples and ethnic groups, was to be applied to all areas subject to the mandate system.
(C) Non-European peoples lacked the preparation to become independent and were assigned to World War I victors for "tutelage."
(D) The Mandate System was administered by the League of Nations.
(E) Britain received Palestine from the former Ottoman Empire.

77. Legalism with its adherents Han Fei Zi (Tzu) and Li Si (Li Ssu) considered that humans were by nature evil. Which of the following is a clear consequence of that system?
(A) The interpretation of history as a dynastic cycle.
(B) The role of a leader is to provide discipline and maintain order.
(C) Chinese society worked best when all citizens understood their places and duties within the system.
(D) Immoral leaders lacked the mandate from heaven.
(E) The best ruler was the one who governed least.

78. In 1935 Hitler instituted the Nuremburg Laws that
(A) began the rearmament of Germany.
(B) organized the Gestapo, the secret police.
(C) provided employment on public work projects like the autobahns.
(D) denied Jews civil and commercial rights.
(E) declared the Treaty of Versailles Treaty null and void.

79. From the Islamic World, western Europe received
(A) glass lenses for magnification.
(B) identification of diseases and their causes in the *Canon of Medicine* by Ibn Sina (Avicenna).
(C) the Chinese inventions of the compass, gunpowder, and paper.
(D) Greek and Roman classics.
(E) all of the above.

80. The term *green revolution* refers to
(A) reforestation of the Third World.
(B) deforestation of the Third World.
(C) expanded irrigation farming due to water-diversion projects.
(D) the assault on the rain forests.
(E) increased agricultural output due to fertilizers and seed breeding.

81. Reasons for a successful communist revolution in Russia included all EXCEPT
(A) Russian losses during World War I.
(B) working conditions in cities.
(C) army support for the czar.
(D) politicized workers' unions.
(E) the czar's abdication.

82. Which of the following statements concerning economic agreements is not correct?
(A) North American Free Trade Agreement in 1994 established a partnership involving the U.S., Canada, and Mexico.
(B) OPEC created an oil cartel among oil-producing countries to set the price of oil.
(C) The Marshall Plan provided economic aid for the rebuilding of western Europe following World War II.
(D) The European Economic Community was founded in response to the pressures of the Cold War.
(E) The International Monetary Fund was organized to provide small loans to the desperately poor (particularly women) in developing countries.

83. Which twentieth-century leader led the way in rapid industrialization by means of top-down, agriculturally capitalized modernization?
(A) Castro
(B) Stalin
(C) Lenin
(D) Mussolini
(E) Hitler

84. The leader of the Red Army in the civil war that lasted from 1918 to 1921 was
(A) V. I. Lenin.
(B) Karl Marx.
(C) Leon Trotsky.
(D) Alexander Kerensky.
(E) Joseph Stalin.

85. Take up the White Man's burden—
Send forth the best ye breed—
Go bind your sons to exile
To serve your captives' need;
To wait in heavy harness,
On fluttered folk and wild—
Your new-caught, sullen peoples,
Half-devil and half-child.

This passage from Rudyard Kipling's "The White Man's Burden" refers to which European motivation for the imperialization of Africa?
(A) the desire to convert African peoples to Christianity
(B) the quest for natural resources
(C) the quest for land and power
(D) the duty to spread the benefits of civilization to native peoples
(E) the desire to give disinherited sons access to land

86. On this map of Africa, the modern states shown are
   (A) Kenya, Ethiopia, and South Africa.
   (B) Ghana, Egypt, and Tanzania.
   (C) Namibia, Nigeria, and Sudan.
   (D) Angola, Ivory Coast, and Mali.
   (E) South Africa, Angola, and Zimbabwe.

87. The U.S. occupation of Japan after World War II resulted in which of the following?
   (A) demilitarization
   (B) industrialization
   (C) rapprochement with China
   (D) collectivization of agriculture.
   (E) U.S. control of industry.

88. Hellenistic Society represented a diffusion and merging of cultural traditions. All of the following are examples of this cultural amalgamation EXCEPT
   (A) India's construction of monuments carved and decorated with stone.
   (B) the Hellenization of the Roman world.
   (C) Bactrian Greek art.
   (D) the development of the trade language of Koine.
   (E) Hellenic style of warfare.

89. As a result of the Truman Doctrine, military aid was offered to
   (A) Greece and Turkey.
   (B) Italy and Germany.
   (C) Britain and France.
   (D) the Soviet Union.
   (E) Iran.

90. Fighting between Hindus and Muslims continued following the partition of the subcontinent with both Pakistan and India claiming the disputed area of
   (A) Punjab.
   (B) Bengal.
   (C) South India.
   (D) Kashmir.
   (E) none of the above.

91. Under the leadership of the Ayatollah Khomeini, Iran became a
   (A) modern secular state with a one-party system.
   (B) fundamentalist Sunni nation.
   (C) radical Shi'ite government isolated from its neighbors.
   (D) military dictatorship.
   (E) liberal, westernized republic.

92. Leaders who implemented the Great Proletarian Cultural Revolution were the
   (A) party officials.
   (B) professors and intellectuals.
   (C) Red Guards.
   (D) peasants.
   (E) Russian advisers.

93. What advantages did sea trade offer?
   (A) few political barriers
   (B) Wind was a free source of fuel.
   (C) Shipping was more efficient.
   (D) new sources of wealth
   (E) all of the above

94. This scene reflects one of world history's greatest demographic disasters. It was
(A) the European Plague of the 14th century.
(B) Amerindian deaths on the heels of the Spanish conquest of the Americas in the 16th century.
(C) the 1917–1918 pandemic.
(D) the bloodbath resulting from the Thirty Years War of the 17th century.
(E) death from poison gas in the World War I trenches.

95. By preferring the support of domestic to that of foreign industry, he intends only his own security; and by directing that industry in such a manner as its produce may be of the greatest value, he intends only his own gain, and he is in this, as in many other cases, led by an invisible hand to promote an end which was no part of his intention.

The "invisible hand" in this passage by Adam Smith refers to
(A) the integrated European market.
(B) government mercantilist policies.
(C) the accumulation of profit.
(D) the free market laws of supply and demand.
(E) the human propensity toward greed.

96. This statue is most closely associated with what culture?
(A) Incan
(B) Polynesian
(C) Chinese
(D) Indian
(E) Persian

97. The most important factor leading to an independent Pakistan was
(A) Great Britain's support for an independent Pakistan.
(B) the existence of Pakistani princely states.
(C) Gandhi's leadership in creating a sovereign Pakistan.
(D) the United Nations peace plan for the area.
(E) the existence of Muslim majority in the area.

98. The wealth and independence of the Byzantine Empire resulted from
(A) a carefully designed defense system for Constantinople that included cisterns, walls, a chain across the harbor, and a small, well-trained army.
(B) the skillful use of intelligence and diplomacy to establish a system of military alliances with Catholic popes and European kings.
(C) Constantinople developing as a western entrepot of the Silk Road.
(D) stimulating the production of luxury products by master craftsmen.
(E) all of the above.

99. The two religions often in conflict in India since independence are
   (A) Jainism and Hinduism.
   (B) Hinduism and Buddhism.
   (C) Buddhism and Islam.
   (D) Islam and Christianity.
   (E) Hinduism and Islam.

100. The Egyptian leader who agreed to recognize Israel in exchange for the Sinai was
   (A) Anwar el-Sadat.
   (B) Yassar Arafat.
   (C) Gamal Abdel Nasser.
   (D) Ussein Ibn Ali.
   (E) none of the above.

101. The Mongol invasion had all of the following consequences EXCEPT
   (A) the reopening of the Silk Road.
   (B) the strengthening of maritime trade in the South China Seas.
   (C) the diffusion of gunpowder technology.
   (D) the demand for European products such as wool, porcelain, sugar, spices, and coffee.
   (E) the rise of the autocracy in Russia.

ANSWER SHEET — MODEL TEST 2

1. Ⓐ Ⓑ Ⓒ Ⓓ Ⓔ	36. Ⓐ Ⓑ Ⓒ Ⓓ Ⓔ	71. Ⓐ Ⓑ Ⓒ Ⓓ Ⓔ
2. Ⓐ Ⓑ Ⓒ Ⓓ Ⓔ	37. Ⓐ Ⓑ Ⓒ Ⓓ Ⓔ	72. Ⓐ Ⓑ Ⓒ Ⓓ Ⓔ
3. Ⓐ Ⓑ Ⓒ Ⓓ Ⓔ	38. Ⓐ Ⓑ Ⓒ Ⓓ Ⓔ	73. Ⓐ Ⓑ Ⓒ Ⓓ Ⓔ
4. Ⓐ Ⓑ Ⓒ Ⓓ Ⓔ	39. Ⓐ Ⓑ Ⓒ Ⓓ Ⓔ	74. Ⓐ Ⓑ Ⓒ Ⓓ Ⓔ
5. Ⓐ Ⓑ Ⓒ Ⓓ Ⓔ	40. Ⓐ Ⓑ Ⓒ Ⓓ Ⓔ	75. Ⓐ Ⓑ Ⓒ Ⓓ Ⓔ
6. Ⓐ Ⓑ Ⓒ Ⓓ Ⓔ	41. Ⓐ Ⓑ Ⓒ Ⓓ Ⓔ	76. Ⓐ Ⓑ Ⓒ Ⓓ Ⓔ
7. Ⓐ Ⓑ Ⓒ Ⓓ Ⓔ	42. Ⓐ Ⓑ Ⓒ Ⓓ Ⓔ	77. Ⓐ Ⓑ Ⓒ Ⓓ Ⓔ
8. Ⓐ Ⓑ Ⓒ Ⓓ Ⓔ	43. Ⓐ Ⓑ Ⓒ Ⓓ Ⓔ	78. Ⓐ Ⓑ Ⓒ Ⓓ Ⓔ
9. Ⓐ Ⓑ Ⓒ Ⓓ Ⓔ	44. Ⓐ Ⓑ Ⓒ Ⓓ Ⓔ	79. Ⓐ Ⓑ Ⓒ Ⓓ Ⓔ
10. Ⓐ Ⓑ Ⓒ Ⓓ Ⓔ	45. Ⓐ Ⓑ Ⓒ Ⓓ Ⓔ	80. Ⓐ Ⓑ Ⓒ Ⓓ Ⓔ
11. Ⓐ Ⓑ Ⓒ Ⓓ Ⓔ	46. Ⓐ Ⓑ Ⓒ Ⓓ Ⓔ	81. Ⓐ Ⓑ Ⓒ Ⓓ Ⓔ
12. Ⓐ Ⓑ Ⓒ Ⓓ Ⓔ	47. Ⓐ Ⓑ Ⓒ Ⓓ Ⓔ	82. Ⓐ Ⓑ Ⓒ Ⓓ Ⓔ
13. Ⓐ Ⓑ Ⓒ Ⓓ Ⓔ	48. Ⓐ Ⓑ Ⓒ Ⓓ Ⓔ	83. Ⓐ Ⓑ Ⓒ Ⓓ Ⓔ
14. Ⓐ Ⓑ Ⓒ Ⓓ Ⓔ	49. Ⓐ Ⓑ Ⓒ Ⓓ Ⓔ	84. Ⓐ Ⓑ Ⓒ Ⓓ Ⓔ
15. Ⓐ Ⓑ Ⓒ Ⓓ Ⓔ	50. Ⓐ Ⓑ Ⓒ Ⓓ Ⓔ	85. Ⓐ Ⓑ Ⓒ Ⓓ Ⓔ
16. Ⓐ Ⓑ Ⓒ Ⓓ Ⓔ	51. Ⓐ Ⓑ Ⓒ Ⓓ Ⓔ	86. Ⓐ Ⓑ Ⓒ Ⓓ Ⓔ
17. Ⓐ Ⓑ Ⓒ Ⓓ Ⓔ	52. Ⓐ Ⓑ Ⓒ Ⓓ Ⓔ	87. Ⓐ Ⓑ Ⓒ Ⓓ Ⓔ
18. Ⓐ Ⓑ Ⓒ Ⓓ Ⓔ	53. Ⓐ Ⓑ Ⓒ Ⓓ Ⓔ	88. Ⓐ Ⓑ Ⓒ Ⓓ Ⓔ
19. Ⓐ Ⓑ Ⓒ Ⓓ Ⓔ	54. Ⓐ Ⓑ Ⓒ Ⓓ Ⓔ	89. Ⓐ Ⓑ Ⓒ Ⓓ Ⓔ
20. Ⓐ Ⓑ Ⓒ Ⓓ Ⓔ	55. Ⓐ Ⓑ Ⓒ Ⓓ Ⓔ	90. Ⓐ Ⓑ Ⓒ Ⓓ Ⓔ
21. Ⓐ Ⓑ Ⓒ Ⓓ Ⓔ	56. Ⓐ Ⓑ Ⓒ Ⓓ Ⓔ	91. Ⓐ Ⓑ Ⓒ Ⓓ Ⓔ
22. Ⓐ Ⓑ Ⓒ Ⓓ Ⓔ	57. Ⓐ Ⓑ Ⓒ Ⓓ Ⓔ	92. Ⓐ Ⓑ Ⓒ Ⓓ Ⓔ
23. Ⓐ Ⓑ Ⓒ Ⓓ Ⓔ	58. Ⓐ Ⓑ Ⓒ Ⓓ Ⓔ	93. Ⓐ Ⓑ Ⓒ Ⓓ Ⓔ
24. Ⓐ Ⓑ Ⓒ Ⓓ Ⓔ	59. Ⓐ Ⓑ Ⓒ Ⓓ Ⓔ	94. Ⓐ Ⓑ Ⓒ Ⓓ Ⓔ
25. Ⓐ Ⓑ Ⓒ Ⓓ Ⓔ	60. Ⓐ Ⓑ Ⓒ Ⓓ Ⓔ	95. Ⓐ Ⓑ Ⓒ Ⓓ Ⓔ
26. Ⓐ Ⓑ Ⓒ Ⓓ Ⓔ	61. Ⓐ Ⓑ Ⓒ Ⓓ Ⓔ	96. Ⓐ Ⓑ Ⓒ Ⓓ Ⓔ
27. Ⓐ Ⓑ Ⓒ Ⓓ Ⓔ	62. Ⓐ Ⓑ Ⓒ Ⓓ Ⓔ	97. Ⓐ Ⓑ Ⓒ Ⓓ Ⓔ
28. Ⓐ Ⓑ Ⓒ Ⓓ Ⓔ	63. Ⓐ Ⓑ Ⓒ Ⓓ Ⓔ	98. Ⓐ Ⓑ Ⓒ Ⓓ Ⓔ
29. Ⓐ Ⓑ Ⓒ Ⓓ Ⓔ	64. Ⓐ Ⓑ Ⓒ Ⓓ Ⓔ	99. Ⓐ Ⓑ Ⓒ Ⓓ Ⓔ
30. Ⓐ Ⓑ Ⓒ Ⓓ Ⓔ	65. Ⓐ Ⓑ Ⓒ Ⓓ Ⓔ	100. Ⓐ Ⓑ Ⓒ Ⓓ Ⓔ
31. Ⓐ Ⓑ Ⓒ Ⓓ Ⓔ	66. Ⓐ Ⓑ Ⓒ Ⓓ Ⓔ	101. Ⓐ Ⓑ Ⓒ Ⓓ Ⓔ
32. Ⓐ Ⓑ Ⓒ Ⓓ Ⓔ	67. Ⓐ Ⓑ Ⓒ Ⓓ Ⓔ	102. Ⓐ Ⓑ Ⓒ Ⓓ Ⓔ
33. Ⓐ Ⓑ Ⓒ Ⓓ Ⓔ	68. Ⓐ Ⓑ Ⓒ Ⓓ Ⓔ	103. Ⓐ Ⓑ Ⓒ Ⓓ Ⓔ
34. Ⓐ Ⓑ Ⓒ Ⓓ Ⓔ	69. Ⓐ Ⓑ Ⓒ Ⓓ Ⓔ	104. Ⓐ Ⓑ Ⓒ Ⓓ Ⓔ
35. Ⓐ Ⓑ Ⓒ Ⓓ Ⓔ	70. Ⓐ Ⓑ Ⓒ Ⓓ Ⓔ	105. Ⓐ Ⓑ Ⓒ Ⓓ Ⓔ

Model Test 2

> *The actual SAT II: World History examination will contain ninety questions. This Model Test includes more than that, in order to give you a more comprehensive practice exam.*

1. Which of the following statements INCORRECTLY links the leader, country, and change following World War I?
   - (A) The Fascists, both antidemocratic and anticommunist, seized power in Italy under Benito Mussolini.
   - (B) Germany's National Socialist party, led by Adolf Hitler, gained a majority in the election of 1933 and abolished the Reichstag.
   - (C) Following the Amritsar Massacre in India, Mohandas Gandhi launched a nonviolent protest against British rule.
   - (D) Supporting President Wilson's 14 Points, the United States became a leader in the League of Nations to make the world safe for democracy.
   - (E) In China Mao Tse-tung and his communist army fled the Nationalist Chinese army of Chiang Kai-shek in their long march to a new stronghold in the north.

2. Which INCORRECTLY links the technology with the people of the fifteenth century?
   - (A) Germans and Koreans—printing press with moveable type
   - (B) Indians—vertical loom, block printing, and spinning wheel
   - (C) Chinese—compass and ocean-going ships
   - (D) Arabs—dhows and lateen sails
   - (E) English—steam engine and spinning jenny

3. Between 1880 and 1900 all of the following European nations established empires in Africa EXCEPT the
   - (A) British.
   - (B) French.
   - (C) Germans.
   - (D) Italians.
   - (E) Spanish.

4. What was the cause of the French Revolution?
   - (A) rising power of the middle class
   - (B) inspiration of the American Revolution
   - (C) threat of national bankruptcy
   - (D) increased taxes paid by the peasants
   - (E) all of the above

5. "It is true that we are called a democracy. . ." "For we are lovers of the beautiful, yet with economy . . ."

   This probably describes the people of which classical city?
   - (A) Athens
   - (B) Sparta
   - (C) Rome
   - (D) Pataliputra
   - (E) Chang-an

6. All of the following were Soviet satellites EXCEPT
   - (A) Poland.
   - (B) Czechoslovakia.
   - (C) Hungary.
   - (D) Yugoslavia.
   - (E) Bulgaria.

7. Why did the discovery of the Americas lead to Spanish impoverishment?
   (A) Much of the gold stayed in the Americas to build churches and missions.
   (B) Bullion was used to pay for Spanish debt and wars.
   (C) Bullion was used to pay for Asian products.
   (D) The importation of so much American gold and silver led to inflation within the Spanish economy.
   (E) all of the above

8. The emerging rulers who gained control of Russian society in the 1500s were
   (A) the Tartars.
   (B) the boyars.
   (C) the serfs.
   (D) the czars.
   (E) the veche.

9. Which of the following INCORRECTLY links the philosopher with his philosophy?
   (A) Locke—All people have the right to life, liberty, and property.
   (B) Hobbes—People gave up their freedom to a ruler who established order.
   (C) Montesquieu—The state should be divided so that no one person or one group have unlimited power.
   (D) Voltaire—people are rarely fit to govern themselves and should, without reservation, submit themselves to the rule of an enlightened monarch.
   (E) Rousseau—men are born free but everywhere are in chains.

10. Leaders of the Taiping Rebellion favored
    I. rapid economic development.
    II. defense of the Amur basin and Manchuria against Russian encroachment.
    III. redistribution of land.
    IV. equality between men and women.
    V. reduction in taxes.

    (A) I, II, and III
    (B) I, III, and V
    (C) II, III, and V
    (D) III, IV, and V
    (E) I, II, and IV

11. Once Lenin seized power, he ordered all EXCEPT
    (A) participation in World War I to continue.
    (B) nationalization of the banks.
    (C) large landed estates redistributed among the peasants.
    (D) worker control of factories.
    (E) confiscation of church properties.

12. In Persia, the new Safavid dynasty (1501–1736) established a state religion that was
    (A) Sunni Islam.
    (B) Shi'ite Islam.
    (C) Eastern Orthodox Christianity.
    (D) Hinduism.
    (E) none of the above.

13. Chinese bronzes of the Shang Dynasty are considered masterpieces worldwide. They are constructed by
    (A) welding decorative pieces to a bronze container.
    (B) using the lost wax process.
    (C) pouring molten bronze between two clay molds to imprint the design.
    (D) using all of these methods.
    (E) using none of these methods.

14. Who was responsible for nationalizing the Suez Canal?
    (A) Anwar Sadat
    (B) Menachem Begin
    (C) Gamal Abdel Nasser
    (D) Queen Victoria
    (E) Lawrence of Arabia

15. Nomadic pastoralists differed from hunter-gatherers because they herded domesticated animals in plains regions of Asia, Africa, and the Americas. Advantages of domesticated animals include all of the following EXCEPT
    I.   a reliable source of power and transport.
    II. a steady source of protein.
    III. a new degree of mobility.
    IV. the continuation of slash-and-burn agriculture.

    (A) I and II
    (B) I, II, and III
    (C) II, III, and IV
    (D) I, III, and IV
    (E) all of the above

16. Classical Chinese thought reflects all EXCEPT
    (A) the search for the "tao."
    (B) the search for truth by following a "middle path."
    (C) the need for social and political harmony.
    (D) the belief in God.
    (E) the necessity for strong government.

17. The "Scramble for Africa" led to the European colonization of the whole African continent EXCEPT
    (A) Egypt and South Africa.
    (B) Liberia and Ethiopia.
    (C) Kenya and Madagascar.
    (D) Morocco and Libya.
    (E) Nigeria and Congo.

18. European influence did not penetrate the interior of Africa until the
    (A) nineteeth century.
    (B) eighteenth century.
    (C) seventeenth century.
    (D) sixteenth century.
    (E) fifteenth century.

19. The most likely explanation for this is
    (A) the military superiority of the Africans.
    (B) the Europeans were not interested in the interior.
    (C) malaria.
    (D) rain forests.
    (E) all of the above

20. This artistic masterpiece was sculpted by
    (A) Leon Battista Alberti.
    (B) Leonardo da Vinci.
    (C) Raphael.
    (D) Michelangelo.
    (E) Corrego.

21. Which battle is INCORRECTLY linked with its consequence?
    (A) Battle of Manzikerk—The Seljuk Turks defeated the Byzantines and claimed land from Palestine to Turkey.
    (B) Battle of Talas River—The Muslims with their Central Asian allies learned the technology for producing paper after defeating the Chinese and their Central Asian allies.
    (C) Battle of Tours—The Muslim advance into eastern Europe ended with this battle.
    (D) The fall of Constantinople—The victory of the Ottoman Turks and the end of the Byzantine Empire
    (E) The fall of Kiev—The founding of Moscow and new city-states in the northeast by the Russians.

22. The Boer War (1899–1902) was fought between
    (A) Great Britain and Afrikaners for control of South Africa.
    (B) France and Britain over the Sudan.
    (C) Germany and Britain for control of East Africa.
    (D) Afrikaners and Zulu for the Orange Free State.
    (E) Germany and France for Morocco.

23. According to Descartes and Bacon,
    (A) reason is the foundation of knowledge.
    (B) reason could be used to interpret the results of experimentation and observation.
    (C) inductive and deductive thought are the basis of reason.
    (D) rationalism is the basis of science.
    (E) all of the above

24. Which of the following geographical advantages was shared by Egypt and Mesopotamia?
    (A) Gradual rise of flood waters with yearly deposits of silt
    (B) Borders protected by natural geographic barriers
    (C) Large deposits of stone
    (D) Access to timber and copper
    (E) Access to water for irrigation

25. In 1453 the Ottoman Turks gained control of
    (A) the Balkans.
    (B) Constantinople.
    (C) the Adriatic Sea.
    (D) Syria, Palestine, and Egypt.
    (E) Vienna.

26. Chinampas were
    (A) subordinate provinces within the Aztec state.
    (B) marketplaces within the city of Tenochtitlan.
    (C) neighboring states that paid tribute to the Aztecs.
    (D) artificial floating gardens that supplied the Aztecs with food.
    (E) pyramids built by the Aztecs to honor their gods.

27. Which architectural form uses the arch?
    I. aqueduct
    II. coliseum
    III. pantheon
    IV. Parthenon
    V. St. Sophia

    (A) I, II, and III
    (B) I, II, and IV
    (C) all except III
    (D) all except IV
    (E) all except V

28. Which port in the Indian Ocean trade is INCORRECTLY linked with its product?
    (A) Mogadishu—gold
    (B) Calicut—cotton
    (C) Ormuz—-carpets
    (D) Jidda—paper
    (E) Hangzhou—porcelain

29. Athenian democracy DIFFERED from modern American democracy in that
   (A) only citizens voted.
   (B) public buildings and the arts were open to all.
   (C) government was a direct democracy.
   (D) juries were chosen by lot.
   (E) the executive branch included the commander-in-chief.

30. Which of the following statements CORRECTLY defines stateless societies?
   (A) indigenous peoples related by bloodlines
   (B) agricultural colonists supported by an organized state
   (C) caravans of Muslim traders who moved from market to market
   (D) culturally and ethnically homogeneous societies with local governments
   (E) none of the above

31. What was the international significance of Italy's invasion of Ethiopia and Japan's invasion of Manchuria?
   (A) the failure of appeasement
   (B) the weakness of the United Nations
   (C) the injustice of the Treaty of Versailles
   (D) the ineffectiveness of the League of Nations
   (E) the formation of the Rome-Berlin-Tokyo axis

32. The *Tale of Genji* is famous because
   (A) it is written in Japanese rather than Chinese.
   (B) describes court life during the Heian period.
   (C) was written by a woman.
   (D) is one of the world's first novels.
   (E) all of the above.

33. Which is NOT a twentieth century art form?
   (A) abstractionism
   (B) impressionism
   (C) romanticism
   (D) socialist realism
   (E) bauhaus

34. Which of the following societies developed a lasting concept of monotheism?
   (A) Hebrew
   (B) Egyptian
   (C) Non Nok Tha
   (D) Hindu
   (E) Chinese

35. Which of the policies advocated by Robert Owen directly resulted in reform legislation?
   (A) Healthy people are better workers.
   (B) Profits should be shared through philanthropy.
   (C) improved wages for all laborers
   (D) better working conditions for women and children
   (E) The community should be the focus of manufacturers.

36. The first maritime power to navigate the Indian Ocean in order to extend political and military power, as well as trade in luxury products, was
   (A) Portugal.
   (B) Spain.
   (C) China.
   (D) France.
   (E) England.

37. All of the following are reactions to the development of nuclear weapons EXCEPT
   (A) fear of MAD, "mutually assured destruction," which led to the suspension of nuclear war.
   (B) the decline in the number of guerrilla wars with their dependence on traditional weapons.
   (C) modern war technology, which was confined to countries that can afford it, often with traumatic consequences to the national economies.
   (D) the space exploration programs of the Soviet Union and the United States, which included a consideration of the use of weapons technology.
   (E) the proliferation of nuclear weapons.

38. "If one break a man's bone, they shall break his bone.
If one destroy the eye of a freeman or break the bone of a freeman, he shall pay one mana silver
If one destroys the eye of a man's slave or break a bone of a man's slave, he shall pay one-half his price."

The source of this quote is most likely
(A) the New Testament
(B) Draco's Code of Law
(C) Hammurabi's Code
(D) Justinian's Code
(E) Laws of Manu

39. "*Red-haired* is a general term for the barbarians of the western islands. Amongst them are the Dutch, French, Spaniards, Portuguese, English, and Yu-su-la (Muslims?), all of which nations are horribly fierce. Wherever they go, they spy around with a view to seize other people's territories."

H. A. Giles

This passage was probably written by
(A) a Chinese official in the sixth century C.E.
(B) an Aztec official in the sixteenth century C.E.
(C) a Chinese official in the eighteenth century C.E.
(D) a Japanese official in the nineteeth century C.E.
(E) a Korean official in the twentieth century C.E.

40. The leaders of India's Congress Party included all of the following EXCEPT
(A) Indira Gandhi.
(B) Jawaharlal Nehru.
(C) Muhammad ali Jinnah.
(D) Rajiv Gandhi.
(E) Mahatma Gandhi.

41. Under the Sun King, Louis XIV, local government was firmly in the hands of
(A) local governors.
(B) church officials.
(C) intendants.
(D) satraps.
(E) parliaments.

42. The Solidarity movement in Poland, which ultimately toppled the communist regime, was helped by what other Polish institution?
(A) the army
(B) the Catholic church
(C) the Polish parliament
(D) the peasantry
(E) the dissident communist party members

43. Of the following foods, which was domesticated in the eastern hemisphere?
(A) corn
(B) potatoes
(C) cocoa
(D) wheat
(E) tomatoes

44. What was behind the ten-year Mexican Revolution and the Civil War?
(A) revenge for the U.S. acquisition of Texas
(B) unification of Mexico and Central America
(C) return to indigenous Indian rule
(D) return to classical liberalism
(E) demand for land reform, voting rights, and the right to organize and strike

45. Central to the beliefs of Zoroastrianism was
(A) monotheism.
(B) polytheistic gods representing elements of nature.
(C) establishment of a theistic state with the king worshipped as a god.
(D) a pantheon of gods with anthropomorphic characteristics.
(E) dualistic beliefs in good and evil.

46. The historical interpretation of the French Revolution as a liberal revolt by the bourgeoisie is challenged by the evidence that
    (A) only 8 percent of France's population was middle class.
    (B) the middle and upper classes were disunited in their objectives.
    (C) the French were governed by a dictator.
    (D) France eventually returned to a partial monarchy.
    (E) all of the above

47. The most influential ruling class in Chinese history was
    (A) soldiers.
    (B) nobles.
    (C) merchants.
    (D) scholars.
    (E) priests.

48. Who said, during the Cold War, that Berlin was the "great testing place of Western courage and will" and "Ich bin ein Berliner" (I am a Berliner)?
    (A) Mikhail Gorbachev
    (B) Helmut Kohl
    (C) Willy Brandt
    (D) Vaclev Havel
    (E) John F. Kennedy

49. The social consequences of industrialization during the 1800s was marked by all of the following EXCEPT
    (A) increasing importance of education.
    (B) beginning of the age of mass consumption and culture.
    (C) increasing migration of workers from cities to the countryside.
    (D) improvement in urban living conditions.
    (E) a new class of urban workers, the proletariat.

50. Pastoral nomads served essential roles as
    (A) agents of change.
    (B) empire builders.
    (C) long-distance traders.
    (D) mercenaries.
    (E) all of the above

51. Karl Marx believed that the Industrial Revolution would lead to
    (A) a world revolution of the working class.
    (B) the overthrow of the bourgeoisie.
    (C) the triumph of communism.
    (D) the state withering away.
    (E) all of the above

52. The U.S. president who withdrew American forces from Vietnam was
    (A) Truman.
    (B) Kennedy.
    (C) Johnson.
    (D) Carter.
    (E) Nixon.

53. What architectural features are unique to gothic architecture?
    (A) flying buttresses and stained glass windows
    (B) domes and steeples
    (C) cross-vaulting and barrel arches
    (D) minarets and calligraphy
    (E) icons and gargoyles

54. The most likely reason that people's republics were established in Central and East Europe after World War II is the
    (A) presence of Soviet troops.
    (B) presence of Tito's troops.
    (C) preference of East and Central European countries for communism.
    (D) preference in Central and East Europe for republicanism.
    (E) treaties signed at Yalta and Teheran.

55. The empires that were linked with one another through trade routes branching from the Silk Road circa 100 C.E. were
  I. Rome
  II. Carthage
  III. Egypt
  IV. Mauryan India
  V. Han China.

  (A) I and V
  (B) II and IV
  (C) I, II, and IV
  (D) I, II, and III
  (E) all of the above

56. Which of the following is arranged in CORRECT chronological order?
  (A) Cuban Missile Crisis, Korean War, World War II
  (B) United Nations Charter, Wall Street Crash, Berlin Wall
  (C) Korean War, Cuban Missile Crisis, Berlin Wall
  (D) Berlin Wall, Korean War, Cuban Missile Crisis
  (E) World War I, United Nations Charter, World War II

57. Christianity became an established religion with many converts in the eastern Mediterranean because of all EXCEPT
  (A) the travel and organization of early churches by Paul of Tarsus.
  (B) communal rituals, like the Eucharist, which were open to all believers.
  (C) the stated purpose for life offered in the Epistles and Gospels.
  (D) its universal appeal to the upper class.
  (E) the opportunity to gain political and economic status.

58. Based on linguistic and physical evidence, all of the following were sites of Polynesian migrations EXCEPT
  (A) Hawaii.
  (B) Australia.
  (C) New Zealand.
  (D) Madagascar.
  (E) Fiji.

59. The medieval Roman Catholic Church often was in conflict with secular rulers over the issue of
  (A) selection of the pope.
  (B) excommunication.
  (C) punishment of heretics.
  (D) lay investiture.
  (E) all of the above

60. Siddhartha Gautama was designated by his followers as the Buddha, which means
  (A) King of Nepal.
  (B) Emperor of Buddhism.
  (C) the Great Teacher.
  (D) the Prophet.
  (E) the "Enlightened" One.

61. World War II began for the Chinese in
  (A) 1910 when the Japanese annexed Korea.
  (B) 1931 when the Japanese invaded Manchuria.
  (C) 1939 when the Japanese invaded China.
  (D) 1941 when the Japanese invaded Singapore.
  (E) 1941 when the Japanese attacked Pearl Harbor.

62. The Mongol army was successful for all of the following reasons EXCEPT
  (A) the unification of Central Asian tribes loyal to one leader.
  (B) the ability of the Mongol commanders to rule all conquered peoples under one law, one language, and one religion.
  (C) the use of intimidation and deception to demoralize the enemy.
  (D) the mobility of the cavalry.
  (E) the division of the army into units of 10, 100, 1000, and 10,000, with commanders at each level responsible for discipline and training.

63. The Sermon on the Mount reflects which fundamental aspect of Christianity?
(A) Love your neighbor and hate your enemy.
(B) Love your neighbor and your enemy.
(C) Love God and follow the Commandments.
(D) Blessed are those who work and lead nations.
(E) The kingdom of heaven belongs to those who are strong and successful.

64. The *Epic of Gilgamesh*
(A) shows man's concern with enduring questions of life and death.
(B) has some parallels to Biblical stories like Noah's Ark and the Tale of Job.
(C) was written about 2000 B.C.E. but probably repeated orally for millennia earlier.
(D) is one of the world's oldest written stories.
(E) all of the above

65. Which of the following men was responsible for the germ theory of diseases?
(A) Albert Schweitzer
(B) Edwin Chadwick
(C) Louis Pasteur
(D) Joseph Lister
(E) Frances Bacon

66. Which of the following statements is inaccurate?
(A) Times of great interaction stimulate new ways of doing things and new habits of thought.
(B) Total wars of the twentieth century have required nations to field large, professional armies, which are entirely separate in their training and deployment from the civilian population.
(C) With modernization have come population pressures, resource depletion, and environmental disequilibrium.
(D) Wars of the twentieth century have produced new technologies and inventions and introduced people to new ways of doing things.
(E) Western culture has continued to set worldwide trends.

67. All of the following are pillars of the Islamic faith EXCEPT
(A) belief in the creed that "There is no God but Allah, Muhammed is His prophet."
(B) prayer five times a day.
(C) almsgiving.
(D) fasting during the holy month of Ramadan.
(E) pilgrimage to Medina.

68. Which of the following predicted that population tends to expand faster than the supply of food?
(A) Adam Smith
(B) Thomas Malthus
(C) David Ricardo
(D) George Hegel
(E) Frederick Engels

69. A social reason for Spanish exploration and conquest was
(A) the development of the caravel.
(B) a demand for spices like nutmeg, mace, ginger, cinnamon, and pepper.
(C) competition and rivalries between the Spanish and other Europeans.
(D) the opportunity for disinherited young Spanish nobles to advance.
(E) the desire to convert pagans to the Roman Catholic faith.

70. Unlike the Russians, the Chinese communists under Mao
(A) depended on foreign aid from the allies following World War II.
(B) envisioned a revolution of peasant guerrilla fighters.
(C) centered their efforts in cities organizing through labor unions.
(D) took the brunt of the fighting against the Japanese invaders.
(E) were discredited among the peasants and workers at the end of World War II because of inflation and corruption.

71. The development of writing led to all of the following advantages for a more complex society EXCEPT
- (A) centralized rule and enforcement of government regulations.
- (B) empowered peasant villages.
- (C) increased body of knowledge passed from one generation to another.
- (D) centralized records of tax payments, land ownership, and contracts.
- (E) creation of a literate bureaucratic class.

72. Between 1865 and 1910,
- (A) the United States surpassed Britain as the major world producer of steel.
- (B) Britain overtook the United States as the major world producer of steel.
- (C) Russia overtook Britain as the major world producer of steel.
- (D) Germany overtook the United States as the major world producer of steel.
- (E) none of the above

73. Famines in India in the late 1880s were the likely result of
- (A) the Sepoy Rebellion.
- (B) the doctrine of lapse.
- (C) British policy to encourage the production of cotton rather than food.
- (D) policies of the Indian National Congress.
- (E) sporadic peasant revolts.

74. Which of the following countries declared war on Japan one week before Japan surrendered in 1945?
- (A) England
- (B) France
- (C) China
- (D) Russia
- (E) India

75. Plantations with African slave labor were established in
- (A) Mauritius.
- (B) Zanzibar.
- (C) Cape of Good Hope.
- (D) Sicily.
- (E) all of the above

76. The most immediate consequence of the Russian defeat in the Crimean War was
- (A) western investment in Russian manufacturing.
- (B) construction of a network of railroads.
- (C) implementation of high tariffs to protect Russian industry.
- (D) banking reform.
- (E) the Emancipation Proclamation, which freed the serfs.

77. The terror phase of the French Revolution is most associated with
- (A) the declaration of the Rights of Man.
- (B) the Tennis Court Oath.
- (C) the Legislative Assembly.
- (D) the Committee on Public Safety.
- (E) the Directory.

78. The *Analects* sought to establish order among people by recognizing
- (A) the family as the basic unit of society.
- (B) that society could be ordered with all individuals exercising proper behavior and fulfilling their duties.
- (C) that families should establish proper relationships.
- (D) any man, either poor or privileged, could become a gentleman with proper conduct or *Li*.
- (E) all of the above

79. Which organizations are centered around economic rather than political activities?
- I. OPEC
- II. NATO
- III. SEATO
- IV. SWAPO
- V. NAFTA

- (A) I and II
- (B) I and V
- (C) III and IV
- (D) II and IV
- (E) IV and V

80. The Magna Carta was significant in English history because it established
    (A) Norman rule as the treaty following the Battle of Hastings in 1066.
    (B) the royal court system with trial by a jury of 12 peers and made English law the common law for all Englishmen.
    (C) the principle of the rule of law and promised that no tax would be imposed without approval by the common council of the kingdom.
    (D) the process the king would use to appoint the archbishop.
    (E) Parliament as a permanent institution with two assemblies, the House of Lords and the House of Commons.

81. Which organization was not associated with twentieth century independence movements?
    (A) Sans Culottes
    (B) African National Congress
    (C) Kuomintang
    (D) Viet Minh
    (E) Muslim League

82. Which of the following men ruled China as the founder of the Yuan dynasty?
    (A) Genghiz Khan
    (B) Ogedei Khan
    (C) Kublai Khan
    (D) Batu Khan
    (E) none of the above

83. Increases in the Irish population up to 1840 were because of
    (A) better public health.
    (B) industrialization and better job opportunities.
    (C) introduction of the potato as a staple for peasants.
    (D) improved education.
    (E) improved economic conditions in the eighteenth and nineteeth centuries.

84. All were reasons for the rapid extension of the Inca Empire EXCEPT
    (A) equal rights for common peasants.
    (B) Quechua, a shared common language.
    (C) an elaborate system of roads, bridges, and tunnels.
    (D) a state religion headed by the Inca.
    (E) a highly trained bureaucracy.

85. All of the following were Muslim centers of Islamic culture and education in the period from 1200 to 1600 C.E. EXCEPT
    (A) Delhi.
    (B) Timbuktu.
    (C) Cairo.
    (D) Cordoba.
    (E) Kiev.

86. The map on page 392 illustrates
    (A) the Byzantine Empire in 565 C.E.
    (B) the Roman Empire in 117 C.E.
    (C) Alexander the Great's Empire in 323 B.C.E.
    (D) the spread of agriculture in Europe.
    (E) Cyrus the Great's Empire in 486 B.C.E.

87. What was the reason Belgium became important to the outbreak of World War I?
    (A) It was part of the Triple Alliance.
    (B) Its mountainous terrain prevented implementation of the Schlieffin Plan.
    (C) Belgium had a defensive alliance with France.
    (D) Belgium was Germany's highway into France.
    (E) Russia had an alliance with Belgium.

88. What is the most likely explanation for the fact that Siam (Thailand) maintained its independence in the nineteenth century when countries all around it were colonized?
    (A) The geography of Thailand offered natural protective barriers.
    (B) The Treaty of Paris prohibited such imperialization.
    (C) The Dutch presence was very powerful.
    (D) The British in Burma and the French in Indochina distrusted each other; Siam (Thailand) provided a buffer zone between the two.
    (E) The Thais, like the Japanese, closed their borders to foreigners.

89. Which of the following were adaptations Lenin made to Marxism?
    I. The revolution was to be led by workers and peasants.
    II. The revolution would be planned and directed.
    III. The new government was to be a "Dictatorship of the Proletariat."
    IV. Capitalists were identified as imperialists and the enemy of all who experienced colonialism.

    (A) I, II, and III
    (B) II, III, and IV
    (C) I, III, and IV
    (D) I, II, and IV
    (E) all of the above

90. The first explorer to sail around the world from 1519 to 1522 was
    (A) Bartholomew Diaz.
    (B) Vasco da Gama.
    (C) Pedro Alvares Cabral.
    (D) Ferdinand Magellan.
    (E) Christopher Columbus.

91. Which of the following issued the Balfour Declaration in 1917 with its contradictory assurances to Jews and Palestinians?
    (A) League of Nations
    (B) United Nations
    (C) The Allies
    (D) Britain
    (E) Ottoman Turkey

92. This Diego Rivera mural emphasizes which aspect of the Mexican Revolution?
    (A) anti-U.S. imperialism
    (B) communist insurgency
    (C) Pancho Villa's insurgency
    (D) machismo
    (E) the peasant insistance on land reform

93. Characteristic of Aztec society was
    I. an upper class of clans of calpulli who regulated social and political life.
    II. an emperor who ruled by inheritance and election.
    III. slaves who owned property and could own other slaves.
    IV. a religion remembered for its benevolent rituals and for its encouragement of education and the arts.

    (A) I and IV
    (B) II, III, and IV
    (C) I, II, and III
    (D) all of the above
    (E) none of the above

94. What was a common physical characteristic of all the earliest civilizations?
    (A) Rivers that could provide water for agriculture.
    (B) Rainfall that encouraged the production of grain crops.
    (C) A steady supply of alluvial soil.
    (D) Rivers that could be navigated easily.
    (E) Geographic barriers that provided protection from invasion.

95. Using scenes of daily life, Japanese woodblock prints or Ukiyo-e like this one by Hokusai was produced as one of many copies for
    (A) peasants.
    (B) laborers.
    (C) samurai.
    (D) the imperial court.
    (E) merchants.

96. Which was NOT a significant factor in British industrialization in the eighteenth century?
    (A) increased agricultural production
    (B) rising population
    (C) river systems to provide a power source
    (D) a growing domestic and colonial market
    (E) the discovery of petroleum

97. The Alliance for Progress was
    (A) the United Nation's attempt to help less developed countries.
    (B) the agreement by Mexico and the United States to lower tariff barriers.
    (C) Teddy Roosevelt's policy of "Speak Softly and Carry a Big Stick."
    (D) John F. Kennedy's program to use economic aid to prevent communism in Latin America.
    (E) Franklin Roosevelt's attempt to keep Latin America in the western camp during World War II.

98. The *Code of Manu* reflects
    (A) Hindu mysticism.
    (B) Aryan beliefs about nature of the cosmos.
    (C) Jainist beliefs in nonviolence.
    (D) Hindu law.
    (E) social aspects of Buddhism.

99. Which European treaty redrew European borders on the balance-of-power principle?
    (A) Berlin
    (B) Vienna
    (C) Versailles
    (D) Paris
    (E) Sevres

100. Classical liberals believed government should
    (A) be the watchdog over environmental problems.
    (B) protect private property.
    (C) supervise and regulate public health.
    (D) establish a graduated income tax.
    (E) provide sewage disposal and street maintenance.

101. The Byzantine Empire and its capital, Constantinople, were originally part of
    (A) Persia.
    (B) the Mauryan Empire.
    (C) Palestine.
    (D) Alexander the Great's kingdom.
    (E) Rome.

102. Which was the first Asian country to industrialize?
    (A) India
    (B) China
    (C) Korea
    (D) Japan
    (E) Iran

103. Which of the newly industrializing countries became economic miracles after the 1970s?
    (A) Czechoslovakia and Poland
    (B) Taiwan and South Korea
    (C) India and Turkey
    (D) Vietnam and China
    (E) Brazil and Bolivia

104. The most likely explanation for economic miracles of question 103 is
    (A) loans from the World Bank.
    (B) education and industrialization.
    (C) democratic governments.
    (D) large amounts of raw materials.
    (E) adequate land.

105. Which of the following agreements is INCORRECTLY identified?
    (A) Treaty of Tordesillas—divided the Spanish and Portuguese claims, with the Spanish receiving most of the Americas except Brazil.
    (B) Treaty of Westphalia—allowed each German state or city to chose to be either Catholic or Protestant.
    (C) Treaty of Nerchinsk—established the boundary between Russia and China.
    (D) Treaty of Paris—recognized British control of Indian trade.
    (E) Council of Trent—recognized the British claims to North America.

This map relates to question 86.

Answers

Unit I
1. C, p. 6
2. C, p. 8
3. E, p. 4
4. C, p. 5
5. D, p. 8
6. D, p. 9
7. D, p. 9
8. E, p. 12
9. E, p. 4
10. E, p. 8

Unit II
1. E, p. 29
2. C, p. 23
3. D, p. 30
4. B, p. 28
5. C, p. 31
6. D, p. 31
7. E, p. 23
8. B, p. 30
9. B, p. 25
10. A, p. 34

Unit III
1. D, p. 56
2. D, p. 52
3. A, p. 55
4. E, p. 56
5. E, p. 59
6. E, p. 62
7. A, p. 69
8. C, p. 70
9. D, p. 71
10. B, p. 71
11. A, p. 68
12. B, p. 77
13. C, p. 75
14. D, p. 83
15. D, p. 84

Unit IV
1. C, p. 112
2. A, p. 112
3. B, p. 117
4. B, p. 113
5. B, p. 122
6. E, p. 122
7. D, p. 124
8. B, p. 123
9. E, p. 124
10. E, p. 122
11. C, p. 127
12. E, p. 122
13. B, p. 128
14. D, p. 132
15. E, p. 133

Unit V
1. B, p. 162
2. B, p. 174
3. E, p. 166
4. D, p. 167
5. A, p. 169
6. B, p. 169
7. E, p. 168
8. D, p. 170
9. C, p. 172
10. E, p. 172
11. C, p. 175
12. E, p. 178
13. E, p. 187
14. E, p. 180
15. B, p. 184
16. E, p. 185

Unit VI
1. D, p. 175
2. D, p. 206
3. E, p. 206
4. A, p. 210
5. E, p. 209
6. E, p. 208
7. B, p. 212
8. A, p. 211
9. E, p. 212
10. B, p. 212
11. E, p. 214
12. E, p. 214
13. A, p. 218
14. **E, p. 222**
15. **C, p. 226**

— Unit VII
1. D, p. 251
2. D, p. 252
3. B, p. 247
4. A, p. 247
5. B, p. 249
6. B, p. 250
7. B, p. 251
8. D, p. 252
9. C, p. 252
10. D, p. 253
11. A, p. 255
12. C, p. 265
13. C, p. 255
14. C, p. 257
15. E, p. 257
16. D, p. 258
17. C, p. 260

Unit VIII
1. A, p. 294
2. B, p. 294
3. E, p. 292
4. A, p. 295
5. E, p. 299
6. D, p. 299
7. C, p. 300
8. C, p. 300
9. B, p. 302
10. D, p. 301
11. C, p. 301
12. E, p. 316
13. E, p. 307
14. D, p. 307
15. B, p. 308
16. D, p. 309
17. B, p. 312
18. C, p. 316
19. E, p. 329
20. A, p. 333

ANSWERS TO MODEL TESTS

Model Test 1

1. **D** See Unit VI, pages 215–216
2. **C** See Unit I, page 13
3. **C** See Unit I , page 12
4. **D** See Unit VI, page 207
5. **B** See Unit II, page 25
6. **E** See Unit VII, page 273
7. **D** See Unit VII, page 254
8. **B** See Unit II, pages 23, 37
9. **A** See Unit VII, page 260
10. **A** See Unit VIII, page 300
11. **C** See Unit II, page 24
12. **E** See Unit V, page 178
13. **A** See Unit VIII, page 292
14. **B** See Unit II, page 30
15. **D** See Unit VII, page 268
16. **C** See Unit V, page 166
17. **E** See Unit III, page 63
18. **C** See Unit III, page 85
19. **B** See Unit VII, page 260
20. **C** See Unit III, page 74
21. **D** See Unit VIII, page 321
22. **D** See Unit III, page 71
23. **B** See Unit VI, page 223
24. **D** See Unit VII, pages 262
25. **C** See Unit III, page 75
26. **C** See Unit VII, page 257
27. **A** See Unit V, page 176
28. **B** See Unit III, page 86
29. **C** See Unit VIII, page 331
30. **D** See Unit III, page 86
31. **C** See Unit VI, page 279
32. **B** See Unit V, page 183
33. **A** See Unit III, page 80
34. **D** See Unit VIII, pages 229, 345
35. **D** See Unit VI, page 216–217
36. **D** See Unit IV, page 113
37. **B** See Unit VIII, page 301
38. **B** See Unit IV, page 148
39. **C** See Unit I, V, pages 9, 162
40. **D** See Unit IV, page 132
41. **A** See Unit VIII, page 299
42. **E** See Unit IV, page 109
43. **B** See Unit VII, pages 261, 278
44. **E** See Unit V, page 162

45. **D** See Unit II, page 22
46. **E** See Unit VI, page 206
47. **A** See Unit VI, page 223
48. **C** See Unit VIII, page 298
49. **A** See Unit V, page 184
50. **D** See Unit VI, page 227
51. **B** See Unit VI, page 225
52. **A** See Unit VI, page 221
53. **E** See Unit VII, page 248
54. **E** See Unit III, page 53
55. **E** See Unit VII, page 249
56. **D** See Unit VI, page 187
57. **E** See Unit VII, page 250
58. **A** See Unit VII, page 257
59. **D** See Unit IV, page 144
60. **A** See Unit VII, pages 248, 277
61. **B** See Unit VII, page 247
62. **A** See Unit VII, page 251
63. **E** See Unit VII, page 254
64. **B** See Unit VII, page 261
65. **E** See Unit VII, page 263
66. **D** See Unit VII, page 263
67. **E** See Unit V, pages 189, 202
68. **C** See Unit VII, page 263–264
69. **A** See Unit II, page 38
70. **D** See Unit VII, page 254
71. **A** See Unit II, page 28
72. **A** See Unit VII, page 264
73. **D** See Unit IV, page 145
74. **C** See Unit VIII, page 293
75. **B** See Unit VIII, page 295
76. **B** See Unit VIII, page 296
77. **B** See Unit III, page 76
78. **D** See Unit VIII, page 299
79. **E** See Unit IV, page 125
80. **E** See Unit VIII, page 324
81. **C** See Unit VIII, page 305
82. **E** See Unit VIII, page 322
83. **B** See Unit VIII, page 320
84. **C** See Unit VIII, page 306
85. **D** See Unit VII, page 279
86. **C** See Unit VII, page 284
87. **A** See Unit VIII, page 321
88. **E** See Unit III, page 52
89. **A** See Unit VIII, page 301
90. **D** See Unit VIII, page 308

91. **C** See Unit VIII, page 309
92. **C** See Unit VIII, page 312
93. **E** See Unit V, page 185
94. **A** See Unit V, page 193
95. **D** See Unit VII, pages 260, 277
96. **D** See Unit III, pages 83, 41
97. **E** See Unit VIII, page 308
98. **E** See Unit IV, pages 133–134
99. **E** See Unit VIII, page 308
100. **A** See Unit VIII, page 310
101. **D** See Unit V, page 164

Model Test 2

1. **D** See Unit VIII, page 296
2. **E** See Unit VII, page 258
3. **E** See Unit VII, page 264
4. **E** See Unit VII, page 249
5. **A** See Unit III, page 96
6. **D** See Unit VIII, page 301
7. **E** See Unit VI, page 227
8. **D** See Unit V, page 167
9. **D** See Unit VII, page 247
10. **D** See Unit VII, page 265
11. **A** See Unit VIII, page 305
12. **B** See Unit V, page 170
13. **C** See Unit II, page 42
14. **C** See Unit VIII, page 302
15. **B** See Unit I, page 9
16. **D** See Unit III, pages 74, 75
17. **B** See Unit VII, page 264
18. **A** See Unit VII, page 263
19. **A** See Unit VII, page 263
20. **D** See Unit VIII, page 307
21. **C** See Unit V, page 123
22. **A** See Unit VII, page 264
23. **A** See Unit VII, page 246
24. **E** See Unit II, page 22
25. **B** See Unit V, page 172
26. **D** See Unit V, page 187
27. **D** See Unit III, page 55
28. **D** See Unit V, page 201
29. **C** See Unit III, page 52
30. **A** See Unit V, page 126
31. **A** See Unit VIII, pages 298–299
32. **E** See Unit V, page 149
33. **C** See Unit VII, pages 254–255
34. **A** See Unit II, page 34
35. **D** See Unit VII, page 261

36. **C** See Unit VI, page 193
37. **B** See Unit VIII, page 293
38. **C** See Unit II, page 37
39. **C** See Unit VII, page 264
40. **C** See Unit VIII, page 308
41. **C** See Unit VI, page 215
42. **B** See Unit VIII, page 327
43. **D** See Unit VI, page 220
44. **E** See Unit VIII, page 307
45. **E** See Unit III, page 57
46. **E** See Unit VII, page 251
47. **D** See Unit III, page 78
48. **E** See Unit VIII, page 301
49. **C** See Unit VII, page 259
50. **E** See Unit V, page 163
51. **E** See Unit VII, page 261
52. **E** See Unit VIII, page 313
53. **A** See Unit IV, page 140
54. **A** See Unit VIII, page 301
55. **C** See Unit III, page 69
56. **D** See Unit VIII, pages 300–301
57. **D** See Unit III, pages 70–71
58. **B** See Unit IV, page 111
59. **E** See Unit IV, pages 139, 140
60. **E** See Unit III, page 84
61. **B** See Unit VIII, page 298
62. **B** See Unit V, page 163
63. **B** See Unit III, pages 97–98
64. **E** See Unit II, page 23
65. **C** See Unit VII, page 259
66. **B** See Unit VIII, page 294
67. **E** See Unit IV, page 122
68. **B** See Unit VII, page 260
69. **D** See Unit VI, page 222
70. **B** See Unit VIII, page 311
71. **B** See Unit II, page 22
72. **A** See Unit VII, page 263
73. **C** See Unit VII, page 264
74. **D** See Unit VIII, page 300
75. **E** See Unit VI, page 224
76. **E** See Unit VII, page 270
77. **D** See Unit VII, page 250
78. **E** See Unit III, pages 74–75
79. **B** See Unit VIII, pages 307, 310
80. **C** See Unit IV, page 141
81. **A** See Unit VII, page 249
82. **C** See Unit V, page 165
83. **C** See Unit VII, page 274
84. **A** See Unit V, page 189

85. **E** See Unit IV, page 145
86. **E** See Unit II, page 42
87. **D** See Unit VIII, page 295
88. **D** See Unit VII, page 265
89. **E** See Unit VIII, pages 304–305
90. **D** See Unit VI, page 221
91. **D** See Unit VIII, page 309
92. **A** See Unit VIII, page 346
93. **C** See Unit V, page 188
94. **A** See Unit II, page 22
95. **A** See Unit IV, page 156

96. **C** See Unit VII, pages 257–258
97. **D** See Unit VIII, page 307
98. **D** See Unit III, page 83
99. **B** See Unit VII, pages 250–251
100. **B** See Unit VII, page 260
101. **E** See Unit IV, page 132
102. **D** See Unit VII, page 268
103. **B** See Unit VIII, page 323
104. **B** See Unit VIII, page 323
105. **E** See Unit VI, page 212

Index